RESEARCH HANDBOOK ON EUROPEAN UNION CITIZENSHIP LAW AND POLICY

RESEARCH HANDBOOKS IN EUROPEAN LAW

This important series presents a comprehensive analysis of the latest thinking, research and practice across the field of European Law. Organised by theme, the series provides detailed coverage of major topics whilst also creating a focus on emerging areas deserving special attention. Each volume is edited by leading experts and includes specially commissioned chapters from distinguished academics as well as perspectives from practice, providing a rigorous and structured analysis of the area in question. With an international outlook, focus on current issues, and a substantive analysis of the law, these *Research Handbooks* are intended to contribute to current debate as well as providing authoritative and informative coverage.

Forming a definitive reference work, each *Research Handbook* will be essential reading for both scholars in European law as well as for practitioners and policymakers who wish to engage with the latest thinking and ongoing debates in the field.

Titles in this series include:

Research Handbook on EU Energy Law and Policy
Edited by Rafael Leal-Arcas and Jan Wouters

Research Handbook on Legal Pluralism and EU Law
Edited by Gareth Davies and Matej Avbelj

Research Handbook on EU Sports Law and Policy
Edited by Jack Anderson, Richard Parrish and Borja García

Research Handbook on the EU's Common Foreign and Security Policy
Edited by Panos Koutrakos and Steven Blockmans

Research Handbook on EU Economic Law
Edited by Federico Fabbrini and Marco Ventoruzzo

Research Handbook on European Union Taxation Law
Edited by Christiana HJI Panayi, Werner Haslehner and Edoardo Traversa

Research Handbook on the Brussels Ibis Regulation
Edited by Peter Mankowski

Research Handbook on EU Environmental Law
Edited by Marjan Peeters and Mariolina Eliantonio

Research Handbook on EU Disability Law
Edited by Delia Ferri and Andrea Broderick

Research Handbook on European State Aid Law
Edited by Leigh Hancher and Juan Jorge Piernas López

Research Handbook on EU Media Law and Policy
Edited by Pier Luigi Parcu and Elda Brogi

Research Handbook on European Union Citizenship Law and Policy
Navigating Challenges and Crises
Edited by Dora Kostakopoulou and Daniel Thym

Research Handbook on European Union Citizenship Law and Policy

Navigating Challenges and Crises

Edited by

Dora Kostakopoulou

Chair of the Scientific Committee of the Fundamental Rights Agency of the European Union and KU Leuven, Belgium

Daniel Thym

University of Konstanz, Germany

With

Felicitas Ernst

University of Konstanz, Germany

Johannes Siegel

University of Konstanz, Germany

RESEARCH HANDBOOKS IN EUROPEAN LAW

Cheltenham, UK • Northampton, MA, USA

© The Editors and Contributors Severally 2022

All rights reserved. No part of this publication may be reproduced, stored in a retrieval system or transmitted in any form or by any means, electronic, mechanical or photocopying, recording, or otherwise without the prior permission of the publisher.

Published by
Edward Elgar Publishing Limited
The Lypiatts
15 Lansdown Road
Cheltenham
Glos GL50 2JA
UK

Edward Elgar Publishing, Inc.
William Pratt House
9 Dewey Court
Northampton
Massachusetts 01060
USA

A catalogue record for this book
is available from the British Library

Library of Congress Control Number: 2022931162

This book is available electronically in the **Elgar**online
Law subject collection
http://dx.doi.org/10.4337/9781788972901

Printed on elemental chlorine free (ECF)
recycled paper containing 30% Post-Consumer Waste

ISBN 978 1 78897 289 5 (cased)
ISBN 978 1 78897 290 1 (eBook)

Printed and bound in the USA

Contents

List of contributors		vii
1	Introduction: challenges and crises of Union citizenship *Daniel Thym*	1
PART I	THEORETICAL EXPLORATIONS	
2	The power of the norm: EU citizenship as constitutional right *Anne Wesemann*	13
3	A social-constructivist approach towards the evolution of EU citizenship *Martin Steinfeld*	32
4	The evolution of citizens' rights in light of the EU's constitutional development *Daniel Thym*	49
5	The genesis of European rights *Willem Maas*	70
6	EU citizenship: a social empathy perspective *Karmelia Yiannakou*	83
7	The relationship between national and EU citizenship: what is it and what should it be? *Martijn van den Brink*	100
PART II	CITIZENS' RIGHTS	
8	Citizenship, territory and COVID-19 *Stephen Coutts*	116
9	The rules on the free movement of workers in the European Union *Adela Boitos and Manuel Kellerbauer*	131
10	Free movement or fundamental rights? EU citizenship as a legal gateway to fundamental rights protection *Adrienne Yong*	149
11	EU citizenship and family reunification: the evolving concept of a European Union territory *Hester Kroeze*	165
12	Using EU citizenship to protect academic freedom: an alternative method *Tamas Dezso Ziegler*	184

13 Does Member State withdrawal automatically extinguish EU citizenship? 201
    Oliver Garner

PART III SOCIAL CITIZENSHIP

14 EU citizenship and the welfare state 225
    Francesco Costamagna and Stefano Giubboni

15 Progression and retrogression of the ECJ case law on access to social benefits 249
    Ségolène Barbou des Places

16 The limits of judicialising transnational welfare: progression and retrogression of the ECJ case law on access to social benefits 265
    Susanne K. Schmidt

17 The outer limits of transnational solidarity between the EU's Member States in a social security setting 282
    Jaan Paju

PART IV EU CITIZENSHIP POST-BREXIT: DIFFERENTIATED CITIZENSHIP REVISITED

18 Differentiated citizenship in the European Economic Area 297
    Christian Franklin and Halvard Haukeland Fredriksen

19 'Citizenship of the Association': the examples of Turkey and Switzerland 320
    Narin Idriz and Christa Tobler

20 Employment and social rights of labour migrants post-Brexit 343
    Herwig Verschueren

21 Irish citizenship law after Brexit: implications for Northern Ireland 364
    Clemens M. Rieder

22 Epilogue: on guest houses and institutional reconfigurations 384
    Dora Kostakopoulou

Index 392

Contributors

Ségolène Barbou des Places is Professor of Public and European Law at the Sorbonne Law School, Paris 1 Panthéon-Sorbonne University and Fellow of the Institut Convergences Migrations.

Adela Boitos is Member of the Legal Service of the European Commission.

Francesco Costamagna is Professor of EU Law at the University of Turin and Fellow at the Collegio Carlo Alberto.

Stephen Coutts is Lecturer in Law at University College Cork.

Christian Franklin is Professor of Law and Joint Manager of the Research Group for EU/EEA, Competition and Market Law at the University of Bergen.

Halvard Haukeland Fredriksen is Professor of EU and EEA Law at the University of Bergen.

Oliver Garner is Maurice Wohl Research Fellow in European Rule of Law at the Bingham Centre for the Rule of Law, British Institute of International and Comparative Law and Editor (Rule of Law) of the CEU Democracy Institute Review of Democracy.

Stefano Giubboni is Professor of Labour Law at the University of Perugia.

Narin Idriz is Researcher at TMC Asser Institute, The Hague, and Member of the Human Rights Committee of the Dutch Advisory Council on International Affairs (AIV).

Manuel Kellerbauer is Legal Adviser at the Legal Service of the European Commission and lecturer at the universities of Saarbrücken and Würzburg.

Dora Kostakopoulou is Professor of European Union Law, European Integration and Public Policy at KU Leuven.

Hester Kroeze is PhD Candidate in the field of EU Citizenship and Family Reunification Rights at the Ghent European Law Institute.

Willem Maas is Jean Monnet Chair and Professor of Political Science, Public & International Affairs, and Socio-Legal Studies at York University (Canada).

Jaan Paju is Senior Lecturer in Constitutional Law and Associate Professor in European Law at Stockholm University.

Clemens M. Rieder is Senior Lecturer in EU Law at Queen's University Belfast (Northern Ireland) and Executive Committee Member at the Centre for European and Transnational Studies.

Susanne K. Schmidt is Professor of Political Science at the University of Bremen.

Martin Steinfeld is College Lecturer in Law, Director of Studies; Affiliated Lecturer at Faculty of Law, University of Cambridge.

Daniel Thym is Professor of Public, European and International Law and Director of the Research Centre Immigration and Asylum Law at the University of Konstanz.

Christa Tobler is Professor of European Law at the Europa Institutes of the Universities of Basel and Leiden.

Martijn van den Brink is British Academy Postdoctoral Fellow at the University of Oxford.

Herwig Verschueren is Professor of International and European Employment and Social Law at the University of Antwerp.

Anne Wesemann is Senior Lecturer in Law and Head of Department at The Open University Law School, UK.

Karmelia Yiannakou LLB, MA Res, PhD is a Registered Advocate and Independent Researcher focusing on EU citizenship, migration, social justice and human rights in law and education.

Adrienne Yong is Senior Lecturer in Law at The City Law School, City, University of London; Co-Director of the Institute for the Study of European Laws (ISEL); and Gender & Sexuality Research Centre (GSRC) Organising Committee Member.

Tamas Dezso Ziegler is Associate Professor and Head of the Department of International Relations and European Studies, Faculty of Social Sciences, Eötvös Loránd University, Budapest.

1. Introduction: challenges and crises of Union citizenship

Daniel Thym

1. NON-LINEAR UNION CITIZENSHIP

European integration came about in the era of high modernity and incorporated the belief in the possibility of progress on the basis of humanism, rationalism, science and technology, as well as economic development.[1] Preambular recitals of the European Treaties epitomise that belief to this date, as do the initial reliance on technocratic institutions, the creation of the European Atomic Energy Community, and reliance on the law as the primary instrument of governance. The process of European integration has traditionally embodied the conviction that economic, social, technological and political progress are possible[2] – and the success of Western Europe during the *trente glorieuses* of the postwar period seemed to justify the conception of linear evolution towards a better life. Arguably, the optimistic vision of 'ever closer union'[3] symbolises the search for constant improvement, where the future will almost inevitably be better than the past.[4]

The modernist vision of progress was resurrected, indirectly at least, after the end of the Cold War by what appeared to be the beginning of an epoch that was aptly described as the 'end of history',[5] to illustrate the widespread expectation that liberal and democratic constitutionalism in the Western tradition would no longer be contested. The gradual disappearance of borders, state sovereignty and ideological struggles was an integral part of the positive narrative about globalisation throughout the 1990s. Union citizenship was created in this overall context by the Treaty of Maastricht.[6] Legal rules and court judgments on the new status and the free movement of persons were interpreted by academic observers to herald the assertion of novel forms of post- or transnational citizenship.[7] It was often assumed at the time that this process would continue and that legal rules and corresponding court judgments would

---

[1] See generally https://en.wikipedia.org/wiki/High_modernism accessed 26 May 2021.
[2] See Articles 2–3 TEU.
[3] Recital 1 of the Preamble of the original EEC Treaty of 1957, the present Treaty on the Functioning of the European Union and the Charter of Fundamental Rights.
[4] See also Chalmers, Damian/Trotter, Sarah: Fundamental Rights and Legal Wrongs: The Two Sides of the Same EU Coin, ELJ 22 (2016), 9, 15–16.
[5] Fukuyama, Francis: The End of History and the Last Man (Free Press, 1992).
[6] See Article 8–8e Treaty establishing the European Community as amended by the Treaty of Maastricht (OJ 1992 C 224/36), adopted 7 February 1992, entered into force 1 November 1993.
[7] See Soysal, Yasemin: Limits of Citizenship. Migrants and Postnational Membership in Europe (University of Chicago Press, 1994), 141–51; and Sassen, Saskia: Losing Control? Sovereignty in an Age of Globalization (Columbia UP, 1996), 88–99.

continue to expand equal treatment and residence security across borders, thus transforming prevailing conceptions of citizenship that had existed at the national level.[8]

For those studying the state of the Union in the 2020s, it can be difficult to grasp the sense of optimism with which colleagues had earlier approached Union citizenship. Enthusiasm has given way to widespread disappointment, scepticism and critique of the institutional practices on free movement and Union citizenship, including court judgments. They are condemned for advancing the rights of economically successful citizens over those in precarious occupations, women and marginal social groups.[9] The positive narrative of individual rights as an instrument of emancipation is complemented by darker perceptions of governmental control and subjectification rewarding good behaviour.[10] Instead of embracing transnational mobility as a force for the good, some highlight the tension, if not conflict, with traditional conceptions of solidarity and democratic belonging.[11] It is palpable that the 'critical turn'[12] has reached EU legal studies and the academic research on Union citizenship.

Legal, political and contextual reasons underlying the critical turn will be discussed throughout this Handbook. From the perspective of the history of intellectual thought, the overlap with the decline of the modernist belief in historical teleology, which had informed the EU's creation, stands out. Modernism has given way to diverse strands of postmodernist thought questioning the assumption of steady betterment. Objective rationality was replaced by critical deconstructivism, and social or legal institutions that had previously been widely accepted are criticised from a feminist or postcolonial angle.[13] The idea of linear progress towards a better future is dethroned by the theoretical equivalence of dead ends, standstill or even decline.[14] That applies to the internal critique of the evolution of Union citizenship, on which most academic writing of EU law experts concentrates, as it does to the external deconstruction of the EU's self-image as a force for the good in light of the postcolonial rejection of the distinction between Union citizens and third country nationals enshrined at Treaty level as a form of neo-colonial 'apartheid'.[15]

---

[8] See Kostakopoulou, Dora: The Future Governance of Citizenship (CUP, 2008); Maas, Willem: Migrant, States and EU Citizenship's Unfulfilled Promise, Citizenship Studies 12 (2008), 583–96.

[9] See O'Brien, Charlotte: Unity in Adversity: EU Citizenship, Social Justice and the Cautionary Tale of the UK (Bloomsbury/Hart, 2017); Carter, Daniel: Inclusion and Exclusion of Migrant Workers in the EU, in: Moritz Jesse (ed.), European Societies, Migration, and the Law. The 'Others' amongst 'Us' (CUP, 2020), 301–20.

[10] See Neuvonen, Päivi Johanna: Retrieving the 'Subject' of European Integration, ELJ 25 (2019), 6–20; Kochenov, Dimitry: The Citizenship of Personal Circumstances in Europe, in: Daniel Thym (ed.), Questioning EU Citizenship: Judges and the Limits of Free Movement and Solidarity in the EU (Bloomsbury/Hart, 2017), 37–56.

[11] See Menéndez, Agustín/Olsen, Espen D.H.: Challenging European Citizenship: Ideas and Realities in Contrast (Palgrave, 2020); Seubert, Sandra: Shifting Boundaries of Membership. The Politicisation of Free Movement as a Challenge for EU Citizenship, ELJ 26 (2020), 48–60.

[12] See generally Editorial Comments: The Critical Turn in EU Legal Studies, CML Rev. 52 (2015), 881–88; Azoulai, Loïc: Solitude, désoeuvrement et conscience critique. Les ressorts d'une recomposition des études juridiques européennes, Politiques européennes 2015, 8–86.

[13] See generally https://en.wikipedia.org/wiki/Postmodernism accessed 26 May 2021.

[14] See Ferguson, James: Decomposing Modernity: History and Hierarchy after Development, in: James Ferguson (ed.), Global Shadows: Africa in the Neoliberal World Order (Duke UP, 2006), 176–93.

[15] See Balibar, Etienne: Nous, citoyens d'Europe: Les Frontières, l'Etat, le people (La Découverte, 2001); see also Thym, Daniel: Deciphering the Role of Migration Law in the Social Construction of 'Otherness', in: Jesse (ed.), *European Societies* (n. 9), 323–55.

Placing emphasis on non-linear evolutionary paths of Union citizenship aims to draw our attention to the social, political and intellectual context of contemporary legal debates. Doing so highlights that – notwithstanding the vision of 'ever closer union' – restrictive tendencies, thematic shifts or changes of direction are conceptually as likely as further expansion. It is important to realise that the emphasis on non-linearity is not meant as a normative preposition that supranational citizenship is bound to fail or that institutional practices are necessarily bad. Rather, it serves as an investigative device to shed light on underlying trends, contextual forces and normative implications of the law and policy of Union citizenship. The outcome of this venture is no foregone conclusion. In that respect, deconstruction and reconstruction go hand in hand. Non-linearity rejects quasi-natural trajectories of perpetual progress in the same way as the prediction of inevitable decline. The future is not pre-determined but depends – like the past – on legal and institutional choices that can change over time.

2. CHALLENGES: NORMATIVE OPEN-ENDEDNESS

When the Treaty of Maastricht introduced Union citizenship, the initial reaction was temperate.[16] Early reactions criticised the rules for not adding much substance. Citizenship was perceived as essentially a label attached to free movement and direct elections to the European Parliament. Commentators highlighted the 'weakness'[17] of the legal framework and castigated the new status as a misnomer bound to remain an 'empty gesture', a sort of 'cynical public relations exercise' on the part of the High Contracting Parties.[18] It is well known that the situation changed from the late 1990s onwards when the Court started interpreting citizens' rights,[19] thus building upon the earlier judicial expansion of the free movement of workers and other persons which had been interpreted generously by the EU legislature and the Court of Justice ever since the 1970s.[20] Court judgments played a prominent role in the initial euphoria about Union citizenship as an embryonic form of supra- or transnational citizenship transforming hitherto prevailing conceptions of state membership.

In one of the first prominent judgments on citizenship, the Court of Justice hinted at the forward-looking potential when stating that Union citizenship 'is *destined to be* the fundamental status'.[21] This prospective dynamism did not come as a surprise. In contrast to the cautious

---

[16] This and the next two sections build on Thym, Daniel: Introduction: The Judicial Deconstruction of Union Citizenship, in: Thym (ed.), *Questioning EU Citizenship* (n. 10), 1, 1–8.

[17] O'Leary, Síofra: The Evolving Concept of Community Citizenship: From the Free Movement of Persons to Union Citizenship (Kluwer, 1996), 304–7.

[18] See Weiler, Joseph H.H.: European Citizenship and Human Rights, in: Jan Winter/Deirdre Curtin/Alfred Kellermann/Bruno de Witte (eds), Reforming the Treaty on European Union (T.M.C. Asser, 1996), 57, 68, 73.

[19] For an overview, see Kochenov, Dimitry: The Essence of EU Citizenship Emerging from the Last Ten Years of Academic Debate: Beyond the Cherry Blossoms and the Moon?, ICLQ 62 (2013), 97–136.

[20] See Kadelbach, Stefan: Union Citizenship, in: Armin von Bogdandy/Jürgen Bast (eds), Principles of European Constitutional Law, 2nd edn (Hart, 2009), 443, 445–8.

[21] ECJ, C-184/99, *Grzelczyk*, EU:C:2001:458, para 31 (emphasis added), which in French, the working language of the Court, read '*a vocation à être*'; the English-language version of later judgments employed 'is intended to be'; see also Jessurun d'Oliveira, Hans Ulrich: Union Citizenship and Beyond, in: Nathan Cambien/Dimitry Kochenov/Elise Muir (eds), European Citizenship under Stress: Social Justice, Brexit and Other Challenges (Brill Nijhoff, 2020), 28, 40–1.

observers mentioned previously, others had predicted early on that the new status would not remain an empty normative shell.[22] They expected the citizenship label to have a transformative impact, as it did for many years. To this day, citizenship judgments constitute one of the most tantalising lines of the ECJ case law, discussed in numerous academic articles and monographs. In doing so, commentators often described the evolution in a transformative manner from (old) 'market citizenship' towards (new) 'real, social or political citizenship', including access to social benefits, voting rights and free movement for those other than workers.[23] To do so reflects the vision of 'ever closer union' and the idea of linear progress.

Union citizenship lends itself to such progressive narratives. Experts of political theory emphasise that the notion of 'citizenship' has a rich history, throughout which it often served as a projection sphere for political visions of a good life and a just society. It is the aspirational openness of the citizenship concept that explains why it has long steered diverse calls for wider social and political inclusion.[24] It served as a normative anchor in debates about the abolition of serfdom and slavery, the gradual extension of the right to vote and the construction of the welfare state.[25] More recently, women, ethnic minorities and gay men and lesbians have fought for emancipation by invoking 'citizenship'.[26] That is not to say that there is a uniform conception of citizenship: its meaning remains theoretically contested and politically disputed.[27] Yet, it is for this reason that rules on citizenship can serve, like human rights, as channels to feed normative arguments into legal debates.[28] The inherent openness of the citizenship concept supports progressive change by means of dynamic interpretation.

Against this background, Union citizenship shares a general characteristic with the European Union: they both defy easy definition. Affirmative recourse to constitutional lan-

---

[22] See Shaw, Jo: Citizenship of the Union: Towards a Post-National Membership?, in: European University Institute (eds), Collected Courses of the Academy of European Law 1995, Volume VI-1 (Kluwer, 1998), 237, 278–96; and Tomuschat, Christian: Staatsbürgerschaft – Unionsbürgerschaft – Weltbürgerschaft, in: Josef Drexl/Karl Kreuzer/Dieter Scheuing/Ulrich Sieber (eds), Europäische Demokratie (Nomos, 1999), 73, 75.

[23] By way of example, see Kochenov, Dimitry: The Citizenship Paradigm, C.Y.E.L.S. 15 (2012–13), 197–226; Shaw, Jo: Citizenship: Contrasting Dynamics at the Interface of Integration and Constitutionalism, in: Paul Craig/Gráinne de Búrca (eds), The Evolution of EU Law, 2nd edn (OUP, 2011), 575–609; Spaventa, Eleanor: Seeing the Wood despite the Trees? On the Scope of Union Citizenship and its Constitutional Effects, CML Rev. 45 (2008), 13–45; Tryfonidou, Alina: Reverse Discrimination in EC Law (Kluwer, 2009), ch 4.

[24] See Dahrendorf, Ralf: Citizenship and Beyond – The Social Dynamics of an Idea, Social Research 41 (1974), 673–701; Sassen, Saskia: Territory, Authority, Rights: From Medieval to Global Assemblages (Princeton UP, 2006), ch 6.

[25] For Europe, see Magnette, Paul: Citizenship: The History of an Idea (ECPR Press, 2005), chs 4, 5; and for the US, see Shklar, Judith N.: American Citizenship: The Quest for Inclusion (Harvard UP, 1991).

[26] See Strasser, Sabine: Rethinking Citizenship: Critical Encounters with Feminist, Multicultural and Transnational Concepts of Citizenship, in: Beatrice Halsaa/Sasha Rosenell/Sevil Sümer (eds), Remaking Citizenship in Multicultural Europe. Women's Movements, Gender and Diversity (Palgrave, 2012), 21–41.

[27] See Bosniak, Linda: Citizenship Denationalized, Indiana Journal of Global Legal Studies 7 (2000), 447, 450–3; Benhabib, Seyla: Claiming Rights across Borders: International Human Rights and Democratic Sovereignty, American Political Science Review 103 (2009), 691, 697–9.

[28] For academic practice, see Thym, Daniel: Frontiers of EU Citizenship. Three Trajectories and their Methodological Foundations, in: Dimitry Kochenov (ed.), EU Citizenship and Federalism: The Role of Rights (CUP, 2017), 705–30.

guage often hides deeper problems in describing the European Union in quasi-statist terms, for which, moreover, diverse traditions exist among the Member States.[29] Crucially, this is not an argument against constitutional terminology. To the contrary, we would miss out on a decisive component of the integration process if we pretended that it is a simple form of intergovernmental cooperation, a sort of advanced free trade area. The European Union is much more, even if it remains notoriously difficult to describe the conceptual underpinning of Union citizenship. The more restrictive turn of recent practices and the ensuing non-linearity complicate the venture further.[30] Against this backdrop, the Handbook introduces readers to the state of the art of the legal debate.

The authors contributing to this Handbook are predominantly legal academics and share an intimate knowledge of legal rules and court judgments. Questions of legal interpretation and the search for systematic coherence are a common thread of the contributions. Yet, the methodology they employ often stretches beyond doctrinal hermeneutics, encompassing various forms of contextual and theoretical analyses that help explain institutional practices. The aspirational openness of the citizenship concept renders norms and ideas particularly relevant for the (re)configuration of Union citizenship.[31] A sound legal–doctrinal exegesis is necessary but benefits from being embedded in broader contextual and theoretical explorations precisely because citizens' rights convey normative values and express basic choices of societies, which can change over time.[32]

3. THE TRADITION OF 'INTEGRATION THROUGH LAW' AND ITS LIMITS

In the European Union, the volatility of the citizenship concept is reinforced by recent weaknesses of the traditional method of 'integration through law', which influenced the making of Union citizenship. In the EU, the law has often been employed as an instrument for change.[33] The belief in the effectiveness of the legally driven modification of social and economic

---

[29] See Jakab, András: European Constitutional Language (CUP, 2016); Walker, Neil: Postnational Constitutionalism and the Problem of Translation, in: Joseph H.H. Weiler/Marlene Wind (eds), European Constitutionalism Beyond the State (CUP, 2003), 27–54.

[30] See generally McCrea, Ronan: Forward or Back: The Future of European Integration and the Impossibility of the Status Quo, ELJ 23 (2017), 66–93; Walker, Neil: The Place of European Law, in: Grainne de Búrca/J.H.H. Weiler (eds), The Worlds of European Constitutionalism (CUP, 2012), 57–104.

[31] On open-endedness and co-creation, see Kostakopoulou, Dora: Ideas, Norms and European Citizenship: Explaining Institutional Change, ML Rev 68 (2005), 233–67; Komárek, Jan: EU Citizens' Duties: Preventing Barriers to the Exercise of Citizens' Rights, in: Sandra Seubert/Oliver Eberl/Frans van Waarden (eds), Reconsidering EU Citizenship: Contradictions and Constraints (Edward Elgar Publishing, 2018), 64, 75–8.

[32] See generally Cover, Robert: Foreword: Nomos and Narrative, Harvard Law Review 97 (1983), 4, 11–44; and von Bogdandy, Armin: Founding Principles of EU Law: A Theoretical and Doctrinal Sketch, ELJ 16 (2010), 95, 98–100.

[33] See the classic account by Cappelletti, Mauro/Seccombe, Monica/Weiler, Joseph: Integration through Law: Europe and the American Federal Experience, in: Mauro Cappelletti, Monica Seccombe and Joseph Weiler (eds), Integration through Law: Europe and the American Federal Experience, Volume I: Methods, Tools and Institutions. Book 1: A Political, Legal and Technical Overview (de Gruyter, 1986), 3–68; and the recent, more sceptical assessment by Azoulai, Loïc: 'Integration through Law' and Us, ICON 14 (2016), 449–63.

realities was strengthened in the 1990s by the success of the single market programme.[34] In retrospect, the quarter century between the Single European Act and the entry into force of the Treaty of Lisbon appears as a period of almost continuous Treaty changes, which reached its climax in efforts to foster the steady advance towards political union through a legally binding Charter of Fundamental Rights and the (unsuccessful) project of a Treaty establishing a Constitution for Europe.[35] The introduction of Union citizenship was an integral part of these endeavours.

When the Treaty of Maastricht introduced the new status, it built upon earlier projects to move towards some sort of federal Europe via incipient forms of citizenship underlying the evolution of the free movement *acquis*.[36] This objective gathered momentum when heads of state or government promoted further integration through citizens' rights in the 1970s, including free movement for those other than workers and direct elections to the European Parliament, thereby laying the groundwork for the later introduction of Union citizenship.[37] To be sure, there was little discussion, let alone widespread agreement, about the contours of the new status besides the focus on specific rights attached to it.[38] Yet, this did not unmake the forward-looking normative potential. While much seemed possible originally, recent developments have nourished a sense of caution – both in the institutional practice and regarding the fate of the European project.

An underlying reason for the recent caution is inherent limits to what 'integration through law' can achieve. Treaty changes, new legislation and innovative court judgments alone are not capable of bringing about an enhanced degree of identificatory pattern or transnational solidarity: establishing a fundamental status called 'citizenship' or enacting a legally binding Charter of Fundamental Rights are not self-fulfilling prophecies.[39] Legal rules, judgments and academic treatises participate in the constant (re)construction of societal self-perceptions but cannot change them single-handedly; they need to be embedded in social practices and political life in order not to remain a 'hollow hope'.[40] Again, this is not to say that judgments and other legal practices are irrelevant. Court judgments can foster social change if they are

---

[34] See van Gestel, Rob/Micklitz, Hans-W.: Revitalizing Doctrinal Legal Research in Europe: What about Methodology?, EUI Working Paper LAW 2011/05, 11–12.

[35] See Walker, Neil: Legal Theory and the European Union: A 25th Anniversary Essay, OJLS 25 (2005), 581, 585; Hunt, Jo/Shaw, Jo: Fairy Tale of Luxembourg? Reflections on Law and Legal Scholarship in European Integration, in: David Phinnemore/Alex Warleigh-Lack (eds), Reflections on European Integration: 50 Years of the Treaty of Rome (Palgrave, 2009), 93, 94.

[36] For the 1960s, see Evans, Andrew: European Citizenship, ML Rev. 45 (1982), 497, 499–504.

[37] On the 1970s and 1980s, see Wiener, Antje: Building Institutions: The Developing Practice of European Citizenship (Westview Press, 1998), chs 2, 3; Maas, Willem: Creating European Citizens (Rowman & Littlefield, 2007), ch 2.

[38] See Magnette, Paul: La Citoyenneté Européenne : Droits, Politiques Institutions (Editions de l'Université de Bruxelles, 1999), ch 5.

[39] See the pointed critique by Weiler, Joseph H.H.: To Be a European Citizen: Eros and Civilization, Journal of European Public Policy 4 (1997), 495–519; and Haltern, Ulrich: Pathos and Patina: The Failure and Promise of Constitutionalism in the European Imagination, ELJ 9 (2003), 14–44.

[40] Rosenberg, Gerald N.: The Hollow Hope. Can Courts Bring about Social Change?, 2nd edn (University of Chicago Press, 2008).

connected to broader debates and social struggles.[41] However, the law will not do the trick by itself.

Against this backdrop, the restrictive turn of recent institutional practices, notably court judgments, can be rationalised, in part at least, as an expression of judges losing faith in the potential of transformative jurisprudence. There was a notable parallel between the aspirational rulings and the rise of the Constitutional Treaty, whose failure might have paved the way for a more careful approach.[42] This trend seems to have been reinforced by the repercussions of the euro crisis, the Brexit referendum, political controversies about migration and the rise of euroscepticism across the continent throughout the 2010s.[43] Note that many controversial judgments concerned economically inactive Union citizens and residence rights of family members holding the nationality of a third state. These matters are politically salient. Moreover, the adoption of the Free Movement Directive 2004/38/EC indicated that the legislature did not support far-fetched equal treatment for those not working. People familiar with the inner workings of the Court emphasise deference towards broader constitutional trends and political processes as an explanatory factor for the restrictive turn.[44]

4. CRISES: POLITICAL, JUDICIAL AND PRAXEOLOGICAL CONTESTATION

Union citizenship has been engulfed in a threefold crisis revolving around political, judicial and social controversies. First, citizens' rights are questioned politically in several Member States. To be sure, free movement had been discussed earlier, for instance during the original Treaty negotiations and regarding posted workers in the 1990s.[45] Yet, the intensity of the discussion increased after the 2004 enlargement. 'Polish plumbers' and the Services Directive became household names in France in the run-up to the unsuccessful referendum on the Treaty

---

[41] See Bonjour, Saskia: Speaking of Rights: The Influence of Law and Courts on the Making of Family Migration Policies in Germany, Law & Policy 38 (2016), 328–48; and Everson, Michelle: A Citizenship in Movement, GLJ 15 (2014), 965, 966–7.

[42] For an instructive categorisation, see Dougan, Michael: The Bubble that Burst: Exploring the Legitimacy of the Case Law on the Free Movement of Union Citizens, in: Maurice Adams/Johan Meeusen/Gert Straetmans/Henri de Waele (eds), Judging Europe's Judges: The Legitimacy of the Case Law of the European Court of Justice Examined (Hart, 2013), 127–54.

[43] See generally Yong, Adrienne: The Rise and Decline of Fundamental Rights in EU Citizenship (Hart, 2019), ch 5; Wesemann, Anne: Citizenship in the European Union: Constitutionalism, Rights and Norms (Edward Elgar Publishing, 2020), ch 6; Giubboni, Stefano: Free Movement of Persons and European Solidarity: A Melancholic Eulogy, in: Herwig Verschueren (ed), Residence, Employment and Social Rights of Mobile Persons: On How EU Law Defines Where They Belong (Intersentia, 2016), 78–88.

[44] See the Court's President Lenaerts, Koen/Gutiérrez-Fons, José: Epilogue on EU Citizenship: Hopes and Fears, in: Kochenov (ed.), *EU Citizenship and Federalism* (n. 28), 751–80; and a former Advocate General, writing jointly with a Spanish law professor, Sarmiento, Daniel/Sharpston, Eleanor: European Citizenship and Its New Union: Time to Move On?, in: Kochenov (ed.), *EU Citizenship and Federalism* (n. 28), 226–42.

[45] See the historic study by Goedings, Simone A.W.: Labor Migration in an Integrating Europe. National Migration Policies and the Free Movement of Workers 1950–1968 (SDU Uitgevers, 2005), chs 3–5; and Davies, Paul: Posted Workers: Single Market or Protection of National Labour Law Systems?, CML Rev. 34 (1997), 571–602.

establishing a Constitution for Europe,[46] and several Member States engaged in contentious practices against Union citizens of Roma ethnicity.[47] The question of welfare benefits was one of the hottest topics in the debate prior to the Brexit referendum.[48] Yet, it was not only the British who were sceptical. The governments of the Netherlands and Austria have repeatedly argued against expansive citizens' rights for family members from third states and what they present as 'welfare tourism', which the German government has also tried to reduce by limiting access to social benefits.[49] Academic commentators have interpreted the cautious contents of the Free Movement Directive 2004/38/EC as a call for judicial restraint.[50]

Second, a number of judgments during the 2010s were perceived by some as a legal challenge of Union citizenship by judges backtracking on the spirit of innovative earlier rulings. Three themes stand out among the multi-faceted case law: access to social benefits by citizens who are not economically active, culminating in the *Dano* and *Alimanovic* judgments;[51] the immigration status of third country national family members in the aftermath of the *Ruiz Zambrano* ruling;[52] and residence rights of criminal offenders.[53] These judicial developments will take centre stage in Parts II and III of this Handbook. They also draw our attention to other trends that receive less attention, although they present crucial aspects of the legal evolution as well. Brexit, by contrast, has not resulted in many court cases. Still, it reinvigorated the interest in various forms of differentiation citizenship and free movement under association agreements. They will be addressed in Part IV.

Third, the normative concept underlying Union citizenship is defined, as we have seen, by an inbuilt instability stemming from the absence of a widely shared understanding of supranational citizenship. Controversial elements include relations between the national

---

[46] See Barnard, Catherine: Unravelling the Services Directive, CML Rev. 45 (2008), 323, 325–31.

[47] See Gehring, Jacqueline S.: Free Movement for Some. The Treatment of the Roma after the European Union's Eastern Expansion, EJML 15 (2013), 7–28; O'Nions, Helen: Roma Expulsions and Discrimination: The Elephant in Brussels, EJML 13 (2011), 361–88.

[48] See Curtice, John: Why Leave Won the UK's EU Referendum, JCMSSI 55 (2017), 19–37; Reynolds, Stephanie: (De)Constructing the Road to Brexit: Paving the Way to Further Limitations on Free Movement and Equal Treatment?, in: Thym (ed.), *Questioning EU Citizenship* (n. 10), 57–88.

[49] See exemplarily Austrian Ministry of the Interior, German Federal Ministry of the Interior, Dutch Ministry of Security and Justice, UK Home Office: Letter to the Irish Presidency of the Justice and Home Affairs Council, March 2013; as well as Blauberger, Michael/Heindlmaier, Anita/Kramer, Dion/Sindbjerg Martinsen, Dorte/Sampson Thierry, Jessica/Schenk, Angelika/Werner, Benjamin: ECJ Judges Read the Morning Papers. Explaining the Turnaround of European Citizenship Jurisprudence, Journal of European Public Policy 25 (2018), 1422–41; and the contributions to Damay, Ludivine/Delledonne, Giacomo/Mercenier, Heidi/Ni Chaoimh, Eadaoin (eds), La libre circulation sous pression. Régulation et dérégulation des mobilités dans l'Union européenne (Bruylant, 2018).

[50] See Coutts, Stephen: The Court, the Legislature and the Co-Construction of a Status of Social Integration, in: Cambien/Kochenov/Muir (eds), *European Citizenship under Stress* (n. 21), 113–34; van den Brink, Martijn: Justice, Legitimacy and the Authority of Legislation within the European Union, ML Rev. 82 (2019), 293–318.

[51] See the contributions to Part IV of this Handbook.

[52] See Yong, *Rise and Decline* (n. 43), chs 3–4; Neier, Christina: Der Kernbestandsschutz der Unionsbürgerschaft (Nomos, 2019); Thym, Daniel: Family as Link: Explaining the Judicial Change of Direction on Residence Rights of Family Members from Third States, in: Herwig Verschueren (ed), *Residence, Employment and Social Rights* (n. 43), 11–38.

[53] See Coutts, Stephen: Citizenship, Crime and Community in the European Union (Hart, 2019); Hamenstädt, Kathrin: Expulsion and 'Legal Otherness' in Times of Growing Nationalism, EL Rev. 45 (2020), 453–70.

and supranational levels[54] and the normative justification for transnational equality.[55] What is more, the praxeological turn of the social sciences away from institutions towards social practices and street-level agency has led to a burgeoning literature on performative citizenship on the ground.[56] The findings of these studies often contrast with the optimistic vision of legal analyses by highlighting that citizenship practices have had a limited impact on identificatory patterns and transnational solidarity.[57] There is no straightforward linkage between such findings and restrictive Court judgments, but they reiterate that 'integration through law' does not always succeed.

5. THE SIMULTANEITY OF PROGRESS AND RETROGRESSION

The incremental approach of the case law complicates the identification of trends and tendencies at a time when there are no major institutional developments besides court judgments (which may be a relevant observation in itself, indicating political preference for the maintenance of the status quo). The Court of Justice tends to build new doctrinal structures 'stone by stone' instead of presenting an overarching plan directly, as the examples of the legal status of third country national family members and the substance of rights test amply illustrate.[58] This incremental and experimental approach has the benefit of allowing judges to take on board feedback and criticism from domestic courts and political actors,[59] but it also means that the degree of novelty and generalisability will become apparent only gradually. The proverbial 'two steps forward, one step back' – or 'two steps back, one step forward' – often define the citizenship case law.

At an intermediate level of abstraction, the notion of non-linearity supports that trend. It corresponds to the idea of non-simultaneity, which is often used in the rhetorical phrase 'the

---

[54] See the contribution by Martijn van den Brink in this Handbook; and Bauböck, Rainer: Why European Citizenship? Normative Approaches to Supranational Union, Theoretical Inquiries in Law 8 (2007), 453–88.

[55] See de Witte, Floris: Justice in the EU. The Emergence of Transnational Solidarity (OUP, 2015); and Sangiovanni, Andrea: Solidarity in the European Union, OJLS 33 (2013), 213–41.

[56] See generally Isin, Engin F.: Performative Citizenship, in: Ayelet Shachar/Rainer Bauböck/Irene Bloemraad/Maarten Vink (eds), The Oxford Handbook of Citizenship (OUP, 2017), 500–23; and Bloemraad, Irene: Theorising the Power of Citizenship as Claims-Making, JEMS 44 (2018), 4-26.

[57] See Recchi, Ettore: Mobile Europe. The Theory and Practice of Free Movement in the EU (Palgrave Macmillan, 2015); Juverdeanu, Cristina: The Different Gears of EU Citizenship, JEMS 49 (2021), 1596–1612; and Menéndez/Olsen, *Challenging European Citizenship* (n. 11), ch 5.

[58] See the case studies by De Somer, Marie: Precedents and Judicial Politics in EU Immigration Law (Routledge, 2018), ch 8; and Langer, Jurian: EU Citizenship from the Cross-Border Link to the Genuine Enjoyment Test. Understanding the 'Stone-by-Stone' Approach of the Court of Justice, in: Jan van der Harst/Gerhard Hoogers/Gerrit Voerman (eds), European Citizenship in Perspective (Edward Elgar Publishing, 2018), 82–102.

[59] See Weiler, Joseph H.H.: Epilogue: Judging the Judges – Apology and Critique, in: Adams/Meeusen/Straetmans/de Waele (eds), *Judging Europe's Judges* (n. 42), 235, 247–8; and Schmidt, Susanne K.: The European Court of Justice and the Policy Process: The Shadow of Case Law (OUP, 2018), chs 3-4.

simultaneity of the non-simultaneous' (German: *Ungleichzeitigkeit des Gleichzeitigen*).[60] It is more than a play on words. It gained popularity through its use by philosopher Ernst Bloch, who coined it as a catchword in his cultural theory rejecting the rational impulse of historical teleology.[61] Bloch emphasised the coexistence of heterogeneous developments that may result in non-synchronous contradictions propelling the evolution of a given society in diverse directions.[62] Alternative outcomes remain conceivable. Union citizenship need not be set on a course of inevitable decline or permanent standstill.

Note that non-linearity means more than the binary confrontation between the expansion of citizens' rights ('two steps forward, one step back') and potential retrogression ('two steps back, one step forward'). Steps to the side or in a different direction are possible. Indeed, academic analyses might lose sight of the novelty factor of citizens' rights by focusing on cross-border mobility only. While it will be difficult for the Court to overrule principled statements on the purely internal situation, the substance of rights or social benefits, other themes might guide Union citizenship.[63] In particular, future innovations may move beyond the transnational by encompassing all Union citizens, not merely those on the move. To be sure, such case law would transcend the citizenship-specific rights listed explicitly in Article 20(2) TFEU. Instead, other rights and duties 'provided for in the Treaties'[64] may take centre stage: the Charter of Fundamental Rights, political participation or the effective realisation of public policy objectives to put flesh on the bones of Articles 2–3 TEU.[65]

Besides fundamental rights, at least four areas have witnessed judicial dynamism in parallel to the noticeable retrogression of the case law on social benefits. First, judges defended the political rights of Union citizens in situations not requiring a cross-border element, thus reinforcing the right to political participation in home states.[66] Second, the Court strengthened the right to acquire Union citizenship via state nationality and maintained that free movement guarantees continue to apply after naturalisation; in doing so, it effectively reinvigorated the responsibility of home states.[67] Third, it reinforced protection against extradition to third

---

[60] The concept was applied to the Union citizenship case law previously by Kostakopoulou, Dora/Thym, Daniel: Conclusion: The Non-Simultaneous Evolution of Citizens' Rights, in: Thym (ed.), *Questioning EU Citizenship* (n. 10), 309–22.

[61] See Bloch, Ernst: Tübinger Einleitung in die Philosophie (Suhrkamp 1964) building on the terminology of the cultural historian Pinder, Wilhelm: Das Problem der Generationen in der Kunstgeschichte Europa (Frankfurter Verlagsanstalt, 1926).

[62] Bloch, Ernst: Erbschaft dieser Zeit (Suhrkamp, 1962), published first in 1935, tried to elucidate the collapse of Germany's Weimar Republic into Nazi dictatorship.

[63] For an ever optimistic outlook, see Kochenov, Dimitry: EU Citizenship: Some Systemic Constitutional Implications, European Papers 3 (2018), 1061–74.

[64] See the first sentence of Article 20(2) TFEU.

[65] For a similar argument, see Sarmiento/Sharpston, 'New Union' (n. 44), 231–41.

[66] See ECJ, C-650/13 *Delvigne*, EU:C:2015:648; as well as Hyltén-Cavallius, Katarina: EU Citizenship at the Edges of Freedom of Movement (Hart, 2020), ch 6; and Shaw, 'Contrasting Dynamics' (n. 23), 597–608.

[67] See ECJ, *Tjebbes et al.*, C-221/17, EU:C:2019:189; and ECJ, *Lounes*, C-165/16, EU:C:2017:862, paras 45–52; as well as Strumia, Francesca: Supranational Citizenship's Enablers: Free Movement from the Perspective of Home Member States, EL Rev. 45 (2020), 507–25; and de Groot, David A.J.G.: Free Movement of Dual EU Citizens, European Papers 3 (2018), 1075–1113; see also Reynolds, Stephanie: Union Citizenship: Placing Limitations on a Human-Centred Approach?, in: Nuno Ferreira/Dora Kostakopoulou (eds), The Human Face of the European Union (CUP, 2018), 155–86.

states, again by emphasising the connection to the state of nationality.[68] Fourth, it extended classic free movement guarantees to family relations that had traditionally been excluded, such as gay marriage or Muslim adoption,[69] and reaffirmed the generous interpretation of existing guarantees regarding, by way of example, financial resources.[70]

None of the above undoes the restrictive tendencies of the judgments on social benefits and the standstill of the case law on residence rights of third country national family members. It indicates, however, that alternative outcomes remain possible. Several chapters in this Handbook chart new directions which the institutional practice might explore in the future.

Finally, even the absence of judicial innovation does not render Union citizenship superfluous. To the contrary, more than ten million Union citizens are permanently residing in a Member State other than that of their nationality, and many more are exercising free movement rights temporarily. The absence of further innovation does not reverse the protective credentials of the case law that is being upheld by domestic courts and the Court of Justice on an almost daily basis throughout the Union. That is a major achievement after more than 50 years of legislative and judicial dynamism. Union citizenship may not have fulfilled some of the initial expectations, but it remains alive and kicking – and a fascinating area of legal research, embedding the doctrinal detail into theoretical and contextual analyses.

---

[68] See ECJ, *Petruhhin*, C-182/15, EU:C:2016:630; ECJ, *Pisciotti*, C-191/16, EU:C:2018:222; Coutts, Stephen: From Union Citizens to National Subjects: *Pisciotti*, CML Rev. 56 (2019), 521–40.

[69] See ECJ, *Coman et al.*, C-673/16, EU:C:2018:385; ECJ, *SM*, C-129/18, EU:C:2019:248.

[70] See ECJ, *Bajratari*, C-93/18, EU:C:2019:809; ECJ, *Subdelegación del Gobierno en Ciudad Real*, C-836/18, EU:C:2020:119.

PART I

THEORETICAL EXPLORATIONS

2. The power of the norm: EU citizenship as constitutional right

Anne Wesemann[1]

1. INTRODUCTION

European Union citizenship has been dragged, almost kicking and screaming, to the forefront of the Brexit debate. It is a shy concept, embracing those holding the status under a cloak, hiding issues such as barriers to movement and access to welfare and social services that others face very visibly. Brexit challenges the political and normative understanding of EU citizenship by threatening that it will become 'a lost status' for some and limiting the effects of the status for others.

The narrow understanding of the norms' functioning fuels these threats, while at the same time seemingly dismissing the constitutional character and influence of EU citizenship. The norms are read as a rigid rule, given precise and narrow effect through secondary legislation. This chapter will, however, discuss Articles 20 and 21 TFEU as open-textured constitutional rights norms, willing to be influenced by external factors in their scope and able to face challenges effectively through a focus on the balancing of individual interests and the consequential re-scoping of the norm itself.

The concept of constitutional rights norms applied here follows Robert Alexy's theory of constitutional rights. This approach focuses on the structure of norms and sees two different norm categories: principles and rules. These co-exist within a constitutional framework but show different characteristics and consequently react differently when in conflict. EU citizenship Treaty norms will be read as principles, meaning their scope will be re-evaluated in each applied scenario. In doing so, the scope of each norm is adjusted according to a balance between the individual's situation and political, treaty-external legal and societal contexts. EU citizenship is therefore a constitutional right, entrenched through constitutional rights norms.

CJEU case law applying Articles 20 and 21 TFEU shows how the Court's reasoning and judgment reflects the constitutional rights norms characteristics of the Treaty provisions. Cases such as *Zambrano* (C-34/09) and *Rottmann* (C-135/08) show a clear resemblance to Alexy's constitutional rights norm characteristics, where the Court seemingly widened the scope of the norms. *Lounes* (C-165/16) is a more recent example of the Court re-evaluating the scope and meaning of EU citizenship in line with societal developments.

Analysing EU citizenship in this way connects constitutionalising efforts with the need for adaptability. EU citizenship as a fundamental status within EU law provides constitutional relevance while at the same time ensuring required flexibility in the light of political and societal challenges. The norm itself consequently provides us with the tools to embrace the challenges ahead.

---

[1] This contribution is based on an excerpt of the monograph *Citizenship in the European Union: Constitutionalism, Rights and Norms* published October 2020 by Edward Elgar Publishing.

While the focus of this chapter will be the establishment of European Union citizenship as a constitutional rights norm within the European Union constitutional framework, the analysis will commence with Alexy's reflections on the German constitutional framework (Grundgesetz – Basic Law). This is because Alexy's approach to norm structure and functionality can be applied to European Union treaty provisions, and European Union citizenship in particular.[2]

2. CONSTITUTIONAL RIGHTS NORMS

Robert Alexy introduces the concept of constitutional rights norms by assessing the possible definition of constitutional rights, and the discourse around norm theory and norm collision. Following this structure, this chapter will prepare the analysis of European Union citizenship as a constitutional rights norm by introducing the aforementioned elements of Alexy's approach. The differentiation of rules and principles, which is part of Alexy's norm theory discourse, is a key element of this analysis and will be given particular attention.

2.1 Constitutional Rights

Constitutional rights are expressed through normative statements.[3] Each normative statement expressing such right is a constitutional rights norm. Constitutional rights are consequently identified through assessment of substance of the norm expressed by the normative statement. Those seeking to define constitutional rights with a focus on the substance of the norm view 'constitutional rights as protecting an extremely broad range of interests but at the same time limitable by recourse to a balancing or proportionality approach'.[4] This applies horizontally, between individual right holders, as well as vertically, between the right holder and a public body or the state itself. Human rights are one example of constitutional rights in many constitutional legal frameworks.[5] Loughlin, in aiming to establish a concept of constitutional rights, discusses how far 'the term should be reserved for that category of natural rights that are retained by the people when the constitution of government is devised' and as such 'are enumerated' within a constitutional document.[6]

It is not just the substance but also the format in which constitutional rights are presented by which the constitutional 'quality' of rights is assessed.[7] Schmitt viewed constitutional rights as a substantive element of 'the foundation of the state'.[8] The purpose of rights is to support

---

[2] Robert Alexy, *A Theory of Constitutional Rights* (OUP 2002) 30.
[3] Alexander Heinold, *Die Prinzipientheorie bei Ronald Dworkin und Robert Alexy* [The principle theory of Ronald Dworkin and Robert Alexy] (Duncker & Humblot 2011) 177.
[4] Ibid 1, 10.
[5] Carl Wellman, *The Moral Dimensions of Human Rights* (OUP 2010) 127 ff.
[6] Martin Loughlin, *Foundations of Public Law* (OUP 2010) 344.
[7] Kai Möller, 'Balancing and the Structure of Constitutional Rights' (2007) 5 International Journal of Constitutional Law 453–68, 453 https://doi.org/10.1093/icon/mom023 accessed 10 January 2020.
[8] Carl Schmitt, 'Verfassungsrechtliche Aufsätze [*Essays in Constitutional Law*]. Grundrechte und Grundpflichten' [*Constitutional Rights and Constitutional Duties*] in Carl Schmitt, *Verfassungsrechtliche Aufsätze* [*Essays in Constitutional Law*] (1973) 190.

and form a liberal state and, within that, qualify as individual liberty.⁹ Schmitt established his approach on the basis of the German Weimar Constitution, which never came to fruition but was manipulated in order to support Hitler's democratic uprising and legalise his actions.¹⁰ The main issue with Schmitt's definition is that it makes the characterisation of constitutional rights dependent on the definition of the State.¹¹

Alexy's approach is itself focused on norm structure and therefore adds little to the debate on substantive characteristics of constitutional rights.¹² It is useful to consider a selection of means to identify these norms, instead of aiming for one clear-cut definition. One group of norms clearly deserving of the title 'constitutional rights provisions' is that of norms expressing the guarantee of a subjective right.¹³ Another indicator is the norm's position within the constitutional text.¹⁴ While the former involves a substantive element, the latter again focuses on structure – albeit of the legal text, not only the norm itself.¹⁵ The characterisation of constitutional rights can therefore be developed around a mix of substantive or formal, even structural, definitions and approaches.

2.2 Derivative Constitutional Rights Norms

The identification remains limited to a specific constitutional text, as the constitutional right entrenched is limited in the same way. In Alexy's case the context is the Basic Law only and it initially focuses on directly expressed constitutional rights. These norms present a right through their open-textured structure, as they aim to secure an 'extremely broad range of interests'.¹⁶ This open-textured norm alone and in of itself cannot, however, provide enough clarity on the right entailed and protected.

This is where Alexy introduces *zugeordnete* constitutional rights norms, translated by Rivers as derivative norms.¹⁷ These derivative norms can be created through case law, in specific circumstances even academic commentary, which defines crucial terminology and consequentially scopes the constitutional right entrenched within the text of the constitution.¹⁸ The example Alexy uses relates to the freedom of sciences as entrenched by Art. 5 (2)

---

⁹ Ibid 206.
¹⁰ Karl Polak, *Die Weimarer Verfassung: ihre Errungschaften und Mängel* [*Weimar's Constitution: Its Accomplishments and Deficiencies*] (Kongressverlag 1948); Christoph Gusy, 'Die Weimarer Verfassung zwischen Überforderung und Herausforderung' [*Weimar's Constitution between Overextension and Challenge*] (2016) 55(3) Der Staat 291–318; Jürgen Brokoff, *Die Apokalypse in der Weimarer Republik* [*The Apocalypse within Weimar's Republic*] (Fink 2001).
¹¹ Alexy (2002) 31.
¹² Ibid. Critical: Kai Möller, *The Global Model of Constitutional Rights* (OUP 2012) 2. Möller views his work as 'a substantive moral theory of rights, [which] can thus be read as offering a constructive response to what [he regards] as deficiencies in Alexy's methodology'.
¹³ Möller (2007) 453; Alexy (2002) 32.
¹⁴ Möller (2007) 453.
¹⁵ Identifying constitutional rights norms in this way has its limitations. Alexy provides one example for the limits of this approach through Article 93 (1) No. 4 of the Basic Law: Alexy (2002) 32.
¹⁶ Möller (2012) 1.
¹⁷ While *derivative* expresses the supposedly secondary nature of these constitutional rights norms, *conjugated* would describe the relationship between constitutional rights norms within the Basic Law and those linked to them more efficiently, as the German term *zugeordnet* does not necessarily express a secondary nature.
¹⁸ Alexy (2002) 33 ff.

GG. This constitutional rights norm is supported by decisions of the Federal Constitutional Court defining the meaning of scientific activity.[19] Derivatives close the open texture of the main norm to some extent, as they are relevant to specific situations only, whereas the full open-texture constitutional rights norm remains applicable generally. Denying these derivative norms constitutional status would be denying their constitutional relevance in relation to the substance and structure of constitutional rights norms.[20] It is the relationship between the constitutional rights norms and their derivatives that clarifies and substantiates the constitutional right(s) entailed. It is the constitutional rights norms' open texture that facilitates this process and consequently awards constitutional character to specific court decisions, which provide substantive and structural qualifications of the relevant norm within the constitution.

This open texture is reflected in the principle character of constitutional rights norms. Alexy differentiates, like others before him, between rules and principles as norm categories or concepts of a norm.[21]

2.3 Rules and Principles

The varying approaches are, however, often confusing, applying inconsistent terminology and contributions to the discourse, using the terms 'norm' and 'principle' almost as opposites – suggesting principles are not norms – or using them interchangeably.[22] This chapter follows Alexy's approach by discussing rules and principles as norm concepts. Both are like norms present in legal texts, whether they are of constitutional quality or not. In that way, the differentiation between rules and principles is not per se a constitutional matter but a norm-theoretical one, proposing a formal and structural norm definition.

There are varying perspectives within norm theory regarding the identification and differentiation of rules and principles.[23] Some view it as a 'superfluous commonplace' that 'unnecessarily complicates' the issues it is seeking to address.[24] Others accept a structural difference between rules and principles but view it as not a fundamental difference, rather a 'gradual

---

[19] Ibid, in reference to BVerfGE 35, 79 (113).
[20] Alexy (2002); Michael Kleiber, *Der grundrechtliche Schutz künftiger Generationen* [*Future Generations' Constitutional Protection*] (Mohr Siebeck 2014).
[21] Among others: Oliver W Holmes, 'The Common Law' (1881) American Bar Association 35, 78 f; Roscoe Pound, 'Common Law and Legislation' (1908) 21(6) Harvard Law Review 383–407; Karl N Llewellyn, *The Common Law Tradition* (Little, Brown and Company 1960); Joseph Raz, 'Legal Principles and the Limits of Law' (1972) 81(5) Yale Law Journal 823–54; Ronald Dworkin, *Taking Rights Seriously* (Harvard University Press 1977); Josef Esser, *Grundsatz und Norm in der richterlichen Fortbildung des Privatrechts* [*Principle and Norm in Judicial Education in Civil Law*] (J.C.B. Mohr 1956).
[22] See on terminology Esser (1956).
[23] Heinold discusses these as *Übereinstimmungsthese* (congruence thesis), *schwache Trennungsthese* (weak partition thesis) and *starke Trennungsthese* (strong partition thesis): Heinold (2011) 182 ff.
[24] Graham Hughes, 'Rules, Policy and Decision Making' (1968) 77(3) The Yale Law Journal 411–39, 419; András Jakab, *European Constitutional Language* (CUP 2016) 369–74.

logical difference'.²⁵ Principles are merely argued to be 'norms of relatively high generality', with rules being perceived as narrower in scope.²⁶

A third group is represented by Alexy's approach, as well as by Dworkin. Both see a clear differentiation between principles and rules as norm categories.²⁷ Alexy introduces principles as 'optimization requirements'.²⁸

2.3.1 Optimization requirements

According to Alexy, norms which 'require something be realized to the greatest extent possible given the legal and factual possibilities' are principles.²⁹ These norms can be satisfied to varying degrees and are seeking to be realised to their optimum. As the circumstances in which the principle is to be realised change, the degree to which it achieves fulfilment will vary. The factually possible is determined through the situation to which we want to apply the principle. The legally possible, however, depends on those norms (principles and rules) that limit the principle at hand, by either contradicting it directly or infringing on its scope by establishing rights that interfere with their substance. These characteristics are evident when analysing the principle in relation to other (conflicting/competing) norms.

In contrast to principles, rules have a binary character. A rule either applies to a situation or not. There is no variation in the degree of satisfaction, fulfilment or generality when it comes to rules: 'In this way rules contain fix points in the field of the factually and legally possible.'³⁰

This is an abstract, structural differentiation, which acknowledges that norms do not fulfil identical purposes and functions and consequently present different characteristics. It is worth noting that the concept of optimization requirements, while alien to other legal frameworks, is by now a well-established perception of norms within the German legal framework. Alexy first discussed the concept of optimization requirements in 1979 and published his constitutional rights thesis in 1985.³¹

In acknowledging that not all norms function equally when applied and interpreted, we accept that there are different norm categories. The advantages of a clear distinction will become more apparent when we explore how rules and principles function in what Alexy calls *Prinzipienkollision* and *Regelkonflikt*.³²

---

²⁵ Heinold (2011) 183; Raz discusses the degree to which Dworkin's differentiation is fitting: Raz (1972) 825 ff. Also: Jan-Reinard Sieckmann, *Regelmodelle und Prinzipienmodelle des Rechtssystems* [*Models of Rules and Principles within the Legal System*] (Nomos 1990).
²⁶ Alexy (2002) 45.
²⁷ Ibid 47 ff; Heinold (2011) 184; Dworkin (1977) 24, 41 ff.
²⁸ Alexy (OUP 2002) 47 ff; Also referred to as 'optimization obligations': Aulis Aarnio, 'Taking Rules Seriously' (1990) 42 Achiv für Rechts- und Sozialphilosophie 180–92, 187 ff.
²⁹ Robert Alexy, 'Zum Begriff des Rechtsprinzips' (1979) 1 Rechtstheorie 59–87, 79 ff; Alexy (OUP 2002) 47.
³⁰ Ibid 48.
³¹ Alexy (1979); Robert Alexy, *Theorie der Grundrechte* (Suhrkamp 1994). Critical: Joachim Englisch, *Wettbewerbsgleichheit im grenzüberschreitenden Handel* [*The Level Playing Field in Transborder Trade*] (Mohr Siebeck 2008) 21 ff; Johannes Dreier, *Die normative Steuerung der planerischen Abwägung* [*Normative Governance in Planning Law Consideration*] (Duncker & Humblot 1995) 121 ff.
³² The discussion of norm collision (*Normenkollision*) is inherent to German constitutional law and German legal theory. Internationally, the discussion is best reflected through international private law.

2.4 Norm Collision

Rules and principles as two norm versions interact differently when opposing norms are relevant to the same scenario. It is this interaction, or norm collision, that highlights the different characteristics of both norms.[33]

2.4.1 Conflicting rules

According to Alexy, principles and rules solve situations of norm collision differently, which in turn serves as evidence that these two norm categories exist and are distinguishable. As rules either apply or do not, there can be no gradual difference to their relevance and applicability to a situation. Where two rules apply but they arrive at contradicting legal ought judgments, either one of the rules can be viewed as the exception to the other, or one rule is declared to be invalid.[34] In a significant difference from principles, the relationship between conflicting rules remains in place even after the specific situation arose. If one rule cannot be the exception to the other, it will need to be 'excised from the legal system'.[35] The invalidity is indefinite and does not depend on the 'factually or legally possible' in any given situation. The relationship between the two rules cannot be altered by the circumstances of differing situations, as it is not one of degree.

2.4.2 Competing principles

Principles act differently in a norm collision, which is a consequence of their ability to present the fulfilment or satisfaction of their scope in varying degrees. In addition, the established relationship between two contradicting or competing principles is not permanent. The defeated principle will not be 'excised' from the legal system, for in a different scenario it may see a different fate.[36] While a collision of rules consequently results in a statement regarding validity, the outcome of a collision of principles is one of 'weight'.[37]

These collision situations are the simplest form of norm collision, as both opponents belong to the same category of norms. The norm collision most interesting for this chapter and the discussion of EU citizenship as constitutional rights norm is that between principles. This collision gives rise to the 'law of competing principles'. Alexy shows how the collision of principles cannot operate in the abstract but does depend on the individual circumstances of each case. He concludes: 'The circumstances under which one principle takes precedence over another constitute the condition of a rule which has the same legal consequences as the principle taking precedence.'[38] The collision of competing principles is solved as soon as one

---

[33] Heinold discusses norm collision in greater depth, albeit Alexy does not see the need for clarification in his approach. Those engaged in the debate disagree on whether rules entailing exceptions prevent a collision from occurring: Heinold (2011) 189 ff.

[34] Alexy (2002) 49.

[35] Ibid. This excision can take different forms, examples being *lex posterior derogate legi priori* (later law repeals an earlier law) or *lex specialis derogate legi generali* (special law repeals general law).

[36] Alexy uses the term *Prinzipienkollision*, while Rivers translates this into 'competing principles'. Rivers' translation focuses on the principal characteristics and speaks well to the weighing and balancing part of the solution process, while Alexy at this point seems to focus on presenting the issue as one of norm collision: Alexy (2002) 50.

[37] Alexy uses Dworkin's 'concept of a dimension of weight' here: Dworkin (1977) 26 f.

[38] Alexy (2002) 54.

of these principles is given effect over the other by establishing a rule. That the result of the principle collision formulates a rule sits well with the common law understanding and application of the doctrine of precedent. A court decision can create a new norm, as a version of the legislated norm. We will see the degree to which the law of competing principles applies to the CJEU jurisprudence in EU citizenship and whether it is reflected in the reasoning and reference to previous case law.

Alexy's law of competing principles is not uncontested. Jakab is adamant that a structural differentiation between rules and principles is 'superfluous', as 'the problems of applying the law it explains can be explained without it'.[39] While he disagrees with any structural differentiation between rules and principles, he proposes that what Alexy discusses as principles are simply rules with a 'scope which is uncertain because of the vague and general expressions contained in their linguistic form'.[40] Jakab consequently agrees with Alexy's assessment of constitutional rights norms as open-textured and needing clarification. He may be critical of a clear structural difference between rules and principles, but his criticism does not survive closer scrutiny, as he overlooks the equality that the norms involved in a collision can hold in a case.[41] When reviewing CJEU cases in the area of EU citizenship, the discussion about rules and principles and their differentiation will continue, aiming to show how this particular norm theory approach enhances the analysis of constitutionally significant case law within the European constitutional framework.

3. EUROPEAN UNION CITIZENSHIP

Before engaging with the relevant case law, we consider the unique concept of EU citizenship itself. It can be positioned in relation to other non-national citizenship concepts and its constitutionalising effect will inform the characterisation of EU citizenship as a constitutional right within the context of constitutional rights norms. Overall, a holistic approach to EU citizenship is needed, encompassing perspectives 'from history, politics, law and sociology'.[42]

EU citizenship is often referred to in connection to discussions of transnational citizenship, or 'citizenship beyond the state'.[43] Post-Maastricht Treaty literature in particular refers to the Union's citizenship concept when discussing valuable, potential or even dismissible concepts of transnational citizenship.[44] Linklater dubbed it a 'weak [starting point] but [...] encouraging

---

[39] Jakab (2016) 374.
[40] Ibid.
[41] Ibid 373 ff.
[42] Dora Kostakopoulou, 'European Union citizenship rights and duties, civil, political and social' in Engin F Isin and Peter Nyers (eds), *Handbook of Global Citizenship Studies* (Routledge 2014) 427–36, 427.
[43] Among others: Andrew Linklater, *The Transformation of Political Community: Ethical Foundations of the Post-Westphalian Era* (Polity Press 1998) 183; Haldun Gülalp, 'Citizenship and Democracy beyond the Nation-state?' (2013) 25(1) Cultural Dynamics 29–47, 42; Jürgen Habermas, 'Citizenship and National Identity: Some Reflections on the Future of Europe' (1992) Praxis International 1–19, 1; John Hoffman, *Citizenship beyond the State* (Sage 2004) 161; Dora Kostakopoulou, 'Union citizenship as a model of citizenship beyond the nation-state: possibilities and limits' in Albert Weale and Michael Nentwich (eds), *Political Theory and the EU* (Routledge 1998) 158–71.
[44] Stefan Kadelbach, 'Union Citizenship' in Armin von Bogdandy and Jürgen Bast (eds), *Principles of European Constitutional Law* (Hart 2010) 443–77, 444.

legal and moral innovations from which more extensive developments may grow'.[45] Habermas asked whether 'there can ever be such a thing as European citizenship', arguing that 'genuine civil rights do not reach beyond national borders'.[46] Habermas' point remains valid. It is the substance of EU citizenship, notwithstanding the Court's proclamations of fundamentality, which determines how far the EU citizenship status is meaningful to those holding it and to those arguing the case for 'citizenship beyond the state'.

3.1 Design and Reality

While EU citizenship was formally established by the Maastricht Treaty in 1993, it took some time for it to be effectively implemented.[47] Owing to the Court's interventions, the concept shifted from *Marktbürgerschaft* to a more meaningful independent status, albeit there still being a long way for the concept to fulfil its full potential.

The concept shifted from a narrow definition of EU citizenship, as creating and enabling the market citizen, towards a subjective rights-based approach focusing on the individual rather than their economic activity.[48] EU law moved from mainly, if not solely, protecting the economic freedom to act to guaranteeing free development of the individual, with a particular focus on free movement.[49] The scope and content of EU citizenship rights, however, remain contested.

While some view the EU citizen as empowered by individually enforceable rights and privileges,[50] others are far more critical of the actual content of EU citizenship.[51] Eleftheriadis argues that there is no meaningful separate status of EU citizenship, and that Member State nationals are rather subject to 'rights under reciprocity, whenever they become active economic agents or stakeholders in another member state'.[52] EU Citizenship is seen as a victim of the EU's flawed structure, as it can only become a meaningful status 'when the Union becomes a multi-national federal state'.[53] MacCormick sees a constitutionalising effect of EU citizenship, but only where there is 'a sense of European civic identity, and therewith a European civic *demos*'.[54]

Whether EU citizenship is of constitutional significance or not seems to depend on the way in which one assesses its value for the individuals holding the status. The more one views the citizen as being empowered through the scope and content of the relevant norms, the more gravitas the status holds within the EU framework. It all depends on the 'dissonance between

---

[45] Linklater (1998) 183.
[46] Habermas (1992) 9.
[47] Reich discusses how EU citizenship, as provided for in the Treaties, is only providing subjective rights in a selective manner. In discussing the subjective rights of EU citizens, he looks for a 'grassroot democracy' enabled through a constitutional structure based on subjective rights: Norbert Reich, *Buergerrechte in der Europaeischen Union* [*Citizen Rights in the European Union*] (Nomos 1999) 48 ff.
[48] Among others: Ibid 53; Kadelbach (2010) 444.
[49] Reich (1999) 53.
[50] Ibid 148 f.
[51] Pavlos Eleftheriadis, 'The Content of European Citizenship' (2014) 15 German Law Journal 777–96.
[52] Ibid 792.
[53] Hoffman (2004) 17.
[54] Neil MacCormick, 'Democracy, Subsidiarity, and Citizenship in the "European Commonwealth"' (1997) 16(4) Law and Philosophy 331–56, 342.

European citizenship's constitutional design and reality'.⁵⁵ To create harmony – or, better still, identity – the legally established rights within the status of EU citizenship need to match citizen expectations and pass the test of reality in the Court when confronted with Member State-attempted limitations of the impact of the status.

EU citizenship has significantly contributed to the transformation of the EU.⁵⁶ At first, the EU's focus was on 'consolidating, rather than constitutionalising' and an 'adaptive stabilisation' of the meaning of EU citizenship, while scholars were vastly critical of even the relevance of the status.⁵⁷ Eventually, 'Union citizenship raised citizen expectations' as conferring and protecting specific rights.⁵⁸ The CJEU saw itself increasingly challenged to clarify the meaning of EU citizenship but also its positioning to other rights and principle provisions like the free movement provisions of the single market, most of all free movement of workers (Article 45 TFEU) and non-discrimination (Article 18 TFEU).⁵⁹ Eventually, the challenges of a post-national citizenship status inextricably linked to national citizenship became more and more apparent, as Member States saw their sovereignty over matters of exclusive competence, such as when to withdraw nationality after naturalisation, threatened.⁶⁰ As the Court outgrew its role as faithful servant of the interests of the Member States,⁶¹ it seemed to transform itself into a citizen court.⁶² Where there was a focus on 'free movement of labour', a shift towards 'equal treatment' and consequently non-discrimination followed.⁶³ Mobility was followed by equality and this is where the allegiance as EU citizens is formed: 'A European public that is freed from nationalistic trappings and mythical foundations, is comfortable with diversity, values inclusion by replacing nationality with domicile, and actively seeks the deepening of democracy at all levels of governance.'⁶⁴ Embracing means of public participation, as and where possible, is one element of that.⁶⁵ We can see EU citizenship as a 'self-actualization [and] for connectivity and reciprocal equal recognition'.⁶⁶ Within that reciprocal recognition

---

⁵⁵ Dora Kostakopoulou, 'Ideas, Norms and European Citizenship: Explaining Institutional Change' (2005) 68(2) Modern Law Review 233–67, 265.
⁵⁶ Ibid 235 ff; Linklater (1998) 188.
⁵⁷ Supra Kostakopoulou (2005) 244 ff, viewing this in the context of politics and appetite for change at the time.
⁵⁸ Ibid 246 in reference to the Second Report from the Commission on Citizenship of the Union, COM (97) 230.
⁵⁹ Case C-85/96 *Maria Martinez Sala v Freistaat Bayern* EU:C:1998:217; Case C-413/99 *Baumbast and R v Secretary of State for the Home Department* EU:C:2002:493; Case C-168/91 *Christos Konstantinidis v Stadt Altensteig – Standesamt and Landratsamt Calw – Ordnungsamt* EU:C:1993:115; Case C-224/98 *Marie-Nathalie D'Hoop v Office national de l'emploi* EU:C:2002:432.
⁶⁰ Case C-184/99 *Rudy Grzelczyk v Centre public d'aide sociale d'Ottignies-Louvain-la-Neuve* EU: C:2001:458; Case C-148/02 *Carlos Garcia Avello v État belge* EU:C:2003:539; Case C-135/08 *Janko Rottmann v Freistaat Bayern* EU:C:2010:104; Case C-34/09 *Gerardo Ruiz Zambrano v Office national de l'emploi (ONEm)* EU:C:2011:124.
⁶¹ A phrase borrowed from Dora Kostakopoulou (2005) 256 in reference to Geoffrey Garrett, Roger Daniel Kelemen and Heiner Schulz, 'The European Court of Justice, National Governments, and Legal Integration in the EU' (1998) 52 International Organisation 149–76.
⁶² Supra Kadelbach (Hart 2010) 443; Dora Kostakopoulou, *Citizenship, Identity and Immigration in the EU: Between Past and Future* (Manchester UP 2001) 68.
⁶³ Ibid 428.
⁶⁴ Ibid 431.
⁶⁵ Kostakopoulou (2005) 240.
⁶⁶ Ibid.

lies the sense, if not duty, of social solidarity.[67] There is transformative capacity within a solidarity approach that can be seen as central in the constitutional arrangements of the EU in general and EU citizenship in particular.[68]

3.2 Constitution and Structure

EU citizenship has real relevance within the constitutional framework of the Union. It is, in an experimental way, pushing the limits of the constitutional understandings of Member States and Union alike.[69] It is seen as a transformative force, enabling as well as demanding institutional and constitutional change.[70] EU citizenship's 'fundamentality' has been shaped by CJEU case law and entrenched by secondary legislation, and continues to be defined through EU citizens themselves in their exercise of rights and responsibilities. It has impacted the 'political constitution of the EU' as much as the 'juridical'.[71] It has led to institutional reform and continues to inspire the Court to inform the EU's constitutional framework.[72] The rights, responsibilities and status of EU citizenship have driven these constitutional developments. The norm itself, however, also provides us with clues regarding its constitutional relevance.

Through its introduction with the Maastricht Treaty, EU citizenship occupied a constitutionally crucial place within the amending Treaty.[73] Introduced as part of the Treaty's constitutional principles, the relevance of the provision for the EU's constitutional framework has been evident from the start.[74] Articles 20 and 21 TFEU sit within part II of the TFEU, together with non-discrimination provisions.

Reviewing EU citizenship as a constitutional rights norm within the EU legal order supports the aforementioned constitutional transformations, developments and reforms through its characteristics and as a source for derivative norms. Its open texture has allowed and required the establishment of a series of derivative constitutional rights norms, be it in the form of case law or directives and regulations.[75] All three categories derive their fundamentality and con-

---

[67] Kostakopoulou (2014) 434.
[68] Malcolm Ross, 'Solidarity – A New Constitutional Paradigm for the EU?' in Malcolm Ross and Yuri Borgmann-Prebil (eds), *Promoting Solidarity in the EU* (OUP 2010) 23–45, 36 f.
[69] Kostakopoulou sees the need for EU citizenship to be experimental: Kostakopoulou (2014) 434.
[70] Linklater (1998) 185; Agustín José Menéndez, 'Which Citizenship? Whose Europe? The Many Paradoxes of European Citizenship' (2014) 15 German Law Journal 907–33, 932; Kostakopoulou (2014); Ross (2010); Reich (1999) 48; Jo Shaw, *The Transformation of Citizenship in the EU* (CUP 2007); Carlos Closa Montero, 'Between EU Constitution and Individuals' Self: European Citizenship' (2001) 20(3) Law and Philosophy 34571; Agustín José Menéndez, 'A Theory of Constitutional Synthesis' in John Erik Fossum and Agustín José Menéndez (eds), *The Constitution's Gift* (Rowman & Littlefield 2011) 45–76, 71. More critical: Antje Wiener and Vincent Della Salla, 'Constitution-making and Citizenship Practice: Bridging the Democracy Gap in the EU?' (1997) 35(4) Journal of Common Market Studies 595–614; Joseph HH Weiler, *The Constitution of Europe* (CUP 1999) 344 f.
[71] Richard Bellamy, 'The "Right to Have Rights": Citizenship Practice and the Political Constitution of the EU' in Richard Bellamy and Alex Warleigh (eds), *Citizenship and Governance in the EU* (Continuum 2001) 41–70, 50 ff.
[72] Kostakopoulou (2014); Closa Montero (2001).
[73] Massimo La Torre, 'Citizenship, Constitution and the EU' in Massimo La Torre (ed.), *European Citizenship: An Institutional Challenge* (Springer 1998) 435–57, 436.
[74] Ibid.
[75] Alexy (2002) 36.

stitutional relevance from the constitutional rights norm established through the TFEU, while they fulfil their clarifying and substantiating function.[76]

The role of the Court in engaging with the gaps between secondary legislation and primary treaty legislation, visualised through cases brought before it, is crucial when analysing the norm structure and constitutional role of EU citizenship. It was, and continues to be, the Court that ensures that a system of rights protections exists where EU citizenship is concerned.[77]

4. EUROPEAN CONSTITUTIONAL RIGHTS NORMS

EU citizenship shifted the focus from economically driven policies towards issues of European democracy, legitimacy and, especially, European constitutionalism.[78] Its constitutionalising characteristic is enabled and reflected by the way its outlining norm is structured, which links to Alexy's approach.

The following sections will view EU citizenship as a constitutional rights norm within the EU legal order, applying the concept as a principle that, in its fundamentality and subjective rights, seeks to be fulfilled to the optimum extent possible, when balanced with other principles, such as intergovernmental considerations, Member State obligations and concerns and institutional effectiveness.[79]

4.1 Rules and Principles

The basis of Alexy's norm differentiation was introduced previously. We need to evidence that European Union citizenship is indeed a principle before we can argue that the principle's characteristics influence the Court's application of the norm. In doing so, we need to ensure that the argument does not become a circular one, as relying on Court reasoning can serve both the differentiation of rules and principles and the evidence of principle functionality. Generally, we will see the characteristics of principles reflected in the way the Court engages with the principle of proportionality and in the balancing and weighing of interests. As these interests are entrenched through right-bearing norms, in our example EU citizenship, the exercise of balancing can be treated as a reflection on their structural characteristics as principles. Additionally, the way in which the Court reasons in cases where it relies on Articles 20 and 21 TFEU and Directives will reflect the open texture of the EU citizenship norms, in line with Alexy's analysis.[80]

In order for us to test the relevance of Alexy's theory of constitutional rights in the context of European Union law, we need to determine whether his differentiation between rules and principles is as visible within the EU legal framework as it is within the context of German constitutional law. The cases of *Rottmann* and *Zambrano* will be our starting point.[81]

---

[76] Ibid 35.
[77] Reich (1999) 56.
[78] Kostakopoulou (2005) 233.
[79] Ibid 48.
[80] Alexy (2002) 33 ff.
[81] Case C-135/08 *Janko Rottmann v Freistaat Bayern* EU:C:2010:104, ECR 2010 I-01449; Case C-34/09 *Gerardo Ruiz Zambrano v Office national de l'emploi (ONEm)* EU:C:2011:124, ECR 2011 I-01177.

4.1.1 *Rottmann* and *Zambrano*

Rottmann, Austrian by birth, was in danger of becoming stateless and losing his EU citizenship as Germany had withdrawn his naturalisation as German due to fraudulent behaviour by Rottmann himself.[82] Rottmann had lost his Austrian citizenship, in accordance with Austrian law, when naturalising as German. Before even discussing the citizenship issue, the Court had to show that it was right to hear and decide the case at all. After all, Rottmann was arguably, until recently, a naturalised German engaged in legal proceedings with German authorities: a purely internal situation, with consequently no reason for the Court to be involved and EU law to be applied.[83]

Zambrano concerns third-country national parents of EU citizen minors who were refused residence rights and working permits in Belgium, risking the Zambrano family's forced removal. Here the question of Court jurisdiction was even more prominent, as the EU citizens of the family had never exercised their free movement rights and were again battling regulations by their Member State of origin.

This is not how the Court views it. Rather, and with using Article 20 TFEU in an almost self-evident manner, the Court in *Rottmann* declares with reference to *Micheletti* that the matter at hand is one within EU law, as 'Member States must, when exercising their powers in the sphere of nationality, have due regard to EU Law'.[84] The EU law to which it explicitly refers is its own ruling on the fundamental status of EU citizenship.[85] The fundamentality of Article 20 TFEU consequently pulls matters of Member State competence into the realm of EU law. While others view this as a judicially activist extension of EU competence, it can just as convincingly be perceived as first evidence for the constitutional rights norm character of EU citizenship.[86]

In *Zambrano* the Court relied heavily on Articles 20 and 21 TFEU in its reasoning and, while they were relevant to the case, made no reference to the right to family life or other provisions. Crucially, the Court held that any measure that 'deprive[s EU citizen minors] of the genuine enjoyment of the substance of the rights attaching to the status of European Union citizen' is prohibited by Article 20 TFEU.[87] While some received *Zambrano* as the 'next logical step' in the Court's attempt to 'increase the scope of EU citizenship step by step' or 'stone by stone', others view it as a fundamental extension of competences and scope.[88]

---

[82] Ibid I – 01481.
[83] Ibid I – 01486 para 38.
[84] Ibid I – 01487 para 45.
[85] Ibid para 43.
[86] Among others: Kristine Kruma, 'A Hopeful Transmission: Searching for Citizenship beyond the State' (2015) 17 European Journal of Migration and Law 361–93, 366 ff; Hans Ulrich Jessurun d'Oliveira, Gerard Rene de Groot and Anja Seling, 'Court of Justice of the European Union: Decision of 2 March 2010, Case C-315/08, Janko Rottmann v. Freistaat Bayern Case Note 1 Decoupling Nationality and Union Citizenship? Case Note 2 The Consequences of the Rottmann Judgment on Member State Autonomy – The European Court of Justice's Avant-Gardism in Nationality Matters' (2011) 7, 1 European Constitutional Law Review 138–60.
[87] *Zambrano* I – 1253.
[88] Guth and Mowlam (2012) 80; Lenaerts (2015) 2 ff; Lenaerts (2013) 1351 ff; Dimitry Kochenov, 'A Real European Citizenship: A New Jurisdiction Test: A Novel Chapter in the Development of the Union in Europe' (2011) 18(1) Columbian Journal of European Law 55–109, 91 ff; Thomas Horsley, 'Reflections on the Role of the Court of Justice as the "Motor" of European Integration: Legal Limits to Judicial Lawmaking' (2013) 50(4) CML Rev 931–64; Anja Lansbergen and Nina Miller, 'Court

4.1.2 EU citizenship as principle

Looking at the norm itself now, Article 20 TFEU clearly states that only those persons holding the nationality of a Member State are citizens of the European Union. The normative statement is clear. The rights awarded in Articles 20 ff are awarded to those that hold the nationality of one of the Member States only. Reading Article 20 TFEU as a rule, we can simplify it to mean: EU citizens are those who are nationals of a Member State. The normative statement is then to be read as a rigid expression of a norm, meaning: only Member State nationals shall be EU citizens. Considering this rule, Rottmann loses his EU citizenship status the moment German citizenship is rescinded, as the rule ceases to apply to him. The Zambrano parents will not fall under the protection of the norm, as they are not EU citizens themselves.

Considering the Court's reasoning in both cases, however, we see no indication that the Court applied these norms with a view to applying rigid rules. Where the Court reasoned the fundamentality of EU citizenship, it made it very clear in *Rottmann* that it was 'by reason of [the situation's] nature and its consequences' that the case was brought into the remit of EU law. The fact that the ultimate loss of rights, with the loss of EU citizenship, was imminent provided the Court with jurisdiction over the case. The nature and consequences of the loss of citizenship concern the Court. It refers to the functionality of the norm within the EU legal order, but also its relevance for the individual affected. While the norm's semantics merely state who can be an EU citizen, the Court reads it also as entailing statements regarding its fundamentality, the rights awarded to the individual in norms following Article 20 TFEU and consequences of its loss. It does not apply the norm in a rigid manner, but rather contextualises it as sitting within a network of provisions influencing one another.

This becomes even more evident when considering *Zambrano*, a case that has significantly impacted the EU's legal framework and free movement law within the EU context.[89] It is a difficult case to examine by focusing on Court reasoning alone, as the Court provides us with 'frustratingly' little.[90] The Court spends all but three pages – ten paragraphs – responding to the questions submitted for preliminary ruling.

It is *Rottmann* that informs the analysis of *Zambrano*, which becomes particularly apparent in AG Sharpston's opinion.[91] AG Sharpston sees *Zambrano* as a next step in relation to *Rottmann*, particularly in overcoming the fact that again the situation is focused on one Member State only, without any cross-border element.[92] We will return to *Zambrano*'s more substantial discussion later and will here focus on the way the Court pulls the scenario into

---

of Justice of the European Union European Citizenship Rights in Internal Situations: An Ambiguous Revolution? Decision of 8 March 2011, Case C-34/09 *Gerardo Ruiz Zambrano v. Office national de l'emploi (ONEM)*' (2011) 7(2) European Constitutional Law Review 287–307.

[89] Case C-34/09 *Gerardo Ruiz Zambrano v Office national de l'emploi (ONEm)* EU:C:2011:124, ECR 2011 I-01177 [*Zambrano*]; Jessica Guth and Edward Mowlam, 'The Evolution of European Union Citizenship – Where Does Zambrano Take Us?' (2012) 46(1) The Law Teacher 75–82; Koen Lenaerts, 'EU Citizenship and the European Court of Justice's "Stone-by-Stone" Approach' (2015) 1 International Comparative Jurisprudence 1–10; Koen Lenaerts, 'How the ECJ Thinks: A Study on Judicial Legitimacy' (2013) 36(5) Fordham International Law Journal 1302–71, 1354 ff; Ferdinand Wollenschläger, 'The Judiciary, the Legislature and the Evolution of Union Citizenship' in Philip Syrpis (ed.), *The Judiciary, the Legislature and the EU Internal Market* (CUP 2012) 302–30.

[90] Lansbergen and Miller (2011) 287.

[91] Opinion of Advocate General Sharpston delivered on 30 September 2010. Case C-34/09 *Ruiz Zambrano* EU:C:2010:560, ECR 2011 I-01177, Opinion of AG Sharpston, I–1206 ff.

[92] Ibid I-1206, para 95.

an EU law context, again arguably widening the scope of the provision and its jurisdiction and therefore showing the principle character of the norm.[93] Whereas in *Rottmann* the Court argued based on the 'nature and consequence' of the loss of citizenship, in *Zambrano* it reasoned that 'Article 20 TFEU precludes national measures which have the effect of depriving citizens of the Union of the genuine enjoyment' of their EU citizen rights.[94] In *Rottmann*, the threat of having EU citizenship withdrawn pulled the case into the Court's jurisdiction, whereas in *Zambrano* the impact on the ability to enjoy the rights conferred through that status were sufficient to achieve the same result.

Were Article 20 TFEU to be read as a rule, the scope of the provision could not be easily widened. Its fundamentality could not be influenced and strengthened by consideration of individual scenarios. The rule would either apply (arguably in *Rottmann* it would not, whereas in *Zambrano* it would) or not. It would then in its scope either award protection in the specific situation, or not. The *Zambrano* case would not have been decided satisfactorily if Article 20 TFEU would have been read as a hard-set rule.

This is a reflection of the open texture of EU citizenship provisions, Article 20 TFEU being the focus. Its fundamentality, rights and functionality only become apparent as they are applied within the wider context of EU law, tested in relation to Member State legal orders and even international law.[95] It is only in this way that the norms come to fulfil their function within the specifics of the legal system to which they are applicable. Otherwise they remain abstract, applicable to the narrowest of cases with limited applicability and functionality – not what the Court views EU citizenship to be.

Now that we can see how characterising Article 20 TFEU as a principle, in norm category terms, is supported by the way the Court enables its application in these cases, we can see whether Articles 20 and 21 TFEU behave like optimisation requirements.

4.2 Competing Optimization Requirements

It is overly simplistic to differentiate between rules and principles by way of their scope alone. Moreover, we need to investigate how far Alexy's characterisation of principles as optimization requirements is reflected by the EU citizenship Treaty norms.

4.2.1 *Zambrano* revisited

The *Zambrano* case appeals to this analysis as the Court decided to widen the scope of the EU citizenship principle in such a way that the norm extends rights beyond the remit of the EU citizen itself. Arguably, the principle of EU citizenship has a different optimum fulfilment in this case than in, for example, *Rottmann*, and consequently the scope is extended to that new optimum scope, within the factually and legally possible.

Within *Zambrano* a conflict of norms arises where the Court reasons with the established fundamentality as opposed to the interests of the Member States and their sovereignty in immigration policy matters. We know the result: the EU citizen rights of the Zambrano children are to be extended, in their effect, to the third-country national parents; but how does the Court

---

[93] Lenaerts (2013) 1342 ff; Horsley (2013) 934 ff.
[94] *Zambrano* I – 1252, para 42, referring to *Rottmann* I – 1487, para 42.
[95] In *Rottmann* the Court gives particular consideration to the Convention on the reduction of statelessness and the Universal Declaration of Human Rights: *Rottmann* I – 1489, paras 52–53.

get to this point? It engages in an exercise of balancing and weighing of opposing principles in order to determine the optimum substance of the principle entailed within the EU citizenship provisions, in line with the factually and legally possible.

The norm principle(s) of EU citizenship, within its core, entails the protection of the rights of the individual EU citizen by awarding them a specific status. In opposition to this stand the norms governing Member States' sovereignty in immigration matters.[96] European Union citizenship is consequently contested by these provisions determining Member State interests.

On the one hand, the Court had to consider the risks for Member States and the impact on their policies and policymaking powers. It had to consider the Member States' arguments regarding the status of the Zambrano parents as undocumented migrants and the consequential irregular employment without a working permit over a considerable time period, as in doing this the Zambranos were in breach of domestic law.[97] On the other hand, it had to consider the rights of the Union citizens, the two Zambrano children born in Belgium. The Court does not, in the little reasoning we are given, diminish the Member State interests or disprove their application to the case at hand. Within the process of balancing, the Court rather declares that depriving 'the genuine enjoyment of the substance' of EU citizen rights derived from the status of EU citizenship itself is prohibited within the scope of the EU citizenship treaty norms.[98] It consequently alters the legally possible, pushing the existing substance of the norm further, extending its scope to outweigh the opposing norm. It extends Article 20 TFEU to mean not only 'EU citizens' but also non-EU citizen 'carers where [the EU citizens] are minors'.[99]

This particular extension of the *ratione personae* speaks partly to Alexy's radiation thesis.[100] He discusses the 'radiating effect' of constitutional rights norms in relation to horizontal effect and his approach is firmly situated within German constitutional rights theory, relying on jurisprudence of the FCC. This part of his approach wants to show how constitutional rights norms influence not only the state–citizen but also the citizen–citizen, or third party, relationship. As another 'effect of constitutional rights and constitutional rights norms on the legal system', this relationship is impacted as well, as these norms 'embody an objective order of values, which applies to all areas of law'.[101] Considering the approach the Court of Justice took in *Zambrano*, it is arguable that a similar radiating effect arises from EU citizenship provisions. Although it remains defensive of rights between the citizen and the state (here Belgium), the provision radiates onto non-right holders in order to prevent the loss of rights for the right holders themselves. The Court significantly expands the core of citizenship and consequently allows this norm principle room to radiate, in its effects, onto individuals who do not qualify as protected individuals themselves. In doing so, it further limits the scope of the opposing norms governing Member State interests. EU citizenship is of such fundamentality that it radiates onto non-EU citizens in order to prevent significant limitation to the fundamental status of

---

[96] No assumption is made on the norm characteristics (rules or principles) of Member State interests.
[97] *Zambrano* I – 1243 ff.
[98] *Zambrano* I – 1252, para 42.
[99] Kochenov (2011) 64 ff.; Chiara Raucea, 'European Citizenship and the Right to Reside: "No One on the Outside Has a Right to be Inside?"' (2016) 22(4) European Law Journal 470–91; Stephen H Legomsky, 'Rationing Family Values in Europe and America: An Immigration Tug of War between States and their Supra-national Associations' (2011) 25(4) Georgetown Immigration Law Journal 807–58.
[100] Alexy (2002) 352 ff.
[101] Ibid 352.

Union citizenship. The Court also provides a limitation of this radiation with the enjoyment principle. Radiation is only triggered where there is the possibility that the core Union citizen be deprived 'of the genuine enjoyment of the substance of the rights conferred by virtue of their status as citizens of the Union'.[102] The principle of Union citizenship therefore does not automatically radiate onto non-protected individuals. Only when a directly protected individual has their rights significantly impacted due to another individual falling out of scope of the protecting norm does this specific radiating effect of the norm become apparent. The Court creates some form of trigger in *Zambrano*, viewing the EU citizen minors' immediate danger of forfeiting the enjoyment of their citizenship rights as the element allowing the radiating effect.

Consequently, our analysis of the legally possible suggests that EU citizenship is optimising its scope through radiation. In line with Alexy's thesis, this result does not render the opposing principle completely and indefinitely invalid, which a conflict between norm rules might. In this particular scenario, the Court decision reflects the optimum fulfilment of the optimisation requirements in the EU citizenship constitutional rights norm. It does, for identical conflicts, create a rule regarding the decision of this case: the genuine enjoyment test.[103]

Zambrano was received as almost revolutionary in furthering EU citizenship rights.[104] We have seen how the interests of the individuals outweighed those of the public authorities and Member States.

4.2.2 *Chavez-Vilchez*

Zambrano left us wondering: where does EU citizenship go from here?[105] *Chavez-Vilchez* promised some insight, as the claimants' situation was comparable: the case saw eight third-country nationals, all mothers to EU citizen minors, claiming a right to reside together with access to child benefits.[106] The Court therefore relied unsurprisingly heavily on *Zambrano* and the genuine enjoyment test in its reasoning.[107] In *Zambrano* the Court constructed 'derivative residence rights' stemming from a 'relationship of strong dependence between third-country nationals and the Union citizen family members'.[108] Applying the theory of constitutional rights norms, we saw a radiation of the children's EU citizenship onto the non-EU citizen parents.[109] In *Chavez-Vilchez* the situation of each of the families involved differed, which Advocate General Szpuna acknowledged by offering solutions under Directive 2004/38 and Articles 20 and 21 TFEU.[110] The Court, however, while agreeing that the situations dif-

---

[102] *Zambrano*. I – 1252 par 42.
[103] Ibid para 45.
[104] Lenaerts (2013) 1351 f; Kochenov (2011) 80 f.
[105] Guth and Mowlam (2012).
[106] Case C-133/15 *H.C. Chavez-Vilchez and Others v Raad van bestuur van de Sociale verzekeringsbank and Others* EU:C:2017:354.
[107] Ibid, paras 36, 49, 53, 60 ff, 65, 69.
[108] Fulvia Staiano, 'Derivative Residence Rights for Parents of Union Citizen Children under Article 20 TFEU: Chavez-Vilchez' (2018) 55(1) CML Rev 225–41, 226.
[109] The term derivative was avoided so not to create a confusion with Alexy's derivative constitutional rights norms.
[110] Opinion of Advocate General Szpunar delivered on 8 September 2016. Case C-133/15 *H.C. Chavez-Vilchez and Others v Raad van bestuur van de Sociale verzekeringsbank and Others* EU:C:2016: 659, Opinion of AG Szpunar, paras 48 ff.

fered, found in each scenario the need to bring the case directly under Article 20 TFEU.[111] It also distinguished its judgment from the AG opinion with its complete silence on any aspects of the principle of proportionality, to which AG Szpuna had devoted a whole section and substantial aspects of his argument.[112]

The lack of direct reference to the principle of proportionality does not mean the Court did not engage in an exercise of balancing and weighing of opposing interests. The norms opposing one another in *Chavez-Vilchez* see EU citizenship on the one side, and the Netherlands' legislation concerning the right to reside and access to child benefits of third-country national parents to EU citizen minors on the other.[113] The domestic legislation also required the consideration of the children's best interest in deciding this case.[114]

We know that any norm conflict establishes with its solution a new rule that can then, should the factually and legally possible be identical, be re-applied to other cases where the same norm conflict arises. The Court saw *Chavez-Vilchez* as such a case, re-applied the *Zambrano* rule of genuine enjoyment to the conflict of norms and found it to solve the norm conflict.[115] While applying the *Zambrano* rule, the Court also offered a more detailed understanding of the norm principle of EU citizenship and the rule itself. It was the first time the Court was able to clarify the *Zambrano* rule in relation to situations where an EU citizen parent was available for care.[116] Instead of taking this as reason to distinguish the case from *Zambrano* and consequently needing to engage in another process of balancing and weighing, it saw the *Zambrano* rule to be applicable, viewing the EU citizenship scope to be applicable in the same way as it was in *Zambrano* and not in any way narrowed.

Chavez-Vilchez allows us to see how the Court works with established rules on norm conflicts. The way the Court refers to *Zambrano* without an explicit process of balancing of interests indicates that it did not see a need to do so, as the result of that process in *Chavez-Vilchez* was pre-determined through the *Zambrano* rule. Legal certainty was created, although at least one of the norms involved was an open-textured principle, requiring optimisation.

4.2.3 *Lounes*

Lounes is a case that was received with particular interest in the UK due to the political climate in which the judgment came through: the case concerned a dual British–Spanish citizen, and only a couple of months before the judgment was passed, the UK had given notice of its intention to withdraw as a Member State.[117]

Lounes, an Algerian national, married Ormazábal, a Spanish citizen by birth who, in addition, naturalised as British. Lounes was served a removal notice from the UK authorities upon applying for a residence card as spouse to an EU national.[118] The case was referred

---

[111] *Chavez-Vilchez*, paras 48–58.
[112] Opinion of Advocate General Szpunar, paras 94–97.
[113] No analysis is offered on the norm character and structure of the domestic norms of the Netherlands.
[114] *Chavez-Vilchez*, paras 70–72.
[115] Ibid, para 72.
[116] Fulvia Staiano (2018) 232.
[117] Case C-165/16 *Toufik Lounes v Secretary of State for the Home Department* EU:C:2017:862.
[118] Summarising the case: Alina Tryfonidou, 'What's wrong with the UK immigration rules governing the rights of dual-British and EU citizens? Comment on the Lounes reference' (2016) EU Law Analysis Blog http://eulawanalysis.blogspot.com/2016/03/whats-wrong-with-uk-immigration-rules

to the CJEU, with the questions focusing on the application of Directive 2004/38, which seemed to limit the Court in its scope. The Court, however, started its judgment outlining the relevance of Article 21 TFEU in the given scenario. It needed to assert the relevance of the Treaty provision, as the Directive could not apply in situations where 'nationals […] enjoy an unconditional right of residence', which was the case for Ormazábal as a British–Spanish citizen.[119] AG Bot assessed how Ormazábal's 'legal situation [had] been profoundly altered, both in EU law and in national law, on account of her naturalisation', leading to the 'paradoxical' exclusion of Ormazábal from the scope of the Directive, as she was now fully integrated into her host Member State.[120] Consequently, Lounes could not rely on the Directive in seeking to establish a derived right to reside from Ormazábal's residency rights.

Integration is the key element of this case. Both the Court and AG Bot focused on the integrational aim of Directive 2004/38. AG Bot assigned the Directive's offering of permanent residency the status of a 'genuine vehicle for integration', taken to 'its logical conclusion' by Ormazábal when she naturalised.[121]

Lounes shows the presence and relevance of integration particularly in relation to EU citizenship, bringing it to the forefront of the 'ever closer Union'. The Court used integration as a means to differentiate Ormazábal's situation from that of non-dual British citizens. It argued:

> it would be contrary to the underlying logic of gradual integration that informs Article 21 (1) TFEU to hold that such citizens, who have acquired rights under [Directive 2004/38] as a result of having exercised their freedom of movement, must forgo those rights […] by becoming naturalised in that Member State.[122]

Ormazábal acquired the permanent right to reside under the Directive while she lawfully resided in the UK. She lost the right to reside as awarded to her by the Directive when she naturalised, as she then gained residency rights intrinsic to her British citizenship status. The Court argued that this differentiates her from a UK–EU citizen who has never exercised free movement rights and consequently cannot rely on EU law.[123]

The case is similar to *Zambrano*, as it widens the scope of the principle of EU citizenship. The Court focused on the integration element within EU citizenship. It argued that integration within the EU and among its people is included within the norm Article 21 TFEU. In EU citizenship cases before *Lounes*, the Court arguably saw no need to explicitly express this part of the principle within Article 21 TFEU. More convincingly, though, the Court extended the scope of Article 21 TFEU in order to close a gap between the Treaty norm and the Directive that would otherwise occur in situations like that in *Lounes*. Following this reasoning, the Court found that Lounes can rely on his wife's EU citizenship status when seeking the right to reside. The scope of the constitutional rights norm of Article 21 and the principle entailed

---

.html accessed 30 March 2021; Steve Peers, 'Dual citizens and EU citizenship: clarification from the ECJ. EU Law Analysis Blog' (2017) EU Law Analysis Blog http://eulawanalysis.blogspot.com/2017/11/dual-citizens-and-eu-citizenship.html?m=1 accessed 30 March 2021; *Lounes,* paras 14–27.

[119] *Lounes*, paras 37, 42.

[120] Opinion of Advocate General Bot delivered on 30 May 2017. Case C-165/16 *Toufik Lounes v Secretary of State for the Home Department* EU:C:2017:407, Opinion of AG Bot, paras 61 ff.

[121] Ibid, para 85.

[122] *Lounes*, para 58.

[123] Sara Iglesias Sánchez, 'Purely Internal Situations and the Limits of EU Law: A Consolidated Case Law or a Notion to be Abandoned?' (2018) 14(7) European Constitutional Law Review 7–36.

also award protection to dual citizens, when the dual nationality is the result of furthered integration.

This is not a case where principles compete; rather, the open texture of the constitutional rights norm in Article 21 TFEU is reflected in the way the Court brings out the integrational elements and seeks to connect the TFEU norm with the Directive. The Court is allowed to do so, as the norm does not make a narrow normative statement that either applies or not. Instead, it expresses a principle, seeking to be fulfilled to the greatest extent possible.

5. CONCLUSION

An objective analysis to complement the assessment of subjective rights can serve as an effective tool in an otherwise politically heated debate, Brexit being one example. European Union citizenship is therefore only one of many constitutional rights norms within the European Union legal framework. Other examples are the single market provisions within the TFEU. Overall, bringing an appreciation of norm structure to the attention of EU legal scholars is an attempt to enhance the analysis of the EU's constitutional order, and Alexy's theory of constitutional rights has proven a valuable asset in assessing EU citizenship's functionality and role within the EU's legal framework.

EU citizenship is a principle that, in its fundamentality and subjective rights, seeks to be fulfilled to the optimum extent possible,[124] when balanced with other principles such as intergovernmental considerations, Member State obligations and concerns and institutional effectiveness. This is reflected by the CJEU's way of working with Articles 20 and 21 TFEU.

The open texture of these norms allows, and requires, norm-external factors to influence their scope. The cases discussed in this chapter only serve as exemplars, as Alexy's criteria for constitutional rights norms are reflected in many other cases.[125] Not all of these cases extend the scope of individual rights protected, which evidences that the norm's open texture can support both the widening and the narrowing of the scope, depending on what is factually and legally possible. This provides these norms with the necessary flexibility to fulfil their constitutional function effectively in an ever changing political European and global climate. The history of European Union citizenship case law shows how the CJEU seems to have taken one step forward and two steps back on various occasions. Reading these cases within the context of the political and societal factors of the time evidences how the norm is required to show a less rigid structure compared to that of other EU norms. EU citizenship's open texture allows the norm to effectively reflect those influences, enabling the CJEU to take these factors into account. In doing so, a structural and formal argument is gained in a debate of EU citizenship that is otherwise focused on rights content and substance. This is the valuable contribution made by an analysis of EU law through the lens of Robert Alexy's constitutional rights thesis: we are able to add objective criteria to an otherwise often subjective discourse.

---

[124] Alexy (2002) 48.
[125] Anne Wesemann, *Citizenship in the European Union: Constitutionalism, Rights and Norms* (Edward Elgar Publishing 2020).

3. A social-constructivist approach towards the evolution of EU citizenship

Martin Steinfeld

1. INTRODUCTION

A holistic examination of the overlap between the law and policy of EU citizenship necessitates a set of methodological approaches that can both explain and help to understand such an evolutionary and crucial concept in the wider context of European integration. This chapter attempts not to explain but to explore, in the sense of providing a framework for scholars in the field to conduct their own research. Supranational citizenship provides fertile ground for social constructivist scholars to explore because of its inherently essentially contested nature. Constructivists arguably commence from a standpoint of epistemological humility. The framework does not presuppose that it has a theoretical monopoly when examining any area of law or policy and, indeed, does not contain one monolithic theoretical and methodological approach, but encourages plurality and diversity within a core, and crucial, set of assumptions. It is a framework that articulates a nuanced social theory of change that can holistically encapsulate the interrelationship between law and policy, that places special emphasis on underlying (and often under-examined) normative propositions and that conceptualises institutions (defined in a multiplicity of ways) as vital sites of norms and identity formation. As a set of theoretical approaches, constructivism takes in various shades of exploration on a spectrum, ranging from a framework predisposed to outlining the development of contested norms to other authors predisposed to (more) critical deconstruction.

One core aspect of social constructivist approaches is that they can conceptualise law better than more black-letter approaches: approaches that struggle to engage law, for instance, in its inherently socio-political context. Constructivist approaches can, in part, conceptually map out the evolution of EU citizenship in terms of its past, present and potential future. Following this brief introduction, this chapter will try to outline EU citizenship studies' potential for constructivist research in three sections, all of which constitute cumulative building blocks upon which to evaluate and assess the potential for research in a particular substantive area of citizenship research. Section 2 will attempt to outline the core tenets of constructivism that are relevant to work in this area of law/policy. Section 3 will examine the need for such research and why it is important to outline such a need prior to any substantive examination using constructivist research methods. The final part of the job is, essentially, the so-called nuts and bolts of any potential project. This will involve outlining a particular version of such methods as adopted by the author, with a view to simply offer various options on the conceptual menu.

2. WHAT ARE THE RELEVANT CORE TENETS OF CONSTRUCTIVISM FOR THE PURPOSES OF EU CITIZENSHIP RESEARCH?

EU citizenship is, as has undoubtedly been repeatedly stated elsewhere in this volume, an inherently multifaceted and contingent concept. It clearly straddles a divide between law and policy/politics, and has normative underpinnings but with practical implications (particularly as elaborated by the CJEU).[1] It also has a past, a present and a future: a veritable kaleidoscope of genealogical research. Thus EU citizenship as a concept provides fertile ground for constructivist research because its core tenets are conducive to such interdisciplinary work, and it has sufficient malleability as a set of methodological approaches to shed new and unthought-of light even on a concept that has become so integral to European integration more generally. In its essence, constructivism encompasses a broad spectrum of theoretical approaches ranging from perspectives more closely aligned to mainstream systemic neoliberal and neorealist standpoints in international relations to those more comparable to poststructuralist discourse theory. In other words, while, as Adler famously stated, constructivism attempted to seize a 'middle ground' between two seemingly irreconcilable approaches in terms of positivist and post-positivist standpoints, the 'middle ground' itself can take various forms.[2] At its heart is the so-called ideational turn in the social sciences, where the study of ideas (not understood in an instrumental or superficial sense) is considered to be fundamental and where, essentially, 'ideas matter'. Constructivists of all shades and shapes, though, elaborate considerably further than this rather simple proposition, because it constitutes a set of theoretical approaches in which institutions and identity also 'matter'; crucially, constructivists attempt to theorise, articulate and elaborate upon the complex and nuanced relationship between these concepts. Equally, what perhaps unites all constructivists is a desire to ensure that the 'ideational turn' embedded in aspects of post-positivism has a lasting legacy in the form of a plurality of research agendas. Its whole purpose is therefore to have 'left the stage of meta-theorising and entered the realm of concrete empirical work'.[3] The conclusions reached as a result of a constructivist research project can and arguably should be illuminating in the sense of critically theorising, explaining and understanding social change in a manner that more straightforward legal or social scientific approaches would struggle with. These core concepts have some specificity to them, which needs to be elaborated upon.

2.1 The Role of the Ideational

For theorists who have embraced the 'ideational turn' in social scientific research, constructivist methodology opens up a hitherto under-theorised social world of possibilities. In order to

---

[1] See, for instance, Case C-184/99 *Rudy Grzelczyk v Centre public d'aide sociale d'Ottignies-Louvain-la-Neuve* EU:C:2001:458 [2001] ECR I 6193 (with clearly practical implications on the social welfare provisions of the applicant's host state) or Case C-34/09 *Gerardo Ruiz Zambrano v Office national de l'emploi (ONEm)* EU:C:2011:124 [2011] ECR I- 1177 (also with clearly practical implications on national immigration and citizenship law).

[2] Emanuel Adler, 'Seizing the Middle Ground: Constructivism in World Politics' (1997) 3(3) European Journal of International Relations, 319–63 at 320.

[3] Thomas Risse, 'Social Constructivism and European Integration' in Antje Wiener and Thomas Diez (eds), *European Integration Theory* (OUP 2004) 173.

truly encapsulate the notion that 'reality' itself is inherently socially constructed, a constructivist methodological framework needs to take into account the interrelationship between three key factors: ideas, material factors (which are not denied) and the crucial role of agency. In a constructivist sense, for 'ideas' to become truly ideational as such (rather than simply just 'words'), they have to have a specificity and resonance in specific contexts. This is a particularly important issue in the context of EU citizenship because of the inherent need for it (and arguably its failure) to derive such a resonance and sense of legitimacy among those who hold such a status.[4] Constructivist theorists vary in their characterisation of the ideational, but all place a crucial emphasis on the interrelationships between material and ideational factors. By suggesting that reality is socially constructed, constructivists claim to recognise that material factors (such as natural disasters) as well as human agency matter, but also that we should recognise that human life is inherently *social*, and therefore that ideas equally 'matter'. For constructivists 'ideas' is a generic term to describe discourse and social 'norms', and therefore, by contrast with conventional approaches, 'we need to take words, language and communicative utterances seriously'.[5] Constructivism claims that individuals ultimately subjectively create and re-create discourse but that, having done so, discourse takes on a life of its own that cannot be pinned down to one particular individual in a truly dialectical relationship. This is termed 'intersubjectivity'[6] and can be seen as an attempt to theorise how a subjective assertion becomes a social truth. Individuals create discourse through articulating subjective principles, but these principles (sometimes) become understood and accepted by others, and it is at this point that it becomes intersubjective: a norm or discourse.[7] This characterisation of 'ideas' is methodologically highly useful because it means that that researchers can outline this process and can do so in a multiplicity of ways. Some might focus on the evolution of a discourse or set of discourses; some might focus on, say, a cascade or diffusion of norms, placing, perhaps, greater emphasis on the instrumentality of their creation.[8] Fundamentally, though, constructivist methodology in all its various shapes or forms not only focuses on the role of the ideational in social life but does so in a way that can be explored, examined, extrapolated and ultimately systematised for the purposes of a concrete research agenda.

---

[4] See, for instance, Ryan Bakker, Liesbet Hooghe, Seth Jolly, Gary Marks, Jonathan Polk, Jan Rovny, Marco Steenbergen and Milada Anna Vachudova, 'Who opposes the EU? Continuity and change in party Euroscepticism between 2014 and 2019' (London School of Economics: 2020) https://blogs.lse.ac.uk/europpblog/2020/06/01/who-opposes-the-eu-continuity-and-change-in-party-euroscepticism-between-2014-and-2019/ accessed 18 September 2020 and Yoo-Duk Kang and Chang-Rhyong Oh, 'Spreading Euroscepticism and Its Macro-Level Determinants: Empirical Analysis of the Eurobarometer Survey in 2004–2017' (2020) 28(3) Journal of Contemporary European Studies, 348–65, 348–9.
[5] Thomas Risse, 'Social Constructivism', p.164.
[6] Ibid.
[7] Ibid.
[8] In terms of the former see Martin Steinfeld, *Fissures in EU Citizenship: The Deconstruction and Reconstruction of the Legal Evolution of EU Citizenship* (CUP 2021), upon which much of the thoughts in this chapter are based. In terms of the latter, see Thomas Risse and Kathryn Sikkink, 'The Socialization of International Human Rights Norms into Domestic Practices: Introduction' in Thomas Risse, Stephen C Ropp and Kathryn Sikkink (eds), *The Power of Human Rights: International Norms and Domestic Change* (CUP 1999) and Antje Wiener, *A Theory of Contestation* (Springer 2004).

2.2 The Iterative Role of the Agency within Institutional Environments

Constructivist research methods do not simply outline and articulate the evolution of norms or discourses (though that is an inherent aspect); they do so in a manner that attempts to extrapolate the nuanced emergence of such norms as created initially by individuals in often complex institutional environments. Constructivism is thus well suited to research on EU citizenship, because the concept has emerged as a result of social construction in a dialectical and iterative sense from a vast array of formal and informal institutional fora within the EU. Agency is important in this process, as 'well placed individuals, with entrepreneurial skills' still make an enormous difference in dictating whether what they say becomes normalised.[9] Nonetheless, constructivism recognises that individuals do not operate prior to society; they are deeply and inexorably immersed in it, and must be recognised as ultimately cognitive ever-changing beings. As Ruggie put it: 'Constructivism is about human consciousness and its role in international life.'[10] Identity, in other words (as will be outlined below), also 'matters', and the methodological individualism that tends to underpin conventional approaches cannot recognise that identities constantly change.[11] Constructivism claims that this happens through discourse in specific contexts – normally a multiplicity of institutional fora. In other words, institutions also 'matter', as they are social environments in which individuals interact and where identities (as well as ideas themselves) are formed.[12] Institutions are considered to be fundamental to constructivist theory because they act as 'conveyor belts for the transmission of norms',[13] which would include 'legal discourse',[14] and are 'effective agents of social construction'.[15] Constructivism also defines institutions broadly as 'a relatively stable collection of practices and rules defining appropriate behaviour for specific groups of actors in specific situations'.[16] A fundamental aspect of institutions as understood by (some) constructivists is the concept of an epistemic community. Haas maintains that 'an epistemic community is a network of professionals with recognized expertise and competence in a particular domain and an authoritative claim to policy-relevant knowledge within that domain or issue area'.[17] Likewise, as Mutschler put it (paraphrasing Haas), 'Epistemic communities have a shared

---

[9] Jeffrey T Checkel, 'Social Construction and European Integration' in Thomas Christiansen, Knud Erik Jørgensen and Antje Wiener (eds), *The Social Construction of Europe* (Sage 2001) 56.

[10] John Ruggie, 'What Makes the World Hang Together? Neo-utilitarianism and the Social Constructivist Challenge' (1998) 52(4) International Organization, 855–85, 856.

[11] Ibid.

[12] Thomas Risse and Antje Wiener, 'The Social Construction of Social Constructivism' in Thomas Christiansen, Knud Erik Jørgensen and Antje Wiener (eds), *The Social Construction of Europe* (Sage 2001) 202.

[13] Michael Barnett and Martha Finnemore, *Rules for the World: International Organizations in Global Politics* (Cornell UP 2004) 33.

[14] Ian Johnstone, 'The Power of Interpretive Communities' in Michael Barnett and Raymond Duvall (eds), *Power in Global Governance* (CUP 2009) 185–204, 201.

[15] Martha Finnemore and Kathryn Sikkink, 'Taking Stock: The Constructivist Research Program in International Relations and Comparative Politics' (2001) 4 Annual Review of Social Science, 391–416, 400.

[16] Martha Finnemore and Kathryn Sikkink, 'International Norm Dynamics and Political Change' (1998) 52 International Organization, 887–917, 891.

[17] Peter Haas, 'Introduction: Epistemic Communities and International Policy Coordination' (1992) 46 International Organization, 1–35, 3.

set of normative and principled beliefs, shared causal beliefs, shared notions of validity and a common policy enterprise'.[18] This methodological approach is particularly advantageous in the context of EU citizenship, because on one level this citizenship is a rather nebulous concept with somewhat opaque origins. While it is true that it was formally created at Maastricht in 1992, its normative roots can be traced to the period prior to its legal creation in both a legal and a socio-political sense and it has evolved considerably since 1992.[19] The advantage of constructivist methodology is that the ebbs and flows of its discursive construction can be thoroughly examined both within and beyond a number of EU institutions: be it the CJEU, the European Parliament, the Commission or indeed as reflected in the views of national parliaments and civic discourse more generally.

2.3 Citizenship as an Identity Construct

While it certainly could be suggested that EU citizenship is a nebulous concept, it is also inherently linked to a normative and emancipatory evolution towards postnational citizenship. It is in effect a global prototype which, if successful, could be exported elsewhere as a concept.[20] Conceptualised as such, constructivism is particularly useful as a set of research methods to examine the evolution of EU citizenship. Constructivism is capable of recognising the notion of citizenship for what it is – an identity practice as well as a legal concept – and it is a methodology that does not display fidelity to any particular institution or agent in examining its construction. Nonetheless, it suggests that institutions are important sites of not only norm construction but identity formation. As Adler maintains: 'Constructivists understand institutions as reified sets of intersubjective constitutive and regulative rules that, in addition to helping coordinate and pattern behaviour and channel it in one direction or another, also help establish new collective identities and shared interests of practices.'[21] In addition, it has the capacity to offer a profound critique of the evolution of EU citizenship. While it is certainly the case that the CJEU has developed an extensive legal portfolio on citizenship, this does not necessarily mean, as has already been stated, that there is an intimate connection between the specific discourse of EU citizenship as it has legally evolved and whether EU citizens themselves positively identify themselves based on their status. In this respect the evolution of the law on EU citizenship suffers from being derived within an epistemic community embedded within a form of technocratic elitism. As Finnemore and Sikkink state:

> Groups with specialized knowledge often have a common set of norms and world views; many scholars would argue that technical knowledge is never value neutral and always comes with an array of shared normative understandings that make it meaningful, therefore powerful, in social life. As they deploy their knowledge, these epistemic communities often disseminate new norms and understandings along with technical expertise. Consequently, they can act as powerful mechanisms of social construction.[22]

---

[18] Max Mutschler, *Arms Control in Space: Exploring Conditions for Preventive Arms Control* (Palgrave Macmillan, 2013) 54.
[19] See further: Steinfeld, *Fissures in EU Citizenship*, 1–36.
[20] See further: ibid, 269–341.
[21] Emanuel Adler, 'Constructivism in International Relations' in Walter Carlsnaes, Thomas Risse and Beth Simmons (eds), *Handbook of International Relations* (Sage 2002) 95–110, 104.
[22] Finnemore and Sikkink, 'Taking Stock', 402.

Indeed, Finnemore and Sikkink are even more critical of this process when they claim: 'Professions often serve as powerful and pervasive agents working to internalize norms among their members. Professional training does more than simply transfer technical knowledge; it actively socializes people to value certain things above others [...] lawyers all carry different normative biases systematically instilled by their professional training.'[23]

However, it is arguably this very process of norm diffusion, followed by dissemination and positive identification within a very specific epistemic community of EU lawyers in which a specific construction of EU citizenship emerged (for instance based on examining (and reifying) seminal cases such as *Grzelczyk* and *Ruiz-Zambrano*) and upon which a particular notion of citizenship as a form of postnational identification emerged.[24] If anything, there appears to be a cognitive dissonance between EU citizenship and identity as understood within such a technocratic environment and the wider world beyond it. Constructivist methodology can at least commence the process of examining why that might be the case in a holistic fashion, and perhaps suggesting that there might be fissures at the heart of a postnational identity construct created within an epistemic community of technocratic (legal) elites.[25]

2.4 A Theory of Social Change

Finally, a core tenet of constructivism is that by examining the evolution of agent-created norms within institutional environments embedding different notions of identification, it can examine the evolution of social change, often over many years. Once again, this standpoint is particularly important in the context of the evolution of and towards EU citizenship because constructivism is a theoretical approach that is perhaps uniquely capable of assessing it in all its socio-political and legal complexity. There are three core (and interrelated) aspects of a constructivist approach to social change that arguably stand it apart from other methodological approaches. First is its ability to lay bare social life for what it is: inherently contingent. Thus what is ultimately meant by the very phrase 'social constructivism' is that reality is what we make of it[26] and that it is therefore 'reformable'.[27] Change is seen to come about through a process of what has been termed 'social learning'[28] – a claim that individuals' identities evolve over time through interaction with others and discourse in a multiplicity of institutional environments.[29] Crucially, though, it is important to recognise that individuals change slowly. The concept of social learning is about theorising the incremental evolution of individual identities through a plethora of hitherto unrecognised and seemingly mundane day-to-day practices and routines.[30] In other words, ideas are seen to have material effects. Second, once inherent contingency is recognised, a whole new social world is opened up in which construc-

---

[23] Finnemore and Sikkink, 'International Norm Dynamics', 905.
[24] For instance in Dimitry Kochenov (ed.), *EU Citizenship and Federalism: The Role of Rights* (CUP 2017), some part of almost every chapter is dedicated to *Ruiz-Zambrano*.
[25] See further: Steinfeld, *Fissures in EU Citizenship*, 269–341.
[26] Alexander Wendt, 'Anarchy Is What States Make of It: The Social Construction of Power Politics' (1992) 46(2) International Organization, 391–425, 410.
[27] Dora Kostakopoulou, *Citizenship, Identity and Immigration in the European Union: Between Past and Future* (MUP 2001) 2.
[28] Checkel, 'Social Construction', 53.
[29] Ibid.
[30] Ibid.

tivism offers a qualitatively different view on the notion of citizenship. For a start, identities need not be monopolised by 'the state'. For Kostakopoulou, 'multiple identity is now normal' and Union citizenship is therefore perfectly possible.[31] Citizenship must therefore be recognised for being an identity practice like any other as it 'entails more than rights [...] it also contains a context-specific meaning which has been developed through social [...] practice' and is 'continually contested and rebuilt over time'.[32] Finally, constructivism simply views the EU differently. All theorists recognise the 'unique *sui generis* nature of the Community'[33] but constructivism goes further and sees it as a perfect example of an enormously complex process of 'social learning in action'. It 'is the most likely case for international institutions to have constitutive effects [...] it is an institutionally dense environment [...] with high levels of transnational [...] normative activity'.[34] Thus, there are several aspects of constructivism that make its approach qualitatively different from conventional approaches and can thus be conceptually useful in examining both the past and present of EU citizenship and projecting towards its future evolution.

In sum, constructivism is concerned with examining and theorising ideas, identity and institutions in tandem as the core elements that constitute social life. It is through doing so that social constructivism claims, perhaps uniquely, to be able to holistically assess and examine social change. Collectively, the (often critical) social context within which EU citizenship emerged and evolves 'matters'.

3. WHY USE CONSTRUCTIVISM FOR RESEARCH ON CITIZENSHIP? THE PROBLEMS WITH CONVENTIONAL APPROACHES

On one level, there is nothing wrong with conventional approaches to studies in EU citizenship. Scholars should be encouraged to embrace a plurality of approaches, be it empirical, legal, policy-orientated, or any other approach to such an important area of study and research. However, it is a core claim of constructivists that conventional approaches, while undeniably of value, are not capable of holistically examining EU citizenship in all its complexity: there is something missing from them. There are arguably five key problems with conventional approaches that need to be recognised.

First, there is often no recognition that all approaches 'tacitly presuppose' certain assumptions about the world in order to engage in any form of analytical endeavour.[35]

Second, because of this, the world is ostensibly and unthinkingly reduced to one consisting solely of autonomous, rational individuals (or agents) acting with a 'given' set of interests and fixed unchanging identities and in which, crucially, ideas play little or no role in constituting

---

[31] Kostakopoulou, *Citizenship, Identity and Immigration*, 2.
[32] Antje Wiener, *'European' Citizenship Practice: Building Institutions of a Non-State* (Westview Press 1998) 26–8.
[33] Michelle Everson, 'The Legacy of the Market Citizen' in Jo Shaw and Gillian More (eds), *New Legal Dynamics of European Union* (Clarendon Press 1995) 73–90, 79 (quoting Diedre Curtin).
[34] Checkel, 'Social Construction', 59.
[35] Alexander Wendt, *Social Theory of International Politics* (CUP 1999) 371 (quoting Alfred North Whitehead).

'reality'.³⁶ It is noticeable, for instance, how often the citizenship provisions of the Treaty were (initially) dismissed as 'a symbolic plaything',³⁷ or as 'grand rhetoric'.³⁸ For constructivists, 'rhetoric' and 'symbolism' should not be so readily cast aside; they are both highly significant potential causal factors worth studying in their own right.

Third, little or no attempt is made to explain how social change comes about especially within legal contexts, except in terms of the development of legal principles on citizenship within the case law of the CJEU.

Fourth, identity plays little role in conventional approaches. This is something that is particularly relevant to any debate on the extent to which citizenship can be seen to have partially emerged from the case law of the CJEU on free movement of persons, as it cannot simply be viewed as 'a formal [...] elaboration of [...] rights attaching to a particular category of persons';³⁹ there is ultimately an inexorable link to debates on an emerging European identity. We need to recognise that true citizenship involves 'a psychological sense of attachment between the peoples of Europe and [...] Union [...] citizenship [...] cannot just be created through legal enactment; it is dependent to a significant extent on the society in which the law exists'.⁴⁰

Finally, conventional methods arguably make little attempt to recognise the inherently social context within which the CJEU in particular operates. The problem is ultimately a methodological one, particularly in a legal context. Haltern contends that the law is 'too often taught as a highly technical set of rules, a dense doctrinal thicket hardly extending beyond "black letter law"'.⁴¹ It is a literal and descriptive approach, portraying law as establishing 'objective facts',⁴² with the end result being the appearance of a seemingly ideologically neutral assessment conducted in a seemingly ideologically neutral legal terrain.⁴³ This has resulted in the CJEU being portrayed as existing in a 'hermetically closed' environment,⁴⁴ which, of course, it is not. Thus, for all of the above reasons, conventional approaches to citizenship lack the ability to holistically assess it, in particular because they are methodologically incapable of seeing it in its inherently social context – so much so that Haltern pleads that it 'virtually cries out to be understood by means of an interdisciplinary approach to law',⁴⁵ which, according to Wincott, 'very few scholars' do.⁴⁶ Thus, to repeat, it is hoped that this chapter will encourage

---

[36] Wendt in ibid.
[37] Hans Ulrich Jessurun D'Oliveira, 'Union Citizenship: Pie in the Sky' in Allan Rosas and Esko Antola (eds), *A Citizen's Europe: In Search of a New Order* (Sage 1995) 82.
[38] Sionaidh Douglas-Scott, *Constitutional Law of the European Union* (Longman 2002) 371.
[39] Jo Shaw, 'Citizenship of the Union: Towards Post-National Membership?' in *Collected Courses of the Academy of European Law – 1995 European Community Law, Vol VI, Book 1, European University Institute, Florence, Academy of European Law* (Martinus Nijhoff Publishers 1998) 248.
[40] Nicholas Barber, 'Citizenship, Nationalism and the European Union' (2002) 27(3) EL Rev, 241–59 at 247.
[41] Ulrich Haltern, 'Integration through Law' in Antje Wiener and Thomas Diez (eds), *European Integration Theory* (OUP 2004) 178.
[42] Ibid, 192.
[43] Anne-Marie Burley and Walter Mattli, 'Europe before the Court: A Political Theory of Legal Integration' (1993) 47(1) *International Organization* 41–76, 45.
[44] Ibid.
[45] Haltern, 'Integration through Law', 178.
[46] Daniel Wincott, 'Political Theory, Law and European Union' in Jo Shaw and Gillian More (eds), *New Legal Dynamic of European Union* (Clarendon Press 1995) 293, 299.

more scholars to engage in such important interdisciplinary research into the evolution of EU citizenship.

4. THE 'NUTS AND BOLTS' OF SOCIAL CONSTRUCTIVIST RESEARCH ON EU CITIZENSHIP

As has already been outlined, constructivist research methodology takes a particular – 'middle ground' – epistemological standpoint to then examine the evolution of ideas in tandem with and in the context of institutional environments in which agency plays a crucial role, but with the ultimate aim to holistically theorise and evaluate social change, including the evolution of identity. What constructivist theorists then claim is that there is a fundamental need to draw particular strands of such a set of perspectives together to form a methodological basis for empirical work. However, in so doing, individual pieces of research are given conceptual space in which to develop a particular method based upon a particular set of *a priori* assumptions. As Finnemore and Sikkink maintain:

> There is no single constructivist method or research design. Constructivism opens up a set of issues, and scholars choose the research tools and methods best suited to their particular question. In some cases, quantitative methods yield particular insight. In other cases, qualitative and interpretative methods are more appropriate. Many research projects have used a combination of these methods to illuminate different parts of a larger puzzle. In this sense, designing constructivist research is not fundamentally different from designing other kinds of research. Constructivists, like any other researchers, use the full array of available tools.[47]

Given the interdisciplinary nature of EU citizenship (with a particular emphasis on the role of language and identity combined with concrete legal rights), such a methodological flexibility is inherently valuable. After having taken a particular standpoint, it is possible to develop a methodological 'toolkit' which can be adapted to numerous aspects of research on citizenship. Such a methodological tailoring is considered to be fundamentally necessary in adapting discourse theory to practical empirical work. As Torfing maintains:

> Discourse theory aims to describe, understand, and explain how and why particular discursive formations were constructed, stabilized, and transformed. In order to reveal the necessary and sufficient conditions for discourse to be shaped and reshaped in a particular way, discourse theory employs a contextualized conceptual tool kit that includes important concepts like dislocation, hegemony, social antagonism etc.[48]

One of potentially many methodological perspectives (and one that will be focused on in this chapter) is derived from a Foucauldian understanding of discourse theory and methodology, combining both qualitative and quantitative research methods dependent upon the particular type of citizenship research being conducted – something which is perfectly conceivable in

---

[47] Finnemore and Sikkink, 'Taking Stock', 396.
[48] Jacob Torfing, 'Discourse Theory: Achievements, Arguments and Challenges' in David Howarth and Jacob Torfing (eds), *Discourse Theory in European Politics: Identity, Policy and Governance* (Palgrave Macmillan 2005) 1–32 at 22.

constructivist methodology.[49] Based upon Foucault's archaeological and genealogical conception of the origins of discourse and the way in which societies are governed by it, it is possible to attempt to 'trace' the subjective origins of the various discursive structures upon which EU citizenship depends and follow their development to the point at which they become a form of social common sense.[50] This method has several fundamental aspects to it but in particular takes a particular stance on discourse (and therefore implicitly the role of ideology in social life), with points of comparison and contrast with other constructivist perspectives and other theoretical perspectives – particularly poststructuralism – manifesting in a number of ways that are particularly relevant from the perspective of a research handbook on EU citizenship.

4.1   Norms as Discourse

A Foucauldian perspective essentially takes what appears to be a rather circular stance. It posits that a particular conception of 'ideas' can and should be discourse. At the same time it distinguishes discourse as understood more broadly and narrows it down to a variant of intersubjectivity. In terms of the former point, as Risse contends: 'If we want to understand and explain social behaviour, we need to take words, language, and communicative utterances seriously.'[51] It is the particular use of language that literally constructs reality. As Finnemore and Sikkink further maintain:

> Speech can also persuade; it can change people's minds about what goals are valuable and about the roles they play (or should play) in social life. When speech has these effects, it is doing important social construction work, creating new understandings and new social facts that reconfigure politics. In one of the pioneering works of the field, Kratochwil (1989) examined the role of legal reasoning in persuasion and other social construction processes.[52]

In other words, there are numerous shades of understanding and conceptualising norms/ideas. However, a Foucauldian approach emphasises language *as* discourse. Kendall and Wickham, for instance, warn of the 'danger' of confusing the term 'discourse' with 'language'.[53] In part, the distinction between 'language' *per se* and discourse is structural. From a Foucauldian perspective, discourse can be understood as 'a corpus of statements whose organisation is regular and systematic'.[54] Likewise, Wæver suggests: 'Discourse can be defined as a system that regulates the formation of statements.'[55] Furthermore, it is the structural nature of discourse that itself constitutes reality. As Ferguson put it: 'discourse is a practice, it is structured, and has real effects which are much more profound than simply "mystification".'[56] Moreover, this conception of discourse then has a practical application in terms of examining the interrela-

---

[49] Finnemore and Sikkink, 'Taking Stock', 395–6. See further: Steinfeld, *Fissures in EU Citizenship*.
[50] Jason Powell, 'The Development of Post-structuralism and Aging' in Jared Jaworski (ed.), *Advances in Sociology: Volume 3* (Nova Science Publishers 2006) 53–68, 57–8.
[51] Risse, 'Social Constructivism', 164.
[52] Finnemore and Sikkink, 'Taking Stock', 402.
[53] Gavin Kendall and Gary Wickham, *Using Foucault's Methods* (Sage 1999) 42.
[54] Ibid.
[55] Ole Wæver, 'Discursive Approaches' in Antje Wiener and Thomas Diez (eds), *European Integration Theory* (OUP 2004) 197–215 at 199.
[56] James Ferguson, *The Anti-Politics Machine: Depoliticization, and Bureaucratic Power in Lesotho* (CUP 1994) 18.

tionship between texts (which would include different court judgments or policy documents on citizenship) and patterns of language within texts. In terms of examining the use of language between texts, Paltridge maintains:

> Discourse analysis focuses on knowledge about language beyond the word, clause, phrase and sentence that is needed for successful communication. It looks at patterns of language across texts and considers the relationship between language and the social and cultural contexts in which it is used. Discourse analysis also considers the ways in which the use of language presents different views of the world and different understandings. It examines how the use of language is influenced by relationships between participants as well as the effects the use of language has upon social identities and relations. It also considers how views of the world, and identities, are constructed through the use of discourse.[57]

Likewise, in terms of patterns of language within texts, Torfing claims that discourse analysis examines the 'form of a chain of statements/expressions, the manner in which they came about (archaeology) [...] [as well as] rule-governed behaviour that leads to a chain of similarly interrelated system of statements'.[58] In its essence, therefore, a concrete research agenda on the evolution of EU citizenship in any institutional context is conceptually possible using this methodology. In particular, it is possible to examine patterns of language across numerous texts on citizenship to then determine the evolution from instrumental and agent-created 'talk' to a more structural notion of citizenship embedded with latent meaning.

4.2 Identifying the 'Nodal Points' of Citizenship

In order to differentiate mere 'talk' from discourse, it is necessary to identify its 'nodal points'. In a citizenship context this can mean that citizenship is the principal discourse, which has various context-dependent and inherently contingent aspects to it. Examples of this might be the notion of social solidarity or that of its 'fundamental status', or, indeed, the protection offered to third country nationals by virtue of a family member holding that status. These are all enunciated within the case law of the CJEU.[59] Alternatively, it is possible to suggest that citizenship itself operates as a macro-discursive construction but depends on several micro or related discursive constructions. In this context the nodal points of EU citizenship are inexorably intertwined with free movement of persons and equal treatment, both of which could be construed as discursive sub-structures of citizenship.[60] From a methodological perspective, though, this type of analysis is inherently structural. As Wæver put it: 'Discourse analysis looks for structures of meaning. "Things" do not have meaning in and of themselves, they only become meaningful in discourse.'[61] It is possible to assess language in terms of examining the point at which it becomes structural or, as has already been stated, a series of statements with

---

[57] Brian Paltridge, *Discourse Analysis: An Introduction* (Continuum 2006) 2.
[58] Torfing, 'Discourse Theory', 26.
[59] See *Grzelczyk*, 6242, at para. 31; Case C-209/03 *The Queen (on the application of Dany Bidar) v London Borough of Ealing, Secretary of State for Education and Skills* EU:C:2005:169 [2005] ECR I 2119; 2170, at para. 56; and *Ruiz Zambrano*. See further: Steinfeld, *Fissures in EU Citizenship*, 100–60 and 269–341.
[60] See further: Steinfeld, *Fissures in EU Citizenship*.
[61] Wæver, 'Discursive Approaches', 198.

a 'corpus' to it. By so doing it is possible to identify the various different aspects – or 'nodal points' – of citizenship.

Crucially, *agency* is a crucial part of the process of identifying the evolution from subjective articulation to intersubjective nodal points. Attempts can be made to examine the types of language used to describe citizenship and emphasis placed by particular 'meaning architects' in order to embed a particular and contingent emphasis within the institutional environments. As Finnemore and Sikkink suggest: 'The meanings of any particular norm and the linkages between existing norms and emergent norms are often not obvious and must be actively constructed by proponents of new norms. Activists work hard to frame their issues in ways that make persuasive connections between existing norms and emergent norms.'[62]

Thus, one aspect of intelligent discourse construction relates to the way in which a new discourse can be developed through being continually associated with pre-existing and pervasive norms that had existed for many years. This is particularly pertinent to attempts to derive contemporary meaning for Union citizenship given its inherent link to early free movement of persons case law, for instance.[63] In addition to linkages made both within and between discourses, it is possible to examine the types of words used and other rhetorical strategies which tend to emphasise the importance of particular concepts within the text. For instance, Stillar maintains that it is important to examine the 'devices that are used to relate parts of one sentence to parts of another across spans of text'.[64] Indeed, Torfing suggests that this is part of a practical application of discourse theory:

> At a more concrete level, discourse can be analysed as an ensemble of cognitive schemes, conceptual articulations, rhetorical strategies, pictures and images, symbolic actions (rituals), and structures (architectures), enunciative modalities, and narrative flows and rhythms. All these things should be analysed both in terms of their ability to shape and reshape meaning.[65]

EU citizenship is arguably richly embedded in all of these elements and thus multiple research agendas are possible using Foucauldian discourse methodology. It should be noted that the importance of putting particular words or phrases under a discursive microscope is that the successful use of such 'devices' leads to textual 'cohesion' which is in turn structural and then discursive.[66] As Stillar continues: 'Cohesion gives text unity, enabling it to be interpreted as a whole, rather than as an unorganized collection of words.'[67] Likewise, Titscher, Meyer, Wodak and Vetter maintain: 'by means of lexical elements, sentence components and other linguistic elements, text structures are formed.'[68] Not only is textual cohesion an important illustration of subjective utterances evolving to become discourse but this is particularly illustrative in a citizenship context, because contemporary understandings of EU citizenship can only be understood in their context. For instance, it is simply not possible to suggest that EU citizenship is simply a generic form of postnational identity which could in effect be easily

---

[62] Finnemore and Sikkink, 'International Norm Dynamics', 908.
[63] See further: Steinfeld, *Fissures in EU Citizenship*.
[64] Glenn Stillar, *Analyzing Everyday Texts: Discourse, Rhetoric and Social Perspectives* (Sage 1998) 49.
[65] Torfing, 'Discourse Theory', 14.
[66] Stillar, *Analyzing Everyday Texts*, 49.
[67] Ibid.
[68] Sefan Titscher and others, *Methods of Text and Discourse Analysis* (Sage 2000) 22.

replicated around the world. It has a shape and form that can only be understood in the wider context of European integration, which itself is dependent on both legal and socio-political developments over many years.

Equally, *repetition* is considered to be fundamental to establishing discourse, and this is particularly relevant to citizenship because simply uttering or speaking citizenship is and should be of relevance from a research perspective. From a constructivist perspective, the more citizenship is spoken of (with a particular emphasis on who utters it and, potentially, why), the more it becomes a form of social truth and constitutes reality. Therefore, instances of repetition of particular phrases or concepts are important to examine. Repetition is fundamental in the context of an holistic approach to norm diffusion as it emphasises both structure and agency in so doing. As has already been outlined, a core tenet of constructivist theory is that a concept is subjectively uttered but then becomes sufficiently pervasive to become intersubjective, that is, discursive. Finnemore and Sikkink, as has been stated above, outline two phases in the process of norm creation, the first of which deals specifically with subjective utterances. It is the second phase, though, that is of most concern to constructivist theorists, in that an assessment of how subjective utterance becomes pervasive simultaneously justifies the *a priori* use of the theory itself: it is part of its 'value-added'. An aspect of this 'second phase' has been termed 'dynamic imitation'.[69] By using the phrase 'dynamic' emphasis is then placed upon the instrumental use of repetition by well-placed individuals in order to consolidate subjective utterances such that they can have the potential to become discursive. In addition, repetition has a structural aspect to it in that it is also important to examine repetition that is made almost unthinkingly, not by 'norm entrepreneurs' but by a number of less dynamic actors within an institutional environment. For Risse in particular, 'the dispersal of cultural values works through mimetic imitation'.[70] It should be noted that such an approach is both quantitative and qualitative in its implications. It is quantitative in the sense that, at times, space can be devoted to the sheer repetition of a particular phrase within a text. However, in addition to so doing, attempts can be made to examine the context in which particular repetitions are made, and thus repetition can also be examined in a qualitative sense.[71]

In addition, as has also been emphasised, one of constructivism's core tenets is to examine social change through discursive evolution. There are a number of ways that this can be achieved and one of them is to examine discursive *snapshots* at particular times: what Powell terms a 'slice through the discursive nexus'.[72] There is both an element of examining a specific period of time combined with examining particular periods of evolution under a discursive microscope. As an example, it is possible to take various 'snapshots' of the legal evolution of EU citizenship, such as when Advocate-General Jacobs uttered the phrase 'civis europeus sum' in *Konstandinidis*, or when the CJEU referred to citizenship being 'destined' to be a 'fundamental status' in *Grzelczyk*, all the way up to citizenship as understood in the post-Brexit era.[73] This is qualitative in the sense that attempts can be made to compare statements made

---

[69] Finnemore and Sikkink, 'International Norm Dynamics', 895.
[70] Thomas Risse, 'Constructivism and International Institutions: Towards Conversations across Paradigms' in Ira Katznelson and Helen Milner (eds), *Political Science as Discipline: Reconsidering Power, Choice and the State of the Century's End* (W.W. Norton 2002) 597–623, 611.
[71] See further: Steinfeld, *Fissures in EU Citizenship*, 203–66.
[72] Kendall and Wickham, *Using Foucault's Methods*, 45.
[73] Case C-168/91 *Konstantinidis v Stadt Altensteig* EU:C:1993:115 [1993] ECR I 1191, 1212.

within the text of CJEU judgments often many years apart in order to demonstrate the fundamental change of the context within which the legal notion of citizenship has evolved over time. This discursive 'snapshot' concept also has an additional practical aspect to it in that it can be limited to examining words on the page of court judgments as they appear, while acknowledging, implicitly, that there is life beyond the framing of a camera lens. In other words, what is not being denied is that various actors may or may not have an influence on the text of a court report without being directly mentioned. Obvious examples of these are the référendaires within the cabinet of a particular judge or Advocate-General. The views of these actors, by necessity, can only be credited to that of the particular judge or Advocate-General (whose role it is to ultimately write and be accountable for a particular opinion or judgment in any case). It may well be, for instance, that highly significant acts of subjective creation commenced with highly confidential discussions and reports within a particular cabinet or, indeed, over lunch at the Court's cafeteria. However, such discussions are, by definition, either confidential and/or un-reportable, thereby being unresearchable. Ultimately what matters are the words as they appear on the page of a particular judgment (or indeed policy document), irrespective of their extra-textual background, and it is in this context that the concept of a 'snapshot' provides a useful practical limitation within which constructivist research into EU citizenship can flourish.

A final aspect of a Foucauldian approach to research on EU citizenship is to focus on what can be termed *failures and resistance*. In terms of failures, Finnemore and Sikkink acknowledge that 'many emergent norms fail to reach tipping point'.[74] In other words, some subjective utterances fail to become intersubjective, or alternatively some early discourses lose resonance over time and remain essentially confined to linguistic history. It is important to examine such 'failures' nevertheless, as they also demonstrate the instrumental contingency that is at the heart of discourse creation. In other words, an alternative 'reality' could perhaps have led to an entirely different outcome. Indeed, such an examination can be seen to be fundamentally in keeping with the essence of Foucault's method, as aspects of law or policy that are now considered to be 'irrelevant' may prove to be far from so in a discursive sense. Likewise, resistance to the emergence of a discourse equally demonstrates the role of agency and contingency. As Finnemore and Sikkink put it: 'People who dislike existing norms and rules […] often band together and try to change them.'[75] Nonetheless, resistance to a particular discursive development is still an important aspect of its development, because 'No discourse can be protected from contestation and contamination as their boundaries are continuously breached and redrawn'.[76] This dialectical process of contamination, contestation and recontestation is fundamental to analysing discourse because by so doing, for instance, a discourse of EU citizenship has developed in a specific context that simply cannot be understood in a sense abstracted from its context and generically compared to other citizenship models. Conversely, resisting voices within the text of the CJEU jurisprudence or policy documents can, ironically, further validate and consolidate the creation of a discourse through simply uttering it: what could be termed being 'entrapped by one's own rhetoric'. Risse and Wiener, for instance, outline the concept of 'entrapment […] to denote that EU member states might comply with certain rules to which

---

[74] Finnemore and Sikkink, 'International Norm Dynamics', 895.
[75] Finnemore and Sikkink, 'Taking Stock', 400.
[76] Torfing, 'Discourse Theory', 19.

they have committed even if these norms contradict their preferences or current interests'.[77] For Risse and Wiener, what is evident in an EU context is that certainly initially resistant Member States became entrapped into uttering concepts that they would not ordinarily have agreed with because the entire context of the utterance had already been 'strategically framed' by other actors, particularly the Commission.[78] Thus, examining both discursive failure and discursive resistance forms part of the methodological 'toolkit' that can be adapted for various research projects into the evolution of EU citizenship.

4.3 The Fundamental Importance of Taking a Critical Approach to Research on EU Citizenship

It has already been suggested that there is a necessity to conduct constructivist research into the evolution of EU citizenship because it adds value to conventional approaches to the subject. It could, perhaps, be left there in terms of elaborating a concrete research agenda based upon the conceptual tools developed from a Foucauldian notion of discourse methodology. However, not only are aspects of constructivist approaches overtly critical; also, taking a critical approach to a fundamental concept (possibly the jewel in its crown) within European integration at a time when it has arguably been challenged in the era of both Brexit and a wider trend towards populism arguably could not be more necessary. For Risse, there is a fundamental need for a critical approach within constructivist empirical work because 'discourse is a process of construction of meaning allowing for certain interpretations while excluding others [...] [in] which constructions of meaning become so dominant that they are being taken-for-granted'.[79] In this respect, devoting time to 'tracing' the social construction of so-called common sense that underpins EU citizenship (the 'taken-for-granted' or 'dull' aspects of case law or policy that are often overlooked by conventional approaches) is an important endeavour. For Finnemore and Sikkink, when 'norm internalization occurs[,] norms acquire a taken-for-granted quality and are no longer a matter of broad public debate'.[80] Instead, a normative aspect of constructivism – a focus on deconstruction – at times critiques such 'common sense', and this is because what is presented as 'value-neutral' is often far from so. As Paltridge maintains: 'The norms and values which underlie texts are often "out of sight" rather than overtly stated [...] the aim of a critical approach to discourse analysis is to help reveal some of these hidden and "often out of sight" values, positions and perspectives'.[81] Therefore, part of the Foucauldian method is devoted to shedding light on aspects of any subject area that hitherto did not form part of mainstream analysis. By so doing, the 'normal' becomes almost surreal. As Chambon put it: 'Foucault often selected the least expected features, those that tend to be overlooked as insignificant, the details that "don't matter". Through dissection, ordinary features of routine activity become exquisite and glaring – at times

---

[77] Thomas Risse and Antje Wiener, 'The Social Construction of Social Constructivism' in Thomas Christiansen, Knud Erik Jørgensen and Antje Wiener (eds), *The Social Construction of Europe* (Sage 2001) 196.
[78] Ibid.
[79] Risse, 'Social Constructivism', 165.
[80] Finnemore and Sikkink, 'International Norm Dynamics', 904.
[81] Paltridge, *Discourse Analysis*, 178.

unbearable.'[82] From the perspective of EU citizenship a critical constructivist perspective can have two fundamental implications. First, the seemingly 'mundane' act of 'tracing' citizenship to its origins inevitably leads to its origins in the early days of free movement of persons and market citizenship. In this respect, for instance, it has been claimed, after painstaking genealogical discourse-theoretical research, that the very notion of citizenship is riddled with latent 'fissures' throughout its construction (for instance, by being linked to a controversial notion of the 'worker' as understood in EU law).[83]

In addition (and second), a critical constructivist perspective by implication examines the borders and limits of discursive construction. In other words, examining 'othering' is vital part of a critical constructivist approach. As Torfing outlines:

> The hegemonic articulation of meaning and identity is intrinsically linked to the construction of social antagonism, which involves the exclusion of a threatening Otherness that stabilizes the discursive system while, at the same time, preventing its ultimate closure [...] Foucault convincingly demonstrated that the limits and unity of discourse cannot be constructed by reference to an inner essence, in terms of a particular theme, style, conceptual framework, etc. Alternatively, we have to look for something outside the discourse in order to account for its limits.[84]

Issues relating to borders are therefore an important aspect of a critical approach, as 'In a concrete analysis of discourse, social antagonism shows itself through the production of political frontiers, which often invoke stereotyped pictures of friends and enemies'.[85] Europe, the European Union and, of course, its citizenship can be considered by some to be fertile ground for 'othering', in the sense of the construction of a threatening 'other' beyond Europe's borders – so much so that Derrida himself wrote an article specifically on this subject.[86] While some may regard the evolution of EU citizenship as a prototype for an emancipatory and non-discriminatory future of postnational citizenship and identity, seen from a critical constructivist perspective what is 'exquisite and glaring' about EU citizenship is what and who is left out by not holding the status of the citizen. This is, in a sense, the hard edge of citizenship, and more attention should be devoted to it. Thus, the final aspect of a social constructivist research agenda into EU citizenship is that it can, and arguably should, take a critical perspective.

5. CONCLUSION

This chapter commenced with the notion that by virtue of its essentially contested (and, indeed, interdisciplinary) nature, there is fertile ground for social constructivist research (in its various shapes and forms) on EU citizenship. It then examined what constructivism is at its core. It outlined an epistemological standpoint occupying a 'middle ground' between

---

[82] Adrienne Chambon, 'Foucault's Approach: Making the Familiar Visible' in Adrienne Chambon, Allan Irving and Laura Epstein (eds), *Reading Foucault for Social Work* (Columbia University Press 1995) 60.
[83] Steinfeld, *Fissures in EU Citizenship*, 39–99.
[84] Torfing, 'Discourse Theory', 15.
[85] Ibid, 16.
[86] Jacques Derrida, *The Other Heading: Reflections on Today's Europe* (Indiana UP 1992).

positivism and post-positivism which has the theoretical potential to systemically outline the evolution of EU citizenship through a complex interaction between norms, identity and institutions. In a sense this is a methodological approach that is ideal for examining the evolution (and possible regression) of EU citizenship by virtue of the way in which citizenship simultaneously occupies conceptual space as a legal/political construct and an ideal and potential form of supranational identity. The chapter then briefly outlined the inherent 'value-added' of constructivist approaches to EU citizenship, particularly in a legal context, by virtue of going considerably beyond conventional approaches to the concept by distinguishing itself from agent-centred and/or black-letter legal approaches to immerse the legal evolution of EU citizenship in its inherent context. The chapter then outlined one of potentially many methodological approaches within constructivist approaches – termed a toolkit – as a way to encourage further research in any aspect of the evolution of citizenship. It is clear that while EU citizenship was formally created by virtue of Treaty amendment at Maastricht in 1992, as a notion it had existed for many years prior to that.[87] It is also clear that an emerging body of case law and policy has emerged post-1992 and continues to emerge and evolve. It thus has a past, present and future, all of which should be the subject of holistic research. A Foucauldian perspective on constructivism was outlined, predisposed to conceiving of ideas as discourse(s). Far from 'meta-theorising', it has been claimed that a Foucauldian perspective contains several aspects that are particularly useful from the perspective of EU citizenship research, with a particular emphasis on articulating and outlining the various 'nodal points' of the discursive construction of citizenship by virtue of examining patterns and repetition within and beyond texts (often over many years), taking discursive 'snapshots' of citizenship over various periods of time and even examining agents outlining subjective concepts that failed as well as those that resisted the evolution towards EU citizenship. These are all concepts that are inherently flexible and could be adapted to a number of methodological approaches. However, the chapter ended critically. The survival of EU citizenship as a meaningful status and concept could not be more challenged in the contemporary environment of Brexit and various waves of populism more generally throughout Europe. The future of EU citizenship needs to examine the inherent fissures or flaws in its past and, indeed, present, with its roots in an economic notion of citizenship and its present troubled by exclusion by virtue of not being European. While it is not mandatory to engage in critical constructivist research on EU citizenship, it is certainly hoped that more such research may emerge in time and that this chapter has helped in some way towards achieving that aim.

---

[87] As early as 1976, Plender famously stated that European citizenship was 'incipient' by virtue of the early case law on free movement of persons. Richard Plender, 'An Incipient Form of European Citizenship' in Francis Jacobs (ed.), *European Law and the Individual* (North Holland Publishing 1976) 39.

4. The evolution of citizens' rights in light of the EU's constitutional development

Daniel Thym[1]

1. INTRODUCTION

The constitutional foundations of Union citizenship are bound to remain unstable due to the doctrinal and conceptual ambiguity of supranational citizens' rights. If that is the case, change need not present linear progress towards 'more' citizenship, reflecting the EU's famous self-description as 'ever closer union'.[2] It could similarly result in friction, dead ends and retrogression. On this basis, this chapter sets out to explain the evolution of citizens' rights as a reflection of broader trends. Our heuristic device for rationalising the constitutional embeddedness will be a juxtaposition of two competing models of the concept of transnational mobility. Their impact on the case law and institutional practice will be exemplified through closer scrutiny of three thematic leitmotifs defining most accounts of citizenship as regards to solidarity, political participation and identity.

Having reminded readers of the underlying reasons for the legal and conceptual ambiguity of Union citizenship, comments in this chapter will demonstrate that institutional practice fluctuates between two models: one based on residence and the other focusing on social integration. As ideal types, these models influence the resolution of specific questions, although positions of policy actors will most likely reflect a blend, thereby reinforcing the overall trend towards constant variation and conceptual indeterminacy (see section 2). The pertinence of this approach will be tested in relation to ongoing disputes about social benefits and transnational solidarity (section 3), political participation and the significance to nationality (section 4) and migration and collective identities (section 5). It will be shown that the evolution of citizens' rights in these areas is intimately connected to broader constitutional trends, such as the euro crisis, the failure of the Constitutional Treaty or arguments about immigration. Answers to specific questions in the case law and the political process can be rationalised as building blocks of an EU that accepts the limits of the federal vision by accommodating the continued diversity among Member States.

---

[1] This chapter was first published in Daniel Thym (ed.) *Questioning EU Citizenship* (Bloomsbury/Hart 2017) 111–34. It is reprinted here with the kind permission of the publisher; the style of the references in the footnotes has been adapted.

[2] Recital 1 of the Preamble of the original EEC Treaty of 1957, the present Treaty on the Functioning of the European Union [2012] OJ C326/47 and the Charter of Fundamental Rights [2012] OJ C326/391.

2. TWO COMPETING MODELS

Citizens' rights are no abstract category: they are intricately connected to a social context. Until recently, in Western thought, this context concerned membership in statal communities; it remains uncertain whether the citizenship concept can be applied to a supranational polity such as the EU and whether doing so requires conceptual adaptation. This question has preoccupied the scholarly literature over the past years and notable differences persist.[3] Against this background, this section suggests rationalising the evolution of citizens' rights through the juxtaposition of divergent visions of transnational mobility whose identification can serve as a heuristic device for reconstructing institutional practices.

This approach builds on the work of the American migration scholar Hiroshi Motomura, who demonstrated that the US perspective on immigration evolved over time by distinguishing between three ways of construing the relationship between incoming migrants and US society: legal rules may be perceived, alternatively, as a quasi-automatic 'transition', as a 'contract' obliging newcomers to comply with certain conditions or as an 'affiliation' when immigrants gradually get involved with the nation's life.[4] Such a constructivist account recognises that different ideals coexist and can change over time. It can be particularly useful in relation to Union citizenship whose significance remains contested.[5]

To identify different visions of transnational membership is not to say that the ECJ or other EU institutions hold a uniform concept of citizenship. Arguably, it is not the function of judges to actively engage in theoretical debate: they should resolve legal disputes.[6] We cannot expect a Grand Chamber of 15 judges to have a uniform understanding or to reflect on it openly in their judgments. Although the standard invocation of Union citizenship as 'fundamental status' may be taken to hint at an underlying theory, it might not exist.[7] This does not, however, prevent academic commentators from reconstructing the theoretical infrastructure. Such academic reconstructions are ideal types which are modelled upon judgments and policy initiatives as legal phenomena and which accentuate theoretical features for analytical purposes. They are not mutually exclusive and the positions of policy actors will most likely reflect a blend, combining elements of different ideal types. Arguably, the discrepancies underlying many free movement rulings can be explained by this mixture: judges drift along.

In this section, I will present the methodological background (section 2.1) and discuss, on this basis, two visions of transnational membership which I shall call the 'residence model' (section 2.2) and the 'integration model' (section 2.3). Their explanatory potential is limited to the EU context, where transnational mobility constitutes the hallmark of supranational citizens' rights to this date. It is not the purpose of this chapter to rationalise the meaning of citizenship more generally. Implications of the two models will be illustrated later in relation to three thematic leitmotifs that feature prominently in contemporary citizenship accounts:

---

[3] For an overview, see Dora Kostakopoulou, 'European Union Citizenship: Writing the Future' (2007) 13 ELJ 623; Dimitry Kochenov, 'The Essence of EU Citizenship Emerging from the Last Ten Years of Academic Debate' (2013) 62 ICLQ 97.
[4] See Hiroshi Motomura, *Americans in Waiting* (OUP 2006).
[5] The argument in this section builds upon Daniel Thym, 'The Elusive Limits of Solidarity' (2015) 52 CML Rev. 17, 33–9.
[6] Cf. Cass R Sunstein, *One Case at a Time* (HUP 1999).
[7] Cf. Andrew Williams, *The Ethos of Europe* (CUP 2011).

social solidarity, political participation and questions of collective identification.[8] Doing so will link the discussion of Union citizenship to broader constitutional trends.

2.1 Methodological Background

There was and remains nothing inevitable in the evolution of Union citizenship. Even within a nation-state context, the notion of citizenship is a prime example of an essentially contested project which lends itself to different visions of what we mean by citizenship. In the European Union, this volatility is reinforced by the transformative character of the European integration process and corresponding uncertainties about its *finalité*, which reinforce the inherent openness of the citizenship concept in the context of EU integration.[9] Methodologically, these characteristics can be integrated into legal accounts on the basis of a contextually embedded doctrinal constructivism which accepts, in contrast to US-style legal realism, that legal concepts can have a semi-autonomous significance.[10]

Corresponding legal analyses are based on a reconstruction of the case law and its doctrinal foundations, thereby ideally supporting a better understanding of the systematic coherence of the law and its internal inconsistencies.[11] Doing so assumes that doctrinal arguments and constraints should be taken seriously in a discursive community involving academics in the constant reconstruction of the legal infrastructure.[12] Meanwhile, abstract legal concepts, such as free movement, citizenship or human rights, require a broader constitutional analysis in a process that Armin von Bogdandy has aptly described as a doctrinal argument about constitutional principles.[13] This chapter follows this approach by extrapolating the constitutional infrastructure guiding the interpretation of rules on Union citizenship.

Such focus on questions of doctrinal interpretation and constitutional reconstruction does not imply that legal debates exist in splendid isolation. To the contrary, constitutional principles such as citizenship convey a set of normative values and express basic choices of societies, which can change over time.[14] Citizens' rights, like human rights, present fields of the law resonating with broader social and political developments. Their conceptual openness was one factor facilitating progressive interpretation by the ECJ described by academic observers as a process of judicial transformation transcending the original rationale of market integration.[15]

---

[8] On recurring themes in debates about citizenship, see Linda Bosniak, 'Citizenship Denationalized' (2000) 7 Ind. J. Global Legal Stud. 447–509; and Richard Bellamy, *Citizenship: A Very Short Introduction* (OUP 2008).

[9] For further comments see Daniel Thym, 'Introduction' in ibid. (ed.) *Questioning EU Citizenship* (Bloomsbury/Hart 2017) sect. II.

[10] See Thomas Horsley, 'Reflections on the Role of the Court of Justice as the "Motor" of European Integration' (2013) 50 CML Rev. 931, 934–54; and Gunnar Beck, *The Legal Reasoning of the Court of Justice of the EU* (Hart 2012).

[11] See Rob van Gestel and Hans-Wolfgang Micklitz, 'Why Methods Matter in European Legal Scholarship' (2014) 20 ELJ 292–316.

[12] See Mattias Kumm, 'On the Past and Future of European Constitutional Scholarship' (2009) 7 ICON 401, 406–11.

[13] See Armin von Bogdandy, 'Founding Principles of EU Law: A Theoretical and Doctrinal Sketch' (2010) 16 ELJ 95, 98–100.

[14] See Robert M Cover, 'Foreword: *Nomos* and Narrative' (1983) 97 Harvard L. Rev. 4, 11–44.

[15] See Eleanor Spaventa, 'From Gebhard to Carpenter' (2004) 41 CML Rev. 743, 764–8; Stefan Kadelbach, 'Union Citizenship' in Armin von Bogdandy and Jürgen Bast (eds) *Principles of European Constitutional Law* (2nd edn, Hart 2009) 435, 461–6.

However, such an outcome was and is no foregone conclusion. The broader social and political context may similarly support restrictive tendencies, thematic shifts or judicial changes of direction.[16] Our analysis will show that the evolution of Union citizenship discloses such reorientation and that political actors and social practices can influence these interpretative metamorphoses.

2.2 'Residence Model'

The novelty factor of Union citizenship lies in its supranational character. It grants rights to transnational movement, equal treatment and political participation across state borders, thereby overcoming the Westphalian model of territorial sovereignty. The individual right to free movement for broadly defined categories of economic activity and corresponding guarantees of equal treatment, which up until now pinpoint the essence of citizens' rights, do not abolish political communities at national level, but oblige them to treat Union citizens similarly to nationals. When Union citizens move, territorial presence often replaces the formal link of nationality as the demarcation line between insiders and outsiders participating in the formation of solidary communities.[17] Below I will discuss the extent to which this model can help us rationalise the evolution of citizens' rights at EU level.

Academic discourse on EU law presents us with two visions behind the residence model that coincide insofar as the rights of Union citizens are concerned, but which can diverge in relation to individuals from outside the EU – reflecting an underlying ambiguity as to how to relate European integration to the rest of the world. While some propagate the emergence of a generic model of stakeholder citizenship that is conceptually not restricted to the EU context and may pave the way for the general realignment of membership,[18] others describe the EU and its citizenship in (con-)federal terms.[19] This discrepancy takes centre stage when we analyse migration law towards third-country nationals,[20] but it is less relevant for the distinction between the 'residence model' and the 'integration model', since both the federal and the universalist frames of reference converge on the treatment of intra-European mobility.

2.3 'Integration Model'

The 'integration model' rejects the quasi-automatic acquisition of citizens' rights whenever someone takes up habitual residence. Instead it highlights qualitative factors connecting individuals to a political community, which often includes an expectation that one should actively pursue incorporation into societal structures. The success or failure of this venture may regu-

---

[16] See Dora Kostakopoulou, 'Co-creating European Union Citizenship' (2012/13) 15 C.Y.E.L.S. 255, 259–66; Jo Shaw and Nina Miller, 'When Legal Worlds Collide' (2013) 38 EL Rev. 137–66.

[17] For an early description of this idea, see Gareth Davies, 'Any Place I Hang My Hat?' (2015) 11 ELJ 43, 47–9.

[18] See esp. Dora Kostakopoulou, *The Future Governance of Citizenship* (CUP 2008) ch. 4; Yasemin Soysal, *Limits of Citizenship* (University of Chicago Press 1994).

[19] This approach is particularly common among scholars from continental Europe, such as Christoph Schönberger, *Unionsbürger* (Mohr Siebeck 2005); Stefan Kadelbach (n 15) 469–75; and Anne Pieter van der Mei, *Free Movement of Persons within the EC* (Hart 2003).

[20] See Daniel Thym, 'Citizens and Foreigners in EU Law' (2016) 22 ELJ 296, 302–6.

late the degree of residence security and equal treatment under EU law.[21] From this perspective, free movement within the European Union is more than an emancipatory 'playground of opportunities'[22] enhancing the freedom of choice of individuals through the pursuit of one's preferences; here it is not the case that anyone residing abroad is automatically considered an insider, as it is under the 'residence model' discussed above. Rather, the 'integration model' emphasises the value of social cohesion as a precondition for democratic allegiance and social solidarity. It makes access to social benefits and other rights associated with membership in a specific community conditional upon certain prerequisites without which equal treatment with nationals will be denied.

It is important to note that there is a variety of theoretical explanations for the significance of social cohesion which can result in different responses to specific questions.[23] In particular, social cohesion does not necessarily imply ethno-cultural closure and may support quite the reverse, namely changing self-perceptions of European societies in response to transnational mobility and cultural diversity. The argument for social cohesion is not about classic nationalism: it recognises, rather, that political communities require a sense of shared identity if our societies are to be more than the sum of their parts.[24] Despite the inherent emphasis on liberty, the doctrinal infrastructure of EU free movement law embraces important expressions of the 'integration model', which the Court has strengthened in a number of controversial judgments concerning access to social benefits and the limits of residence security in recent years. A central objective of this chapter is to try to clarify this reorientation of the case law.

3. SOCIAL BENEFITS AND TRANSNATIONAL SOLIDARITY

Equal access to social benefits has received much attention in scholarly treatises on Union citizenship over the years. Judgments delivered by the ECJ on cases such as *Martínez Sala*, *Grzelczyk*, *Förster* or, most recently, *Dano* and *Alimanovic* feature prominently in academic accounts of Union citizenship. Moreover, the issue presents itself as a perfect thematic prism to elucidate the conceptual (re-)orientation of supranational citizenship, since welfare provision represents a core ingredient of modern statehood and corresponding citizens' rights.[25] It epitomises the component of individual rights which lies at the heart of many citizenship theories, in particular those written by legal academics. Our analysis will proceed in two steps, highlighting the Court's position first (section 3.1) and discussing contextual factors that may explain the change of direction thereafter (3.2).

---

[21] See Loïc Azoulai, 'Transfiguring European Citizenship' in Dimitry Kochenov (ed.) *EU Citizenship and Federalism* (CUP 2017) 178–203.
[22] Dimitry Kochenov (n 3) 130.
[23] For an overview see Margaret Moore, 'Cosmopolitanism and Political Communities' (2006) 32 Soc. Theor. & Practice 627–58; Sarah Song, 'Three Models of Civic Solidarity' in Rogers M Smith (ed.) *Citizenship, Borders, and Human Needs* (Penn Press 2011) 192–207.
[24] See Christian Joppke, *Citizenship and Immigration* (Polity Press 2010) ch. 4.
[25] See Thomas H Marshall, *Class, Citizenship and Social Development* (Doubleday 1964).

3.1 Judicial Change of Direction

Access to social benefits is a perfect test case to highlight the pertinence of the 'residence model' and the 'integration model' described above, since their distinct features coincide with changing parameters of the free movement rules. There is a noticeable difference between the classic position of EU law on the equal treatment of those who are economically active (section 3.1.1) and the integration requirements for other citizens, which have been fortified in a number of more recent judgments (3.1.2).[26]

3.1.1 Residence model

The classic foundation of the residence model can be found in the recitals of implementing legislation on the free movement of workers: widespread equal treatment is perceived as a means to facilitate social integration, thus allowing migrant workers to enjoy the same rights from day one as a matter of principle.[27] On this basis, the Court reaffirmed in a number of judgments delivered over the past decades that Union citizens who are working in another Member State 'shall enjoy the same social and tax advantages as national workers'.[28] This trend towards residence-based equality was reaffirmed by the social security coordination regime that links special non-contributory cash benefits to the place of residence through legislation. This also applies to individuals other than workers.[29] The ECJ endorsed this approach by the legislature in light of primary law, since non-contributory benefits are 'closely linked with the social environment'.[30] This has important ramifications for our topic: mobility is perceived to entail a changing of the guard in the realm of welfare benefits, since the state of residence is expected to take over whenever someone moves across borders.

A strict version of the residence model would focus, in line with social security coordination, on the place of 'habitual residence' to determine the state bearing responsibility for social assistance: the crucial question would be 'where the habitual centre of their interests is to be found'.[31] We would have to distinguish, for that matter, between temporary 'visitors', who are physically present but retain habitual residence elsewhere, and 'residents', who relocate their centre of interests enduringly.[32] Social security experts maintain that the ECJ should

---

[26] The argument in this section builds upon Daniel Thym (n 5) 33–9.

[27] Cf. Recital 5 Council Regulation (EEC) 1612/68 of 15 October 1968 on freedom of movement for workers within the Community [1968] OJ L257/2 and today's Recital 6 European Parliament and Council Regulation (EU) 492/2011 of 5 April 2011 on freedom of movement for workers within the Union Text with EEA relevance [2011] OJ L141/1; see also C-186/87, *Cowan*, EU:C:1989:47, paras 16–17.

[28] Art. 7(2) Regulation (EU) 492/2011 on freedom of movement for workers within the Union Text with EEA relevance [2011] OJ L141/1 in line with Regulation (EEC) 1612/68 on freedom of movement for workers within the Community [1968] OJ L257/2.

[29] See Art. 70 of European Parliament and Council Regulation (EC) 883/2004 of 29 April 2004 on the coordination of social security systems [2004] OJ L166/1.

[30] Case C-537/09, *Bartlett et al.* EU:C:2011:278, para 38; for further reading see Michael Dougan, 'Expanding the Frontiers of European Union Citizenship' in Catherine Barnard and Okeoghene Odudu (eds) *The Outer Limits of European Union Law* (Hart 2009) 119, 144–50.

[31] Definition of the term 'habitual residence' in Case C-90/97, *Swaddling* EU:C:1999:96, para. 29; for details see Anne Pieter van der Mei (n 19) 161–4.

[32] For practical examples see Commission, *Practical Guide: The Legislation that Applies to Workers* (Dec. 2013) sect. 3.

have moved down this road in *Brey* and *Dano* when it had to decide on the equal treatment of citizens residing abroad without being economically active there.[33]

Things turned out differently. Instead of relying on the residence-based rationale of Regulation (EC) No. 883/2004 to resolve the dispute, the ECJ effectively diminished its relevance by arguing that the Social Security Coordination Regulation should be construed, first and foremost, as a coordination instrument that identifies the legal order applicable and does not harmonise national rules governing access to specific social benefits.[34] This meant that other rules took over. The latter gave more flexibility to the Court on the basis of the EU Treaties and the Citizenship Directive 2004/38/EC, although their contents had often been applied in a manner which effectively extended domestic welfare systems to all those who are physically present as residents. *Martínez Sala*, *Trojani* and *Grzelczyk* are the most pertinent examples of such residence-based reasoning by the ECJ on the basis of the regular rules on the free movement of persons.[35] However, this was not the only possible outcome: the same rules could be interpreted in a way that directs the case law in a different direction.

3.1.2 Integration model

In the *Förster* ruling the ECJ embarked upon its first full-fledged version of the 'integration model' when it made equal access to study grants conditional upon 'a certain degree of integration',[36] thereby denying equal access to study grants to Union citizens who had resided in the host state for less than five years.[37] To be sure, the integration criterion had been developed by the Court in a number of earlier judgments, but these had employed it in a way that focused on territorial presence in line with the 'residence model'.[38] *Förster* departed from this line of reasoning by making equal treatment conditional upon other qualitative factors.

The essence of the integration model concerns the rejection of equal treatment whenever someone fails to satisfy the 'real/genuine link'[39] or 'certain degree of integration'[40] standard established by the Court.[41] Doctrinally, it is construed as an objective consideration for justifying unequal treatment under Article 18 TFEU, Article 24 Directive 2004/38/EC, Article 4 Regulation (EC) No. 883/2004 or Article 7 Regulation (EU) No. 492/2011, which the Court

---

[33] See Herwig Verschueren, 'Preventing "Benefit Tourism" in the EU' (2015) 52 CML Rev. 363, 377–81; Anuscheh Farahat, 'Solidarität und Inklusion' [2015] Die Öffentliche Verwaltung 45, 47–9.

[34] See Case C-140/12 *Brey* EU:C:2013:565, paras 39–43; reaffirmed by Case C-308/14 *Commission v the United Kingdom* EU:C:2016:436, paras 63–67; and the critique by Herwig Verschueren, 'Free Movement or Benefit Tourism' (2014) 16 EJML 147, 159–64.

[35] See Case C-85/96 *Martínez Sala* EU:C:1998:217; Case C-456/02 *Trojani* EU:C:2004:488; Case C-184/99 *Grzelczyk* EU:C:2001:458.

[36] Case C-158/07 *Förster* EU:C:2008:630, para. 49.

[37] Cf. Art. 24(2) European Parliament and Council Directive 2004/38/EC of 29 April 2004 on the right of citizens of the Union and their family members to move and reside freely within the territory of the Member States [2004] OJ L158/77, whose compatibility with primary law the ECJ reaffirmed in *Förster*, ibid, paras 51–55.

[38] See, in particular, Case C-138/02 *Collins* EU:C:2004:172, para. 72; Case C-209/03 *Bidar* EU:C: 2005:169, paras 58-62; and Case C-258/04 *Ioannidis* EU:C:2005:559, para 35.

[39] Case C-224/9 *D'Hoop* EU:C:2002:432, para. 38; and *Collins* (n 38) para. 67 for jobseekers.

[40] *Bidar* (n 38) para 57 for other Union citizens.

[41] On the emergence of a coherent concept, see Moritz Jesse, 'The Value of "Integration" in European Law' (2011) 27 ELJ 172, 17–82.

interprets in parallel.[42] Nonetheless, it is difficult to identify clear patterns on the basis of the ECJ case law about how the integration criterion should be applied to specific scenarios.[43]

The inherent difficulties in the application of the real link standard to individual cases may have been one deciding factor for the Court to opt for a clear-cut answer in *Dano* and *Alimanovic* when it flatly denied equal treatment to certain categories of Union citizens irrespective of the circumstances of the individual case, since it construed the rejection of equal treatment to flow directly from Directive 2004/38/EC[44] – a conclusion it justified, among others, by the high degree of legal certainty and transparency for domestic authorities and individuals concerned.[45] It is difficult to imagine a more radical deviation from the residence model: territorial presence is deemed irrelevant under EU law; unlawful presence in another Member State brings about no legally significant link to the host society.[46]

It should be noted that the integration model has implications for both incoming and outgoing citizens when it comes to social benefits. While the former may be excluded from welfare provision (as in *Förster*), the latter can rely on the integration argument to 'export' benefits when moving abroad. Conceptually, limitations on incoming citizens and generosity for outgoing nationals are two sides of the same coin if social affiliation, not territorial presence, guides the scope of transnational rights.[47] Against this background, it was conceptually coherent that in a number of judgments throughout the years the ECJ allowed students to export study grants, which host societies can withhold from incoming foreigners. It delivered a remarkable line of rulings emphasising the responsibility of the home state through benefits' exportation in various domains.[48]

3.2 Constitutional Context

There are at least three contextual factors which help to rationalise the move towards the integration model in light of the broader constitutional outlook. First, the Court may have yielded to the EU legislature, since it should be remembered that the initial enthusiasm for equal treatment was shared by the legislature, whose generous interpretation of the Treaty regime throughout the 1960s preceded later Court judgments.[49] That is not to say that the Court wasn't innovative: it certainly was, but its attention mostly focused on national rules in domestic legal orders. Judges often corrected Member States, but there were few instances throughout the years in which it positioned itself consciously against the EU legislature in free movement

---

[42] See Daniel Thym (n 5) 23–4.
[43] See Michael Dougan, 'The Bubble that Burst' in Maurice Adams et al. (eds) *Judging Europe's Judges* (Hart 2013) 127, 140–5; and Daniel Thym (n 5) 45–9.
[44] See Case C-333/13 *Dano* EU:C:2014:2358, para. 77; Case C-67/14 *Alimanovic* EU:C:2015:597, paras 59-60; Niamh Nic Shuibhne, 'Limits Rising, Duties Ascending' (2015) 52 CML Rev. 889, 908–11.
[45] *Alimanovic* (n 44) para 61; Case C-299/14 *Garcia-Nieto et al.* EU:C:2016:114, para. 49.
[46] See also Daniel Thym, 'When Union Citizens Turn into Illegal Migrants' (2015) 40 EL Rev. 248, 256–8.
[47] See Rainer Bauböck, 'Global Justice, Freedom of Movement and Democratic Citizenship', (2009) 50 European Journal of Sociology 1, 19–22; Gareth Davies (n 17) 49–54.
[48] See Nicolas Rennuy, 'The Emergence of a Parallel System of Social Security Coordination' (2013) 50 CML Rev. 1221, 1232–50; Michael Dougan (n 30) 136–62.
[49] See Daniel Thym, 'Family as Link' in Herwig Verschueren (ed.) *Residence, Employment and Social Rights of Mobile Persons* (Intersentia 2016) 11, 16–18; Simone AW Goedings, *Labor Migration in an Integrating Europe* (SDU Uitgevers 2005).

cases. The most prominent examples are *Grzelczyk* and *Baumbast*, when it scrutinised free movement legislation in light of primary law.[50]

It went along these lines in *Vatsouras*, although judges shied away from declaring the restriction in Article 24(2) of the Citizenship Directive to be an outright violation of the EU Treaties.[51] Corresponding uncertainties about the implications of the judgments ultimately led to another reference by the same German court in *Alimanovic*, in response to which the ECJ decided to cease challenges to the exemption on the basis of primary law.[52] The same holds for *Förster*, where judges indirectly confirmed statutory rules on not granting study grants before the acquisition of permanent residence status.[53] In *Dano*, the ECJ was confronted with deliberate ambiguity on the part of the EU legislature and opted for a conservative standpoint.[54] Doing so had the side effect of rendering it easier to satisfy the demands of the British government in the run-up to the Brexit referendum.[55] It could be interpreted, therefore, as an act of defiance towards the potential future will of the EU legislature on a highly politicised topic. In short, the restrictive turn could be an expression of judicial restraint.[56]

Second, the doctrinal infrastructure of the free movement rules for workers and those who do not work may be similar, but their constitutional context differs markedly. While the former (Articles 45, 49, 56, 59 TFEU) have been an integral part of the common market ever since the original Treaty of Rome, the latter (Article 21 TFEU) are closely linked to the concept of Union citizenship brought about by Treaty of Maastricht. Its introduction reiterated the political dream of building some sort of federal Europe, which culminated in the move towards the Constitutional Treaty. Against this background, it can be argued that both the initial enthusiasm of the Court's early citizenship case law and its later hesitation reflect a broader integrationist reorientation,[57] in particular for those who are not economically active. Potential feedback loops between the Court's case law and the evolution of political union will be discussed below.

Third, there is no uniform concept of solidarity underlying equal access to social benefits, since we have to distinguish between work-related benefits and broader social assistance to anyone, defining most domestic welfare systems. Granting equal treatment to workers was and is largely uncontroversial, since most Member States gradually embraced territoriality instead of nationality as the door-opener for various forms of social benefits after the Second World War.[58] Equal treatment for incoming workers was also meant to prevent downward pressure on

---

[50] See Micheal Dougan, 'The Constitutional Dimension to the Case Law on Union Citizenship' (2016) 31 EL Rev. 613–41.
[51] Cf. Joined Cases C-22/08 and 23/08 *Vatsouras and Koupatantze* EU:C:2009:344, paras 33 seq.
[52] See the contribution by Ferdinand Wollenschläger, 'Consolidating Union Citizenship' in Daniel Thym (ed.) *Questioning EU Citizenship* (Bloomsbury/Hart 2017) 171–90.
[53] ECJ (note 35) para 55 notes Art. 24(2) Directive 2004/38/EC, which did not apply directly to the case *ratione temporis*.
[54] See Paul Minderhoud and Sandra Mantu, 'Back to the Roots?' in Daniel Thym (n 52).
[55] See Stephanie Reynolds, '(De)constructing the Road to Brexit' in Daniel Thym (n 52) 57–88.
[56] See Koen Lenaerts, 'The Court's Outer and Inner Selves' in Maurice Adams et al. (n 43) 13, 17–28; Michael Dougan (n 43) 145–53; Vassilis Hatzopoulos, 'Actively Talking to Each Other' in Mark Dawson et al. (eds) *Judicial Activism at the European Court of Justice* (Edward Elgar Publishing 2013) 102–41.
[57] See Michael Dougan (n 43) 150–1.
[58] See Maurizio Ferrera, *The Boundaries of Welfare* (OUP 2005); Thomas Kingreen, *Soziale Rechte und Migration* (Nomos 2010).

legislation, protecting the domestic population.[59] One may certainly question the outer limits of this equality, such as in-work benefits for part-time workers or the level of payments for children living abroad.[60] But such disputes about the fringes should not distract from the essentially economic rationale of equal treatment for workers in line with classic free movement law and corresponding equal treatment guarantees for those who are economically active.

By contrast, there may be no solid normative vision of how transnational solidarity should be construed outside the labour market (it certainly does not follow from the basic agreement on how to treat workers). Floris de Witte has shown that the equal treatment of workers, which one may reconstruct theoretically as an expression of a Durkheimian organic solidarity, does not necessarily pre-empt our position on transnational solidarity for those in need.[61] Similar rights for those who are economically inactive require a broader vision of social justice beyond the paradigms of the single market. To be sure, the Court could have constructed such vision, but it could not draw, when doing so, on the basic political consensus for workers. Again, it may be no surprise, therefore, that the innovative judgments were delivered during a period of optimism in the late 1990s and early 2000s, while the more restrictive turn coincided with the economic crisis which engulfed the Eurozone after 2010.[62] At that time it became more visible that the EU lacked a meaningful social policy, the emergence of which commentators had been cautiously optimistic about a decade earlier.[63]

4. MEMBERSHIP IN POLITICAL COMMUNITIES

In recent Western thought, citizenship has most commonly been associated with membership in political communities.[64] These communities have traditionally been states and the transfer of the citizenship idea to the European Union may therefore necessitate conceptual translation exploring the degree to which established patterns of state membership can be applied to the EU.[65] Recent events reinforced the uncertainty as to whether such conceptual translation may succeed. This section explores corresponding changes (section 4.1) and relates them to broader constitutional trends characterising the ongoing crisis of the European project (4.2).

---

[59] See Simone AW Goedings (n 49) 122–6; Síofra O'Leary, 'Free Movement of Persons and Services' in Paul Craig and Gráinne de Búrca (eds) *The Evolution of EU Law* (OUP 2011) 499, 508–11.

[60] Both questions featured prominently in the reform package agreed upon in the run-up to the Brexit referendum: see Stephanie Reynolds, '(De)constructing the Road to Brexit' in Daniel Thym (n 52) 57–88.

[61] See Floris de Witte, *Justice in the EU* (OUP 2015) ch. 3.

[62] Cf. Stefano Giubboni, 'Free Movement of Persons and European Solidarity' in Herwig Verschueren (n 49) 78, 80–1.

[63] Cf. Catherine Barnard, 'EU "Social" Policy' in Paul Craig and Gráinne de Búrca (n 59) 641–86.

[64] See Dominique Leydet, 'Citizenship' in *Stanford Encyclopedia of Philosophy* (Fall 2011 edition) http://plato.stanford.edu/entries/citizenship>.

[65] Cf. Neil Walker, 'Postnational Constitutionalism and the Problem of Translation' in Joseph H H Weiler and Marlene Wind (eds) *European Constitutionalism Beyond the State* (CUP 2003) 27–54.

4.1 Evolution of Citizens' Rights

The most visible expression of membership in a political community is the right to vote, but it also presupposes the status defining someone as a member of this community and giving her a basic right to remain.[66] In both respects, we can observe a reorientation of supranational citizens' rights in the evolution of the EU Treaties and case law. While residence abroad appeared as the central axis for political participation and the right to remain for many years (section 4.1.1), attachment to the state of origin was reinforced more recently (4.1.2).

4.1.1 Residence model

The Treaty of Maastricht endowed the newly established category of Union citizenship with distinct rights, including the right to vote in municipal and European elections while living in another Member State.[67] This transnational right to vote presents an obvious move towards residence as the decisive factor for political participation. At the time, it could be expected that the voting rights in municipal and European elections might be followed by further moves towards a European democracy. A legal expression of this forward-looking dynamic was today's Article 25 TFEU, which called on the EU institutions 'to strengthen [Union citizenship] or to add to the rights' by means of a simplified Treaty revision procedure.[68] In contrast to the original excitement,[69] the provision turned out to be a dead letter and was not activated once over the past 25 years.

To be sure, the Lisbon Treaty intended to strengthen political participation through, among other things, the introduction of a citizens' initiative and more ambitious Treaty language,[70] but, as discussed below, this did not change much in practice. Regarding the right to vote, attempts to move further towards the residence model failed.[71] Luxembourg rejected voting rights for EU citizens in national elections in a referendum,[72] and the Commission adopted a recommendation requesting Member States to retain the right to vote for nationals living abroad[73] – instead of taking up the citizens' initiative to extend transnational participation in the country of residence.[74] This episode may not be of crucial relevance, but it presents anecdotal evidence for the decline of the 'residence model'.

Along similar lines, EU citizenship was not considerably reinforced as a basic status. Its official designation as 'Citizenship *of the Union*' may relate the individual to the Union's

---

[66] See Linda Bosniak (n 8) 456–63, 470–9.
[67] See today's Article 22 Treaty on the Functioning of the European Union [2012] OJ C326/47.
[68] Art. 25 Treaty on the Functioning of the European Union [2012] OJ C326/47 in line with the original Art. 8e(2) as amended by the Treaty of Maastricht [1992] OJ C224/36.
[69] Cf. Síofra O'Leary, *The Evolving Concept of Community Citizenship* (Kluwer 1996) 308–14.
[70] See Paul Craig, *The Lisbon Treaty* (OUP 2010) 66–71; Jo Shaw, 'Citizenship' in Paul Craig and Gráinne de Búrca (n 59) 575, 597–608.
[71] For corresponding proposals, see Federico Fabbrini, 'Voting Rights for Non-citizens' (2011) 7 EuConst 392, 404–5.
[72] Cf. on the 2015 referendum, Michèle Finck, 'Towards an Ever Closer Union Between Residents and Citizens?' (2015) 11 EuConst 78–98.
[73] See Commission Recommendation 2014/53/EU of 29 January 2014 addressing the consequences of disenfranchisement of Union citizens exercising their rights to free movement [2014] OJ L32/34.
[74] Cf. the Citizens' Initiative 'Let me vote' (No. ECI(2013)000003), which failed to gather enough signatures in 2013/14.

territory as a whole,⁷⁵ but this does not unmake the primary relevance of state nationality. It is sometimes forgotten that corresponding concerns were one of the reasons for the initial Danish rejection of the Maastricht Treaty: Danish voters worried that the EU would interfere with nationality laws.⁷⁶ As a result the European Council adopted a decision, which was integrated into primary law five years later, that EU citizenship 'shall complement and not replace national citizenship'.⁷⁷ It is true that this was reformulated by the Treaty of Lisbon in line with the erstwhile Constitutional Treaty, although it remained unclear whether the semantic shift from Union citizenship 'complement[ing]' to 'be[ing] additional' to nationality implied substantive change.⁷⁸

Against this background, it did not come as a surprise that the Court trod carefully when scrutinising nationality laws. In *Rottmann* it may have obliged Member States to take into account the consequences of any deprivation of nationality for citizens' rights under EU law, while being cautious not to limit state discretion extensively.⁷⁹ Notwithstanding the need for a proportionality test, it reaffirmed the domestic prerogative for acquiring or losing Union citizenship together with nationality in light of international law.⁸⁰ This seemed to change when the *Ruiz Zambrano* judgment set out to reinforce the legal significance of Union citizenship by proclaiming that citizens may invoke the status against measures of their home state depriving citizens of the genuine enjoyment of the substance of rights⁸¹ – a criterion reformulated later as relating to situations 'where [Union citizens] would have to leave the territory of the Union'.⁸² Deriving from Union citizenship a quasi-automatic guarantee to remain on EU territory presented us with a rich expression of the 'residence model'.

4.1.2 Integration model

It is well known among experts of EU law that the Court may have positioned itself for a great leap forward in *Ruiz Zambrano*, but changed direction in later rulings, thereby retreating from the initial move towards the residence model.⁸³ The practical relevance of the 'substance of rights test' was effectively limited to the situation of minor citizens with third-country national family members.⁸⁴ Moreover, the conceptual significance of the new approach was restricted when the Court emphasised that the guarantee to remain in the Union did not imply that a family could stay in Luxembourg where it was residing, since the children held a French

---

⁷⁵ See Loïc Azoulai (n 21) sect. I.
⁷⁶ See David Howarth, 'The Compromise on Denmark and the Treaty on European Union' (1994) 31 CML Rev. 765, 772–3.
⁷⁷ Article 17(1) EC Treaty as amended by the Treaty of Amsterdam [1997] OJ C340/173 differed from Article 8(1) EC Treaty as amended in Maastricht (n 68).
⁷⁸ See Annette Schrauwen, 'European Citizenship in the Treaty of Lisbon' (2008) 15 Maastricht Journal 55, 59–60; Jo Shaw (n 70) 598–600.
⁷⁹ Case C-135/08 *Rottmann* EU:C:2010:104, para. 40 noted the decision of the European Council in response to the first Danish referendum.
⁸⁰ Cf. *Rottmann* (n 79) para 39; and Case C-369/90 *Micheletti* EU:C:1992:295, para. 10.
⁸¹ Cf. Case C-34/09 *Ruiz Zambrano* EU:C:2011:124, para. 42.
⁸² Case C-256/11 *Dereci et al.* EU:C:2011:734, para. 65.
⁸³ For an overview, see Dimitry Kochenov, 'The Right to Have What Rights?' (2013) 19 ELJ 502–16; Mattias Wendel, 'Aufenthalt als Mittel zum Zweck' [2014] *Die Öffentliche Verwaltung* 133–43.
⁸⁴ See Niamh Nic Shuibhne, 'Integrating Union Citizenship and the Charter of Fundamental Rights' in Daniel Thym (n 52) 209–41; Daniel Thym (n 49) 25–8.

passport and could be expected, therefore, to return to France.[85] Union citizenship may connect the individual to Union territory, but the residual responsibility rests with the home state, in line with the public international law.[86] Thus judges accentuated social affiliation instead of territorial presence as the guiding principle for citizens' rights, in line with its conclusion on the EU–Turkey association agreement that 'the acquisition of the nationality of the host Member State represents, in principle, the most accomplished level of integration'.[87]

Along similar lines, the ECJ realigned the significance of social affiliation in an area that had defined much of its early case law on free movement: the public policy exception on the basis of which Member States can expel Union citizens. Judges employed the concept of social integration to interpret the legal position of mobile citizens under the newly established permanent residence status in Directive 2004/38/EC: if citizens disappoint the integration objective, they obtain fewer rights and can be expelled more easily in light of 'integration-based reasoning'.[88] In *Dias*, this implied that formal factors (presence of national residence certificates) are outweighed by qualitative considerations (absence of sufficient resources) because 'the integration objective [...] is based not only on territorial and time factors but also on qualitative elements'.[89] This approach has been reaffirmed in other (but not all) judgments on permanent residence.[90]

The ECJ also employed the integration criterion to bolster its novel approach to the issue of public security.[91] This was manifest in the conclusion in *G* that the seemingly precise ten-year rule for enhanced protection against expulsion should be understood as a proxy for a complex assessment of qualitative factors as a result of which periods of imprisonment need not to be taken into account.[92] The doctrinal impact of these judgments should not be overestimated, since they primarily concern those residing for more than five years and have no immediate bearing on the ECJ's well-established case law on other scenarios.[93] Yet, they signal a conceptual shift away from residence-based equality towards an output-oriented assessment that links citizens' rights to the degree of integration.[94]

---

[85] Cf. Case C-86/12 *Alokpa & Moudoulou*, EU:C:2013:645, para. 34.

[86] See Case C-434/09 *McCarthy* EU:C:2011:277, para. 29; for a thorough analysis, see Maria Florentina Haag, 'Die Letztverantwortung des Herkunftsmitgliedstaates im Unionsbürgerrecht' in Daniel Thym and Tobias Klarmann (eds) *Unionsbürgerschaft und Migration im aktuellen Europarecht* (Nomos 2017) 15–39.

[87] Case C-171/13 *Demirci et al.* EU:C:2015:8, para. 54.

[88] Case C-162/09 *Lassal* EU:C:2010:592, para. 37 following AG Trstenjak, ibid. para. 80.

[89] Case C-325/09 *Dias* EU:C:2011:498, para. 64.

[90] Contrast Case C-378/12 *Onuekwere* EU:C:2014:13, paras 34–36 and Case C-469/13 *Tahir* EU:C:2014:2094, paras 33–34 to Case C-244/13 *Ogieriakhi* EU:C:2014:2068.

[91] See Loïc Azoulai (n 21).

[92] Cf. Case C-400/12 *G* EU:C:2014:9, paras 29–36.

[93] Doctrinally, the new approach remains limited – so far, at least – to Arts 16 and 28, not to Arts 7 and 27 of Directive 2004/38/EC.

[94] Similarly, see Sophie Robin-Olivier, 'Libre circulation des travailleurs' [2011] Revue trimestrielle de droit européen 599, 604–7; Niamh Nic Shuibhne (n 44) 916–26; and Eleanor Spaventa, 'Once a Foreigner, Always a Foreigner' in Herwig Verschueren (n 49) 89–110.

4.2 Constitutional Context

Two contextual factors may help rationalise the move towards the integration model in light of the broader constitutional outlook. They concern the limited bearing of the traditional method of integration through law in the realms of democracy (below 1.) and the general crisis of legitimacy in which the EU has been engulfed in recent years (2.).

4.2.1 The limits of 'integration through law'

The process of EU integration has always relied on the transformative potential of 'integration through law' by employing the law as an instrument for change.[95] Union citizenship was an integral part of this endeavour: a special status for citizens with direct elections to the European Parliament and free movement for those other than workers had been an integral part of the political dream of building some sort of federal Europe through successive Treaty amendments and institutional practices,[96] which also informed the move towards Union citizenship in the Treaty of Maastricht.[97] We can perceive, on this basis, the introduction of citizens' rights as an effort of social engineering to enhance the democratic legitimacy of the European project by way of constitutional fiat. If that is correct, the counter-argument is apparent: it highlights failures and pitfalls of the legal rules in practice.[98] Establishing a fundamental status called 'citizenship' is not a self-fulfilling prophecy. Citizens' rights need to be embedded into social structures and political life in order to fill the legal rules with substance.

It could be argued more convincingly at the time of the Treaty of Maastricht than today that transnational voting rights might be a first move towards a supranational democracy based on enhanced participation and a genuine political culture with pan-European political parties and public discourses.[99] Success was certainly no foregone conclusion, but a cautious optimism prevailed among many observers at the time.[100] The experience of comparative federalism showed that citizens' rights can have unifying effects.[101] Yet there is nothing automatic in such a process: whether and, if so, to what extent Union citizenship commands centripetal forces cannot be deduced from a simple comparison with nineteenth-century state-building. Contextual factors may prevent history repeating itself – and these factors seem to have pointed in the opposite direction in recent years.

It was mentioned earlier that there is a notable parallel between the aspirational Court judgments on Union citizenship and the rise of the Constitutional Treaty, whose failure might have paved the way for a more restrictive turn.[102] This trend seems to have gathered momentum as

---

[95] See Daniel Thym, 'Introduction' in ibid. (ed.) *Questioning EU Citizenship* (Bloomsbury/Hart 2017) sect. III.

[96] Cf. Antje Wiener, *Building Institutions* (Westview 1998) chs 2, 3; Ferdinand Wollenschläger, *Grundfreiheit ohne Markt* (Mohr Siebeck 2007) 90–101.

[97] See, again, Daniel Thym (n 95) sect. III.

[98] See Ulrich Haltern, 'Pathos and Patina' (2003) 9 ELJ 14, 26–32; Jiří Přibáň, 'The Juridification of Identity' (2009) 16 Constellations 44, 47–53.

[99] For the original optimism, notwithstanding principled caveats, see the German Federal Constitutional Court, Judgment of 12 Oct. 1993, Cases 2 BvR 2134/92 & 2159/92, *Treaty of Maastricht*, BVerfGE 89, 155, 184–5.

[100] See, by way of example, Jürgen Habermas, 'Remarks on Dieter Grimm's "Does Europe Need a Constitution?"' (1995) 1 ELJ 303–7.

[101] See the comparison by Christoph Schönberger (n 19).

[102] See Michael Dougan (n 43) 150–1.

a result of the euro crisis and the rise of euroscepticism across the continent. Arguably, events over the past years have shown that even an ideal institutional setting for voting rights and other participatory elements would not necessarily give rise to a meaningful European democracy. Empirical studies show that citizens either do not use their rights in the first place or do not identify with the supranational polity when doing so.[103] Citizens' rights have resulted in a limited degree of shared feelings of mutual belonging among the citizens of Europe capable of sustaining, as an identificatory infrastructure for solidarious communities, broader redistributive policies.[104] From an empirical perspective, the *legal* construction of Union citizenship need not coincide with the *social* construction of European identity.

4.2.2 A vision for the Union as a whole

An initial analysis of the Brexit referendum reveals a division between mobile and immobile citizens, since it was the latter who disproportionately supported the 'leave' campaign.[105] This coincides with earlier findings that those exercising their free movement rights are inclined to be more supportive of EU integration, while those who do not tend to be more critical.[106] By contrast, much of the academic literature focused on the mobile citizen living in another Member State, while ignoring the broader societal and political effects of the decision by many citizens to stay at home[107] – which, coincidentally, was a crucial consideration in the Spaak report paving the way for the Treaty of Rome.[108] A holistic analysis will have to overcome this primary attention to those crossing borders. The doctrinal proposal to apply citizens' rights to purely internal situations was rejected by the Court for reasons which arguably concerned the preservation of the federal balance of power.[109] The challenge remains how to relate the analysis of citizens' rights to wider effects for societies as a whole.

Such a broader outlook would connect discussions about transnational mobility to the state of the Union as a whole. Indeed, the citizenship case law is not the only area in which judges in Luxembourg shied away from fostering a supranational vision of social justice by means of Treaty interpretation: not assessing austerity measures in light of the Charter of Fundamental Rights is another example.[110] Thus the reticence on the part of the Court to further explore the constitutional potential of Union citizenship may reflect a more general concern that guarantees in the EU Treaties cannot resolve the problems with which the EU is confronted at this juncture. The Court may have decided implicitly not to develop a thick reading of constitutional rules on either citizenship or monetary union at time of profound economic and political crisis. Anyone trying to change this will have to engage, therefore, in a general undertaking to

---

[103] See Adrian Favell, 'European Citizenship in Three Eurocities' (2010) 30 Politique européenne 187, 191–202.

[104] Cf. Richard Bellamy, 'Evaluating Union Citizenship' (2008) 12 Citizenship Studies 597, 601–6; Gerard Delanty, 'European Citizenship' (2007) 11 Citizenship Studies 63–72.

[105] See Rainer Bauböck, 'Freedom of Movement under Attack' (2016 EUDO Citizenship Forum).

[106] See Ettore Recchi, 'The Engine of "Europeanness"?' in Daniel Thym (n 52) 135–48; Theresa Kuhn, *Experiencing European Integration* (OUP 2015) ch. 7; Neil Fligstein, *Euro-Clash* (OUP 2010).

[107] For a rich discussion see Sara Iglesias Sánchez, 'A Citizenship Right to Stay?' in Dimitry Kochenov (n 21) 371–93.

[108] Cf. Editorial Comments (2014) 51 CML Rev. 729, 730; Simone AW Goedings (n 49) 121–3.

[109] For more detail see Daniel Thym, 'Frontiers of EU Citizenship' in Dimitry Kochenov (n 21) 705, 719–22.

[110] See Agustín José Menéndez, 'Which Citizenship?' (2014) 15 GLJ 907, 928–31.

develop a vision of social justice for the Union as a whole, not only for those moving across borders.¹¹¹

This leaves us with the overall impression of both the EU institutions and the Union's highest Court retreating from earlier attempts at constitutional engineering by means of enhanced citizens' rights and progressive constitutional adjudication. That need not be understood as resignation. It could be presented positively as a move towards a more confederal understanding of European integration which restrains the vision of some sort of federal Europe and accepts that the Member States will remain the primary political communities in years to come.¹¹² Doing so would not be a return to the closed nation-state, but would build the European Union on domestic communities within a broader supranational structure of mutual respect and responsiveness.¹¹³ The move away from residence-based voting rights and the strengthening of national citizenship in recent case law can be perceived as building blocks of such a European Union based on domestic political communities instead of promoting a quasi-federal vision of the EU.

5. MIGRATION, MOBILITY AND SOCIAL COHESION

Citizenship can have many meanings. Most accounts seem to concur, nonetheless, that it embraces questions of membership and belonging, although authors might disagree about how the element of identity is to be construed normatively.¹¹⁴ The European Union is no exception, since it has been an integral part of the redefinition of statehood after the Second World War. More recently, this 'post-national' conception of Union citizenship was confronted with the increasing salience of migration from third-states, which became a prominent feature of EU activities and domestic policy debates. This section will explore the interaction between both developments by linking the institutional practice on citizens' rights (section 5.1) to debates about migration at European and national level (5.2).

5.1 Evolution of the Citizens' Rights

Considering controversial citizenship cases, the residence status of family members of Union citizens holding the passport of a third state appears as a common thread in judgments such as *Baumbast*, *Carpenter*, *Akrich*, *Metock*, *Ibrahim*, *Ruiz Zambrano*, *Dereci* and *Alokpa*. This linkage between Union citizenship and migration law helps us rationalise the shift, on the part of the ECJ, from enhanced residence rights (section 5.1.1) to a renewed focus on questions of social integration (section 5.1.2).

---

¹¹¹ The 'Conclusion' by Dora Kostakopoulou and Daniel Thym in Daniel Thym (ed.) *Questioning EU Citizenship* (Bloomsbury/Hart 2017) explores trends in this direction.
¹¹² See the contribution by Francesca Strumia, 'European Citizenship and Transnational Rights' in Daniel Thym (n 52) 149–69.
¹¹³ See Kalypso Nicolaïdis, 'European Demoicracy and Its Crisis' (2013) 51 JCMSt. 351–69; Richard Bellamy, 'An Ever Closer Union of Peoples' (2013) 35 J Eur. Integration 499–516.
¹¹⁴ See Karin De Vries, 'The Integration Exception' in Daniel Thym (n 52) 267–86 and Clíodhna Murphy, 'Membership without Naturalisation?' in Daniel Thym (n 52) 287–308.

5.1.1 Residence model

The introduction of Union citizenship has been an integral part of the redefinition of statehood. It was meant to symbolise the benefits which EU integration brings to the individual, thereby supporting the '*rapprochement* of peoples who wish to go forward together'.[115] Union citizenship can be said, therefore, to have a 'post-national' character. It appeared as a vehicle for overcoming the close nation-state with its traditional ethno-cultural definition of belonging.[116] Citizens' rights could be construed, on this basis, as emancipatory in character, giving the individual the option to choose different life plans and to pursue her happiness beyond her home state. It presented, in essence, an instrument to overcome established meanings of belonging. To find conclusive evidence that such vision motivated judges is inherently difficult, but cannot be excluded.[117]

It is much easier, by contrast, to trace the interaction between Union citizenship and the residence rights of third-country national family members. Their status came into the ambit of ECJ case law only indirectly, since third-country nationals cannot rely on citizens' rights. They benefit from free movement in the form of 'derived rights'[118] as family members of a sponsor holding an EU passport. As a result, corresponding judgments were not primarily about movement for economic purposes, which constituted the formal doctrinal basis for the Court's intervention, but revolved around questions of family unity in substance.[119] For some years, it seemed as if judges in Luxembourg were protecting family unity as an end in itself. The formal linkage to free movement rights was given little attention.[120] Residence-based equality for Union citizens and third-country national family members appeared as the new hallmark of transnational citizens' rights.

5.1.2 Integration model

In recent years, the Court of Justice has shown noticeable sensitivity when dealing with family members from third countries. Judgments concerned diverse doctrinal scenarios, but they had one thing in common: they revealed an interpretative shift from a judicial style of argumentation based on the telos (purpose) and constitutional principles (human rights, free movement) to an examination of the wording and the general scheme of the rules in question. This conclusion extends to judgments on social benefits and the more restrictive follow-up to *Ruiz Zambrano* discussed earlier in the same way, as it concerns third-country national family members.

The Court found, for instance, that a derived residence right after divorce does not come about if the partner left the Member State before initiating divorce proceedings,[121] and that parents living across the border in another Member State cannot invoke derived rights.[122] It

---

[115] European Union, Report by Mr Leo Tindemans to the European Council, Bulletin of the EC Supplement 1/76, 27 (emphasis in the original).
[116] See Dora Kostakopoulou (n 18) ch. 4; Yasemin Soysal (n 18).
[117] For instructive reading, see Bruno de Witte (n 61) 22–37; Joseph HH Weiler, 'To Be a European Citizen' in ibid. (ed.) *The Constitution of Europe* (CUP 1999) 324–57.
[118] *Dereci et al* (n 82) para. 55.
[119] For further comments, see Daniel Thym (n 49) 20–31.
[120] See Eleanor Spaventa (n 15) 764–8; Alina Tryfonidou, 'Family Reunification Rights of (Migrant) Union Citizens' (2009) 15 ELJ 634–53.
[121] See Case C-218/14 *Singh et al.* EU:C:2015:476.
[122] See Case C-40/11 *Iida* EU:C:2012:2405, paras 46–65.

also concluded that family members do not benefit from a derived residence status whenever a Union citizen moves abroad, marries there and returns to his home state before a period of three months has elapsed, since free movement has not been exercised effectively in such a scenario.[123] It is noticeable that such a conclusion puts less emphasis on family unity as an end in itself, reinforcing instead the classic concept of transnational mobility as the hallmark of free movement.[124] This did not undo the generosity of the earlier case law, which judges did not overturn, but it emphasised that citizens' rights do not bring about indefinite equal treatment whenever residing abroad.

The perspective of migration law towards third-country nationals allows us to elucidate another element of the free movement case law: the qualitative approach to the 'integration' yardstick in recent rulings on social benefits and the public policy justification discussed above. Generally, the notion of 'integration' is used more frequently for cross-border movements of third-country nationals than for Union citizens. It became a central term in debates about immigration policy at national and European level from the mid-2000s onwards.[125] In the context of immigration law, the concept soon developed a life of its own, emphasising the value of social cohesion besides residence-based quality; secondary legislation often employed the term in the context of opening clauses allowing Member States to make the residence status of foreigners conditional upon, for instance, integration requirements by promoting the knowledge of the national language.[126] The ECJ subscribed to this contextual approach in two judgments.[127]

5.2 Constitutional Context

There are at least three contextual factors which help to rationalise the move towards the integration model in light of the broader constitutional outlook. First, EU law had addressed cross-border movements of people mainly from the perspective of Union citizenship for many years. This may have changed given the newly found prominence of immigration from third countries both in political debates and in the EU Treaties, which have comprised supranational competences for law-making on immigration law sensu stricto since the Treaty of Amsterdam, on the basis of which the EU legislature adopted a number of legislative instruments that can have a direct bearing on citizenship cases.[128] On closer inspection, various judgments on family members discuss these instruments alongside free movement rules,[129] although the ECJ

---

[123] See Case C-456/12 *O & B* EU:C:2014:135, para. 52.

[124] See Eleanor Spaventa, 'Family Rights for Circular Migrants and Frontier Workers' [2015] 52 CML Rev. 753, 764–78; Etienne Pataut, 'Citoyenneté de l'Union européenne' [2014] Revue trimestrielle de droit européen 781, 791.

[125] For a reliable overview, see Sergio Carrera, *In Search of the Perfect Citizen?* (Martinus Nijhoff 2009); Karin De Vries (n 114).

[126] See Moritz Jesse (n 41) 182–8; Sergio Carrera (n 125) ch. 4.

[127] See Case C-579/13 *P & S* EU:C:2015:369 and Case C-153/14 *K & A* EU:C:2015:453; and the analysis by Clíodhna Murphy; and Daniel Thym, 'Towards a Contextual Conception of Social Integration in EU Immigration Law' (2016) 18 EJML 89–111.

[128] See Thomas Horsley (n 10) 956–63; Anja Lansbergen and Nina Miller, 'European Citizenship Rights in Internal Situations' (2011) 7 EuConst 287, 300–1.

[129] See esp. ECJ (n 82) paras 71–72; ECJ (n 122) paras 78–81; Case C-87/12 *Ymeraga et al.* EU:C:2013:291, para. 42.

had brushed aside a related argument some years before.[130] These new rules on third-country nationals differ markedly from Union citizenship – mirroring discrepancies between citizens' rights and the EU–Turkish association acquis in relation to which the Court explicitly recognised that it pursued different objectives than EU citizenship and that, therefore, 'the two legal schemes in question cannot be considered equivalent'.[131] In short, the change could be the result of an adaptation, on the part of judges, to a modified legal and constitutional context.

Second, the distinction between Union citizenship and immigration law in relation to third-country nationals has constitutional implications, since the latter leaves the EU legislature more discretion.[132] When adopting corresponding rules, the Member States rejected a transfer of the residence-based logic of the (early) citizenship regime to immigration law. Instead, they promoted the more contextualised meaning of social integration mentioned earlier. It can be argued that the qualitative realignment of the 'integration' yardstick in the more recent citizenship case law integrates this immigration-based logic into free movement rules (while many commentators had expected the influence to run in the opposite direction[133]). The language used by the British government before the Brexit referendum did the same: it constantly branded Union citizens as 'migrants' and warned against instances of 'benefits tourism', thereby tearing down the semantic wall between the 'mobility' of EU citizens and the 'immigration' status of third-country nationals which the Commission had tried to erect in its official communications.[134]

Third, the Court may have responded to calls from national governments after intense reactions to both the *Metock* judgment and the *Ruiz Zambrano* ruling had signalled fundamental concerns.[135] We should be careful, however, not to equate this call for proactive integration policies with right-wing populism even if it can be (mis)used for this purpose. Allowing Member States to pursue integration policies within certain limits need not contradict the 'post-national' orientation of Union citizenship, which helped overcome the closed nation-state. Supranational rules would continue to direct the reconfiguration of collective identities away from traditional notions of ethno-cultural essentialism to embrace diversity and non-discrimination,[136] without however preventing Member States from seeking a new sense of mutual trust and collective belonging on the basis of some sort of rights-based and discourse-oriented constitutional patriotism, be it at national level or for an emerging European democracy.[137] Such outlook would suit earlier findings that the EU institutions started to recognise the value of social cohesion at a time when the financial crisis and Brexit indicated that some sort of political union at supranational level would not be forthcoming.

---

[130] Despite calls to the contrary by AG Geelhoed, Case C-127/08 *Metock* EU:C:2008:449, para. 66 neglected the immigration dimension.

[131] Case C-371/08 *Ziebell* EU:C:2011:809, para. 74.

[132] See Daniel Thym, 'EU Migration Policy and Its Constitutional Rationale' (2013) 50 CML Rev. 709, 716–25.

[133] See Moritz Jesse (n 41) 188–9; Kees Groenendijk, 'Recent Developments in EU Law on Migration' (2014) 16 EJML 313–35.

[134] Cf. Daniel Thym (n 46) 256.

[135] See Niamh Nic Shuibhne and Jo Shaw, 'General Report' in Ulla Neergaard et al. (eds) *Union Citizenship. The XXVI. FIDE Congress* (DJØF 2014) 65, 139–50.

[136] See Christian Joppke (n 24) ch. 4; Daniel Thym (n 20) 314–15.

[137] See Jürgen Habermas, 'Staatsbürgerschaft und nationale Identität' in ibid., *Faktizität und Geltung* (Suhrkamp 1992) 632–60; Gerard Delanty (n 104) 67; Jan Werner Müller, *Constitutional Patriotism* (Princeton UP 2007).

6. CONCLUSION

While the legal rules on Union citizenship have been relatively stable, their interpretation has changed markedly and remains subject to intense debates about Court judgments and wider institutional practice. This chapter set out to rationalise these arguments in light of broader constitutional trends defining the state of the European integration process at this juncture. It employed two distinct visions of how to construe supranational citizenship as a heuristic device for reconstructing discussions on diverse subject matters such as welfare benefits, political participation, nationality law, residence security and interaction with immigration law towards citizens of third countries. Doing so allowed us to highlight a common trend underlying Court judgments and institutional practice: they epitomise a drift away from residence-based equality towards a novel emphasis on the value of social cohesion when the meaning of citizens' rights is intricately connected to the degree of integration in host societies.

How to explain this normative reconfiguration of supranational citizenship? This chapter argues that the volatile character of Union citizenship and the move towards the 'integration model' can be rationalised by the constitutional context. Although each scenario is defined by specific circumstances discussed above, there are three overarching themes connecting the evolution of citizens' rights to broader constitutional trends. First, the ECJ's restrictive turn on social benefits and family members can be explained by greater deference to the legislature, which had always sent out mixed signals when it came to social benefits for Union citizens who do not work and to the immigration status of third-country nationals. Although judges in Luxembourg had emphasised the dynamic potential of Union citizenship in earlier cases, new judgments are defined by a conservative style of argumentation which accentuates the limits of Union law and recognises the significance of the new provisions on immigration law.

Second, there is a notable parallel between shifting institutional practices and the rise and fall of the Constitutional Treaty. The latter arguably presented the high point of the 'integration through law' concept which employed EU law as an instrument for political and social change. Union citizenship was an integral part of these endeavours, since it had always been aimed at fostering the link between the European project and its citizens. The momentum behind this idea seems to have been lost. This is most visible in discussions on political participation and the significance of nationality in relation to which the initial drive towards transnational equality based on residence gave way to a fortification of membership and democratic legitimacy in the Member States. Institutional practices emphasising the value of social integration appear as epitaphs of a Union losing self-confidence as a supranational polity, emphasising instead the continued significance of solid political communities at national level.

Third, there is nothing automatic in the projection of a legal solution from one policy field to another. Thus, the equality-based reasoning behind economic market integration cannot justify access to social benefits across borders for those who do not work. To do so requires a distinct normative vision of social justice. In this respect, a general deficit of European constitutionalism became apparent in recent years. The Court of Justice hesitates to develop a thick normative understanding of supranational rules that may guide the resolution of intricate political questions. Union citizenship is not the only area in which the Court trod carefully, not least in the run-up to the Brexit referendum. It similarly showed constraint in the context of the euro crisis. The novel emphasis on social integration in the citizenship case law need not contradict this tendency. It can be explained as an expression of institutional practices which accept the limits of supranational constitutionalism while recognising that the Union should be built on functioning communities at national level. The evolution of citizens' rights can be construed as an integral part of this wider trend.

5. The genesis of European rights
Willem Maas

1. CITIZENSHIP, EUROPEAN RIGHTS AND EUROPEAN INTEGRATION

The genesis of European rights has not been adequately explained.[1] Contrary to what many believe, arguments over European rights have been present since the start of European integration. This means that existing accounts of European Union citizenship do not adequately capture its origins and growth. European rights have political origins. A rights-based approach – breaking citizenship down into its constituent rights in order to examine their origins – explicates the politics surrounding the introduction and expansion of European rights. It thereby clarifies the nature of an important aspect of European integration, showing that European rights did not originate from the slow accretion of functional spill-overs, but rather resulted from agreements reached by government negotiators.

The existing literature on European rights can be divided into two general categories. The first comprises legalistic narratives of the gradual development of treaties, directives, regulations and court cases. This literature is typically divorced from any deep consideration of the political and economic context of the legal documents under consideration.[2] The second category of literature reflects the recent surge in interest in citizenship and has proliferated since the 'introduction' of European Union citizenship in the Maastricht Treaty of 1992. Existing work on EU citizenship presents it as a recent phenomenon whose precursors date from the 1980s,[3] or at the most from the mid-1970s.[4] By contrast, this chapter elucidates the political genesis of the key rights of EU citizenship, those concerning free movement of workers, in the initial negotiations that established the foundations of European integration in the early 1950s.

---

[1] This chapter was previously published in JCMS the Journal of Common Market Studies (2005) 43(5) 1009–25. Parts of earlier versions of this article were presented at conferences of the International Studies Association 2002; the Canadian Political Science Association 2002; and the European Union Studies Association 2003. My debts for assistance with the larger research project on EU citizenship on which this chapter draws are too numerous to mention. For comments specifically on this chapter, however, I thank Alan Milward, Gilles Grin, Christopher Chivvis and the anonymous referees. Any remaining shortcomings are my own.

[2] F. Burrows, *Free Movement in European Community Law* (Clarendon Press 1987); John Handoll, *Free Movement of Persons in the EU* (Wiley 1995).

[3] Hans Ulrich Jessurun d'Oliveira, 'Union Citizenship: Pie in the Sky?' in Allan Rosas and Esko Antola (eds), *A Citizen's Europe: In Search of a New Order* (Sage 1995); Epaminondas A. Marias, 'From Market Citizen to Union Citizen' in Epaminondas A. Marias (ed), *European Citizenship* (European Institute of Public Administration 1994); Jo Shaw, 'The Many Pasts and Futures of Citizenship in the European Union' (1997) 22(6) European Law Review 554.

[4] Elizabeth Meehan, *Citizenship and the European Community* (Sage 1993); Carlos María Bru, *La Ciudadanía Europea* (Editorial Sistema 1994); Antje Wiener, *European Citizenship Practice: Building Institutions of a Non-State* (Westview 1998).

The virtue of a rights-based analysis of citizenship is that it connects and extends the two literatures discussed above: the work of legal scholars who trace the evolution of treaties, directives, regulations and court decisions, and the work of scholars who focus on contemporary EU citizenship.[5] The focus is on the origins of European rights of free movement, because freedom of movement represents the core of contemporary EU citizenship.[6] The analysis has important implications for our understanding of European Union citizenship, which ceases to be a contemporary phenomenon that dates only from the Maastricht Treaty,[7] becoming instead a recent expression of the same kinds of political tensions and resolutions that have characterized the entire history of European integration.

The political push for rights predates the Schuman plan which led to the 1951 European Coal and Steel Community Treaty (ECSC; Treaty of Paris), but supranational rights in Europe originated in this Treaty's provisions for the free movement of coal and steel workers. In a political compromise, these provisions were included at the insistence of the Italian delegation, although other Member States delayed their implementation. The 1957 Treaty establishing the European Economic Community (EEC; Treaty of Rome) extended free movement rights to much wider categories of workers and specified in far greater detail how these rights would be realised.

Most commentators view the Treaty of Rome as the 'birth of Europe', yet the earlier Treaty of Paris not only established the Community's basic institutional framework,[8] but also established the first legal provisions concerning free movement of labour. While free movement did not figure prominently in the ECSC Treaty negotiations, the promise of these rights provided the key incentive for Italian participation in the Community. Determining how these rights would be exercised took years to negotiate and even longer to implement, ultimately being outpaced by the wider category of free movement rights contained in the Treaty of Rome. Although it significantly broadened the scope of free movement rights, the Treaty of Rome's announcement of the free movement of workers – one of the four freedoms that comprise the internal market agenda – was reproduced from the Treaty of Paris. Thus, the Treaty of Rome should be viewed as simply the expansion of an already established framework of politically negotiated provisions that granted free movement rights. The rights that today form the core of EU citizenship date from the free movement provisions of the European Coal and Steel Community.

---

[5] This chapter thus extends back the work of legal scholars who have perceptively argued that the Treaty of Rome's free movement provisions established an 'incipient' form of European citizenship: Richard Plender, 'An Incipient Form of European Citizenship' in Francis Geoffrey Jacobs (ed), *European Law and the Individual* (Elsevier/North Holland 1976) or that Union citizenship is the effect rather than the cause of increased mobility rights: Patrick Dollat, *Libre circulation des personnes et citoyenneté européenne: enjeux et perspectives* (Bruylant 1998).

[6] European Commission, *Report of the High-Level Panel on the Free Movement of Persons (Veil Report)* (Office for Official Publication of the European Communities 1998).

[7] Joseph H.H. Weiler, *The Constitution of Europe* (Cambridge University Press 1999).

[8] Berthold Rittberger, 'Which Institutions for Post-war Europe? Explaining the Institutional Design of Europe's First Community' (2001) 8(5) Journal of European Public Policy 673–708.

2. FROM THE SCHUMAN PLAN TO THE ECSC TREATY

A rights-based view of citizenship allows us to break citizenship down into its constituent parts and thereby to examine the rise of citizenship from the very beginnings of European integration. Today it is conventional wisdom that freedom of movement had to be introduced in order to ensure a common market.[9] The logic is clear for free movement of goods and capital. But even if it is conceded that individual mobility is a desirable goal in an economic community, it does not automatically follow that free movement provisions should be enshrined as individual rights. The assertion that an EU citizen who moves to live or work in another Member State is exercising a new transnational right is incontrovertible.[10] Because extending European rights to individuals constrains Member States to respect those rights,[11] states should prefer not individual rights but rather bilateral or multilateral agreements as a means of enhancing individual mobility. It is thus not easy to explain why national governments should be willing to grant rights to individuals rather than simply working out intergovernmental bargains on an ad hoc basis.[12]

The political push for specific European rights predates the Schuman plan. In Italy in 1943, the Movimento Federalista Europeo envisaged the creation of a European 'continental' citizenship alongside national citizenship, consisting of direct political and legal relationships with a European federation. The 'Milan programme' – drawn up by Giovanni Gronchi, later President of the Italian Republic; Count Stefano Jacini; and labour union leader Achille Grandi – called among other things for the legal equality of the citizens of all states and the 'option to take out European citizenship in addition to national citizenship'.[13] Similarly, the Dutch 'European Action' group called for European citizenship to supplement national citizenship, and the 1948 Hague Congress of the European Movement resolved that an essential ingredient of union was direct access for citizens to redress before a European court of any violation of their rights under a common charter.[14]

In this context, the first concrete steps to European integration were initiated with the announcement by French minister Robert Schuman on 9 May 1950 – the tenth anniversary of the German invasion of France, the Netherlands, Belgium and Luxembourg – of a plan for an

---

[9] Frits Bolkestein, 'De uitbreiding en het effect ervan op de vrijheden van de interne markt' *Beraad voor de bouw* (2000) http://europa.eu.int/comm/internal_market/en/speeches/spch363nl.pdf.

[10] Commission of the European Communities, *Freedom of Movement for Persons in the European Community* (OOPEC 1982).

[11] Lisa J. Conant, *Justice Contained: Law and Politics in the European Union* (Cornell University Press 2002).

[12] Alan Milward argues that 'when Italian governments selected emigration as a priority policy choice, an interdependent international order advanced such policies better than an integrationist one', in *The European Rescue of the Nation-State* (Routledge 1992) 437, but this is a politically incomplete picture. The policy choice of emigration is much better served through supranational institutions than ad hoc bargains. In terms of the historical record, as will be shown below, Italian negotiators pushed very hard to achieve an integrationist solution: they were primarily responsible for including free movement rights in the treaties.

[13] Piero Malvestiti, 'There Is Hope in Europe' in Addresses delivered on the occasion of the inauguration of the High Authority of the European Coal and Steel Community, 16–23 September (Publications Department of the European Communities 1959) 58.

[14] Gary T Miller, 'Citizenship and European Union: A Federalist Approach' in Lloyd C Brown-John (ed), *Federal-type Solutions and European Integration* (University Press of America 1995) 371–2.

ECSC. Some believed that the Schuman plan would narrow the scope for independent state action and possibly herald the eventual demise of state sovereignty.[15] Nevertheless, negotiators focused almost exclusively on economic issues. Free movement of labour played a minor role in the bargaining between the potential Member States in the summer and autumn of 1950. The sole exception was Italy, for which the issue was of enormous importance: the promise of free movement for workers was a key reason for Italian participation in the ECSC.[16] Although political support for the 'European idea' and the economic desire to acquire raw materials cheaply also figured, the principal incentive for Italian participation in the Schuman plan was 'to permit export of its surplus labor'.[17] Indeed, for 'at least fifteen years after the war, the primary interest of most Italians in a European federation was the hope of finding an outlet for the emigration of large numbers of their excess population'.[18]

The issue of labour migration was broached by Taviani, the Italian negotiator, who later wrote that free movement rights for workers constituted a fundamental principle of the Community. Its realisation was the key condition for Italian participation, and Taviani even envisioned creating a European ministry of labour.[19] During the negotiations, Taviani pushed for a better deal on migration by raising the spectre of a High Authority with the power to set and enforce wage levels across the Community.[20] As this was an important issue for the other potential Member States, the negotiations proceeded with 'the Italians using the issue as a bargaining counter for a resolution on the migration question and the Dutch and Germans resolute in keeping HA powers to an absolute minimum'.[21] Because Dutch and German negotiators were concerned that the High Authority would overturn the delicate compromises that had been achieved domestically, they were ready to capitulate to the Italian demand for a flexible resolution to the migration question.[22] Like Italy, the Netherlands and Germany were labour-exporting countries in the early 1950s, and thus did not foresee any problems.[23]

Opposition might have come from the only potential Member States which had significant numbers of foreign coal workers: Belgium (70,594 foreign workers in 1951) and France (56,535). In Belgium, more than two out of every five coal workers were non-Belgian, primarily Italian. In France, the proportion was half that of Belgium: foreigners accounted for

---

[15] Paul-Henri Spaak, 'The Integration of Europe: Dreams and Realities' (1950) 29(1) Foreign Affairs 95.
[16] Giuseppe Pella, *La Comunità Europea del Carbone e dell'Acciaio: Risultati e Prospettivo* (Edizioni 5 Lune 1956); Vedi F Serra, 'Alcune osservazioni sulla presenza della rappresentanza degli interessi nella delegazione italiana al Piano Schuman' in Andrea Ciampani (ed), *L'altra via per l'Europa: Forze sociali e organizzazione degli interessi nell'integrazione europea (1947–1957)* (Franco Angeli 1995) 132.
[17] Henry L. Mason, *The European Coal and Steel Community: Experiment in Supra-nationalism* (Martinus Nijhoff 1955) 5.
[18] F. Roy Willis, *Italy Chooses Europe* (Oxford University Press 1971) 150.
[19] Paolo Emilio Taviani, *Solidarietà atlantica e comunità europea* (Edizioni Atlante 1954) 176–80.
[20] Ruggero Raniero, *Italy and the Schuman Plan Negotiations* (European University Institute 1986) 22.
[21] Richard T. Griffiths, 'The Schuman Plan Negotiations: The Economic Clauses' in Klaus Schwabe (ed), *Die Anfänge des Schuman-Plans, 1950/51* (Nomos 1988) 42.
[22] Albert Kersten, 'A Welcome Surprise? The Netherlands and the Schuman Plan Negotiations' in Klaus Schwabe (ed), *Die Anfänge des Schuman-Plans, 1950/51* (Nomos 1988) 296.
[23] Daniel Vignes, *La Communauté européenne du charbon et de l'acier : Un exemple d'administration économique internationale* (Georges Thone 1956).

one out of every five coal workers.²⁴ Most of these workers were Polish, and thus unaffected by any potential ECSC Treaty provisions. Bolstered by strong public support for the Schuman plan, and intent on forging a deal, the French delegation under the leadership of Jean Monnet was willing to grant concessions.²⁵ The Belgian position was a pragmatic one, concerned more with the fate of its ailing coal and steel industries than the prospect of even more immigration of workers.²⁶ Indeed, if coal mines were to close, it seemed likely that foreign workers would return to their countries of origin.

The Italian delegation was keen to promote the freedom of movement of its nationals elsewhere in Europe. In the earlier Organization for European Economic Co-operation (OEEC) and Franco–Italian customs union negotiations, Italy had presented emigration requests for large numbers of unskilled workers, but received only limited offers for skilled workers. Since there were already between 70,000 and 80,000 Italian coal and steel workers in the other five prospective ECSC Member States, the Italian negotiators argued that, failing labour mobility on a general scale, it should surely be possible to achieve a sectoral arrangement.²⁷ The delegation received strong support from Italian parliamentarians such as Christian Democrat Deputy Bima and Grupo Misto Senator Merzagora, who regarded the ultimate outcome of the negotiations as the achievement of a political goal they had long desired.²⁸ The Italian delegation was successful in its effort to include free movement rights in the draft Treaty, and the first steps to free movement rights for workers in the area that would become the European Economic Community were enshrined in the ECSC Treaty. Article 69 of the final Treaty announced that 'Member States undertake to remove any restriction based on nationality upon the employment in the coal and steel industries of workers who are nationals of Member States and have recognised qualifications in a coalmining or steelmaking occupation, subject to the limitations imposed by the basic requirements of health and public policy'.

Because of these limitations, the Italian success in including freedom of movement for labour was thus tempered. Here in nascent form were the restrictions on freedom of movement for the purposes of health and public policy that still today provide Member States with the power to limit free movement rights.²⁹ Rather than being forced to admit workers, Member

---

²⁴ Communauté Européenne du Charbon et de l'Acier, *Recueil Statistique de la Communauté Européenne du Charbon et de l'Acier* (Haute Autorité 1953) 54.

²⁵ As early as October 1950, French public opinion favoured the Schuman plan by a margin of two to one, despite being rather ill-informed about its contents: Institut français de l'opinion publique, *Sondages: Revue française de l'opinion publique* (1951) 13(1) 23; Raymond Racine, *Vers une Europe nouvelle par le plan Schuman* (La Baconnière 1954); Jean Monnet, *Mémoires* (Fayard 1976).

²⁶ Michel Dumoulin, 'La Belgique et les débuts du Plan Schuman (mai 1950–février 1952)' in Klaus Schwabe (ed), *Die Anfänge des Schuman-Plans, 1950/51* (Nomos 1988); Alan Milward, 'The Belgian Coal and Steel Industries and the Schuman Plan' in Klaus Schwabe (ed), *Die Anfänge des Schuman-Plans, 1950/51* (Nomos 1988).

²⁷ William Diebold, *The Schuman Plan: A Study in Economic Cooperation 1950-1959* (Council on Foreign Relations 1959); Ruggero Raniero, *Italy and the Schuman Plan Negotiations* (European University Institute 1986) 22–3.

²⁸ Communauté Européenne du Charbon et de l'Acier, *Le Traité C.E.C.A. devant les Parlements Nationaux* (Assemblée Commune, Division Etudes, Information et Documentation 1958).

²⁹ Thus Articles 39 and 46 of the Treaty of Amsterdam (on free movement of workers and the right of establishment, respectively) specify that these rights continue to be 'subject to limitations justified on grounds of public policy, public security or public health'. The point is not teleological; the current utility of these restrictions clearly cannot explain their inclusion at the beginning of the process of integration. Rather, free movement provisions have been subject to restrictions from their inception, although the

States could invoke health issues or public policy in order to limit access to domestic labour markets. Another potential source of restriction was the ambiguous definition of 'recognised qualification'. Section 2 of Article 69 provided that 'Member States shall draw up common definitions of skilled trades and qualifications therefor', which left significant room for restrictive interpretation. Finally, a key institutional barrier was the fact that the role of the High Authority was limited to co-ordinating and advising: according to the Treaty, the Member States were responsible for drafting and implementing the Treaty's free movement provisions. One reason for this arrangement may have been the Italian preference for announcing principles in the treaties, while postponing the details about administration and implementation.[30]

3. RATIFICATION AND IMPLEMENTATION

As was true during the negotiations – where only the Italian delegation placed much emphasis on labour mobility – the question of the free movement of workers remained a minor one during the various national debates on the ratification of the ECSC Treaty.[31] Still, some parliamentarians, such as Communist members of the French Assemblée Nationale Bonte and Patinaud, Communist member of the French Conseil de la République Primet, and Communist Belgian Senator Glineur, reproached the Treaty's authors for desiring to bring about a 'deportation' of labour. Communists were worried that workers would 'become nothing more than simple merchandise'.[32] Indeed, Communist parties in all the parliaments of the Member States were opposed to the proposed Treaty. For example, the French Communists saw the Treaty as a tool of American foreign policy.[33] Dutch Christian Democrats argued that free movement of workers would create moral problems as families were uprooted.[34] A German socialist member of the Bundestag pointed out that Article 69 was unclear about whether workers in

---

legal and practical restraints on freedom of movement have been gradually disappearing since these first attempts in the 1950s.

[30] Giacinto della Cananea, 'L'Italia e l'Europa: la politica "comunitaria" nel periodo iniziale del processo di integrazione (1952–1967)' in Erik Volkmar Heyen (ed), *Die Anfänge der Verwaltung der Europäischen Gemeinschaft* (Nomos 1992).

[31] Communauté Européenne du Charbon et de l'Acier, 1958 (n 28).

[32] Communauté Européenne du Charbon et de l'Acier, 1958 (n 28) 131.

[33] Americans 'would again deport French workers with the aid of the Treaty's clauses guaranteeing free movement of labour. American capital and its tool, the Ruhr industrialists, would soon control the [High Authority]. A huge army of French unemployed would be created to provide slave labor for American bases in France, where atom bombs and bacteriological weapons would be stored', according to Henry L. Mason, *The European Coal and Steel Community: Experiment in Supra-nationalism* (Martinus Nijhoff 1955) 30. Beyond the rhetoric, the key concern was that the freedom of movement provisions would equate workers with goods and capital and make them ripe for exploitation. French communists had long remained opposed to European unification. A September 1957 public opinion survey found that 55 per cent of French communists thought that a union of France with the other five ECSC/EEC states was of little or no use (5 per cent thought it was indispensable; 25 per cent thought it was somewhat or very useful; 15 per cent did not respond), compared to only 11 per cent of socialists (31 per cent indispensable; 46 per cent somewhat or very useful; 12 per cent no response) and single digits of partisans of the other parties: results from Institut français de l'opinion publique, *Sondages: Revue française de l'opinion publique* (1957) 19(3) 12–13.

[34] Representatives Maenen (KVP) in the Second Chamber and Vixseboxse (CHU) in the First Chamber according to Communauté Européenne du Charbon et de l'Acier, *Le Traité C.E.C.A. devant*

the coal and steel industries who moved to another Member State would be authorised to seek alternative employment in the host state if their employment were disrupted by strikes.[35] In the end, though, none of these concerns prevented the Treaty of Paris from being ratified in all the Member States.

Ratification did not automatically mean that coal and steel workers could freely move within ECSC territory. Goods had been immediately subject to free movement. In contrast, Article 69's commitment to worker mobility could be implemented only by unanimous agreement between the Member States. Negotiations over its detailed provisions began in March 1953 as the High Authority appointed a committee of experts to propose the best means of implementing Article 69. The committee reported in November, when the High Authority endorsed its findings and called an intergovernmental conference.[36] The HA's efforts to facilitate worker mobility among the six Member States were spearheaded by the social affairs commission. One of the High Authority's four general commissions, the social affairs commission was responsible for a panoply of policies intended to raise the standard of living, only one of which was freedom of movement. On the basis of the work done by the committee of experts the previous autumn, the social affairs commission took a first step towards co-ordination on Article 69 by convening an intergovernmental conference of the labour ministers of the six Member States in May 1954. Although the meeting reportedly took place in a 'cordial atmosphere', its only outcome was 'to raise certain imperfections in the Treaty and to partially make clear how Article 69 should be revised', although the Commission heralded the meeting as 'a first step towards a new and fruitful process of interinstitutional collaboration'.[37] Nevertheless, the draft agreement did provide the basis for further discussions over the summer and autumn.

These discussions ended in a relatively narrow interpretation of Article 69. The Italians had continued to push for wider interpretation while opposition grew elsewhere as industries in the other states, particularly France and Luxembourg, underwent technical conversions which reduced the demand for coal and steel workers.[38] This caused the Italians to focus efforts on creating a more general market for labour that would not be restricted to coal and steel workers.[39] The HA's report at the conclusion of the negotiations lamented their prolonged

---

les Parlements Nationaux (Assemblée Commune, Division Etudes, Information et Documentation 1958) 131.

[35] The representative, Birkelbach, was concerned about workers' rights in the event of a strike : reported by Communauté Européenne du Charbon et de l'Acier, *Le Traité C.E.C.A. devant les Parlements Nationaux* (Assemblée Commune, Division Etudes, Information et Documentation 1958) 132. The focus of this kind of concern later shifted to the question of whether or not a worker originally admitted to work in the coal and steel industry could later change occupation: reported by High Authority of the European Coal and Steel Community, *Second General Report on the Activities of the Community* (Publications Service of the European Coal and Steel Community 1954) 171.

[36] High Authority of the European Coal and Steel Community, *Second General Report on the Activities of the Community* (Publications Service of the European Coal and Steel Community 1954) 169.

[37] Communauté Européenne du Charbon et de l'Acier, 'Rapport sur l'application du traité instituant la Communauté européenne du charbon et de l'acier pendant la période du 1er Janvier au 30 avril 1954' (Assemblée Commune, Service d'études et de documentation 1954) 9.

[38] European Coal and Steel Community, *Bulletin from the European Community for Coal and Steel* (Publications Service of the European Coal and Steel Community 1954) 168.

[39] The HA co-operated with the International Labour Office to convene a meeting of experts in Geneva to study a draft European social security convention for migrant workers, according to High Authority of the European Coal and Steel Community, *Third General Report on the Activities of the Community* (Publications Service of the European Coal and Steel Community 1955) 159. And the Spaak

nature but presented the agreement 'as a first step towards the creation of a "common market" for labour'.[40] The Council of Ministers approved the revised draft agreement on 8 December 1954, although its implementation would depend on parliamentary ratification in each of the Member States.[41] Administrative details were finalized in the months that followed, and a final agreement on free movement was reached in more than twice the time it had taken to negotiate the Treaty itself. The High Authority reassured anyone worried about potential mass migrations that 'comparatively few workers [would] immediately avail themselves' of the labour cards. Rather, it estimated that any significant labour migration would have to be preceded by 'reconversions and marked technical changes [to] area labour markets'.[42]

Although the HA and the Italian government had strongly urged that the definition of worker qualifications be interpreted broadly, other governments succeeded in limiting the application of the Treaty to certain skilled workers: only 300–400,000 of the Community's 1.4 million coal and steel workers qualified for the international work permits which would allow them to move freely. The international permit allowed these skilled workers to seek employment in other Member States without being held up by the red tape generally governing the immigration of labour. A contemporary American observer reported enthusiastically on early efforts made to 'enable these workers to enjoy all the social security benefits of the receiving country, thus preventing the discriminations that have frequently been practised against aliens in the past' and to 'improve co-ordination between the various employment organizations in the Member States so that workers in one country may know more easily whether jobs are available elsewhere'.[43]

Despite such optimistic assessments immediately following the agreement on Article 69's provisions, full implementation of the agreement was delayed until after all the Member States had ratified it. Italy, Belgium, France and the Netherlands ratified the agreement by the end of 1955. However, the German Bundestag delayed ratification until May 1956 and Luxembourg stymied the entire process by postponing its ratification until June 1957.[44] As a result, the agreement on free movement of workers finally took effect in September 1957, four and a half years after work on it had begun. This delay proved a constant irritant to the Italians between

---

subcommittee favourably assessed the various efforts of the Council of Europe, the European Political Community and the OEEC to facilitate worker mobility, concluding that the establishment of a common European labour market should be introduced gradually, according to Comité intergouvernemental créé par la Conférence de Messine, *Inventaire des organismes existants dans les domaines visés par la résolution de Messine* (European Community for Coal and Steel 1955).

[40] High Authority of the European Coal and Steel Community, *Third General Report on the Activities of the Community* (Publications Service of the European Coal and Steel Community 1955) 157–8.

[41] Henry L. Mason, *The European Coal and Steel Community: Experiment in Supra-nationalism* (Martinus Nijhoff 1955) 101–2.

[42] European Coal and Steel Community (n 38).

[43] Derek Curtis Bok, *The First Three Years of the Schuman Plan* (Princeton University Press 1955) 56.

[44] Luxembourg's contemporary resistance on matters of migration has deep historical roots. For example, in 1953 the Luxembourg Christian Socialist deputy Margue feared 'a rash and unreasonable migration which would do more harm than good to both the labour market and the standard of living of the workers', according to the Meeting of the Common Assembly, 13 May 1953, p.83, cited in Dirk Spierenburg and Raymond Poidevin, *The History of the High Authority of the European Coal and Steel Community: Supranationality in Operation* (Weidenfeld and Nicolson 1994) 175.

1952 and 1957. Most of the speeches by Italian members of the Common Assembly concerned the migration issue, in particular the delay in working out Article 69's provisions.[45]

The Italian preoccupation with migration may be explained by these numbers: ECSC officials calculated in 1954 that

> present labour migration across frontiers within the Community is confined to Italian agricultural labourers employed in Belgian coal mines. Some 40,000 of the 150,000 miners in Belgium are Italians. Most of the Italian workers in the Belgian mines, however, regard their employment as temporary. The other main group of migrants are some 12,000 workers who live near frontiers of the Community nations and now can cross at will for work without encountering obstacles.[46]

Though some Italian economists discouraged the idea that 'opening the frontiers could free a massive emigration of Italian workers and eliminate unemployment in a flash',[47] the political interest shown during the ECSC negotiations persisted.

The delayed introduction of free movement raised such ire that the Common Assembly included the issue in its constitutional proposals for rewriting the ECSC Treaty as a result of the negotiations taking place on the European Economic Community. The question of free movement rights was the *only* policy issue in a document otherwise solely concerned with the relationship between the High Authority and the new institutions that the proposed new treaties would introduce. Dissatisfied with the application of Article 69, the Common Assembly concluded that the Member States were acting too slowly to implement free movement rights for coal and steel workers. Therefore, it proposed that the High Authority should take over from the Member States the responsibility to establish 'common definitions of skilled trades and qualifications', propose immigration rules and settle 'any matters remaining to be dealt with in order to ensure that social security arrangements do not inhibit labour mobility'.[48] The Common Assembly further proposed to insert into the Treaty a new article giving the High Authority the power to propose measures to address possible disproportionalities between the supply of and demand for labour.[49]

The Common Assembly's faith in the High Authority may have been somewhat misplaced. Encouraging greater free movement of labour did not appear to be a key priority for the High Authority. Instead, it focused on combating unemployment and constructing adequate housing for coalminers and steelworkers. President of the High Authority Jean Monnet saw free movement of workers as only one of a number of ways to achieve better living and working conditions for workers across the six Member States.[50] This was true despite Monnet's earlier, well-known rhetoric about uniting Europeans by focusing not on states but on peoples. Nevertheless, the social affairs commission was persistent in the face of Member

---

[45] Mason (n 41) 100.

[46] European Coal and Steel Community, *Bulletin from the European Community for Coal and Steel* (Publications Service of the European Coal and Steel Community 1954).

[47] Confederazione Italiana Sindicati Lavoratori, *La politica sociale della Comunità Economica Europea: Atti del terzo convegno di studi di economia e politica del lavoro* (1959) 70–1; F Roy Willis, *Italy Chooses Europe* (Oxford University Press 1971).

[48] Gerhard Kreyssig, *Révision du Traité instituant la Communauté Européenne du Charbon et de l'Acier* (Communauté Européenne du Charbon et de l'Acier 1958) 24–5.

[49] Kreyssig (n 48).

[50] Jean Monnet, *Les États-Unis d'Europe ont Commencé: La Communauté Européenne du Charbon et de l'Acier, Discours et Allocutions 1952–1954* (Robert Laffont 1955).

State intransigence and delay, its efforts duly reported in the Common Assembly's updates.[51] These effects were favourably received. The social affairs commission noted with satisfaction that the EEC Treaty offered the chance to correct the restrictions which had been placed on free movement of workers on the basis of a restrictive interpretation (especially by the Council decision of 8 December 1954) of Article 69 of the ECSC Treaty.[52]

4. FROM PARIS (ECSC) TO ROME (EEC)

Despite the slow progress on liberalising restrictions on the movement of workers, mainstream political actors across Europe were united in supporting the ECSC's striving for 'efficiency and distribution of labour' in order to achieve the goal of a 'sound economy based on a rational distribution of labour in a free market'.[53] This goal was seen as a desirable objective, and one that could be expanded to other economic sectors. In 1954, the governments of the six Member States began to consider a new economic initiative that would complement the ECSC. The Dutch were pressing for a general economic common market, against the view of the Belgian government – supported by French ministers, Jean Monnet, and others – that further co-operation should occur by economic sector, extending the ECSC into transport and forms of energy other than coal and steel. On 20 May 1955, the Benelux governments presented a joint proposal combining the sectoral and common market approaches. This proposal was considered at the special meeting of the ECSC Council of Ministers at Messina on 2 and 3 June 1955. At Messina, the ministers established an intergovernmental committee headed by Belgian Foreign Minister Paul-Henri Spaak to prepare a report on the feasibility of a common customs union and a common atomic energy agency. They further agreed to adopt the Benelux programme, modified for more gradual implementation.[54]

The Benelux itself represented a successful experiment in the free movement of workers. Even though a *de facto* common market in labour had been operational in the Benelux since the end of the Second World War, no Treaty had been signed to formalise this arrangement

---

[51] Communauté Européenne du Charbon et de l'Acier, 'Rapport fait par Mlle M.A. Klompé sur les relations extérieures de la Communauté et le développement de celle-ci envisagé à la lumière de l'évolution politique actuelle (Document no. 4)' (Assemblée Commune, Service d'études et de documentation 1954).

[52] Communauté Européenne du Charbon et de l'Acier, 'Rapport de M. Bertrand sur la migration et la libre circulation des travailleurs dans la CECA. Rapport no. 5, novembre 1957' (Assemblée Commune, Service d'études et de documentation 1957); Assemblée parlementaire européenne, 'Rapport sur le règlement relatif aux premières mesures pour la réalisation de la libre circulation des travailleurs dans la Communauté, Document 67' (1960) 8–9.

[53] Council of Europe, *First Joint Meeting of the Members of the Consultative Assembly of the Council of Europe and of the Members of the Common Assembly of the European Community of Coal and Steel, Official Report of the Debate, 22 June 1953* (Consultative Assembly 1953) 71.

[54] For some governments, including that of the United States, establishing a common approach to atomic energy was more important than any other form of co-operation. Thus, according to Secretary of State John Foster Dulles, the United States did not attach to the common market proposals the same 'immediate security and political significance as [it did] to Euratom', although it also recognised that a common economic market might 'contribute constructively to European integration', which was useful in tying Germany to western Europe according to Peter M.R. Stirk and David Weigall, *The Origins and Development of European Integration: A Reader and Commentary* (Pinter 1999).

by the time the ECSC foreign ministers met in Messina. Furthermore, the number of workers making use of this common labour market remained relatively small. Nevertheless, a Benelux social affairs commission was working on a proposal which would formally eliminate the need for worker and employer permits, regulate labour shortages and surpluses and introduce the principle of equal treatment for nationals of any Benelux country.[55] This proposal acquired legal force in 1957, thereby establishing the first coordinated system for the free movement of workers within the future EEC.

As the ECSC free movement provisions continued to be obstructed, proponents of greater European integration pushed instead for expanding rights to many more categories of workers in the approaching Treaty establishing the EEC. A large part of the impetus for the growing focus on workers' freedom of movement can be found in the report submitted by the Spaak committee. The report argued that undistorted competition would lead to monetary stability, economic expansion, social protection, a higher standard of living and quality of life, economic and social cohesion, and solidarity among the Member States.[56] In the Spaak committee's view, these goals depended on the undistorted competition of which freedom of movement for workers formed an integral part. Free movement of workers was required for the other objectives to be achieved, and the committee argued that '[w]e should not overestimate the scale of movements of labour that would occur in a common market without any barriers'.[57] The committee's recommendations contain the genesis of the 'market citizen'[58] who bears rights as an economic rather than political actor.

While the Treaty of Paris had limited freedom of movement to workers with 'recognised qualifications in a coalmining or steelmaking occupation', the final text of the Treaty of Rome expanded the scope of the free movement provisions to cover all workers, with the exception of those employed in the public service. Freedom of movement for workers now entailed

> the right [...] to accept offers of employment actually made; to move freely within the territory of the Member States for this purpose; to stay in a Member State for the purpose of employment [...] [and] to remain in the territory of a Member State after having been employed in that State. (Article 48 EEC)

The Treaty of Rome did leave room for Member States to restrict these rights in implementing regulations: Member State governments could avoid implementing free movement rights based on public policy, health or security grounds. Still, the new rights went well beyond any arrangements provided for in bilateral agreements. Although bilateral agreements were clearly more important in the early years,[59] the experience of negotiating the ECSC provisions laid the groundwork for the Treaty of Rome's free movement provisions. This is clear from the Treaty negotiating drafts referring extensively to ECSC Article 69, from the fact that many

---

[55] Comité intergouvernemental créé par la Conférence de Messine, *Commission du Marché Commun des Investissements et des Problèmes sociaux, sommaire de conclusions no 3* (European Community for Coal and Steel 1955) 94.

[56] Comité intergouvernemental créé par la Conférence de Messine, *Rapport des Chefs de Délégation aux Ministres des Affaires Étrangères* (European Community for Coal and Steel 1956).

[57] *Rapport des Chefs de Délégation aux Ministres des Affaires Étrangères* (n 56) 88.

[58] Michelle Everson, 'The Legacy of the Market Citizen' in Jo Shaw and Gillian More (eds), *New Legal Dynamics of European Union* (Oxford University Press 1995).

[59] Federico Romero, *Emigrazione e integrazione europea 1945–1973* (Edizioni Lavoro 1991).

negotiators had participated in the ECSC negotiations and from the Spaak committee's earlier work examining the ECSC provisions on freedom of movement.[60] Unlike the Treaty of Paris, the Treaty of Rome set a clear deadline for implementing free movement. Article 49 of the Treaty of Rome provided that as 'soon as this Treaty enters into force, the Council shall, acting on a proposal from the Commission and after consulting the Economic and Social Committee, issue directives or make regulations setting out the measures required to bring about, by progressive stages, freedom of movement for workers'. The article therefore granted the Commission – rather than the Member States, as was the case with the ECSC Treaty – the power and the responsibility to propose measures required to bring about freedom of movement for workers. The Treaty of Rome thus contained an expanded version of the labour provisions originally announced in the Treaty of Paris six years previously.

5. CONCLUSION

European Union citizenship is often presented as a recent invention. By breaking citizenship down into its constituent rights, however, we can trace its genesis back to the earliest years of European integration. Although the political push for European rights predates the Schuman plan, the European Coal and Steel Community Treaty contained the foundation of what today forms the core of right of Union citizenship: freedom of movement. The political origins of European rights are evident from the ECSC Treaty negotiations and ratification and implementation debates. Article 69 of the Treaty provided that Member States would remove all restrictions based on nationality on the employment in the coal and steel industries of workers who were citizens of Member States and who had recognised qualifications in a coalmining or steelmaking occupation. The determination of what constituted a recognised qualification, however, was left to intergovernmental bargaining: Member States had to agree to common definitions, and the resulting agreement then had to be ratified by each of the Member States before it would come into effect. In the final agreement reached in 1954, only 300,000 of the

---

[60] Thus, for example, the 22 January 1957 negotiating draft discusses who should be covered under the term 'national worker' and suggests adopting the interpretation of ECSC Article 69, Chefs de Délégation document 257, replacing document 156 of 10 January 1957, reported in Comité intergouvernemental pour le Marché Commun et l'Euratom, *Rédaction approuvée par le Comité des Chefs de délégation le 22 janvier 1957 concernant Titre III Chapitre 3 La libre circulation des travailleurs* (European Community for Coal and Steel 1957). Furthermore, the Italian delegation once again tied the issue of free movement of workers to another sensitive issue, this time by threatening to block agreement on the free movement of capital unless a safeguard clause proposed by the delegations from France and Luxembourg was removed (Chefs de Délégation meetings of 1, 8–9 and 17–18 February 1957). Several members of the Italian delegation had participated in the ECSC negotiations or the work of the OEEC according to F. Roy Willis, *Italy Chooses Europe* (Oxford University Press 1971) 56. Earlier, the Spaak committee had noted that the experience of the ECSC established that it was not necessary to eliminate economic distortions before lowering the barriers to the free movement of workers, according to Comité intergouvernemental créé par la Conférence de Messine, *Commission du Marché Commun des Investissements et des Problèmes sociaux, sommaire de conclusions no 3* (European Community for Coal and Steel 1955), 8 September 1955, Document 191. And a sub-committee of the Spaak committee extensively studied the ongoing ECSC experience according to Comité intergouvernemental créé par la Conférence de Messine, *Rapport présenté par M.J. Doublet au nom de la sous-commision des problèmes sociaux* (European Community for Coal and Steel 1955), 23 September 1955, Document 277.

Community's 1.4 million coal and steel workers were deemed qualified to move freely, and the agreement was not ratified by all the Member States until 1957. The delay frustrated many participants, particularly the Italian negotiators, whose primary interest in European integration was facilitating the emigration of large numbers of Italian workers to the rest of Europe. The difficulties in reaching a common definition of who would qualify for freedom of movement, and the slow ratification of the intergovernmental agreement after it had finally been reached, may help explain the much stronger free movement provisions of the Treaty of Rome. This expanded the scope of the free movement provisions to all workers, with the exception of those employed in the public service, and granted the Commission – rather than the Member States, as was the case with the ECSC Treaty – the power and the responsibility to propose measures required to bring about freedom of movement for workers. Furthermore, the Treaty of Rome set a clear deadline for the implementation of the free movement of workers, who gained the right to move freely within the territory of the Member States to accept offers of employment, to stay in a Member State to work, and to remain there after having been employed in that state. The obligation placed on governments to eliminate distinctions based on nationality (Paris) thus became the right of workers to free movement (Rome), which continues today to form the nucleus – subsequently expanded and transformed – of EU citizenship.

6. EU citizenship: a social empathy perspective
Karmelia Yiannakou

1. INTRODUCTION

The ancient Greek philosopher Heraclitus expressed that 'the only constant in life is change'. Similarly, Aristotle's theory of motion (*kinesis*), which was developed to understand change in the natural world, was explained as the actuality (*entelecheia* (+*energeia*)) of a potentiality (*dynamis*). By analogy, this suggests that any conception of actualising a potentiality always involves an active element of being-at-work (*energeia*) which, it can be argued, does not necessarily imply a *telos* in the sense of end but rather one in terms of *purpose*. The constant of change, which inevitably leaves us exposed to uncertainty and vulnerability, is sometimes more intensely felt at the social level when it follows a crisis that is driven, for example, by demands for social, political, economic and other readjustments. The EU has not been unaccustomed to crises, as it was itself born out of one of the biggest crises the world has witnessed.

Following the Second World War, the pooling of coal and steel industries was not merely a move to revive a collapsed economy but a move towards reviving the shaken spirit of European societies through an emphasis on solidarity and world peace by making future war 'not merely unthinkable, but materially impossible'.[1] Since then, there have been a series of legal treaties and the adoption of a vast number of binding and non-binding legal instruments to secure economic growth and protect against war. These can no longer operate as the only legitimising factor for the EU, especially following the introduction of EU citizenship whereby every person holding the nationality of a Member State has become a Union citizen (Article 20 TFEU). A series of crises during the last decade urge us, now more than ever, to pose the much-needed *Quo vadis Europe?* The rise of populist rhetoric in Europe, the tensions concerning socio-economic welfare following the sovereign debt crisis and the lead-up to Brexit and the failures of adequate protective mechanisms in asylum and migration, coupled with the anxieties and uncertainties of the recent global health crisis within the broader domestic political climate on the future of Europe, continue to remind us that EU citizenship, like every other institution, is woven into a very complex and multi-layered environment.

It is, therefore, not difficult to see how change – in terms of constitutional and institutional development (substantial or more trivial), but also a shift in individual and collective consciousness – is often the response to critical events and crises. As Kostakopoulou put it: 'Transformations, be they in society, social sciences or ourselves, essentially commence as re-orientations. Things suddenly look different. From this standpoint, new explorations are possible, new meanings can be discovered and the fine-structure of a relation to which things can be added is revealed.'[2]

---

[1] Schuman Declaration.
[2] Dora Kostakopoulou, *Institutional Constructivism in Science and Law: Frames of Mind, Patterns of Change* (CUP 2018) 5.

Change is thus in flux, involving a matrix of complex relations which cannot be disconnected from one another unless zooming in to understand a particular aspect or explore a specific feature. When we, therefore, talk about change in the context of EU citizenship, as rightly advocated by many scholars and legal practitioners, we are zooming in to understand a minor aspect of change within the broader socio-political context, not only within the EU but within the global environment. Although this interconnectivity may be self-evident, it is often omitted or detached from the examination of EU citizenship. It is important that we make a conscious effort to contextualise our subject of analysis despite its often being a Herculean task, because that is how we can better reflect upon our expectations and anchor them to a broader purpose that allows us to live together better.

This contribution suggests that we are at a juncture where a reorientation towards societal transformation is not only desired but necessary. Therefore it offers a lens, both methodological and normative, through which we may explore aspects of EU citizenship going beyond an analysis of legislation and judicial decisions and offering instead an additional alternative framework that allows us to focus on the subject *qua* citizen and her relationship to the legal structures. This chapter can be situated in the context of more recent calls by experts, socio-legal scholars and practitioners for a new narrative of European integration and EU citizenship.[3] It follows an institutional constructivist approach as developed by Kostakopoulou and it converges this and Kostakopoulou and Ferreira's thesis for a humanist shift within EU law and policy by concentrating on the affective and relational dimension of EU citizenship as a social institution capable of transforming and constructing social realities. My contribution has an interdisciplinary orientation and introduces a social empathy approach that derives from the practice-based discipline of social work, while incorporating and fusing elements from sociology, social psychology and political philosophy. The aims are twofold: first, the chapter defends the need for a creative multidisciplinary approach to exploring questions of EU citizenship and social justice by shifting our focus towards human-centred citizenship; second, it hopes to inspire further research concerning the relationality of EU citizenship and citizens as they experience it in their everyday lives through interdisciplinary research.

The structure of this chapter is as follows. It provides a bird's-eye view of the main controversies within the current state of affairs in the context of EU citizenship, albeit in a very limited manner, as extensive analyses of case law and the status quo have been provided elsewhere.[4] Subsequently, it reflects upon EU citizenship as a matrix of relations drawing upon institutional constructivism. It then introduces the social empathy approach as a prism that enables us to reflect upon the different relations, practices and injustices involved and as a way to re-orientate our approach to EU citizenship and social justice in the EU.

---

[3] Nathan Cambien, Dimitry Kochenov, Elise Muir (eds), *European Citizenship Under Stress: Social Justice, Brexit and Other Challenges* (Brill|Nijhoff 2020); Charlotte O'Brien, *Unity in Adversity: EU Citizenship, Social Justice and the Cautionary Tale of the UK*, (Hart Publishing 2017); Nuno Ferreira, Dora Kostakopoulou (eds) *The Human Face of the European Union: Are EU Law and Policies Humane Enough?* (CUP 2016).

[4] Daniel Thym (ed.), *Questioning EU Citizenship: Judges and the Limits of Free Movement and Solidarity in the EU* (Hart Publishing 2017).

2. BIRD'S-EYE VIEW OF THE STATUS QUO

Many EU law scholars have systematically explored EU citizenship as this has developed from its embryonic phase, through special rights for citizens,[5] to its codification in the Maastricht treaty and its judicial interpretation during different stages of the European integration.[6] Throughout the years the EU itself has been approached from different angles and has been explained and described using different terms such as 'superstate',[7] 'cosmopolitan empire',[8] 'network polity'[9] and, inter alia, 'superpower'.[10] Similarly, commentators have criticised European citizenship and underlined its weakness, particularly when compared to its national counterparts,[11] as well as, with caution, considering it from a democratic legitimacy perspective and in terms of the idea of a *demos*.[12] However, it has also been explored with reserved optimism regarding its potential.[13] It is this optimism that allows us to seek creativity even in one of the most rigid disciplines, law, and in the most controversial subtopic within EU law, namely citizenship.

Currently, this optimism is clouded by the strong orientation of citizenship towards economic activity within the internal market, the persisting migratory element still needed in the majority of cases to activate citizenship and the Charter, and the uncertainties associated with the loss of EU citizenship in the light of Brexit.

The Court's recent case law, which will not be analysed here, indicates the construction of a marginalised group of citizens – those who are 'static', 'non-mobile' or 'economically

---

[5] Commission of the European Communities, Towards European Citizenship COM (75) 321 final (2 July 1975).
[6] Spaventa, for example, identifies four periods, namely 'market citizen' phase, constituent phase, consolidation phase and reactionary phase. Eleanor Spaventa, 'Earned Citizenship – Understanding Union Citizenship through Its Scope', in Dimitry Kochenov (ed.), *EU Citizenship and Federalism: The Role of Rights* (CUP 2017) 204–25.
[7] Glyn Morgan, *The Idea of a European Superstate: Public Justification and European Integration* (Princeton University Press 2009).
[8] Ulrich Beck, Edgar Grande, *Cosmopolitan Europe* (Polity 2007).
[9] Barrie Axford, Richard Huggins, 'Towards a post-national polity: the emergence of the Network Society in Europe' (2000) 48 (S1) The Sociological Review 173.
[10] Robert J. Guttman (ed), *Europe in the New Century: Visions of an Emerging Superpower* (Lynne Rienner Publishers 2001).
[11] Hans Ulrich Jessurun d'Oliveira, 'Union Citizenship: Pie in the Sky?', in Allan Rosas and Esko Antola (eds), *A Citizens' Europe: In Search of a New Order* (Sage 1995); Hans Ulrich Jessurun d'Oliveira, 'European Citizenship: Its Meaning, Its Potential', in Renaud Dehousse (ed.), *Europe after Maastricht: An Ever Closer Union?* (Springer 1994); Siofra O'Leary, *The Evolving Concept of Community Citizenship* (Kluwer 1996).
[12] Cris Shore, *Building Europe: The Cultural Politics of European Integration* (Routledge 2000); Cris Shore, 'Whither European citizenship: Eros and civilization revisited' (2004) 7(1) European Journal of Social Theory 27; Simon Hix, *What's Wrong with the European Union & How to Fix It* (Polity Press 2008) cf: Andrew Moravcsik, 'In defence of the "democratic deficit": reassessing the legitimacy in the European Union' (2002) 40 (4) Journal of Common Market Studies 603.
[13] Theodora Kostakopoulou, 'Towards a theory of constructive citizenship in Europe' (1996) 4 (4) Journal of Political Philosophy 337, 346; Carlos Closa, 'The concept of citizenship in the Treaty on European Union' (1992) 29 (6) Common Market Law Review, 1137; Antje Wiener, 'Assessing the constructive potential of Union citizenship – a socio-historical perspective' (1997) 1 (17) European Integration Online Papers.

inactive'.[14] Although the controversy regarding issues of access to the national welfare systems has been particularly salient since the economic crisis,[15] the Court's formalistic and laconic interpretation of citizenship in the line of *Dano* case law reflects a judicial stasis[16] which appears contrary to its earlier more ambitious and normative trajectory.[17] Although this does not mean that EU citizenship has no future or that the Court is bound to follow the same administrative logic in the future, it does suggest that for a more substantial change to take place we need more than judicial imagination. As Thym has pointed out in the context of *Dano*, 'the hesitation on the side of the Court to become involved with wider political disputes presents a powerful reminder of the limits of transformative integration through law'.[18]

The reaction to the Court's approach in *Dano*,[19] *Alimanovic*,[20] *Garcia Nieto*[21] and *Commission v United Kingdom*[22] shows a mixed approach in the literature: while some suggest that the Court has essentially abandoned any form of social and meaningful citizenship based on equality and inclusion,[23] others argue that the Court has not departed significantly from its earlier jurisprudence and has instead provided legal certainty.[24] Even if the Court's interpretation of citizenship provisions in such cases is hermeneutically justified, there is still a longing shared by the majority of socio-legal scholars within this area for (more) inclusive citizenship if the latter is to amount to anything that goes beyond the confines of the market.[25] This derives from the fact that the EU has long ceased to be considered as a merely economic and political organisation and, as a result, certain expectations have been formed. These are connected to the EU's responsibilities – legal or otherwise – towards its citizens and others within its sphere of influence. The Court, as we know, has played a major role in paving this path in cases like

---

[14] See for example Anita Heindlmaier, Michael Blauberger, 'Enter at your own risk: free movement of EU citizens in practice' (2017) 40 (6) West European Politics 1198-1217; Daniel Thym, 'The elusive limits of solidarity: residence rights of and social benefits for economically inactive Union citizens' (2015) 52 (1) CML Rev 17–50; Moritz Jesse, Daniel William Carter, 'Life after the "Dano-Trilogy": Legal Certainty, Choice and Limitations in EU Citizenship Case Law' in Cambien, Kochenov, Muir (n 3).

[15] Agustín José Menéndez, 'The existential crisis of the European Union' (2013) 14 (5) German Law Journal 453–526.

[16] Although, as we will see, this perceived stasis can be understood, as Kostakopoulou explained, in terms of regression.

[17] See further Urška Šadl, Suvi Elina Sankari, 'Why Did the Citizenship Jurisprudence Change?' in Thym (n 4), 89–109; see also Niamh Nic Shuibhne, 'Limits rising, duties ascending: The changing legal shape of Union citizenship' (2015) 52(4) CML Rev 889–937.

[18] Daniel Thym, 'When Union citizens turn into illegal migrants: the Dano case' (2015) 40 EL Rev 248–61, 260.

[19] C-333/13 *Elisabeta Dano and Florin Dano v Jobcenter Leipzig* EU:C:2014:2358.

[20] C-67/14 *Jobcenter Berlin Neukölln v Nazifa Alimanovic and Others* EU:C:2015:597.

[21] C-299/14 *Vestische Arbeit Jobcenter Kreis Recklinghausen v Jovanna García-Nieto and Others* EU:C:2016:114.

[22] Case C-308/14 *Commission v UK*, EU:C:2015:666.

[23] More characteristically see criticism by Charlotte O'Brien, 'Civis capitalist sum: class as the new guiding principle of EU free movement rights' (2016) 53 (4) CML Rev 937–77; Charlotte O'Brien, 'The ECJ sacrifices EU citizenship in vain: Commission v. United Kingdom' (2017) 54 (1) CML Rev 209–43.

[24] Moritz Jesse, Daniel William Carter, 'Life after the "Dano-Trilogy"': Legal Certainty, Choices and Limitations in EU Citizenship Case Law' in Cambien, Kochenov, Muir (n 3).

[25] O'Brien (n 3); Kochenov, 'EU citizenship: some systemic constitutional implications' (2018) 3(3) European Papers 1061–74, 1073, 4; Ferreira and Kostakopoulou (n 3).

Martinez Sala,[26] *Grzelczyk*,[27] *Baumbast*[28] and *Bidar*,[29] not least due to a more individualised approach towards the applicants[30] and the construction of important doctrinal principles in the context of family unity in judgments such as *Zhu*,[31] *Singh*[32] and *Metock*,[33] among others.

The Court's approach in the line of *Dano* case law rested upon the argument that applicants such as Ms Dano could not be brought within the scope of *ratione personae* of the non-discrimination principle under Article 24(2) of Directive 2004/38 as, in that case, Ms Dano did not fulfil the residence criteria set out in Article 7(1)(b) of the said directive.[34] What becomes problematic from the Court's reasoning is not the rejection of access to social benefits in the host Member State per se; instead, it is the implications regarding legal residence and non-discrimination for non-economically active citizens merely on the basis of criteria provided in Article 7(1)(b), along with the thinning of proportionality assessment and the Court's reversal of the need to examine individual circumstances,[35] both of which were entirely omitted from the *Dano* judgment.[36] Non-economically active citizens who fail to fulfil the residence criteria on the basis of the directive alone are essentially left in limbo because, on the one hand, they cannot invoke the Charter, since according to the Court the rules on social assistance fall outside the scope of EU law,[37] and on the other hand, these citizens are unlikely to be expelled merely on the basis of unlawful residence. As Thym has pointed out, 'people without a right to remain may continue to reside unlawfully, and domestic authorities could try to effectively "starve them out" by denying access to social benefits'.[38] Although citizens like Ms Dano could theoretically be brought within the scope of the equality provision by becoming economically active, this would reflect a purely instrumentalist form of citizenship contrary to the substantive and meaningful vision of EU citizenship that is 'destined to be the fundamental status of nationals'[39] so eagerly previously promulgated by the Court. This instrumentalist form of citizenship that has been accused of being 'conditional upon wealth,

---

[26] Case C-85/96 *María Martínez Sala v Freistaat Bayern* EU:C:1998:217.
[27] Case C-184/99 *Rudy Grzelczyk v Centre public d'aide sociale d'Ottignies-Louvain-la-Neuve* EU:C:2001:458.
[28] Case C-413/99 *Baumbast and R v Secretary of State for the Home Department* EU:C:2002:493.
[29] Case C-209/03 *The Queen, on the application of Dany Bidar v London Borough of Ealing and Secretary of State for Education and Skills* EU:C:2005:169.
[30] Spaventa (n 6).
[31] Case C-200/02 *Kunqian Catherine Zhu and Man Lavette Chen v Secretary of State for the Home Department* EU:C:2004:639.
[32] C-218/14 *Kuldip Singh and Others v Minister for Justice and Equality* EU:C:2015:476.
[33] Case C-127/08 *Blaise Baheten Metock and Others v Minister for Justice, Equality and Law Reform* EU:C:2008:449.
[34] *Dano* (n 19) paras 66–69.
[35] For an analysis of these issues see Niamh Nic Shuibhne, 'What I tell you three times is true: lawful residence and equal treatment after Dano' (2016) 23 (6) Maastricht Journal of European and Comparative Law 908–36; Daniel Carter, Moritz Jesse, 'The "Dano evolution": assessing legal integration and access to social benefits for EU citizens' (2018) 3 (3) European Papers 1179–1208.
[36] In *Alimanovic* the Court, rather than ignoring proportionality, simply presumed it without further justifying it (para 61); regarding individual circumstances it stated that it is not individual claims that would place an unreasonable burden on the state but rather 'the accumulation of all the individual claims which would be submitted': para 62. The same was reinforced in *Garcia Nieto*, paras 49–50.
[37] *Dano* (n 19) para. 90 Judgment; point 146 in the Opinion of the Advocate General.
[38] Thym (n 18) 258.
[39] C-184/99 *Rudy Grzelczyk* (n 27).

health, and good behaviour',[40] and which 'punish[es] and undermin[es] [...] the life-chances of those citizens who fail to qualify as "good enough"',[41] is highly problematic for a more aspirational and meaningful type of transnational/supranational citizenship and one that provides legitimacy for European integration.

An instrumentalist form of citizenship risks depreciating other important developments concerning the individual as the legal subject of EU law, as it can be said that it has gradually contributed to the construction of a marginalised group of citizens within Young's definition of marginalisation as a form of oppression which has implications for social justice. In Young's words, '[m]arginals are people the system of labor cannot or will not use', including those who are laid off from work and cannot find a new job, those who become involuntarily unemployed and single mothers and their children, among others.[42] Marginalisation, according to Young, 'is perhaps the most dangerous form of oppression'.[43] Although one could counter-argue that mechanisms are in place in the context of free movement, and exceptionally citizenship, for working mothers (*Saint Prix*,[44] *Dakneviciute*[45]), those previously self-employed (*Gusa*,[46] *Dakneviciute*[47]) and children who have not exercised their freedom to move (*Zambrano*,[48] *C.S.*,[49] *Rendón Marín*[50]), or in the context of the protection of derivative rights of family members (*Coman*,[51] *Chenchooliah*[52]), these may not be considered sufficient if we take into account the complex contemporary realities of people's lives that are not connected to their free movement rights.

O'Brien's active-led ethnography is a reminder of this, as she highlights that in the everyday experience of EU citizenship, groups and individuals who may be in more need of protection and who may find themselves in vulnerable situations are those that are more likely to 'fall through the gaps'.[53]

The administrative rules and protective safeguards in this sense may easily exclude individuals as they become conditional upon criteria that may not be controlled by them. At the same time, final assessment left to the discretion of the Member States' authorities risks operating against the welfare of certain individuals and groups, particularly within the current political climate, if the protection of individual rights clashes with public interests. Relevant to this is that even in the context of fundamental rights related to family and children's rights (Articles

---

[40] Speventa (n 6) 13, 14.
[41] Kochenov (n 25) 1064; For more general critique of the concept of citizenship see Dimitry Kochenov, *Citizenship* (MIT Press 2019).
[42] Iris Marion Young, *Justice and the Politics of Difference* (Princeton University Press 1990) 53.
[43] Ibid.
[44] Case C-507/12 *Jessy Saint Prix v Secretary of State for Work and Pensions* EU:C:2014:2007.
[45] Case C-544/18 *The Commissioners for Her Majesty's Revenue & Customs v Henrika Dakneviciute* EU:C:2019:761.
[46] Case C-442/16 *Florea Gusa v Minister for Social Protection and Others* EU:C:2017:1004.
[47] Case C-544/18 *Dakneviciute* (n 45).
[48] Case C-34/09 *Gerardo Ruiz Zambrano v Office national de l'emploi (ONEm)* EU:C:2011:124.
[49] Case C-304/14 *Secretary of State for the Home Department v CS* EU:C:2016:674.
[50] Case C-165/14 *Alfredo Rendón Marín v Administración del Estado* EU:C:2016:675.
[51] Case C-673/16 *Relu Adrian Coman and Others v Inspectoratul General pentru Imigrări and Ministerul Afacerilor Interne* EU:C:2018:385.
[52] Case C-94/18 *Nalini Chenchooliah v Minister for Justice and Equality* EU:C:2019:693.
[53] O'Brien (n 3) 2827–41.

7 and 24 Charter), which are also general principles of EU law,[54] the current judicial reasoning does not fully embrace the protection of family life and unity or children's rights in their own right. Instead these become conditional, and increasingly less generous when placed in the context of the welfare state. For example, issues may arise in the context of cases involving new mothers where, although they are temporarily entitled to take time away from work for pregnancy, childbirth and caregiving, this becomes conditional upon their return to work within a reasonable time.[55] This is not problematic in itself, but considering that the logic behind it is the effectiveness of the labour market rather than, or equal to, the protection of rights related to family, children or the wellbeing of individuals, questions can be raised about the gendered aspect of free movement and the cost on human wellbeing, especially concerning unpaid care work.[56] Even if this scenario may not apply to the majority of women, who will be protected – assuming they are employed – by the Pregnant Workers' Directive, it still points to some of the potential weaknesses in terms of protection for specific groups of people.

In *Chavez-Vilchez*,[57] for example, the Court ruled that in assessing whether children who are Union citizen would be obliged to leave the Union's territory and thus be deprived of the genuine enjoyment of the substance of their rights, along the lines of *Zambrano*, the relationship of dependency with the third-country national parent had to be assessed in light of the best interests of the child in spite of the fact that the other parent, a Union citizen, 'is actually able and willing to assume sole responsibility'. This case involved eight different applicants who were third-country national mothers living in the Netherlands with their Dutch children whose fathers were EU citizens. The Court expanded the Netherlands' restrictive interpretation of *Zambrano* and provided guidance by invoking Article 7 (family life) and Article 24(2) (best interests of the child) of the Charter and submitting the following:

> In reaching such a conclusion, account must be taken, in the best interests of the child concerned, of all the specific circumstances, including the age of the child, the child's physical and emotional development, the extent of his emotional ties both to the Union citizen parent and to the third-country national parent, and the risks which separation from the latter might entail for that child's equilibrium.[58]

The same approach was followed in *K.A.*,[59] where the Court ruled that the relationship of dependency with a third-country national needs to be assessed based on all the specific circumstances, 'including the age of the child, the child's physical and emotional development, the extent of his emotional ties to each of his parents, and the risks which separation from the third-country national parent might entail for that child's equilibrium'.[60] While this development is positive from a legal perspective, as it enhances the application of the Charter and provides for a case-by-case analysis anchored in the best interest of children, if we were

---

[54] Case C-11/70 *Internationale Handelsgesellschaft mbH v Einfuhr- und Vorratsstelle für Getreide und Futtermittel* EU:C:1970:114, para. 4.
[55] O'Brien provides several case studies involving mothers and the administrative obstacles to claiming rights: see O'Brien (n 3) ch. 8.
[56] See commentary in the case of Saint-Prix, Nicole Busby, 'Crumbs of comfort: pregnancy and the status of "Worker" under EU law's free movement provisions' (2015) 44 (1) ILJ 134–45.
[57] C-133/15 *H.C. Chavez-Vilchez and Others v Raad van bestuur van de Sociale verzekeringsbank and Others* EU:C:2017:354.
[58] Ibid, para. 71.
[59] C-82/16 *K.A. and Others v Belgische Staat* EU:C:2018:308.
[60] Ibid, para 72.

to switch lenses and see this case through the eyes of different individuals we may realise that it is more nuanced than it first appears. If we take into account the complexity of social reality, the changing norms around gender roles and the many different forms of family, we may legitimately wonder about the normative claims made by the Court or the national courts in each case, and question how to assess care and dependency in specific situations. Article 9 of the Convention on the Rights of the Child states, among others, that a state should not separate children from their parents except where this is 'necessary for the best interests of the child'. This, however, is not the Court's starting point. The latter may place quite a heavy load on parents to prove their relationship and bond with their children – save in exceptional circumstances, this is a socially recognised bond that is assumed to be in a child's best interest. This could potentially become problematic in those cases where a Member State unofficially opts for more conservative interpretations of family and gender roles (which within the current climate of populism and authoritarian regimes is not unlikely), giving space for authorities to discriminate against specific social groups. The latter may, among others, include fathers or step-parents, who are less likely to be considered as providing primary care and who may therefore more easily become subject to deportation without further regard to the psychological impact on children, or family unity more generally.[61] This more nuanced approach suggests that proportionality holds a key role in determining cases, but that better safeguards may need to be put in place in order to prevent potential abuse or marginalisation of specific groups of people by making more explicit commitments to gender equality beyond the market and to children's welfare in their own right.[62]

The remainder of the chapter attempts to put in place a methodological and normative framework which can help us re-orientate our approach to citizenship. This approach may not be shared by those who still interpret EU law within the traditional and binary frames of intergovernmentalism and supranationalism, but it may resonate with those who are seeking alternative, slightly more creative, and normative frameworks through which to explore citizenship, which are not strictly confined to legal, political and economic accounts.

3. CITIZENSHIP AS A MATRIX OF RELATIONS, NOT JUST A STATUS AND A BUNDLE OF RIGHTS

In the previous section, we glimpsed at the limits of legal instruments and their judicial interpretation in the context of citizenship. This section will attempt to show how EU citizenship can benefit from a multidisciplinary framework beyond its legal, political and economic confines by bringing in the more affective sciences. Citizenship is, as O'Brien shows, a lived experience, the impact of which does not always reach the courts, yet influences the lives of people.[63] At the same time, Kostakopoulou reminds us that institutions are not 'monolithic

---

[61] For example, the Court in Joined Cases C-356/11, C-357/11 *O and S v Maahanmuuttovirasto and Maahanmuuttovirasto v L* EU:C:2012:776 decided that EU citizen children were not 'legally, financially or emotionally dependent' on their third-country national stepfathers, who thus could not derive residence rights because EU citizenship would not be jeopardised by a refusal of a right to reside thus obliging the children to move (para 56); see also C-40/11 *Yoshikazu Iida v Stadt Ulm* EU:C:2012:69.

[62] See also O'Brien (n 3) 7162.

[63] O'Brien (n 3).

and soulless entities' outside of our world but have a dynamic relationality.[64] As institutions become inseparable from the realities and lives of people, it is the latter's actions, claims and practices that point towards the need for improvement and change and, consequently, towards a normative orientation.[65]

The above depicts the fluidity of laws and institutions and rationalises, to an extent, the well-established paradox of European integration that builds on an inclusive and exclusive regime.[66] The complex and relational links between free movement, citizenship and the individual can be seen as a relationship of power:

> In itself the exercise of power is not violence; nor is it a consent which, implicitly, is renewable. It is a total structure of actions brought to bear upon possible actions; it incites, it induces, it seduces, it makes easier or more difficult; in the extreme it constrains or forbids absolutely; it is nevertheless always a way of acting upon an acting subject or acting subjects by virtue of their acting or being capable of action. A set of actions upon other actions.[67]

Although Foucault's notion of power is most commonly used in the field of migration to illustrate the biopolitical dimension within the discourses of security and control, power itself as defined above is not necessarily a coercive mechanism but rather a historical enquiry into 'how human beings are made subjects'.[68] In the context of the EU, viewing free movement and citizenship through the lens of power allows us to explore how individuals become subjects within this legal–constitutional order which extends beyond political and legal frameworks – although these have unquestionably contributed to the granting and deepening of rights and freedoms, not least within the context of the common market through workers' rights, family rights, citizens' rights and, increasingly, human rights.

This angle of free movement and citizenship allows us to recognise that actors qua individuals qua citizens have been co-creators of the European project rather than passive recipients of the status quo, revealing the interaction and relationality between structure and agency rather than their mutual exclusivity. It is this interaction and relationality upon which this contribution focuses, arguing for a shift in thought and practice towards a more affective and socio-psychological dimension of EU citizenship.

Giddens explains that '[t]he most important aspects of structure are rules and resources recursively involved in institutions. Institutions by definition are the more enduring features of social life. In speaking of the structural properties of social systems I mean their institutionalized feature, giving "solidity" across time and space.'[69]

Kostakopoulou builds on this idea of institutions as inextricably entangled with our social realities through her institutional constructivism and *connexio rerum* model, which captures this complex interaction between structure, agency, co-construction of reality and

---

[64] Kostakopoulou (n 2) 69.

[65] Ibid, 79–80.

[66] Diego Acosta Arcarazo, Jacopo Mertire, 'Trapped in the lobby: Europe's revolving doors and the other as Xenos' (2014) 39 (3) EL Rev 362.

[67] Michel Foucault, 'Why study power? The question of the subject' (1982) 8 (4) Critical Inquiry 777–95, 789.

[68] Ibid, 777.

[69] Andrew Giddens, *The Constitution of Society: Outline of the Theory of Structuration* (Polity Press 1984) 24.

knowledge.⁷⁰ As she explains, 'structure, agency, institutions and discourse all intersect and interact in specific locations at a given time'.⁷¹ One manifestation of this may be said to be the perceived stasis of the Court, mentioned earlier, and the susceptibility of citizenship to political and economic aspects as well as Eurosceptic, anti-migrant and populist rhetoric. As Kostakopoulou explains, in this situation 'change takes the form of regression or the reversal of institutional choice'.⁷²

The *connexio rerum* then is explained as 'depict[ing] an unbroken world of conjunctions and interactions among elements that are co-implicated but can also be distinguished from each other [...] [it] uncovers a world of relations, mutual entanglement and synergy'.⁷³

Drawing from that, EU citizenship can be explored as an institution characterised by 'rules, practices, processes, routinized processes, functions, roles, norms, a set of relations and procedures'.⁷⁴ Its relation to the individual cannot be consequently constrained to a legal and practical framework of the rights and freedoms to move, reside, and work but must take in all those micro-processes attached to a person's identity, life choices, vulnerabilities and relations with the state and others. In other words, there is a human element inherent in the constitutional and institutional design of EU citizenship that we simply cannot overlook. The inclusive and exclusive regime of citizenship, regardless of its legal foundations, does not merely permit or reject access to certain rights and freedoms but makes claims about an 'ideal' subject, while it normalises specific modes of living and identifies, implicitly and explicitly, our legal and moral norms. The citizenship regime, therefore, undoubtedly has an impact on the socio-psychological part of individuals, who may be required to abandon friends, families and bonds they have created, or may be rejected and left unsupported when they most need this support. This does not diminish the significant developments of citizenship and the contribution of the Court in enhancing the position of individuals qua citizens within EU law; instead, it emphasises this non-linear and complex reality of citizenship and the need to acknowledge its socio-psychological dimensions that transcend its conceptualisation as a legal status associated with the provision of a bundle of rights.

Any form of social justice that we may therefore advocate for the EU must embrace this affective, behavioural and human aspect within the actual everyday living and experiencing of citizenship. This includes reflecting upon our responsibilities towards each other, which go beyond legal obligations. Such a new model for social justice should, therefore, recognise the relationship between law/justice and emotion/behaviour, rather than either explicitly or implicitly dismissing it. This relationship has long been recognised by moral and political philosophers who nodded towards the need for empathy in the conception of justice.

In the context of developing the faculty of moral thinking, Rawls recognised that 'acquiring a morality of association [...] rests upon the development of the intellectual skills required to regard things from a variety of points of view and to think of these together as aspects of one system of cooperation'.⁷⁵ Smith's concept of sympathy further indicated this need to recognise other's plight as a form of justice. He said: '[t]o seem to not be affected by the

---

⁷⁰ Kostakopoulou (n 2) 109.
⁷¹ Ibid, 19.
⁷² Ibid, 179.
⁷³ Ibid, 34.
⁷⁴ Ibid, 65.
⁷⁵ John Rawls, *A Theory of Justice (Revised Edition)* (Belknap Press/Harvard UP 1999) 410.

joy of our companions is but want of politeness; but to not wear a serious countenance when they tell us their afflictions, is real and gross inhumanity.'[76] More contemporary scholars such as Nussbaum recognised the role of emotions such as love in the context of justice and the common good.[77] At the same time, Solomon argued that principles of justice are 'utterly meaningless without that fundamental human sense of caring and the ability to understand and personally care about the wellbeing of other human beings and other creatures who may be very far away and personally quite unknown to us'.[78] More recently, in the context of the EU, Ferreira and Kostakopoulou have argued for 'a compassionate, empathic, inter-connected and caring "right way" of doing and living politics and norms'.[79] Their humanistic thesis paves the way for further reflection on the complex relations between institutions such as citizenship and the actual lives of people, and provides a new lens through which to assess and explore current practices. O'Brien's legal action research could be viewed in this light, as it examines obstacles to citizenship in its practical everyday context, providing valuable insight into the experiential dimension of citizenship.

The following section introduces social empathy as both a normative and a methodological approach to EU citizenship, in the wider context of the Area of Freedom, Security and Justice, in the hope that this may contribute to further reflection on the relational and more affective dimension of EU citizenship and as a step towards addressing some of its weaknesses and pitfalls by anchoring it to the wellbeing and autonomy of individuals and societies.[80] This approach can be linked to the normative values and principles safeguarded in Article 2 TEU which states that '[t]he Union is founded on the values of respect for human dignity, freedom, democracy, equality, the rule of law and respect for human rights, including the rights of persons belonging to minorities'. The primary focus is to introduce, rather than comprehensively conceptualise, social empathy as a prism through which to reflect upon the various relations, practices and injustices in the context of citizenship and as one way of reconfiguring social justice in the EU.

4. A SOCIAL EMPATHY LENS

Social empathy was introduced by Segal to expand interpersonal empathy to include a deeper awareness about structural inequalities and to cultivate the ability to engage in other-orientated perspective-taking.

Social empathy applies empathy to social systems to better understand the experiences of different people, communities and cultures. Social empathy is the combination of: (1) experiencing empathy to its fullest extent, (2) gaining deep insight and knowledge about historical

---

[76] Adam Smith, Sálvio Marcelo Soares (eds) *The Theory of Moral Sentiments* (6th edn, first published 1790, MεταLibri 2006) 10.

[77] Martha Nussbaum, *Political Emotions: Why Love Matters for Justice* (Belknap Press/Harvard University Press 2013) 145.

[78] Robert Solomon, *A Passion for Justice: Emotions and the Origins of the Social Contract* (Rowman & Littlefield Publishers 1995) 33.

[79] Nuno Ferreira, 'Introduction' in Ferreira, Kostakopoulou (n 3).

[80] Autonomy is here understood in line with Castoriadis' account, as both individual and collective, which cannot be mutually exclusive: Cornelios Castoriadis, Η φαντασιακή θέσμιση της κοινωνίας [The imaginary Institution of Society] (Kedros 1978) 150–63.

and socio-economic contexts, particularly about inequality and disparity; and (3) embracing the importance of social responsibility.[81]

Although space does not allow for an analysis of the very complex notion of interpersonal empathy upon which social empathy builds, for present purposes it suffices to say that interpersonal empathy involves at least three aspects, namely affective, cognitive and somatic, which may occur simultaneously. Empathy has been approached from different scientific disciplines, including neuroscience,[82] social neuroscience[83] and social work,[84] and has been defined, among others, as 'a capacity, a cognitive ability, a skill, a feeling, understanding, a disposition, a process'.[85] In other words, empathy is as much an embodied experience as it is cognitive and affective.[86]

Social empathy, which builds on the cognitive processes that can be developed and cultivated, takes this a step further by suggesting that an inability or unwillingness to understand the perspective of others – their historical and socio-economic contexts and life experiences – may lead to divisions, prejudice and distrust. Segal and others have explained that social empathy involves 'the application of empathy on and by larger systems, such as organizations that are responsible for decisions and policies that impact large groups of people'.[87] In assessing empathy, Segal and others have provided an index which measures individuals' social empathy towards others. However, the application I wish to suggest here goes even further: I believe that there is value in reflecting upon social empathy in the context of institutions which are, according to the 'polycentric epistemology'[88] of *connexio rerum*, capable of 'shap[ing], influenc[ing] and guid[ing] peoples' actions, reactions, revised responses and recurrent actions'.[89] Although an equivalent index may not be necessary to assess or explore social empathy in the context of EU citizenship (or other institutions and policy fields), there are useful elements we can identify that can be used as guides in our inquiry into normative pathways to reconceptualise our understanding and future of EU citizenship.

Central to social empathy is the notion of *contextual understanding of systemic barriers*, which encompasses an understanding of the historical situation of specific groups.[90] This indicates a reflexive process rather than automatic assumptions about the situation of others.

---

[81] Elizabeth Segal, 'Social empathy: a model built on empathy, contextual understanding, and social responsibility that promotes social justice' (2011) 37 Journal of Social Service Research 266, 267–8.

[82] Marco Iacoboni, *Mirroring People: The Science of Empathy and How We Connect with Others* (Picador 2009).

[83] Claus Lamm, Jasminka Majdandžić, 'The role of shared neural activations, mirror neurons, and morality in empathy – a critical comment' (2015) 90 Neuroscience Research 15; Haakon G. Engen, Tania Singer, 'Empathy circuits' (2012) 23 (2) Current Opinion in Neurobiology 275.

[84] Karen E. Gerdes, 'Empathy, sympathy, and pity: 21st century definitions and implications for practice and research' (2011) 37 (3) Journal of Social Service Research 230.

[85] Ibid.

[86] See also a recent multivariate study that confirms this point: Leonardo Cristov-Moore, Nicco Reggente, Pamela K Douglas, Jamie D Feusner, Marco Iacoboni, 'Predicting empathy from resting state brain connectivity: a multivariate approach' (Frontiers in Integrative Neuroscience 14 February 2020).

[87] Elizabeth A. Segal, Karen E. Gerdes, Cynthia A. Lietz, M. Alex Wagaman, Jennifer M. Geiger, *Assessing Empathy* (Columbia UP 2017) 24.

[88] Kostakopoulou (n 2).

[89] Ibid, 65.

[90] Segal, Gerdes, Lietz, Wagaman, Geiger (n 87) 26.

The second crucial element is the *macro self-other awareness/perspective-taking*. As Segal et al explain, this macro-level perspective-taking

> asks us to walk in the shoes of another, but with an eye toward the impact of external factors that impact experience. By putting ourselves in the situations of others with different characteristics of group identity, such as race, gender, sexual orientation, ability, age, and class background, we can develop broader empathic insight, which is social empathy.[91]

These two components of social empathy are interlinked with a third element which consists of more than the utilisation and cultivation of interpersonal empathy and more than an informed understanding of the life experiences and historical circumstances of groups and individuals in a diverse society, namely social responsibility, which is connected to positive social action and change and is, therefore, inextricably linked to social justice.[92]

The question that can be raised at this point is whether there is a place for social empathy in the reconceptualisation of EU citizenship and, if so, what the tools could be that would allow us to develop a more empathic, more human-centred approach to citizenship that would further enhance the polity's legitimacy and still be grounded in law. There are some central features of social empathy that are important to note and which converge with other theories that advocate social justice.

First, as social empathy rests upon interpersonal empathy, which at its core respects individual human beings as ends in themselves, we could say that it recognises their inherent dignity and value because it presupposes that we see each person as a distinct individual but also a member of social groups' society. In the context of moral equality, Sangiovanni has introduced the concept of social cruelty to describe 'the unauthorized, harmful, and wrongful use of another's vulnerability to attack or obliterate their capacity to develop and maintain an integral sense of self'.[93] Although Sangiovanni gives the extreme examples of torture and genocide as manifestations of social cruelty, his definition and particularly his references to 'vulnerability' and 'integral sense of self' are crucial in the context of social justice more generally. These can be influential and guiding in more mundane contexts and practices because it presupposes the inherent value and autonomy of the self, its sociality, interdependency and interaction with its social environment.[94] For example, if we were to apply this in the context of citizenship, we could question, first, whether we would be correct in suggesting, as I did earlier, that the current legal framework contributes to the marginalisation of specific groups of people, that is, the economically inactive or those who cannot fulfil the criteria of Article 7 Directive 2004/38/EC; and second, whether this marginalisation qua oppression impacts the individual's integral sense of self and whether their vulnerability is exacerbated as a result of the current legal and judicial framework of citizenship. Based on institutional constructivism, with an emphasis on relations rather than clear-cut structures, we could very well argue that this is a high possibility, especially for those who are in vulnerable situations, or those whose strong links to the host state are disregarded. Although this by no means suggests that it falls within Sangiovanni's definition of social cruelty, it nevertheless raises interesting questions about the normative ori-

---

[91] Ibid., 27.
[92] Segal (n 81) 266–77, 269–73.
[93] Andrea Sangiovanni, *Humanity without Dignity: Moral Equality, Respect, and Human Rights* (Harvard UP 2017) 75.
[94] Ibid, 132.

entation of citizenship and European integration. Social empathy's premise rests therefore on acknowledging the significance of one's inherent need to be recognised as the author of one's life within the broader social context, yet avoiding the moral position of individualism that views the individual as above the state. Instead, it reflects the relational nature of individual, society and laws and justice.

The above is connected to the second central element of social empathy, namely the recognition of the condition of vulnerability, which holds a central place in many feminist-orientated theories of justice and ethics.[95] Fineman, for example, who defined vulnerability as 'universal and constant, inherent in the human condition', recognises social and state responsibility in addressing vulnerability.[96] She acknowledges the relational nature of institutions and society, both of which reproduce inequalities, and explains that 'because neither inequalities nor the systems that produce them are inevitable, they can also be objects of reform'.[97] According to Fineman, vulnerability can prove 'valuable in constructing critical perspective on political and societal institutions, including law'.[98] Vulnerability is at the heart of social empathy, as it is embraced here, because it requires institutions, states and other individuals to actively identify any structural inequalities, to understand the external dimension of disparities and to actively and proactively provide support through social responsibility. This is lastly connected to the aspect of solidarity, on which there is an extensive literature in the context of the EU, and which will not be looked at in detail here.[99]

Solidarity can be identified as being the result or the process of applying social empathy, either implicitly or explicitly. By applying a *contextual understanding of systemic barriers* along with *macro self-other awareness/perspective-taking*, the conditions for social responsibility are created or become more obvious. If social responsibility is then taken up, we are likely to witness a strengthened form of solidarity that depends neither on functional and economic reasons nor on emotional reasons stemming from common identity and shared goals; instead, it would be based on a balance and harmonisation of individual and public needs based on their relationality. Sangiovanni has provided an interesting interpretation of the phenomenon of solidarity as acting in solidarity with others when we 'commit ourselves to the formation and maintenance of a political organisation that will help us to prevent the worst evils of the state of nature'.[100] For this, we need to consider how the EU and EU citizenship purport to do that, and whether the European polity therefore warrants our support, which will then justify our acting in solidarity with one another and committing ourselves to protecting our political organisations. It suffices for the current purposes to suggest that Article 2 TEU

---

[95] See generally Catriona Mackenzie, Wendy Rogers, Susan Dodds (eds), *Vulnerability: New Essays in Ethics and Feminist Philosophy* (OUP 2014); in the context of EU employment law see Nicole Busby, *A Right to Care? Unpaid Work in European Employment Law* (OUP 2011).

[96] Martha A. Fineman, 'The Vulnerable Subject: Anchoring Equality in the Human Condition' (2008) 20 (2) Yale Journal of Law and Feminism 1.

[97] Ibid.

[98] Ibid, 9.

[99] For transnational perspectives see Veronica Federico, Christian Lahusen (eds) *Solidarity as a Public Virtue? Law and Public Policies in the EU* (Nomos 2018); see also Andrea Biondi, Eglė Dagilytė, Esin Küçük (eds), *Solidarity in EU Law: Legal Principles in the Making* (Edward Elgar Publishing 2018); Floris De Witte, *Justice in the EU: The Emergence of Transnational Solidarity* (OUP 2015).

[100] Andrea Sangiovanni, 'Solidarity as Joint Action' (2015) 31(4) Journal of Applied Philosophy 340–59, 354.

becomes central to this as it provides the normative foundations of the European polity, to which all laws and policies should refer back. Even though these values and principles function as general legal standards and are broad in nature, they provide protective safeguards for EU citizens (and others) and have been utilized by the Court in defining the scope of citizenship, especially in earlier case law. Upholding the rule of law, one of the fundamental values of the Union, enshrined in Article 2 TEU, could be used as an example that legitimises our commitment to the maintenance of democratic governance and the prevention of its demise, generating good reasons for acting in solidarity with one another, and seeking to preserve our democratic values but also to remedy the ills that threaten to undermine them.

5. FACILITATING SOCIAL EMPATHY THROUGH THE GENERAL PRINCIPLES OF EU LAW

The preceding sections identified three important aspects that are at the heart of social empathy, namely: the recognition of dignity or the significance of 'an integral sense of self'; the acknowledgement of the condition of vulnerability; and solidarity as a commitment to our political and social institutions[101] that promote individual and societal autonomy.

Application of the strands of *contextual understanding of systemic barriers* along with *macro self-other awareness/perspective-taking* would need to be adjusted depending on the specific issue we want to tackle, and in order to identify elements that would allow us to assess systemic barriers. For example, non-economically active citizens, those in vulnerable situations, the poor, the stateless, those with alternative lifestyles or those – primarily women – who take a break from work to care for others could be said to be facing structural obstacles to realising their citizenship or fundamental rights due to exclusion and marginalisation which result from systemic weaknesses that need to be addressed. We would need tools that enable us to engage in other-orientated perspective-taking on an institutional level, as we could not simply expect, for example, judges to invoke their emotional sensitivities and personal experiences to express *interpersonal* empathy towards applicants.[102] Instead, social empathy, as embraced here, suggests that we could utilise or develop mechanisms grounded in law that would help us to re-orientate our frames of thinking towards cultivating a sense of social responsibility on an institutional level.

In the context of EU citizenship and its interpretation by the Court of Justice, constitutional provisions and general principles of EU law are of central significance. Such principles derive mainly from the normative provisions of the EU treaties such as those enshrined in Article 2 TEU.[103] These can be initially identified as closely connected to the rule of law but extend beyond that, including, but not limited to, proportionality, fundamental rights and non-discrimination. These would need to be interpreted and applied following a reflexive process whereby the limitations to an individual or constitutional right should only be justified by referring back to the values and principles in Article 2 TEU as these have been further

---

[101] Ibid., 356.
[102] Although studies exploring judicial empathy have been conducted.
[103] See also Kalaitzaki, who also sees Article 2 TEU as key to enhancing fundamental rights: Katerina Kalaitzaki, 'EU Citizenship as a Means of Broadening the Application of EU Fundamental Rights: Developments and Limits', in Cambien, Kochenov, Muir, (n 3).

developed by the Court, as well as being linked to the wider purpose of the legal system as a whole and not only on secondary law, as is currently the trend. However, general principles, as tools used by the Court, are not always explicitly mentioned when weighing conflicting constitutional and fundamental rights and freedoms.[104]

In engaging with the general principles as part of understanding systemic or other barriers to justice and the protection of rights in order to 'fully understand the lived experiences of groups [and individuals]',[105] we should be able to clearly identify and stand by the values and principles of the European polity in more explicit terms.

Proportionality plays a crucial role in the process of social empathy as it is the element that allows the Court to engage with and examine the circumstances of each applicant and to decide or provide guidance to the national courts as to whether personal rights and freedoms are justifiably limited.[106] In the context of balancing rights and justifications of limiting laws, Barak identifies 'the social importance' as the 'rule according to which the weight of each of the scales should be determined'.[107] In this light, the thinning of proportionality as a general principle of EU law is problematic as it automatically tips the scales against certain individuals and, therefore, does not promote social responsibility.[108] By halting consideration for personal circumstances, at least in cases of social welfare, and more strictly assessing legal residence based on secondary law without anchoring this to the broader purpose of the treaties, it leaves individuals exposed and downplays a human-centred citizenship, thereby affecting human flourishing and wellbeing. As O'Brien argued, proportionality should be not only strengthened but also more clearly codified to be used as a means towards the redefinition of fairness and function as a guide for national courts.[109] Equally, the scope of EU law and, consequently, the applicability of the Charter based on an emphasis on conditionality and duties that are tied to secondary legislation do not currently extend equal protection to all EU citizens. This is enhanced by the uncertainties concerning, on the one hand, the applicability of Article 20 TFEU combined with the *Zambrano* principle as safeguarding the substance of citizenship rights and, on the other, the different legal basis deriving from Article 21 TFEU in conjunction with Directive 2004/38.

---

[104] For example, in balancing a fundamental right and a public interest, or in delineating the scope of EU law, the Court will resort to constitutional and general principles such as proportionality and fundamental rights or will engage in a balancing exercise without explicit reference to these principles. The judgment in *Zambrano* illustrates this point, particularly when we consider the elaborate opinion of Advocate General Sharpston, who examined in detail the aspects of proportionality, reverse discrimination and fundamental rights while the Court made no clear reference to neither of these principles. Yet it developed, quite innovatively, its doctrine on the genuine enjoyment of the substance of the citizenship rights to find in favour of the applicant. *Zambrano*, para 44.

[105] Segal, Gerdes, Lietz, Wagaman, Geiger (n 87) 26.

[106] Aharon Barak, *Proportionality: Constitutional Rights and their Limitations* (CUP 2012) 340.

[107] Ibid, 349.

[108] It may be useful to note that proportionality is used differently in the context of asylum, where fundamental/human rights more clearly bring applicants within the scope of the Charter.

[109] See O'Brien (n 3) ch. 9.

6. CONCLUSION

This contribution has suggested that we must take moral obligations that are substantiated into law more seriously, and this requires a humanistic lens along the lines proposed by Ferreira and Kostakopoulou. A social empathy approach draws upon the humanist thesis and supports the view that the institution of citizenship is woven within a matrix of complex relations and lived experiences. Because of that, the legal and judicial framework of citizenship needs to acknowledge this relationality and shift orientation towards a 'human face' if we are to remedy structural weaknesses and potential injustices as a common effort to maintain democratic principles and values. Social empathy as a normative prism encourages us to engage in a reflexive process concerning the different relations, discourses and structures within the citizenship regime and explore potential injustices by re-orientating ourselves towards more empathic, fair and human-centred institutions that exist to improve rather than obstruct human flourishing.

7. The relationship between national and EU citizenship: what is it and what should it be?

Martijn van den Brink

1. INTRODUCTION

The relationship between national and EU citizenship is fraught with tensions and subject to increasing contestation. Whereas shortly after the introduction of EU citizenship in 1993 it was assumed by most observers that this status was in all respects subordinate to national citizenship,[1] the three decades that have followed have repeatedly shown that their relationship is not as straightforward as it once seemed. The Court of Justice of the EU (CJEU) has been nibbling away at Member State sovereignty in the domain of nationality and disputes over the proper relationship between the nationalities of the Member States and EU citizenship seem to be growing in frequency as well as intensity. In addition to the already existing conflicts over national rules that led to the deprivation of their EU citizenship, UK nationals are currently challenging their loss of EU citizenship and associated rights in various courts at national and EU level, and the Commission has launched infringement proceedings against Member States running investor citizenship programmes for undermining the essence of EU citizenship.[2]

This raises two questions: what is the relationship between national and EU citizenship legally speaking, and what should it be normatively speaking? These two are separate and distinct questions, contrary to the apparent belief of many scholars and practitioners of EU citizenship law that the positive law can be made synonymous with what it ought to be. They seem to believe that EU citizenship law can mean exactly what they wish it to mean, especially when it comes to the relationship between national and EU citizenship.[3] Those opposed to the loss of EU citizenship by UK nationals try to construe EU citizenship law broadly so as to allow for the retention of this status and the rights attaching thereto;[4] those opposed to allowing individuals to acquire citizenship in exchange of a monetary investment want to read

---

[1] For a more general discussion of this relationship, Gerard-René de Groot, 'Towards a European Nationality Law' (2004) 8 Electronica Journal of Comparative Law; Karolina Rostek and Gareth Davies, 'The Impact of Union Citizenship on National Citizenship Policies' (2006) 10 European Integration Online Papers; Dimitry Kochenov, 'Rounding Up the Circle: The Mutation of Member States' Nationalities under Pressure from EU Citizenship' [2012] EUI RSCAS Working Paper.

[2] These cases will be discussed in further detail below.

[3] But not only when it comes to this relationship. A similar conflation of considerations of law and considerations of justice has happened in the area of social assistance as I show in Martijn van den Brink 'The European Union's Demo*i*cratic Legislature' (2021) 19 *International Journal of Constitutional Law* 914.

[4] Dora Kostakopoulou, '*Scala Civium*: Citizenship Templates Post-Brexit and the European Union's Duty to Protect EU Citizens' (2018) 56 Journal of Common Market Studies 854; Volker Roeben and others, *The Feasibility of Associate EU Citizenship for UK Citizens Post-Brexit: A Study for Jill Evans MEP* (Swansea University 2017).

a principle of genuine link into EU citizenship law to outlaw this practice;[5] and those opposed to denaturalisation argue that the boundaries of national citizenship should be pushed back so far as to avoid this.[6] In this chapter, I wish to challenge these ideas and argue that we should consider the legal relationship between national and EU citizenship independently of our normative appraisal of what it should become.

Good lawyers are sometimes said to be those who can make creative use of the law. There is, no doubt, an important element of truth in this statement, but it also seems to me that good lawyers know the law and the limits thereof. Attempts to align the positive law with our sense of justice or decency can impair our capacity to understand the law and evaluate legal argumentation, but also cloud our moral judgment as to whether and how the law should be amended. Let me explain the second point. The contemporary political and academic debate on the relationship between national and EU citizenship often focuses on singular instances of this relationship. Having identified a problem, efforts are made to interpret existing law in a way that precisely addresses the problem, without always looking at the broader practical or normative implications of the chosen approach. The legal proceedings launched by the European Commission against the investor citizenship schemes of Malta and Cyprus are a case in point. The Commission advocates the introduction of a 'genuine link' requirement as a condition for the acquisition of EU citizenship in order to combat such schemes,[7] seemingly without considering the far-reaching implications the application of this requirement would have for the relationship between national and EU citizenship more generally.[8] To avoid such ill-considered proposals, we need to have a more comprehensive vision of what the relationship between national and EU citizenship should become, while allowing for the possibility that our ideals may not be realisable within the boundaries of the law as they currently exist.

This chapter examines successively the legal and the normative dimensions of the relationship between national and EU citizenship. The legal analysis will focus on EU Treaty law and the relevant jurisprudence on the CJEU and shows some important tensions between these two sources of law. The legal reasoning of the CJEU does not even seem capable of justifying the very minimal restrictions the case law has so far imposed on the authority of the Member States to determine the rules on the acquisition and loss of national citizenship. If this analysis is correct, then it follows that the Treaties certainly do not justify some of the more far-reaching restrictions discussed above, such as outlawing investor citizenship or allowing UK nationals to retain their EU citizenship. It will be difficult to change the relationship between national and EU citizenship, therefore, without Treaty amendment. Whether the Treaties should be amended depends on whether this relationship is in need of change. The

---

[5] Report from the Commission to the European Parliament, the Council, the European Economic and Social Committee and the Committee of the Regions of 23 January 2019 on Investor Citizenship and Residence Schemes in the European Union, (COM(2019) 12 final) 6. See also Sergio Carrera, 'The Price of EU Citizenship: The Maltese Citizenship-for-sale Affair and the Principle of Sincere Cooperation in Nationality Matters' (2014) 21 *Maastricht Journal of European and Comparative Law* 406.

[6] See, for example, Dimitry Kochenov, 'The Tjebbes Fail' (2019) 4 *European Papers* 319.

[7] Report from the Commission (n 5); European Commission Press Release, 'Investor Citizenship Schemes: European Commission opens infringements against Cyprus and Malta for "selling" EU citizenship' (20 October 2020) available at: https://ec.europa.eu/commission/presscorner/detail/en/ip_20_1925 accessed 9 March 2021.

[8] Martijn van den Brink, 'Revising Citizenship within the European Union: Is a Genuine Link Requirement the Way Forward?' (2022) 23 *German Law Journal* 171.

second part of the chapter discusses this question and explains why it would be desirable for the EU to have greater influence over the conditions relating to the loss and acquisition of national and EU citizenship, in particular to offer third-country nationals with developed social ties to their society of residence a credible path to citizenship.

2. WHAT IS THE RELATIONSHIP BETWEEN NATIONAL AND EU CITIZENSHIP?

Three dimensions define the relationship between national and EU citizenship: linkage, derivation and access. Linkage concerns the question of whether there should be a connection between EU citizenship and nationality. Derivation is about the causal direction between the two; about which enjoys primacy over the other. Access refers to who decides on the criteria of acquisition and loss of citizenship.[9] The EU Treaties establish the primacy of national over EU citizenship. More specifically, they establish a linkage between national and EU citizenship and treat the latter as the derivative status. In addition, Member States enjoy responsibility over the conditions on the acquisition and loss of national *and* EU citizenship. Article 20 TFEU states this most clearly: 'Every person holding the nationality of a Member State shall be a citizen of the Union. Citizenship of the Union shall be additional to and not replace national citizenship.' This provision was joined by three Declarations that also emphasise that decisions on the attribution of nationality are for the Member States to take,[10] including Declaration No 2 on nationality of a Member State, which states expressly that 'the question whether an individual possesses the nationality of a Member State will be settled solely by reference to the national law of the Member State concerned'.

It is therefore undisputed, as the CJEU has confirmed several times, that 'the rules on the acquisition and loss of nationality fall within the competence of the Member States'.[11] Moreover, as EU citizenship is derivative of Member State nationality, it follows logically that the EU has no competence to determine who is a citizen of the Union.[12] And yet, there is considerable debate about the legal dimension of the relationship between EU and national citizenship, such as whether nationals of a country withdrawing from the EU have the right to retain their EU citizenship or whether Member States can be required not to offer their citizenship in exchange for money. The reason why this relationship is highly contested has been aptly articulated by the former Vice-President of the European Commission, Viviane Reding: 'naturalisation decisions taken by one Member State are not neutral with regard to

---

[9] The criteria of 'linkage', 'derivation', and 'access' are borrowed from Rainer Bauböck, 'Why European Citizenship? Normative Approaches to Supranational Union' (2007) 8 Theoretical Inquiries in Law 453.

[10] For critical discussion, AC Evans, 'Nationality Law and the Free Movement of Persons in the EEC: With Special Reference to the British Nationality Act 1981' (1982) 2 Yearbook of European Law 173, 177–8; Gerard-René de Groot (n 1); Dimitry Kochenov, '*Ius Tractum* of Many Faces: European Citizenship and the Difficult Relationship between Status and Rights' (2008) 15 Colum. J. Eur. L. 169.

[11] Case C-135/08 *Rottmann* EU:C:2010:104, para 37; Case C-221/17 *Tjebbes and others* EU:C: 2019:189.

[12] Daniel Sarmiento and Martijn van den Brink, 'EU Competence and Investor Migration' in Dimitry Kochenov and Kristin Surak (eds), *The Law of Citizenship and Money* (CUP (forthcoming)).

other Member States *and* to the EU as a whole.'[13] Given that the status of EU citizenship brings with it the right to cross-border movement, the rules on acquisition and loss of nationality of one Member State may indeed have an impact on others. However, the fact that the deprivation of national citizenship can lead to the loss of EU citizenship has in particular been given as a reason to limit the powers of Member States in the field of citizenship. Is there reason to think, therefore – contrary to what the Treaties suggest – that the primacy of national over EU citizenship is subject to significant restrictions?

Prior to the introduction of EU citizenship, the CJEU had already decided that, in laying down the conditions for the acquisition and loss of nationality, national authorities must have 'due regard to EU law'.[14] It has relied on this in subsequent cases to impose additional limits on the powers of national governments to determine who their citizens are. The case law imposes two restrictions on Member State powers in the domain of nationality.[15] The first concerns the *recognition* of nationality. The judgments in *Micheletti* and *Garcia Avello* provide that it is impermissible for Member States 'to restrict the effects of the grant of the nationality of another Member State by imposing an additional condition for recognition of that nationality'.[16] The second concerns the *loss* of nationality. The judgments in *Rottmann* and *Tjebbes* make clear that a decision placing EU citizens 'in a position capable of causing him to lose the status [of EU citizenship] and the rights attaching thereto falls, by reason of its nature and its consequences, within the ambit of European Union law'.[17] While the CJEU still leaves national authorities extensive leeway, they are under an obligation 'to determine whether the loss of the nationality of the Member State concerned, when it entails the loss of citizenship of the Union and the rights attaching thereto, has due regard to the principle of proportionality'.[18] That means, concretely, that the relevant rules should allow for 'an individual examination of the consequences of that loss for the persons concerned from the point of view of EU law';[19] in particular that they do not 'disproportionately affect the normal development of his or her family and professional life'.[20] These decisions do not concern the *acquisition* of nationality, but the CJEU has been asked in *JY v Wiener Landesregierung* (pending) whether such situations can exceptionally also fall within the scope of EU law.[21]

These decisions were certainly ground-breaking from a legal point of view, but their practical importance is easy to overstate. *Micheletti* and *Garcia Avello* did not challenge national rules on the loss and acquisition of national citizenship; *Rottmann* and *Tjebbes* did, but to a very limited extent. *Tjebbes* led the Dutch authorities to complement the rules on the loss of nationality with an individual assessment, but not to amend them.[22] And despite the

---

[13] 'Citizenship must not be up for sale'. Speech by Viviane Reding on 15 January 2004, available at < http://europa.eu/rapid/press-release_SPEECH-14-18_en.htm > accessed 9 March 2021. Italics added.
[14] Case C-369/90 *Micheletti* EU:C:1992:295, para 10.
[15] See also, Jo Shaw, 'Citizenship: Contrasting Dynamics at the Interface of Integration and Constitutionalism' (2020) RSCAS Working Paper 2020/33, 31-35.
[16] *Micheletti*, para 10; Case C-148/02 *Garcia Avello*, EU:C:2003:539, para 28.
[17] *Rottmann*, para 42; *Tjebbes and others*, para 32.
[18] *Tjebbes and others*, para 40.
[19] *Tjebbes and others*, para 41.
[20] *Tjebbes and others*, para 44.
[21] Case C-118/20 *JY v Wiener Landesregierung* (pending).
[22] Raad van State, Uitspraak 201504577/2/A3, 201507057/2/A3, 201508588/2/A3, 201601993/2/A3, 201604943/1/A3 en 201608752/1/A3 (12 February 2020) NL:RVS:2020:423.

revolutionary nature of *Rottmann*, the applicant lost his Member State nationality and became stateless due to having acquired it fraudulently.²³ Still, there is a widespread belief that these judgments provide a solid and sound legal basis for transforming EU citizenship into a more autonomous status that would further limit Member States' competence in the field of citizenship, for example by introducing legal principles intended to resist denaturalisation or investor citizenship, or even the loss of EU citizenship by UK nationals after Brexit.²⁴

These arguments seem highly questionable as a matter of EU law. Those who take the position that additional limits can be placed on national competence in the area of nationality must believe that the justification for decisions such as *Rottmann* and *Tjebbes* is legally sound *and* that these decisions (or another provision of EU law) provide a sound basis for (say) outlawing investor citizenship or extending EU citizenship to UK nationals. The problem, it seems to me, is that not even the first is true; the legal justification for *Rottmann* and *Tjebbes* is rather weak. To see this, we need to examine the argumentation of both judgments in more detail.

2.1 A Reappraisal of Existing Case Law

According to the principle of conferral, 'the Union shall act only within the limits of the competences conferred upon it by the Member States in the Treaties to attain the objectives set out therein. Competences not conferred on the Union in the Treaties remain with the Member States.'²⁵ However, it is settled case law that Member States must, in areas falling within their competence, exercises their powers in a manner consistent with EU law.²⁶ For example, the organisation of the armed forces is a national competence, but one that must, according to the ruling in *Kreil*, be exercised with due regard to EU non-discrimination law.²⁷ Likewise, although the EU shall not prejudice the status under national law of churches and other religious associations or communities,²⁸ the CJEU held in *Egenberger* that domestic norms cannot prejudice the right to non-discrimination guaranteed under EU law.²⁹

The CJEU invoked the same line of reasoning in its EU citizenship case law: it is within the competence of the Member States to establish rules on the acquisition and loss of nationality, but these powers must be exercised 'having due regard to EU law'. This argument works well with respect to the decisions in *Micheletti* and *Garcia Avello* that Member States must recognise the grant of nationality of another. The acquisition and loss of the status of EU citizenship, and thereby also the rights attached to this status, depend on the acquisition and loss of a Member State nationality. The enjoyment of these rights could be jeopardised if Member

---

[23] See also Nathan Cambien, 'Case C-135/08, Janko Rottmann v. Freistaat Bayern' (2011) 17 Colum. J. Eur. L. 375; Dimitry Kochenov, 'Case C-135/08, Janko Rottmann v. Freistaat Bayern, Judgment of the Court (Grand Chamber) of 2 March 2010' (2010) 47 CML Rev 1831.

[24] See the literature referred to in the introduction.

[25] Article 5(2) TEU. For further discussion, Rene Barents, 'The Internal Market Unlimited: Some Observations on the Legal Basis of Community Legislation' (1993) 30 C M L Rev 85; Kieran Bradley, 'The European Court and the Legal Basis of Community Legislation' (1988) 13 E L Rev 379.

[26] Case C-267/06 *Maruko*, EU:C:2008:179, para 59; Case C-443/15 *David L. Parris* EU:C:2016: 897, para 58. For further discussion, Bruno de Witte, 'Exclusive Member State Competences – Is There Such a Thing?' in Sacha Garben and Inge Govaere (eds), *The Division of Competences between the EU and the Member States: Reflections on the Past, the Present and the Future* (Hart Publishing 2017) 61–2.

[27] Case C-285/98, *Kreil* EU:C:2000:2, para 16. See also *David L. Parris*.

[28] Article 17 TFEU.

[29] Case C-414/16 *Egenberger* EU:C:2018:257. See also Case C-68/17 *IR v JQ* EU:C:2018:696.

States were allowed to refuse to recognise the nationality – and with that EU citizenship – granted by other Member States.[30] That is the reason why the CJEU decided in *Lounes* that 'Member States cannot restrict the effects that follow from holding the nationality of another Member State, in particular the rights which are attendant thereon under EU law and which are triggered by a citizen exercising his freedom of movement'.[31] In other words, this limitation of national powers was necessary to prevent Member States from evading their obligations under EU citizenship law, just as the limitation of national powers in relation to defence and religious organisations, in *Kreil* and *Egenberger*, was necessary to prevent Member States from evading their obligations under EU non-discrimination law.

The same argument does not work with respect to *Rottmann* and *Tjebbes*, contrary to what the CJEU claims. At first sight, the disputes in these cases seem to be structured similarly to those in *Kreil* and *Egenberger* – involving a clash between a national competence on the one hand and a right conferred and protected by EU law on the other hand. More specifically, *Rottmann* and *Tjebbes* seem to stem from a conflict between the national competence in the field of nationality on the one hand and the rights that EU law confers on EU citizens on the other, just as *Kreil* and *Egenberger* involved a clash between national competences in the fields of defence and religion, respectively, and the right to non-discrimination under EU law. However, where the exercise of national competence in *Kreil* and *Egenberger* was incompatible with EU (non-discrimination) law, the exercise of the power to lay down the rules on the loss and acquisition of nationality in *Rottmann* and *Tjebbes* was not. To the contrary, although a decision to withdraw the nationality of a Member State may lead to the loss of EU citizenship, this is a result that is consistent with, and indeed expressly required by, EU law – by the derivative nature of EU citizenship and its conditionality on Member State nationality.

This difference was entirely disregarded by the CJEU in *Rottmann* and later in *Tjebbes*. Instead, it justified its decision to limit national competence in the area of nationality on the basis of a few loose remarks about EU citizenship which do not hold water. First of all, it reiterated the statement made in earlier judgments that 'citizenship of the Union is intended to be the fundamental status of nationals of the Member States'.[32] It is not even clear whether this is a legal argument, but to the extent that it is, Weiler has correctly observed that it cannot be squared with the 'text, teleology and legislative history' of the Treaties.[33] If anything, Article 20 TFEU suggests that national citizenship is intended to be the fundamental status of Member State nationals.

The second, and seemingly more important, argument concerned the meaning of the proviso having due regard to EU law in respect of the national power to lay down the conditions for the acquisition and loss of nationality. It was said in *Rottmann* that this proviso

> enshrines the principle that, in respect of citizens of the Union, the exercise of that power, in so far as it affects the rights conferred and protected by the legal order of the Union, as is in particular the case

---

[30] Which justifies the CJEU's rejection of applying the *Nottebohm* judgment of the International Court of Justice under EU law. See further Martijn van den Brink (n 8).
[31] Case C-165/16 *Lounes* EU:C:2017:862, para 55.
[32] Case C-184/99 *Grzelczyk* EU:C:2001:458; Case C-34/09 *Ruiz Zambrano* EU:C:2011:124.
[33] For more general criticism of the 'destined to be the fundamental status' slogan, Joseph HH Weiler, 'Epilogue: Judging the Judges – Apology and Critique' in Maurice Adams and others (eds), *Judging Europe's Judges: The Legitimacy of the Case Law of the European Court of Justice* (Hart 2013) 248.

of a decision withdrawing naturalisation such as that at issue in the main proceedings, is amenable to judicial review carried out in the light of European Union law.[34]

With all due respect, this argument is unintelligible. One expects the CJEU to mention a substantive principle of law to which national authorities must have due regard, but instead it suggests that having due regard to EU law requires the possibility of judicial review. Presumably, this process is intended to ensure that due regard is had to EU law, but *Rottmann* failed to specify which principles of EU law. *Tjebbes* may have been an attempt to clarify this; the CJEU specified that Member States must have 'due regard to the principle of proportionality',[35] but this is not very illuminating either. Proportionality is the second stage of a two-pronged review procedure that follows the first stage, in which a claimant must demonstrate a possible unlawful interference with legally guaranteed rights.[36] The unanswered question remains which right(s) guaranteed by EU law may be unlawfully interfered with by a decision to withdraw a Member State nationality.

The CJEU mentions the status of EU citizenship and the rights attaching thereto, but while a decision to withdraw nationality may affect these rights, this result is not unlawful but is prescribed by EU law. The CJEU assumes that the withdrawal of the status of EU citizenship is in itself sufficient to subject denaturalisation decisions to review under EU law,[37] but this view runs into the problem discussed above, namely that this status is not supposed to affect or replace Member State nationality. Whatever way we look at it, *Rottmann* and *Tjebbes* seem too weakly reasoned to support their far-reaching legal ramifications. It remains unclear which substantive principles of EU law are violated by a decision to withdraw a Member State nationality. It may entail the loss of EU citizenship status, and the rights conferred thereby, as a direct implication, not violation, of EU law.

2.2 Can EU Law Affect Conditions for Acquisition and Loss of National Citizenship?

This is not to say that the possibility of national rules on the loss and acquisition of national citizenship being in conflict with rights or obligations laid down in EU law can be ruled out completely. We already saw that the decision by the CJEU to oblige Member States to recognise each other's grant of nationality is justified in order to guarantee the right to free movement and residence. In the same vein, Member States can be expected to have due regard to EU free movement law when deciding whom to grant to or deprive of their nationality.[38] Therefore, the deprivation of EU citizenship may be contrary to EU free movement law if the withdrawal of a nationality or the refusal to grant it is linked to or results from the exercise of the right to free movement.[39] Moreover, it is not just EU free movement law that may be relevant to determining the lawfulness of the domestic rules on the loss and acquisition of nationality. As AG Maduro once said, 'any rule of the Community legal order may be invoked if the conditions

---

[34] *Rottmann*, para 48.
[35] *Tjebbes*, para 40.
[36] Moshe Cohen-Eliya and Iddo Porat, *Proportionality and Constitutional Culture* (CUP 2013) 16.
[37] *Rottmann*, para 46.
[38] See, in this respect, also, Case C-135/08 *Rottmann*, Opinion of AG Maduro EU:C:2009:588.
[39] The two cases that are relevant in this respect are *Rottmann* and *JY v Wiener Landesregierung* (pending).

for the acquisition and loss of nationality laid down by a Member State are incompatible with it'.[40] For example, the Commission argues that the investor citizenship schemes of Cyprus and Malta violate the duty of sincere cooperation laid down in Article 4(3) TEU.[41]

Yet EU law does not seem to provide a legal justification for the imposition of far-reaching restrictions on conditions for the acquisition and loss of national citizenship. Situations where the deprivation of EU citizenship is linked to the exercise of free movement are far and few between. Furthermore, even if the Commission were able to prove that the investor citizenship schemes of Malta and Cyprus violate the duty of sincere cooperation, this finding would most likely only relate to the excesses associated with these arrangements, such as money laundering or corruption, and not to the practice as such.[42] Barring exceptional situations, national rules on the acquisition and loss of nationality will be in accordance with the provisions of EU law.

For example, the Commission's idea that nationality cannot be awarded 'absent any genuine link to the country or its citizens',[43] meaning that citizenship must be reserved for individuals with sufficiently strong social ties to the state, does not appear to have any basis in EU law. The introduction of a genuine link requirement would have sweeping implications for the relationship between national and EU citizenship; it would outlaw the practice of investor citizenship, as the Commission intends, but also, inter alia, discretionary and remedial naturalisation schemes.[44] So far, the Commission has not been able to demonstrate persuasively that naturalisation schemes that are not premised upon the principle of genuine link are incompatible with EU law.[45] Second, Article 20 TFEU says clearly that EU citizenship is 'additional to' and dependent on Member State nationality. This should be sufficient to reject the argument that UK nationals have a claim to EU citizenship following the UK's departure from the EU.[46] There are currently three cases pending before the CJEU questioning the legality of the withdrawal agreement, among other reasons because it deprives UK nationals of their EU citizenship status.[47] These were recently joined by two preliminary references that directly ask the CJEU whether UK nationals can retain their EU citizenship.[48] These claims should be dismissed on the basis of Article 20 TFEU.

---

[40] Opinion of AG Maduro (n 38) para 28.
[41] European Commission Press Release, 'Investor Citizenship Schemes: European Commission opens infringements against Cyprus and Malta for "selling" EU citizenship' (20 October 2020) available at: https://ec.europa.eu/commission/presscorner/detail/en/ip_20_1925 accessed 9 March 2021.
[42] For further discussion, Martijn van den Brink (n 8); Daniel Sarmiento and Martijn van den Brink (n 12).
[43] Report from the Commission to the European Parliament, the Council, the European Economic and Social Committee and the Committee of the Regions of 23 January 2019 on Investor Citizenship and Residence Schemes in the European Union (COM(2019) 12 final) 6.
[44] See further, Martijn van den Brink (n 8).
[45] Ibid. See also, Dimitry Kochenov, 'Genuine Purity of Blood: The 2019 Report on Investor Citizenship and Residence in the European Union and Its Litigious Progeny' [2020] LEQS Paper No. 164/2020.
[46] For a general discussion of the idea of granting UK nationals EU citizenship following Brexit, Martijn van den Brink and Dimitry Kochenov, 'Against Associate EU Citizenship' (2019) 57 Journal of Common Market Studies 1366.
[47] Case T-252/20 *Silver and Others* (pending); Case T-198/20 *Shindler and Others* (pending); Case C-298/20 P(R) *Price and Others* (pending).
[48] Case C-673/20 *Préfet du Gers* (pending); Case C-32/21 *Institut national de la statistique* (pending).

In their current relationship, national citizenship enjoys primacy over EU citizenship. In light of what the EU Treaties and the attached Declarations say, it is somewhat puzzling that there is so much disagreement on that issue. No doubt some will promote contrary ideas solely for legal or political gain, but there are at least two other reasons that explain why the relationship between EU and national citizenship is so contested. The first is that the foggy CJEU jurisprudence may give the impression that more sweeping restrictions on national competence in matters of national citizenship can easily be justified under EU law. The second is the belief that their current relationship is inadequate and needs to be reformed in order to remedy these shortcomings. As I explain below, there are good reasons to reconsider and revise the relationship between national and EU citizenship but, given what this relationship is according to EU Treaty law, implementing proposals for reform will be hard to accomplish without Treaty amendment.

3. WHAT THE RELATIONSHIP BETWEEN NATIONAL AND EU CITIZENSHIP SHOULD BE

There are various ways in which the relationship between national and EU citizenship can be reformed. Before discussing whether, and if so which, reform is desirable, the different options will briefly be examined.[49] In the previous section we saw that this relationship is defined by three dimensions: linkage, derivation and access. Each of these dimensions can be modified. First, the derivative relationship between national and EU citizenship can be reversed, to establish the primacy of EU over national citizenship, akin to the relationship between the central and local citizenships in most federal states.[50] Second, it is possible to remove, in part or in full, the linkage between national and EU citizenship and establish the latter as a status enjoying (partial) autonomy from nationality. Third, control over access can be modified by giving the EU greater influence over the conditions relating to the loss and acquisition of national and thereby EU citizenship. The first and most ambitious possibility, reversing the derivative relationship, has to the best of my knowledge never been contemplated seriously, so will not be discussed in what follows.[51] Instead, the discussion will first focus on arguments in favour of the autonomy of EU citizenship status, before explaining that modifying the access dimension is the most promising solution where there are reasons to reform the relationship between national and EU citizenship.

3.1 EU Citizenship as an Autonomous Status

Calls for EU citizenship to be autonomous from national citizenship have grown stronger in recent years. This intensification is largely a consequence of Brexit and the concomitant loss

---

[49] This section builds on but also improves the argument made previously in Martijn van den Brink, 'A Qualified Defence of the Primacy of Nationality over European Union Citizenship' (2020) 69 IC L Q 177.

[50] For an insightful study that highlights some of EU citizenship's federal characteristics: Christoph Schönberger, 'European Citizenship as Federal Citizenship: Some Citizenship Lessons of Comparative Federalism' (2007) 19 Revue Européenne de Droit Public 61.

[51] I consider some of its drawbacks in Martijn van den Brink (n 49).

of EU citizenship by British nationals, which led to calls for an associate EU citizenship status for nationals of a withdrawing Member State. There are, however, also more ambitious and, I will argue, more thoughtful proposals for an autonomous status that are not centrally concerned with the UK's departure from the EU. Proponents of the autonomy of EU citizenship rarely call for full autonomy, that is, a complete disconnection from nationality, but prefer partial autonomy: nationals of Member States are EU citizens by definition, but non-nationals are offered an additional European route to EU citizenship.

Fears that UK nationals would lose their EU citizenship status against their will as a result of Brexit led several prominent politicians and scholars to float the idea of an associate citizenship for UK nationals to safeguard their EU citizenship status and rights.[52] Exponents of associate EU citizenship proposed an autonomous EU citizenship for nationals of withdrawing Member States alone. While undoubtedly well-intentioned, these proposals are, in my view, among the most ill-advised with regard to EU citizenship that I am aware of. Associate EU citizenship is contrary both to the EU's own interests and to important democratic principles. On the first point, the EU's responsibility should lie primarily with its own citizens. If nationals of a former Member State could retain their EU citizenship rights as associate EU citizens should they so wish, the EU would be deprived of a powerful tool to force a withdrawing state to offer an equally favourable arrangement for EU citizens. For this reason the EU must insist on reciprocity in its dealings with withdrawing states, so that a settlement is reached that is fair both to the citizens of the withdrawing state and to its own. A second reason why associate EU citizenship runs counter to the EU's interests is that withdrawal becomes more attractive to other countries if their nationals can enjoy the benefits of EU citizenship without accepting the burdens of EU membership.[53]

Proposals for associate EU citizenship also raise deeper normative democratic problems. First, if all nationals of a withdrawing state were allowed to retain their EU citizenship rights as associate citizens, it would be close to impossible to guarantee their right to vote in elections to the European Parliament. After all, where are associated citizens who are not citizens or residents of an EU Member State supposed to cast their vote? More importantly, it is unclear why nationals of a withdrawing state who are not resident in the EU should be included in political processes that do not affect or coerce them (or not nearly as much as individuals resident within the EU). There seems no reason to believe that it is wrong to deprive UK nationals living in the UK of their right to vote in elections to the European Parliament.[54] A narrower conception of associate EU citizenship, which reserves the possibility of acquiring this status for nationals of a withdrawing state residing in an EU Member State, avoids this problem.[55] Yet, it raises another concern of fairness and justice: why should the EU grant the rights of EU citizenship only to UK nationals and not to all other long-term resident third-country nationals? Past legal membership of the EU (the possession of EU citizenship) seems a weak criterion for determining who should be an EU citizen in the present, especially when compared to an alternative criterion: present social membership, that is, actual social ties with EU Member States.

---

[52] These proposals and their subtle differences are discussed in detail in Martijn van den Brink and Dimitry Kochenov (n 46).
[53] For a more detailed discussion of these objections, ibid 1373–6.
[54] See further on these points ibid 1376–8.
[55] The leading account avoiding this problem is that by Dora Kostakopoulou (n 4).

Proposals for an autonomous EU citizenship status do not run into this problem. By decoupling EU citizenship from nationality and leaving decisions on national citizenship to the Member States, while granting the EU the prerogative to decide on the possession of EU citizenship, the EU would be able to draw its boundaries of inclusion more democratically. It could allow all third-country nationals with significant social ties to the EU to become EU citizens, even if they are not eligible for naturalisation under national law. In order to achieve a more inclusive EU citizenship, proponents of an autonomous status advocate only EU citizenship's partial decoupling from national citizenship.[56] Logically, Member State nationals should be EU citizens by default, if only because the EU political system builds on national political structures and presupposes that national institutions and citizens are bound by the political outcomes produced by EU institutions. Kostakopoulou has therefore proposed that EU citizenship must be decoupled from national citizenship as regards the acquisition of this status, so that EU citizenship can be granted to individuals without a Member State nationality.[57] In her view, third-country nationals must have a legal claim to EU citizenship once they 'have been residing on a lawful and permanent basis in the territories of the EU for five years'.[58] The apparent benefit of these proposals is the realisation of not just a more inclusive but also a 'more cosmopolitan political community',[59] premising the EU 'upon the unity of the peoples of Europe'.[60]

The desire to prevent unjust exclusion from citizenship is right (see more below), but an autonomous EU citizenship status is not the answer. All proposals for an autonomous citizenship, no matter their form, face one seemingly insurmountable obstacle, which I have called 'the problem of partial political participation'.[61] EU citizens are represented in EU decision-making processes both directly by the European Parliament and indirectly by national representatives in the Council, who are accountable to national parliaments. Suppose that individuals could acquire EU citizenship without having the nationality of a Member State. This would create a category of second-class EU citizens who are represented by the European Parliament but not indirectly by national representatives in the Council. An autonomous EU citizenship status would therefore not achieve what its proponents hope for, namely a more inclusive and cosmopolitan European community.

---

[56] Garner explores the possibility of full autonomy but recognises its disadvantages. Oliver Garner, 'The Existential Crisis of Citizenship of the European Union: The Argument for an Autonomous Status' (2018) 20 Cambridge Yearbook of European Legal Studies 116, 144.

[57] Others have proposed to disconnect the two in respect of the loss of EU citizenship, but these proposals are concerned with the status of UK nationals after Brexit and are subject to the same limitations as the proposals for associate EU citizenship discussed above. See, for example, Mark Dawson and Daniel Augenstein, 'After Brexit: Time for a further Decoupling of European and National Citizenship?' https://verfassungsblog.de/brexit-decoupling-european-national-citizenship/ accessed 9 March 2021.

[58] Dora Kostakopoulou, 'European Union Citizenship: Writing the Future' (2007) 13 European Law Journal 623, 644.

[59] Dora Kostakopoulou (n 4) 857.

[60] Mark Dawson and Daniel Augenstein (n 57).

[61] Martijn van den Brink (n 49) 190.

3.2 Shared EU Conditions for the Loss and Acquisition of National and EU Citizenship

It is thus undesirable to loosen the linkage between national and EU citizenship. The acquisition and loss of EU citizenship should thus follow that of national citizenship, just as it does right now. A radical rupture with the status quo that would come from reversing or disconnecting the derivative relationship between national and EU citizenship seems both unnecessary and undesirable. As far as the current relationship between national and EU citizenship raises problems that call for its revision, reconsidering the dimension of 'access' is more promising than that of 'linkage' or 'derivation'. Before discussing this dimension, however, it is necessary to examine more closely what, if anything, justifies a revision of this relationship.

Three different reasons have been offered. The first is the need to protect the integrity of EU citizenship – its 'essence' or 'very concept', as the European Commission and Parliament put it respectively in their objections to the investor citizenship programmes run by several Member States.[62] These statements may be rhetorically appealing, but they leave enormous ambiguity as to what exactly the essence or very concept of EU citizenship entails. Furthermore, they overstate the importance of EU citizenship as an independent concept. It is merely complementary to national citizenship, and serves mainly to mediate the relationship of Member State nationals with Member States of which they are not nationals – the rights to free movement and non-discrimination offer EU citizens access to rights derived from national citizenship rather than a set of independent European rights.[63] In practice, little would change if EU citizenship were abolished tomorrow. Nationals of Member States would retain the rights and entitlements they currently enjoy as EU citizens, but then simply as Member State nationals; Malta and Cyprus would no longer be able to 'sell' EU citizenship, but investors could still acquire the full set of free movement rights based on the nationality of these states; and rendering someone stateless would no longer result in the loss of EU citizenship, but still deprive that person of the rights enjoyed under EU law by virtue of being a Member State national. In other words, the added value of EU citizenship over and above Member State nationality is so minimal that this concept alone provides no justification for restricting the authority of Member States with regard to the criteria of acquisition and loss of citizenship.

The second reason put forward for a revision of the relationship between national and EU citizenship is that national rules on the acquisition and loss of EU citizenship can potentially have negative implications for other Member States. Because EU citizenship is parasitic upon national citizenship and the acquisition of these statuses comes with the right to move and reside freely across the EU, 'naturalisation decisions taken by one Member State are not neutral with regard to other Member States'.[64] This argument has some strength but should be used carefully and sparingly. Every acquisition of a nationality leads to the acquisition of EU citizenship, so no decision to grant a nationality is by definition neutral with regard to other Member States. The purely hypothetical possibility that national rules on access to nationality

---

[62] Report from the Commission; European Parliament, 'Joint Motion for a Resolution on EU Citizenship for Sale' (14 January 2014) available at: www.europarl.europa.eu/sides/getDoc.do?reference =P7-RC-2014-0015&type=MOTION&language=EN&redirect accessed 9 March 2021.

[63] Richard Bellamy, *A Republican Europe of States: Cosmopolitanism, Intergovernmentalism and Demoicracy in the EU* (CUP 2019) chapter 5.

[64] Speech by Viviane Reding (n 13).

may cause negative externalities that affect other states does not appear to be a valid reason for restricting the Member States' competence in this area. National rules must be demonstrably highly likely to have such an effect. It has been suggested that this threshold could be met by Member States engaging in 'an unjustified mass naturalisation of nationals of non-member States',[65] or by investor citizenship programmes that pose significant security risks such as money laundering or corruption.[66] In particular, naturalisation rules which demonstrably put other Member States at risk may be considered contrary to the principle of sincere cooperation. However, this was already mentioned in the previous section as a principle of EU law that may be capable of restricting Member State competence in the area of nationality. Therefore, as the EU already seems to have the legal capacity to deal with naturalisation conditions that can burden other Member States, these situations do not call for a revision of the relationship between national and EU citizenship. If these problems can be shown to exist, they can be addressed under the current framework of EU law.

The third reason is the strongest one, and was already touched upon above when discussing the argument for the autonomy of EU citizenship. While many states have facilitated the acquisition of citizenship for the lucky few, including persons with the financial means to acquire citizenship by investment or with special ancestral ties to a particular state, the path to national citizenship has become more difficult for many migrants in recent years.[67] A European Union committed to democratic fairness has an interest in ensuring that migrants are not excluded permanently, or for an excessively long period, from national and EU citizenship.[68] The exclusion of third-country nationals with strong social ties from citizenship not only constitutes a democratic wrong at national level; it also affects the EU's own legitimacy, first of all because national representative processes are key to the legitimisation of EU policies, but also because national citizenship goes hand in hand with EU citizenship and the right to vote for and stand in elections to the European Parliament. To address this deficit, the EU should be granted the powers to provide for minimum standards on access to national and EU citizenship.

In recent years the debate about who is entitled to be an EU citizen has focused for the most part on the unjust inclusion rather than the unjust exclusion of third-country nationals, especially when considering the EU institutions' fight against investor citizenship. The scope of this debate is too narrow. What we need is a more comprehensive discussion on the proper boundaries of EU citizenship,[69] focusing both on privileges of the lucky few and on the plight of the larger group of third-country nationals with a difficult path to citizenship. If anything, the predicament of the latter should be a priority in this discussion, if we accept that under-inclusive naturalisation conditions are of greater concern than over-inclusive rules. Simply put, all things being equal, the exclusion of citizenship of third-country nationals with

---

[65] Opinion of AG Maduro (n 38) para 30.

[66] Report from the Commission; Transparency International and Global Witness, 'European Getaway: Inside the Murky World of Golden Visas' (2018), available at www.globalwitness.org/ru/campaigns/corruption-and-money-laundering/european-getaway/.

[67] For a discussion of these contradictions: Ayelet Shachar, 'The Marketization of Citizenship in an Age of Restrictionism' (2018) 32 Ethics & International Affairs 3; Liav Orgad, 'Naturalization' in Ayelet Shachar and others (eds), *The Oxford Handbook of Citizenship* (1st edn, OUP 2017).

[68] This paragraph draws on Martijn van den Brink (n 8).

[69] For my attempt, Martijn van den Brink (n 49). See further, Rainer Bauböck (n 9); Oliver Garner (n 56).

significant social ties to their country of residence is more problematic than the inclusion of wealthy investors without social ties. Let me briefly explain why this is the case.[70]

The boundaries of citizenship are determined by 'the accident of birth within particular geographical borders [or] the sheer luck of descent',[71] which explains why citizenship provides a morally arbitrary concept for the allocation of rights and duties. Migrants often have the same social connections to a particular state as its citizens but are not recognised as full members and deprived of important rights, in particular certain political rights. They may have grown up there or have built up a relationship with their state of residence over an extended period of time, and they cooperate and participate with fellow residents in the production of collective societal goods. Still, they may not be in a position to become full members of their society. It is increasingly accepted that this is problematic, and that such social connections ought to be recognised as giving migrants a moral claim to the rights and ultimately status of citizenship.[72] In particular, as the class of rights closely tied to citizenship is that of political rights, the moral wrong in denying migrants with genuine links the right to obtain citizenship is in large part a democratic wrong. Therefore, migrants who have been resident for an extended period of time and have become social members of society have a moral claim to legal inclusion. It follows that individuals without social membership – without substantial social ties – do not have a moral claim to citizenship and the rights that come with this status. However, it does not follow from the fact that it is morally permissible to deny persons without social ties citizenship that it is morally impermissible to grant them citizenship (for investment or for another reason).[73] This is why under-inclusive naturalisation rules are morally more problematic than over-inclusive rules.

To be clear: this does not show that over-inclusive naturalisation conditions are never objectionable. Investor citizenship, or another over-inclusive naturalisation programme, may be so for one or another reason. However, given how sensitive the Member States are towards increasing the EU's powers in the domain of nationality, in order to have any chance of improving the relationship between national and EU citizenship it will be necessary to set certain priorities on the basis of what is most necessary and feasible. Granting the EU the power to introduce shared minimum conditions with regard to access to national and EU citizenship will require Treaty amendment and thus be difficult to achieve in itself. If the EU also wants to ban practices that are profitable for the Member States and which seem to have gained in popularity in recent years, it will become impossible to introduce even the most desirable changes. Therefore, it seems better to me to aim for EU minimum standards that make naturalisation conditions less under-inclusive rather than less over-inclusive.

4. CONCLUSION

This chapter has sought to clarify what the relationship between national and EU citizenship is, and what it ought to be. As to the first question, it was shown that the EU Treaties establish

---

[70] The more extensive argument is developed in Martijn van den Brink (n 8) section C.2.
[71] Ayelet Shachar, *The Birthright Lottery: Citizenship and Global Inequality* (Harvard UP 2009) 7.
[72] Joseph H Carens, *The Ethics of Immigration* (OUP 2013) chapter 8.
[73] For a similar argument, Javier Hidalgo, 'Selling Citizenship: A Defence' (2016) 33 Journal of Applied Philosophy 223.

the primacy of national over EU citizenship and that restrictions on national competence regarding the conditions relating to the loss and acquisition of nationality are justified only if the exercise of that competence may unlawfully interfere with the rights or obligations laid down in EU law. The CJEU has failed to recognise the limits established by the Treaties and has allowed EU law to unjustifiably encroach upon the competence of the Member States in the area of nationality, namely also in those situations where they exercise their competence in a manner consistent with EU law. As to the second point, the relationship between national and EU citizenship is not what it should be. Although the more radical proposals for a revision of this relationship, and in particular proposals for an associated or autonomous EU citizenship, seem undesirable from a democratic point of view, so too is the current relationship, which perpetuates the unjustified exclusion of third-country nationals with strong social ties from national and EU citizenship. This defect can be addressed by granting the EU the powers to enact shared minimum rules that condition access to national and EU citizenship.

PART II

CITIZENS' RIGHTS

8. Citizenship, territory and COVID-19
Stephen Coutts

1. INTRODUCTION

The COVID-19 crisis posed a direct threat to the construction of the European Union as 'an area of freedom, security and justice in which the free movement of persons is assured' to be 'offered to Union citizens'.[1] Mobility was seen as facilitating the spread of the virus and the achievement of the Union in removing borders and achieving frictionless movement suddenly presented itself as a threat to the life and health of the populations of the Member States. In response to the virus, all Member States took measures to restrict the mobility of persons, relying haphazardly on the legal derogations contained in the Schengen Border Code and the Free Movement Directive.[2] As with the euro crisis, it seems that EU law, with its division of competences between the Member States and the Union, might be ill equipped to manage unforeseen crisis. This did result in certain legal tensions, although an assessment regarding the legality or otherwise of Member State measures in light of Union law is not clear cut.

This chapter, while addressing questions regarding the legality of Member State measures in relation to the free movement and Schengen legal frameworks, will largely focus on the impact of the COVID-19 crisis on the emerging notion of territory in Union citizenship legal studies and what the various responses – both Member State and Union – reveal about the state of territoriality and the interaction between Member State and Union notions of territory. It will argue that the legal responses to COVID-19 paradoxically reaffirmed the centrality of 'hard' Member State territoriality and the 'soft' nature of Union spatiality and yet saw the emergence of certain features of EU territoriality and, separately, the Europeanisation of national categories of belonging. What the COVID-19 crisis has revealed is that in the area of citizenship, Member States remain central as political–territorial units, yet at the same time this is layered with an emerging notion of EU territoriality.

2. UNION TERRITORY, FREE MOVEMENT AND CITIZENSHIP

2.1 Territory and Citizenship

Territory performs a number of functions in relation to citizenship.[3] Citizenship is first and foremost a status of membership, and one that carries with it legal rights and a sense of belong-

---

[1] Treaty on the Functioning of the European Union (TFEU), art. 3.
[2] European Parliament and Council Directive 2004/38/EC of 29 April 2004 on the right of citizens of the Union and their family members to move and reside freely within the territory of the Member States [2004] OJ L158/77.
[3] For a general overview see Neil Walker, 'The Place of Territory in Citizenship' in Rainer Bauböck and others (eds), *The Oxford Handbook of Citizenship* (OUP 2017).

ing to the political community.⁴ All of these elements draw upon territoriality in one sense or another.

National territory can be an important element in constructing a common identity, central to most forms of state-based citizenship today.⁵ The notion of the 'homeland' is a powerful one, and affiliation with and affection for the homeland can be a significant element in a shared identity.⁶ It is a common element in a national narrative and commitment to the homeland is frequently used as a proxy for commitment to the community as a whole, integrated into different patriotic narratives. It is also a powerful underpinning to the inter-generational dimension of a political community and points to, and can act as a proxy for, a persistence of the community through time.⁷ As with all markers of group identity, commitment and symbolic attachment to the national territory is a characteristic that must be shared among the group, and moreover must be one that is perceived to be shared by other members of the group – that is, it is not enough that everyone recognises the national territory as such; they must know or believe that other members of the group hold similar beliefs.⁸

Linked to this identity function – territory as an abstract symbol for the community – is a related notion of territory as simply the shared space in which a particular political community collectively exists.⁹ The members are brought together and engage in the collective practice of living together, institutionalised through law and other social institutions, over a particular space or part of the world. Their shared lives are built on this territory as a physical space and this has political significance for the group for the collective life they build together on it. As Arendt puts it:

> 'territory' as the law understands it, is a political and a legal concept and not merely a geographical term. It relates not so much and not primarily, to a piece of land as to the space between individuals in a group whose members are bound to, and at the same time separated and protected from each other by all kinds of relationships, based on a common language, religion, a common history and laws. Such relationships become spatially manifest insofar as they themselves constitute the space wherein the different members of the group relate to and have intercourse with each other.¹⁰

Territory is also important from a narrower legal sense, as jurisdiction. Jurisdiction and territory do not perfectly align, with states increasingly exercising some forms of extra-territorial jurisdiction.¹¹ Nonetheless, most legal systems define most elements of their jurisdiction in

---

⁴ There are various ways of conceiving of citizenship and its different dimensions. For a review see Jo Shaw, *The Transformation of Citizenship in the European Union: Electoral Rights and the Restructuring of Political Space* (CUP 2007) ch. 1. See also Rainer Bauböck, *Recombinant Citizenship* ((1999) 67 Political Science Series, Institute for Advanced Studies, Vienna).
⁵ See Neil Walker (n 3).
⁶ David Miller, *On Nationality* (Clarendon 1995) ch. 2.
⁷ See Charles S Maier, 'Being There: Place, Territory and Identity' in Seyla Benhabib, Ian Shapiro and Danilo Petranovich (eds), *Identities, Affiliations and Allegiances* (CUP 2007).
⁸ See David Miller (n 6) ch. 2.
⁹ And over which they may hold collective rights: see Margaret Moore, *A Political Theory of Territory* (OUP 2015) ch. 3.
¹⁰ Speaking of the state of Israel. See Hannah Arendt, *Eichmann in Jerusalem: A Report on the Banality of Evil* (Penguin Classics 1963) 262–3.
¹¹ For example in criminal law. See for example European Parliament and Council Directive 2011/93/EU of 13 December 2011 on combating the sexual abuse and sexual exploitation of children and child pornography, and replacing Council Framework Decision 2004/68/JHA of 22 December 2003 on

relation to the territory of the state. This of course is no mistake, it being the space over which the state can exercise coercive force and also the territory on which any particular legal and political community is located. It is the unity of the different elements of the modern state: sovereignty, authority and control, territory and people. As Doyle puts it, law is 'the law of a [particular] community; [its] spatial dimension is the geographic distribution of that community. Law is necessarily territorial.'[12]

This necessarily territorial characteristic of law is linked to citizenship in a more particular way. A core element of citizenship is the granting of certain rights to the individual as a member of the community, with a view towards equality with co-members. It is, famously, the right to have rights.[13] Enforceable rights are creatures of law and law is deployed over a given territory linked to the particular legal system. While some citizenship rights are enjoyed extra-territorially, the vast majority of rights granted to individuals in any particular community are exercisable only within the territory of that community – a fact which flows naturally from the treatment of jurisdiction mentioned in the previous paragraph. The right to access that territory is therefore crucial. Indeed, the unconditional right to access and even remain on the territory, largely guaranteed in international and frequently constitutional law, is one of the few rights clearly linked to [national] citizenship, including under Union law.[14] As noted by Brubaker, it is at the border that the distinction between citizen and non-citizen becomes apparent.[15] Citizenship as a right to access territory is therefore the concrete manifestation of Arendt's right to have rights.[16] It is, however, broader than legal rights, but relates to the various public goods that any political community creates for its members, be they social, economic or political.[17] To put it another way, rights over and within any particular territory and the community occupying that territory are coded by membership. This can take different forms in today's world of migration[18] but it is citizenship which is the 'gold standard' and which provides (relatively) unconditional access[19] to the national territory and all that entails.

---

combating the sexual exploitation of children and child pornography [2011] OJ L355/1, art. 17(1) which mandates extraterritorial jurisdiction based on nationality for sexual offences against children.

[12] Oran Doyle, 'Spatial Statism: Afterword to the Foreword by Ran Hirschl and Ayelet Shachar' (2020) 18 ICON 29, 30.

[13] Hannah Arendt, *The Origins of Totalitarianism* (first published 1951, Schoken Books 2004) 293.

[14] Unlike nationals, Member States retain the right to expel Union citizens, albeit under the control of Union law. While protection increases over time, this is never absolute.

[15] Rogers Brubaker, *Citizenship and Nationhood in France and Germany* (Harvard University Press 1992) 30, noting that borders are nowadays projected beyond the state as well as operating within a state's physical borders. See also Linda Bosniak, *The Citizen and the Alien: Dilemmas of Contemporary Membership* (Princeton UP 2006) for the various ways in which states impose borders – both internal and external – sorting members from non-members.

[16] Hannah Arendt (n 13) 293.

[17] Michael Walzer, *Spheres of Justice: A Defense of Pluralism and Equality* (Basic Books 1984) ch. 1, noting that membership is itself a public good and considerations of justice should apply when determining how it should be distributed.

[18] See Tomas Hammar, *Democracy and the Nation State: Aliens, Denizens and Citizens in a World of International Migration* (Ashgate 1990) and Neil Walker, 'Denizenship and Deterritorialisation in the European Union' in Hans Lindahl (ed.), *A Right to Inclusion and Exclusion: Normative Faultlines of the EU's Area of Freedom, Security and Justice* (Hart 2009).

[19] Although we should be cognisant of the resurgent practice of citizenship deprivation. See Audrey Macklin and Rainer Bauböck, 'The Return of Banishment: Do the New Denationalisation Policies Weaken Citizenship?' (2015) EUI Working Papers, RSCAS 2015/14 and Milena Tripkovic,

In short, citizenship still matters in a world where states are still territorially organised and rights and public goods associated with states are deployed on that territory, and citizenship grants unconditional access to that territory.[20]

2.2 Union Citizenship and EU Territory

The European Union does not have a territory in a legal sense.[21] Indeed, a fixed territory, along with a stable population and a monopoly over the legitimate use of force, is the classic Weberian definition of a *state*,[22] and the European Union is not a state. Where territory is mentioned in the context of EU law it is generally with reference to the territories of the Member States, and refers more prosaically to the field of application of any area of Union law.[23] Indeed, one can question whether such a thing as a European territory can be said to exist, taking Maier's concept of territory as an inherently political and legal bounded and controllable space premised on state sovereignty.[24] This notion of 'hard territoriality', including within it the exercise of coercive force, control over borders and the enforcement of law, remains a feature of the Member States in today's EU.[25] The Union deploys on the other hand a 'soft' form of territoriality or, to put it more accurately, spatiality, where space refers simply to an internally unbounded surface (possibly enclosed where appropriate) upon which social, political and economic forces operate and interact. It is apposite that the Union refers to its various constructs as 'areas' or 'spaces'.[26] As noted by Pullano, in its spatial dimension the Union is not so much constructing a hard territory, claiming a particular legal territory and claiming some ability to exercise force over it; rather it is concerned with the management of flows – economic and social – throughout the space it constructs.[27] 'Rather than being primarily concerned with state-building or the institutionalisation of governance structures, the EU is centrally concerned with the construction of European spaces. Put simply the EU actively constructs European spaces, which it alone is capable of governing.'[28] This development of a (soft) European spatiality has significant implications for the territoriality of Member States and the relationship of those states to their territory, constraining their ability under normal

---

'Transcending the Boundaries of Punishment: On the Nature of Citizenship Deprivation' (forthcoming 2021) Brit J Criminol DOI: 10.1093/bjc/azaa085.

[20] See Ayelet Shachar, 'The Worth of Citizenship in an Unequal World' (2007) 8 Theoretical Inquiries in Law 367.

[21] See Luis María Díez-Picazo, 'What Does It Mean to Be a State within the European Union?' [2002] Riv Ital Dir Pubbl Communitario 651.

[22] See Richard Swedberg and Ola Agevall, *The Max Weber Dictionary: Key Words and Central Concepts* (Stanford University Press 2005) (ES:901).

[23] Teresa Pullano, 'The Evolving Category of Territory: From the Modern State to the European Union' (2009) GARNET Working Paper No 64/09,5.

[24] Charles S Maier (n 7).

[25] See Teresa Pullano (n 23).

[26] See the old wording of the treaties where an 'internal market shall comprise an area without internal frontiers' (TEC, art. 14(2) [version applicable after the Treaty of Nice]), overtaken in the Treaty of Lisbon by Article 3(2) TEU in which the Union shall offer its citizens 'an area of freedom, security and justice'.

[27] Teresa Pullano (n 23).

[28] Chris Rumford, 'Rethinking European Spaces: Territory, Borders and Governance' (2006) 4 Comparative European Politics 127, 128.

circumstances to exclude certain actors from their territory and their economic and social systems. And indeed, as the Union develops more coherent external border policies with greater involvement of supranational institutions, Member State territoriality continues to be affected. The spaces constructed by the Union and the corresponding controls and constraints of Union law certainly impact on the nature of that territoriality. Nonetheless, it remains the case that territoriality in the hard sense remains a feature of Member States.

And yet, this absence of territoriality on the part of the Union sits uneasily with the notion of citizenship and the attempt by the supranational institutional actors to construct a meaningful citizenship of the European Union. Given the link between community, territory, rights and citizenship outlined above, there is perhaps a natural tendency for a status of citizenship, properly substantiated, to develop as an outgrowth some concept of territory. The encouragement of circulation and flow throughout the 'space' of the European Union, constructed from its various Member State components, is far from insignificant. Indeed, as pointed out by Kostakopoulou,[29] it renders borders between national communities more porous and, especially in its more intense form as a 'status of social integration',[30] reforms categories of national belonging in the Union, making them more inclusive. Nonetheless, what is absent from this picture is a sense of a political bond, identity, and a sharing of a common space which, as indicated above, seems so important to the notion of citizenship as the institutional manifestation at an individual level of the political community.[31]

There have been some indications of the emergence of a thicker form of territoriality on the part of the Union in judgments of the Court of Justice on Article 20 TFEU, developing the famous *Zambrano* doctrine under which Member States are precluded from expelling a third country-national carer parent of a Union citizen if the result would be the removal of the Union citizen from the 'territory of the Union', thereby denying him or her the genuine enjoyment of the substance of the rights of Union citizenship.[32] Azoulai noted the reference to Union territory as a supranational reference point at the time of *Zambrano*.[33] I have argued elsewhere that the Article 20 TFEU right effectively embodies a right to the territory of the Union,[34] akin in some ways to the general right of national citizenship to access the national territory, with all that entails. In this view the territory of the Union now represents a common place of social integration, albeit disaggregated by Member State territory. Importantly from a doctrinal and conceptual perspective, this right emerges *from* the rights of free movement and residence which are of course deployed across the Member States, emphasising that this European territory emerges from the territories of the Member States. It is a citizenship terri-

---

[29] Dora Kostakopoulou, 'European Citizenship: Writing the Future' (2007) 13 ELJ 623, 642.

[30] Loïc Azoulai, 'La Citoyenneté Européenne, un Statut d'Intégration Sociale' in Gérard Cohen-Jonathan and others (eds), *Chemins d'Europe: Mélanges en l'honneur de Jean Paul Jacqué* (Dalloz 2010).

[31] On this see Michel Rosenfeld, *The Identity of the Constitutional Subject: Selfhood, Culture and Community* (Routledge 2010).

[32] Case C-34/09 *Gerardo Ruiz Zambrano v Office national de l'emploi* (ONEm) EU:C:2011:124, para. 42.

[33] Loïc Azoulai, '"Euro-Bonds": The Ruiz Zambrano Judgment or the Real Invention of EU Citizenship' (2011) 3 Perspectives on Federalism 31, 33.

[34] Stephen Coutts, 'The Shifting Geometry of Union Citizenship: A Supranational Status from Transnational Rights' (2019) 21 CYELS 318, 333 ff. Similarly see Chiara Raucea, 'European Citizenship and the Right to Reside: "*No One on the Outside has a Right to be Inside?*"' (2016) 22 ELJ 470.

tory emerging from the European space of free movement. The turn to territory has been noted by other scholars in the field of Union citizenship studies. Níc Shuibhne notes the varying ways in which territory is being deployed by the Court of Justice and associated problems of coherence.[35] Mantu, speaking more directly of free movement rights, notes the reordering of national territory as a consequence of Union citizenship.[36]

This is far from a thick territoriality associated with national political communities. As noted above, it is built on Member State territories, now accessible to Union citizens via Article 21 TFEU rights. Moreover, it clearly lacks the thicker historical and social attachments between national citizenship and the national territory that enable the territory to act as an important reference and symbol for the community as a whole. It is a rather bare legal construction of a European citizenship territory, developed on the basis of legal rights, and one that is imbricated with or layered upon national territories.

To this we must add the additional and highly complementary construction of the Schengen zone, which, while not limited to Union citizens – in the sense that all individuals circulating in the Schengen states benefit – is linked to Union citizenship in at least two ways. First, in a very practical sense it facilitates the right of free movement by the removal of a very pervasive, if minimally important from a practical point of view (for Union citizens), restriction on the free movement of persons – that is, border checks. It is in this sense a classic flanking policy of the internal market. It is additionally important from a symbolic point of view: borders are important symbolic divisions and border checks, with all their state paraphernalia, are important physical reminders of the existence of borders and boundaries between states.[37] Even without being presented with physical borders in one's immediate surroundings, the existence of such borders can give a sense of closure to the population at large and create the national space as a 'secure space'.[38] The abolition of internal border checks therefore contributes to the actual and symbolic construction of that space of free movement associated with Union citizenship, as recognised by AG Cosmas in his Opinion in *Wijsenbeek* when he stated that 'recognition of the possibility of moving (in principle) unchecked within the geographic area corresponding to a legal order is inherent in the status of citizen covered by that legal order'.[39] Similarly, the construction of a common external border can contribute towards the creation of this feeling of closure at a European level.

---

[35] Niamh Níc Shuibhne, 'The "Territory of the Union" in EU Citizenship Law: Charting a Route from Parallel to Integrated Narratives' (2019) 38 YEL 267.

[36] Sandra Mantu, *EU Citizenship and Territory: Unsettling the National, Embedding the Supranational* (Brill Nijhoff 2020).

[37] In some sense a reflection of what Michael Billing has called 'banal nationalism'. See Michael Billing, *Banal Nationalism* (Sage 1995).

[38] Daniel Thym and Jonas Bornemann, 'Schengen and Free Movement Law During the First Phase of the COVID-19 Pandemic: Of Symbolism, Law and Politics' (2020) 5 European Papers 1143, 1155.

[39] Case C-378/97 *Criminal proceedings against Florus Ariël Wijsenbeek* EU:C:1999:144, Opinion of AG Cosmas, para. 101.

3. COVID-19 AND EUROPEAN TERRITORY

3.1 The Endurance of National Territoriality

While it is clear that European Union law has restructured national territory and has constrained in important ways the manner in which states exercise jurisdiction over their territories, especially regarding exclusion, it is also clear that European Union law does not supplant in a general sense the territorial role of Member States, especially in its hard sense in terms of exercising force. As noted above, the 'hard territoriality' enjoyed by Member States as described by Pullano,[40] in the sense of exercising coercive force over their territory and in particular their borders, remains. This must be placed alongside the general division of labour between the Union and the Member States in the provision of public goods. As noted above, the Union constructs spaces and manages social and economic flows, hopefully *contributing* to prosperity, individual freedom and security, among other possible public goods. Member States retain their status and character as states in the classic Weberian definition and, importantly for present purposes, for the provision of core state functions of the security and health of the population.[41] And indeed, those core state functions are recognised at numerous points in EU law. Article 72 states that the Area of Freedom, Security and Justice 'shall not affect the exercise of the responsibilities incumbent upon Member States with regard to the maintenance of law and order and the safeguarding of internal security'. Article 347 TFEU imposes a duty of consultation on Member States and possible coordination ('with a view to taking together steps') but accepts in the same paragraph that

> a Member State may be called upon to take in the event of serious internal disturbances affecting the maintenance of law and order, in the event of war, serious international tension constituting a threat of war or in order to carry out obligations it has accepted for the purposes of maintaining peace and international security.

And while phrased as an obligation of consultation and possible coordination, it has been interpreted as constituting a possible derogation from the strictures of supranational law.[42]

In a more particular sense, this enduring role for Member States in providing public security and the link with territory is reflected in appropriate derogations in the areas of free movement and the Schengen Border Code (SBC)[43] to allow for restrictions on free movement and the reintroduction of border controls, respectively, for reasons of public security, public policy and public health in the case of the free movement of Union citizens, and for public security and public policy in the case of the SBC. As is discussed in more detail below, the onset of

---

[40] Teresa Pullano (n 23) 22.
[41] For a reading of state formation focused on these core functions in the modern period see Michel Foucault, *Security, Territory, Population: Lectures at the College de France 1977–1978* (Arnold I Davidson ed, Graham Burchell tr, Palgrave Macmillan 2004).
[42] Daniel Thym, 'Travel Bans in Europe: A Legal Appraisal' (*Verfassungsblog*, 2020) https://verfassungsblog.de/travel-bans-in-europe-a-legal-appraisal/ accessed 11 January 2020 citing Case C-423/98 *Alberto Albore* EU:C:2000:401.
[43] European Parliament and Council Regulation 2016/399/EU of 9 March 2016 on a Union code on the rules governing the movement of persons across borders (Schengen Border Code) [2016] OJ L77/1, arts 25 and 28.

the COVID-19 crisis led to the use of these derogations in a wholesale manner, and with a corresponding impact on the European space of free movement and the tentative European citizenship territory described above. The effect, however, has, perhaps surprisingly, not been uniform, and there are elements of fragmentation on national lines *alongside* the emergence of a common European territory and the Europeanisation of access to national territory.

3.2 Re-Emergence of the National Territory as a Safe Space

The initial phase of the COVID-19 crisis in Europe was characterised by national retrenchment, with the rapid proliferation of border controls and wide-ranging entry bans on virtually all travel leading to an uncoordinated and complex system of national restrictive measures throughout the Union, and with Union institutions initially caught off guard in their response.[44]

Under the Schengen Border Code restrictions were rapidly introduced, with Austria introducing the first such restrictions from certain severely affected Italian regions on 11 March 2020. Within weeks border controls had been re-introduced and various forms of passenger travel suspended throughout the Schengen area.[45] The rapid reintroduction of borders caught the Union institutions somewhat by surprise and the Commission's initial response was the issuance of guidance to facilitate the continued free flow of border traffic, particularly in relation to essential goods and supply chains, but also for frontier and other essential workers.[46]

Questions have been raised concerning the legality of the reintroduction of borders under Articles 25 and 28 of the Schengen Border Code. To begin with, public health is not listed as an applicable ground for the reintroduction of borders under the SBC, it having been removed during the legislative process.[47] Nonetheless, a convincing case can be made that a public health threat of pandemic proportions such as COVID-19, with all the social and economic disruption it entails and, more importantly, its profound impact on the lives of Member State populations, can fall under the general category of public policy and public security.[48] Further concerns were raised regarding the 'nonchalant handling of procedural rules',[49] in particular the notification requirements and the switching between different legal bases for derogations to extend border controls beyond the periods envisaged in the SBC.[50] Perhaps more serious

---

[44] Daniel Thym and Jonas Bornemann (n 38). See also Sergio Carrera and Ngo Chun Luk, *In the Name of COVID: An Assessment of the Schengen Internal Border Controls and Travel Restrictions in the EU* (Study for the LIBE Committee of the European Parliament, 2020).

[45] For a detailed overview see Sergio Carrera and Ngo Chun Luk, *Love thy Neighbour? Coronavirus Politics and Their Impact on EU Freedoms and Rule of Law in the Schengen Area* (CEPS Paper in Liberty and Security 2020-04, 2020) and Sergio Carrera and Ngo Chun Luk (n 44).

[46] Communication from the Commission on the assessment of the application of the temporary restriction on non-essential travel to the EU, 8/04/2020 COM(2020) 148 final.

[47] Sergio Carrera and Ngo Chun Luk (n 44) 57.

[48] See for example the recent definition of public security in Joined Cases C-331/16 and 366/16 *K v Staatssecretaris van Veiligheid en Justitie and HF v Belgische Staat* EU:C:2018:296 (albeit under free movement law rather than the SBC) as something which may be affected by 'a direct threat to the peace of mind and physical security of the population as a whole' (para. 42). See also Daniel Thym and Jonas Bornemann (n 38) 1148 and Stefano Montaldo, 'The COVID-19 Emergency and the Reintroduction of Internal Border Controls in the Schengen Area: Never Let a Serious Crisis go to Waste' (2020) 5 European Papers 523, 527.

[49] Thym and Bornemann (n 38) 1148.

[50] Carrera and Ngo Chun Luk (n 44) 54–5. See also Stefano Montaldo (n 48) at 528.

from the point of view of the legality of the reintroduction of border controls is the question of objective justification and the related requirement of proportionality. The effectiveness of border closures (and other travel restrictions) can be doubted when the virus is already circulating within the community and so such measures would not appear to be suitable to attain the proclaimed objective.[51] Nonetheless, against this we must place the precautionary principle and the ability of Member States to act in situations of scientific uncertainty.[52]

Corresponding with the reintroduction of border controls[53] in the early stage of the COVID-19 crisis, Member States also responded by introducing travel bans, banning travel from particular Member States, or even, in the case of Hungary, from *all* Member States.[54] In line with international law, most states exempted nationals, but also exempted Union citizen (and often third country-national) residents and persons transiting their territory on their return to their place of residence.[55] Later in the year, in conjunction with Union-level coordination, most Member States removed border controls and relaxed outright entry bans, replacing them with less onerous restrictions on free movement such as testing requirements, the completion of passenger locator forms and, especially, mandatory quarantine, depending on the region or state from which an individual was coming.

As with the reintroduction of borders under the Schengen Border Code, the legality of these measures could be questioned, although a clear conclusion of illegality is not evident. Restrictions on free movement on the ground of public health (unlike the situation under the SBC) are provided for under article 29 Directive 2004/38/EC, which refers specifically to 'diseases of epidemic potential as defined by the instruments of the World Health Organisation'.[56] Unlike in the case of restrictions based on the grounds of public policy and public security, an individual threat does not need to be identified and so general measures such as those described above would appear to be possible. However, notification and possible appeals are to be provided for by Member States,[57] and it is unclear to what extent these requirements have been met. As with the reintroduction of border controls, the real questions arise regarding compliance with the general principles of non-discrimination and proportionality.

The issue of non-discrimination is not problematic for the legality of entry bans. Nationals have a right under international law to return to their state of nationality, a fact acknowledged by EU law.[58] Indeed, some EU law instruments use nationality as a means of identifying the most appropriate Member State to receive an individual.[59] However, there is no similar objec-

---

[51] See Sergio Carrera and Ngo Chun Luk (n 44), 68 ff.
[52] See Gareth Davies, 'Does Evidence-based EU Law Survive the COVID-19 Pandemic? Considering the Status in EU Law of Lockdown Measures which Affect Free Movement' (2020) 2 Frontiers in Human Dynamics Article 584486, 3.
[53] It is important from the point of view of legal analysis to separate out the issue of border checks and controls on the one hand from entry restrictions on the other, the former being an inconvenience but hardly an insurmountable barrier for most Union citizens, the latter prohibiting in law entry (or other travel restrictions) as such.
[54] For a detailed overview see Sergio Carrera and Ngo Chun Luk (n 44).
[55] For an overview see ibid.
[56] Directive 2004/38/EC (note 2) art. 29.
[57] See ibid, arts 30 and 31.
[58] C-41/74 *van Duyn v Home Office* EU:C:1974:133, para. 22.
[59] See for example the Council Framework Decision 2008/909/JHA of 27 November 2008 on the application of the principle of mutual recognition to judgements in criminal matters imposing custodial sentences or measures involving deprivation of liberty for the purposes of their enforcement in the

tive justification for treating national and non-national Union citizens differently with regard to other travel restrictions, including mandatory quarantine and testing requirements. While there is evidence of variation in treatment in some specific circumstances,[60] for the most part Member States do appear to have applied these restrictions in a non-discriminatory manner.

The proportionality assessment is more difficult and must take into account appropriate variation among Member States in terms of risk tolerance and uncertainty or incompleteness in scientific evidence.[61] One difficulty that does emerge is the national frame of reference of the majority of such travel restrictions. Measures must be suitable for achieving their objective and if restrictions are applied to free movement between Member States, comparable restrictions should be in place within a Member State.[62] Where there is no significant variation in the epidemiological situation between two states compared to within a particular state, it is difficult to see the suitability or policy coherence requirement being met for the imposition of travel restrictions (such as mandatory quarantine) between the two states but not between, say, regions in a particular state. As Thym and Bornemann put it: 'why should a journey from Berlin to Frankfurt be permitted, while travelling from Luxembourg to Frankfurt is not, even though both destinations currently constitute high risk areas?'[63] Of course, travel restrictions must operate according to some geographic criteria; some geographic unit must be selected and at a sufficient level of detail any such selection will appear arbitrary from the point of view of the disease (what if certain areas of a city had higher levels of the disease?). However, in larger states, particularly with more developed levels of regional and local government, selecting the *national* rather than regional or local geographical units for the operation of travel restrictions does reflect a certain epidemiological nationalism.

Thus, perhaps of greater significance than the narrow epidemiological function of supressing transmission of the virus is the symbolic function these measures might serve. Both of these sets of measures – especially border controls combined with entry bans, but also mandatory quarantine and testing requirements – represent the national territory as a 'safe space', physically separated and protected from a more dangerous and threatening outside. Borders themselves are powerfully symbolic and, as noted above, are physical manifestations of state power, closure and control over territory. The use of the state as the reference point for travel restrictions, including travel bans, fragments the space of free movement and European territory created by Union citizenship along national lines. In the terms we outlined above, the 'hard territoriality' of Member States, rendered less visible and conditioned in normal times, re-emerges forcefully in times of crisis. The core (Member) state functions of assuring the security and health of the (national) population deploys itself both physically (in the case of

---

European Union [2008] OJ L327/27, art 4 which indicates nationality as a criteria for transferring an individual serving a custodial sentence (alongside residence). See also Directive 2004/38/EC (note 2) art. 27(4) providing that '[t]he Member State which issued the passport or identity card shall allow the holder of the document who has been expelled on grounds of public policy, public security or public health from another Member State to re-enter its territory without any formality'.

[60] For example, Lithuania allows nationals to opt for a post-entry test rather than obliging them to have proof of a negative COVID test before entering the state. See Sergio Carrera and Ngo Chun Luk (n 44) 30.

[61] See Gareth Davies (n 52).

[62] See Joined Cases C-115/81 and 116/81 *Adoui and Cornuaille v Belgium* EU:C:1982:183, para. 8 on the regulation of sex work.

[63] Daniel Thym and Jonas Bornemann (n 38) 1168.

border controls) and legally (in the case of travel restrictions) along national territorial lines, disrupting and fragmenting the European space of free movement.

3.3 Emerging EU Territory: The EU Travel Ban

At the same time, COVID-19 saw the emergence of a potent symbol of EU territoriality in the adoption of a common external EU travel ban. Initially sceptical of the use of travel bans,[64] the European institutions quickly reversed their policy and announced the introduction of a European-wide travel ban on all non-essential travel into the European Union. This ban initially took the form of a Communication from the European Commission, addressed to Member States and calling on them to use their competence under the SBC to enforce such a ban.[65] This was later elaborated upon in a more formalised and legally weighty, but still soft law, instrument of a Council Recommendation in June 2020.[66] While initially exceptions were limited to essential travel and repatriating Union citizens, their family members and third country-national residents, later in the summer the ban was relaxed with respect to a number of third states presenting a low risk of COVID-19 transmission. The number of such states exempted from the ban was limited and the criteria for essential travel somewhat vague.[67]

The introduction of the EU travel ban, much like the national travel bans and border closures, was perhaps more important for its symbolic function, effecting closure but this time at a European level and presenting the European Union as a 'safe place', than for any role it may have played in combating transmission of the virus. The European Commission's initial communication admitted that 'travel restrictions are generally not seen by the World Health Organisation as the most effective way of countering a pandemic'.[68] (Particularly, it should be said, when Europe was already at that point the epicentre of the pandemic.) And yet '[t]he EU's external border has to act as a security perimeter for *all Schengen States*'.[69] The policy, with its nod to securitisation, echoes more recent trends in EU border policy and, indeed, the political direction of the current Commission towards a 'Europe that protects'.[70] For the purposes of the present chapter, there is an assertion of European territoriality in the sense of

---

[64] For example when reacting to the US travel ban announced by Donald Trump. See Sergio Carrera and Ngo Chun Luk (n 45) 16.
[65] Communication from the Commission on COVID-19: Temporary Restrictions on Non-Essential Travel to the EU COM(2020) 115 final of 16 March 2020 and for implementation see European Commission, *COVID-19 Guidance on the implementation of the temporary restriction on non-essential travel to the EU, on the facilitation of transit arrangements for the repatriation of EU citizens and on the effects on visa policy* C(2020) 2050 final (2020).
[66] Council Recommendation 2020/912 of 30 June 2020 on the temporary restrictions on non-essential travel into the EU and the possible lifting of such restriction [2020] OJ L208 I/1.
[67] Daniel Thym and Jonas Bornemann (n 38) 1160.
[68] Communication from the Commission on COVID-19: Temporary Restrictions on Non-Essential Travel to the EU (n 65) 1.
[69] Ibid, 1 (emphasis in original). It should be noted that despite the reference to the Schengen area, the ban was not applied to non-Schengen EU states, applying instead to the curious term EU+ states (EU Member States, Schengen states and, until the end of the Brexit transition period, the UK). Council Recommendation on the temporary restrictions on non-essential travel into the EU and the possible lifting of such restriction (n 66), recital (1) and footnote (1).
[70] Daniel Thym and Jonas Bornemann (n 38) 1156.

exercise of legally bounded and controllable space[71] and an attempt by the European Union to assert a place in the provision of security for its community through use of its territory.

At the same time, we should note the nature of the European Union's and the supranational institutions' involvement in the implementation of this policy. The external borders of the Schengen area are still Member State borders and their management remains the responsibility of the Member States. The Communications from the Commission were non-binding and while the Recommendation from the Council does carry more legal weight and could be considered a more formalised and authoritative source of soft law, it too is non-binding. Member States did, perhaps surprisingly, largely comply with this policy, but it was as much a matter of the Member States acting collectively in establishing this European territory as one of the Union institutions exercising any legal authority to do so.[72] Thym and Bornemann are right to point to the importance of the inter-governmentalism in constructing the Union response[73] and, in this instance, the creation of a (supranational?) European territory through inter-governmental means.

The purpose of the EU travel ban was not only to construct an external border to provide 'security' for the Union and its peoples; it was also intended to create the necessary conditions for the 'lifting of internal border control measures':[74] closure and hardening of the outside was to be accompanied by opening and softening of the inside. As with the external EU travel ban, this was largely successful, with Member States for the most part removing their border controls in the summer of 2020.[75] This was accompanied by a relaxation of travel restrictions, especially travel bans, with most Member States replacing them with measures such as quarantine. As noted above, these still operated along national lines and as such do represent an assertion of national territoriality. But there was a certain degree of coordination at a European level, with the Council issuing recommendations in October 2020 on a common approach towards the lifting (and possible reintroduction) of restrictions based on common criteria.[76] This is entirely fitting with the Union's function in facilitating flows in the European economic and social space and coordinating Member State action to that effect.[77] In that sense it represents something of a success – albeit perhaps limited – for the affirmation of European space, again noting that this is the opening of national territory and the European coordination of the exercise of national power over borders and territory. And yet this space of common free movement is linked to the project of European integration and the 'European way of life'. The Council Recommendations open with a reference to Union citizenship[78] and the Commission communication which marks one of the opening documents in European-wide coordination

---

[71] See Charles S Maier (n 7).
[72] Echoing a point made by Daniel Thym and Jonas Bornemann regarding the importance of inter-governmental action in saving the Schengen system and the corollary of the quasi-failure of supranational institutions to control Member State actions in re-introducing border controls.
[73] Daniel Thym and Jonas Bornemann (n 38) 1151 ff.
[74] Communication from the Commission on COVID-19: Temporary Restrictions on Non-Essential Travel to the EU (n 65) 2.
[75] There have been some re-introductions at the time of writing, in early 2021, in response to surging case numbers and new, more transmissible variants of the virus.
[76] Council Recommendation 2020/1475/EU of 13 October 2020 on a coordinated approach to the restriction of free movment in response to the COVID-19 pandemic [2020] OJ L337/3.
[77] See section I.
[78] Council Recommendation 2020/1475/EU of 13 October 2020 on a coordinated approach to the restriction of free movment in response to the COVID-19 pandemic, recital (1).

refers to how various travel restrictions 'harm our European way of life where citizens can travel freely across borders, whether as workers, students, family members, or tourists. We must work to restore this key achievement of European integration.'[79] There is an effort here to reference the European Union as a space across which citizens can live their lives and pursue different activities; doing so somehow represents the 'European way of life'.

It is worth pausing to consider the combined effect of the external EU travel ban and the partially successful reopening of internal travel restrictions. Together these create a genuinely distinctive European space, clearly differentiated from the outside world; a space in which the European way of life – of which internal travel is such an important part – can exist. The emergence of a distinct European territory is visible, and yet it is clearly and significantly intertwined and achieved through the ongoing exercise of (hard) Member State territoriality and the coordination of Member State action.

3.4 Europeanisation of National Belonging

The final manner in which the COVID-19 crisis has revealed how territoriality and citizenship function in the European Union is the extension of the phenomenon of Europeanisation of national categories of belonging, recognised for some time as one of the core effects of Union citizenship. As noted above, Union citizenship as a status of social integration[80] is intended to render the boundaries between national political communities more porous;[81] Union citizens become quasi-nationals of another Member State, particularly over time.[82] Categories of national belonging become Europeanised. What is remarkable – and remarkable because so little commented upon – is how seamlessly Union citizens and their family members were included within national categories in the operation of entry bans, in particular. As noted above, it is at the border that differences between nationals and non-nationals become apparent; access to territory is coded by membership. And yet all Member States in this great sorting exercise included Union citizens and their family members. Even Hungary, which announced a ban on all non-nationals, did in fact in the final regulations extend this to include non-national Union citizen residents. And a number of states introduced entry bans only for third country nationals.[83] Indeed, the common repatriation of Union citizens from outside the Union was another manifestation of this inclusive and common approach.[84] The Commission rightly stressed the importance of non-discrimination in the operation of any travel restrictions, and indeed this principle does appear to have been largely respected. Indeed, as Mantu has demonstrated, in some elements of the response to the virus European citizens continued to be treated as privileged migrants, albeit as economic actors within the single market.[85] It is important to note that this is not somehow the creation of a European community but is

---

[79] Communication from the Commission Towards a phased and coordinated approach for restoring freedom of movement and lifting internal border controls – COVID-19 [2020] OJ C169/03, C-169/30.
[80] Loïc Azoulai (n 30).
[81] Dora Kostakopoulou (n 29).
[82] On the importance of time in Union citizenship law see Alexander Somek, 'Solidarity Decomposed: Being and Time in European Citizenship' (2007) 32 EL Rev 787.
[83] Sergio Carrera and Ngo Chun Luk (n 45) 9.
[84] Daniel Thym and Jonas Bornemann (n38) 1156.
[85] Sandra Mantu, 'EU Citizenship, Free Movement and COVID-19 in Romania' [2020] Frontiers in Human Dynamics Article 594987.

rather the opening of national communities and the national territory, even in times of closure, to certain Union citizens. It is a Europeanisation of the national community and of national categories of belonging.

4. CONCLUSION

If travelling as a tourist, worker or service provider within the common space of movement created by rights of free movement associated with Union citizenship and the elimination of borders as a consequence of Schengen reflects the 'European way of life', what does the COVID-19 crisis, the response to which has entailed a dramatic curtailment of non-essential travel and the reintroduction of borders, tell us about the relationship between territory and citizenship in the Union and its relationship with Member State territoriality? A complex picture emerges.

On the one hand there is a clear assertion of 'hard' Member State territoriality, as described by Pullano, with concomitant importance for the construction of citizenship and community within the Union. Member States have exercised their sovereign powers over borders and mobility in attempts to ensure the security and health of their populations. In doing so they have operated along national frames of reference both for the reintroduction of borders and for the imposition of travel restrictions. The result is a physical but also symbolic closure of national territoriality; the construction of the national territory as a safe space and the fragmentation of the Union space of free movement – the space of rights and mutually open plurality of communities associated with Union citizenship. Access to other Member States' territory, a key element of Union citizenship and indeed the innovation of Union citizenship (in the sense of opening up the territories and societies of other Member States to Union citizens), is suspended in a wholesale manner in the face of imperative reasons of Member State security and policy.

At the same time, particularly after the initial stage of the crisis, a distinction emerged quite clearly between intra- and extra-EU movement and closures. Member States, while still operating quite severe travel restrictions, did display a *relative* openness vis-à-vis other EU (and 'EU+') states) compared with the rest of the world. Indeed, the distinction is quite marked, with a quasi-total travel ban being imposed vis-à-vis the outside world but travel with restrictions allowed between EU+ states.[86] Moreover, the effect of Europeanising national categories of belonging, so long a feature of Union citizenship, operated smoothly during the crisis, extended to the coordination of the repatriation of Union citizens abroad. There is a clear privileging of other EU states, resulting in a distinct European space within which the 'European way of life' can unfold, albeit differentiated to a much greater extent than under normal circumstances.

---

[86] This is a generalisation. The application of travel bans towards the rest of the world and indeed towards EU states did vary in some details, particularly in relation to the third states from which travellers were permitted. Some states, such as Denmark, applied the same criteria to EU and non-EU states when deciding whether to permit or forbid travel. For an overview of the different internal travel restrictions and the implementation of the EU travel ban across Member States see Sergio Carrera and Ngo Chun Luk (n 44) 3–4. For travel restrictions imposed by Denmark see p.25.

This softening on the inside is powerfully complemented by a hardening of the outside, increasing the distinction between inside and outside and constructing the European space of movement as a more clearly bounded and controlled European territory, providing security for its population. And yet, as with the (incomplete) coordination of internal restrictions and the re-elimination of border controls, this is achieved largely through Member State action, co-ordinated at a Union level. A European space of movement incrementally develops some territory-like features, associated with Union citizenship and a 'European way of life', and yet this is built through the exercise of Member State powers and is layered upon a reassertion of Member State territoriality.

9. The rules on the free movement of workers in the European Union

Adela Boitos and Manuel Kellerbauer[1]

1. INTRODUCTION

The free movement of workers is one of the four fundamental freedoms and, hence, one of the pillars on which the EU internal market reposes. It is true that its economic importance may be questioned in the light of the relatively low number of Union citizens taking advantage of the opportunity to seek employment in other Member States: among the EU citizens of working age, solely 3.3 per cent resided in an EU country other than that of their citizenship in 2019.[2] Nevertheless, free movement of workers may have greater benefits for the process of creating an *ever closer union among the peoples of Europe*[3] than any other fundamental freedom. Employment is a crucial instrument in terms of facilitating integration of Union citizens into another country's society, and literature suggests that mobile workers directly contribute to shaping individuals' attitudes towards other Member States' cultures and help dismantle prejudice.[4] At the same time, the influx of a great number of workers from other Member States has not always been greeted with enthusiasm, especially where it has occurred in a short time-frame and concerned workers from new Member States in which the levels of salary appeared more competitive.

In 1956 the Spaak report,[5] which set out a plan for establishing the common market, highlighted that the free movement of workers may bring about such challenges. It remarked not only on the possibly insufficient incentives for workers to seek employment in other Member States but also on the need to combat the prejudices that workers from other Member States might face when they moved abroad. Exactly 60 years later, in the run-up to the UK referendum on EU membership, free movement of persons became one of the key issues which crystallised anti-EU sentiment. It speaks of the importance of this fundamental freedom that the Union was willing to risk the withdrawal of one of its largest Member States rather than make greater concessions that might have undermined its protection.[6]

---

[1] The authors work in the Legal Service of the European Commission. They express their personal views, which are not to be construed as being those of the European Commission.
[2] Eurostat, 'EU citizens living in another Member State – statistical overview' (Statistics explained, June 2020) https://ec.europa.eu/eurostat/statistics-explained/index.php/EU_citizens_living_in_another_Member_State_-_statistical_overview accessed 13 January 2021.
[3] As directed by Article 1 TEU.
[4] See e.g. Cornelius Cappelen and Yvette Peters, 'The impact of intra-EU migration on welfare chauvinism' (2018) Journal of Public Policy, 38(3), 389–417.
[5] Comité intergouvernemental, *Rapport des chefs de délégation aux ministres des Affaires étrangères* (Bruxelles, 21 avril 1956).
[6] Prior to the referendum, the British Prime Minister negotiated with the other EU Member States and the EU institutions to establish a 'new settlement' between the UK and the Union that would have convinced British citizens that staying in the Union was the better option. While the negotiations resulted

Article 45(1) TFEU provides that free movement of workers shall be 'secured' throughout the EU. Individuals seeking to benefit from this protection must demonstrate that their case fulfils the following requirements.

First, it needs to be established whether a given situation falls within the scope of the free movement of workers. To this effect, the following questions need to be answered:

- Is the person concerned a Union citizen or a third country national eligible in view of their family ties with a Union citizen or on the basis of an international agreement concluded between the Union and a third country?
- Is the person concerned a 'worker' as defined in the Court of Justice of the EU's (hereafter 'the Court') case law?
- Is there an element relating to at least one Member State other than the one whose nationality the person concerned holds?
- Is Article 45 TFEU inapplicable because employment in the public service is concerned?

Second, a restriction of the free movement of workers needs to be established. Such a restriction can result either from direct or indirect discrimination against the worker in question or from a so-called obstacle that is liable to render the exercise of this freedom less attractive.

Third, not all restrictions of the free movement of workers are unlawful. Rather, it must be examined whether restrictive measures are justified in the individual case because they serve legitimate reasons in the public interest, are appropriate and do not go beyond what is necessary to attain the legitimate aim they pursue.

The following explanations are structured in accordance with the above three points.[7]

2. THE SCOPE OF THE FREE MOVEMENT OF WORKERS

2.1 Union Citizenship as a General Requirement

The personal scope of Article 45 TFEU is at the outset limited to 'workers of the Member States'.[8] While workers from third countries thus generally cannot invoke this fundamental freedom, there are two notable exceptions.

First, family members of Union citizens may come within the ambit of the free movement of workers under certain circumstances. Although not explicitly mentioned in Article 45 TFEU, this is intuitive since Union citizens might refrain from taking up employment in another Member State if doing so came at the price of tearing up their family. Nowadays, the rights

---

in EU commitments to amend EU secondary legislation in the fields of free movement and access to social benefits for EU workers, the outcome was largely considered as unlikely to significantly curb free movement of persons into the UK. An in-depth analysis of the New Settlement by an European Parliament think tank is accessible at www.europarl.europa.eu/thinktank/en/document.html?reference=EPRS_IDA(2016)577983 accessed 1 March 2021.

[7] Due to the brevity of the present contribution, the rules governing the adoption of 'measures required to bring about freedom of movement for workers' pursuant to Article 46 TFEU and 'measures in the field of social security' necessary to ensure the free movement of workers pursuant to Article 48 TFEU, as well as the provisions of Article 47 TFEU on encouraging the exchange of young workers, will not be addressed.

[8] Article 45(2) TFEU.

of family members of Union citizens that work in other Member States are mainly laid down in EU secondary legislation, and in particular Directive 2004/38[9] and Article 10 Regulation 492/2011.[10]

Second, international agreements concluded between the Union and third countries may extend the free movement of workers to third country nationals or grant them rights comparable to Union citizens. One may think first and foremost of the EEA Agreement that brings together the EU Member States and three of the EFTA States, namely Iceland, Liechtenstein and Norway.[11] Similarly, the association agreement concluded between the EU and Turkey provides for free movement of workers, although the rights granted do not fully equal those afforded under Article 45 TFEU.[12] The principle of free movement of workers is also enshrined in a bilateral Treaty concluded with Switzerland.[13] By contrast, it was the UK's declared aim to end free movement of persons with the Union when it withdrew from the EU, and the EU–UK Trade and Cooperation Agreement[14] does not contain any guarantees to UK or EU citizens in this regard.[15]

2.2 The Autonomous EU Concept of Worker

2.2.1 The *Lawrie-Blum* criteria and their exhaustiveness

The Treaty itself does not provide a definition of the term 'worker'. The Court held early on that the Treaty attributes an autonomous EU meaning to that concept,[16] thus precluding Member States from establishing their own criteria for qualifying certain persons as workers and excluding others.

---

[9] European Parliament and Council Directive 2004/38/EC of 29 April 2004 on the right of citizens of the Union and their family members to move and reside freely within the territory of the Member States amending Regulation (EEC) No 1612/68 and repealing Directives 64/221/EEC, 68/360/EEC, 72/194/EEC, 73/148/EEC, 75/34/EEC, 75/35/EEC, 90/364/EEC, 90/365/EEC and 93/96/EEC [2004] OJ L158/77.

[10] European Parliament and Council Regulation (EU) 492/2011 of 5 April 2011 on freedom of movement for workers within the Union [2011] OJ L141/1.

[11] See Articles 28–30 of the Agreement on the European Economic Area [1994] OJ L1/3 and Chapter 18 of this volume, Christian N.K. Franklin and Halvard H. Fredriksen, Differentiated Citizenship in the European Economic Area.

[12] The Court has inferred from the relevant provisions of the EU–Turkey Association Agreement that the principles laid down in the context of Article 45 TFEU must be extended, so far as is possible, to Turkish nationals who enjoy the rights conferred by Association Council Decision 1/80 of 19 September 1980 on the development of the association. See, to that effect, Case C-136/03 *Dörr* EU:C:2005:340, para 62 and the case-law cited. See also Chapter 19 of this volume, Narin Idriz and Christa Tobler, 'Citizenship of the Association': The Examples of Turkey and Switzerland.

[13] See [2002] OJ L114/6. Pursuant to Article 1(d), the Agreement aims 'to accord the same living, employment and working conditions' to Union citizens and Swiss nationals. See also Chapter 19 of this volume, Narin Idriz and Christa Tobler, 'Citizenship of the Association': The Examples of Turkey and Switzerland.

[14] OJ L 149, 30.04.2021, p. 10-2539.

[15] An overview of the EU-UK Trade and Information Agreement is given at https://ec.europa.eu/info/sites/info/files/eu-uk_trade_and_cooperation_agreement-a_new_relationship_with_big_changes-brochure.pdf accessed 1 March 2021.

[16] Case C-75/63 *Unger v Bedrijfsvereniging voor Detailhandel en Ambachten* EU:C:1964:19.

In its landmark judgment *Lawrie-Blum*,[17] the Court established an exhaustive list of three objective criteria which distinguish an employment relationship from other types of economic activities:

- A person performs services for a certain period of time;
- for and under the direction of another person;
- in return for which he or she receives remuneration.

The concept of worker in EU law, and, hence, the above three criteria, are to be construed broadly.[18] Furthermore, they are exhaustive. Union law does not impose conditions related to the contractual form of the employment relationship, which may be that of a traineeship,[19] or have a sui generis status in national law.[20] Nor is it necessary for the worker to be employed by an undertaking, as opposed to, for example, a sporting association[21] or a religious community.[22] All that is required is 'the existence of, or the intention to create, an employment relationship'.[23]

Since the Union law definition of the term 'worker' is confined to the three *Lawrie-Blum* criteria, it follows from the primacy of Union law and the direct effect of Article 45 TFEU[24] that Member States may not add additional requirements where they apply Article 45 TFEU or EU secondary law based on the same concept.

Even where Union law refers to the concept of 'worker' as defined in national law, Member States are precluded from ignoring the *Lawrie-Blum* criteria, as in doing so they may undermine the *effet utile* of EU rules.[25]

2.2.2 Performing services for a certain period of time

The first *Lawrie-Blum* criterion requires that the employment relationship must exist 'for a certain period of time'.[26] However, the fact that employment is of short duration cannot, in itself, exclude that employment from the scope of Article 45 TFEU.[27] Rather, the short duration of the contract and the low salary for providing services may be without relevance where other factors show the genuine and effective character of the work, such as the right to paid leave, to the continued payment of wages in the event of sickness, to a contract of employment which is subject to the relevant collective agreement or to the payment of contributions.[28]

---

[17] *Lawrie-Blum*.
[18] Case C-53/81 *Levin v Staatssecretaris van Justitie* EU:C:1982:105; Case C-171/91 *Tsiotras v Landeshauptstadt Stuttgart* EU:C:1993:215.
[19] *Lawrie-Blum*; Case C-27/91 *URSSAF v Hostellerie Le Manoir* EU:C:1991:441, para 8.
[20] Case C-344/87 *Bettray v Staatssecretaris van Justitie* EU:C:1989:226, paras 14–15.
[21] Case C-415/93 *Union royale belge des sociétés de football association and Others v Bosman and Others* EU:C:1995:463, para 74.
[22] Case C-196/87 *Steymann v Staatssecretaris van Justitie* EU:C:1988:475, paras 11- 12.
[23] *Bosman*, para 74.
[24] On which, see section 3.2.
[25] See, for instance regarding European Parliament and Council Directive 2008/104/EC Case C-216/15 *Betriebsrat der Ruhrlandklinik* EU:C:2016:883, paras 27–42.
[26] *Lawrie-Blum*, para 17.
[27] Case C-413/01 *Ninni-Orasche* EU:C:2003:600, para 32.
[28] Case C-432/14 *O* EU:C:2015:643, paras 24–25.

Thus, having worked for as little as two and a half months[29] or even four days[30] may confer the status of worker.

Similarly, the fact that a person only works part-time,[31] ten hours a week[32] or with low productivity[33] does not exclude an employment relationship if elements such as the overall length of the contractual relationship or the social advantages granted demonstrate a real and genuine professional activity.[34]

2.2.3   For and under the direction of another person

As opposed to a self-employed person, a worker provides services 'for and under the direction of another person'. The term 'worker' within the meaning of Article 45 TFEU thus does not encompass self-employed persons, whose relationship with the person receiving the services is not one of subordination.[35] It follows that the freedom of movement of workers on the one hand and the freedom to provide services as well as the freedom of establishment on the other are in principle mutually exclusive.[36]

Features typical of self-employment, such as the freedom to choose one's own schedule, the place and the content of one's work,[37] to recruit one's own assistants[38] or to participate in the employer's commercial risks[39] exclude a person from an employment relationship. Most obviously, the director of a company is not a 'worker' where he or she is the sole[40] or majority shareholder.[41]

Finally, the classification of a person as self-employed under national legislation does not exclude their qualification as a 'worker' for the purposes of EU law.[42]

---

[29] *Ninni-Orasche*, para 32.
[30] *O*, paras 24-25.
[31] *Levin*, para 17; Case C-139/85 *Kempf v Staatssecretaris van Justitie* EU:C:1986:223.
[32] Case C-171/88 *Rinner-Kühn v FWW Spezial-Gebäudereinigung* EU:C:1989:328.
[33] *Bettray*, para 15.
[34] Case C-14/09 *Genc* EU:C:2010:57, paras 25–28.
[35] Case C-107/94 *Asscher v Staatssecretaris van Financiën* EU:C:1996:251, para 26; Case C-337/97 *Meeusen v Hoofddirectie van de Informatie Beheer Groep* EU:C:1999:284, para 15.
[36] See Case C-35/19 *Belgian State (Indemnité pour personnes handicapées)* EU:C:2019:894, para 20: 'Where a national measure affects both the free movement of workers and the freedom to provide services the Court will, in principle, examine it in relation to only one of those two fundamental freedoms where it is shown that, in the circumstances of the case, one of them is entirely secondary in relation to the other and may be considered together with it (see, to that effect, judgment of 14 October 2004, Omega, C 36/02, EU:C:2004:614, paragraph 26 and the case-law cited)'; see also Case C-55/94 *Gebhard v Consiglio dell'Ordine degli Avvocati e Procuratori di Milano* EU:C:1995:411, para 20. By contrast, regarding the recognition of a diploma for a profession that can be exercised both independently and as a worker, the Court has recently left open whether Article 45 or 49 applies; see Case C-218/19 *Onofrei* EU:C:2020:1034, para 23.
[37] Case C-256/01 *Allonby* EU:C:2004:18, para 72; Case C-270/13 *Haralambidis* EU:C:2014:2185, para 33.
[38] *Haralambidis*, para 33.
[39] Case C-3/87 *The Queen v Ministry of Agriculture, Fisheries and Food, ex parte Agegate* EU:C:1989:650, para 36.
[40] *Asscher*, para 26.
[41] Case C-138/13 *Dogan* EU:C:2014:2066, para 31.
[42] *Allonby*, para 79.

2.2.4 Against remuneration

The requirement that workers provide services against remuneration would seem to distinguish workers from economically inactive persons and volunteers, who become active in pursuit of non-materialistic aims.

The concept of remuneration needs to be construed broadly. The Court has repeatedly held that the source of the funds received (including subsidies from public funds) does not have any impact on the qualification of remuneration.[43] Payment in kind also constitutes remuneration: activities performed by members of a religious community constitute economic activities insofar as the services which the community provides to its members may be regarded as the indirect 'quid pro quo' for genuine and effective work.[44] Nor is it necessary for the employer to carry out its activities for profit.[45]

When assessing whether payment received in exchange for a service constitutes remuneration, the Court is more interested in the predictability and regularity of the payment,[46] which is indicative of an employment relationship, than in the particular conditions relating to its minimum amount. Notably, a maintenance allowance for a trainee position qualifies as remuneration even if it constitutes only assistance allowing them to meet their minimum needs.[47] Even the fact that a worker's earnings do not cover all their needs, and must be complemented by other means of subsistence such as property[48] or State financial assistance,[49] cannot exclude his or her situation from falling within the scope of Article 45 TFEU.[50]

Nevertheless, the activities pursued must be effective and genuine. This requirement has in the past been satisfied by activities as diverse as traineeships,[51] apprenticeships,[52] professional or semi-professional football[53] or prostitution.[54] However, it excludes activities on such a small scale as to be regarded as purely marginal and ancillary, as well as work pursued as a means of rehabilitation or reintegration, whose purpose is to enable the person concerned to take up ordinary employment or to lead a as normal as possible a life sooner or later.[55]

The Court has explicitly rejected in recent case law the establishment of a threshold below which an activity would always have to be regarded as being marginal and ancillary.[56] As for duration, it has recalled that, independently of the limited amount of remuneration for the activity in question, the possibility cannot be ruled out that, following an overall assessment of the employment relationship in question, that activity may be considered by the national

---

[43] *Bettray*, para 15.
[44] *Steymann*, para 12.
[45] Case C-301/14 *Pfotenhilfe-Ungarn* EU:C:2015:793, para 30.
[46] *Haralambidis*, para 36.
[47] Case C-109/04 *Kranemann* EU:C:2005:187, para 16.
[48] *Levin*, para 17.
[49] *Kempf*, para 14.
[50] Case C-213/05 *Geven* EU:C:2007:438, para 27; Case C-444/93 *Megner and Scheffel v Innungskrankenkasse Vorderpfalz* EU:C:1995:442, para 18.
[51] *Kranemann*, para 18; Case C-229/14 *Balkaya* EU:C:2015:455, para 52.
[52] Case C-188/00 *Kurz* EU:C:2002:694, paras 33–36; Case C-3/90 *Bernini v Minister van Onderwijs en Wetenschappen* EU:C:1992:89, paras 15–17.
[53] Case C-13/76 *Donà v Mantero* EU:C:1976:115, para 12; *Bosman*, para 73.
[54] Case C-268/99 *Aldona Malgorzata Jany and Others v Staatssecretaris van Justitie* EU:C:2001:616, para 33.
[55] *Bettray*, para 17.
[56] *Genc*, paras 29–30.

authorities to be real and genuine, thereby allowing its holder to be granted the status of 'worker' within the meaning of Article 45 TFEU.[57]

2.2.5 The special case of jobseekers and those who are or no longer employed

Strictly speaking, jobseekers do not meet the *Lawrie-Blum* conditions under which persons qualify as a worker. In particular, they do not yet perform services for remuneration. Nevertheless, Article 45 itself suggests that jobseekers may infer certain rights from the free movement of workers, given that its paragraph 3 specifically mentions the possibility to move freely within the territory of Member States for accepting offers of employment. Nowadays, case law on the free movement of workers accords jobseekers a right of residence in other Member States for a reasonable amount of time (generally six months, and potentially longer where the job search continues to have chances of success)[58] as well as a limited right to equal treatment concerning benefits granted for the job search during the same period.[59] Article 45 TFEU also precludes the State of origin from obstructing the freedom of one of its nationals to accept and pursue employment in another Member State.[60]

Those who no longer work equally do not fulfil the *Lawrie-Blum* criteria. However, instantly depriving them of the rights that Article 45 TFEU is intended to accord would strongly discourage Union citizens from taking up work in another Member State in the first place and thus defeat the purpose of this Treaty provision. Accordingly, pursuant to Article 45(3)(d) TFEU, EU legislation grants former workers a right of residence and right to equal treatment, which, depending on the duration of work, is either transitory or definitive.[61]

2.2.6 The extension of the personal scope of Article 45 TFEU to employers

Nothing in the wording of Article 45 TFEU prevents other categories, and in particular employers, from relying on it,[62] even if they are not explicitly mentioned in the text of that article. The Court held that workers' rights could be deprived of all meaning if a Member State

---

[57] See section 2.2.2.

[58] Article 14(4)(b) of European Parliament and Council Directive 2004/38 specifically determines the conditions governing the retention of the right of residence of Union citizens who leave their Member State of origin with the intention of seeking employment in the host Member State. The Court held that that provision was adopted by the EU legislature with a view to codifying the guidance arising from the judgment of 26 February 1991, *Antonissen* (Case C-292/89 *The Queen v Immigration Appeal Tribunal, ex parte Antonissen* EU:C:1991:80) on the right of residence of jobseekers based on Article 45 TFEU (see Case C-710/19 *G.M.A. v État belge* EU:C:2020:1037, para 33). In this context, the Court held that it is only after a reasonable period of time has elapsed that a jobseeker may be required to provide evidence not only that he or she is continuing to seek employment but also that he or she has a genuine chance of being engaged.

[59] See Joined Cases C-22/08 and 23/08 *Vatsouras and Koupatantze* EU:C:2009:344, para 32. By contrast, jobseekers generally enjoy no right to social assistance; see Case C-67/14 *Alimanovic* EU:C:2015:597.

[60] Case C-544/11 *Petersen* EU:C:2013:124, para 36 and the case-law cited.

[61] For instance, in *Tarola* the Court inferred from Article 7(1) and (3)(c) of European Parliament and Council Directive 2004/38, on account of an activity pursued for a period as brief as two weeks, that a Union citizen retains his status of worker for a period of no less than six months provided that he has registered as a jobseeker with the relevant employment office; see Case C-483/17 *Tarola* EU:C:2019:309, para 54.

[62] Case C-350/96 *Clean Car Autoservice v Landeshauptmann von Wien* EU:C:1998:205, para 19; Case C-379/11 *Caves Krier Frères* EU:C:2012:798, para 28.

could circumvent the prohibitions which they contain by imposing on employers restrictions to freedom of movement which they know to be prohibited if imposed directly on workers.[63] The right of employers to engage workers in accordance with the rules governing the freedom of movement of workers therefore exists as a necessary corollary of the right to free movement of workers.[64]

2.3 The Public Service Exception

According to Article 45(4) TFEU, the provisions of Article 45 'shall not apply to employment in the public service'. This 'public service exception' shows deference to the legitimate interest Member States may have in reserving to their own nationals a range of posts which 'presume on the part of those occupying them the existence of a special relationship of allegiance to the State and reciprocity of rights and duties which form the foundation of the bond of nationality'.[65] As an exception to the rule of unfettered free movement, one expects the scope of Article 45(4) TFEU to be construed narrowly, and indeed the Court has limited its scope to what is strictly necessary for safeguarding the interests that the provision allows the Member States to protect.[66] The following limitations are key in this respect.

First, 'public service' within the meaning of Article 45(4) TFEU only covers posts which involve direct or indirect participation in the exercise of powers conferred by public law and duties designed to safeguard the general interests of the State or of other public authorities.[67] Accordingly, people working for the national railway company;[68] teachers, even if they decide which pupils will make it to the next class;[69] and even sworn private security guards recruited by security firms to arrest offenders do not fall under the derogation of Article 45(4) TFEU.[70]

Second, recourse to Article 45(4) TFEU cannot be justified on the sole ground that powers of a public authority are attributed under national law. It is also necessary that those powers be in fact exercised on a regular basis by the worker in question and do not constitute a minor part of his duties.[71]

Third, even where a post generally falls within the category of public service within the meaning of Article 45(4) TFEU, once admitted into the public service of a Member State mobile workers are entitled to the full application of the provisions contained in Article 45(1) to (3) TFEU.[72] For instance, a Member State may reserve certain posts in its armed forces to its own nationals. However, once it admits Union citizens from other Member States to such

---

[63] *Clean Car*, para 21; Case C-474/12 *Schiebel Aircraft* EU:C:2014:2139, para 26.
[64] *Clean Car*, para 20; *Caves Krier Frères*, para 28.
[65] See Case C-20/16 *Bechtel* EU:C:2017:488, para 35; Case 152/73 *Sotgiu v Deutsche Bundespost* EU:C:1974:13, para 4; Case C-149/79 *Commission v Belgium* EU:C:1980:297, para 10.
[66] See Case C-405/01 *Colegio de Oficiales de la Marina Mercante Española* EU:C:2003:515, para 41.
[67] See *Haralambidis*, para 44 and the case law cited.
[68] Case 149/79 *Commission v Belgium* EU:C:1982:195, para 10. The question was left open for certain posts, though, namely head technical office supervisor, principal supervisor, works supervisor, stock controller and night watchman.
[69] *Lawrie-Blum*, paras 24–28.
[70] See Case C-283/99 *Commission v Italy* EU:C:2001:307, para 21; the Court pointed out that such guards have no more power to arrest offenders than any other ordinary member of the public.
[71] *Haralambidis*, para 58.
[72] Case C-392/05 *Alevizos* EU:C:2007:251, para 70 and the case-law cited.

posts, there is no justification under Article 45(4) TFEU to discriminate against them in terms of salaries or taxes.

Fourth, the public service exception concerns only the access of nationals of other Member States to certain posts in a host Member State's public service.[73] Member States can never invoke Article 45(4) to justify restriction of the free movement of workers regarding their own nationals,[74] for instance due to the fact that they acquired relevant qualifications in another Member State.

2.4 The Requirement of a Cross-Border Element

As with all fundamental freedoms guaranteed under Union law, the free movement of workers cannot be applied to situations that are confined in all respects within a single Member State.[75] In practical terms, this means individuals must have their residence,[76] or, in the case of frontier workers,[77] their employment, in a Member State other than the State of which they are nationals, or, in the case of jobseekers, must move to another State in order to seek such employment.[78] This was not the case, for example, for Spanish nationals residing in Spain who set up business in Spain as estate agents without the required professional qualifications and authorizations.[79] By contrast, a national of a Member State who married an Indian national, resided with him in another Member State as a worker and then returned to her home Member State came within the scope of the provisions of the TFEU on freedom of movement for workers.[80] Indeed, the Court found that EU citizens might be deterred from exercising their right to free movement if the conditions they would meet upon return to their home Member State 'were not at least equivalent to those which [they] would enjoy under the Treaty or secondary law in the territory of another Member State'.[81]

Requiring a cross-border element has been criticised as falling short of ensuring effective free movement within the entirety of the Union.[82] However, the above outlined case law exists for good reason. The Union rules on the fundamental freedom are intended to abolish internal frontiers to ensure the free movement of goods, persons, services and capital between Member States.[83] Addressing matters that are purely internal to one and the same Member State therefore exceeds their objectives.

---

[73] See Case C-443/93 *Vougioukas v Idryma Koinonikon Asfalisseon* EU:C:1995:394, para 19; Case C-248/96 *Grahame and Hollanders v Bestuur van de Nieuwe Algemene Bedrijfsvereniging* EU:C:1997: 543, para 32; Case C-15/96 *Schöning-Kougebetopoulou v Freie und Hansestadt Hamburg* EU:C:1998:3, para 13; and Case C-195/98 *Österreichischer Gewerkschaftsbund* EU:C:2000:655, para 36.
[74] See Case C-298/14 *Brouillard* EU:C:2015:652, para 33.
[75] See to that effect Case 20/87 *Ministère public v Gauchard* EU:C:1987:532, paras 12 and 13, and Case C-18/95 *Terhoeve* EU:C:1999:22, para 26, and the case-law there cited. See also Case C-97/98 *Jägerskiöld* EU:C:1999:515, para 42, and Case C-60/00 *Carpenter* EU:C:2002:434, para 28.
[76] See e.g. *Lawrie-Blum*.
[77] See e.g. Case C-830/18 *Landkreis Südliche Weinstraße* EU:C:2020:275.
[78] Case C-370/90 *The Queen v Immigration Appeal Tribunal and Surinder Singh I*:EU:C:1992:296.
[79] Case C-330/90 *López Brea and Hidalgo Palacios* EU:C:1992:39.
[80] *Singh*.
[81] *Singh*, para 19.
[82] See, for instance, AG Sharpston, opinion in Case C-212/06 *French Community and Walloon Government v Flemish Government* EU:C:2007:398, Opinion of AG Sharpston, para 116.
[83] See Article 26(2) TFEU.

The cross-border requirement is applied with considerable 'souplesse', though. Any link regarding another Member State, such as the professional experience acquired abroad, may suffice. For example, the criterion is met for a dentist who is a Belgian national, established in Belgium, and who practises in Belgium, provided that a number of his patients come from other Member States.[84]

By contrast, the mere fact that a subsidiary which employs a worker is controlled by a parent company established in a Member State other than that in which that subsidiary is established is not sufficient in order to establish a link in the situations contemplated by Article 45 TFEU.[85] Similarly, a situation in which the prospect of a cross-border element is merely speculative, such as the opportunity to eventually apply for a post in a different Member State,[86] does not fall under Union law.

3. RESTRICTIONS OF THE FREE MOVEMENT OF WORKERS

Similar to other fundamental freedoms, restrictions of the free movement of workers may come in two different forms: discriminations and obstacles. However, Article 45 TFEU presents a particularity. It may not be restricted only by Member States, those on whom Member States confer public powers or those in a position collectively to regulate the freedom in question, such as trade unions and employers' organisations acting through collective agreements.[87] Rather, any employer in the Union is required to respect the free movement of workers. In the following, the explanations as to the two forms of restrictions are thus preceded by a brief digression on the so-called direct vertical and horizontal effect of Article 45 TFEU.

3.1 Direct Vertical and Horizontal Effect

Restrictions of the free movement of workers may result from measures adopted by a Member State or by private employers.

As regards measures adopted by a Member State, those entitled may find it easier to invoke Article 45 TFEU due to its 'vertical direct effect'. The Court recognised early on that, while Union law is generally rendered binding on private persons through implementation measures in the national legal order, in light of the precise obligations which it imposes, Article 45 TFEU should be applied directly in Member States even in the absence of such measures.[88]

---

[84] Case C-339/15 *Vanderborght* EU:C:2017:335, paras 54–56.
[85] Case C-566/15 *Erzberger* EU:C:2017:562, para 29.
[86] Case C-180/83 *Moser v Land Baden-Württemberg* EU:C:1984:233.
[87] Other fundamental freedoms also require private actors to refrain from restrictions where they establish rules which, albeit not public in nature, are designed to regulate collectively the freedom in question. Otherwise, the abolition as between Member States of such restrictions would be compromised if the abolition of State barriers could be neutralised by obstacles resulting from the exercise of their legal autonomy by associations or organisations not governed by public law. See, for instance, Case C-36/74 *Walrave and Koch* EU:C:1974:140, para 17; *Donà*, para 17; *Bosman*, para 82; Joined Cases C-51/96 and 191/97 *Deliège* EU:C:2000:199, para 47; Case C-281/98 *Angonese* EU:C:2000:296, para 31; Case C-309/99 *Wouters and Others* EU:C:2002:98, para 120; and Case C-438/05 *International Transport Workers' Federation and Finnish Seamen's Union, 'Viking Line'* EU:C:2007:772, para 33.
[88] Case C-41/74 *Van Duyn* EU:C:1974:133, paras 6–7.

As a consequence, Article 45 TFEU takes precedence over any national measure which might conflict with it[89] and gives rise to rights for its beneficiaries which national courts must protect.[90] Another important consequence of the direct effect of this Treaty provision is that legal acts of the EU institutions cannot fall short of the rights conferred to workers in Article 45 TFEU. Due to the precedence that primary EU law takes over acts adopted by the EU institutions, the guarantees enshrined in Article 45 TFEU would prevail in such a case.

Furthermore, Article 45 TFEU can be invoked against measures adopted by non-State actors ('horizontal direct effect'). In this regard, the Court noted early on that the principle of non-discrimination set out in the Treaty provision is drafted in general terms and not specifically addressed to the Member States.[91] The Court considered that the freedom of movement of workers would be frustrated if 'the abolition of State barriers could be neutralised by obstacles resulting from the exercise of their legal autonomy by associations or organisations not governed by public law'.[92]

In the preliminary ruling *Angonese*, the Court held for the first time that any private employer was precluded from restricting Article 45 TFEU, in that case by requiring applicants to hold a particular language diploma, issued by a single province of that Member State.[93]

3.2 Discriminatory Measures

3.2.1 The areas covered: employment, remuneration and other work conditions

'Securing' the free movement of workers[94] translates into the abolition of any discrimination based on nationality between workers of the MS 'as regards employment, remuneration and other conditions of work and employment'.[95]

The Court considers that access to employment cannot be limited to conditions obtained 'before an employment relationship comes into being'.[96] For example, the prospect of receiving family credit may encourage an unemployed worker to accept low-paid work, with the result that the benefit is related to considerations governing access to employment.[97]

With regards to remuneration, the Court has held that the principle of equal treatment would be rendered ineffective if it could be undermined by discriminatory national provisions on income tax[98] or social security contributions.[99]

As to 'other conditions of work', the Court has held that the concept cannot be limited to working conditions which are set out in the contract of employment or applied by the employer in respect of a worker's employment.[100] For example, the entitlement to paid annual

---

[89] Case C-118/75 *Watson* EU:C:1976:106.
[90] Case C-179/90, *Merci Convenzionali Porto di Genova v Siderurgica Gabrielli* EU:C:1991:464.
[91] Case C-36/74 *Walrave v Union Cycliste Internationale* EU:C:1974:140, para 17.
[92] *Walrave*, para 18, and *Bosman*, para 83.
[93] *Angonese*, paras 21–35.
[94] Article 45(1) TFEU.
[95] Article 45(2) TFEU.
[96] Case C-116/94 *Meyers v Adjudication Officer* EU:C:1995:247, para 22.
[97] *Meyers*, para 22.
[98] Case C-175/88 *Biehl v Administration des contributions* EU:C:1990:186, para 12; Case C-279/93 *Finanzamt Köln-Altstadt v Schumacker* EU:C:1995:31, para 23; Case C-512/13 *Sopora* EU:C:2015:108, para 22.
[99] *Hostellerie Le Manoir*, para 12.
[100] *Meyers*, para 24.

leave conferred on workers 'unquestionably' forms part of the field of employment and work conditions.[101] A benefit such as family credit, which is necessarily linked to an employment relationship, also constitutes a working condition.[102]

Discrimination may also arise in other fields and where it is not contrary to Article 45(2) TFEU as such, it may break rules of EU secondary legislation. In particular, Article 7(2) of Regulation No 492/2011 provides that a worker who is a national of a Member State is to enjoy, in the territory of another Member State, the same social and tax advantages as national workers. Recalling that this regulation is a particular expression, in the specific area of the grant of social advantages, of the principle of equal treatment enshrined in Article 45 TFEU, the Court has recognised that it must be 'accorded the same interpretation as that provision'.[103]

3.2.2 Direct discrimination

Direct discrimination, that is, unequal treatment on grounds of nationality of a worker, is the most obvious restriction of the free movement of workers. Member States can be expected to resort to directly discriminating measures only where they are convinced that such restrictions are justified on grounds of public policy, public security and public health.[104]

However, it is important to bear in mind that direct discrimination does not only occur where a Member State treats its nationals more favourably than the nationals of another Member State.

Rather, Article 45 TFEU also prohibits discrimination between nationals of Member States other than the host Member State, such as, for instance, France treating Belgian workers better than Spanish workers. Having regard to the wording of Article 45(2) TFEU, which seeks to abolish all discrimination based on nationality 'between workers of the Member States', read in the light of Article 26 TFEU, the Court held that freedom of movement of workers also prohibits discrimination between non-resident workers if such discrimination leads to nationals of certain Member States being unduly favoured in comparison with others.[105]

By contrast, under settled case law, so-called 'reverse discriminations' – whereby a host Member State treats its own nationals less advantageously than the nationals of another Member State – are not covered by Article 45 TFEU or any other fundamental freedoms of the Treaty. Any difference in treatment between Union citizens governed by purely internal circumstances and those falling within the freedom of movement of workers would be justified by the fact that both are not in a comparable situation.[106]

3.2.3 Indirect discrimination

While discrimination on grounds of nationality is usually easily identifiable, limiting Article 45 TFEU to such forms of restriction would fall short of ensuring its *effet utile*. Disparity in treatment between workers from different Member States can arise not only from a condition related to nationality, but also from criteria which 'reveal a connection to a given Member

---

[101] Case C-437/17 *Gemeinsamer Betriebsrat EurothermenResort Bad Schallerbach* EU:C:2019:193, para 17.
[102] *Meyers*, para 24.
[103] Case C-703/17 *Krah* EU:C:2019:850, para 2; *Landkreis Südliche Weinstraße*, para 29; Case C-401/15 *Depesme and Kerrou* EU:C:2016:955, para 35.
[104] See Article 45(3) TFEU and the explanations below, section 4.1.
[105] *Sopora*, para 25.
[106] Case C-127/08 *Metock* EU:C:2008:449, para 78.

State, focusing on characteristics of that State'[107] and which may achieve the same effect as the criterion of nationality. In other words, Article 45 TFEU also forbids covert forms of discrimination where conditions under national law are indistinctly applicable but can more easily be satisfied by national workers than by migrant workers, or where there is a risk that they may operate to the particular detriment of migrant workers.[108]

Criteria which do not directly refer to nationality but which may, in practice, particularly disadvantage non-nationals can relate to residence,[109] place of origin,[110] the place where professional experience was acquired,[111] the place where the linguistic knowledge was acquired,[112] the place where the diploma was awarded,[113] the national education system of the trainee,[114] and so on.

Interestingly, for a measure to be discriminatory it is not required to place at a disadvantage only nationals of other Member States while reserving the more favourable treatment to all nationals of the host Member State. This first followed from the case law in *Angonese*, regarding a language certificate required for employment that had to be obtained in the Italian province of Bolzano. This requirement arguably also disadvantaged other nationals of the host Member State, given that many Italians acquired their language certificate in parts of Italy other than Bolzano. Nevertheless, the Court found a discrimination

> notwithstanding that the requirement in question affects Italian nationals resident in other parts of Italy as well as nationals of other Member States. In order for a measure to be treated as being discriminatory on grounds of nationality under the rules relating to the free movement of workers, it is not necessary for the measure to have the effect of putting at an advantage all the workers of one nationality or of putting at a disadvantage only workers who are nationals of other Member States, but not workers of the nationality in question.[115]

More recently, regarding the comparable concept of discrimination in the context of EU secondary legislation, the Court held that a national measure making reimbursement of school transport costs subject to a requirement of residence in a German region (*Land*) constitutes indirect discrimination towards frontier workers, regardless of the fact that national workers resident in other German regions (*Länder*) were also adversely affected by that national measure.[116]

---

[107] Case C-437/17 *Gemeinsamer Betriebsrat EurothermenResort Bad Schallerbach* EU:C:2018:627, Opinion of AG Saugmandsgaard Øe, para 26.
[108] Case C-237/94 *O'Flynn* EU:C:1996:206, para 18.
[109] *Schumacker*, para 28; *Clean Car*, para 29.
[110] *Sotgiu*, para 11.
[111] Case C-514/12 *Zentralbetriebsrat der gemeinnützigen Salzburger Landeskliniken* EU:C:2013:799, para 28.
[112] Case C-379/87 *Groener* EU:C:1989:599, para 23; *Angonese*, paras 39–42.
[113] Case C-147/03 *Commission v Austria* EU:C:2005:427, paras 43, 46 and 47.
[114] *Hostellerie Le Manoir*, para 11.
[115] *Angonese*, para 41.
[116] *Landkreis Südliche Weinstraße*, paras 33–34.

3.3 Obstacles to Free Movement

According to its wording, Article 45(2) TFEU only seeks the abolition of discrimination between Member States' workers and it was only in 1993 that the Court held for the first time that the provision also banned obstacles to the free movement of workers.[117] In 1995, in its landmark ruling in *Gebhard*, the Court clarified that the general prohibition of such obstacles applied to all fundamental freedoms alike.[118]

It is worth noting that the Court applies the concepts 'discrimination' and 'obstacle' as being fully independent; that is, a measure can represent an obstacle to the free movement of workers even in the absence of any discrimination.[119] The proposition that an obstacle cannot be found without an assessment of factors such as differentiation and comparability,[120] both factors typically being of importance when assessing discrimination, has thus not been heeded by the Court. In fact, the Court has referred to 'non-discriminatory obstacles to the freedom of movement for workers'.[121]

Obstacles are defined as 'any national measure which is capable of hindering or rendering less attractive the exercise by EU nationals of the fundamental freedom' in question.[122] Applying this new 'obstacle-based' approach has greatly widened the scope of Article 45 TFEU, as an individual seeking to rely on it is not required to demonstrate different treatment of two comparable situations, but simply that a measure may discourage him or her from exercising his or her freedom of movement.

The potential breadth of this definition might seem striking in view of the abundance of measures that could be argued to render it less attractive for Union nationals to take advantage of the fundamental freedoms that Union law accords them.[123] If taken to extremes, regulations on business closing hours could be considered obstacles to the free movement of goods since they render it less attractive for economic operators from other Member States to sell their products at any desired point in time. Regarding free movement of goods, in its famous *Keck* judgment the Court generally narrowed down the term 'obstacle' by excluding from its scope selling arrangements that applied equally to all measures in fact and in law.[124]

No comparable case law exists in the field of free movement of workers. Nevertheless, the Court applies two more specific limitations to avoid an overly wide interpretation of the concept of obstacle.

---

[117] Case C-19/92, *Kraus* EU:C:1993:125, para 32.
[118] *Gebhard*, para 37.
[119] See e.g. Case C-190/98 *Graf* EU:C:2000:49, para 23. The Court's case-law on this point is less obvious where national provisions relate to tax or social security; see Case C-272/17 *Zyla v Staatssecretaris van Financiën* EU:C:2019:49, para 26.
[120] As argued in Opinion of Advocate General Bobek in Case C-703/17 *Krah* EU:C:2019:450, Opinion of AG Bobek, para 74.
[121] *Zyla*, para 26.
[122] Case C-710/18 *WN v Land Niedersachsen* EU:C:2020:299, para 25; *Krah*, para 41; *Erzberger*, para 33.
[123] See for example Advocate General Tizzano's criticism in his Opinion in Case C-442/02 *CaixaBank France* EU:C:2004:187, Opinion of AG Tizzano, applicable to all fundamental freedoms.
[124] See to this effect Joined Cases C-267 and 268/91 *Keck and Mithouard* EU:C:1993:905, para 16.

First, no restriction of Article 45 TFEU occurs where an event is too uncertain and indirect to be regarded as liable to hinder freedom of movement for workers.[125] The first instance in which the Court applied this limitation was the *Graf* judgment, concerning a rule providing for the loss of compensation on termination of employment where the worker himself terminates the contract. Although this might have rendered it less attractive for workers to terminate the contract with a view to seeking employment in other Member States, the Court found no obstacle because the compensation depended on a 'future and hypothetical event, namely the subsequent termination of his contract without such termination being at his own initiative or attributable to him'.[126] The possibility of losing such entitlement was 'too uncertain and indirect a possibility for legislation to be capable of being regarded as liable to hinder freedom of movement for workers'.[127]

Second, the Court held that disadvantages merely resulting from disparities between the Member States' social rules and tax legislation are immaterial in terms of establishing an obstacle to the free movement of workers. The idea behind this limitation is that primary EU law can offer no guarantees to a worker that moving to a Member State other than his country of origin will be neutral in terms of social security or tax rules. In view of the disparities between the Member States' legislation not harmonised by EU law, such a move may be more or less advantageous for the person concerned in that regard.[128]

4. JUSTIFICATIONS OF MEASURES PROHIBITED UNDER ARTICLE 45(2) TFEU

While barriers to the free movement of workers are, as a rule, prohibited by Article 45 TFEU,[129] they do not result in infringements of this Treaty provision in all cases. Rather, they may be justified if they meet three conditions: they must (1) pursue an objective in the public interest; (2) be appropriate for attaining this objective; and (3) be limited to what is necessary to attain it.[130] It is worth highlighting that it is for the Member State invoking the justification to submit an analysis of the appropriateness and proportionality of the restrictive measure adopted and provide precise elements to substantiate its arguments.[131]

---

[125] *Graf*, para 22, referring to case law regarding the free movement of goods; Case C-69/88 *Krantz v Ontvanger der Directe Belastingen* EU:C:1990:97, para 11; and Case C-44/98 *BASF v Präsident des Deutschen Patentamts* EU:C:1999:440, paras 16 and 21. Despite this limitation, restrictions on freedom of movement are prohibited even if they are of limited scope or minor importance (see Case C-315/13 *De Clercq and Others* EU:C:2014:2408, para 61).

[126] *Graf*, para 24.

[127] *Graf*, para 25.

[128] See Case C-95/18 *Sociale Verzekeringsbank v F. van den Berg and Giessen* EU:C:2019:767, paras 57–59; *Erzberger*, paras 33–35. The Court has also referred, by analogy, to *Alevizos*, para 76 and the case-law cited, and Case C-187/15 *Pöpperl* EU:C:2016:550, para 24.

[129] See, for instance, Case C-137/04 *Rockler* EU:C:2006:106, para 20.

[130] Settled case-law since the 1990s; see Case C-259/91 *Allué and Coonan and others v Università degli studi di Venezia and Università degli studi di Parma* EU:C:1993:333, para 15; *Pöpperl*, para 29.

[131] Case C-8/02 *Leichtle* EU:C:2004:161, para 45; *Rockler*, paras 25–26.

4.1 Reasons in the Public Interest

The Court is relatively generous when it comes to accepting objectives in the public interest invoked for justifying restrictions of the fundamental freedoms. Apart from the written grounds of justification set out in Article 45(3) TFEU ('public policy, public security and public health'),[132] many other legitimate interests have been accepted by the Court, such as:

- protecting the effectiveness of fiscal supervision;[133]
- ensuring the effective organisation of the school system;[134]
- combating the risk of seriously compromising the financial equilibrium of a social security system;[135]
- maintaining, on grounds of public health, a balanced medical and hospital service open to all;[136]
- ensuring that the public has a supply of medicinal products which is reliable and of good quality;[137]
- maintaining the cohesion of a tax system;[138]
- maintaining a financial and competitive balance between sport clubs and encouraging the recruitment and training of young players;[139]
- ensuring the proper functioning of the public authorities.[140]

By contrast, aims of a purely administrative or economic nature, such as an increase in financial burdens or possible administrative difficulties, cannot justify restrictions of the fundamental freedoms.[141]

4.2 Appropriateness

Measures restricting the fundamental freedoms must be appropriate for ensuring the attainment of the objective that they pursue. This translates into the requirement that such measures genuinely reflect a concern to attain that objective in a consistent and systematic manner.[142] The appropriateness test often functions as a sincerity check. If Member States are indeed interested in furthering the legitimate aim put forward, their actions should reflect a genuine concern and a planned approach in terms of attaining this objective. Where a rule presents

---

[132] See in this regard the implementing rules on restricting free movement of Union citizens and their family members on grounds of public policy, public security or public health laid down in Articles 27-33 European Parliament and Council Directive 2004/38.
[133] Case C-15/15 *New Valmar* EU:C:2016:464, para 51.
[134] *Landkreis Südliche Weinstraße*, para 41.
[135] Case C-419/16 *Simma Federspiel* EU:C:2017:997, para 42.
[136] *Simma Federspiel*, para 42.
[137] Case C-465/18 *AV and BU v Comune di Bernareggio* EU:C:2019:1125, para 46.
[138] Case C-300/15 *Kohll* EU:C:2016:361, para 60.
[139] *Bosman*, para 106.
[140] *Pöpperl*, para 30.
[141] *Rockler*, para 24; *Kohll*, para 59; Case C-55/00 *Gottardo* EU:C:2002:16, para 38; Case C-400/02 *Merida* EU:C:2004:537, para 30; Case C-172/11 *Erny* EU:C:2012:399, para 48; Joined Cases C-501/12 to 506/12, 540/12 and 541/12 *Specht and Others* EU:C:2014:2005, para 77.
[142] See, to this effect, Case C-169/07 *Hartlauer* EU:C:2009:141, para 55; Joined Cases C-171/07 and 172/07 *Apothekerkammer des Saarlandes and Others* EU:C:2009:316, para 42.

significant loopholes or falls short of attaining its aims for other reasons, it fails the appropriateness test. For example, forcing a civil servant to resign in order to work in another Member State, and therefore lose a significant part of his retirement pension, is not an appropriate measure for attaining the aim of ensuring the proper functioning of the public authorities.[143]

4.3   Necessity Test

While the appropriateness test may be argued to examine whether measures show enough commitment in terms of attaining the reasons in the public interest invoked, the third step of the justification assessment examines whether Member States or employers overshoot the mark, that is to say, whether there are measures less restrictive of the fundamental freedom which would enable the objective to be attained just as effectively.[144]

The necessity test also precludes disregarding qualifications acquired in other Member States. In particular, where, under national law, access to a profession depends upon the possession of a diploma or a professional qualification or periods of practical experience, a Member State must take into consideration all of the diplomas, certificates and other evidence of qualifications and relevant experience by comparing the specialised knowledge and abilities so certified, and that experience, with the knowledge and qualifications required by the national legislation.[145]

5.   CONCLUSIONS

The above outline of the EU rules on free movement of workers illustrates the far-reaching rights from which mobile workers in the internal market benefit, even vis-à-vis private employers. The Court has made a broad interpretation of the scope of Article 45 TFEU and a narrow reading of its exceptions, and it is now widely known that any discrimination against workers from other Member States and any measure rendering the exercise of free movement less attractive are generally prohibited. It has sometimes been considered that the growing importance EU law has afforded to EU citizenship, and its link with Article 45 TFEU,[146] accounted for the Court's willingness to remove any elements susceptible to discouraging workers to exercise their free movement, in a departure from the 'predominantly commercial'[147] focus of the four liberties.

However, despite the ever more extensive rights granted by the Union Court in its elaborate case law, the greatest challenges to the free movement of workers are still identical to those identified in the Spaak report more than 60 years ago. Union citizens have yet to fully grasp the advantages they may gain when drawing from the treasure that work opportunities in other

---

[143] *Pöpperl* paras 36–38.
[144] See, to that effect, *AV*, para 47; *Apothekerkammer des Saarlandes and Others*, paras 25 and 52.
[145] *Brouillard*, para 54; Case C-340/89 *Vlassopoulou v Ministerium für Justiz, Bundes- u. Europaangelegenheiten Baden-Württemberg* EU:C:1991:193, para 16; Case C-234/97 *Fernández de Bobadilla* EU:C:1999:367, para 31; Case C-31/00 *Dreessen* EU:C:2002:35, para 24; and Case C-313/01 *Morgenbesser* EU:C:2003:612, paras 57 and 58.
[146] Catherine Barnard, *The Substantive Law of the EU: The Four Freedoms* (4th edn, OUP 2013) 302.
[147] Paul Craig and Gráinne de Búrca, *EU Law: Texts, Cases and Materials* (4th edn, OUP 2007) 806.

Member States present, and the prejudice that mobile workers face, in particular when they move to more affluent Member States, still needs to be dismantled.

Those who feared that the UK's withdrawal from the Union would sound the death knell for free movement of persons in Europe may find comfort in the initial fallout from Brexit. The voices of those deploring the loss of this fundamental freedom already grow louder, and UK artists wanting to tour Europe and UK employers seeking EU fruit pickers are only some of them. Furthermore, the UK's decision to abolish EU free movement of workers has not brought down the number of migrants entering UK territory but merely led to its workforce being predominantly sourced from other, non-EU countries.[148] It would thus appear that UK rules geared towards reducing incentives for foreign workers seeking job opportunities have proven as imperfect as the EU rules aimed at encouraging their mobility.

---

[148] See the official migration statistics available at www.ons.gov.uk/peoplepopulationandcommunity/populationandmigration/internationalmigration/bulletins/migrationstatisticsquarterlyreport/august2020 accessed 3 March 2021. According to these data, EU net migration had been falling following peak levels in 2015 and 2016 and stabilised recently. However, non-EU net migration has been gradually increasing since 2013 and, as at year ending March 2020, is at some of the highest levels seen since International Passenger Survey records began for this group in 1975.

10. Free movement or fundamental rights? EU citizenship as a legal gateway to fundamental rights protection

Adrienne Yong[1]

1. INTRODUCTION

This chapter offers the view that the status of EU citizenship can only truly become the 'fundamental status'[2] it was hailed to be if the scope of the protection of rights offered as part of being an EU citizen refocuses more explicitly on fundamental rights protection. The main argument is based on the claim that EU citizenship status should be a legal gateway to fundamental rights protection, rather than a gateway to free movement rights. When EU citizenship was first established in the Maastricht Treaty in 1993,[3] rights to free movement and residency were the mainstay of the Treaty's substantive citizenship rights provision, now under Article 21 TFEU. However, this chapter argues that this focus on free movement rights puts EU citizenship status under the umbrella of the internal market's four fundamental freedoms, which raises questions about citizenship being market-based rather than fundamental rights-based.[4] This is of pertinence now because the discourse on market citizenship and free movement rights has re-emerged in recent case law, putting into question the role of fundamental rights in EU citizenship status' future. Existing literature on EU citizenship status' recent trajectory has noted a trend in CJEU case law that favours conferral of free movement rights under Article 21 TFEU as the primary substance of EU citizenship, rather than protecting fundamental rights.[5] This chapter's contribution to the literature is to clarify why these cases should have adopted a fundamental rights discourse instead through EU citizenship status – hence being a 'legal gateway' for fundamental rights protection. This argument is based on the claim that the Court of Justice of the EU (CJEU) has protected fundamental rights through EU citizenship initially through Article 18 TFEU, then relying on the European Convention on Human Rights (ECHR) and eventually the Charter of Fundamental Rights.[6] This chapter adopts a primarily doctrinal approach, whose analysis will then be placed within a wider judicial context to offer reasons

---

[1] This chapter considers case law up until 15 September 2020.
[2] Case C-184/99 *Grzelczyk* EU:C:2001:458, para 31.
[3] Article 8, Treaty of Maastricht on the European Union [1992] OJ C191/01, now Article 20, Consolidated Version of the Treaty on the Functioning of the European Union [2008] OJ C115/47.
[4] Michelle Everson, 'The Legacy of the Market Citizen' in Jo Shaw and Gillian More (eds), *New Legal Dynamics of the European Union* (OUP 1995); Niamh Nic Shuibhne, 'The Resilience of EU Market Citizenship' (2010) 47 CML Rev 1597.
[5] Niamh Nic Shuibhne, 'The "Territory of the Union" in EU Citizenship Law: Charting a Route from Parallel to Integrated Narratives' (2019) 38 YEL 267; Stephen Coutts, 'The Shifting Geometry of Union Citizenship: A Supranational Status from Transnational Rights' (2019) 21 CYELS 318.
[6] Adrienne Yong, *The Rise and Decline of Fundamental Rights in EU Citizenship* (Hart Publishing 2019).

for the judicial choices made by the CJEU. It highlights the structural inequalities associated with a free movement analysis, giving weight to the argument that more attention should be given to fundamental rights through EU citizenship. This has affected certain marginalised groups and promoted a narrow view of the ideal EU citizen.

The chapter is structured as follows. First, it offers a brief outline of the development of EU citizenship status through a fundamental rights lens, with the intention of distinguishing it from the free movement discourse that dominates most of the commentary. Second, it analyses the recent case law to show how the discourse is not showing EU citizenship status as the legal gateway for fundamental rights. Two main groups of recent case law are identified, one concerning third-country nationals (TCNs), the other on the Citizens' Rights Directive 2004/38. Finally, it will clarify why a free movement approach to EU citizenship case law is undesirable by way of highlighting structural inequalities and discrimination embedded when adopting this judicial approach.

2. FREE MOVEMENT OR FUNDAMENTAL RIGHTS?

EU citizenship status has famously been criticised as an afterthought to the provisions on the free movement of persons, which were originally focused on workers' rights under Article 45 TFEU and the predecessor to Regulation 492/2011.[7] Criticism centred on the CJEU's interpretation of EU citizenship as being only a cosmetic change upon its introduction in the Maastricht Treaty, because existing workers' rights were not distinguished clearly enough from EU citizenship rights.[8] Since then much has changed, with the history of EU citizenship being well documented. This chapter will not attempt to revisit these details in their entirety.[9] However, a particular view of its development needs to be highlighted in light of this chapter's objective to reframe the citizenship discourse from a fundamental rights lens in order to distinguish it from free movement. It thus becomes possible to understand why this chapter argues in favour of the CJEU accepting that EU citizenship should be a legal gateway to fundamental rights. This section elucidates the claim that the EU citizenship discourse has been underlined by fundamental rights protection from the outset. It also distinguishes the free movement narrative, to explain why this should not be the trajectory the CJEU favours in future.

---

[7] Council Regulation 492/2011 of 5 April 2011 on freedom of movement for workers within the Union [2011] OJ L 141/1. See previously, Regulation (EEC) No 1612/68 of the Council of 15 October 1968 on freedom of movement for workers within the Community OJ L257/2.

[8] Case C-59/85 *Reed* EU:C:1986:157; Case C-370/90 *Singh* EU:C:1992:296. See Carole Lyons, 'A Voyage around Article 8: An Historical Evaluation on the Fate of European Union Citizenship' (1997) 17 YEL 135; Jo Shaw, 'The Interpretation of European Union Citizenship' (1998) 61 MLR 293.

[9] See for a non-exhaustive early selection: À Castro d'Oliveira, 'Workers and Other Persons: Step-by-Step from Movement to Citizenship – Case Law 1995–2001' [2002] CML Rev 77; Eleanor Spaventa, 'From *Gebhard* to *Carpenter*: Towards a (Non-) Economic European Constitution' (2004) 41 CML Rev 743; Michael Dougan, 'The Constitutional Dimension to the Case Law on Union Citizenship' (2006) 5 Inter Alia 77; Eleanor Spaventa, 'Seeing the Wood Despite the Trees? On the Scope of Union Citizenship and its Constitutional Effects' (2008) 45 CML Rev 13; Niamh Nic Shuibhne, 'The Third Age of EU Citizenship' in Phil Syrpis (ed.), *The Judiciary, the Legislature and the EU Internal Market* (CUP 2012).

2.1 Foundations of Free Movement (of Workers)

It is pertinent to begin by outlining why fundamental rights and free movement are competing within the EU citizenship sphere. There is a longer history of rights under free movement explaining why it dominated the discussion surrounding citizenship status in the beginning. However, tensions arose because the EU was born out of the four fundamental freedoms under the internal market, and there was initially no intention of protecting non-economic rights. When Maastricht introduced social and political rights, it was met with some hesitance.[10] However, it could equally have been argued that these social and political rights were a logical (and unavoidable) extension of economic rights.[11] This politically sensitive area explained the CJEU's tentative approach to expanding the scope of citizenship rights early on. Reference to free movement and other more established and accepted general principles dominated early on as the basis of conferral for citizenship rights, leading to protection only for the economically active and their families.[12] However, it created a problematic distinction between workers and citizens.[13]

The CJEU addressed this in the seminal *Sala* case by clarifying how EU citizenship status was separate from worker status.[14] It was not just the economically active EU citizen who could benefit from citizenship rights, but also EU citizens who were legal residents. The CJEU clarified that EU citizenship rights included protection under Article 18 TFEU, non-discrimination on the grounds of nationality. This chapter argues that direct recourse to Article 18 TFEU is where protection of fundamental rights was first tentatively introduced to the jurisprudence, given that equal treatment is a general principle of EU law. This is seen as an early link to fundamental rights protection through application of the general principles, of which fundamental rights are also part.[15] EU citizens who are legal residents in host Member State territory should thus be treated equally to nationals because of their EU citizenship status. It was thus understandable for the CJEU to begin by basing EU citizenship on legal residency in light of the novelty of introducing non-economic rights in Maastricht.

After decades of the European Economic Community,[16] the case law for some years after *Sala* relied on the exercise of free movement as the main factor determining whether one could benefit from EU citizenship rights.[17] The CJEU also attached black letter criteria to rights

---

[10] Wolfgang Wessels, 'Rationalizing Maastricht: The Search for an Optimal Strategy of the New Europe' (1994) 70 International Affairs 445; Simon Usherwood and Nick Startin, 'Euroscepticism as a Persistent Phenomenon' (2013) 51 JCMS 1.

[11] Jason Coppel and Aidan O'Neill, 'The European Court of Justice: Taking Rights Seriously?' (1992) 12 Legal Studies 227; Philip Alston and Joseph Weiler, 'An "Ever Closer Union" in Need of a Human Rights Policy: The European Union and Human Rights' in Philip Alston (ed.), *The EU and Human Rights* (OUP 1999).

[12] Case C-224/98 *D'hoop* EU:C:2002:432; Case C-413/99 *Baumbast* EU:C:2002:493; Case C-456/02 *Trojani* EU:C:2004:488; Case C-138/02 *Collins* EU:C:2004:172.

[13] HU Jessurun d'Oliveira, *European Citizenship: Pie in the Sky* (Sage Publications 1995); Ulrich K Preuss, 'Two Challenges to European Citizenship' (1996) 44 Political Studies 534; Jo Shaw, 'The Many Pasts and Futures of Citizenship in the European Union' (1997) 22 EL Rev 554.

[14] Case C-85/96 *Martinez Sala* EU:C:1998:217.

[15] Yong (note 6) 24–5.

[16] Treaty of Rome (Treaty establishing the European Economic Community).

[17] Primarily crossing borders and/or economic activity. See Joined Cases C-64/96 and 65/96 *Uecker and Jacquet* EU:C:1997:285 and cases in n 12.

conferral, so it was usually the worker or ex-worker who moved and had sufficient resources and comprehensive health insurance for him and his family to satisfy the criteria for protection under EU citizenship.[18] While it may have perhaps been a gentle introduction to more social and political rights when EU citizenship was first introduced, the main thrust of the argument in this chapter is that there is less appetite for tiptoeing around the main substance of EU citizenship, which should be fundamental rights protection. It is all the more so as this chapter perceives EU citizenship development as having been underscored by fundamental rights protection from the start.

2.2 Towards a Legal Gateway for Fundamental Rights Protection

This chapter argues that the black letter criteria of proving sufficient resources and comprehensive health insurance – which later became part of Directive 2004/38, Article 7 – inherently encourages a free movement analysis over a fundamental rights one when conferring EU citizenship rights.[19] These conditions derive from those applied to workers' rights, which were created to recognise the economically active under EU law. The EU appears to support a very traditional view of what work is, and applied this to the detriment of those who do not contribute economically, or are engaged in non-traditional or atypical work.[20] This is an inherently gendered view of the ideal EU citizen,[21] affecting women disproportionately as they are more likely to fall into both categories of non-worker status. This is another reason why promoting a fundamental rights agenda in the CJEU jurisprudence going forward becomes more important, as discussed later. It is part of addressing this disproportionate impact on certain marginalised groups – especially important given the increase in family reunification cases.

It is understandable that the CJEU had to strike a careful balance between promoting greater social and political rights and respecting its unfamiliarity to Member State authorities early on in citizenship's history. However, as it transpired that it was indirectly discriminating between groups of citizens as outlined above, the CJEU begun to take more steps to attempt to remedy this. While the discourse on fundamental rights protection in early case law was not as explicit, given it mainly manifested as equal treatment and non-discrimination, it seemed a logical consequence – as in the case of workers' rights – that EU citizens' families also needed protection – if for nothing else, to facilitate free movement. As with most of EU citizenship, this is how family rights were first introduced into the discourse. This was most evident in the controversial *Carpenter* case,[22] where only a potential obstacle to cross-border free movement of services was enough to trigger the Treaty and protect the working Union citizen and his family from being separated. A fundamental rights interpretation of *Carpenter*

---

[18] *Baumbast*.
[19] Council Directive on 2004/38/EC of 29 April 2004 on the right of citizens of the Union and their family members to move and reside freely within the territory of the Member States amending Regulation (EEC) 1612/68 and repealing Directives 64/221/EEC, 68/360/EEC, 72/194/EEC, 73/148/EEC, 75/34/EEC, 75/35/EEC, 90/364/EEC, 90/365/EEC 93/96/EEC [2004] OJ L158/77, Article 7.
[20] Case C-66/85 *Lawrie-Blum* EU:C:1986:284, which requires work not to be marginal or ancillary. See further, Isabel Shutes and Sarah Walker, 'Gender and Free Movement: EU Migrant Women's Access to Residence and Social Rights in the UK' (2018) 44 Journal of Ethnic and Migration Studies 137.
[21] Charlotte O'Brien, 'I Trade, Therefore I Am: Legal Personhood in the European Union' (2013) 50 CML Rev 1643.
[22] Case C-60/00 *Carpenter* EU:C:2002:434.

would conclude that the CJEU sought to facilitate family reunification. The easier, more palatable option was chosen, though, in terms of framing the decision under the free movement of services. However, this creative line of reasoning has garnered some criticism for being too far-reaching.[23]

The criticism of the CJEU in *Carpenter* for its confusing messaging as to the scope of EU citizenship is another reason to support an explicit fundamental rights discourse in EU citizenship. The majority of cases after *Carpenter* where fundamental rights were significant mostly concerned rights to family reunification, with some important ones on rights to a name.[24] One of the most notable is *Garcia Avello*,[25] an early example of when fundamental rights were arguably instrumental to the final judgment, but not so explicitly. Parents of dual national Belgian–Spanish children sought to register their children's surnames in Belgium in the traditional Spanish way, inclusive of both parents' surnames. Belgium did not recognise this and the CJEU held it was contrary to EU law. Free movement under EU citizenship would be impeded if the surnames were inconsistent in different Member States. Perhaps at the time a free movement approach was chosen to err on the side of caution, reconciling a potentially low political appetite for explicit deference with fundamental rights reasoning in case law.

However, the CJEU had already stated that 'the requirements flowing from the protection of fundamental rights in the Community legal order are also binding on Member States when they implement Community rules'.[26] In this vein, and also given that the Charter of Fundamental Rights was established in 2000, the CJEU in *Garcia Avello* could have been more forthright about explicitly mentioning fundamental rights. Subsequent case law, most notably the *Chen*[27] and *Metock*[28] cases, did, however, demonstrate the CJEU's increasing willingness to accept a more explicit fundamental rights discourse. Both were specifically about third-country nationals (TCNs) remaining on EU territory and relying on derived rights from Union citizen family members. The *Chen* decision allowed a TCN mother to stay with her Union citizen infant who needed her to remain in the EU territory to care for her. Family reunification was even clearer in *Metock*, where the CJEU clarified the scope of Directive 2004/38's conditions for accompanying and joining EU citizen family members. These cases led smoothly to *Ruiz Zambrano*,[29] where it was finally accepted that EU citizenship did not need to be reliant on a cross-border test to trigger the Treaty rights. Instead, the status was now an independent legal basis for rights.

By doing away with what had come to be criticised as highly arbitrary,[30] the cross-border test would now be replaced with the deprivation of genuine enjoyment test from *Ruiz Zambrano*. In what seemed to be positive signs towards embracing a fundamental rights discourse – especially in light of the Lisbon Treaty's guarantees of greater fundamental rights protection

---

[23] Samantha Besson and André Utzinger, 'Introduction: Future Challenges of European Citizenship – Facing a Wide-Open Pandora's Box' (2007) 13 ELJ 573, 574.
[24] Case C-208/09 *Sayn-Wittgenstein* EU:C:2010:806; Case C-391/09 *Runevic-Vardyn and Wardyn* EU:C:2011:291; Case C-353/06 *Grunkin and Paul* EU:C:2008:559.
[25] Case C-148/02 *Garcia Avello* EU:C:2003:539.
[26] Case C-292/97 *Karlsson* EU:C:2000:202, para 37.
[27] Case C-200/02 *Zhu and Chen* EU:C:2004:639.
[28] Case C-127/08 *Metock and Others* EU:C:2008:449.
[29] Case C-34/09 *Ruiz Zambrano* EU:C:2011:124.
[30] Charlotte O'Brien, 'Real Links, Abstract Rights and False Alarms: The Relationship between the ECJ's "Real Link" Case Law and National Solidarity' (2008) 33 EL Rev 643.

through Article 6 TEU – the CJEU in *Ruiz Zambrano* allowed a Colombian father with derived rights of residency to remain in Belgium with his Belgian children, who were born there and had never moved. However, what was less satisfactory was the CJEU's careful choice not to mention fundamental rights. Instead, it focused entirely on the fact that 'a refusal would lead to a situation where those children, citizens of the Union, would be forced to leave EU territory with their parents'.[31] Failing to mention fundamental rights left open the question of whether these rights were conferred as part of an independent legal basis for rights.[32] Disappointingly, subsequent case law confirmed that this was not the case.

3. MOVING BACKWARDS ON FUNDAMENTAL RIGHTS OR FORGING AHEAD WITH FREE MOVEMENT?

It is clear now, close to three decades after the introduction of EU citizenship status, that EU citizenship status differs – and was intended to differ – from worker status. The scope of EU citizenship has arguably taken on a shape of its own, characterised by more explicit references to fundamental rights. It culminated in *Ruiz Zambrano*, where EU citizenship status was finally emancipated from the cross-border test, becoming an independent legal basis for rights. For a fleeting moment, this may have marked a more permanent departure from the internal market's free movement approach in case law, and towards a fundamental rights discourse being the dominant factor for the CJEU in deciding rights under EU citizenship.[33] However, this was quickly usurped by cases decided shortly after *Ruiz Zambrano* that clarified that EU citizenship was not the legal gateway for fundamental rights protection, but rather that some rights – particularly those under Directive 2004/38 – were still dependent on exercising free movement and intended to remove obstacles to it.[34]

The idea of being a legal gateway for fundamental rights protection comes out of the claim that EU citizenship is now an independent legal basis for rights. Without cleaving to free movement *per se*, this should have opened a 'gateway' to claiming protection of fundamental rights simply by virtue of one's citizenship status.[35] This would have been a significant departure from the market-based roots of EU citizenship, distinguishing it from worker status. However, the recent judicial trend is for a fundamental rights element to be presented as a free movement issue instead. This section will analyse case law from the recent past in two broad categories – cases on third-country nationals, and cases on application of Directive 2004/38. This elucidates the current situation in EU citizenship case law, demonstrating how a free movement approach is becoming dominant, and offering the alternative fundamental rights perspective where appropriate.

---

[31] *Ruiz Zambrano*, para 44.
[32] Niamh Nic Shuibhne, 'Seven Questions for Seven Paragraphs' (2011) 36 EL Rev 161; Hanneke van Eijken and Sybe de Vries, 'A New Route into the Promised Land? Being a European Citizen after *Ruiz Zambrano*' (2011) 36 EL Rev 704.
[33] Armin von Bogdandy and others, 'Reverse Solange: Protecting the Essence of Fundamental Rights against EU Member States' (2012) 49 CML Rev 489.
[34] Case C-434/09 *McCarthy* EU:C:2011:277; Case C-256/11 *Dereci* EU:C:2011:734.
[35] Case C-34/09 *Ruiz Zambrano* EU:C:2011:560, Opinion of AG Sharpston.

3.1 Third-Country Nationals

The most prominent trend in recent case law is cases involving TCNs and family reunification rights. The increase in cases on TCNs can explain why the CJEU has adopted a free movement over a fundamental rights approach, as it has been said that 'the CJEU will most likely not decide in favour of TCNs, either in the area of free movement or immigration policies, as well as national security'.[36] The reasons for this, however, are varied. National security and immigration both arguably fall under the umbrella of the Area of Freedom, Security and Justice (AFSJ), which has been plagued by criticism of Fortress Europe; EU citizenship highlights this by drawing a starker divide between those within the EU and those outside.[37] This is exacerbated by focusing on free movement, which is too often rooted in the internal market and does not adequately address wider fundamental rights issues. This section argues that certain circumstances in case law on TCN family reunification have indeed influenced the choice of a free movement analysis over a fundamental rights one.

The first cases concern spousal divorce rights. These situations highlight how embedded the free movement analysis is in the CJEU's approach to citizenship of late. TCNs marry EU citizens who then leave them after the marriage breaks down. If the EU citizen leaves before divorce is official, Article 7(2) of Directive 2004/38 no longer applies to protect their (now former) TCN spouse.[38] It becomes clear that the situation is very much one that can have disproportionate effects on women, as *NA* exemplifies. The TCN wife was subject to domestic violence then abandoned by her spouse, with custody of the children. Rights were only conferred to her because her ex-spouse had worked and his children (and their primary carer – their non-EU mother) enjoyed an independent right of residence based on the children's right to education.[39] Though the CJEU appeared to be protecting the fundamental rights of the TCN mother through her EU children in *NA*, in reality it was the children deriving rights from their father who benefited from worker status.

Interestingly, however, upon considering patterns in the case law, it does seem that there may have been another influential factor for the CJEU deciding in favour of the mother in *NA*: the fact that children were involved. While *NA* does not so explicitly refer to the children's best interests, children have been central to the CJEU's considerations in many cases since. This is where EU citizenship status had the opportunity to become a legal gateway to fundamental rights protection because of explicit links between care for children and family reunification. *Rendón Marín*[40] and *CS*[41] present an interesting dilemma concerning TCN parents with criminal convictions. The CJEU had to balance competing views of the individual: on the one hand, a good parent that wants to stay to care for their EU children; on the other, a bad TCN with

---

[36] Urška Šadl and Mikael Rask Madsen, 'Did the Financial Crisis Change European Citizenship Law? An Analysis of Citizenship Rights Adjudication Before and After the Financial Crisis' (2016) 22 ELJ 40, 44.

[37] Sionaidh Douglas-Scott, 'The Rule of Law in the European Union: Putting the Security into the Area of Freedom, Security and Justice' (2004) 29 EL Rev 219; Sarah Fine, 'Whose Freedom of Movement Is Worth Defending?' in Rainer Baubock (ed), *Debating European Citizenship* (Springer 2019). See also Case C-247/17 *Raugevicius* EU:C:2018:898.

[38] Case C-218/14 *Singh and Others* EU:C:2015:476; Case C-115/15 *NA* EU:C:2016:487.

[39] *NA*, paras 57–59.

[40] Case C-165/14 *Rendón Marin* EU:C:2016:675.

[41] Case C-304/14 *CS* EU:C:2016:674.

a criminal conviction. In both cases the CJEU stressed that TCNs do not enjoy any autonomous rights deriving from EU citizenship, but deporting both sets of parents would amount to a deprivation of genuine enjoyment. However, what ultimately looked like a fundamental rights decision because of family reunification is actually underscored by a free movement analysis because of reliance on the deprivation of genuine enjoyment test from *Ruiz Zambrano*, which has become mostly about removing obstacles to free movement.

While the Charter is mentioned in both *Rendón Marín* and *CS*, it was ultimately the fact that the children would be forced to leave the EU territory if their parents were deported that was the deciding factor for the CJEU. In *Chavez-Vilchez*, even less mention of the Charter is made in considering rights of non-working TCN mothers of dependent Dutch children who had Dutch fathers.[42] The determining factor was, again, a free movement interpretation of the deprivation of genuine enjoyment, which allowed national authorities to consider if the other parent – often the EU national father – is 'actually able and willing to assume sole responsibility for the primary day-to-day care of the child'[43] before confirming that the child would otherwise be forced to leave the territory of the Union. While this has the effect of keeping a family together, it cements the post-*Ruiz Zambrano* position of EU citizenship status not being a legal gateway to fundamental rights. While the outcome is one of protecting fundamental rights, again it is the free movement emphasis in the grounds of the judgment itself that is problematic.

Conferring derived rights to TCN parent(s) from their Union citizen children often requires an assessment of the extent of the child's dependency. As *Chavez-Vilchez* confirms, the level of dependency determines if there is an obstacle to free movement that confers protection under EU citizenship. Subsequent case law sees some variation in personal circumstances but little variation in the approach adopted by the CJEU. *Altiner and Rayn* considers the dependency of a Turkish son on his father's new Danish wife. The son, living with his mother in Turkey, sought residency in Denmark as a family member of his father's wife upon their return from living in Sweden. Questions in the case surrounded whether the son entered Denmark 'as a natural consequence' of his stepmother returning home, given that he did not habitually live with them.[44] The most important claim made by the CJEU in *Altiner and Ravn* is that 'any right of residence in an EU Member State of a third-country national derives from the exercise of freedom of movement by a Union citizen'.[45] Therefore, though not decisive, these 'natural consequences' of movement were a factor that the CJEU was at pains to highlight, thus overshadowing any family reunification discourse that may have been relevant.

Slowly but surely, the overall message from the CJEU about EU citizenship is that of it being about free movement, with fundamental rights protection as an added bonus. The fact that children are involved may somewhat factor into the final decision implicitly, but it is not enough to reframe the analysis from an explicit fundamental rights lens. Even without children, in *Lounes*, *KA and others* and *RH* the CJEU allowed TCNs to derive rights from their family members,[46] but the entire focus was on dependency and proving a sufficient link with

---

[42] Case C-133/15 *Chavez-Vilchez* EU:C:2017:354.
[43] *Chavez-Vilchez*, para 71.
[44] Case C-230/17 *Altiner and Ravn* EU:C:2018:497 para 25.
[45] *Altiner and Ravn*, para 30.
[46] Case C-165/16 *Lounes* EU:C:2017:862; Case C-82/16 *KA and Others* EU:C:2018:308; Case C-836/18 *RH* EU:C:2020:119.

the Union citizen family member so that deprivation of genuine enjoyment is clear in the sense of being forced to leave the EU territory. Furthermore, the CJEU persistently repeats that the Treaty and its citizenship provisions by no means confer any autonomous rights on TCNs, and that any rights enjoyed are derived. This repeated emphasis seems to put distance between EU citizenship and an inherent fundamental rights discourse, especially in light of the fact that cases on family reunification rights are the most prevalent manifestation of fundamental rights, and these almost always involve TCNs.

In this vein, criticism of the EU's traditional view of gendered family relationships exists,[47] but recent cases have shown the CJEU's willingness to accept non-traditional families. Here is where there is most potential for a fundamental rights discourse; situations sit squarely within the scope of protecting the right to private and family life.[48] *Coman* set the precedent: a TCN spouse of Romanian in a same-sex marriage sought residency in Romania, where same-sex marriages are not recognised.[49] The CJEU held that non-recognition of a same-sex marriage cannot be the sole reason for refusing derived rights. Another non-traditional family situation was seen in *SM*, where the Algerian *kafala* system of child 'adoption' undertaken by a French couple residing in the UK was not recognised by national authorities, thereby denying the child entry to the UK.[50] In *Coman*, the CJEU stated that denying rights would mean 'a Union citizen may be denied the possibility of returning to the Member State of which he is a national together with his spouse'.[51] This is despite preliminary observations noting that there was family life because of being married that could have been cited as a factor in the final outcome.[52] In *SM*, though the CJEU eventually allowed the child to enter the UK, the situation itself was devoid of any assessment of fundamental rights protection.

The important takeaway from *Coman* and *SM* is the CJEU's broader recognition of a wider definition of family life, more consistent with the approach taken by the European Court of Human Rights.[53] However, what is becoming clearer is how the norm in EU citizenship cases is that of free movement and removing obstacles to it. The CJEU's wider definition of family and thus interferences to family life are to be applauded, but the approach taken to protecting family life is not often through EU citizenship status. Instead, EU citizenship has become a status facilitating free movement and residence, rather than seeking to protect one's fundamental rights. For example, in *Coman*, a fundamental rights analysis would argue that rights for same-sex TCN spouses are akin to preserving rights to one's identity and avoiding an interruption to the EU citizen's private life under Article 7 Charter. This preference for a free

---

[47] Eleonore Kofman, 'Gendered Migrations, Livelihoods and Entitlements in European Welfare Regimes' in Nicola Piper (ed.), *New Perspectives on Gender and Migration: Livelihood, Rights and Entitlements* (Routledge 2008).

[48] Alina Tryfonidou, 'The EU Top Court Rules that Married Same-sex Couples Can Move Freely Between EU Member States as "Spouses": Case C-673/16, Relu Adrian Coman, Robert Clabourn Hamilton, Asociaţia Accept v Inspectoratul General pentru Imigrări, Ministerul Afacerilor Interne' (2019) 27 Feminist Legal Studies 211.

[49] Case C-673/16 *Coman and Others* EU:C:2018:385.

[50] Case C-129/18 *SM* EU:C:2019:248.

[51] *Coman and Others*, para 40.

[52] Cf. Case C-89/17 *Banger* EU:C:2018:570, where a TCN in an unmarried cohabiting couple was denied residency. The CJEU, citing *Coman*, required extensive reasons for any refusal not to recognise unmarried partners, especially when the Treaty was triggered by the EU citizen family member moving to work.

[53] *Marckx v Belgium* (1979) 2 EHRR 330.

movement analysis becomes even more prominent in cases on Directive 2004/38 on rights other than those associated with TCNs.

3.2 Directive 2004/38

The two main groups of recent cases under Directive 2004/38 concern benefits and expulsion. Both areas have been plagued by increasing hostility from national authorities towards an overly liberal interpretation of conferring benefits and protection against expulsion.[54] It is argued that this is temporally consistent with the rise of right-wing populist parties in Europe and uproar concerning benefit tourism and allowing foreign criminals to remain in host Member States.[55] Unlike in the cases on TCN family reunification above – which may have adopted a free movement analysis but were ultimately decided favourably – these cases on benefits and expulsion are a little more nuanced and a little less generous. As such, details are ever more important, as the specific substance of the cases arguably plays a role in the CJEU's final judgments. Benefits have been discussed widely, mostly around the *Dano* case and subsequent cases.[56] Expulsion has been of note as well, as protection against expulsion is slowly becoming less and less robust.[57]

Cases on benefits concern the definition of special non-contributory benefits and whether this amounted to social assistance under Article 24, Directive 2004/38. If they were, national authorities would not be obliged to confer them. More recently, *Alimanovic* and *Garcia-Nieto* both confirmed the narrow approach taken in *Dano*, that special non-contributory benefits were a form of social assistance enjoyed only by legal residents.[58] As such, in both cases the non-economically active citizens were held to the high standards of the Directive and its black letter criteria. Without sufficient resources, claimants were not entitled to any assistance. Contrast the approach in these cases to *Gusa* and *Tarola*, on Romanians working in Ireland.[59] In both, claimants were economically 'active' through either job-seeking or former worker status, so the CJEU decided to allow them to retain worker status, thereby conferring equal treatment to benefits. These were by and large straightforward cases because of

---

[54] Hostility is evident from the British media, especially in light of the UK's withdrawal from the EU. In particular, see David Cameron, *A New Settlement for the United Kingdom in a Reformed European Union* (10 November 2015); Adrienne Yong, 'Human Rights Protection as Justice in Post-Brexit Britain: A Case Study of Deportation' in Tawhida Ahmed and Elaine Fahey (eds), *On Brexit: Law, Justices and Injustices* (Edward Elgar Publishing 2019).

[55] Gregor Aisch, Adam Pearce and Rousseau Bryant, 'How Far Is Europe Swinging to the Right?' *The New York Times* (23 Oct 2017) www.nytimes.com/interactive/2016/05/22/world/europe/europe-right-wing-austria-hungary.html accessed 3 Aug 2018.

[56] Case C-333/13 *Dano* EU:C:2014:2358; Case C-140/12 *Brey* EU:C:2013:565. See Herwig Verschueren, 'Preventing "Benefit Tourism" in the EU: A Narrow or Broad Interpretation of the Possibilities Offered by the ECJ in *Dano*?' (2015) 52 CML Rev 363; Daniel Thym, 'When Union Citizens Turn Into Illegal Migrants: The *Dano* Case' (2015) 40 EL Rev 249.

[57] Article 28, Directive 2004/38. See Dora Kostakopoulou and Nuno Ferreira, 'Testing Liberal Norms: The Public Policy and Public Security Derogations and the Cracks In European Union Citizenship' (2013) 20 ColumJEurLaw 167.

[58] Case C-67/14 *Alimanovic* EU:C:2015:597 para 44; Case C-299/14 *Garcia-Nieto and Others* EU:C:2016:114 para 39.

[59] Case C-442/16 *Gusa* EU:C:2017:1004; Case C-482/17 *Tarola* EU:C:2019:309.

movement related to economic activity.[60] In contrast, in *Dano*, *Alimanovic* and *Garcia-Nieto*, non-economically active citizens were not granted protection.

The trend of economically active individuals being 'deserving' citizens applies also to cases on expulsion.[61] Protection against expulsion had the potential to be one of EU citizenship's most effective forms of protection, with enhanced protection granted the more integrated a citizen is in their host Member State.[62] The recent trend in expulsion cases, however, exhibits a lowering of the high level of protection that the original provision in Directive 2004/38 seemingly intended to offer.[63] This has always been grounded in free movement because protection against expulsion is arguably seen as removing the ultimate obstacle to free movement. The recent case law on expulsion has sought to clarify what may have been perceived to be becoming a broad-brush approach to the factors in Article 28, Directive 2004/38 requiring consideration before expelling an EU citizen. In doing so, striking a balance between security around borders and citizenship and fundamental rights becomes relevant.

E and *B and Vomero* both concerned EU citizens who had been imprisoned or detained for criminal offences.[64] An expulsion order with a ten-year entry ban was issued for E, an Italian in Spain. He claimed he was no longer a genuine and present threat to society justifying expulsion because he had been in prison for 6 years serving his 12-year sentence.[65] The CJEU decided that being imprisoned when the expulsion decision is taken does not necessarily mean the individual cannot be a present and genuine threat.[66] In *B and Vomero*, a similar issue was considered for a Greek permanent resident of Germany who was subject to expulsion and an entry ban despite qualifying for enhanced protection under Article 28(3)(a), Directive 2004/38. It was held that his imprisonment did not automatically break any integrative links or nullify enhanced protection,[67] but the CJEU left open the possibility that detention *could* break links and amount to a break in continuity of residency, based on 'the duration of residence and the degree of integration of the citizen concerned in the host Member State'.[68] These cases demonstrate that more discretion is being given to Member States when justifying deportation.

Following these limitations on protection against expulsion was *K and HF*, a damning judgment confirming that past conduct could be taken into account under Article 28, Directive 2004/38, adding further nuance to the provision. Asylum was sought in the Netherlands for two individuals (one EU citizen, one TCN) and their families but were rejected on the basis of their having previously committed war crimes. The CJEU decided that public security justifications for expulsion included both internal and external security,[69] or 'direct threat to the peace of mind and physical security of the population'. Therefore, previous war crimes were

---

[60] In Case C-308/14 *Commission v UK* EU:C:2016:436, the CJEU allowed the UK to require a right to reside as part of the conditions for claiming social assistance. In *Gusa*, recognition of self-employed work was made clear and in *Tarola*, it was the obligation to register for jobseeker status.

[61] Eleanor Spaventa, 'Earned Citizenship: Understanding Union Citizenship through Its Scope' in Dimitry Kochenov (ed), *EU Citizenship and Federalism: the Role of Rights* (CUP 2015).

[62] Yong (n 54).

[63] Loic Azoulai and Stephen Coutts, 'Restricting Union Citizens' Residence Rights on Grounds of Public Security: Where Union Citizenship and the AFSJ Meet' (2013) 50 CML Rev 553.

[64] Case C-193/16 *E* EU:C:2017:542; Case C-316/16 *B and Vomero* EU:C:2018:256.

[65] As per Case C-30/77 *Bouchereau* EU:C:1977:172, para 28.

[66] *E*, para 24.

[67] *B and Vomero*, para 71.

[68] *B and Vomero*, para 82.

[69] Case C-331/16 *K and HF* EU:C:2018:296, para 42.

relevant. Where in *Bouchereau* it was held that previous convictions should only be relevant where conduct becomes a present threat,[70] what this case now suggests is that it is much broader due to threats to one's peace of mind. While a free movement analysis is not necessarily so prominent in these cases, it is what is absent that is more troublesome. The CJEU has strictly upheld the criteria under the Directive to the great disadvantage of these EU citizens without considering fundamental rights implications of their decisions.[71] By and large, they fall into an 'undeserving' category because of past indiscretions or non-economically active status. Perhaps it is this which explains why fundamental rights have been largely absent or brushed aside in the overall holistic assessment of proportionality when conferring citizenship.

4. (NOT) MAKING WAY FOR FUNDAMENTAL RIGHTS PROTECTION

Sadly, it is all too true that it is 'naïve to believe that Member States will act in a way in which they will always respect fundamental rights'.[72] Therefore, questions around EU fundamental rights protection had been posed from around the time that the EU itself began to emerge as a social and political actor, as well as an economic entity. Whether fundamental rights *would* play a role in EU citizenship's future was a question that the commentary widely speculated on (and still speculates on), based on the jurisprudence of the CJEU;[73] whether it *should* play a role was a normative question debated by scholars from the very start; and whether it *could* play a role was a legal question debated notably by Advocates General.[74] This chapter advocates that EU citizenship's future *should* be one where fundamental rights are an inherent part of the rights under the status' scope, and that it *could* do so because EU citizenship status should be a legal gateway to these rights. The CJEU *would* incorporate fundamental rights into citizenship discourse to create an ever closer Union of peoples.[75] It had begun to show signs of doing so in the mid- to late 2000s, but the tone has changed in CJEU jurisprudence, bringing into question EU citizenship's role as the legal gateway for fundamental rights – as the cases above show.

This author has previously argued that there is a correlation between the political climate and the CJEU judgments themselves, in that the CJEU's legal culture of decision-making seems to be affected by the political environment within which it makes decisions, and

---

[70] *Bouchereau* (n 65).
[71] Cf. in Case C-94/18 *Chenchooliah* EU:C:2019:693, a TCN wife of a Portuguese national sought protection against expulsion from Ireland after losing derived rights when her husband was imprisoned in Portugal. The CJEU decided any expulsion order had to be compliant with procedural protection under Articles 30, 31 and 15, so the Irish expulsion order could not require her to be expelled *and* subject to an entry ban.
[72] Ermioni Xanthopoulou, *Fundamental Rights and Mutual Trust in the Area of Freedom, Security and Justice: A Role for Proportionality?* (Bloomsbury Publishing 2020) 24.
[73] *Chen*; Bernard Hofstotter, 'A Cascade of Rights, or Who Shall Care for Little Catherine? Some Reflections on the *Chen* Case' (2005) 30 EL Rev 548.
[74] See AG Jacobs in Case C-168/91 *Konstantinidis* EU:C:1992:504, Opinion of AG Jacobs; AG Sharpston in Case C-456/12 and Case C-457/12 *O and B; S and G* EU:C:2013:842, Opinion of AG Sharpston and *Ruiz Zambrano*, and extrajudicially, Francis G Jacobs, 'Citizenship of the European Union: A Legal Analysis' (2007) 13 ELJ 591.
[75] Preamble, Consolidated Version of the Treaty on European Union [2008] OJ C115/13.

these decisions make an impact.[76] As others noted in the context of the eurozone debt crisis, it 'would exacerbate the tendency of the CJEU to yield to national (state) sensitivities and reach pro Member State outcomes to the detriment of private (individual) interests at stake or the pro-integration interests of the Commission and its traditional alliance with the Court'.[77] Indeed, the above case law seems to suggest that the CJEU has succumbed to this pressure as well as other pressures from other crises befalling the EU, including the migration crisis, the rule of law crisis and the UK's withdrawal from the EU.[78] All this has contributed to what this author has called a decline in fundamental rights protection in EU citizenship case law. This decline in fundamental rights has been coupled of late with a return to considering obstacles to free movement.

There are significant issues with the apparent decision not to make EU citizenship status the legal gateway for fundamental rights. There are structural inequalities that this free movement approach promotes without realising. It has become of greater concern with the rise in cases on fundamental rights that manifest mainly as issues of private and family life, especially family reunification. As mentioned, there are some gendered elements to the judgments which are undesirable. It is the primary reason for promoting a fundamental rights lens applied to EU citizenship status' scope rather than a free movement one. If protection is more easily granted to economic migrants with sufficient resources and comprehensive health insurance, this effectively benefits wealthy working men. This raises the issue of whether it is respecting the general principle in EU law of equal treatment and other values in Article 2 TEU, particularly 'human rights, including the rights of persons belonging to minorities'.

In this vein, despite the obvious disproportionate effects on disadvantaged women and families seeking rights outlined above, there may be a more political explanation for the CJEU choosing not to make EU citizenship the legal gateway for fundamental rights. Indeed, there have been signs that this is not the way the CJEU wanted to go, since post-*Ruiz Zambrano* case law confirmed that the deprivation of genuine enjoyment test was entirely about removing obstacles to free movement. Criticism came fast and hard when the case law trends appeared to suggest an increasingly restrictive scope of EU citizenship rights after a period of expansion in scope which was argued to have been driven by the constitutionalisation of the fundamental rights discourse.[79] However, almost a decade after *Ruiz Zambrano*, the CJEU seems to have changed its tone once again. In what seems to be an attempt to balance criticism of excessive restriction of the scope with respect for national authorities' dissatisfaction as to an excessively liberal expansion of scope, the CJEU has decided to base EU citizenship primarily on rights to free movement. On the surface, decisions appear to broadly benefit EU citizens. However, the judicial reasoning applied actually undermines the fundamental status of EU citizenship, at least from the perspective of fundamental rights protection.

The cases on family reunification rights provide especial food for thought in the context of gendered notions of families and parental roles related to the TCN seeking residency under EU

---

[76] Yong (n 6) 150.

[77] Šadl and Madsen (n 36) 57.

[78] Adrienne Yong, 'The Future of EU Citizenship Status during Crisis: Is There a Role for Fundamental Rights Protection?' (2020) 7(2) Journal of International and Comparative Law 471.

[79] Niamh Nic Shuibhne, 'Limits Rising, Duties Ascending: The Changing Legal Shape of Union Citizenship' (2015) 52 CML Rev 889; Eleanor Spaventa, 'Striving for Equality: Who "Deserves" to be a Union Citizen?' in Antonio Tizzano and others (eds), *Scritti in Onore di Giuseppe Tesauro* (Editoriale Scientifica 2014).

citizenship. As mentioned, the non-traditional same-sex marriage and *kafala* system of 'adoption' saw the CJEU adapt its traditional notions of family and grant residency rights in both cases. While in general this was argued to have been progressive,[80] applying a feminist lens to *Chavez-Vilchez*'s assessment of assumption of parental responsibility from eight different situations where TCN mothers were primary carers of Dutch children who had Dutch fathers highlights the potential disproportionate effect on women of an analysis entirely concerned with free movement. The focus in the case was around dependency and whether the fathers could assume sole responsibility in order to amount to a deprivation of genuine enjoyment. While ultimately this was not on its own sufficient as a ground to deny residency, it was still a relevant factor and an additional burden to the mothers seeking residency with their children. The CJEU highlights that 'contact between the children and their fathers was, variously, frequent, seldom or even non-existent'.[81] In this situation, there is a more pressing need to ensure that fundamental rights to private and family life are not breached because of the inability to rely on the EU citizen fathers.

There have been quite a number of recent cases in which the TCN mother of a Union citizen child has faced difficulties in retaining residency of late. The CJEU's insistence on finding a link with free movement – often through economic activity – affects these individuals more because of the likelihood that they are not working, or are doing unpaid work such as care. As such, it becomes clear that not only is it not desirable to be a TCN, but also being a non-working carer – a woman – makes rights conferral more elusive. This has been most starkly evident in the benefit saga, with the claimants in *Dano*, *Alimanovic* and *Garcia-Nieto*[82] being three non-economically active women with children who exercised free movement rights, but who did not work and therefore were not conferred welfare benefits. In contrast, the economically active men in *Gusa* and *Tarola* did not face the same obstacles, with the implication being that, as before, being a worker is a privileged position as compared to simply being an EU citizen. Given that EU citizenship status should have done away with this distinction, it is a step backwards to restrict the scope of fundamental rights protection through EU citizenship to what appears to be a re-emergence of market citizenship and free movement principles.

The problem with a return to market citizenship principles under EU citizenship is the fact that this begins to clearly demarcate limitations for who is considered a deserving or non-deserving citizen. This is separate to the feminist arguments and speaks more widely to an undermining of fundamental rights protection. Cases on expulsion and under Directive 2004/38 exemplify this best. While cases on TCN family reunification sometimes fail to mention the Charter, there is a more prominent trend in the expulsion cases that often do not involve TCNs where no mention of the Charter is made at all. It seems to suggest, overall, that the picture of the 'bad' EU citizen dominates the assessment, creating a hierarchy of who has earned or deserves protection through good behaviour – often amounting to economic activity. This becomes especially problematic for EU citizens who have engaged in criminal activity.[83]

---

[80] Amanda Spalding, 'Where Next after *Coman*?' (2019) 21 European Journal of Migration and Law 117, 118.

[81] *Chavez-Vilchez*, para 43.

[82] Note that in *Garcia-Nieto*, residency for the father was also sought and they were an unmarried couple. The case still highlights inequalities for disadvantaged low-income families.

[83] Stephen Coutts, 'Union Citizenship as Probationary Citizenship: *Onuekwere*' (2015) 52 CML Rev 531.

Indeed, this is contrary to the Charter's scope being engaged when EU law is being implemented.[84] It is also against the spirit of the fundamental status of EU citizenship as understood in this chapter as a legal gateway to fundamental rights.

It remains now only to analyse one the most interesting cases of the past few years, the *Tjebbes* case, which does not fit into either of the two aforementioned categories.[85] It would be remiss not to mention it given its relevance in light of what the fundamental status of EU citizenship means in terms of free movement or fundamental rights. In *Tjebbes*, Dutch nationals who had spent ten years continuously outside the Netherlands were set to lose their Dutch nationality and with it, EU citizenship. Like the earlier *Rottmann* case where, despite nationality being an exclusive Member State competence, nationality laws affecting EU citizenship status fell within the scope of EU law,[86] the CJEU decided that it was acceptable for a Member State to require a genuine link, such as an uninterrupted period of long residence within the territory. However, it must consider if this is proportionate to loss of EU citizenship status. This case appears to seek to highlight the fundamentality of EU citizenship status, which, in the political context of the UK's withdrawal from the EU and requisite loss of citizenship, is highly pertinent.[87] In terms of fundamental rights protection, the CJEU mentions that family life must be considered as part of the proportionality assessment. However, as expected, it is still in the context of limits to free movement and travel to and from an EU Member State to see family or work.[88]

Many may argue that the free movement analysis should not be criticised given that it has garnered mostly positive outcomes, especially rights for TCNs and acceptance of non-traditional families.[89] In *Tjebbes* this certainly proved true, and is considered a fair balance between Member State and EU interests.[90] In almost all the cases on TCNs discussed above, claimants were granted protection under EU citizenship despite adopting free movement analyses. Some have even suggested a precedent for the CJEU becoming more progressive in modern situations of family life. However, this chapter has sought to look beyond just the case outcomes to EU citizenship being a true legal gateway for fundamental rights, and what it perceives being a 'fundamental status' of EU citizenship to mean. While the positive outcomes are commendable, this chapter sought to look more closely at the CJEU rhetoric. It reveals issues such as those raised above as to a disproportionate effect on women and low-income families, and restrictive application of progressive decisions that undermine their original effectiveness. It no longer appears to be enough to simply exercise free movement, especially if other factors make your situation less 'desirable'. This promotes the image of undeserving EU citizens that should not be protected and undermines fundamental rights protection, but also the fundamental status of EU citizenship.

---

[84] Article 52 Charter. See Case C-617/10 *Fransson* EU:C:2013:105.
[85] Case C-221/17 *Tjebbes* EU:C:2019:189.
[86] Case C-135/08 *Rottmann* EU:C:2010:104.
[87] Martijn van den Brink, 'Bold, but Without Justification? *Tjebbes*' (2019) 4 European Papers 409.
[88] *Tjebbes*, paras 45–46.
[89] Floris De Witte, 'Freedom of Movement Needs to Be Defended as the Core of EU Citizenship' in Rainer Baubock (ed.), *Debating European Citizenship* (Springer 2019).
[90] Hanneke van Eijken, 'Tjebbes in Wonderland: On European Citizenship, Nationality and Fundamental Rights' (2019) 15 European Constitutional Law Review 714.

5. CONCLUSION

Free movement or fundamental rights? This was the question posed at the outset in the context of the future of EU citizenship status. The hope was that the answer would be fundamental rights, and that EU citizenship status would be the legal gateway to it. Free movement, an analysis adopted previously under a market-based citizenship, was how the CJEU originally approached cases under EU citizenship, rewarding citizens for economic activity. This was eventually replaced by a more citizen-centric approach through EU citizenship status supported by fundamental rights protection. This chapter argued that threads of fundamental rights protection have run throughout the EU citizenship discourse from the very beginning, which had been substantiated as EU citizenship also gained relevance. However, recent case law has shown that the CJEU has retreated to a free movement analysis in its case law, arguably as a response to criticism of post-*Ruiz Zambrano* liberation of the status of EU citizenship as an independent legal basis for rights from the cross-border test.

This chapter argued that the case law from the past five years has exemplified that free movement is dominant once again, and EU citizenship does not appear to be a legal gateway to fundamental rights protection. While the outcomes pay lip service to fundamental rights protection by way of favourable decisions that grant right to third-country national family members, looking more closely at the implications of the decision-making shows that structural inequalities are more embedded. This is because free movement promotes a very specific view of the ideal and deserving EU citizen, which has been exemplified in cases on rights under Directive 2004/38 particularly on benefits and protection against expulsion. This has a disproportionate impact on women, low-income families and individuals with a criminal conviction. This chapter argued that if EU citizenship status was a legal gateway to fundamental rights protection, it would relieve pressure on EU citizens added by a free movement analysis applied to EU citizenship status. However, despite the potential and the clear fundamental rights undertones to case law, the choice made so far is clear – free movement still dominates.

11. EU citizenship and family reunification: the evolving concept of a European Union territory

Hester Kroeze

1. INTRODUCTION

Family reunification in the EU covers all situations in which a person who does not enjoy lawful residence in the European Union (hereafter: a third-country national) obtains a residence right under EU law to join a family member who is an EU citizen or a lawful resident of one of the Member States. The principle is always the same: someone from outside the EU enters a Member State for the purpose of family reunification. The applicable rules, however, vary strongly according to the legal status of the family member who already resides in the European Union and sponsors the application.[1] A crucial circumstance is whether the family member who sponsors the application is an EU citizen or a third-country national. Family reunification between *two third-country nationals* is governed by European migration law.[2] Directive 2003/86 on family reunification[3] between two third-country nationals is the most important legislative instrument in this field, although some third-country nationals may benefit from more lenient rules as well. Decision 1/80 which applies to Turkish nationals residing in the European Union, for instance, provides them with more favourable family reunification rights than other third-country nationals legally residing in the EU.[4] Family reunification between *EU citizens and third-country nationals* is part of European constitutional law. The acknowledgement of family reunification rights to EU citizens is connected to the establishment of the internal market and intended to stimulate free movement of persons. In the early years of European integration these free movement rights were only granted to economically active Member State nationals (now EU citizens), who would be less inclined to exercise these rights if they were forced to leave their families behind in their home Member State. The acknowledgement of family reunification rights should facilitate their mobility and therewith contribute to the establishment of the European internal market and economic

---

[1] Cathryn Costello, *The Human Rights of Migrants in European Law* (OUP 2016) 103; Daniel Thym, 'Family as Link: Explaining the Judicial Change of Direction on Residence Rights of Family Members from Third States' in Herwig Verschueren (ed.), *Residence, Employment and Social Rights of Mobile Persons: On How EU Law Defines Where They Belong* (Intersentia 2016) 11, 12.

[2] The European Union first obtained the competence to issue legislation in the field of European migration law at the entry into force of the Amsterdam Treaty in 1999.

[3] Directive 2003/86/EC of 22 September 2003 on the right to family reunification [2003] OJ L 251/12.

[4] Anne Staver, 'Free Movement and the Fragmentation of Family Reunification Rights' (2013) 15(1) European Journal of Migration and Law 69; Stanislas Adam and Peter Van Elsuwege, 'Citizenship Rights and the Federal Balance between the European Union and Its Member States: Comment on Dereci' (2012) 37(2) EL Rev 176; Kees Groenendijk, 'Family Reunification as a Right under Community Law' (2006) 8(2) European Journal of Migration and Law 215.

prosperity among the Member States.⁵ This chapter focuses on this type of family reunification between EU citizens and their third-country national family members and disregards family reunification between two third-country nationals.

The interconnectedness between family reunification and the internal market implies that any obstacle to family reunification that hinders the exercise of free movement rights should be abolished.⁶ This principle allows for a broad interpretation of family reunification rights under EU law, but also conditions the right to family reunification. If there is no exercise of free movement rights, there can be no right to family reunification, which excludes EU citizens who remain in their home Member State as beneficiaries of the EU rules on family reunification. Their legal position is governed by national law. The Member State has discretion to determine the requirements for family reunification that apply under national law.⁷ This chapter demonstrates how the Court of Justice (hereafter: the Court) interprets the scope of family reunification under EU law in a broad manner, which diminishes Member States' competence to regulate family reunification of their nationals. The Court's interventions are nevertheless justified: first, because through its case-law, the Court remediates a mismatch between the purpose of art. 21 TFEU⁸ to facilitate free movement of persons, and the applicable criterion to come within the scope of EU law. Second, the development in the scope of family reunification under EU law can be understood in the light of an ongoing paradigm shift, in which the EU citizen's right to reside on the territory of the European Union as a whole is increasingly important.

Section 2 of this chapter explains the European constitutional context in which family reunification rights for EU citizens are positioned. Section 3 discusses the active personal scope of family reunification, and distinguishes three situations in which an EU citizen can rely on EU law for the purpose of family reunification: cross-border situations, post-cross-border situations, and non-cross-border situations. Section 4 discusses the passive personal scope of family reunification, which concerns the definition of family members of EU citizens who are eligible for family reunification, once EU law is applicable. The fifth and final section reflects on the evolving concept of a European Union territory and its influence on the Court's case-law on the active and the passive personal scope of the right to family reunification under EU law.

---

[5] Chiara Berneri, *Family Reunification in the EU: The Movement and Residence Rights of Third Country National Family Members of EU Citizens* (Bloomsbury Publishing 2017) 27; Elspeth Guild, Steve Peers and Jonathan Tomkin, *The EU Citizenship Directive: A Commentary* (2nd edn, OUP 2019) 56; Catherine Barnard, *The Substantive Law of the EU: The Four Freedoms* (6th edn, OUP 2019) 29; Pieter Boeles, Maarten Den Heijer, Gerrie G. Lodder and Cornelis Wolfram Wouters, *European Migration Law* (2nd edn, Intersentia 2014).

[6] E.g. Case C-370/90 *Surinder Singh* EU:C:1992:296, [1992] ECR I-04265, paras 19–20; Case C-413/99 *Baumbast and R.* EU:C:2002:493, [2002] ECR I-07091, para 52; Case C-127/08 *Metock* EU:C:2008:449, [2008] ECR I-06241, para 68; Thym (n 1) 18–19.

[7] Arts 4(1) and 5(1–2) of the Consolidated Version of the Treaty on European Union [2012] OJ C 326/13 (TEU).

[8] Consolidated Version of the Treaty on the Functioning of the European Union [2012] OJ C 326/47 (TFEU).

2. THE CONFLICT OF COMPETENCES

An important catalyst for the Court's case-law on the right to family reunification between EU citizens and third-country national family members under EU law is the earlier mentioned distinction in legal position between EU citizens who exercise their free movement rights, and those who stay in the Member State of which they are a national. The distinction in itself is due to the division of competences between the EU and the Member States. The European Union is only competent to regulate in areas that have been attributed to it on the basis of the principle of conferral.[9] In the context of establishing the internal market, this competence only extended to issues that would benefit the internal market. Therefore the European Union could only regulate the right to family reunification where it facilitated movement between the Member States, leaving so-called purely internal situations untouched.[10] The coexistence of the two regimes allows for the emergence of reverse discrimination, which occurs when EU law provides more lenient conditions for family reunification than national law.[11] The discrepancy urges EU citizens who cannot fulfil the requirements for family reunification under national law to search for alternative routes that allow them to benefit from the profitable rules of EU law, and dispute the applicability of national law before the Court of Justice. This litigation has led to an extensive body of case-law. This case-law exposes a gap between the purpose of EU law to ensure the effectiveness of free movement rights, and the choice of criteria that secondary legislation uses to confer residence rights to family members of EU citizens. Art. 3 of Directive 2004/38[12] reads that the Directive applies 'to all Union citizens who move to or reside in a Member State other than that of which they are a national'. Art. 21 TFEU, which is the Directive's legal basis, on the other hand, protects the exercise of free movement rights, regardless of nationality. In light of this principle, the Court grants family reunification rights to EU citizens who reside in a Member State of which they are a national when they can

---

[9] Arts 4(1) and 5(1–2) TEU; Peter Van Elsuwege, 'The Phenomenon of Reverse Discrimination: An Anomaly in the European Constitutional Order?' in Lucia Serena Rossi and Federico Casolari (eds), *The EU after Lisbon: Amending or Coping with the Existing Treaties?* (Springer 2014) 161.

[10] E.g. Case 115/78 *Knoors* EU:C:1979:31, [1979] ECR 399, para. 24; Cases 35/82 and 36/82 *Morson and Jhanjan* EU:C:1982:368, [1982] ECR 3723, para. 18; Cases C-64/96 and C-65/96 *Uecker and Jacquet v Nordrhein Westfalen* EU:C:1997:285, [1997] ECR I-03171, para. 16; Berneri (n 5) 27; Niamh Nic Shuibhne, 'Free Movement of Persons and the Wholly Internal Rule: Time to Move On' (2002) 39 CML Rev 731; Siofra O'Leary, 'The Past, Present and Future of the Purely Internal Rule in EU Law' (2009) 13 *Irish Jurist* 1966; Alina Tryfonidou, 'Reverse Discrimination in Purely Internal Situations: An Incongruity in a Citizens' Europe' (2008) 35(1) Legal Issue of Economic Integration 43.

[11] Reverse discrimination is the situation in which citizens of a Member State enjoy fewer rights, or a weaker legal position, than EU citizens who have moved to that Member State. Adam and Van Elsuwege (n 4); Van Elsuwege (n 9); Alina Tryfonidou, *Reverse Discrimination in EC Law* (Vol. 64. Kluwer Law International BV 2009); Dominik Hanf, '"Reverse Discrimination" in EU Law: Constitutional Aberration, Constitutional Necessity, or Judicial Choice?' (2011) 18(1–2) Maastricht Journal of European and Comparative Law 29; Valérie Verbist, 'Reverse Discrimination In The European Union: A Recurring Balancing Act' (Doctoral Thesis KU Leuven 2016); Hester Kroeze, 'Distinguishing Between Use and Abuse of EU Free Movement Law: Evaluating Use of the "Europe-route" for Family Reunification to Overcome Reverse Discrimination' (2018) 3(3) EP 1209, 1216.

[12] Directive 2004/38/EC of 29 April 2004 on the right of citizens of the Union and their family members to move and reside freely within the territory of the Member States amending regulation (EEC) No 1612/68 and repealing Directives 64/221/EEC, 68/360/EEC, 72/194/EEC, 73/148/EEC, 75/34/EEC, 75/35/EEC, 90/364/EEC, 90/365/EEC and 93/96/EEC [2004] OJ L 158/77.

demonstrate movement prior to residence in their home Member State, directly on the basis of art. 21 TFEU.[13] This contribution qualifies these situations as 'post cross-border situations',[14] which exist in addition to the traditional 'cross-border situations'.[15]

On top of 'cross-border situations' and 'post-cross-border situations', this chapter discusses 'non-cross-border situations'. Non-cross-border situations lack a connection with free movement rights. The applicant in such a situation always resided in the Member State of which he is a national, without crossing a border between Member States at any time. In those situations, family reunification rights cannot be derived from art. 21 TFEU, because the acknowledgement of these rights does not benefit the exercise of free movement rights. In *Ruiz Zambrano*, however, the Court of Justice recognized art. 20 TFEU as an additional ground for family reunification if the refusal of a residence right to a family member of an EU citizen would deprive that EU citizen of the genuine enjoyment of the substance of the rights that are attached to being an EU citizen, in particular the right to reside on the territory of the European Union as a whole.[16] The judgment has considerable impact on the Member States' competence to determine the requirements for family reunification for nationals who did not exercise their free movement rights, because a refusal of a residence right that might deprive an EU citizen of his citizenship rights is now subject to EU law review. From the perspective of the division of competences, *Ruiz Zambrano* was therefore more controversial than the Court's decisions in post-cross-border situations,[17] but can nevertheless be understood – through the development of the concept of a European Union territory.[18]

---

[13] See art. 3 of Directive 2004/38 (n 12).
[14] *Surinder Singh* (n 6); Case C-456/12 *O. and B.* EU:C:2014:135; Case C-165/16 *Lounes* EU:C: 2017:862.
[15] Case C-60/00 *Carpenter* EU:C:2002:434, [2002] ECR I-06279; *Baumbast and R.* (n 6); Case C-200/02 *Zhu and Chen* EU:C:2004:639, [2004] ECR I-09925.
[16] Case C-34/09 *Ruiz Zambrano* EU:C:2011:124, [2011] ECR I-01177; Case C-434/09 *Shirley McCarthy* EU:C:2011:277, [2011] ECR I-03375; Case C-256/11 *Dereci* EU:C:2011:734, [2011] I-11315; Case C-356/11 *O. S. and L.* EU:C:2012:776; C-86/12 *Alokpa and Moudoulou* EU:C:2013: 645; Case C-165/14 *Rendón Marín* EU:C:2016:675; Case C-304/14 *CS* EU:C:2016:674; Case C-133/15 *Chavez-Vilchez* EU:C:2017:354; Case C-82/16 *K.A.* EU:C:2018:308; Case C-836/18 *Ciudad Real v RH* EU:C:2020:119.
[17] E.g. Kay Hailbronner and Daniel Thym, 'Case C-34/09, Gerardo Ruiz Zambrano v. Office national de l'emploi (ONEm), Judgment of the Court of Justice (Grand Chamber) of 8 March 2011' (2011) 48 CML Rev 1253; Peter Van Elsuwege, 'Shifting the Boundaries: European Union Citizenship and the Scope of Application of EU Law – Case No. C-34/09, Gerardo Ruiz Zambrano v. Office National de l'Emploi' (2011) 38 Legal Issues of Economic Integration 263; Hanneke Van Eijken and Sybe De Vries, 'A New Route into the Promised Land? Being a European Citizen after Ruiz Zambrano' (2011) 5 EL Rev 704; Dimitry Kochenov, 'A Real European Citizenship: A New Jurisdiction Test – A Novel Chapter in the Development of the Union in Europe' (2011) 18 Columbia Journal of European Law 55; Niamh Nic Shuibhne, '(Some of) the Kids are Alright: Comment on McCarthy and Dereci' (2012) 49 CML Rev 349; Martijn van den Brink, 'EU Citizenship and EU Fundamental Rights: Taking EU Citizenship Rights Seriously' (2012) 39 Legal Issues of Economic Integration 273.
[18] See section 5 of this chapter.

3. SITUATIONS IN WHICH EU CITIZENS FALL WITHIN THE SCOPE OF EU LAW

The scope of family reunification between EU citizens and third-country nationals under EU law has two dimensions. This section discusses the active personal scope, which determines whether an EU citizen can rely on EU law for the purpose of family reunification. Section 4 focuses on the passive personal scope of family reunification, which determines which family members of EU citizens are eligible for family reunification, once the EU citizen falls within the reach of EU law.

3.1 Cross-border Situations

Directive 2004/38 on the right to free movement of European citizens and their family members is the main legal framework for family reunification between EU citizens and their family members in the European Union. Art. 3 of the Directive reads that it applies to European citizens who 'move to or reside in' a Member State of which they are not a national and to their family members, but this criterion is not entirely clear. Is it sufficient to *either* 'move to' *or* 'reside in' another Member State? Or might it be that 'moving to' and 'residing in' are cumulative criteria?[19]

The purpose of Directive 2004/38 to facilitate movement between Member States and the provisions that follow up on its art. 3 indicate that, at the very least, EU citizens who *both* move to *and* reside in another Member State benefit from family reunification rights derived from the Directive. Art. 5 of Directive 2004/38 provides EU citizens with a right to exit their home Member State, art. 6 entitles them entry into another Member State for a period of up to three months and art. 7 sets the conditions under which they can reside in the Member State they entered on the basis of art. 6 for a period of more than three months. Moving to and residing in another Member State are thus logical steps in the systemic design of Directive 2004/38, which establishes an entitlement to family reunification in the Member State of destination. The Court itself confirms in *Carpenter* that '[i]t follows both from the objective of the Directive and the wording [...] that it applies to cases where nationals of Member States leave their Member State of origin and move to another Member State in order to establish themselves there'.[20]

It is less clear whether an EU citizen who *did not move* between Member States, but nevertheless *resides* in a Member State of which he is not a national, benefits from family reunification rights derived from Directive 2004/38. This situation occurs when an EU citizen is born in a Member State of which he is not a national. It follows from the Court's ruling in *Zhu and Chen* that this situation also falls within the scope of Directive 2004/38.[21] Chen was a Chinese national who gave birth to her baby Zhu in Northern Ireland, through which Zhu obtained Irish nationality. Northern Ireland is part of the jurisdiction of the United Kingdom,

---

[19] *Ruiz Zambrano* (n 16), Opinion of AG Sharpston EU:C:2010:560, para 86.

[20] *Carpenter* (n 15), paras 32–33, quote from para 32, see infra. The directive referred to is Directive 73/148 on the abolition of restrictions on movement and residence within the Community for nationals of Member States with regard to establishment and the provision of services [1973] OJ L 172/14, which is one of the predecessors of Directive 2004/38.

[21] *Zhu and Chen* (n 15).

so Zhu was born an Irish citizen in a Member State of which she was not a national – the United Kingdom – without ever moving between Member States. The Court of Justice ruled that mother Chen could derive a residence right from the predecessor of Directive 2004/38,[22] even if there hadn't been movement prior to residence of an EU citizen in a Member State of which she was not a national, provided that baby Zhu complied with the criteria for residence in the United Kingdom set by Directive 2004/38.[23]

What happens when an EU citizen *moves* to another Member State, *without residing* there? This happens, for instance, when frontier workers reside in their own Member State, but move daily to another Member State to work there. This case differs from the situation in which there is residence in another Member State without prior movement, because residence in the Member State of which someone is a national is unconditional and thus *cannot* be regulated by EU law.[24] In *Carpenter*, the Court of Justice held that family members of an EU citizen can only derive a residence right when they accompany the EU citizen in the exercise of their Treaty rights 'by moving to or residing in a Member State other than their Member State of origin'.[25] The Directive does not govern residence rights of family members of an EU citizen in his Member State of origin, where frontier workers reside.[26] Frontier workers do, however, exercise their Treaty freedoms under art. 45 TFEU (workers) or art. 56 TFEU (services),[27] so their family members derive a residence right from primary EU law, unless a refusal of that right is justified and proportional.[28] The outcome of *Carpenter* and *S. and G.* in part reconciles the mismatch between the purpose of Directive 2004/38 to facilitate free movement, and the applicable criterion to come within its scope.

3.2   Post-cross-border Situations

The mismatch between the purpose of Directive 2004/38 to facilitate free movement and the nationality criterion that applies in order to fall within the Directive's scope is also the reason for the case-law on the 'post-cross-border situation'. Post-cross-border situations occur when an EU citizen exercises free movement rights and finds himself in a Member State of which

---

[22]   Directive 90/364 of 28 June 1990 on the right of residence [1990] L 180/26.
[23]   *Zhu and Chen* (n 15); Thym (n 1) 21; Alina Tryfonidou, 'C-200/02, Kunquian Catherine Zhu and Man Lavette Chen v. Secretary of State for the Home Department: Further Cracks in the Great Wall of the European Union' (2005) 11 EPL 527; Jean-Yves Carlier, 'Case C-200/02, Kunqian Catherine Zhu, Man Lavette Chen v. Secretary of State for the Home Department, Judgment of the Court of Justice (Full Court) of 19 October 2004' (2005) 42 CML Rev 1121.
[24]   *Surinder Singh* (n 6), para 22; Case C-291/05 *Eind* EU:C:2007:771, [2007] ECR I-10719, para 31; *Shirley McCarthy* (n 16), paras 29, 50.
[25]   *Carpenter* (n 15), para 34.
[26]   *Carpenter* (n 15), para 36; Case C-457/12 *S. and G.* EU:C:2014:136, para 34.
[27]   *Carpenter* (n 15), para 37; *S. and G.* (n 26), para 39.
[28]   *Carpenter* (n 15), paras 38–45; *S. and G* (n 26), paras 40–41; Helen Toner, 'Comments on Mary Carpenter v. Secretary of State, 11 July 2002 (Case C-60/00)' (2003) 5 European Journal of Migration Law 163; Eleanor Spaventa, 'From Gebhard to Carpenter: Towards a (Non-)economic European Constitution' (2004) 41 CMLR 743; Eleanor Spaventa, 'Family Rights for Circular Migrants and Frontier Workers, Annotation on O and B (C-456/12) and S and G (Case C-457/12)' (2015) 52 CMLR 753; Sarah Schoenmaekers and Alexander Hoogenboom, 'Singh and Carpenter Revisited: Some Progress but No Final Clarity (C-456/12+ C-457/12)' (2014) 21(3) Maastricht Journal of European and Comparative Law 464; Nathan Cambien, 'Cases C-456/12 O. and B. and C-457/12 S. and G.: Clarifying the Inter-state Requirement for EU Citizens?' [2014] European Law Blog.

he is not a national, followed by a change in his situation as a result of which he is (again) a national of the Member State where he resides. The clearest example is when an EU citizen moves to another Member State and then returns to his home Member State. This is called a 'return situation'.[29] Another example is when an EU citizen moves to another Member State and obtains the nationality of the host Member State.[30] In both situations the EU citizen finds himself in a Member State of which he is a national, where – as *Carpenter* and *S. and G.* made clear – in principle he cannot benefit from EU law family reunification rights.[31] In both cases, however, the EU citizen did exercise his free movement rights prior to residence in a Member State of which he is a national. The Court ruled that even though Directive 2004/38 does not apply, the prospect of losing family members' residence rights obtained in the host Member State might hinder the EU citizen's exercise of his free movement rights under art. 21 TFEU in the first place.[32] So to ensure the effectiveness of art. 21 TFEU, the EU citizens' family members could derive a residence right *post* movement as well, directly on the basis of art. 21 TFEU.[33] EU law continues to be applicable where previously Member States applied their national laws on family reunification. The case-law on post cross-border situations thus strongly impacts Member State competence to set the requirements for family reunification for their own nationals.

The return situation and naturalization in the host Member State resemble each other to the extent that both situations change a cross-border situation into a seemingly internal situation. In other words, although the EU citizen exercises free movement rights and temporarily resides in a Member State of which he is not a national, he (again) finds himself in a Member State of which he is a national. In both cases, the Court acknowledges the earlier exercise of free movement rights and ensures continued applicability of EU law and the retention of family reunification rights. Both situations are thus qualified as *post*-cross-border, because an EU citizen residing in his own Member State falls within the scope of EU law *after* movement between Member States has taken place. There is, however, an important distinction between return and naturalization. For the return situation, the Court of Justice ruled that residence rights can only be retained upon return to the home Member State if the EU citizen and his family member demonstrate that they created or strengthened their family life during their

---

[29] *Surinder Singh* (n 6); Case C-109/01 *Akrich* EU:C:2003:491, (2003) ECR I-09607; *Eind* (n 24); *Metock* (n 6); *O. and B.* (n 14); Case C-673/16 *Coman* EU:C:2018:385; Case C-89/17 *Rozanne Banger* EU:C:2018:570; Case C-230/17 *Altiner and Ravn* EU:C:2018:497; Thym (n 1) 23–5; Spaventa 2015 (n 28); Kroeze (n 11); Schoenmakers and Hoogenboom (n 28); Cambien (n 28); Elaine Fahey, 'Going Back to Basics: Re-embracing the Fundamental of the Free Movement of Persons in Metock' [2009] 36 Legal Issues of Economic Integration 83.

[30] *Lounes* (n 14); Elena Gualco, 'Is Toufik Lounes Another Brick in the Wall? The CJEU and the On-going Shaping of the EU Citizenship' (2018) 3(2) EP 911; David De Groot, 'Free Movement of Dual EU Citizens' (2018) 3(3) EP 1075; Hester Kroeze, '*Toufik Lounes* – De relatie tussen (dubbele) nationaliteit en EU burgerschapsrechten' (2018) 5 *SEW* 225.

[31] *Carpenter* (n 15), para 36; *S. and G.* (n 26), para 34.

[32] *Surinder Singh* (n 6); *Akrich* (n 29); *Eind* (n 29); *Metock* (n 6); *O. and B.* (n 14); *Coman* (n 29); *Rozanne Banger* (n 27); *Altiner and Ravn* (n 24); *Lounes* (n 14). The Court's reasoning in *Lounes* was slightly different and predominantly focused on the fact that becoming a national of the host Member State is an act of integration, which is one of the purposes of EU free movement law. It would be counterintuitive to 'punish' integration with a loss of rights. Therefore Mrs Ormazabal could still derive a residence right for her spouse from EU law, even after she became a British citizen.

[33] Directive 2004/38 applies by analogy.

residence in the host Member State.³⁴ In the case about naturalization, on the other hand, the EU citizen – Mrs Ormazabal – and her husband – Mr Lounes – only met after she obtained the nationality of the host Member State – the United Kingdom. As a result, not only can existing residence rights be retained, but new family reunification rights can be derived from EU law as well.³⁵

3.3 Non-cross-border Situations

The scope of family reunification under EU law was further extended by the *Ruiz Zambrano* line of case-law.³⁶ Ruiz Zambrano was a Colombian national who lived and worked in Belgium without a residence right. Two of his three children obtained Belgian nationality, because otherwise their father's (intentional) failure to register them at the Colombian embassy would have left the children stateless. The Court of Justice ruled that Ruiz Zambrano could derive a residence right from art. 20 TFEU, because the refusal of a residence right would force his children to leave the territory of the European Union with their parents. This forced departure would deprive the children, who were European citizens,³⁷ from the genuine enjoyment of the substance of their EU citizenship rights, and this would run counter to the institution of European citizenship itself. The case lacked a link with the right to free movement, because the children resided in the Member State of which they were nationals, so Directive 2004/38 could not apply.³⁸ Nor had the children ever before exercised their free movement rights, so the Court's case-law on the direct applicability of art. 21 TFEU in post-cross-border situations did not apply either. *Ruiz Zambrano* thus brought a seemingly 'non-cross-border' or 'purely internal situation' within the scope of EU law. Similar to the case-law on post-cross-border situations, *Ruiz Zambrano* and subsequent case-law strongly impacted the competence of the Member States to issue rules on family reunification for their own nationals. Now even nationals who do not exercise their free movement rights at all may benefit from EU family reunification rights as well, if a refusal of this right would deprive the EU citizen of the genuine enjoyment of the substance of his EU citizenship rights.³⁹ 'The Court is taking legal possession of the territories of the Member States. Granting a residence right to a person not covered by art. 21 TFEU necessarily implies a loss of control by Member States over immigration flows, entry and access to their territory.'⁴⁰

Subsequent case-law sheds more light on the meaning of being deprived of the substance of EU citizenship.⁴¹ The Court of Justice has made clear that this deprivation only occurs in

---

[34] *O. and B.* (n 14); Kroeze (n 11).
[35] It is not clear why this distinction exists. For a discussion of different possibilities see Kroeze (n 30).
[36] *Ruiz Zambrano* (n 16); Thym (n 1) 25–8; Hailbronner and Thym (n 17); Van Elsuwege (n 17); Van Eijken and De Vries (n 17); Kochenov (n 17); Shuibhne (n 17); Van Den Brink (n 17).
[37] Art. 20 TFEU.
[38] *Carpenter* (n 15), para 36; *S. and G.* (n 24), para 24; *Ruiz Zambrano* (n 16), para 39.
[39] Hailbronner and Thym (n 17); Dora Kostakopoulou, 'When EU Citizens become Foreigners' (2014) 4 EJL 447, 449.
[40] Loïc Azoulai, 'Transfiguring European Citizenship: From Member State Territory to Union Territory' in Dimitry Kochenov (ed.), *EU Citizenship and Federalism: The Role of Rights* (CUP 2017) 178, 197.
[41] Hester Kroeze, 'The Substance of Rights: New Pieces of the Ruiz Zambrano Puzzle' (2019) 2 EL Rev 238.

exceptional circumstances[42] of legal, financial or emotional dependency[43] to such an extent that the departure of the third-country national would indeed force the EU citizen to leave with his family member.[44] For adults, such dependency is 'conceivable only in exceptional cases' because as a rule they are capable of living their lives independently. Deprivation of the substance of citizenship rights for adults as a result of expulsion of a family member is only possible when 'there could be no form of separation' between the EU citizen and the family member on whom he is dependent.[45]

For minor EU citizens, the question was raised whether the departure of a third-country national parent or family member would still deprive the EU citizen from the substance of his EU citizenship rights when there is another parent or family member with the nationality of a Member State who is able and willing to take care of the child. The Court of Justice ruled that this factor is indeed relevant, but not decisive to determine whether a relationship of dependency exists between the child and the third-country national family member that would entitle that family member to a residence right under art. 20 TFEU. This relationship should be assessed independently and take account of all the specific circumstances of the case, including the age of the child, the child's physical and emotional development, the extent of his emotional ties both to the EU citizen parent and to the third-country national parent, and the risks which separation from the latter might entail for the child's equilibrium.[46] Furthermore, it was determined that residence rights derived from art. 20 TFEU are not absolute and can be limited in the interest of public order or public security in a similar way as rights derived from art. 21 TFEU or Directive 2004/38 can be limited.[47]

4. FAMILY MEMBERS ELIGIBLE FOR FAMILY REUNIFICATION ON THE BASIS OF EU LAW

The previous section discussed the active personal scope of family reunification under EU law, which determines whether an EU citizen who seeks family reunification with his family members can rely on EU law. This section focuses on the passive personal scope of family reunification under EU law, which determines which family members of EU citizens are eligible for a residence right, once EU law is applicable.

---

[42] *Dereci* (n 16).
[43] *O. S. and L.* (n 16).
[44] *Chavez-Vilchez* (n 16).
[45] *K.A.* (n 16) para. 65; *Ciudad Real v RH* (n 16) para 56; Kroeze (n 41).
[46] *Chavez-Vilchez* (n 16) paras 69–71; Hester Kroeze, '*Chavez-Vilchez v. SVB Nederland* – The Child's Interest becomes the Central Element in the Ruiz Zambrano Genuine Enjoyment Test' in Aniel Pahladsingh and Ramona Grimbergen (eds), *The Charter and the Court of Justice of the European Union: Notable Cases from 2016–2018* (WLP 2019) 137; Hanneke Van Eijken and Pauline Phoa, 'The Scope of Article 20 TFEU Clarified in Chavez-Vilchez: Are the Fundamental Rights of Minor EU Citizens Coming of Age?' (2018) 6 EL Rev 949.
[47] *Rendón Marín* (n 16); *CS* (n 16); *K.A.* (n 16); arts 27–28 Directive 2004/38; Päivi Johanna Neuvonen, 'EU Citizenship and Its "Very Specific" Essence: Rendón Marín and CS' (2017) 54 CML Rev 1201; Hester Kroeze, 'Rendón Marín and CS: A Reflection on Proportionality and Fundamental Rights in EU Citizenship Law' in Pahladsingh and Grimbergen (n 46) 161.

4.1 Family Members Eligible for Family Reunification under Article 21 TFEU

In cross-border situations, art. 2(2) of Directive 2004/38 defines which family members of EU citizens are automatically entitled to derive a residence right in the host Member State. These family members include the spouse or registered partner, the children of both partners under the age of 21, and older children and the parents of both partners who are dependent on the EU citizen.[48] Art. 3(2)(a) of Directive 2004/38 allows for family reunification with other family members as well if they are part of the household of the EU citizen, financially dependent or in need of medical care. The unmarried and unregistered partner of an EU citizen with whom he enjoys a durable relationship is eligible for family reunification on the basis of art. 3(2)(b) of Directive 2004/38.[49] In post-cross-border situations Directive 2004/38 applies by analogy,[50] so the definition of family members who are eligible for family reunification is the same.

Arts 2(2) and 3(2) of Directive 2004/38 define which family members of EU citizens are entitled to a residence right derived from EU law, but do not specify substantive criteria to be qualified as a family member. Spouses, for instance, are eligible for family reunification, but Directive 2004/38 fails to mention whether the conclusion of the marriage should meet specific criteria, such as being a state marriage rather than a religious marriage, or an opposite-sex rather than a same-sex marriage. Defining the criteria under which a relationship between an EU citizen and a third-country national qualifies as a family member within the meaning of Directive 2004/38 is regulated by national family law. The recognition of family relationships that were established in a different Member State or outside of the European Union is regulated by the Member States' national rules of private international law.[51] In recent case-law, however, the Court of Justice has set foot on the terrain of posing minimum conditions to the recognition of family relationships, for the purpose of deriving a residence right as a family member of an EU citizen under EU law.

The first question dealt with by the Court of Justice is whether the relationships that are protected by EU law also include same-sex relationships. The applicable legislation does not define the concepts of spouse, marriage or relationship, so the literal text allows for a broad interpretation and acknowledgement of EU family reunification rights to spouses and (registered) partners of all genders. In 2001 the Court found in *D. v Sweden* that there was insufficient consensus about same-sex relationships among the Member States to include them within the protection of EU law.[52] In 2018 in *Coman*, the Court took a different approach.[53]

---

[48] Case C-1/05 *Jia* EU:C:2007:1, [2007] ECR I-00001; Case C-423/12 *Reyes* EU:C:2014:16.
[49] Case C-83/11 *Rahman* EU:C:2012:519; *Banger* (n 27); Family members in art. 2(2) of Directive 2004/38 benefit from an automatic conferral of derived residence right, directly on the basis of the directive. Residence rights derived from art. 3(2) of Directive 2004/38 are subject to the discretion of the Member States to assess the situation and decide whether or not a residence right is awarded on the basis of the merits of the case, but should be facilitated within the normal meaning of the concept of 'facilitation'.
[50] E.g. *Eind* (n 24), para 39; *O. and B.* (n 14), para 50; *Coman* (n 29), para 25.
[51] Barbara Stark, *International Family Law: An Introduction* (Routledge 2017) 1–3; Maria Rosaria Marella, 'The Non-subversive Function of European Private Law: The Case of Harmonisation of Family Law' (2006) 12(1) European Law Journal 78, 78–9; Ann Laquer Estin, 'Families and Children in International Law: An Introduction' (2002) 12(2) Transnational Law & Contemporary Problems 271, 271–3.
[52] Case C-122/99 *D. and Sweden v. Council* EU:C:2001:304, [2001] ECR I-04319.
[53] *Coman* (n 29).

The Court of Justice concluded that consensus in the Member States had developed in such a way that same-sex relationships are now also protected by European Union law and same-sex partners are equally entitled to rights derived from EU law as opposite-sex partners.[54] The fact that a Member State – in this case Romania – has a constitutional prohibition on same-sex marriage in place does not stand in the way of the acknowledgement of rights derived from EU law, because the obligation to recognize same-sex relationships is only due where EU rights are at stake. The Court does not oblige Member States to introduce same-sex marriage in their national legislation, but introduces a functional recognition of same-sex marriage for the application of rights derived from EU law only.[55]

The Court substantiated its decision with a reference to the case-law of the European Court of Human Rights (ECtHR) on the right to enjoy family life that is protected by art. 8 of the European Convention on Human Rights (ECHR). The case-law of the ECtHR includes same-sex relationship within the protection of art. 8 ECHR, and imposes the obligation to instal a form of legal recognition for same-sex relationships.[56] Pursuant to art. 52(3) of the EU Charter of Fundamental Rights, art. 7 of the Charter, which protects the right to enjoy family life, should offer the same protection as art. 8 ECHR. If same-sex relationships are protected by the ECHR, the European Union is obliged to offer the same protection, provided that the situation falls within the scope of EU law.[57]

The second relevant case of the Court of Justice for the definition of family members eligible for family reunification under art. 21 TFEU and Directive 2004/38 sheds light on the definition of the parent–child relationship, and the definition of family members for whom access and residence should be facilitated under art. 3(2)(a) of Directive 2004/38. *SM* concerns the request for family reunification between an Algerian child placed under *kafala* and its legal guardians, French citizens residing in the United Kingdom.[58] *Kafala* is an Islamic type of foster care which must be distinguished from adoption, because, differently from adoption, *kafala* does not establish kinship.[59] The Court of Justice therefore held that a child placed under *kafala* cannot be considered to be a direct descendent of its legal guardians within the meaning of art. 2(2c) of Directive 2004/38, which otherwise would have given the child an

---

[54] *Coman* (n 29).

[55] Laura Gyeney, 'Same Sex Couples' Right to Free Movement in Light of Member States' National Identities: The Legal Analysis of the Coman Case' (2018) 14 *Iustum Aequum Salutare* 149; Václav Stehlík, 'The CJEU Crossing the Rubicon on the Same-Sex Marriages? Commentary on Coman Case' (2018) 18(2) ICLR 85; Alina Tryfonidou, 'The ECJ Recognises the Right of Same-Sex Spouses to Move Freely Between EU Member States: The Coman Ruling' (2019) 5 EL Rev 663; Dimitry Kochenov and Uladzislau Belavusau, 'Same-Sex Spouses: More Free Movement, but What about Marriage? Coman: Case C-673/16' (2020) 57 CML Rev 227; Barbara Safradin and Hester Kroeze, 'Een overwinning voor vrij verkeersrechten van regenboogfamilies in Europa: het langverwachte Coman arrest' (2019) 1–2 NtEr 51.

[56] *Orlandi and others v Italy* App nos. 26431/12, 26742/12, 44057/12 and 60088/12 (ECtHR 14 December 2017).

[57] *Coman* (n 29). Coman exercised his free movement rights by moving from Romania to Belgium and back, so he found himself in a post-cross-border situation. The acknowledgment of family reunification rights should therefore take account of art. 7 Charter, which protects heterosexual and same-sex couples alike.

[58] Case C-129/18 *SM* EU:C:2019:248.

[59] *SM* (n 58), para 45; Julie Malingreau, 'International Kafala: Right for the Child to Enter and Stay in the EU Member States' (2014) 16(2) European Journal of Law Reform 401.

automatic right to family reunification under EU law. The child can, however, derive a residence right in the capacity of 'other family member' for whom entry to and residence in the Member States should be facilitated on the basis of art. 3(2)(a) of Directive 2004/38.[60] As in *Coman*, the Court substantiated its decision in *SM* by referencing the case-law of the ECtHR which includes children placed under *kafala* within the protection of art. 8 ECHR. The earlier explained EU obligation in art. 52(3) Charter as a result of which the Charter must offer the same minimum protection as the ECHR implies that ECtHR protection of children placed under *kafala* poses an obligation on the European Union to also protect them. In the context of family reunification rights under EU law, this protection may extend to confer a derived residence right to such a child. To determine whether a residence right must be acknowledged, the national authorities of the host Member State of the EU citizen legal guardian(s) should take account of all the relevant circumstances of the case.[61]

Considering the importance of the ECtHR case-law in the reasoning of the Court of Justice, it may be concluded that the definition of family members of EU citizens who are eligible for family reunification under EU law is increasingly shaped by the protection of the family under the ECHR. If the relationship between an EU citizen who falls within the scope of EU law by exercising free movement rights and a third-country national is protected by art. 8 ECHR, EU law confers a residence right on that family member on the basis of art. 2(2) or 3(2) of Directive 2004/38 or the analogous application thereof.

4.2 Family Members Eligible for Family Reunification under Article 20 TFEU

In contrast to family reunification on the basis of art. 21 TFEU and Directive 2004/38, there is no legal framework that defines which family members are eligible for family reunification on the basis of art. 20 TFEU.[62] Furthermore, the distinction between determining whether the EU citizen falls within the scope of this provision and whether a family member is eligible for family reunification on the basis of art. 20 TFEU is less clear than for family reunification on the basis of art. 21 TFEU. Section three explained that reliance on art. 20 TFEU for family reunification does not require cross-border movement, so potentially all EU citizens fall within its scope. Whether or not art. 20 TFEU applies is dependent on the question whether the EU citizen is able to live his or her life independently and separate from his or her family member(s). Only family members on whom the EU citizen is dependent are eligible for family reunification on the basis of art. 20 TFEU, and it is this relationship of dependency that brings the EU citizen within the scope of EU law. Consequently, whereas the applicability of art. 21 TFEU could in theory authorize family reunification with the whole family, art. 20 TFEU only grants a residence right to the person on whom the EU citizen is dependent. The relationship between the EU citizen and the person on whom he is dependent is not defined. Principally, the parent(s) or primary carer of a minor EU citizen can derive a residence right from art. 20 TFEU

---

[60] *SM* (n 58).
[61] *SM* (n 58), para 69; Francesca Strumia, 'The Family in EU Law after the SM Ruling: Variable Geometry and Conditional Deference' (2019) 4(1) EP 389; Katarzyna Woch, 'Gloss to the Judgement of the Court of Justice of the European Union in Case C 129/18, SM versus Entry Clearance Officer, UK Visa Section' (2020) 40 Review of European and Comparative Law 189; Sarah Den Haese and Hester Kroeze, 'The "Right" of a Child Placed under Kafala Care to Reside within the EU with his Guardian (s): The Emergence of a European Family Law?' (2020) 1 *Tijdschrift@ipr.be* 74.
[62] Kroeze (n 41).

if consideration of the facts along the lines of *Chavez-Vilchez* requires so.[63] At the same time, it is not evident that the person on whom an EU citizen is dependent should be a parent or even a family member by blood, as long as the departure of the third-country national care-taker would force the EU citizen to leave the territory of the European Union as well.[64]

5. TOWARDS A EUROPEAN UNION TERRITORY?

The case-law on the active as well as the passive personal scope of the right to family reunification between EU citizens and third-country nationals under EU law reveals a change in perspective in the Court's assessment of the existence of a right to family reunification. Until the Lisbon Treaty was adopted, the Court of Justice's reasoning for the acknowledgement of family reunification rights was to benefit the establishment of the internal market by abolishing any hindrances to the exercise of free movement rights. Since the Lisbon Treaty's entry into force this approach has been shifting towards a more principled protection of European citizens and their right to reside on the territory of the European Union as a whole.[65] The clearest example of this development can be found in *Ruiz Zambrano*, where the Court found an additional ground for family reunification in art. 20 TFEU that is meant to avoid an EU citizen being forced to leave the territory of the Union.[66] *Dereci* complements that phrase with the additive 'as a whole'.[67] If an EU citizen were forced to leave the territory of the European Union as a whole, this would deprive him of the genuine enjoyment of the substance of his citizenship rights.

SM concerns the definition of an EU citizen's family members who are eligible for family reunification and mirrors *Ruiz Zambrano* on the part of the importance of the right to reside on European territory. The Court rules that if the child placed under *kafala* and its legal guardians 'are called to lead a genuine family life and that child is dependent on its guardians', the child should be granted a residence right in the host Member State of its legal guardians.[68] 'This applies a fortiori where [...] those guardians are in fact prevented from living together in that Member State because one of them is required to remain, with the child, in that child's third country of origin in order to care for the child.'[69] 'Being forced to leave' the territory of the Union and 'being prevented from living' on the territory of the European Union seem to be two sides of the same coin – the coin being the right to reside on the territory of the European Union as a whole. The difference between *Ruiz Zambrano* and *SM* is that the legal guardians of *SM* exercised their free movement rights and fell within the scope of art. 21 TFEU rather than art. 20 TFEU. This difference should not give reason to ignore the resemblance in the Court's reasoning. In fact, the similarity is a reason to potentially generalize a change in the Court's perspective from a cross-border logic towards a European territory-oriented logic. In addition, the resemblance between the Court's reasoning in both cases may indicate that a third-country

---

[63] *Chavez-Vilchez* (n 16).
[64] *O. S. and L.* (n 16); Den Haese and Kroeze (n 61).
[65] Some authors (e.g. Azoulai, n 40) distinguish between a European territory and a territory of the Union. For the purpose of this chapter, the different expressions are used interchangeably.
[66] *Ruiz Zambrano* (n 16), para 44.
[67] *Dereci* (n 16), para 66.
[68] *SM* (n 56), para 71.
[69] *SM* (n 56), para 72.

national biological or foster child of an EU citizen may derive a residence right from art. 20 TFEU in the home Member State of that EU citizen as well. Otherwise, the parents who are EU citizens are prevented from living on the territory of the European Union, because they have to take care of their child outside of the EU.

Being able to reside on the territory of the European Union as a whole is thus a citizenship right which EU citizens may in principle not be deprived of, except when public order or public safety are at stake.[70] This right must be distinguished from the right to free movement in art. 21 TFEU. Art. 21 TFEU only grants the right to move and reside in the Member States, whereas the right to reside on the European territory is broader than only the right to move and reside. The European territory is thus more encompassing than merely the sum of the territory of the Member States, and must be conceptually distinguished.

5.1 Conceptualizing the European Union Territory

How should this 'European Union territory' be conceptualized? The territorial scope of the Treaties is defined as the sum of the territories of the Member States.[71] Art. 21 TFEU formulates the right to move and reside freely to be applicable 'within the territory of the Member States'. The definition of the territory of the European Union is thus strongly intertwined with the definition of the territory of the Member States. The centrality thereof is highlighted by the fact that the host society is still able to expel a national of another Member State to protect its own territory.[72] Member State territory thus continues to be the dominant paradigm in constructing EU rights.[73] In that context, Loïc Azoulai questions how there can be a meaningful concept of European citizenship 'if there is no way to connect citizenship to Europe as a whole'. According to him, '[a] proper citizenship regime would constitute not only a right to free movement, but also a right to enjoy the community of values anywhere within the European Union, regardless of territory'.[74] This 'Union of values' is institutionalized in *Ruiz Zambrano*. The forced departure which the Court of Justice aims to prevent implies a departure not only from the geographical space of the European Union, but also from 'a community of ideals and values […] it means being deprived of a certain mode of existence corresponding to the standards of European society'. Understood in this way, 'the territory of the Union "transcends" the "territorial framework of national communities" […] a "European way of life"'.[75] The idea fits in a broader paradigm shift from an economic Union towards a Union of its citizens, which Dimitry Kochenov calls 'the citizenship paradigm of European integration'.[76]

---

[70] *Rendón Marín* (n 16) ; *CS* (n 16).
[71] Art. 52 TEU and art. 355 TFEU; see Azoulai (n 40), 178–9.
[72] Arts 27–28 of Directive 2004/38.
[73] Azoulai (n 40) 179–80.
[74] Azoulai (n 40) 180.
[75] Azoulai (n 40) 181, with reference to Case C-499/06 *Nerkowska* EU:C:2008:300, [2008] ECR I-03993, Opinion of AG Maduro EU:C:2008:132, para 1.
[76] Dimitry Kochenov, 'The Citizenship Paradigm' (2013) 15 *Cambridge Yearbook of European Legal Studies* 197; Thym (n 1) 29. For a more theoretical reflection on European citizenship see: Dora Kostakopoulou, 'European Union Citizenship: Writing the Future' (2007) 13(5) European Law Journal 623.

In his view, non-deportability is the essence of citizenship, and the *Ruiz Zambrano* case-law reaffirms this principle in a European Union context.[77]

Sara Iglesias Sánchez reviews the right to reside on the territory of the Union as a whole from the perspective of the right to stay. She links a strengthening as well as a weakening of the right to stay at home in the European Union to the introduction and importance of free movement rights.[78] Free movement rights entitle EU citizens to reside in all of the Member States and therewith enlarges the scope of the right to stay for EU citizens to the territory of all the Member States and thus, indeed, the territory of the Union as a whole. After *Ruiz Zambrano* it became clear that the concept of a European territory also strengthens EU citizens' right to stay in their home Member State. If a Member State fails to undertake the necessary steps to accommodate the possibility for an EU citizen to stay at home – by refusing family reunification with a family member on whom this EU citizen is dependent, for instance – EU law intervenes on the basis that the refusal of a derived residence right deprives the EU citizen of his rights under EU law.[79] Where genuine enjoyment of EU rights

> is threatened by national action, the veil of internal situations may legitimately be pierced. The protective shield of EU citizenship will then kick in to secure a right of home State residence for Union citizens and the family members on whom they are dependent. There is no need to establish any additional connecting factor to EU law [...] In *Ruiz Zambrano*, the Treaty provision invoked as the basis for this new test was Art. 20 TFEU. [...] [P]rimary Union law confers a very open right to reside 'within the territory of the Member States'. In other words, there is no 'except in your own State' proviso in the Treaty itself.[80]

The competence to presume the existence of a right to reside on the territory of the European Union as a whole can be found in the Treaty provision that establishes European citizenship, because the right to reside on the territory of the European Union as a whole and stay there 'is a basic prerequisite for the enjoyment of all the other rights attached to the status of EU citizenship'.[81] The disclaimer to the importance of the right to reside on the territory of the Union as a whole is that it can only be relied on in exceptional circumstances in case a Member State fails to appropriately protect the right to stay at home. Art. 20 TFEU only functions as a subsidiary remedy, when national measures or lack of measures result in a situation where the EU citizen is forced to leave the territory of the Union as a whole, outside of his own choice.[82]

---

[77] Dimitry Kochenov and Benedikt Pirker, 'Deporting the Citizens within the European Union: A Counter-Intuitive Trend in Case C-348/09, P.I. v. Oberbürgemeisterin der Stadt Remscheid' (2013) 19 Columbia Journal of Euopean Law 369, 376; Kostakopoulou (n 39) 457.

[78] Sara Iglesias Sánchez, 'A Citizenship Right to Stay? The Right Not to Move in a Union Based on Free Movement' in Kochenov (n 40) 371; Niamh Nic Shuibhne 'The "Territory of the Union" in EU Citizenship Law: Charting a Route from Parallel to Integrated Narratives' (2019) 38 *Yearbook of European Law* 267, 269–70 and 281–91.

[79] Iglesias Sánchez (n 78) 377–80.

[80] Shuibhne (n 17) 365.

[81] Iglesias Sánchez (n 78) 377–8.

[82] Iglesias Sánchez (n 78) 378–9.

5.2 Implications of a Changing Perspective

The increasing importance of European Union territory as a whole in its understanding of a European Union of values has an inevitable impact on the relationship between the European Union and its Member States on the one hand, and the European Union and its citizens on the other. First, a shift in approach towards protecting the right to reside on the territory of the European Union as a whole deteriorates the importance of the right to reside in your home Member State. Importantly, the right to reside on the territory of the European Union as a whole does not grant the right to stay in a particular part of this territory or in one of the Member States particularly.[83] In *Alokpa*, the Court ruled that the third-country national mother of French children who were born in Luxembourg and had never been in France could be refused a residence right if she did not comply with the conditions set in Directive 2004/38. The refusal of a residence right would not force the children of Mrs Alokpa, who were EU citizens, to leave the territory of the European Union as a whole, because according to the Court Mrs Alokpa and her children could move to France and derive a residence right from art. 20 TFEU there.[84] Vice versa, a residence right derived from art. 20 TFEU in the home Member State of an EU citizen might be refused if the third-country national on whom the EU citizen is dependent legally resides in another Member State of the European Union.[85] In *Shirley McCarthy*, the Court of Justice gives a suggestion that indicates the legitimacy of such reasoning. It concludes that the circumstances of the case do not imply that the refusal of a residence right to Mrs McCarthy's spouse has the effect of depriving her of the genuine enjoyment of the substance of her citizenship rights. Indeed, the refusal to acknowledge a residence right 'in no way affects her in her right to move and reside freely within the territory of the Member States, or any other right conferred on her by virtue of her status as a Union citizen'.[86] The Court's reasoning in this case could indicate that if Mrs McCarthy wants to benefit from family reunification rights under EU law, she has the possibility to move to another Member State, so she is not forced to leave the territory of the European Union as a whole.[87] An EU citizen thus might be forced to leave his home Member State to reside with his family member in another Member State, as long as he does not need to leave the territory of the European Union as a whole.[88] Further evidence for this perspective can be found in the case of *Rendón Marín* – a Colombian national who resided in Spain with his Polish daughter and Spanish son. Päivi Johanna Neuvonen states that 'the fact that, if Mr Rendón Marín and his children could move to Poland, they could not invoke a derived right to residence under Art. 20 TFEU in Spain seems to imply that the substance of the right to residence does not include the right to

---

[83] Iglesias Sánchez (n 78) 383–4.
[84] *Alokpa and Moudoulou* (n 16); Kroeze (n 41); Iglesias Sánchez (n 78) 381–4.
[85] The Dutch Hague Court of First Instance decided a case in this way where the third-country national mother of Dutch children enjoyed international protection in Germany and Bulgaria – Rb Den Haag 06-02-2020 AWB 19/7020, NL:RBDHA:2020:1203. The Court of Justice has not yet dealt with such a situation.
[86] *Shirley McCarthy* (n 16), para 49.
[87] Shuibhne (n 17) 358, 368–72. It is, by the way, unclear why the Court did not use the same reasoning for Ruiz Zambrano, whose Belgian children could have moved with their parents to another Member State as well. See 367–8 in the same contribution.
[88] Kochenov and Pirker (n 77) 377; Kostakopoulou (n 39) 458–60.

reside in a specific (host) Member State'.⁸⁹ The right to reside on the territory of the European Union as a whole thus deteriorates the importance of residing in your own Member State.

Niamh Nic Shuibhne reflects on the impact of the evolution of a 'Union of values' on the relationship between the European Union and its citizens. She connects the growing significance of the territory of the Union to the concept of 'place-hood' that complements the idea of 'personhood' in EU law that was established through the introduction of European citizenship. She then questions 'what *kind* of legal place the territory of the Union constitutes', and in deciphering how the European Union territory should be understood, she distinguishes three narratives.⁹⁰ According to her, *Ruiz Zambrano* must be understood as 'the *foundational narrative* of territory in EU citizenship law'.⁹¹ It is on the basis of this case-law that the territory of the Union became a legally meaningful concept.⁹² The second and third narratives observed by Shuibhne in fact concern the impact of the evolution of a European Union territory on the relationship between the European Union and its citizens.

On the one hand there is the *protective narrative*, which mirrors the right to reside in the European Union and comes down to the right not to be expelled. The reasoning upon which the Court relies to construct this *protective narrative* 'entrench[es] the idea of Union territory as a legal place underpinned by common values; and as a place where the EU legal order is engaged to protect Union citizens'.⁹³ The clearest example of this narrative can be found in the case of *Petruhhin*, which concerned a Russian extradition request issued for an Estonian national residing in Latvia. The Court ruled that in such a situation, the Member State of residence should inform the Member State of which the EU citizen is a national and give this Member State the opportunity to issue a European arrest warrant so the EU citizen can be prosecuted by his Member State of nationality. When the Member State of nationality issues a European arrest warrant, the Member State of residence should prioritize the European arrest warrant over the extradition request.⁹⁴ This 'neat solution […] ensured insofar as possible that the individual remained on the territory of the Union, thereby protecting his or her rights to free movement and residence, whilst at the same time ensuring that he or she faced justice'.⁹⁵

The *protective narrative* can be contrasted with the *systemic narrative*.⁹⁶ This narrative is characterized by the prevalence of systemic values within the European Union over the individual's right to reside on the territory of the European Union. Whereas the *protective narrative* is justified by the individual's taking part in and benefiting from the European Union's shared values, defying those values may justify the deprivation of the right to reside on Union territory. In that case, 'the primacy concern is systemic, that is, for the functioning and continued health of the EU legal order more abstractly'.⁹⁷ The concern for 'a greater systemic good' fits with the idea that 'the borders of the Union are normative as well as physi-

---

⁸⁹ Neuvonen (n 47) 1211. She refers to *Rendón Marín* (n 16), para 79, which refers to *Alokpa and Moudoulou* (n 16), paras 34–5.
⁹⁰ Shuibhne (n 78) (T) 267–8, original italics.
⁹¹ Shuibhne (n 78) 270, original italics.
⁹² Shuibhne (n 78) 270, 281–91.
⁹³ Shuibhne (n 78) 270, 291–305.
⁹⁴ Case C-182/15 *Petruhhin* EU:C:2016:630; Shuibhne (n 78) 293–9.
⁹⁵ Stephen Coutts, 'From Union Citizens to National Subjects: *Pisciotti*' (2019) 56 CMLR 521, 522–3.
⁹⁶ Shuibhne (n 78) 271, 305–15.
⁹⁷ Shuibhne (n 78) 305–6.

cal'.[98] An example of a case that falls within this narrative is *Pisciotti*.[99] Pisciotti was an Italian national for whom a US extradition request was issued in connection with anticompetitive behaviour. While travelling from Nigeria to Italy, he made a stopover in Frankfurt and got arrested at the airport. The Court referred to *Petruhhin* and ruled that if the German authorities give the Italian authorities the opportunity to issue a European Arrest Warrant and the Italian authorities do not use that possibility, nothing stands in the way of extradition, despite the fact that this extradition compromises the right to reside on European Union territory. The Member State which extradites the EU citizen may investigate the possibility to prosecute the EU citizen itself, but it is not obliged to.[100] According to Stephen Coutts we are thus 'left not so much with a right of the Union citizen to remain on the territory of the Union, but a right of the Member State of nationality to assert its jurisdiction' or not.[101]

6. CONCLUDING REMARKS

This chapter dealt, in a nutshell, with the development of family reunification between EU citizens and third-country nationals under EU law. The competence to regulate this field of law is divided between the European Union and the Member States, and in principle delineated by the definition of the scope of applicability of Directive 2004/38 on free movement of EU citizens and their family members. Art. 3(1) of that directive declares that it can only be applicable to EU citizens 'who move to or reside in' a Member State of which they are not a national, and their family members as defined in its arts 2(2) and 3(2) (cross-border situations). Case-law of the Court of Justice shows that this criterion is too restricted to properly protect the right to move freely in the European Union, conferred upon all EU citizens by virtue of art. 21 TFEU. For cases where EU citizens reside in their own Member States but previously exercised free movement rights, in particular, the Court of Justice decided that EU law continues to be applicable (post-cross-border situations). Otherwise these EU citizens might be hindered from moving in the first place. The Court's case-law that establishes this principle limits the competence of the Member States to set family reunification rules for their own nationals, but is justified by the need to ensure the effectiveness of art. 21 TFEU.

Additionally, this chapter demonstrated how the paradigm which sustains the acknowledgements of family reunification under EU law shifts from a functional internal market approach towards a more principled protection of the European territory as a whole. In this context the Court of Justice ruled that EU citizens who have never exercised free movement rights can still rely on EU law for the purpose of family reunification, if the refusal of a residence right would force the EU citizen to leave the territory of the Union as a whole and deprive him of the substance of his citizenship rights (non-cross-border situations). The Court of Justice thus demonstrates a strong sense of territoriality, which contrasts with the case-law on the right to family life as protected by art. 8 ECHR. The European Court of Human Rights ruled that art. 8 ECHR does not impose an obligation on the Member States of the Council of Europe to respect

---

[98] Shuibhne (n 78) 306; Azoulai (n 40) 187.
[99] Case C-191/16 *Pisciotti* EU:C:2018:222.
[100] Shuihbne (n 78) 306–8.
[101] Coutts (n 95) 523.

a family's preference of country in which to exercise their family life.¹⁰² European Union law, on the other hand, protects EU citizens' right to reside, which requires the acknowledgement of family reunification rights, if the refusal thereof compromises the exercise of the EU citizen's right to reside on the territory of the European Union.¹⁰³ In this narrative 'the Court progresses its understanding of Union territory as the place where Union citizens *ought to be*',¹⁰⁴ because the European Union is the 'right place' for EU citizens.¹⁰⁵ The new paradigm, however, also changes the assessment that is carried out to determine whether this right to reside merits protection in an individual case. European Union territory is constructed in a geographic as well as a normative sense.¹⁰⁶ Membership of a 'Union of values' legitimizes a Union-wide right to reside, and if necessary a right to family reunification, but defying those values may lead to legitimate expulsion.¹⁰⁷ It is worth noting, however, 'that the Court [...] still does not speak of a *positive* right to live in the Union territory, in the way that Advocate-General Sharpston did in *Ruiz Zambrano*; it prefers a *negative* casting of the right not to be forced to leave it'.¹⁰⁸

---

¹⁰² *Abdulaziz, Cabales and Balkandali v United Kingdom* App nos. 9214/80, 9473/81 and 9474/81 (ECtHR 28 May 1985), para 68; *Rodrigues da Silva and Hoogkamer v Netherlands* App no. 50435/99 (ECtHR 31 January 2006), para 39; *Jeunesse v Netherlands* App no. 12738/10 (ECtHR 3 October 2014), para 107. For more information about the case-law of the ECtHR on family reunification under art. 8 ECHR see Daniel Thym, 'Respect for Private and Family Life under Article 8 ECHR in Immigration Cases: A Human Right to Regularize Illegal Stay?' (2008) ICLQ 87.
¹⁰³ Den Haese and Kroeze (n 61) 85.
¹⁰⁴ Shuibne (n 78) 291.
¹⁰⁵ Coutts (n 95) 539.
¹⁰⁶ Coutts (n 95) 539.
¹⁰⁷ Azoulai (n 40); Shuibhne (n 78).
¹⁰⁸ Shuibhne (n 19) 366.

12. Using EU citizenship to protect academic freedom: an alternative method[1]

Tamas Dezso Ziegler

1. RISING AUTHORITARIANISM AND ACADEMIC FREEDOM

This chapter highlights a dynamic interpretation of the institution of EU citizenship, which could enable us to defend, at least partially, academic freedom Europe-wide. It is based on the fact that EU citizenship has evolved greatly in its history, and this process could probably continue. The topic has special relevance because of two problems. First is the marketization of academia,[2] which has a strong effect on academic freedom.[3] Second, in Hungary and Poland issues related to the authoritarian turn of their governments and the techniques of autocratic legalism[4] have resulted in a systemic limitation of academic freedom. In response, the EU could find itself competency to act in these cases through interpreting academic citizens as EU citizens with fundamental rights in the higher education sector.

In Hungary, the changes made between 2010 and 2018 led to a nationalistic palingenesis (complete rebirth) of the legal system: all of the crucial laws were replaced.[5] As the new governmental system is based on strong anti-Enlightenment sentiment,[6] it disrespects pluralism,

---

[1]   I would like to thank Anna Unger, Balázs Majtényi and Zsolt Körtvélyesi for their observations regarding the first draft of this chapter.

[2]   Michael A Olivas, 'The Growing Role of Immigration Law in Universal Higher Education: Case Studies of the United States and the EU' (2015) 37 Houston Journal of International Law 401; Les Levidow, 'Marketizing Higher Education: Neoliberal Strategies and Counter-strategies' in Kevin Robins and Frank Webster (eds), *The Virtual University? Knowledge, Markets and Management* (OUP 2002) 227–48.

[3]   Elise S Brezis and Joël Hellier, 'Social Mobility at the Top and the Higher Education System' (2018) 52 EJ Pol Econ 37; Craig Brandist, 'The Risks of Soviet-Style Managerialism in UK Universities' www.timeshighereducation.com/comment/the-risks-of-soviet-style-managerialism-in-united-kingdom-universities; Kathleen Lynch and Mariya Ivancheva, 'Academic Freedom and the Commercialisation of Universities: A Critical Ethical Analysis' (2015) 15 Ethics in Science and Environmental Politics; Luke Martell, 'The Marketisation of Our Universities Is Fragmenting the Academic Workforce at the Students' Expense' http://blogs.lse.ac.uk/impactofsocialsciences/2013/12/04/the-marketisation-of-our-universities/.

[4]   Roger Daniel Kelemen, 'Europe's Other Democratic Deficit: National Authoritarianism in Europe's Democratic Union' (2017) 52 Government and Opposition, Special Issue 2 (Democracy without Solidarity: Political Dysfunction in Hard Times) 211–38; Laurent Pech and Kim Lane Scheppele, 'Illiberalism Within: Rule of Law Backsliding in the EU' (2017) 19 Cambridge Yearbook of European Legal Studies 3–47.

[5]   To mention only a few major examples, see the new constitution (Fundamental law), Act C. of 2012 on the new Penal Code, Act V. of 2013 on the new Civil Code, Act XXXVI. of 2013 on the Electoral Procedure; Act CCIII. of 2011 on the Elections of the Members of the Parliament; Act CLXII of 2011 on the legal status and remuneration of judges; Act CIV of 2010 on the freedom of the press and the fundamental rules on media content; Act CLXXXV. of 2010 on media services and mass media.

[6]   Zeev Sternhell, *The Anti-Enlightenment Tradition* (Yale UP 2010).

attacks those who criticize governmental actions and tries to extort a uniform worldview by dividing society into 'friends and enemies', in a Schmittian manner. As a side effect of this tendency, dozens of regulations have been introduced that limit academic freedom either directly or indirectly. The Sargentini Report adopted by the European Parliament in September 2018 called on the Council to use the Art. 7 TEU procedure and determine that a clear risk of fundamental rights breaches had occurred in Hungary.[7] In its separate part on 'academic freedom' (Points 33–36), it mentioned certain recent government actions such as the expulsion of the Central European University (CEU), the government ban on gender studies and discrimination against Roma students in primary and secondary schools. However, it did not follow a more holistic approach and did not analyse deeper changes in education governance.

In Poland, several major laws have been repealed or modified.[8] At the end of 2017 the European Commission triggered the Art. 7 TEU procedure against Poland,[9] and the European Parliament supported this action in March 2018.[10] In 2018 a new law on higher education was adopted, which prompted widespread protests demanding 'democratic universities', 'autonomy' and 'sovereign academia'.[11]

---

[7] Report (4 July 2018) on a proposal calling on the Council to determine, pursuant to Article 7(1) of the Treaty on European Union, the existence of a clear risk of a serious breach by Hungary of the values on which the Union is founded. PE 620.837v02-00 A8-0250/2018.

[8] The scope of these changes was not as wide as in Hungary. However, changes were made to the 1984 Polish Press Law; see also Law of 30 December 2015 amending the Broadcasting Law, published in Official Journal on 7 January 2016, item 25; Law of 30 December 2015 amending the Law on Civil Service and certain other acts, published in Official Journal on 8 January 2016, item 34; Law of 15 January 2016 amending the Law on Police and other laws, published in Official Journal on 4 February 2016, item 147; Law of 28 January 2016 on the Prosecutor's Office, published in Official Journal on 15 February 2016, item 177; Law of 28 January 2016 – Regulations implementing the Act – Law on the Prosecutor's Office, published in Official Journal on 15 February 2016, item 178; Law of 18 March 2016 on the Ombudsman and amending certain other laws. For their background see Commission Recommendation of 21.12.2016 regarding the rule of law in Poland complementary to Commission Recommendation (EU) 2016/1374. Com(2016) 8950 final; a law on the Public Prosecution Office; a law on the role of police; and a law on the judiciary. At the centre of the disputes was the restructuring of institutions such as the Constitutional Tribunal and the Supreme Court. 'European Commission Refers Poland to the European Court of Justice to Protect the Independence of the Polish Supreme Court', European Commission Press Release, Brussels, 24 September 2018, IP 18 5830.

[9] Proposal for a Council Decision on the Determination of a Clear Risk of a Serious Breach by the Republic of Poland of the Rule of Law (COM [2017] 835 final).

[10] European Parliament Resolution of 1 March 2018 on the Commission's decision to activate Article 7(1) TEU as regards the situation in Poland (2018/2541[RSP]); Armin von Bogdandy, Piotr Bogdanowicz, Iris Canor, Maciej Taborowski and Matthias Schmidt, 'A Potential Constitutional Moment for the European Rule of Law: The Importance of Red Lines' (2018) 55 CML Rev 1–14.

[11] Jack Grove, 'Student Protests in Poland Delay "Authoritarian" Law' www.timeshighereducation.com/news/student-protests-poland-delay-authoritarian-law; Marysia Ciupka, 'This Is Our Space: Students at Polish Universities Unite in Protest against New Higher Education Reform' http://politicalcritique.org/cee/poland/2018/polish-reform-higher-education-gowin-protest/; 'Protesting Polish Students Stall Controversial Bill That Would Clamp Down on Academic Freedom' https://globalvoices.org/2018/06/26/protesting-polish-students-stall-controversial-bill-that-would-clamp-down-on-academic-freedom/.

2. THE FRAGMENTS OF EU COMPETENCY

If we unravel the EU's role in academia, we can see that its exercise of power can be separated into three major areas. First, it does not have the competency to adopt decisions on certain matters, such as the financing of universities, as they fall into exclusive member state competencies. Second, it has the power to help member states to cooperate (supporting competency). A good example of this is the framework of the Erasmus cooperation. Third, in a number of cases, a clear EU competency exists to adopt laws. This is the case, for example, regarding the recognition of diplomas.[12]

The legal background also shows this fragmentation. Art. 6 TFEU states that the Union only has the competence to support, coordinate or supplement the actions of the member states in education. Art. 165 of the TFEU also explains this power.[13] Moreover, Art. 166 of the TFEU provides a detailed list of jobs, such as the strengthening of the 'European dimension' in education, encouraging the mobility of students and professors and promoting cooperation between educational establishments. The list seems to be exhaustive, narrowing down actions in other fields.[14] It is worth keeping in mind that this cooperation does not necessarily mean the adoption of EU legislation. For example, the Bologna cooperation is based on a simple declaration by the member states, which is not even published in the *Official Journal*.[15] This can cause problems as students do not necessarily receive enforceable rights, because a declaration is not a legal act and has no direct effect.[16] In other cases (such as the European Qualifications Network), this competency has been practised through recommendations.[17]

Contrary to the above, we find acts that were adopted based on certain provisions of the TFEU, which clearly give the EU the competency to govern certain areas. For example, Art. 53 TFEU states that the EU has the right to govern the mutual recognition of diplomas, certificates and other qualifications.[18] Beyond this, the directive on the free movement of students has also been adopted with a competency background rooted in the free movement of citizens.[19] Furthermore, decisions of the Court of Justice have developed certain fields, such

---

[12] Directive 2005/36/EC of the European Parliament and of the Council of 7 September 2005 on the recognition of professional qualifications [2005] OJ L255, 30 September, 22–142; Paul Craig and Grainne De Búrca, *EU Law: Text, Cases, Materials* (PUP 2011) 809 et seq.

[13] Sacha Garben, *EU Higher Education Law* (Kluwer Law International 2011) 55–97.

[14] Marion Simm, 'AEUV Artikel 165, 166' in Jürgen Schwarze, Ulrich Becker, Armin Hatje and Johann Schoo (eds), *EU-Kommentar* (Nomos 2012) 1734.

[15] The Bologna Declaration of 19 June 1999 – Joint declaration of the European Ministers of Education www.magna-charta.org/resources/files/BOLOGNA_DECLARATION.pdf.

[16] Sacha Garben, 'The Bologna Process: From a European Law Perspective' (2010) 16 European Law Journal 208.

[17] Recommendation of the European Parliament and of the Council of 15 February 2006 on further European cooperation in quality assurance in higher education [2006] OJ L64/60; Sacha Garben, *EU Higher Education Law* (n 13) 152.

[18] Directive 2005/36/EC of the European Parliament and of the Council of 7 September 2005 on the recognition of professional qualifications [2005] OJ L255/22.

[19] Council Directive 90/366/EEC of 28 June 1990 on the right of residence for students [1990] OJ L180/30, repealed by Directive 2004/38/EC of the European Parliament and of the Council of 29 April 2004 on the right of citizens of the Union and their family members to move and reside freely within the territory of the Member States amending Regulation (EEC) 1612/68 and repealing Directives 64/221/EEC, 68/360/EEC, 72/194/EEC, 73/148/EEC, 75/34/EEC, 75/35/EEC, 90/364/EEC, 90/365/EEC, and 93/96/EEC (text with EEA relevance) [2004] OJ L158/77.

as access to higher education, support and grants[20] or the free movement of services of private educational institutions.[21] In addition, in the field of justice and home affairs, some rules also govern the member states' relationship with third-country nationals.[22]

While one could find implied powers for the EU to broaden the scope of its actions,[23] until now there have only been deliberate actions to do so. One could also argue that university titles (such as habilitation or MCF) pose great obstacles to the free movement of EU citizens, but this interpretation is not supported by the present stage of EU law. As a result of the fragmented background, certain issues, such as avoiding discrimination against students or students' right to access grants, are addressed, while others, such as students' and professors' fundamental rights in public universities, are not.[24] Moreover, EU law handles education and research separately. Regarding the latter, Art. 4(3) and Art. 179(2) TFEU say that the EU shall only encourage and support research cooperation, and should not interfere with member state power. As a result, in this field we have the same competency problem as in the case of higher education.

Finally, EU citizenship and academic citizenship are not connected in EU legislation at all, and the idea that the two could be connected is missing completely from the legal sources.

---

[20] Case C-147/03 *Commission of the European Communities v Republic of Austria* EU:C:2005: 427 [2005] ECR I-05969; Joined Cases C-11/06 and C-12/06 *Rhiannon Morgan v Bezirksregierung Köln (C-11/06) and Iris Bucher v Landrat des Kreises Düren (C-12/06)* EU:C:2007:626 [2007] ECR I-09161; Case C-73/08 *Nicolas Bressol and Others and Céline Chaverot and Others v Gouvernement de la Communauté français* EU:C:2010:181 [2010] ECR I-02735; Case C-293/83 *Françoise Gravier v City of Liège* EU:C:1985:69 [1985] ECR 593; Case C-209/03 *Dany Bidar v London Borough of Ealing and Secretary of State for Education and Skills* EU:C:2005:169 [2005] ECR I-2119; Case C-158/07 *Jacqueline Förster v Hoofddirectie van de Informatie Beheer Groep* EU:C:2008:630 [2008] ECR I-8507; Case C-184/99 *Rudy Grzelczyk v Centre public d'aide sociale d'Ottignies-Louvain-la-Neuve* EU:C:2001:458 [2001] ECR I-06193; Koen Lenaerts, 'European Union Citizenship, National Welfare Systems and Social Solidarity' (2011) 18 Jurisprudencija – Jurisprudence 405 et seq.; Susann Bartels, 'Students as Subject of EU Law' https://essay.utwente.nl/60302/1/BSc_S_Bartels.pdf.

[21] Case C-9/74 *Donato Casagrande v Landeshauptstadt München* EU:C:1974:74 [1974] ECR 77; Case C-76/05 *Herbert Schwarz and Marga Gootjes-Schwarz v Finanzamt Bergisch Gladbach* EU:C: 2007:492.

[22] Directive (EU) 2016/801 of the European Parliament and of the Council of 11 May 2016 on the conditions of entry and residence of third-country nationals for the purposes of research, studies, training, voluntary service, pupil exchange schemes or educational projects, and au pairing [2016] OJ L132/21; Case C-491/13 *Mohamed Ali Ben Alaya v Bundesrepublik Deutschland* EU:C:2014:2187.

[23] Koen Lenaerts, 'Education in European Community Law after Maastricht' (1994) 31 CML Rev 11.

[24] Sacha Garben, 'The Failure to Protect Education as an Inalienable Policy Domain of EU Member States: A Critical Assessment of Article 165 TFEU on Education and Suggestions for Reform' in Thomas Giegerich, Oskar J Gstrein and Sebastian Zeitzmann (eds), *The EU between 'an Ever Closer Union' and Inalienable Policy Domains of Member States* (Nomos 2014) 528; Paul P Craig, 'Competence: Clarity, Conferral, Containment and Consideration' (2004) 29 European Law Review 323. See also Paul P Craig, 'Competence and Member State Autonomy' in Hans-W Micklitz and Bruno de Witte (eds), *The European Court of Justice and the Autonomy of the Member States* (Intersentia 2012) 11–34.

3. ACADEMIC FREEDOM OF EU CITIZENS AND ACTIONS LIMITING THIS FREEDOM

Contrary to the above, this chapter argues that academic freedom should not be viewed as a policy matter, but as an issue related to fundamental rights. Art. 13 of the Charter of Fundamental Rights of the EU (in the section on 'Freedom of the arts and sciences') says that 'the arts and scientific research shall be free of constraint. Academic freedom shall be respected.'

In Art. 14 the Charter also adds several other rights, such as the right to receive free compulsory education, the freedom to found educational establishments with respect for democratic principles and the right of parents to ensure their own religious, philosophical and pedagogical convictions in education. These are 'in accordance with the national laws governing the exercise of such freedom and right'. This last phrase is especially important as, unlike Art. 51 of the Charter, it seems to suggest that national laws must also conform with these rights. The rights mentioned in the Charter are universal, in the sense that they do not differentiate between EU citizens and third-country nationals. However, if taken seriously, they can be used as a shield to protect EU citizens.

In the following, this chapter recaps the changes in higher education in Poland and Hungary. It tries to cover open or clandestine measures that limit individual or institutional freedom of EU citizens.[25] Institutional freedom is important, as institutional autonomy and individuals' academic freedom are closely connected. Placing a government limit on an institution's teaching, research or financial autonomy can have a negative effect on individual academic freedom, and as such limits EU citizens' academic freedom as well.[26] This can occur if an EU citizen works in the academic environment outside his or her home country, but also in purely domestic situations, where the state acts against the established domestic academic elite. Academic freedom can be understood as a collection of rights 'granted to academic (non-administrative) teaching and research staff in Universities to enable them to undertake their teaching and research activities to the highest possible professional standards'.[27] This also applies to institutions. In their case, it may be defined as the right to 'decide freely and independently how to perform their tasks'.[28]

3.1 Distorting Pluralism: Denying Equality of Universities

In both Hungary and Poland, some governmental actions have selected certain universities and put them in monopoly positions. In Hungary this is especially problematic, as the state diverts

---

[25] James D Gordon, 'Individual and Institutional Academic Freedom' (2010) 49 Brigham Young University Studies 43–7.
[26] Jogchum Vrielink, Paul Lemmensa and Stephan Parmentier, 'Academic Freedom as a Fundamental Right and the LERU Working Group on Human Rights' (2011) 13 Procedia Social and Behavioral Sciences 117–41; Earl Hunt, 'The Rights and Responsibilities Implied by Academic Freedom' (2010) 49 Personality and Individual Differences 264–71; Terence Karran, 'Academic Freedom in Europe: Time for a Magna Charta?' (2009) 22 Higher Education Policy 163–189.
[27] Terence Karran (n 26) 170.
[28] Terence Karran (n 26) 169.

support from other institutions.[29] For example, the National University of Public Service (governed by the Prime Minister's Office) was cut out of the higher education system and received four times as much financial support for students per capita as other universities[30] (interestingly, EU funding allocated through the government even boosts this exceptional position). Furthermore, only graduates of this university may work for (central and local) government, and certain programmes (for example, international public administration) can be taught only at this university.[31] While Corvinus University, the foremost university of economics, was recently privatized (it must work as a private fund in the future), the Hungarian National Bank founded a university (Pallasz Athéné University, later renamed János Neumann University) because its head (a former government minister) was unsatisfied with the way 'orthodox liberal' economists teach. This university also receives extensive state support. In 2020–1, around half of the public universities were privatised.[32]

The landscape of research institutions also changed in Hungary: the government cut out the research institutes of the most important research institution of the country, the Hungarian Academy of Sciences, thereby affecting the research of thousands of scholars. A new research centre was created with a name borrowed (or stolen) from Eötvös Loránd University, one of Hungary's leading universities: the Eötvös Loránd Research Network (ELKH), governed by a commission in which government delegates have a majority. The president of the new structure is Miklós Maróth, a supporter of PM Viktor Orbán, who made a name for himself in the Hungarian press recently for jokingly claiming at a conference that Muslims should be tied into pig skin in order to integrate into European societies. Moreover, many GoNGOs and think tanks have been founded with the purpose of spreading government propaganda.

In Poland, a wider restructuring happened in the Act adopted in 2018 on higher education (called Bill 2.0 in the media). According to the new bill, funding for universities and the power to award degrees will depend on the scores they receive for their research performance, and additional funding will be available only for the top universities. For smaller regional universities, this change could remove their right to offer PhD programmes and reduce their student

---

[29] Public spending on education dropped to 3.8 per cent of GDP, which is one of the lowest percentages among the OECD countries (the OECD average is 5 per cent; the EU average is 4.5 per cent). Only three OECD countries spent proportionately less (Russia, Luxembourg and Ireland). The country spends 0.9 per cent of its GDP on tertiary education, which is approximately half of the OECD average. The number of people holding university degrees dropped: there are 8.8 per cent fewer in Hungary than the European average. The number of students also drastically dropped, from 370,000 in 2010 to 287,000 in 2016. Extensive tuition fees were introduced in 2011, even though, in a national referendum in 2008, 82.2 per cent of voters opposed their introduction. The decline of Hungarian universities in international rankings (many of them lost hundreds of places) also shows the effect of these policies; see 'Education at a Glance – 2018 OECD Indicators' http://webexchanges.oecdcode.org/F0w3Shjh/EAG2018_final_embargo.pdf 258; https://qubit.hu/2018/09/11/magyarorszag-kulonosen-keveset-kolt-oktatasra-a-tanarok-fizetese-toredeke-az-oecd-atlagnak; Márton Gerő, 'Radical Changes in Higher Education' www.eurofound.europa.eu/sr/publications/article/2012/radical-changes-in-higher-education; https://444.hu/2017/05/13/tobb-evtizedes-melyponton-a-magyar-felsooktatasban-hallgatok-szama.

[30] György Unyatyinszki, 'Ömlik a pénz a közszolgálati egyetemnek' [Money flows to the National University of Public Service] https://mno.hu/belfold/omlik-a-penz-a-kozszolgalati-egyetemnek-2418324.

[31] Moreover, state-financed studies here do not count in the 12-semester limit on state-funded studies in the general higher education system.

[32] Erudera College News, 'Half of Hungarian Universities Privatized by Government' https://collegenews.org/half-of-hungarian-universities-privatized-by-government/.

numbers, which could have a devastating effect on them.³³ This divide will be strengthened by the fact that only the largest universities have the right to call themselves universities; others receive the title of 'professional academies'.

In both countries, the changes have produced a kind of academic oligarchization and existential insecurity for those working in the academic sector.³⁴ Apart from domestic (EU) citizens' rights, this can also limit the rights of EU citizens living and working in the academic sector in other countries: as a result of oligarchization, after a while it will become harder to find academic partners in these countries.

3.2 Intrusion into Universities' Decision Making: The Change of Governance

In Hungary, financial directors were appointed by the government to control university finances. Later, so-called university consistoriums were established, which have a crucial role in accepting the budget of the university and approving its development plans. The majority of its members are delegated by the responsible minister. Furthermore, a new institution, the chancellor, was introduced (which, just like the rector, is also delegated by the responsible minister), and many of the rector's powers were transferred to it. Chancellors control spending, the usage of university facilities, recruitment, promotions and salaries.³⁵ Furthermore, after the privatization of Corvinus University, faculties were turned into 'institutes' as of 1 February 2020. As a consequence, autonomous faculty boards were abolished. Furthermore, at the universities freshly privatized in 2020–1, the members of the new foundations' supervising bodies were delegated solely by the government. Many include former and present high-ranking government politicians.³⁶ The biggest outcry resulted from the structural changes at the University of Theatre and Film Arts: protesting students occupied university buildings and teaching ceased for a period.³⁷ The changes resulted in Hungarian higher education dropping from 'sixth position to 28th (one from bottom) on the European University

---

[33] Matthew Reisz, 'Higher Education "Turned Upside-Down" by Polish Reforms' www.timeshighereducation.com/news/higher-education-turned-upside-down-polish-reforms; Marysia Ciupka, 'This is Our Space. Students at Polish Universities Unite in Protest against New Higher Education Reform' http://politicalcritique.org/cee/poland/2018/polish-reform-higher-education-gowin-protest/.

[34] Dorota Dakowska, 'Higher Education in Poland: Budgetary Constraints and International Aspirations' in Jon Nixon (ed.), *Higher Education in Austerity Europe* (Bloomsbury 2017) 79–91.

[35] '[I]n a number of European states, however, universities have decision-making bodies that partially or even pre-dominantly are made up of external representatives and not by academic staff [...] It is clear that in such situations there is a need for counterbalancing safeguards.' Paul Lemmens, Stephan Parmentier, Jogchum Vrielink and Laura Keustermans, 'Academic Freedom as a Fundamental Right', *League of European Research Universities' Advice Paper* No. 6 (December 2010) 19 fn. 50: Terence Karran, 'Academic Freedom in Europe: Reviewing UNESCO's Recommendation' (2009) 57 British Journal of Educational Studies 204. See also decisions No. 41/2005 and No. 39/2006 of the Hungarian Constitutional Court.

[36] Inotai Edit, 'FIDESz Makes Hungary's Universities An Offer They Can't Refuse' https://balkaninsight.com/2021/02/23/fidesz-makes-hungarys-universities-an-offer-they-cant-refuse; Tímea Drinóczi, 'Loyalty, Opportunism and Fear: The Forced Privatization of Hungarian Universities', VerfBlog, 2021/2/05 https://verfassungsblog.de/loyalty-opportunism-and-fear.

[37] Lydia Gal, 'Hungary Continues Attacks on Academic Freedom' www.hrw.org/news/2020/09/03/hungary-continues-attacks-academic-freedom.

Association's financial autonomy scorecard between 2011 and 2017'.[38] A possible effect of the new rules is that some university decisions may be the result of political demands. Perfect examples of this are the University of Debrecen giving Vladimir Putin a special distinction[39] and Abdel Fattah el-Sisi receiving the title *doctor honoris causa* from the National University of Public Service.

In Poland, Bill 2.0 tried to

> diminish the power of university senates made up of students and staff in favour of new university councils whose membership would have had a majority of individuals from outside the institution. These would have the power to set the university's strategy and appoint the rector, with critics warning that appointees to the panels were likely to be 'corporate representatives and politicians'.[40]

Later, an amended version of the changes was adopted, which limited the council's rights concerning university strategy and the election of university rectors. However, the new law gave more power to rectors, who control funding and will have extensive rights to reshape universities' scientific organization. Moreover, faculty boards representing the interests of academic staff were abolished.[41]

3.3 Attacking Freedom of Thought: Banning Academic Programmes

In a number of cases, the direct influence of politics can be even more easily traced regarding the list of university programmes.[42] A perfect example of this is the Hungarian government banning (erased from the list of programmes available to accredit and start) some BA programmes, such as communication and media studies, social studies and cultural anthropology. In 2018 it also banned gender studies,[43] and the start of a 'family studies counter course' was

---

[38] David Matthews, 'The State of Higher Education in Hungary' www.timeshighereducation.com/features/the-state-of-higher-education-in-hungary; Enora B Pruvot and Thomas Estermann, 'University Autonomy in Europe III: The Scorecard 2017' https://eua.eu/resources/publications/350:university-autonomy%C2%A0in-europe-iii-%C2%A0the-scorecard-2017.html.

[39] In this case, the rector warned the university community that he would start disciplinary proceedings if they protested against the decision.

[40] 'Higher Education "Turned Upside-Down" by Polish Reforms' www.timeshighereducation.com/news/higher-education-turned-upside-down-polish-reforms.

[41] 'The Nerds' Turn: Battling for a Democratic Academia in Poland' http://allegralaboratory.net/the-nerds-turn-battling-for-a-democratic-academia-in-poland/.

[42] In a number of cases, attacks against NGOs also affected academia; see 'CEU Suspends Programs for Refugees, Asylum Seekers' https://bbj.hu/news/ceu-suspends-programs-for-refugees-asylum-seekers_154078.

[43] See Government Decree 188 of 2018 amending Government Decree 283 of 2012 on teachers' education, specialization, and the list of teachers' education and amending Government Decree 283 of 2012 on the list of obtainable degrees in higher education and the transcription of new programs; Andrea Pető, 'Report from the Trenches: The Debate around Teaching Gender Studies in Hungary' www.boell.de/en/2017/04/10/report-trenches-debate-around-teaching-gender-studies-hungary.

announced by the Ministry of Human Resources.[44] Furthermore, universities must receive prior permission from the minister if they want to start teaching a programme.[45]

3.4 Limitation of Free Speech through Direct Attacks against Professors

Both countries have experienced different forms of direct attacks against university professors. In Hungary, professors are regularly sought out individually or collectively in the media. A good example of this is the case of *Figyelő*, a pro-government weekly that published the names of hundreds of intellectuals, including academics and even university students, who were the 'agents of George Soros'.[46] Moreover, government-critical scholars were expelled in dramatic ways,[47] it became easier to revoke leadership roles in academia[48] and students were recruited by a government-friendly website to report whether their professors were critical towards the government.[49] In this milieu, several conference programmes about 'sensitive questions', such as gender equality or migration, were cancelled.[50]

Freedom of thought and free speech were also limited in Poland when the country banned academic discussion of the Polish people's participation in the Holocaust. As a result, there were plans to strip Jan T. Gross, a professor at Princeton University, of the Knight's Cross of the Order of Merit of Poland.[51] Later, the bill was changed and the criminal sanctions were erased from it, but Polish researchers were still attacked in Paris at a conference in 2019.[52] Furthermore, Bill 2.0 regulates retirement ages differently between men (65) and women (60). Beside limiting academic freedom, this provision discriminates between people based on their sex, thereby also violating EU citizens' rights.[53]

---

[44] 'Hungary's University Ban on Gender Studies Heats up Culture War' www.dw.com/en/hungarys-university-ban-on-gender-studies-heats-up-culture-war/a-45944422; Sargentini Report, Point (36); 'EUA Condemns Hungarian Government Plan to Ban Gender Studies' https://eua.eu/news/130:eua-condemns-hungarian-government-plan-to-ban-gender-studies.html.

[45] See Art. § 71/B of Act No. CCIV of 2011 on higher education.

[46] 'Hungary's Viktor Orban Targets Critics with "Soros Mercenaries" Blacklist' www.dw.com/en/hungarys-viktor-orban-targets-critics-with-soros-mercenaries-blacklist/a-43381963.

[47] 'Policy Solutions: Political Discrimination in Hungary' www.policysolutions.hu/userfiles/elemzes/265/political_discrimination_in_hungary.pdf 26.

[48] See Act CLXXV of 2010 on the modification of Act XXXIII of 1992 on public servants.

[49] 'Recruiting Student Informers against Disloyal Professors'. Hungarian Spectrum http://hungarianspectrum.org/tag/attacks-on-faculty/.

[50] 'Hungarian Academy of Sciences Rejects Conference Proposals on Political Grounds' hungarianfreepress.com/2018/10/02/hungarian-academy-of-sciences-rejects-conference-proposals-on-political-grounds/.

[51] Hank Reichmann, 'Academic Freedom Threatened in Poland' https://academeblog.org/2016/02/19/academic-freedom-threatened-in-poland/.

[52] Marc Santora, 'Poland's Holocaust Law Weakened after "Storm and Consternation"' www.nytimes.com/2018/06/27/world/europe/poland-holocaust-law.html; Katarzyna Markusz, 'Polish Holocaust Researchers Attacked at Paris Shoah Research Conference', *The Jerusalem Post* (25 February 2019) www.jpost.com/Diaspora/Antisemitism/Polish-Holocaust-researchers-attacked-at-Paris-Shoah-research-conference-581687.

[53] Art. 157 TFEU; Directive 2006/54/EC of the European Parliament and of the Council of 5 July 2006 on the implementation of the principle of equal opportunities and equal treatment of men and women in matters of employment and occupation [2006] OJ L204, 26 December 2006 23; Case C-43-75 *Gabrielle Defrenne v Société anonyme belge de navigation aérienne Sabena* EU:C:1976:56 [1976] ECR 455; Case C-36/74 *B.N.O. Walrave and L.J.N. Koch v Association Union cycliste internationale,*

3.5 The Case of Scholarship Contracts in Hungary

In a small number of cases, EU infringement procedures have been started against Hungary.

The first of such measures (a pilot procedure) was connected with the student agreements introduced in 2012.[54] According to the changes, state-funded students had to conclude a contract with the state, which stipulated that they would have to pay the entire sum of their tuition fee were they to leave the country permanently after their studies.[55] The European Commission began to investigate the case, as it violated Art. 45 of the TFEU. Later, the Hungarian Constitutional Court found the related provisions to be unconstitutional and annulled them.[56] After this, a new rule introduced similar provisions.[57] However, this time, students have to make a statement about their tuition fees and, in the future, only those who chose to be state-funded will have to pay the tuition fee if they leave the country and have not worked in Hungary for a period of time at least as long as that of their studies. This new 'optional form' was mistakenly found to conform to the letter of EU law by the Commission. Apart from the general ban on the limitation of freedom of movement,[58] in the *d'Hoop* case, the European Court of Justice (ECJ) ascertained that

> it would be incompatible with the right of freedom of movement were a citizen, in the Member State of which he is a national, to receive treatment less favourable than he would enjoy if he had not availed himself of the opportunities offered by the Treaty in relation to freedom of movement.[59]

In the *Graf* case it was stressed that 'provisions which, even if they are applicable without distinction, preclude or deter a national of a Member State from leaving his country of origin in order to exercise his right to freedom of movement [...] constitute an obstacle to that freedom'.[60] Even if such measures can be justified if they are intended to fulfil a legitimate aim and are proportionate – like the existence of Belgian[61] and Austrian[62] quota systems for medical

---

Koninklijke Nederlandsche Wielren Unie et Federación Española Ciclismo EU:C:1974:140 [1974] ECR 1405; Ian Loveland, *Constitutional Law, Administrative Law, and Human Rights* (OUP 2012) 375.

[54] Government Decree 2 of 2012 on the student contracts on state scholarship and partial scholarship.

[55] During a 20-year period, they had to work for a period at least twice as long as the time of their education in Hungary.

[56] Constitutional Court Decision No. 32 of 2012.

[57] See Section b) of Art. 48/A, Act CCIV of 2011 on national higher education.

[58] Case C-293/85 *Commission of the European Communities v Kingdom of Belgium* EU:C:1988:40 [1988] ECR 305; Case C-147/03 *Commission of the European Communities v Republic of Austria* EU:C:2005:427 [2005] ECR I-05969; Case C-184/99 *Rudy Grzelczyk v Centre public d'aide sociale d'Ottignies-Louvain-la-Neuve* EU:C:2001:458 [2001] ECR I-6193; Case C-18/95 *F.C. Terhoeve v Inspecteur van de Belastingdienst Particulieren/Ondernemingen buitenland* EU:C:1999:22 [1999] ECR I-345; Case C-109/04 *Karl Robert Kranemann v Land Nordrhein-Westfalen* EU:C:2005:187 [2005] ECR I-2421; Case C-520/04 *Pirkko Marjatta Turpeinen* EU:C:2006:703 [2006] ECR I-10685.

[59] Case C-224/98 *Marie-Nathalie D'Hoop v Office national de l'emploi* EU:C:2002:432 [2002] ECR I-06191.

[60] Case C-190/98 *Volker Graf v Filzmoser Maschinenbau GmbH* EU:C:2000:49 [2000] ECR 2000 I-493.

[61] Case C-73/08 *Nicolas Bressol and Others and Céline Chaverot and Others v Gouvernement de la Communauté française* EU:C:2010:181 [2010] ECR 2010 I-2735.

[62] 'Commission Endorses Austria's Quota System for Medical Studies as Necessary to Protect the Austrian Health Care System, but Asks Austria to End the Quota Imposed on Dental Studies', European Commission Press Release IP/17/1282.

students – a holistic system like the Hungarian one is probably not in line with these general rules of EU law.

3.6 The Case of the Central European University

In 2017 the Hungarian government introduced a law making it impossible for one of the best universities in Hungary – CEU, an American–Hungarian private university – to function in the counrty.[63] The new law introduced two important provisions. First, the activity of any foreign university functioning in Hungary must be based on an agreement between the foreign country and Hungary. Second, foreign universities operating in Hungary must be 'present and offer programs in the country in which they are accredited'.[64] The law triggered protests within and outside Hungary; it was mentioned in the Sargentini Report; and, upon request from the Commissioner of Fundamental Rights, the Constitutional Court started a procedure to review it. One of the most plausible legal arguments against governmental actions was expressed by a group of scholars (including László Sólyom, the former president of Hungary),[65] who wrote an amicus curiae for the Constitutional Court explaining why the new law is unconstitutional.

In response, the European Commission launched an infringement procedure against Hungary.[66] The Hungarian Constitutional Court suspended its procedure – a widely criticized move.[67] Later, a reasoned opinion was sent to Hungary.[68] In December 2017 the Commission referred the case to the Court of Justice of the EU,[69] and in October 2018 CEU announced that it would leave the country and move to Vienna, as the Hungarian government had not signed

---

[63] See Act XXV of 2017 and Art. 76 of the Law on national higher education; European Commission for Democracy through Law (Venice Commission) Hungary Preliminary Opinion on Act XXV of 4 April 2017 on the Amendment of Act CCIV of 2011 on National Tertiary Education; Anne Corbett and Claire Gordon, 'Academic Freedom in Europe: The Central European University Affair and the Wider Lessons' (2018) 58 History of Education Quarterly 467–74; Renáta Uitz, 'Academic Freedom in an Illiberal Democracy: From Rule of Law through Rule by Law to Rule by Men in Hungary' https://verfassungsblog.de/academic-freedom-in-an-illiberal-democracy-from-rule-of-law-through-rule-by-law-to-rule-by-men-in-hungary/; Zsolt Enyedi, 'Democratic Backsliding and Academic Freedom in Hungary' (2018) 16 Perspectives on Politics 1067–74.

[64] Petra Bárd, 'The Open Society and Its Enemies: An Attack Against CEU, Academic Freedom and the Rule of Law' CEPS Policy Insight No. 2017/14 p.2.

[65] András Jakab, Miklós Lévay, Zoltàn Szente and Làszló Sólyom, 'Amicus Curiae az Alkotmánybírósághoz' http://public.mkab.hu/dev/dontesek.nsf/0/af27b40ba3b0b821c1258109003f9b19/$FILE/II_1036_5_2017_%C3%A1ll%C3%A1sfoglal%C3%A1s.002.pdf/II_1036_5_2017_%C3%A1ll%C3%A1sfoglal%C3%A1s.pdf.

[66] European Commission, *Daily News* (26 April 2017) http://europa.eu/rapid/press-release_MEX-17-1116_en.htm.

[67] Gábor Halmai, 'The Hungarian Constitutional Court Betrays Academic Freedom and Freedom of Association' https://verfassungsblog.de/the-hungarian-constitutional-court-betrays-academic-freedom-and-freedom-of-association/.

[68] European Commission, 'Hungary: Commission Takes Second Step in Infringement Procedure on Higher Education Law', Press Release IP/17/1952.

[69] European Commission, 'Commission Refers Hungary to the European Court of Justice of the EU over the Higher Education Law', Press Release IP/17/5004.

the necessary treaty with the US.⁷⁰ The ECJ delivered its judgment in the case in October 2020, and upheld the decision of the Commission.⁷¹

The argumentation of the Commission, and also, partly, the final judgment, deserves some attention. Based on its logic, the Commission only starts a procedure in cases that violate internal market rules or other EU law. In such cases, as a connecting factor to EU law exists, the Commission is able to use the rules of the EU Charter of Fundamental Rights. According to this scheme, for example, when judges were expelled in Hungary, the EU started a procedure not because of an attack against the judiciary but because of age discrimination.⁷² The same is true in the CEU case: here, academic freedom and university autonomy were at stake; however, to trigger the application of the Charter of Fundamental Rights, universities have to be interpreted as businesses. This approach focuses solely on internal market violations, and it leaves a wide grey zone for those programmes that are financed partly by the students and partly by the state at public universities, as well as for those that are partly financed by the state at private universities. According to the *Humbel* case, publicly funded education is not a service under EU law, so it is not possible to find grounds for actions.⁷³ This narrow interpretation could allow a complete shutdown of a public, state-funded university based on political reasons. This raises the question: how could we still resolve an obviously discriminatory, unfair situation, against all odds, with the tools of EU law? One possible answer would be to re-interpret EU citizenship as an institution that also contains fundamental rights. Through this, we could forget the fixation on competency and could re-interpret the problem of academic freedom as a fundamental rights issue rather than a policy-related problem.

4. EU CITIZENSHIP AS A CONNECTING FACTOR BETWEEN ACADEMIC CITIZENS AND FUNDAMENTAL RIGHTS

In its more than two decades of history, EU citizenship was constructed step-by-step and changed from a narrowly interpreted phenomenon into a more complex institution. As a result of ECJ judgments, more and more fundamental rights were attached to citizenship.⁷⁴ In this process, which could probably be marked by the symbolic *Ruiz Zambrano* judgment,⁷⁵ the re-interpretation extended over a strict interpretation of the black letter law, especially in

---

⁷⁰ 'CEU to Open Vienna Campus for U.S. Degrees in 2019; University Determined to Uphold Academic Freedom' www.ceu.edu/article/2018-10-25/ceu-open-vienna-campus-us-degrees-2019-university-determined-uphold-academic.

⁷¹ Case C-66/18 *European Commission v Hungary* ECLI:EU:C:2020:792

⁷² Case C-286/12 *European Commission v Hungary* EU:C:2012:687; Csongor István Nagy, 'Do European Union Member States Have to Respect Human Rights? The Application of the European Union's "Federal Bill of Rights" to Member States' (2017) 27 Indiana International & Comparative Law Review 9 et seq. For similar critique regarding the CEU case, see Laurent Pech and Kim Lane Scheppele (n 3) 13.

⁷³ Case C-263/86 *Belgian State v René Humbel and Marie-Thérèse Edel* EU:C:1988:451 [1988] ECR 5365.

⁷⁴ Dora Kostakopoulou, *Institutional Constructivism in Social Sciences and Law* (CUP 2018) 105 et seq.

⁷⁵ Case C-34/09 Judgment of the Court (Grand Chamber) of 8 March 2011 *Gerardo Ruiz Zambrano v Office national de l'emploi* (ONEm) EU:C:2011:124 ECR 2011 I-01177.

fields such as the free movement of persons.[76] Today, however, several commentators see a decline in the fundamental rights aspects of EU citizenship (see, for example, the *McCarthy*[77] and *Dereçi*[78] cases), especially because some fundamental rights such as 'the right to respect family life appeared to be not sufficient [alone] to bring the cases within the scope of EU law'.[79]

Based on the development of EU citizenship, though, one could argue that European institutions could re-interpret EU citizenship so that it could host a broader framework of fundamental rights (a renewed 'substance of the rights' formula), including rules on academic freedom.[80] Through such a method, citizenship in the same way that connecting factors are used in conflict-of-laws: if an EU citizen is affected in the case, this could trigger the application of certain fundamental rights, as set in Art. 2 TEU or the Charter of Fundamental Rights. If we accept the view that EU citizenship moved from a completely supplemental institution towards a fundamental one, even if it did not reach a final, comprehensive level, one could argue that adding fundamental rights to it would be the next step in its development. This approach would have the advantages that it would not leave EU citizens without basic rights. it would refuse to accept the concept of reverse discrimination[81] and it would handle the EU as a mature institution, an actual community with enforceable laws. Moreover, it could put the stress back on citizens, instead of the market and its special rationality.

However, using EU citizenship as a shield could also have disadvantages. First, just as national citizenship can have an exclusivist character, it could exclude those who are not citizens of a member state – highly unfair treatment, of, for example, university professors or students from third countries. This exclusivist aspect of (EU) citizenship is mentioned by many commentators; it is not a new phenomenon.[82] Second, such a solution could lead to a partial protection: individual academic freedom could be granted, but whether it could cover institutional freedom as well is questionable. As we have seen above, a high number of cases were related to the curtailment of freedom of institutions, not individuals. Probably, however, under a broader interpretation, EU citizenship could also cover this area. From this perspective, institutional freedom could be interpreted as something stemming from the collective: the

---

[76] Case C-184/99 *Rudy Grzelczyk v Centre public d'aide sociale d'Ottignies-Louvain-la-Neuve* EU:C:2001:458 European Court Reports 2001 I-06193; Case C-300/04 *M. G. Eman and O. B. Sevinger v College van burgemeester en wethouders van Den Haag* EU:C:2006:545 ECR 2006 I-08055; Case C-135/08 *Janko Rottmann v Freistaat Bayern* EU:C:2010:104 ECR 2010 I-01449.

[77] Case C-434/09 *Shirley McCarthy v Secretary of State for the Home Department* EU:C:2011:277, [2011] ECR I-3375.

[78] Case C-256/11 Judgment of the Court (Grand Chamber) of 15 November 2011 *Murat Dereci and Others v Bundesministerium für Inneres* EU:C:2011:734.

[79] Chiara Raucea, 'Fundamental Rights: The Missing Pieces of European Citizenship?' (2013) 14 German Law Journal 2036; Adrienne Yong, *The Rise and Decline of Fundamental Rights in EU Citizenship* (Hart 2019).

[80] Dominik Düsterhaus, 'EU Citizenship and Fundamental Rights: Contradictory, Converging or Complementary?' in Dimitry Kochenov (ed.), *EU Citizenship and Federalism* (CUP 2017) 651 *et seq.*; 'Article 20 TFEU precludes national measures which have the effect of depriving citizens of the Union of the genuine enjoyment of the substance of the rights conferred by virtue of their status as citizens of the Union' Judgment in *Ruiz Zambrano*, para 42.

[81] Alina Tryfonidou, 'Reverse Discrimination in Purely Internal Situations: An Incongruity in a Citizens' Europe' (2008) 35 Legal Issues of Economic Integration 43–67.

[82] Dora Kostakopoulou, *The Future Governance of Citizenship* (CUP 2008) 102.

common rights of individuals. However, in this case the connection would be slightly looser than optimal, especially from a legal perspective. On the other hand, such an approach would still enable us to proceed in most cases in which academic freedom is harmed.

5. EU FUNDAMENTAL RIGHTS AND ACADEMIC FREEDOM

If we go further, we find numerous methods that could work well to defend academic freedom. Some of them are connected to the institution of EU citizenship; others could be linked to it, but could also be used in a more universal way to include foreign nationals.

First, according to the Reverse Solange approach,[83] if states abolish certain universities or ban programmes for political reasons, and such actions fit among other systemic fundamental rights violations made by these states, such violations could reach an 'essence' of rights that must be protected. This method links fundamental rights strictly to EU citizenship. However, using it would also have disadvantages,[84] such as limiting answers to problems when systemic deficiencies occur, and it would not defend fundamental rights from all kinds of violations, only those that reach the essence of these rights.[85] Moreover, the concept of systemic violations can pick up rather shady contours.[86] Finally, narrowing down its scope to EU citizenship could also be questioned, just as we have seen above. However, it nevertheless could be a tool to defend academic freedom in Europe.

Second, through a case-by-case analysis, the European Commission could use more progressive interpretations than its widely criticized practice does today, and it could interpret damages to academic freedom as fundamental rights violations. This would be especially the case if the persons in question are European citizens. As a result, the Commission could start procedures for the violation of the values set in Art. 2. TEU and could express that the values codified there are part of the Union acquis and are enforceable.[87] However, in my opinion, at present not only practitioners but also the majority of scholars mistakenly prefer a narrow interpretation of Art. 2 of the TEU and believe that a breach of values should be bound to the Art. 7 TEU procedure.[88]

---

[83] Armin von Bogdandy, Matthias Kottmann, Carlino Antpöhler, Johanna Dickschen, Simon Hentrei and Maja Smrkolj, 'Reverse Solange – Protecting the Essence of Fundamental Rights against EU Member States' (2012) 49 CML Rev 515.

[84] Dimitry Kochenov, 'On Policing Article 2 TEU Compliance: Reverse Solange and Systemic Infringements Analyzed' [2014] Polish Yearbook of International Law 153–62.

[85] Armin von Bogdandy and Michael Ioannidis, 'Systemic Deficiency in the Rule of Law: What It Is, What Has Been Done, What Can Be Done' (2014) 51 CML Rev 59–96.

[86] Case C-216/18 PPU *Request for a Preliminary Ruling from High Court (Ireland)* ECLI:EU:C: 2018:586; Kim Lane Scheppele, 'Rule of Law Retail and Rule of Law Wholesale: The ECJ's (Alarming) "Celmer" Decision' https://verfassungsblog.de/rule-of-law-retail-and-rule-of-law-wholesale-the-ecjs-alarming-celmer-decision/.

[87] Dimitry Kochenov, 'The Acquis and Its Principles: The Enforcement of the "Law" versus the Enforcement of "Values" in the European Union' in András Jakab and Dimitry Kochenov (eds), *The Enforcement of EU Law and Values* (OUP 2017) 12 *et seq*.

[88] Jürgen Schwarze, 'EUV Artikel 2' in Hans von der Groeben, Jürgen Schwarze and Armin Hatje (eds), *EU Kommentar* (Beck 2012) 66; Christian Calliess, 'Art. 2. EUV' in Christian Calliess and Martin Ruffert (eds), *EUV/AEU* (C.H. Beck 2016) 48; Olivier De Schutter, 'Infringement Proceedings as a Tool for the Enforcement of Fundamental Rights in the European Union' www.opensocietyfoundations

Third, to solve the problem of systemic breaches, Kim Lane Scheppele suggests that the Commission should start systemic infringement procedures. Such bulk actions would cover several procedures in the same field at once.[89] Without such an approach, in a number of cases – such as the above-mentioned systemic changes of university governance – there is a high chance that we would not be able to grasp the concatenation of problems without an overview of the whole area, and EU actions will have to be limited to the most obvious fundamental rights breaches. Dimitry Kochenov adds that, based on Art. 259 of the TFEU, member states could also start such procedures (he calls this 'biting intergovernmentalism').[90]

Fourth, András Jakab suggests that the EU Charter of Fundamental Rights should be applied, contrary to its Art. 51(1), which excludes its application in domestic cases.[91] While one might be surprised that this would be possible against the black letter of the law,[92] this method is not as irrational as it seems. If we analyse the relationship of Art. 2 and the Charter, the latter can be interpreted as an exposition of the former. In the *Janah v Libya Benkharbouche v Sudan* case, the proceeding UK courts stressed the importance of the general principles of EU law and applied the Charter, even though, under a strict interpretation, they had to refuse to do so.[93] The Charter, in its Art. 13, claims that the arts and scientific research shall be free of constraints, and it stresses that academic freedom shall be respected. Its Art. 14 emphasizes that everyone has the right to education and to have access to vocational and continuing training. It also grants the freedom to found educational establishments with due respect for democratic principles (*sic!*) and parents' right to ensure the education and teaching of their children in conformity with their religious, philosophical and pedagogical worldview. Applying these rules, even if they are not codified in Title V on EU Citizens' Rights, would be

---

.org/sites/default/files/infringement-proceedings-as-tool-for-enforcement-of-fundamental-rights-in-eu-20171214.pdf; Dimitry Kochenov and Laurent Pech, 'Monitoring and Enforcement of the Rule of Law in the EU: Rhetoric and Reality' (2015) 11 European Constitutional Law Review 519.

[89] Kim Lane Scheppele, 'Enforcing the Basic Principles of EU Law through Systemic Infringement Actions' in Carlos Closa and Dimitry Kochenov (eds), *Reinforcing Rule of Law Oversight in the European Union* (CUP 2016) 122 *et seq.*

[90] Dimitry Kochenov (n 87) 20; Laurent Pech and Kim Lane Scheppele (n 1) 39.

[91] András Jakab, 'Supremacy of the EU Charter in National Courts in Purely Domestic Cases' https://verfassungsblog.de/the-eu-as-a-community-of-human-rights/.

[92] 'Where a legal situation does not fall within the scope of Union law, the Court has no jurisdiction to rule on it, and any Charter provisions relied upon cannot, of themselves, form the basis for such jurisdiction'. Case C-265/13 *Emiliano Torralbo Marcos v Korota SA and Fondo de Garantía Salarial* EU:C:2014:187; see also Case C-206/13 *Cruciano Siragusa v Regione Sicilia — Soprintendenza Beni Culturali e Ambientali di Palermo* EU:C:2014:126; Case C-40/11 *Yoshikazu Iida v Stadt Ulm* EU:C:2012:691; Case C-87/12 *Kreshnik Ymeraga and Others v Ministre du Travail, de l'Emploi et de l'Immigration* EU:C:2013:291; Case C-198/13 *Víctor Manuel Julian Hernández and Others v Reino de España (Subdelegación del Gobierno de España en Alicante) and Others* EU:C:2014:2055; for similar hostility concerning the application of the Strasbourg Law outside EU competency, see Joined Cases C-60 and 61/84 *Cinéthèque SA and Others v Fédération nationale des cinémas français* EU:C:1985:329 [1985] ECR 2605; Case C-299/95 *Friedrich Kremzow v Republik Österreich* EU:C:1997:254 [1997] ECR I-2629.

[93] *Benkharbouche v Secretary of State for Foreign and Commonwealth Affairs*; *Libya v Janah* [2017] UKSC 62; Joshua Rozenberg, 'Never Mind Human Rights Law, EU Law is Much More Powerful' www.theguardian.com/law/2013/oct/09/human-rights-eu-law-powerful; for the first instance decision, see www.scribd.com/doc/173329607/Janah-v-Libya-Benkharbouche-v-Sudan.

a great step forward. It would also solve the conundrum that while we have rules on academic freedom, they cannot be applied to most universities.

Fifth, the EU could create a Magna Carta of Academia, as proposed by Terence Karran.[94] This document could be drafted similarly to the works on a common EU private law,[95] and it could implement many different sources on academic freedom.[96] In the future, it could serve as a substratum of enforceable academic rights of EU citizens.

6. CONCLUSIONS: PSEUDO-ORIGINALISM VERSUS PROGRESSIVE APPROACHES

The preceding discussion has demonstrated that one could find many ways to defend academic freedom in the present system of EU law, including through re-interpretation of EU citizenship. However, right now, the mainstream of EU law scholarship seems to accept that this cannot be done, because enforcing human rights in the EU would be an extension of the rules on EU citizenship as well as of Art. 2 TEU and Art. 52 of the Charter of Fundamental Rights. As a result, this pseudo-originalism does not allow a more forward-looking interpretation of Art. 2 TEU, adheres to an extremely narrow interpretation of direct effect, limits the scope of the Charter and blocks the creation of a proper EU citizenship with fundamental rights. This misinterpretation relies on the political ineffectiveness (in fact: political paralysis) of the EU institutions, which is then ideologized by scholars. The impression is given that this would be the only available form of cooperation, based on some kind of 'proper' interpretation of EU law. As the root cause of this problem lies in intra-EU politics, new institutions (such as a new, special commission on human rights and rule of law)[97] will not be effective either, as the roots of the issues can be traced back to member state politicians, who are interested in maintaining an underperforming system.[98]

---

[94] Terence Karran, 'Academic Freedom in Europe: Time for a Magna Charta?' (2009) 22 Higher Education Policy 163–89.

[95] Nils Jansen and Reinhard Zimmermann, '"A European Civil Code in All But Name": Discussing the Nature and Purposes of the Draft Common Frame of Reference' (2010) 69 Cambridge Law Journal 98–112; Christian von Bar and Eric Clive, *Principles, Definitions and Model Rules of European Private Law – Draft Common Frame of Reference (DCFR)* (Sellier 2010).

[96] This could cover the International Covenant on Economic, Social, and Cultural Rights, the UNESCO recommendation concerning the status of higher education teaching personnel, the Magna Charta Universitatum from 1988, and decisions of the European Court of Human Rights, among others; see Tamas D Ziegler, 'Academic Freedom in the European Union: Why the Single European Market is a Bad Reference Point', Max Planck Institute for Comparative Public Law & International Law (MPIL) Research Paper No. 2019-03, p.25.

[97] Jan-Werner Müller, 'Should the EU Protect Democracy and the Rule of Law inside Member States?' (2015) 21(2) European Law Journal 141–60.

[98] As Posner put it regarding Hungary, '[i]f Europeans cannot even compel a small, financially dependent country in their midst to comply with human rights, then one must infer that they do not care enough about human rights to devote substantial resources to them'. Eric Posner, *The Twilight of Human Rights* (OUP 2014) 106. To put it sharply: states deliberately undermine human rights for economic interests. See e.g. Nik Martin, Ben Knight, 'German Arms Exports Shoot to Record High, Hungary Biggest Buyer' Deutsche Welle (27 Dec. 2019) www.dw.com/en/german-arms-exports-shoot-to-record-high-hungary-biggest-buyer/a-51806849.

While scholars tend to argue against more progressive approaches as 'inappropriate', 'unscientific' or 'unlawful', it is not set in stone that Art. 2 TEU cannot be applied directly, or that EU citizens cannot have enforceable fundamental rights in academia. If we interpret Article 2 TEU as some kind of a legal text, turning a blind eye to human rights breaches seems to be in conflict with it. It is also not as obvious that concepts such as legal pluralism, multi-level constitutionalism or national identity should be allowed to be abused to support authoritarian tendencies.[99] In this regard, US constitutional reasoning, with its brave stance against injustices, could serve as a model for Europe.[100] There, if constitutional provisions were not re-interpreted regularly, minorities still would not have fundamental rights, black people would not be permitted to vote and schools would still be segregated. Law always developed through re-interpretations; the question is simply which direction we take. If we are serious about forming a joint European community based on common values, this cannot proceed through allowing constitutional authoritarianism, wherever it occurs in the EU. By accepting lower standards, the EU gradually empties the content of fundamental rights and rule of law, thereby weakening the institution of EU citizenship and the academic freedom of EU citizens.

---

[99] Kim Lane Scheppele and Gábor Halmai, 'The Tyranny of Values or the Tyranny of One-party States?' VerfB (25 Nov. 2019) https://verfassungsblog.de/the-tyranny-of-values-or-the-tyranny-of-one-party-states/; Julio Baquero Cruz, 'An Area of Darkness: Three Conceptions of the Relationship between European Union Law and State Constitutional Law' in Neil Walker, Jo Show and Stephen Tierney (eds), *Europe's Constitutional Mosaic* (Bloomsbury 2011) 55; Julio Baquero Cruz, 'Another Look at Constitutional Pluralism in the European Union' (2016) 22(3) European Law Journal 356–74; Julio Baquero Cruz, 'The Legacy of the Maastricht-Urteil and the Pluralist Movement' (2008) 14(4) European Law Journal 389–422; Roger Daniel Kelemen, 'The Dangers of Constitutional Pluralism' in Gareth Davies and Matej Avbelj (eds), *Research Handbook on Legal Pluralism and EU Law* (Edward Elgar Publishing 2018) 402; Gábor Halmai, 'Abuse of Constitutional Identity: The Hungarian Constitutional Court on Interpretation of Article E) (2) of the Fundamental Law' (2018) 43 *Review of Central and East European Law* 23–42.

[100] Michael Rosenfeld, 'Comparing Constitutional Review by the European Court of Justice and the U.S. Supreme Court' (2006) 4 I CON, 634 *et seq.*; Eric Foner, *The Story of American Freedom* (Picador 1999).

13. Does Member State withdrawal automatically extinguish EU citizenship?

Oliver Garner

1. INTRODUCTION: THE REVIVAL OF A HYPOTHETICAL LEGAL QUESTION

On 7 February 2018 the District Court in Amsterdam made a decision to send a preliminary reference to the Court of Justice of the European Union.[1] The District Court asked whether the United Kingdom's withdrawal from the European Union automatically leads to the loss of the status and rights of EU citizenship for UK nationals. It referred the further question of whether conditions or restrictions should be imposed as a matter of EU law on the maintenance of EU citizenship rights in the event that EU citizenship is lost. A Court of Justice judgment on these questions had the potential to resolve the ambiguity that has enshrouded the existential nature of EU citizenship since its creation nearly 30 years ago. This had the potential of emancipatory consequences for the role of individuals in the EU constitutional order.[2]

However, this constitutional crossroads was avoided by the decision of the Amsterdam Appeal Court on 19 June 2018 to reverse the decision of the District Court.[3] The Appeal Court decided not to uphold the preliminary reference request because the questions were declared 'insufficiently concrete' in light of the hypothetical nature of the complaint. Furthermore, it is reported that the Appeal Court found that 'given that the Brexit negotiations [were] ongoing, there is a good chance the European court would rule the case inadmissible'.[4] The United Kingdom confirmed its withdrawal from the European Union on 31 January 2020, at which point EU citizenship was ostensibly extinguished for all UK nationals. As it proved in the fast-tracking of the *Wightman* decision,[5] the Court of Justice was willing to address politically and temporally sensitive legal questions pertaining to Brexit before withdrawal

---

[1] C/13/640244 / KG ZA 17-1327 of the Rechtbank Amsterdam of 7 February 2018 – NL: RBAMS: 2018:605, available at https://uitspraken.rechtspraak.nl/inziendocument?id=ECLI:NL:RBAMS:2018: 605 accessed 10 December 2019 (hereafter 'the Amsterdam Case').
 For an English translation, see Jolyon Maugham, 'Decision of the District Court in Amsterdam' (Waiting for Godot, 13 February 2018) https://waitingfortax.com/2018/02/13/decision-of-the-district-court-in-amsterdam accessed 10 December 2019.

[2] See Oliver Garner, 'The Existential Crisis of Citizenship of the European Union: The Argument for an Autonomous Status' (2018) 20 Cambridge Yearbook of European Legal Studies 116.

[3] C/13/640244 / KG ZA 17-1327 of the Gerechtshof Amsterdam NL:RBAMS:2018:605 of 19 June 2018. For a summary in English see 'Appeal judges reject British EU citizenship claim, won't refer to EU court' (*DutchNews.nl*, 19 June 2018) www.dutchnews.nl/news/2018/06/appeal-judges-reject-british-eu-citizenship-claim-wont-refer-to-eu-court/?utm_campaign=shareaholic&utm_medium=linkedin&utm_source=socialnetwork accessed 10 December 2019.

[4] ibid.

[5] Order of the President of the Court in Case C-621/18, *Wightman v Secretary of State for Exiting the European Union* (President of the Court, 19 October 2018).

was confirmed. The General Court, however, confirmed this juridical reality in the *Shindler v European Commission*[6] case by finding that an application for the adoption of a decision to maintain EU citizenship for certain UK nationals was manifestly inadmissible. Arguably, political expedience dictated the Court's legal reasoning, due to the explosive ramifications of throwing the legality of the Withdrawal Agreement into doubt after its conclusion.

This chapter will consider the legal arguments regarding the retention of EU citizenship by former Member State nationals in the event of the counter-factual if the Court of Justice had been posed the preliminary reference before Brexit, or had considered the question admissible after the Withdrawal Agreement came into force. Section 2 will provide a preliminary overview of how the issue of EU citizenship was addressed during the Brexit negotiations, including political arguments that UK nationals should retain their EU citizenship despite the withdrawal of their Member State of nationality. The next section will consider the reasoning of the District Court in its decision to refer the question. The Appeal Court's Decision to overturn the reference will be criticised on the basis that the appropriate time for resolution of the question would have been before the consequences of withdrawal took hold. The arguments for and against automatic extinction will be presented on the basis of the underpinning interpretative methodologies. This section will conclude by considering a potential compromise on the question. The final section will move on to consider the broader normative implications of a judicial decision that EU citizenship is not automatically extinguished upon the withdrawal of a Member State. The argument will be made that such a decision would be a transformative emancipation of EU citizenship and a transformation into a fully autonomous political and legal status. Such a reconstruction of the EU constitutional settlement should only take place through the exercise of self-determination by constituent individuals in accordance with political processes, rather than through a legal judgment.[7]

2. THE ROAD TO AMSTERDAM: THE PLACE OF EU CITIZENSHIP IN THE BREXIT NEGOTIATIONS

2.1 The Brexit Negotiations

The value of EU citizenship was not a central tenet of the 'remain' campaign in the 2016 referendum. Rather than making a positive case for the benefits of EU citizenship, the government's campaign focused on the negative economic consequences of a vote to leave the EU. For example, one UK government leaflet does not make a single reference to 'EU citizenship'. The only implicit reference is found in the statement that '[m]illions of UK citizens travel to Europe each year. The EU has made this easier and cheaper.'[8] EU citizenship and its associated rights did become a central feature of withdrawal negotiations. This arose through the EU

---

[6] *Shindler v European Commission* [2020] OJ T-627/19.

[7] Oliver Garner, 'Does Member State Withdrawal from the European Union Extinguish EU Citizenship: C/13/640244 / KG ZA 17-1327 of the Rechtbank Amsterdam ("The Amsterdam Case")' (European Law Blog, 19 February 2018) http://europeanlawblog.eu/2018/02/19/does-member-state-withdrawal-from-the-european-union-extinguish-eu-citizenship-c13640244-kg-za-17-1327-rechtbankamsterdam-the-amsterdam-case accessed 10 December 2019.

[8] HM Government, 'Why the Government believes that voting to remain in the European Union is the best decision for the UK' https://assets.publishing.service.gov.uk/government/uploads/system/

institutions' political choice to prioritise protecting citizens' rights as one of the three crucial issues for negotiation. The UK Prime Minister exercised the legal power to notify the intention to withdraw from the European Union under Article 50(2) TEU on 29 March 2017.[9] The letter provides a list of principles for the discussions. Principle ii addresses citizens, and outlines the objective to 'aim to strike an early agreement about their [citizens of the remaining Member States living in the United Kingdom, and UK citizens living elsewhere in the European Union] rights'.[10]

The official European Council guidelines for the negotiations, adopted under Article 50(2) TEU on 29 April 2017, further elucidate this objective. Paragraph 8 declares that the arrangements concerning citizens' rights are a core tenet of the objective of ensuring an 'orderly withdrawal'. It states:

> The right for every EU citizen, and of his or her family members, to live, to work or to study in any EU Member State is a fundamental aspect of the European Union. Along with other rights provided under EU law, it has shaped the lives and choices of millions of people. Agreeing reciprocal guarantees to safeguard the status and rights derived from EU law at the date of withdrawal of EU and UK citizens, and their families, affected by the United Kingdom's withdrawal from the Union will be the first priority for the negotiations. Such guarantees must be effective, enforceable, non-discriminatory and comprehensive, including the right to acquire permanent residence after a continuous period of five years of legal residence. Citizens should be able to exercise their rights through smooth and simple administrative procedures.[11]

This set the stage early for a limitation on the scope of protection. The rights to 'live, work, or study' narrow the remit to the juridical rights of free movement granted by Article 20(2)(a) TFEU and Article 21 TFEU.[12] The guidelines do not explicitly outline that negotiations would seek to preserve the political rights for citizens to vote in European Parliament and local elections granted by Article 20(2)(b) TFEU and Article 22 TFEU.[13] The guidelines are thus ambiguous over whether the Withdrawal Agreement would seek merely to preserve the rights of UK citizens, or whether it would seek more holistically to also preserve the status of EU citizenship for those who hold it through their nationality of a withdrawing Member State.

The European Parliament resolution on negotiations with the United Kingdom published on 5 April 2017 is more ambitious on this question. Paragraph 27 states that the European Parliament

> [t]akes note that many citizens of the United Kingdom have expressed strong opposition to losing the rights they currently enjoy pursuant to Article 20 of the Treaty on the Functioning of the European

---

uploads/attachment_data/file/525022/20160523_Leaflet_EASY_READ_FINAL_VERSION.pdf accessed 10 December 2019.

[9] Prime Minister of the United Kingdom, 'Prime Minister's letter to Donald Tusk triggering Article 50', published 29 March 2017 www.gov.uk/government/publications/prime-ministers-letter-to-donald-tusk-triggering-article-50 accessed 10 December 2019.

[10] ibid.

[11] European Council, 'Special meeting of the European Council (Art.50)(29 April 2017) – Guidelines', Brussels, 29 April 2017 (OR.en) EUCO XT 20004/17, para 8.

[12] Consolidated Version of the Treaty on the Functioning of the European Union [2008] OJ C326/01, art.20 and 21. (Hereafter 'TFEU')

[13] ibid, arts 20(2)(b) and 22.

Union; proposes that the EU-27 examine how to mitigate this within the limits of Union primary law whilst fully respecting the principles of reciprocity, equity, symmetry and non-discrimination.[14]

As negotiations commenced, however, it became clear that this 'mitigation' for UK nationals would indeed be limited to the preservation of the juridical rights concerning free movement. This was confirmed in the publication of the joint report[15] of the United Kingdom and the European Union on the first phase of withdrawal negotiations and the accompanying Communication[16] from the Commission to the European Council on 8 December 2017. The latter document confirms the scope of protection:

> [T]he principles underlying the Union's position are that the Withdrawal Agreement should protect the rights of Union citizens, United Kingdom nationals and their family members who, at the date of withdrawal, have enjoyed rights relating to free movement under Union law, as well as rights which are in the process of being obtained and the rights the enjoyment of which will intervene at a later date.[17]

Agreement on citizens' rights was confirmed by the 'green' colour coding of Part II on citizens' rights in the draft Withdrawal Agreement of 19 March 2018.[18]

2.2 The Withdrawal Agreement

The Withdrawal Agreement[19] extensively preserves the disparate threads of the legal rights that individuals derive from EU citizenship.[20] The legal interpretation of the provisions offered here asserts that the Agreement ossifies a conception of the status as one of mere juridical objectivity. This operates to the detriment of a conception of EU citizenship as a status that enables political self-determination. This partial preservation of the existential significance of EU citizenship for UK citizens would inform the legal challenge in the Amsterdam case. Furthermore, it is precisely the text of the Withdrawal Agreement and its implementation by Member States that is the action which the litigants claimed violates the Treaties. If EU citi-

---

[14] European Parliament resolution of 5 April 2017 on negotiations with the United Kingdom following its notification that it intends to withdraw from the European Union (2017/2593(RSP)).

[15] Joint report from the negotiators of the European Union and the United Kingdom Government on progress during phase 1 of negotiations under Article 50 TEU on the United Kingdom's orderly withdrawal from the European Union, 8 December 2017, TF50 (2017) 19 – Commission to EU27.

[16] Communication from the Commission to the European Council (Article 50) on the state of progress of the negotiations with the United Kingdom under Article 50 of the Treaty on European Union, Brussels 8.12.2017, COM(2017) 784 final.

[17] ibid, section 4(a).

[18] Draft Agreement on the withdrawal of the United Kingdom of Great Britain and Northern Ireland from the European Union and the European Atomic Energy Community highlighting the progress made (coloured version) in the negotiation round with the UK of 16–19 March 2018, 19 March 2018, TF50 (2018) 35 – Commission to EU27, Part II.

[19] Agreement on the withdrawal of the United Kingdom of Great Britain and Northern Ireland from the European Union and the European Atomic Energy Community, OJ CI 66/1.

[20] See Oliver Garner, 'Citizens' Rights in the UK–EU Withdrawal Agreement: Ossifying EU Citizenship as a Juridical Status?' (*GLOBALCIT*, 28 November 2018) http://globalcit.eu/citizens-rights-in-the-uk-eu-withdrawal-agreement-ossifying-eu-citizenship-as-a-juridical-status/ accessed 10 December 2019.

zenship were not automatically extinguished by Member State withdrawal, then the removal of the political rights, and termination of the hereditary nature of the status, by this act of the EU would be contrary to Article 20 TFEU and the other primary and secondary law establishing and maintaining EU citizenship.

The preamble to the Agreement establishes the purpose of the citizens rights chapter: to provide reciprocal protection in the situation of the exercise of free movement rights before a date set by Agreement, and to ensure that the rights are enforceable and based on the principle of non-discrimination. The temporal starting point for protection is the exercise of free movement rights before the end of the transition period. However, this is complicated by additional temporal exceptions provided for in the text, in addition to the complexities regarding the scope of who is protected by the agreement.

Part II of the Withdrawal Agreement has been described by Stijn Smismans as a 'copy and paste of substantive EU law norms and EU procedural principles'.[21] Therefore, this functions as a transplant of the binding application of these norms from the source of the EU legal order to the new source of the international agreement between the UK and the EU. This transplant would be an unlawful displacement of the rights of UK nationals in the event that EU citizenship persisted for nationals beyond the withdrawal of a Member State. Title II Chapter I implements the provisions of the citizens' rights Directive;[22] Chapter II transposes the Regulation on the free movement of workers;[23] Chapter III covers the Directive on the recognition of professional qualifications;[24] and Title III transplants the Regulation on the co-ordination of social security systems.[25] A crucial initial point is that the transposition of these provisions only preserves the rights of residence of UK nationals within their host Member State. The free movement rights to move between the borders of the EU-27 Member States are not preserved. The only partial rights of movement preserved for UK nationals are for those who fulfil the definition of 'frontier worker' in one or more states beyond the host State as defined in Article 9(b) of the Withdrawal Agreement. As the 'core' of EU citizenship as a juridical status,[26] the removal of these free movement rights for UK nationals would be the most materially deleterious effect if the legal reality were that they retained the status of EU citizenship.

Beyond the substance of these provisions, there are a number of features that are specific to the new regime, which marks a departure for UK nationals from the status quo of EU citizenship. The definition of 'host State' in Article 9(c) establishes the new default temporal grounding for the retention of residence rights. This condition is their exercise coming before the end of the transition period and continuing residence thereafter. An important temporal

---

[21] Stijn Smismans, 'EU Citizens' Rights Post Brexit: Why Direct Effect beyond the EU Is Not Enough' (2018) 14 European Constitutional Law Review 443, 473.

[22] European Parliament and Council Directive 2004/38/EC of 29 April 2004 on the rights of citizens of the Union and their family members to move and reside freely within the territory of the Member States [2004] OJ L158/77.

[23] European Parliament and Council Regulation (EU) No 492/2011 of 5 April 2011 on the freedom of movement for workers within the Union (codification) [2011] OJ L141/1.

[24] European Parliament and Council Directive 2005/36/EC of 7 September 2005 on the recognition of professional qualifications [2005] OJ L255/22.

[25] European Parliament and Council Regulation No 883/2004 of 29 April 2004 on the coordination of social security systems [2004] OJ L166/1.

[26] Floris de Witte, 'Freedom of Movement Needs to Be Defended as the Core of EU Citizenship' in Rainer Bauböck (ed.), *Debating European Citizenship* (Springer 2019).

point is that Article 15 confirms that periods of legal residence or work in accordance with Union law both before and after the end of the transition period are included in the calculation of the qualifying period necessary to acquire the right of permanent residence.

Article 10(1)(e)(ii) identifies certain categories of individuals who will be protected by the provisions even if they exercise their rights after the end of the transition period. These are direct relations of an EU national in the UK or a UK national in the EU who resided outside the host State before the end of the transition period and who fulfil the conditions established in point (2) of Article 2 of Directive 2004/38, in addition to individuals who are born to or legally adopted by covered individuals after the end of the transition period. Therefore, this functions as a generational clause which ensures the continuing protection of offspring so as to ensure continuity of legal rights in order to preserve family unity. Article 39 of the Agreement confirms the 'life-long protection' of the rights provided for in the Titles, which may only be revoked if the conditions are fulfilled for their revocation as established in Article 20 on the restrictions of the rights of residence and entry. Within an interpretation of surviving and inheritable EU citizenship, this is the clause that would be argued to illegitimately terminate the EU citizenship rights of a UK national upon their death.

On the theme of enforcement procedures, the Agreement provides for an extensive regime for the judicial protection of the substance of the rights in Part II. Article 158 provides for the continuation of the preliminary reference procedure from United Kingdom courts to the Court of Justice of the European Union for cases that commenced at first instance within a period of eight years after the end of the transition period. Article 159 establishes a new independent 'Authority' within the United Kingdom to monitor the implementation and application of Part Two. The contours of this Independent Monitoring Authority are detailed in Schedule 2 to the implementing legislation of the EU (Withdrawal Agreement) Act 2020.

This authority has powers equivalent to the European Commission's to conduct enquiries, to receive complaints from affected individuals and to bring a legal action before a competent court. The 'Authority' may only be disbanded by a decision of the Joint Committee overseeing the Agreement. Article 165(1)(a) establishes a specialised Committee on Citizens' Rights as one of the constituent parts of this Joint Committee overseeing the 'interpretation and application' of the Agreement and meeting at least once a year. Finally, with regard to enforcement, Article 178(2)(a) insulates Part II on citizens' rights from the remedy of temporary suspension of obligations by one of the parties to the Agreement following a failure to implement a ruling of the Joint Committee. This recognises that the protection of citizens' rights forms part of the substantive 'core' of the new legal order established by the Withdrawal Agreement. Accordingly, these provisions must be afforded comprehensive judicial protection and cannot be affected by the use of coercive remedial measures in public international law.

Although Part II of the Withdrawal Agreement preserved the substance of rights grounded in Article 20(2)(a) and Article 21 TFEU, it does not preserve the political rights to vote and stand as candidates in European Parliament and municipal elections provided for by Article 20(2)(b) and Article 22 TFEU. With regard to these political rights, it remains within the discretion of the United Kingdom to enfranchise EU nationals in local elections, and accordingly it remains within the discretion of individual EU Member States to enfranchise UK nationals to vote in local elections as third-country nationals.[27] The right for UK nationals to vote in

---

[27] Conditions for Electoral Rights 2019 database (*GLOBALCIT*, 2019) http://globalcit.eu/conditions-for-electoral-rights/ accessed 11 December 2019.

European Parliament elections in their Member State of residence is also not retained in the Withdrawal Agreement. Within the argument that EU citizenship is retained after Member State withdrawal, this provision would terminate the means for UK nationals to express their direct political will in the election of the co-legislators of the European Union's constitutional order.

Beyond the immediate practical question of whether the Withdrawal Agreement is legally entitled to transform the rights of UK nationals, the silence of the Withdrawal Agreement on political rights may ossify the conception of the status as one that individuals utilise for the passive acquisition and exercise of legal rights, rather than a status that empowers individuals to engage in self-determination through participation in democratic procedures.[28] The final point to make about Part II of the UK–EU Withdrawal Agreement is that, in addition to not preserving political rights, it also obviously does not preserve the status of EU citizenship for UK nationals. The negotiators on both the UK and the EU sides have relied implicitly on the interpretation of the Treaties whereby the withdrawal of a Member State automatically leads to the extinction of EU citizenship for those holding the nationality of that State.

This is based on the assumption that the condition for the acquisition of EU citizenship, nationality of a Member State, also functions as the condition for its extinction. Following the conclusion of the Withdrawal Agreement this question has become undeniably relevant, as the consequences of withdrawal have moved from the hypothetical to reality. Indeed, such a possibility may have been recognised by the General Court on Monday 26 November 2018 in its dismissal of the claim in the *Shindler* case that the European Council's recommendation for a decision to commence withdrawal negotiations did not directly affect the legal situation of UK citizens.[29] The press release states that this is 'merely a preparatory act and draws the consequences of the UK's notification of its intention to withdraw. It is therefore only at the end of the Article 50 TEU procedure that the rights of the applicants are liable to be affected.' This end of the process was confirmed with the extinction of EU citizenship for UK nationals through the coming into force of the Withdrawal Agreement on 31 January 2020.

2.3 Academic and Political Arguments to Preserve EU Citizenship for UK Nationals

The final Withdrawal Agreement provides for an extensive regime of legal protection for UK citizens in EU Member States and EU citizens within the United Kingdom. Before this focus on citizens' rights as an essentially juridical issue was settled, however, there were academic and political attempts to encourage a more holistic approach that would have seen EU citizenship preserved for UK nationals through political processes. The failure of such a political settlement to materialise left judicial proceedings as the only recourse for UK nationals to argue that their EU citizenship is not terminated upon the withdrawal of their Member State. Following the referendum, calls were made in academia to engage in a 'further decoupling of European and national citizenship'.[30] Daniel Augenstein and Mark Dawson argued in July

---

[28] Garner, 'Citizens' Rights in the Withdrawal Agreement' (n 20).
[29] T-458/17 *Shindler and Others v Council* (GC, 26 November 2018).
[30] Mark Dawson and Daniel Augenstein, 'After Brexit: Time for a Further Decoupling of European and National Citizenship?' (*Verfassungsblog*, 14 July 2016) https://verfassungsblog.de/brexit-decoupling-european-national-citizenship/ accessed 11 December 2019.

2016 that a 'further de-coupling of EU citizenship from national membership would allow the Union to replicate the emancipatory move of *Van Gend en Loos* – to liberate individuals from the preference of their states. De-coupling would signify a constitutional recognition that rights acquired as European citizens really are "fundamental".'[31]

Similarly, Dora Kostakopoulou has forwarded an argument for an autonomous 'Eurozenship'. The normative impulse behind the proposal is not limited to the consequences of Brexit, and covers the precarious position of third-country nationals also. However, Kostakopoulou does address withdrawal as a *problematique*: 'Brexit and the likelihood of mass deprivation of Eurozenship rights […] highlight the need for a reform. More than one million UK citizens who have activated their fundamental right to free movement and residence will be deprived of their EU rights without their consent.'[32]

An institutional expression of these academic positions was evident early in the Brexit negotiations. The MEP Charles Goerens' Amendment to a European Parliament Committee on Constitutional Affairs draft report advocated the insertion of 'associate European citizenship':

> A European associate citizenship for those who feel and wish to be part of the European project but are nationals of a former Member State; offers these associate citizens the rights of freedom of movement to reside on its territory as well as being represented in the [European] Parliament; Emphasises that involving citizens in the political processes of their country of residence helps to build European democracy, and therefore calls for the electoral rights of citizens residing in a Member State of which they are not nationals […] to be extended to include all remaining elections.[33]

Such a proposal seems to be a descendant, but at the individual level, of a proposal for the original withdrawal clause put forward by the MEP Andrew Duff and colleagues at the time of the draft constitutional treaty. They argued for the insertion of 'associate membership' of the EU on the basis that '[t]he Constitution makes a greater imposition on Member States […] so it makes sense to permit a Member State to choose a looser partnership in preference to full membership'.[34] However, like Duff's proposal, Goerens' argument for associate European citizenship would never come to fruition. The MEP retracted his amendment to the report, instead arguing via email correspondence that the European Parliament's Spring 2017 resolution[35] would be 'the best opportunity to give Brexit negotiator Guy Verhofstadt the possibility to enforce the Associate EU Citizenship'.[36] As was seen above, the European Parliament resolution only hinted at such a possibility, and the institution was unable to convert this position into the Council's negotiating directives and the Commission's negotiating strategy. Goerens'

---

[31] ibid.

[32] Dora Kostakopoulou, 'Who Should Be a Citizen of the Union? Towards an Autonomous European Union Citizenship' in Liav Orgard and Jules Lepoutre (eds) 'Should EU Citizenship be Disentangled from Member State Nationality?' (2019) EUI Working Papers RSCAS 2019/24 https://cadmus.eui.eu/bitstream/handle/1814/62229/RSCAS%202019_24rev2.pdf?sequence=1&isAllowed=y accessed 11 December 2019.

[33] Amendment 882 to Motions for a European Parliament Resolution on possible evolutions of and adjustments to the current institutional set-up of the European Union (2014/2248(INI)).

[34] Convention on the Future of Europe, Suggestion for amendment of Article: I-59 bis (New): Associate Membership by Members: Mr Andrew Duff, Mr Lamberto Dini, Mr Paul Helminger, Mr Rein Land, Lord Maclennan http://european-convention.europa.eu/docs/Treaty/pdf/46/46_Art%20I%2059a%20Duff%20EN.pdf accessed 11 December 2019.

[35] European Parliament resolution (n 14).

[36] Email from Charles Goerens MEP to author and others (20 December 2016).

correspondence with interested parties pointed them towards a mechanism beyond the EU institutions by which attempts were made to preserve EU citizenship for UK nationals through political processes.

A number of European Citizens Initiatives (ECIs) were registered during negotiations pertaining to EU citizenship: on 11 January 2017 an initiative arguing for a 'European Free Movement Instrument';[37] on 27 March 2017 an initiative for 'EU Citizenship for Europeans: United in Diversity in Spite of *jus soli* and *jus sanguinis*';[38] on 2 May 2017 an initiative titled 'Retaining European Citizenship';[39] and on 23 July 2018 an initiative on 'Permanent European Union Citizenship'.[40] The first of these ECIs is more narrow in its focus. It effectively sought to address the lacuna that would manifest itself in the Withdrawal Agreement regarding the preservation of the right of UK nationals to move freely between EU Member States.[41] The other three initiatives were more ambitious and holistic, advocating that 'facing Brexit, citizenship and nationality must be separated',[42] seeking 'to retain the rights of EU citizenship for all those who have already exercised their freedom of movement prior to the departure of a Member State leaving the Union'[43] and requesting the Commission to 'propose means to avoid risk of collective loss of EU citizenship and rights, and assure all UK citizens that, once attained, such status is permanent and their rights acquired'.[44]

None of the ECIs relating to EU citizenship reached the minimum threshold of one million signatures from a minimum of one quarter of all of the Member States in order to reach the stage of a hearing before the European Commission.[45] However, a relevant point for the wider argument here can be extracted from the fact that all of the initiatives were registered. Article 2 of the Regulation on the citizens' initiative establishes the condition for registration that 'the proposed citizens' initiative does not manifestly fall outside the framework of the Commission's powers to submit a proposal for a legal act of the Union for the purpose of

---

[37] European Citizens Initiative 'European Free Movement Instrument', Commission registration number: ECI(2017)000001, Date of registration: 11 January 2017 https://ec.europa.eu/citizens-initiative/public/initiatives/obsolete/details/2017/000001 accessed 11 December 2019.

[38] European Citizens Initiative 'EU Citizenship for Europeans: United in Diversity in Spite of jus soli and jus sanguinis', Commission registration number: ECI(2017)000003, Date of registration: 27 March 2017 https://ec.europa.eu/citizens-initiative/public/initiatives/obsolete/details/2017/000003 accessed 11 December 2019.

[39] European Citizens Initiative 'Retaining European Citizenship', Commission registration number ECI(2017)000005, Date of registration: 2 May 2017 https://ec.europa.eu/citizens-initiative/public/initiatives/obsolete/details/2017/000005 accessed 11 December 2019.

[40] European Citizens Initiative 'Permanent European Union Citizenship', Commission registration number: ECI(2018)000003, Date of registration: 23 July 2018 https://ec.europa.eu/citizens-initiative/public/initiatives/obsolete/details/2018/000003 accessed 11 December 2019.

[41] For further analysis, see Oliver Garner, 'The European Citizens Initiative on a European Free Movement Mechanism: A New Hope or a False Start for UK Nationals after Brexit?' (*European Law Blog*, 23 February 2017) https://europeanlawblog.eu/2017/02/23/the-european-citizens-initiative-on-a-european-free-movement-mechanism-a-new-hope-or-a-false-start-for-uk-nationals-after-brexit/ accessed 11 December 2019.

[42] 'EU Citizenship for Europeans' (n 38).

[43] 'Retaining European Citizenship' (n 39).

[44] 'Permanent European Union Citizenship' (n 40).

[45] European Parliament and Council Regulation (EU) No 211/2011 of 16 February 2011 on the citizens' initiative [2011] OJ L65/1, art 2.

implementing the Treaties'.[46] The Commission Decision of 22 March 2017 on the '*jus soli* and *jus sanguinis*' initiative is instructive regarding the Commission's position on the legal question of EU citizenship and withdrawal, and its own competences in relation thereto. The Decision states that '[t]here is no legal basis in the Treaties which would empower the EU institutions to adopt a legal act of the Union for the purpose of implementing the Treaties aiming at granting citizenship of the Union to persons who do not hold the nationality of a Member State of the Union'.[47] The preamble goes on to clarify the Commission's opinion that UK nationals will fall under the category of third-country nationals after Brexit:

> Nevertheless, a legal act of the Union for the purpose of implementing the Treaties can be adopted in the field of rights of third-country nationals residing legally in a Member State, including the conditions governing freedom of movement and of residence in other Member States of the EU. Such a legal act may therefore confer certain similar rights to those linked to citizenship of the Union on citizens of a State that has withdrawn from the Union pursuant to Article 50 TEU.[48]

This clarifies explicitly that the Commission holds the view that EU citizenship is extinguished upon the withdrawal of a Member State. Therefore, even if any of the ECIs had passed the procedural hurdles, it seems clear that the Commission would not have gone further than proposing legislation to preserve the rights of UK nationals as third-country nationals. The Commission would not have legislated so as to preserve the status of EU citizenship for UK nationals. This means that the only recourse for UK nationals seeking to resist the loss of EU citizenship was to challenge this status quo legal position.

3. THE LEGAL ARGUMENTS FOR AND AGAINST AUTOMATIC EXTINCTION

3.1 The Admissibility of the Question

This section will analyse the substance of the legal questions considered by the Amsterdam District Court. Before the reference was declared inadmissible, the District Court referred the following questions:

(1) Does the withdrawal of the United Kingdom from the EU automatically lead to the loss of EU citizenship of [United Kingdom] nationals and thus to the elimination of rights and freedoms deriving from EU citizenship, if and in so far as the negotiations between the European Council and the United Kingdom are not otherwise agreed [sic]?
(2) If the answer to the first question is in the negative, should conditions or restrictions be imposed on the maintenance of the rights and freedoms to be derived from EU citizenship?[49]

---

[46] ibid art 3.
[47] Commission Decision of 22 March 2017 on the proposed citizens' initiative entitled 'EU Citizenship for Europeans: United in Diversity in Spite of jus soli and jus sanguinis' Brussels 22.3.2018 C (2017) 2001 final.
[48] ibid.
[49] The Amsterdam Case (n 1), para 5.27.

As a preliminary point, the delivery of the leading case on Article 50 TEU of *Wightman*[50] in December 2018 may be used to criticise the Appeal Court's Decision to overturn the preliminary reference. The question of admissibility was raised in this case concerning whether a Member State could unilaterally revoke notification under Article 50. Similarly to the Appeal Court in the Amsterdam case, the *Wightman* preliminary reference request was originally refused at first instance before the Outer House of the Scottish Court of Session on the basis that the issue was hypothetical because the United Kingdom government had stated that it did not intend to revoke notification. Furthermore, the court of first instance argued that the conditions for a referral under EU law had not been met as the facts were not ascertainable and the issue was hypothetical.[51] The Inner House of the Court of Session overturned this judgment and made a preliminary reference.[52] Relevantly, the presiding domestic judge argued that the question of revocation was neither academic or hypothetical because '[n]otification of withdrawal has been made [...and] in the absence of intervening events [...] take[s] effects in about six months' time'.[53] The same reasoning may be applied to the question of the extinction of EU citizenship as this is a direct legal effect of the operation of Article 50, which had already been set in motion by the time the Amsterdam case was considered. The claim of inadmissibility was reprised by the UK government before the Court of Justice in *Wightman*. It relied upon the argument that the 'question referred addresses events that have not occurred and may not occur' because there was no government policy to revoke Article 50 notification.[54] Arguably, therefore, the claim in the Amsterdam case was less hypothetical than *Wightman* due to the fact that the legal acts – conclusion of the Withdrawal Agreement or a no-deal withdrawal if this failed – that would lead to the claimed illegal result of the termination of EU citizenship were the explicit policy of both the UK government and the EU institutions.

The Court of Justice found that 'questions relating to EU law enjoy a presumption of relevance'.[55] It confirms this presumption with the argument that 'it concerns the interpretation of a provision of EU law – primary law, in this case – and that question is precisely the point at issue in the dispute in the main proceedings'.[56] Despite the fact that it may be argued that these arguments could and should equally have been applied to the question of whether Member State withdrawal extinguishes EU citizenship, the Court of Justice could not have intervened directly in the Amsterdam case due to the deference it displays to national courts: '[i]t is not for the Court to call into question the referring court's assessment of the admissibility of the action [...] which falls, in the context of the preliminary ruling proceedings, within the jurisdiction of the national court.'[57] Nevertheless, it is possible to conclude that, if the Appeal Court had proceeded with the preliminary reference, then the Court of Justice would have applied the presumption of relevance and found the case admissible. Furthermore, the Advocate General Opinion in *Wightman* provides further normative and practical arguments as to why the question of EU law should have been addressed before the treaties ceased to apply to the

---

[50] Case C-621/18 *Wightman v Secretary of State for Exiting the European Union* EU:C:2018:999 (Grand Chamber, 10 December 2018).
[51] *Wightman and Others v Secretary of State for Exiting the European Union* [2018] CSOH 61.
[52] *Wightman and Others v Secretary of State for Exiting the European Union* [2018] CSIH 62.
[53] ibid [31].
[54] *Wightman* (n 50) para 21.
[55] ibid, para 27.
[56] ibid, para 33.
[57] ibid, para 30.

UK. Advocate General Campos Sánchez-Bordona argued that 'it seems to me that the relevant time to dispel doubts [over the legal question] is before, not after, Brexit has occurred and the United Kingdom is inexorably immersed in its consequences'.[58] This logic should also have applied to the issue of EU citizenship extinction. Now that UK nationals are immersed in the consequences of the loss of their EU citizenship, it would be far more difficult to remedy the situation if the Court of Justice were to find that the EU institutions and the UK government acted improperly in terminating the EU citizenship of UK nationals. As argued above, this may have driven the General Court's decision that the question in the 2020 *Shindler* case was inadmissible.[59]

3.2 The District Court Decision

A point of interest in the original District Court reference is the conditional nature of the plaintiff's claim. In the event that EU citizenship were retained following Brexit, the claim was that the Dutch State and the Municipality of Amsterdam would have had to respect, protect and guarantee the rights arising therefrom.[60] In the converse event that the withdrawal of the United Kingdom led to the citizens of the State losing EU citizenship, the plaintiffs made an alternative claim that the Dutch State should not restrict the rights arising therefrom without an individual assessment of the proportionality principle first being carried out. The manifestation of such an assessment for particular plaintiffs includes a claim that the Dutch State would be prohibited from insisting on the relinquishment of British nationality, and the claim that the Municipality of Amsterdam must insist to the State that multiple nationality be facilitated for a person who applies for Dutch nationality. These diverging conditional pathways informed the manner in which the District Court formulated its reference questions. Furthermore, the claims arising in the event of the second option shift the facts into the territory of *Rottmann*[61] and *Lounes*[62] on individual deprivation of EU citizenship through the loss of nationality, as opposed to merely drawing upon these cases by analogy. These claims are relevant for the post-Brexit situation insofar as they relate to the responsibilities of Member State authorities towards UK nationals beyond implementation of the terms of the Withdrawal Agreement.

Paragraph 5.1 of the District Court judgment delineated the three grounds for the plaintiff's claims: (i) the doctrine of acquired rights; (ii) the EU citizenship of Article 20 of the TFEU; (iii) Article 8 of the ECHR. The legal analysis here will focus mainly on the second claim, while touching upon the first claim in the discussion of the 'Option III compromise'. Paragraph 5.2 presents the defendant's defences that (i) the proceedings constituted an undesirable breach of the political negotiation process on Brexit and (ii) the plaintiffs set up a notional dispute exclusively intending to have the case put forward to the ECJ.

Paragraphs 5.3–5.9 and paragraph 5.10 respectively dismissed these defences. The former reasoning may be encapsulated in the statement in paragraph 5.4 that '[t]he simple fact that

---

[58] *Wightman* (n 50) Opinion of Advocate General Campos Sánchez-Bordona, point 42.
[59] *Shindler* (n 6).
[60] The Amsterdam Case (n 1), para 3.1.
[61] Case C-135/08 *Rottmann v Freistaat Bayern* EU:C:2010:104 [2010] ECR I-01449.
[62] Case C-165/16 *Lounes v Secretary of State for the Home Department* EU:C:2017:862 [2017] (Grand Chamber, 14 November 2017).

proceedings are surrounded by political sensitivity is insufficient in this context';[63] the latter may be encapsulated in the paragraph 5.10 statement that '[t]he plaintiffs have credibly demonstrated that the case relates in part to a very real threat and in part to existing infringements of their fundamental rights and freedoms at an individual level'.[64] Of particular interest are the statements in paragraph 5.7, which may provide a connecting thread to the *Rottmann* and *Lounes* case-law because the consequence of naturalisation as a Dutch citizen could be the loss of UK nationality. Finally, the statements pertaining to the degree of protection of those in the minority within a democratic legal state in terms of social or political morality shall be picked up again in the normative analysis of the claim below. On a critical note, it may be suggested that such dicta by the national court of a Member State in relation to the internal constitutional processes of another Member State – regardless of its status as withdrawing – may be construed as encroaching into unwarranted appraisal of 'fundamental structures, political and constitutional' of a Member State as protected by Article 4(2) TEU.[65]

The remainder of the judgment proceeded to assessment of the claims and the 'ground(s)' on which they are based. This parenthetical pluralisation is indicative of the holistic manner in which the District Court conflates the different claims and the legal sources upon which they were predicated. The District Court's framing of Article 20 TFEU is relevant for the substance of the dispute. The Court stated that '[t]he construction of this provision implies a link between the citizenship of a Member State and EU citizenship'.[66] The statement that the Treaty text merely 'implies' a link between nationality and EU citizenship underrepresents the nature of this connection. Member State nationality is the condition *sine qua non* for the acquisition of the status of EU citizenship. The recognition in the next sentence that 'the acquisition of EU citizenship, with its associated rights and freedoms, is reserved for subjects of the Member States of the EU'[67] remedies this understatement, to a certain extent. The final sentence of this paragraph provides a summary of the two perspectives on the crux of the dispute: 'In this light, it is defensible that, as a downside of this, the loss of the status of a citizen of an EU member state leads to the loss of EU citizenship. In view of the following however, this conclusion is not necessarily compelling.'[68]

'The following' consists of consideration of two of the grounds delineated in paragraph 5.1. Consideration of the third ground of art.8 ECHR is absent, at least in the English translation from which this chapter draws. Paragraphs 5.15 to 5.16 consider 'the doctrine of acquired rights',[69] and paragraphs 5.19 to 5.21 consider the '[b]road interpretation of EU citizenship and rights deriving therefrom'.[70] The latter will form the basis of the consideration of 'Option I' and 'Option II' below, and the former shall be drawn upon in consideration of the compromise 'Option III'. Before the delivery of the 'Result' from paragraphs 5.25 to 5.28, the Court delivers a series of paragraphs on themes which do not fit coherently within the three grounds

---

[63] The Amsterdam Case (n 1), para 5.4.
[64] ibid, para 5.10.
[65] Consolidated Version of the Treaty on European Union [2008] OJ C115/13, art 4(2) (hereafter 'TEU').
[66] The Amsterdam Case (n 1), para 5.14.
[67] ibid.
[68] ibid.
[69] ibid, paras 5.15–5.16.
[70] ibid, paras 5.19–5.21.

elucidated by the plaintiffs. These are: 'Protection of the minority against the majority',[71] 'Solidarity between EU citizens and between them and the Member States'[72] and '[c]omplications in the case of young children who are EU citizens'.[73] The sudden and unexpected manifestation of such abstract considerations of general constitutional theory could be construed as falling within Alexander Somek's conception of judicial 'emancipative dissonance'.[74] As such, the content of these paragraphs will be considered within the auspices of the judicial methodology of 'teleological interpretation' in the analyses of 'Option II' and 'Option III' below.

3.3 Three Options on the Substance of the Question

In the abstract, one could present the dispute in question as being rooted in the different answers provided by different judicial methodologies for interpreting the relevant legal sources. Purely textual interpretation[75] of the Treaties may produce the conclusion that nationals of a departed Member State necessarily lose the status and rights of EU citizenship. By contrast, the teleological interpretation[76] of the Treaties that has been developed and employed extensively by the Court of Justice of the European Union could produce the opposite conclusion – automatic loss of EU citizenship upon withdrawal of the Member State of nationality would undermine the purpose for which this status was created and the development it has undergone over the course of its existence. This iterative constructive development has arisen from the necessity for the Court of Justice to play an interstitial gap-filling role[77] as individuals came to bring claims on the basis of factual situations which did not immediately fall under the 'core of certainty'[78] established by the wording of Article 20 TFEU and related secondary law. The cases in which these precedents were established are relevant for the argument that, although Article 20 TFEU establishes the condition for acquisition of EU citizenship, it does not follow as a matter of logical necessity that its text along with Article 50 TEU also exhausts the ambit of the conditions for the retention or loss of the status.

3.3.1 Option I: the argument for automatic extinction upon withdrawal

The former argument, rooted in the text of the Treaty provisions, is relatively simple. The congruent first sentences of Article 20 TFEU and Article 9 TEU both establish the legal condition for acquisition of the status of EU citizenship. This condition is 'holding' the 'nationality of a Member State'. The disclaimer in the next sentence delineates the 'additionality' of EU

---

[71] ibid, para 5.22.
[72] ibid, para 5.23.
[73] ibid, para 5.24.
[74] Alexander Somek, 'The Emancipation of Legal Dissonance' in Henning Koch, Karsten Hagel-Sørensen, Ulrich Haltern and Joseph H.H. Weiler (eds), *Europe: The New Legal Realism: Essays in Honour of Hjalte Rasmussen* (DJØF Publishing 2010).
[75] See, *inter alia*, Antonin Scalia, *A Matter of Interpretation: Federal Courts and the Law* (Princeton University Press 1997).
[76] See, *inter alia*, Miguel Poiares Maduro, 'Interpreting European Law: Judicial Adjudication in a Context of Constitutional Pluralism' (2007) 1(2) European Journal of Legal Studies 137.
[77] See Timothy Endicott, 'Raz on Gaps: The Surprising Part' in Lukas H. Meyer, Stanley L. Paulson and Thomas W. Pogge (eds) *Rights, Culture and the Law: Themes From the Legal and Political Philosophy of Joseph Raz* (Oxford University Press 2003).
[78] H.L.A. Hart, *The Concept of Law* (3rd edn, OUP 2012).

citizenship and confirms that it shall 'not replace national citizenship'.[79] Consequently, Article 20 TFEU establishes that, in contrast to modes of 'naturalisation' that are possible for the acquisition of many national citizenships, EU citizenship cannot be acquired by any means other than the prior holding or acquisition of nationality of a Member State of the European Union. The Amsterdam District Court recognises this argumentation in the statement that 'it is defensible that, as a downside of this [EU citizenship being reserved for subjects of the Member States of the EU], the loss of the status of citizen of an EU Member State leads to the loss of EU citizenship'.[80]

For the purposes of EU law, the prior acquisitive condition of 'nationality of a Member State' is determined by Article 49 TEU[81] – governing accession to the European Union – and Article 50 TEU[82] – governing withdrawal. The first limb of the condition – 'nationality' – should be regarded as determinable by the law of the respective Member States' constitutional orders. This picture has been complicated somewhat by the decision of the Court of Justice in *Rottmann*[83] that when Member States determine the conditions for the removal of this status from specific individuals they act within the scope of EU law, and thus their executive action must fulfil the conditions of the principle of proportionality. This case shall be considered more extensively in the argument against automatic loss below – however, disentanglement of the two constitutive elements of the condition for acquisition of EU citizenship may disentangle the facts of the Amsterdam case from *Rottmann*.

Whereas the latter case addressed the removal of the former element of 'nationality' of a Member State, the present one addresses the revocation of the latter element of the 'membership' of the EU by the state of nationality. Along these lines, Gareth Davies has distinguished the *Rottmann* facts from the facts of the UK's withdrawal on the basis of the distinction between the conditions for 'State membership' and 'individual membership' of the European Union.[84]

Returning to Article 49 TEU and Article 50 TEU, the former provision delineates the condition for acquisition of the status of 'Member' for a State, and the latter provision delineates the conditions for (elective) withdrawal from this status. The acquisitive condition is the ratification of an agreement between the Member State and the candidate State in accordance with the respective constitutional requirements of the contracting States. The primary condition for withdrawal is the date of entry into force of a Withdrawal Agreement between the European Union and a Member State which has notified the European Council of its intention following a decision to withdraw from the Union made in accordance with its own constitutional requirements. The secondary residual condition is the lapse of two years after the notification referred to above, in the absence of a unanimous decision in the European Council to extend. Article 50(3) TEU clarifies that '[T]he Treaties shall cease to apply to the State in question'.[85] The Treaties referred to include the provisions for the acquisition of EU citizenship delineated in

---

[79] TFEU art 20.
[80] The Amsterdam Case (n1), para 5.14.
[81] TEU art 49.
[82] TEU art 50.
[83] *Rottmann* (n 61).
[84] Gareth Davies, 'Union Citizenship – Still Europeans' Destiny after Brexit?' (*European Law Blog*, 7 July 2016) https://europeanlawblog.eu/2016/07/07/union-citizenship-still-europeans-destiny-after-brexit/ accessed 11 December 2019.
[85] TEU art 50(3).

Article 20 TFEU. Concurrently, the lapse of the conditions for being a 'Member State' of the European Union may be concluded to extinguish the condition of holding 'nationality' of such a state for the purpose of continuing to be a Citizen of the European Union.

The reasoning may be summarised in the following syllogism:

(1) The condition to be an EU citizen is holding nationality of a Member State of the European Union (Article 20 TFEU);
(2) This condition may be extinguished through a decision taken in accordance with the constitutional requirements of a State holding this Membership (Article 50 TEU);
(3) Therefore, upon the extinction of State Membership of the European Union, the status of EU citizenship for those individuals who have acquired and retained it through nationality of the departing Member State will concordantly be extinguished.

3.3.2 Option II: the argument against automatic loss of EU citizenship

This teleological argument against automatic loss of EU citizenship is preceded by a meta-textual argument: although Article 20 TFEU is explicit on the condition for the acquisition of EU citizenship, it is silent on the condition for extinction. It is not possible to infer the logical necessity of such extinction from this text. This is reinforced by an argumentative move to consideration of the purposes for which the text was promulgated. By reference to Article 1 TEU and Article 2 TEU,[86] this telos may be construed as the creation of an 'ever closer union amongst the peoples of Europe'.[87] *Wightman* may provide further support for such a holistic approach in the specific interpretation of Article 50 TEU. The Court provides a paradigmatic statement of the teleological approach: 'the interpretation of a provision of EU law requires that account be taken not only of its wording and the objectives it pursues, but also of its context and the provisions of EU law as a whole.'[88]

The judgment reiterates that the 'treaties have as their purpose the creation of an ever closer union among the peoples of Europe'.[89] This is supplemented by references to the values of liberty and democracy in the Treaties and the argument that these values 'form part of the very foundations of the European Union legal order'.[90] This has echoes of the Amsterdam District Court's approach of raising issues pertaining to majoritarianism as a relevant fact. Of more explicit relevance to the question under consideration here, the Court of Justice introduces citizenship of the Union as a component of its holistic method: 'any withdrawal of a Member State from the European Union is liable to have a considerable impact on the rights of all Union citizens, including, *inter alia*, their right to free movement, as regards both nationals of the Member State concerned and nationals of other Member States.'[91] This dicta may be advanced as a hook for whether such a 'considerable impact' is permissible with regard to the purposes and values that underpin the judicial concept of EU citizenship.

The argument would conclude that it would run contrary to the purposes for which EU citizenship has been created if it were to be automatically extinguished for all nationals of a Member State that has embarked upon withdrawal from the European Union in accordance

---

[86] TEU art 2.
[87] TEU art 1.
[88] *Wightman* (n 50) para 46.
[89] ibid, para 62.
[90] ibid.
[91] ibid, para 64.

with Article 50 TEU. The teleological argument that Member State withdrawal does not necessarily lead to the extinction of EU citizenship for the nationals of that State is predicated upon the judicial dicta of the Court of Justice in the cases cited in paragraphs 5.19 and 5.20 of the Amsterdam District Court decision. The District Court provides a delineation of the conception of EU citizenship: 'the CJEU has ruled that citizenship of the Union should be the primary status of nationals of the EU Member States and that, on that basis, subject to explicit legal exceptions, [they] are entitled to equal treatment in law.'[92] A subtle yet significant aspect of this statement is that it is posed in contrast as opposed to congruence with the positive law sources discussed in Option I. This is evident in the conjunction used in the sub-clause: '*[w]hile* Article 20 TFEU states that citizenship of the Union comes alongside national citizenship'.[93] This could be regarded as preparing the scene for an 'emancipatory dissonant'[94] move whereby the judicial dicta that is ostensibly grounded within the purpose underlying the promulgated text is in fact utilised to come to a conclusion that stands in contradistinction to the positive law.

The District Court cites the judgments in *Grzelczyk*,[95] *D'Hoop*,[96] *Wittgenstein*[97] and *Runevič-Vardyn and Wardyn*[98] in support of this statement. It may be suggested that the District Court has taken an expansive interpretation of the (in)famous statement that 'Union citizenship is destined to be the fundamental status of nationals of the Member States, enabling those who find themselves in the same situation to enjoy the same treatment in law irrespective of their nationality, subject to such exceptions as are expressly provided for'.[99]

The inference is that the District Court has taken the first clause of the above statement to mean that EU citizenship will eventually become the primary political and legal source of rights and duties for individuals even outside the scope of EU law. A more conservative interpretation of the dicta would hold that the Court of Justice was merely referring to the eventual goal for Article 20 TFEU to become the primary source of these rights and incipient duties within the boundaries of the EU legal order. This would be a future desideratum in distinction to the piecemeal approach before the Treaty of Maastricht whereby individuals' legal rights and duties were grounded in disparate primary and secondary law sources.[100]

The District Court supplements this judicial conception of EU citizenship with the further conditions regarding the loss thereof that have been established in the *Rottmann* and *Lounes* cases: 'Once lawfully acquired, EU citizenship is an independent source of rights and obligations that cannot be simply reduced or affected by national government actions.'[101] The next

---

[92] The Amsterdam Case (n 1) para 5.19.
[93] ibid (emphasis added).
[94] Somek, 'Legal Dissonance' (n 74).
[95] Case C-184/99 *Rudy Grzelczyk v Centre public d'aide sociale d'Ottignies-Louvain-la-Neuve* EU:C:2001:458 [2001] ECR I-06193.
[96] Case C-224/98 *Marie-Nathalie D'Hoop v Office national de l'emploi* EU:C:2002:432 [2002] ECR I-06191.
[97] Case C-208/09 *Ilonka Sayn-Wittgenstein v Landeshauptmann von Wien* EU:C:2010:806 [2010] ECR I-13693.
[98] Case C-391/09 *Malgožata Runevič-Vardyn and Łukasz Paweł Wardyn v Vilniaus miesto savivaldybės administracija and Others* EU:C:2011:291 [2011] ECR I-03787.
[99] *Rudy Grelczyk* (n 95) para 31.
[100] See Paul Craig and Gráinne de Búrca, *EU Law: Text, Cases, and Materials* (6th edn, OUP 2015), ch 23 'Citizenship of the European Union'.
[101] The Amsterdam Case (n 1) para 5.20.

sentence delineates the conclusion that 'with regard to the withdrawal of the nationality of a citizen of an EU Member State [...] an assessment of the principle of proportionality should take place'.[102] The District Court therefore advances a particular conception of EU citizenship as an independent and incipiently fundamental status that guarantees conditional equal treatment for all nationals of the Member States and that cannot be extinguished by executive actions without a judicial assessment of proportionality.

A teleological argument for the retention of the status notwithstanding withdrawal may be formulated from this conception. Article 20 TFEU may have created citizenship of the Union as a status predicated upon Member State nationality mandating a limited and conditional set of legal rights to free movement, local and European suffrage, petition of the representative and regulatory institutions and residual consular assistance. However, the iterative development of the nature of the status and the rights created therein during the 'destiny era'[103] of its case-law has led to a whole that is qualitatively more than the sum, and origin, of its parts.

Consequently, the argument could be posited that action by a withdrawing Member State and the EU institutions under Article 50 TEU that secures withdrawal without protection of the status violates EU law. Specifically, this would violate the equality guaranteed for nationals of that Member State through their prior acquisition of EU citizenship. I would suggest that the District Court's 'dissonant' introduction of theoretical concepts that have no explicit grounding in the text of primary or secondary EU law – such as the protection of the minority against the majority,[104] solidarity between EU citizens horizontally and between citizens and institutions vertically[105] and the 'derived rights' doctrine for third-country national parents of EU citizens[106] – was an attempt to provide the raw materials with which to construct such a conclusion. One could also envisage that further relevant 'sources' – such as the values contained within Article 2 TEU – could have been advanced in support of arguments before the Court of Justice, similarly to how these sources were advanced in the *Wightman* judgment.

This reasoning may be summarised in the following syllogism:

(1) Article 20 TFEU establishes the condition for the acquisition of EU citizenship. However, it is silent on the condition for its extinction. It cannot be implied as a logical necessity that this condition is the converse of acquisition;

(2) The judicial dicta in the cases deciding the ambit and scope of the status of EU citizenship and rights contained therein has established that the telos of the positive law is to create a fundamental and autonomous status of equality for all Member State nationals which guarantees a set of political and economic rights implemented via secondary legislation;

(3) This purpose means that the purposes for which EU citizenship was established would be undermined if the nationals of a withdrawing Member State were to lose this status upon the disapplication of the Treaties in accordance with Article 50 TEU.

---

[102] ibid.
[103] Garner, 'Existential Crisis of EU Citizenship' (n 2).
[104] The Amsterdam Case (n 1) para 5.22.
[105] ibid, para 5.23.
[106] ibid, para 5.24.

3.3.3 Option III: a compromise? Conditional extinction of EU citizenship

The argument for a potential compromise between the dichotomy of either automatic extinction or retention of EU citizenship for nationals of a departing Member State can be situated in relation to the second question referred by the District Court. This concerned whether any 'conditions or restrictions' should be imposed on the maintenance of the rights and freedoms to be derived from the status of EU citizenship. This wording could be interpreted as referring solely to the maintenance of the rights and freedoms 'to be derived from' EU citizenship. Alternatively and more expansively, the wording could be interpreted as referring both to the maintenance of these substantive positive law rights and to the political and legal status of EU citizenship within which they are agglomerated.

This is far from a moot point, as many of the 'rights and freedoms' contained within Article 20(2) TFEU are already replicated for third-country nationals in secondary legislation.[107] This is supplemented by the extensive regime of protection in the Withdrawal Agreement, which preserves the majority of the rights deriving from EU citizenship, excluding the right to onwards free movement and the political rights. However, if the latter, more expansive interpretation is followed, this could mean that the removal of EU citizenship is subject to conditions imposed upon the Member States and EU institutions.

The argument could be predicated upon the observations of the District Court in paragraph 5.18. The court observes that the UK national claimants could not have foreseen that a vote to leave in the 23 June 2016 referendum would lead to a necessary loss of their rights to live and work in other EU Member States. The District Court claims that the Court of Justice has 'repeatedly ruled on the doctrine of acquired rights' and that '[i]n principle [they] cannot be withdrawn by subsequent decisions. This follows on specifically from the general legal principles which form the basis of EU law, such as the principle of legal certainty and the principle of protection of legitimate expectations.'[108] The District Court's synthesis of the acquired rights and legitimate expectations points could be utilised for an argument that UK nationals have a claim for some minimal protection of their EU citizenship status and rights.

Such an argument would hold that it was not a foreseeable consequence flowing from the referendum result on 23 June 2016 that all UK nationals would lose the status and rights deriving from Article 20 TFEU. This is rooted in the factual context that there is no precedent for a Member State withdrawing from the European Union,[109] and could be supplemented further by the absence of any confirmation or denial thereof by the leave campaign or the United Kingdom government, in addition to the guarantees provided by both the United Kingdom and the EU negotiating sides with regard to the preservation of citizens' rights. Consequently, it may be suggested that UK nationals had a legitimate expectation that the retention of their rights and status should, at the very least, be considered as a possibility in the negotiations between the UK and the EU.

This may be regarded as the establishment or recognition of a residual and minimal legal 'safety net' that could be regarded as binding upon the conduct of both named parties.[110]

---

[107] For example, see Council Directive 2003/109/EC of 25 November 2003 concerning the status of third-country nationals who are long term residents [2004] OJ L16/44.
[108] The Amsterdam Case (n 1) para 5.15.
[109] ibid, para 5.17.
[110] Christophe Hillion, 'This Way, Please! A Legal Appraisal of the EU Withdrawal Clause' in Carlos Closa (ed.) *Secession from a Member State and Withdrawal from the European Union: Troubled Membership* (CUP 2017).

Furthermore, in relation to the fact that the claim in the Amsterdam case is directed towards the State and municipal authorities of another Member State, it could be extrapolated further that these institutions are bound *mutatis mutandis* in their national implementation of the relevant provisions of the Withdrawal Agreement.

At the maximum extent of judicial activism this could have resulted in the finding of a duty binding upon the political actors on the basis of the *telos* of Article 20 TFEU and Article 50 TEU. At the minimum extent of judicial restraint, this could have manifested itself in a non-binding but persuasive imploration from the Union's judicial institution to its political counterparts and the withdrawing Member State to continue to negotiate in good faith so as to find a solution which preserves the rights and status of EU citizenship so far as is possible, thus minimising the disruption to the individual and collective life-plans of affected citizens that may result from Brexit. Part II of the Withdrawal Agreement can be forwarded as evidence that the EU institutions and the withdrawing Member State have fulfilled this obligation. This compromise solution would have been more practically salient if there had been a continued failure to ratify the Withdrawal Agreement and thus a no-deal withdrawal at the end of the (extended) negotiation period. In this situation, the argument for a conditional extinction of EU citizenship on the basis of legitimate expectations could have been forwarded to claim that there is an obligation upon the EU institutions and the withdrawing Member State either to create legislation unilaterally to protect the rights of citizens, and/or to conclude a separate international agreement specifically for the purpose of protecting these rights.[111]

This reasoning may be summarised in the following syllogism:

(1) A Member State's withdrawal from the European Union necessarily extinguishes the EU citizenship of that State's nationals on the basis of the disconnection of the condition for acquisition of the status (Article 20 TFEU and Article 50 TEU).
(2) Regardless of its extinction, EU citizenship is still a status of conditional equality for all of those individuals holding it, and cannot be revoked by executive action without a proportionality assessment (*Grzelczyk*; *Rottmann*).
(3) Part II of the Withdrawal Agreement may be argued to fulfil this requirement. However, regardless of whether the Withdrawal Agreement had been ratified, the government of the United Kingdom and the European Union institutions would have been bound by the relevant general principles of EU law to negotiate in good faith so as to find a political solution in order to fulfil so far as possible the status and rights of those who are losing the status of EU citizenship.

4. THE RAMIFICATIONS OF EMANCIPATIVE LEGAL CONSTITUTIONALISM

It is hoped that the preceding sections have provided a legal doctrinal delineation of the potential arguments and outcomes if a case had come before the Court of Justice arguing that EU citizenship should be retained for nationals of a withdrawing Member State. To evoke David

---

[111] cf Steve Peers, 'Staring into the Abyss: Citizens' Rights after a No Deal Brexit' (*EU Law Analysis*, 6 December 2018).

Hume's well-worn 'is vs. ought' distinction,[112] the aim has been to provide an account of 'what is and what could have been'. By contrast, this penultimate section will indulge in some tentative normative consideration of 'what ought to be'. At the time of the Amsterdam case, Ronan McCrea forwarded the opinion that

> it is very sad for UK citizens who feel the same attachment as many of their fellow EU citizens to their European citizenship. But the appropriate place for them to channel these feelings into action is in the political arena [...] For the Court of Justice to intervene in the way that it has been asked to would be a major error.[113]

I would qualify this final statement with the opinion that the mere act of providing a binding interpretation of EU law on this point would not have been an error in itself. This is all that the Court of Justice would have done had the Amsterdam case preliminary reference been heard. Indeed, this would have provided welcome legal clarity before withdrawal was affected and the political consequences of such a judgment were not overwhelming. However, I would fully endorse McCrea's warning if the Court of Justice had followed the stated purpose of the convenors of the case, and decided on the basis of teleological interpretation that UK nationals should retain the status and rights contained within Article 20 TFEU. To do so would have been to take an emancipative leap of faith.[114] This would have gone beyond judicial activism into the realms of constituent power through the transformative reconstruction of EU citizenship from a set of disparate political and economic rights into a fundamental constituent status.

To embark upon the creation of what may be regarded as a 'constitutional moment'[115] through judicial means would be to exhaust and breach the limits of what should be achieved through 'legal constitutionalism'.[116] The 'output legitimacy'[117] of a body composed of experts who do not enjoy the 'input legitimacy' of election by the individuals who are the political subjects of the constitutional order would be insufficient. The fact that such an emancipative step would be taken in direct contravention to, and ostensible frustration of, a national electoral result would have been an egregious manifestation of Neil Walker's claim that the original sin of the European project is a lack of popular legitimacy.[118] Such a decision would add fuel to the incendiary question that has reared its head with the end of the 'permissive consensus'[119] for European integration since Maastricht: wither (national) democracy on the altar of the (European) technocracy, or in more classic terminology, aristocracy? If EU citizenship is to fulfil the destiny ostensibly claimed for it by the Court of Justice, then the

---

[112] David Hume, *A Treatise of Human Nature, reprinted from the Original Edition in three volumes* (Clarendon Press 1896).

[113] Ronan McCrea, 'Brexit EU Citizenship Rights of UK Nationals and the Court of Justice' *(UK Constitutional Law Association Blog*, 8 February 2018).

[114] See Garner, 'Existential Crisis of EU Citizenship' (n 2).

[115] See Bruce Ackerman, *We the People: Foundations* (Harvard University Press 1991).

[116] See Cormac Mac Amhlaigh, 'Putting Political Constitutionalism in Its Place' (2016) 14 International Journal of Constitutional Law 175.

[117] Fritz Scharpf, *Governing in Europe: Effective and Democratic?* (Oxford University Press 1999).

[118] Neil Walker, 'The EU's Constitutional Overabundance?' (2016) Edinburgh School of Law Research Paper No.2016/14, Europa Working Paper No 2016/07 https://papers.ssrn.com/sol3/papers.cfm?abstract_id=2776800 accessed 11 December 2019.

[119] Liesbet Hooghe and Gary Marks, 'A Postfunctionalist Theory of European Integration: From Permissive Consensus to Constraining Dissensus' (2009) 39 British Journal of Political Science 1.

only legitimate means by which this could be achieved would be through an act of democratic self-determination by individual citizens. The choice would be to retain, acquire or indeed reject EU citizenship as a constituent status. I would conclude that only through such an individual and collective 'leap of faith' could the legitimate transformation of a Union of States, with its foundations in international Treaty law, into a Union of citizens, with its foundations in a constitution, be achieved. Although the likelihood remains remote, the Conference on the Future of Europe could provide a vehicle for such will-expression.

The only situation that would warrant the disconnection of EU citizenship from Member State nationality would be for the status to become a means of exercising constituent power. This would serve as a reconstruction of the foundations of the European Union. These foundations are currently based upon mixed legitimation by individuals as nationals and individuals as EU citizens.[120] In its place, a singular European constituent power would be created through individuals being given the choice to be EU citizens. This would provide the basis for the creation of a new constitutional settlement within the European Union.

Such a revolutionary disruption could be envisaged as a reaction to the hypothetical progression of a domino effect from Brexit cascading into disintegration of the European Union.[121] A constitutional decision to withdraw from the European Union represents the end of the consensus on 'levelling up' constituent power to the supranational level.[122] A fissure is opened between those nationals who do regard their EU citizenship as a means for self-determination and those who do not. This majority-and-minority dynamic towards European integration lurks under the surface for all Member States who have not held a referendum on membership. Although unlikely, there remains a remote possibility of multiple Member States withdrawing from the EU. On the basis of national democratic majorities, this would extinguish the EU citizenship of all, including those who regard it as integral to their political and social identity.

In the face of such a fault-line among the population of Europe with regard to integration, one could formulate an argument for those entitled to EU citizenship being given the choice as to whether they wish to hold the status or not.[123] Those who choose to be European citizens would then form the nucleus of a constitutional convention to determine the design of a future European constitutional polity. Clearly such a constitutional moment would go far beyond the ambit of the current Treaty structure of the European Union.

The repatriation of constituent power by domestic electorates could provide the impetus for a counter-movement establishing constituent power at the European level. This would serve to preserve the achievements of integration for those who regard their European identity as a means of self-determination. If we accept the argument that the original sin of European integration was a lack of popular legitimacy, it may be argued that such a leap of faith is a necessary step to either validate or invalidate the European project in the current climate of

---

[120] Jürgen Habermas, *The Crisis of the European Union: A Response* (Polity 2012).

[121] Markus Patberg, 'Can Disintegration Be Democratic? The European Union Between Legitimate Change and Regression' (2019) Political Studies first published online 10 September 2019 https://journals-sagepub-com.ezproxy.eui.eu/doi/pdf/10.1177/0032321719870431 accessed 11 December 2019.

[122] Markus Patberg, 'The Levelling Up of Constituent Power in the European Union' (2017) 55 Journal of Common Market Studies 203.

[123] Garner, 'Existential Crisis of EU Citizenship' (n 2).

stagnation.[124] The creation of such a status through judicial decision, however, would be an illegitimate means to conduct this endeavour.

5. CONCLUSION

This chapter has sought to demonstrate that the space for a legal challenge concerning the automatic extinction of EU citizenship upon Member State withdrawal was opened up by the focus in the Withdrawal Agreement negotiations on the preservation of the juridical rights derived from EU citizenship, rather than the status itself. This was exacerbated by the failure of political initiatives of the European Parliament and citizens of the EU to address this issue. The root cause of the problem may be laid at the feet of the drafting of Article 50 TEU, which is bereft of any explicit reference to EU citizenship.[125] This creates a penumbra of uncertainty over whether the existence of the status is contained within the general condition of the EU Treaties ceasing to apply to a withdrawing Member State. For the purpose of legal certainty before the consequences of Brexit took hold, it would have been desirable for the original Amsterdam District Court preliminary reference to have been heard by the Court of Justice of the European Union. The most recent case-law on the issue indicates that the Court of Justice would have endorsed a presumption of relevance that the issue was admissible.

The chapter then sought to provide rigorous arguments for three options: that EU citizenship is automatically extinguished upon Member State withdrawal; that it continues to exist for nationals of a former Member State; or, finally, a compromise option whereby EU citizenship is extinguished, but this is conditional upon obligations to maintain the rights deriving therefrom. The final section of the chapter engaged in a normative analysis of the undesirability of EU citizenship being emancipated from Member State nationality through a court decision. The argument is advanced that the only legitimate way for the status to be made autonomous would be through an act of constituent power by an incipient citizenry of Europe.

---

[124] This analysis draws upon Oliver Garner, 'EU Citizenship as an Autonomous Status of Constituent Power' in Liav Orgard and Jules Lepoutres (eds) 'Should EU Citizenship Be Disentangled?' (n 32).
[125] See further, Oliver Garner, 'Seven Reforms to Article 50 TEU' (2021) 46 E.L. Rev 784.

PART III

SOCIAL CITIZENSHIP

14. EU citizenship and the welfare state[1]
Francesco Costamagna and Stefano Giubboni

1. INTRODUCTION

In what we vaguely used to identify with the emphatic and ephemeral formula of the 'European social model',[2] welfare and citizenship are deeply interlinked dimensions: 'social protection is an expression of social justice and a precondition for social inclusion',[3] and both are a cornerstone of that unique concept of democratic citizenship, which in Western Europe was unevenly and painstakingly built during the golden age of the national welfare state.[4] But that unique construction was essentially premised upon a bounded idea of social solidarity, centred on the redistributive efforts of the single welfare state communities,[5] while the very concept of European citizenship has since its inception been built on the opposite stance of free movement of persons and the opening up of national borders in order to further and expand supranational integration.[6]

Thus, European citizenship and the welfare state are premised on an unstable equilibrium of inter-connecting and, at the same time, inevitably conflicting dynamics. Inasmuch as these dynamics are perceived as following a congruent path, such an equilibrium could be preserved with acceptable trade-offs. But this inherent tension is destined to resurface in times of economic and political crisis,[7] when free movement of persons has indeed inescapably become one of the most cherished and most despised features of the European integration process.

On the one side, the combined rights to free movement, residency and equal treatment are still unique in the world with regard to both their scope and their political commitment to sol-

---

[1] The chapter is the outcome of joint efforts of the two authors. However, sections 1, 2, 3 and 9 can be attributed to Stefano Giubboni, while sections 4, 5, 6, 7 and 8 can be attributed to Francesco Costamagna.

[2] For a recent critical re-assessment see Colin Crouch, *Social Europe: A Manifesto* (Social Europe Publishing 2020).

[3] Charlotte O'Brien, *Unity in Adversity: EU Citizenship, Social Justice and the Cautionary Tale of the UK* (Hart Publishing 2017) 9.

[4] Suffice it here to refer to the superb synthesis offered by Tony Judt, *Postwar: A History of Europe since 1945* (Vintage Books 2006), especially in Part 2. For a recent comparative overview see Carlo Trigilia (ed.), *Capitalismi e democrazie. Si possono conciliare crescita e uguaglianza?* (il Mulino 2020).

[5] Cf. Maurizio Ferrera, *The Boundaries of Welfare: European Integration and the New Spatial Politics of Social Protection* (OUP 2005); Stefano Giubboni, *Diritti e solidarietà in Europa. I modelli sociali nazionali nello spazio giuridico europeo* (il Mulino 2012).

[6] Cf. *ex multis* Dimitry Kochenov, 'Growing Apart Together: Solidarity and Citizenship in Europe' in Frans Pennings and Gijsbert Vonk (eds), *Research Handbook on European Social Security Law* (Edward Elgar Publishing 2015) 32; Agustín José Menéndez and Espen DH Olsen, *Challenging European Citizenship: Ideas and Realities in Contrast* (Palgrave Macmillan 2020) Part II.

[7] Stefano Giubboni, 'European Citizenship and Social Rights in Times of Crisis' (2014) 15 German Law Journal No. 5 935.

idarity.⁸ On the other side, these rights now face strong opposition, as they have increasingly been perceived as encouraging social tourism and posing an unsustainable burden on national social protection systems.⁹ The possibility that free movement, associated with equal access to social protection for the movers, could represent a cost for national welfare systems is not a novel concern.¹⁰ But the debate over the budgetary impact of intra-EU mobility vehemently reignited after the EU's eastward enlargements of 2004 and 2007. The financial and economic crisis further exacerbated it, fostering welfare nationalism on the back of mounting xenophobic and racist sentiments. The Brexit debate over these issues represents a good point in case:¹¹ the leave campaign obsessively reiterated the need to 'curb the costs of uncontrolled migration', without providing any meaningful data to back their claims.

This chapter will explore this conflictual relationship by following the tortuous and contradictory paths of the case-law of the Court of Justice on the crucial question of cross-border access to social assistance by mobile European citizens.¹² Although the 'market legacy'¹³ of European citizenship has never disappeared from the scene, in the ascending phase of its case-law the Court of Justice infused the expansive application of the principle of equal treatment in favour of economically inactive EU citizens accessing national social assistance systems with a constitutional tone (§§ 2 and 3). Such approach was essentially framed as an extension of some classic tenets of the free movement of workers into a sphere of the freedom of movement only remotely connected with the dominant rationale of economic integration. However, this expansionary move was short-lived (§ 4), since the great crisis spurred the counter-movement (§§ 5–6) that still dominates the current landscape, with some interesting, albeit limited, exceptions (§§ 7–8).

---

⁸ E.g. Andrew Geddes, *Immigration and European Integration: Toward European Fortress* (MUP 2008).
⁹ For a recent (and disappointed) *resumé* Stefano Giubboni, 'La solidarietà come scudo. Il tramonto della cittadinanza sociale transnazionale nella crisi europea' (2018) Quaderni costituzionali 591.
¹⁰ E.g. Stefano Giubboni, 'Free Movement of Persons and European Solidarity' (2007) 13 European Law Journal No. 3 360, and, more recently, Francesca Strumia, 'European Citizenship and Transnational Rights: Chronicles of a Troubled Narrative' in Daniel Thym (ed.), *Questioning EU Citizenship: Judges and the Limits of Free Movement and Solidarity in the EU* (Hart Publishing 2017) 149 ff.
¹¹ Stephanie Reynolds, '(De)constructing the Road to Brexit: Paving the Way to Further Limitations on Free Movement and Equal Treatment?' in Daniel Thym (ed.) (n 10) 57 ff.
¹² See recently the overview by Philippe Minderhoud and Sandra Mantu, 'Back to the Roots? No Access to Social Assistance for Union Citizens Who Are Economically Inactive' in Thym (ed.) (n 10) 190 ff.
¹³ Michelle Everson, 'The Legacy of the Market Citizen' in Jo Shaw and Gillian More (eds), *New Legal Dynamics of European Union* (Clarendon Press 1995) 73 ff.

2. THE ASCENDING PHASE OF EU SOCIAL CITIZENSHIP: ENSURING ACCESS TO NATIONAL WELFARE STATES BY CIRCUMVENTING THE LIMITS SET BY SECONDARY LEGISLATION

2.1 The Limits Set by Secondary Legislation to Access to Welfare Systems in the Early Days of European Citizenship

The perception that granting full access to social benefits to economically inactive mobile citizens could endanger the financial and political sustainability of national welfare states is a concern that predates the introduction of EU citizenship. This concern found expression in Directive 90/364/EEC, which introduced for the first time a right of movement and residence to citizens who, not being engaged in any economic activity, did not benefit from the freedoms established in the founding Treaties. The act made the right of residence conditional on two circumstances, requiring economically inactive persons to have sufficient resources and comprehensive sickness insurance.[14] The same applied with regard to specific categories of economically inactive persons, such as students. Article 1 of Directive 93/96/EEC confirmed that students from other Member States enjoyed a right of residence only if they had sufficient resources to avoid becoming a burden, and sickness insurance. Moreover, Article 3 explicitly excluded that the right of residence could entitle students to obtain maintenance grants. The limits set by the EU legislator found recognition in the restrictive wording used by the Treaty of Maastricht in the codification of the rights of free movement and residence of European citizens. Then Article 8a EC made these rights 'subject to the limitations and conditions laid down in this Treaty and by the measures adopted to give it effect'.

All these elements were taken 'as powerful evidence of a political consensus that residency and equal treatment is a privilege to be enjoyed by those who can afford it'.[15] Indeed, EU law has traditionally granted equal access to social benefits to workers, primarily in their capacity as economic agents,[16] but also as a reward for their participation in the financing of the welfare system by paying taxes and social contributions in the host State. Yet, it must be emphasised that the Court had moved beyond such a mercantile logic by adopting a very broad definition of worker and, thus, also enabling persons working a few hours a week or earning less than the statutory minimum salary to claim access to social advantages. This evolution has been complemented by the extension of the guarantee of equal treatment to the worker's family members.[17]

---

[14] See Maurizio Ferrera, 'Towards an Open Social Citizenship? The New Boundaries of Welfare in the European Union' in Grainne De Burca (ed.), *EU Law and the Welfare State: In Search of Solidarity* (OUP 2005) 31. The author defined them as a 'sort of reverse means test (or affluence test)'.

[15] Michael Dougan, 'The Constitutional Dimension of the Case Law on Union Citizenship' (2006) 31 EL Rev 613, 624.

[16] Charlotte O'Brien, 'I Trade, Therefore I Am: Legal Personhood in the European Union' (2013) 50 CML Rev 1643.

[17] On this evolution see, *ex multis*, Eleanor Spaventa, *Free Movement of Persons in the European Union. Barriers to Movement in their Constitutional Context* (Kluwer Law International 2007).

2.2 Circumvention of the Limits Set in the Secondary Legislation by Relying on Treaty Equality Provisions

Despite the existence of apparently clear legislative indications to the contrary, the Court sought to close the gap between workers and economically inactive citizens with regard to access to social benefits, levelling up the position of the latter toward that of the former. This move was premised on the idea that citizenship of the EU confers in itself an autonomous entitlement to social rights. From this perspective, the status of being a citizen of the Union actually had a fundamental (or maybe a founding) status,[18] ushering in a new paradigm of social solidarity. This form of solidarity was different from the functional one that had traditionally dominated the construction of the internal market.[19] Indeed, it was meant to operate beyond the circle of those taking part in market processes and, at the same time, beyond the boundaries of national communities,[20] making European citizenship a *'statut d'intégration sociale'*.[21]

The opening up of new avenues of access to national welfare systems for EU citizens not engaged in any economic activity has been pointedly described as a process of judge-made social engineering,[22] redefining the boundaries of welfare systems and redistributive communities.[23] In the absence of a supranational welfare system, this case-law was considered as a force that could lead to the horizontal federalisation of national welfare states.[24]

This judicially induced evolution took place through two interconnected moves. First, the Court heavily relied on Treaty anti-discrimination provisions to circumvent the limits set by secondary legislation. Second, it excluded that the sufficient resources criterion could be read as entailing an automatic exclusion from lawful residence and, thus, from social assistance benefits. Instead the Court required national authorities to carry out an individualised assessment, so to determine whether the exclusion from the required benefit was proportionate. As observed by Dougan, by so doing the Court indirectly subjected EU secondary legislation to

---

[18] Cf. Stefano Giubboni, 'A Certain Degree of Solidarity? Free Movement of Persons and Access to Social Protection in the Case Law of the European Court of Justice' in Malcolm Ross and Yuri Borgmann-Prebil (eds), *Promoting Solidarity in the European Union* (OUP 2010) 181.

[19] Giubboni (n 18) 190–1, where the author defines this form of solidarity as 'organic solidarity', adapting Durkheim's famous conceptualisation.

[20] On the contested notion of transnational solidarity see especially Floris De Witte, *Justice in the EU: The Emergence of Transnational Solidarity* (OUP 2016). For the theoretical ground of transnational solidarity see among others Jens Beckert, Julia Eckert, Martin Kohli and Wolfgang Streeck (eds), *Transnationale Solidarität. Chancen und Grenzen* (Campus Verlag 2004); Hauke Brunkhorst, *Solidarity: From Civic Friendship to Global Legal Community* (MIT Press 2005).

[21] Loïc Azoulai, 'La citoyenneté européenne, un statut d'intégration sociale' in Gérard Cohen-Jonathan and others (eds), *Chemins d'Europe. Mélanges en l'honneur de Jean Paul Jacqué* (Dalloz 2010) 1 ff. See also in a similar vein Dagmar Schiek, 'Perspectives on Social Citizenship in the EU: From *Status Positivus* to *Status Socialis Activus* via Two Forms of Transnational Solidarity' in Dimitry Kochenov (ed.), *EU Citizenship and Federalism. The Role of Rights* (CUP 2017) 341.

[22] Dougan (n 15) 18–19.

[23] Herwig Verschueren, 'European (Internal) Migration Law as an Instrument for Defining the Boundaries of National Solidarity Systems' (2007) 9 European Journal of Migration and Law, 307. For a more critical approach see Michael Dougan and Eleanor Spaventa, 'Wish You Weren't Here ... New Models of Social Solidarity in the European Union' in ibid (eds), *Social Welfare and EU Law* (Hart Publishing 2005).

[24] Justine Lacroix, 'Is Transnational Citizenship (Still) Enough?' in Dimitry Kochenov, Grainne De Búrca and Andrew Williams (eds), *Europe's Justice Deficit?* (Hart Publishing 2015) 177.

a strict proportionality review.²⁵ Indeed, the national rules put under scrutiny were, in most of the cases, the faithful transposition into the domestic legal orders of the limits set forth by the EU legislation analysed above.

Martínez Sala is the judgment that laid the groundwork for the edification of a transnational form of solidarity, allowing non-economically active citizens to rely upon the principle of non-discrimination in order to get access to social assistance benefits. The key question of the case was whether national authorities were entitled to require a specific residence permit before granting such an allowance or whether such a request was to be considered discriminatory under EU law. The German government argued that the principle of non-discrimination was not applicable in the present case, since Ms Martínez Sala's residence was based upon national law and not EU law. The Court rejected this argument, by stating that the scope *ratione materiae* of the principle of equal treatment covers all cases where a European citizen legally resides in a Member State.²⁶ Albeit not openly, the Court came to disconnect the principle of equal treatment from the right of residence and, more importantly, from the secondary pieces of legislation giving effect to the limitations and conditions now envisaged by Article 21 TFEU.²⁷

In *Baumbast* the Court went a step further, by affirming that the right to reside 'is conferred on every citizen of the Union by a clear and precise provision of the EC Treaty'²⁸ and thus has direct effect. This means that a citizen can directly rely on the right of residence provided for by the Treaty to challenge national discriminatory measures. By so doing, the Court transformed Directive 90/364 from an instrument granting freedom of movement and residence, as it was originally conceived, to one setting limitations on its exercise. Moreover, it made clear that 'any limitations and conditions imposed on that right do not prevent the provisions of Article 18(1) EC from conferring on individuals rights which are enforceable by them and which the national courts must protect'.²⁹

2.3 Opening Up New Avenues of Access to National Welfare Systems by Economically Inactive Citizens: The Case of Students

The Court followed the same approach in situations directly concerning cross-border access to national welfare systems by economically inactive citizens and, more specifically, students.³⁰

Grzelczyk represents a leading case in this regard. The judgment concerned the decision by Belgian authorities to withdraw a minimum subsistence allowance (minimex) from a French

---

²⁵ Dougan (n 15) 620–1.
²⁶ Case C-85/96 *Martínez Sala* EU:C:1998:217, paras 62–63. For a highly critical analysis of this reasoning see Kay Hailbronner, 'Union Citizenship and Access to Social Benefits' (2005) 42 CML Rev 1245.
²⁷ Oxana Golynker, 'Jobseekers' Rights in the European Union: Challenges of Changing the Paradigm of Social Solidarity' (2005) 30 E L Rev 111, 120.
²⁸ Case C-413/99 *Baumbast* EU:C:2002:493, para. 84.
²⁹ *Baumbast*, para. 86.
³⁰ Financial assistance for students is a politically sensitive and economically costly issue that has attracted much attention also in the legal literature. See, *ex multis*, Stine Jørgensen, 'The Right to Cross-Border Education in the European Union' (2009) 46 CML Rev 1567; Michael Dougan, 'Fees, Grants, Loans and Dole Cheques: Who Covers the Costs of Migrant Education in the EU?' (2005) 42 CML Rev 943; Anne-Pieter van der Mei, 'EU Law and Education: Promotion of Student Mobility versus Protection of Education Systems' in Dougan and Spaventa (eds) (n 23) 219.

student that was requested and initially obtained after their having studied in Belgium for three years. Several states decided to intervene before the Court to defend the Belgian decision, arguing that the situation fell outside the scope of application of the Treaty equality provisions and that, in any case, the legislative framework was fully in line with Directive 93/96/EEC. The Court seemed rather unimpressed by the strong show of unity by the Member States.

First, it rejected the idea that the aid granted to students for maintenance could be considered as falling outside the scope of application of the Treaty,[31] even though it admitted this was the position it took in previous judgments.[32] But this *revirement* was somewhat warranted by the fact that in the meanwhile the Treaty had introduced the citizenship of the European Union. In that regard, the Court pointed out: 'there is nothing in the amended text of the Treaty to suggest that students who are citizens of the Union, when they move to another Member State to study there, lose the rights which the Treaty confers on citizens of the Union.'[33] Despite its tautological character, this statement reiterates the distinction between the applicability of Treaty provisions on equal treatment and those on the right to reside in another Member State, shielding the former from the limits posed by secondary legislation.

Second, the Court read into the institution of EU citizenship the acceptance of 'a certain degree of solidarity between nationals of a host Member State and nationals of other Member States'.[34] Therefore, national authorities cannot rely upon a blind application of the affluence test enshrined in secondary legislation, by mechanically assuming that anyone seeking assistance is bound to become a burden and, consequently, can be denied the right to reside. Construing the safeguard of national social systems' sustainability as an exception to be narrowly interpreted was the highest point of the judicial trajectory pointing towards the universalisation of the logic of social integration.

This logic is very much present also in *Bidar*, a judgment concerning the British authorities' refusal to grant a subsidised student loan to a French citizen who, after having lived in the UK for three years, enrolled at University College London. The judgment started by confirming that economic aid granted to students falls within the scope of EU law and, more specifically, the principle of non-discrimination.[35] Quite interestingly, even the Commission argued against such a conclusion, pointing to the fact that Article 3 Directive 93/96/EEC expressly excluded the right to payment of maintenance grants on the part of students. The Court admitted that students 'who go to another Member State to start or pursue higher education there'[36] are prevented from seeking aid, but added that this is not the case for 'a national of a Member State who […] is lawfully resident in the territory of another Member State where he intends to start or pursue higher education'.[37] Admittedly, the distinction between the two categories of students sounds quite artificial, but for the Court was enough to adopt an interpretative approach that led to the *de facto* abrogation of the rule contained in the secondary legislation.[38]

---

[31] Case C-184/99 *Grzelczyk* EU:C:2001:458, paras 29–46.
[32] Case C-197/86 *Brown* EU:C:1988:323; Case C-39/86 *Lair* EU:C:1988:322.
[33] *Grzelczyk*, para. 35.
[34] *Grzelczyk*, para. 44.
[35] Case C-209/03 *Bidar* EU:C:2005:169, paras 28–48.
[36] *Bidar*, para. 45.
[37] *Bidar*, para. 46.
[38] On this point see Jean-Philippe Lhernould, 'L'accès aux prestations sociales des citoyens de l'Union Européenne' (2001) Droit Social 1103, 1105.

The Court then evaluated whether the requirements set forth by the domestic legislation could be justified on objective considerations, such as preserving the financial sustainability of the whole system.[39] The Court admitted that this may represent a valid reason to limit access to financial aid, but it excluded that national authorities can rely on formal criteria, such as the duration of the residence, instead having to take into considerations also other aspects such as the existence of 'a genuine link with the society of the State'.[40] Quite remarkably, the entire reasoning was premised on the assumption that Member States 'must, in the organization and application of their social assistance systems, show a certain degree of financial solidarity with nationals of other Member States',[41] morphing what was in *Grzelczyk* only a possibility accepted by EU secondary legislation into a full-fledged legal obligation.

3. THE ADOPTION OF DIRECTIVE 2004/38/EC AS A (SUCCESSFUL) ATTEMPT TO REIN IN THE ACTIVISM OF THE COURT IN GRANTING ACCESS TO NATIONAL WELFARE SYSTEMS TO MOBILE EU CITIZENS

At the beginning of the 2000s, the Commission launched a process of reform of the legal framework governing free movement so to adapt it to the 'new legal and political environment' created by the introduction of EU citizenship.[42] One of the purposes was to consolidate into a single legal instrument all the arrangements for the exercise of the right of freedom of movement, remedying the 'sector-by-sector, piecemeal approach'[43] that had prevailed until that moment. From that perspective, the adoption of a new directive was meant to support the process of convergence between different categories of mobile citizens spurred by the Court.[44] Yet, other actors harboured different expectation. Member States – or, at least, most of them – wanted to react to the activism of the Court and reaffirm that only economically active citizens could claim equal treatment.

---

[39] For a comprehensive analysis of the relationship between integration and access to social benefits see Nicolas Rennuy, 'The Trilemma of EU Social Benefits Law: Seeing the Wood and the Trees' (2019) 56 CML Rev 1549, 1552–8.

[40] *Bidar*, para. 63. For a critical take on this see Catherine Barnard, 'Case C-209/03, R (on the application of Danny Bidar) v. London Borough of Ealing, Secretary of State for Education and Skills' (2005) 42 CML Rev 1465, 1477–80.

[41] *Bidar*, para. 56.

[42] Para 1.3 of the Proposal for a European Parliament and Council Directive of 23 May 2001 on the right of citizens of the Union and their family members to move and reside freely within the territory of the Member States, COM(2011) 257.

[43] Recital 4 Directive 2004/38/EC of the European Parliament and of the Council of 29 April 2004 on the right of citizens of the Union and their family members to move and reside freely within the territory of the Member States amending Regulation (EEC) No 1612/68 and repealing Directives 64/221/EEC, 68/360/EEC, 72/194/EEC, 73/148/EEC, 75/34/EEC, 75/35/EEC, 90/364/EEC, 90/365/EEC and 93/96/EEC [2004] OJ L158.

[44] In this sense Daniel Thym, 'The Elusive Limits of Solidarity: Residence Rights of and Social Benefits for Economically Inactive Union Citizens' (2015) 52 CML Rev 17, 18.

The final version of Directive 2004/38/EC is a compromise between these two opposing views.[45] Article 7 of the Directive reiterates that economically inactive citizens have a right of residence in the territory of another Member State for a period longer than three months only if they have comprehensive sickness insurance and sufficient resources, so to avoid becoming a burden on host State's social assistance system. The legislator decided to retain here the same expression used in the pre-citizenship Directive, confining to the Preamble the more demanding formulation of 'unreasonable burden' adopted by *Grzelczyk* and *Bidar*.[46]

The tension between the two poles is apparent also with regard to Article 24 of the Directive. In the original Commission proposal, the provision contained an unqualified statement on equal treatment, but the Council pushed hard to make this treatment 'subject to such specific provisions as are expressly provided for in the Treaty and secondary law'. The drafting of paragraph 2 provoked similar tensions, despite following a contrary trajectory. The original proposal read as follows: '[b]y way of derogation from paragraph 1, until they have acquired the right of permanent residence, the host Member State shall not be obliged to confer entitlement to social assistance on persons *other than those engaged in gainful activity in an employed or self-employed capacity.*'[47] Subsequently the Commission changed the formulation of the provisions, restricting the possibility of derogating from the principle of equal treatment only to the cases of citizens having resided in a country for less than three months and of students' maintenance aid. Quite remarkably, the Commission made clear that '[t]he Council has accepted this amendment',[48] and thus the fact that citizens not in gainful activity cannot be automatically excluded from social assistance.

It was doubtful whether the Directive could effectively hold back the expansive case-law on access to social benefits or whether the Court would have continued 'to rewrite the rules laid down in secondary Community law'.[49]

Förster represented a first test in that regard, showing that, for all its contradictions, the message sent by the legislator had reached its main target: the Court. The case concerned the Dutch legislation on student financial aid and, more specifically, its provision according to which students holding the nationality of an EU Member State are eligible to obtain the aid only if they have been lawfully resident in the Netherlands for an uninterrupted period of at least five years.

AG Mazák approached the case by following in the footsteps of *Bidar*.[50] More specifically, he held that relying the five-year continuous residence requirement would be disproportionate. The recourse to a 'substantive' notion of integration, as opposed to the 'formal' one under-

---

[45] For a detailed analysis of the act, see Elspeth Guild, Steve Peers and Jonathan Tomkin (eds), *The EU Citizenship Directive: A Commentary* (2nd edn, OUP 2019).
[46] Niamh Nic Shuibhne, 'Limits Rising, Duties Ascending: The Changing Legal Shape of Union Citizenship' (2015) 52 CML Rev 889, 898.
[47] Emphasis added.
[48] Communication from the Commission to the European Parliament pursuant to the second subparagraph of Article 251(2) of 30 December 2003 of the EC Treaty concerning the common position of the Council on the adoption of a European Parliament and Council Directive on the right of citizens of the Union and their family members to move and reside freely within the territory of the Member States, SEC(2003), 7.
[49] Hailbronner (n 26), 1251.
[50] Case C-158/07 *Förster* EU:C:2008:399, Opinion of AG Mazák.

pinning the Dutch residence requirement,[51] was, once again, premised on primary law, which, according to AG Mazák, is not affected by the explicit exclusion of students' maintenance grants from the scope of application of equal treatment provided for in Article 24 of Directive 2004/38/EC.[52]

The Court followed the line of reasoning proposed by AG Mazák, only taking a different path when it came to the very last step. Indeed, it held that the five-year residence condition is 'appropriate for the purpose of guaranteeing that the applicant for the maintenance grant at issue is integrated into the society of the host Member State'.[53] The judgment is very deferential towards the choices made at legislative level, ushering in a new compromise between the creation of an embryonic form of transnational solidarity in the EU and Member States' concerns on the financial implications of free movement on national welfare systems.[54]

4. ABANDONING THE EXPANSIVE LOGIC OF EU CITIZENSHIP TO COPE WITH THE SPECTRE OF SOCIAL TOURISM

The financial crisis that stormed the EU in 2010 put under severe pressure the conceptual construction built by the Court, altering the factual and political landscape. The dramatic economic situation faced by many Mediterranean countries forced many of their residents to move to Northern Member States, which in turn proved to be less and less inclined to host them.[55] Such a negative perception was further compounded by the fact that in those very years the EU eastward enlargement became fully operational with the end of the transitional period.

In 2013, four Member States – the UK, Austria, Germany and the Netherlands – formally asked the Commission to propose the amendment of Directive 2004/38/EC, in order to provide national authorities with more effective tools to combat a 'type of immigration [that] burdens the host societies with considerable additional costs'.[56] The 'burden on public finance' became a key aspect in the wider public debate on migration. As some commentators admit, this development has transformed this issue into a symbol that has progressively 'outgrown the empirical relevance of the matter'.[57] To put it more bluntly, reliance upon this argument looks

---

[51] See generally Stephen Coutts, 'The Absence of Integration and the Responsibilisation of Union Citizenship' (2018) 3 European Papers 761; Moritz Jesse, 'The Value of Integration in European Law – The Implications of the *Förster* Case on the Legal Assessment of Integration Conditions for Third-country Nationals' (2011) 17 European Law Journal 172.

[52] *Förster*, Opinion of AG Mazák, para. 131.

[53] Case C-158/07 *Förster* EU:C:2008:630, para. 52.

[54] On this aspect, for a rightly critical analysis of the judgment, see Anne Pieter van der Mei, 'Union Citizenship and the Legality of Durational Residence Requirements for Entitlement to Student Financial Aid' (2009) 16 Maastricht Journal of European and Comparative Law 477.

[55] For a comprehensive analysis, see Jean-Michel Lafleur and Mikolaj Stanek, *South–North Migration of EU Citizens in Times of Crisis* (Springer 2017). On the demise of the notion of solidarity in the response to the financial crisis and with regard to European citizenship see Agustín José Menéndez, 'Which Free Movement? Whose Free Movement?' in Silvia Borelli and Andrea Guazzarotti (eds), *Labour Mobility and Transnational Solidarity in the European Union* (Jovene editore 2019) 46–52.

[56] Available at http://docs.dpaq.de/3604-130415_letter_to_presidency_final_1_2.pdf. accessed 27 May 2021.

[57] Thym (n 44) 20.

misplaced if one considers the available empirical evidence, which shows that the overwhelming majority of citizens moving to another Member State are economically active[58] and that intra-EU mobility tends to have positive economic effects on receiving states.[59] This notwithstanding, the need to take action against what has come to be known as 'social tourism' has quickly become part of the dominant narrative.[60] The use of the term 'tourism' has a moralistic overtone, conveying the idea that people moving to another State just to enjoy the bounty of their welfare state without contributing to their financing do not deserve protection.

The spectre of benefit tourism[61] has been seen also in the EU legal order, where the Court tried to reassure Member States by sacrificing the expansive logic of Union citizenship as a fundamental status of European citizens. The retreat materialised in a series of judgments that 'appear to roll back decades of citizenship construction'.[62] Such a negative take on the evolution of the Court's case-law contrasts with the position expressed by other commentators, considering it a logical and predictable turn that helped to make the whole legal framework more clear and coherent[63] or even a welcome sign of judicial restraint, as the Court finally abandoned a position that risked 'rousing further nationalism and decreas[ing] solidarity across the Union'.[64] The idea that the adoption of a more restrictive approach has been a decisive step forward in terms of logical and legal coherence is a bit of an overstatement if evaluated in the light of the many key questions that the Court left unanswered. In any case, one cannot but admit that the pursuit of greater legal certainty has had heavy implications at

---

[58] See European Commission, 2019 Annual Report on Intra-EU Labour Mobility (Publications Office of the European Union 2020) 12. The report indicates that, in 2019, 83 per cent of the 11.7 millions movers of working age were economically active movers.

[59] See, with regard to Denmark, Dorte Sindbjerg Martinsen and Gabriel Pons Rotger, 'The Fiscal Impact of EU Immigration on the Tax-Financed Welfare State: Testing the Welfare Burden Thesis' (2017) 18 European Union Politics 620, and, with regard to Germany, Nadine Absenger and Florian Blank, 'From Social Myths to Legal Reality: Limiting the Freedom of Movement of EU Citizens' (2017) Politiche Sociali 469.

[60] On these dynamics, with a specific focus on Germany and Denmark, see Jack Mullan, 'Freedom of Movement at a Crossroads: Welfare Governance and the Boundaries of Belonging in the European Union' (2017) Politiche Sociali 447. This approach has been labelled as 'welfare chauvinism', to identify a populist agenda seeking to shield generous welfare benefits against access by immigrants. See Frederik Hjorth, 'Who Benefits? Welfare Chauvinism and National Stereotypes' (2016) 17 European Union Politics 3; for a prescient analysis of the class-conflict dimension of free movement rights in the EU see Neil Fligstein, *Euroclash: The EU, European Identity and the Future of Europe* (OUP 2008).

[61] See Case C-181/19 *Jobcenter Krefeld* EU:C:2020:377, Opinion of AG Pitruzzella, para. 29. The AG uses this expression to criticise 'the German Government's failure – whether in its written observations or at the hearing before the Court when it was questioned specifically on that point – to provide precise figures capable of illustrating the threat to the German social security system' posed by a restrictive interpretation of the material scope of application of the limits set by Article 24.2 Directive 2004/38/EC to the principle of equal treatment.

[62] Charlotte O'Brien, 'Civis Capitalist Sum: Class as the New Guiding Principle of EU Free Movement Rights' (2016) 53 CML Rev 937.

[63] Daniel Carter and Moritz Jesse, 'The *Dano* Evolution: Assessing Legal Integration and Access to Social Benefits for EU Citizens' (2018) European Papers 1179, 1181.

[64] Michael Blauberger and Susanne K Schmidt, 'Welfare Migration? Free Movement of EU Citizens and Access to Social Benefits' (2014) Research and Politics 1, 6. See also Susanne K Schmidt, 'Extending Citizenship Rights and Losing it All: Brexit and the Perils of Over-constitutionalisation' in Thym (ed.) (n 10) 17, and ibid, 'Building Social Europe Requires Challenging the Judicialisation of Citizenship' in Rainer Bauböck (ed.), *Debating European Citizenship* (Springer 2018) 205–9.

both individual and systemic levels.⁶⁵ As for the first dimension, the retreat from the notion of a modicum of financial solidarity between European citizens contributed to poverty and social exclusion,⁶⁶ turning citizens who were not economically self-sufficient into illegal migrants at risk of being expelled or starved out.⁶⁷ On a systemic level, the approach taken by the Court questions the postulates of the freedom of movement of persons, since the Court has extended the restrictive approach with regard to access to welfare well beyond social tourism.

Operatively, the new judicial course was premised upon the reconsideration of the role of Directive 2004/38/EC, by making it the new fulcrum of the whole legal framework governing the relationship between free movement and national welfare states. This evolution developed along two main lines that will be discussed in the next two paragraphs. On the one side, the Court shifted its focus from the rights enshrined in Treaty provisions on EU citizenship to the Directive, which became the sole yardstick to evaluate the compatibility with EU law of the restrictions posed by Member States to the access to their welfare. On the other side, it progressively extended the scope of application of the limits to the right to reside set in the Directive by adopting an increasingly broad reading of the notion of 'social assistance'.

5. MAKING SECONDARY LIMITATIONS PREVAIL OVER PRIMARY RIGHTS BY REVERSING THE OBJECTIVE OF DIRECTIVE 2004/38/EC

5.1 From *Brey* to *Dano*

In response to the above-described change in the political landscape of free movement, the Court embarked upon what has been aptly dubbed as a process of de-constitutionalisation of citizenship rights.⁶⁸ The Court sidelined Treaty provisions, relying exclusively on Directive 2004/38/EC to assess legal residence and equal treatment rights. This led to the reversal of the objective of the whole legal framework,⁶⁹ making what used to be an exception – safeguarding national welfare systems' financial sustainability – the new priority. This deviation was instrumental to justify a strictly literal interpretation of the provisions of the Directive, allowing Member States to almost automatically exclude citizens who are not self-sufficient from social benefits. This evolution is very much evident in the passage from *Brey* to *Dano*.

---

⁶⁵ As duly admitted also by some of the authors that give a positive evaluation of the new judicial course: see Carter and Jesse (n 63) 1199–1202.
⁶⁶ Herwig Verschueren, 'Preventing Benefit Tourism in the EU: A Narrow or a Broad Interpretation of the Possibilities Offered by the ECJ in *Dano*?' (2015) 52 CML Rev 363, 384.
⁶⁷ Daniel Thym, 'When Union Citizens turn into Illegal Migrants: The *Dano* Case' (2015) 40 E L Rev 249.
⁶⁸ Elise Muir, 'EU Citizenship, Access to Social Benefits and Third-Country National Family Members: Reflecting on the Relationship Between Primary and Secondary Rights in Times of Brexit' (2018) European Papers 1353, 1358–66.
⁶⁹ Thym (n 44) 25.

The *Brey* judgment has an ambiguous character,[70] having been considered both as marking the first separation from the expansive logic of EU citizenship[71] and as 'an outlier inspired by the older purposive approach'.[72] At least with regard to the assessment of equal treatment rights, the decision is very much in line with previous ones. The Court admitted that the exercise of the right of residence for citizens can be subordinated to the legitimate interests of the Member States, such as their public finances. However, national authorities cannot take an application for a benefit as the final evidence that a person has insufficient resources and, thus, can be denied the right of residence.

Moving from principles to practice, this means that national authorities cannot automatically exclude economically inactive citizens from welfare benefits, as they have first to assess whether they would represent an unreasonable burden. In doing so, they have to take 'into account a range of factors in the light of the principle of proportionality'.[73] In that regard, *Brey* went even further than previous decisions, combining the need for an individual assessment with the call for a systemic evaluation. According to the Court, national authorities can reject the application of a social assistance benefit made by an economically inactive person only after having assessed 'the specific burden which granting that benefit would place on the social assistance system as a whole'.[74] Admittedly, if taken at face value, such requirement would place upon national authorities an evidentiary burden almost impossible for them to discharge, and thus 'the individual right to free movement [would] prevail regularly'.[75] Indeed, there is no case in which a State could ever prove that the granting of 'that benefit' would make the system collapse. Even if taken in a more relaxed form, saying that what matters is not the single benefit but the cumulative effects of the granting of several of them, the requirement would pose significant difficulties when it comes its practical application.[76] As pointedly observed by Verschueren, the *Brey* judgment 'increased, rather than alleviated, legal uncertainty and confusion'[77] with regard to the determination of what an unreasonable burden is.

Just a few months after the Third Chamber adopted the *Brey* judgment, the Grand Chamber issued the *Dano* decision, definitively overturning the expansive constitutional dynamic described above. The Court seized the occasion to answer to the concerns expressed by some Member States about benefit tourism and its negative impact on the long-term prospects of national welfare states.[78] This is very much evident in the description of the factual background of the case, where the Court took great care in painting Ms Dano as the prototypical example of a social tourist.[79]

In answering the question on the legality of the rejection of Ms Dano's request, the Court started by saying that EU citizens can claim equal treatment with regard to access to social

---

[70] Herwig Verschueren, 'Free Movement and Benefit Tourism: The Unreasonable Burden of Brey' (2014) 16 European Journal of Migration and Law 147.
[71] Stefano Giubboni, 'EU Internal Migration Law and Social Assistance in Times of Crisis' (2016) Rivista del diritto della sicurezza sociale 247, 2577.
[72] Carter and Jesse (n 63) 1187.
[73] *Brey*, para. 72.
[74] *Brey*, para. 64.
[75] Thym (n 44) 29.
[76] Carter and Jesse (n 63) 1187.
[77] Verschueren (n 66) 367. See also Shuibhne (n 46) 907.
[78] O'Brien (n 62) 946.
[79] *Dano*, para. 39.

benefits only if they have a right of residence under Article 7 Directive 2004/38/EC. This provision, by subordinating the right of residence to financial self-sufficiency, seeks 'to prevent economically inactive Union citizens from using the host Member State's welfare system to fund their means of subsistence'.[80] This is a broad understanding of the clause, reading into it a preclusion that has not been made explicit by the legislator. The interpretation is premised upon a sort of teleological reduction. Contrary to *Brey*, here the Court referred to only one of the objectives of the Directive, that is, 'preventing Union citizens who are nationals of other Member States from becoming an unreasonable burden on the social assistance system of the host Member State', without even mentioning the promotion of the right of free movement.

Moving on from this background, the Court concluded that Member States are fully entitled to refuse to grant social benefits to 'economically inactive Union citizens who exercise their right to freedom of movement solely in order to obtain another Member State's social assistance although they do not have sufficient resources to claim a right of residence'.[81] Lastly, the Court maintained that, in order to determine whether the applicant falls into the category of those who can be excluded, the State has to take into consideration the financial situation of the person concerned. The test adopted is, thus, much lighter than the proportionality appraisal seen in *Brey* and previous case-law.[82] This evolution is very much in line with the choice to prioritise one of the objectives of the Directive – avoiding mobile citizens becoming a burden on national social assistance systems – over promoting intra-EU mobility. Requesting that national authorities carefully evaluate the position of the concerned person and his/her links with the host State was indeed an attempt to strike a balance between these competing interests.[83]

5.2 Allowing Member States to Automatically Exclude Non-self-sufficient Mobile Citizens from Their Welfare Systems: *Alimanovic* and *Garcia-Nieto*

In *Alimanovic*, the Court pushed forward the involution set in motion by *Dano*. The case concerned a Swedish mother and her three daughters; the mother and elder daughter worked in Germany for 11 months until losing their job and applying for social minimum subsistence benefits. German authorities rejected the application on the basis that Ms Alimanovic and her daughter could no longer rely on a right of residence as workers, having lost this status according to the German law that transposed Article 14 Directive 2014/38/EC. The key question was whether the loss of the status was enough to automatically exclude them from the benefit or whether German authorities had to take into consideration the specific situation of Ms Alimanovic and her family. The Court went for the first option,[84] focusing exclusively

---

[80] *Dano*, para. 76.
[81] *Dano*, para. 78.
[82] See Maria E Bartoloni, 'Libera circolazione dei cittadini UE e principio di solidarietà europea: cronaca di una morte annunciata' in Borelli and Guazzarotti (eds) (n 55) 60-61.
[83] See Eleanor Spaventa, 'The Constitutional Impact of Union Citizenship' in Ulla Neergaard, Ruth Nielsen and Lynn Roseberry (eds), *The Role of Courts in Developing a European Social Model: Theoretical and Methodological Perspectives* (DJOF Publishing 2010) 146; Charlotte O'Brien, 'Real Links, Abstract Rights and False Alarms: the Relationship Between the ECJ's Real Link Case Law and National Solidarity' (2008) 33 ELR 643.
[84] Case C-67/14 *Alimanovic* EU:C:2015:597.

on Directive 2004/38/EC and on the limits to the right of residence and equal treatment set therein.

The Court acknowledged that, according to its previous decisions, the Directive would require national authorities to carry out an individual assessment to determine whether the concerned person may represent an unreasonable burden for the social assistance system. However, it held that no such assessment was due in the case at hand. The reason for departing from its own case-law lies in the 'gradual system' established by Directive 2004/38/EC with regard to the retention of the status of worker. Article 7.3 provides that Union citizens having worked for less than one year in the host State retain the status for at least six months. According to the Court, this mechanism already takes into due consideration the personal situation of the concerned person and makes the proportionality test redundant.[85] Admittedly, graduality and proportionality are often in the eye of the beholder, but it is hard to see how legislation that does not allow access to social benefits to citizens who have been working in a country for 11 months and who have strong personal ties with it can meet these requirements. This approach has paradoxical consequences, placing jobseekers with a strong link with the labour market of the host State in a worse position than the much-despised 'social tourists'.

The Court adopted the same approach in *García-Nieto*, which concerned the refusal by German authorities to grant a subsistence benefit to a Spanish national, Mr Peña Cuevas, who had entered Germany with his son to join his partner, Ms García-Nieto, and their daughter. The rejection was based on the fact that, at the time of the application, Mr Peña Cuevas and his son had resided in Germany for less than three months.

The Court did not even consider the possibility that Mr Peña Cuevas could derive a right of residence and equal treatment from being a family member of a worker – Ms García-Nieto was employed as a kitchen assistant – addressing the case as one concerning an economically inactive person.[86] Consequently, it found no difficulty in bringing into play the limitations set in Article 24 Directive 2004/38/EC with regard to economically inactive citizens in their first three months of residence.[87]

Following *Alimanovic*, the Court excluded that national authorities can be required, in a case like the one at hand, to perform any individual assessment before excluding the person from the social assistance system. The conclusion is premised on an argument that, at least from a logical perspective, seems unassailable: if an automatic exclusion from social benefits is admitted in the case of jobseekers, the 'same applies *a fortiori*'[88] with regard to persons that have no previous links with the host State's job market.

---

[85] *Alimanovic*, paras 59–62.
[86] Case C-299/14 *García-Nieto* EU:C:2016:114, para. 41.
[87] *García-Nieto*, para. 43.
[88] *García-Nieto*, para. 48.

6. BEYOND SOCIAL ASSISTANCE AND BEYOND SOCIAL TOURISM: PROMOTING STATUS CONVERGENCE À REBOURS

6.1 Beyond Social Tourism: Treating Jobseekers and Even Workers as Economically Inactive Citizens

When *Dano* was adopted some authors proposed a narrow interpretation of the decision, so as to limit the damage to the idea that citizenship could be a catalyst for transnational solidarity in the EU legal order. Verschueren, in particular, claimed that the restrictive approach adopted by the Court aimed only at curbing social tourism and not the right of equal access to social benefits by all economically disadvantaged citizens. Indeed, when dealing with Member States' capacity to refuse the granting of social benefits, the Court specifically referred to those citizens who 'exercise their right to freedom of movement solely in order to obtain another Member State's social assistance'.[89]

Subsequent decisions proved that this reading was too optimistic, as the Court applied the restrictive approach developed in *Dano* in situations that had nothing to do with social tourism.[90] Nazifa and Sonita Alimanovic, in particular, were not trying to abuse the German welfare system, but only to obtain some help at a moment in which they had lost their previous, precarious jobs and were looking for new work. Yet, as seen above, the Court approached their case by assimilating their condition with that of economically inactive persons. In this sense *Alimanovic* broke with *Collins*, where the Court, '[i]n view of the establishment of citizenship of the Union', held that jobseekers cannot be excluded from the protection from discrimination offered by what is now Article 45 TFEU, at least with regard to benefits that aim to facilitate access to employment.[91]

The extension of the restrictive turn on welfare access from economically inactive persons to other categories of mobile citizens is a worrying sign of the fact that European citizenship has not only lost traction in promoting upward status convergence between the two categories of citizens, but has become a factor pushing in the opposite direction.[92]

The judicial turn was very much in touch with the prevailing political climate, well exemplified by the *New Settlement for the United Kingdom within the European Union*, agreed in February 2016.[93] Here jobseekers were treated under the heading of Article 21 TFEU,

---

[89] *Dano*, para. 78.
[90] This evolution has been envisaged as a possibility, and duly explored, also by Verschueren in his analysis of *Dano*: see again Verschueren (n 66) 377–81.
[91] Case C-138/02 *Collins* EU:C:2004:172, paras 60–67. However, the Court admitted that the host State can exclude jobseekers not having a sufficiently close link with its labour market (see paras 69–70). On this point, see Catherine Jacqueson and Frans Pennings, 'Equal Treatment of Mobile Persons in the Context of Social Market Economy' (2019) 15 Utrecht Law Review 64, 73.
[92] On this in-evolution, see the seminal work by O'Brien (n 3) 91 ff. See also Araceli Turmo, 'The Pernicious Influence of Citizenship Rights on Workers' Rights in the EU: The Case of Student Finance' (2018) European Papers 1115; Kees Groenendijk, 'Access for Migrants to Social Assistance: Closing the Frontiers or Reducing Citizenship?' in Elspeth Guild, Sergio Carrera and Katharina Eisele (eds), *Social Benefits and Migration: A Contested Relationship and Policy Challenge in the EU* (Centre for European Policy Studies 2013) 22–30.
[93] European Council Decision of 19 February 2016 of the Heads of State or Government, meeting within the European Council, concerning a new settlement for the United Kingdom within the European Union, EUCO 1/16.

alongside economically inactive persons, and not under Article 45 TFEU. Furthermore, the Decision established that

> Member States may reject claims for social assistance where EU citizens from other Member States do not enjoy a right of residence or are entitled to reside on their territory solely because of job-search. This includes claims [...] for benefits [that] are also intended to facilitate access to the labour market of the host Member States.[94]

The Decision went even further down this regressive path by allowing Member States to pull an emergency brake so as to limit newly arriving EU workers' access to in-work benefits for a period of up to four years.

Although the prospective UK deal on EU membership never entered into force, the readiness of the EU to compromise on equal access to welfare services by economically active citizens encouraged certain Member States to follow suit.[95] Austria, for instance, decided in 2019 to introduce the indexation of family benefits, by adjusting their amount to the costs of living in the State where the child resides.[96] In January 2019 the Commission launched an infringement procedure against Austria regarding this measure. However, it is worth observing that the same measure was foreseen in the pre-Brexit UK–EU settlement, where the Commission undertook to submit a proposal to amend Regulation 883/2014 and introduce the possibility for Member States to index child benefits.

A similar involution also took place with regard to frontier workers, that is, individuals pursuing an economic activity in one Member State while living in another, to which they return at least once a week. According to Regulation 492/2011 these workers have the same status of 'ordinary' ones, but some judicial decisions have put this commonality of rights under strain. In particular, the Court accepted that Member States can subordinate the access to social benefits by frontier workers or their family members to conditions proving their level of integration in the State of employment.[97] As pointedly observed by Montaldo, the application of these conditions 'plays a permissive function in favour of the interest of Member States',[98] giving them a margin of discretion when it comes to determining the openness of their welfare systems in order to cope with the perceived threat of what is termed here 'study grant forum shopping'.[99]

---

[94] Ibid., Section D(1)(b).
[95] Reynolds (n 11).
[96] See Michael Blauberger, Anita Heindlmaier and Carina Kobler, 'Free Movement of Workers under Challenge: the Indexation of Family Benefits' (2020) Comparative European Politics 925.
[97] Case C-410/18 *Aubriet* EU:C:2019:582; paras 35-47; Case C-238/15 *Bragança Linares Verruga* EU:C:2016:949, para. 69; Case C-20/12 *Giersch* EU:C:2013:411, paras 78–80.
[98] Stefano Montaldo, 'Frontier Workers and Access to Welfare Benefits in the Member State of Employment: Too Much of a Strain?' (2017) Politiche Sociali 489, 500. See also Catherine Jacqueson, 'Any News from Luxembourg? On Student Aid, Frontier Workers and Stepchildren: *Bragança Linares Verruga* and *Depesne*' (2018) 55 CML Rev 901, 913–15.
[99] *Giersch*, para. 21.

6.2 Beyond Social Assistance: Expanding the Material Scope of Application of the Limits set by Directive 2004/38/EC

The evolution analysed above is closely intertwined with the progressive expansion of the scope *ratione materiae* of the Directive and, in particular, of its restrictive right-to-reside test. The expansion came about by first adopting a broad reading of the notion of 'social assistance', referred to in Articles 7 and 24 of Directive 2004/38/EC, and then projecting it into the social security field. By so doing the Court ended up granting a 'normative super-status' to the Directive,[100] giving it precedence over Regulation 883/2004 and transforming it into a gateway to equal treatment rights for mobile EU citizens with regard to virtually any type of social benefit.

The evolution started in *Brey*, where the referring court asked whether a pension's compensatory supplement was to be considered as social assistance and, thus, whether Member States could exclude non-self-sufficient persons from having access to it. The key issue was whether this supplement, a special non-contributory cash benefit (SNCB) in accordance with Article 70 Regulation 883/2004,[101] could be also regarded as falling under the scope of application of Directive 2004/38/EC. The Court answered in the affirmative, maintaining that the same benefit can fall under both regimes and can be defined in a different way by each of them. By so doing, the Court imported the right to residence under Directive 2004/38/EC into the social security coordination regime, so to allow Member States to exclude from their enjoyment people who have a right to obtain them according to Article 70 Regulation 883/2004. Indeed, this provision establishes that SNCBs are to be provided by the State of residence, an expression that refers only to the place where the claimants live or have the main centre of their interests and not to their legal status or their financial situation.

The Court followed the same interpretive line in *Alimanovic*. Here, it held that a subsistence allowance for the long-term unemployed has to be regarded as 'social assistance' for the purposes of Directive 2004/38/EC.[102] To this end it carried out a gravity test, claiming that one of the functions of the benefit – covering the minimum subsistence costs necessary to lead a life in keeping with human dignity – prevailed over the other: facilitating access to the labour market. This finding is as unsubstantiated as it is crucial for the result that the Court wanted to achieve. Painting the benefit as a social assistance one functions to assimilate Ms Alimanovic's situation to that of economically inactive persons rather than workers. In this regard it is worth noting that this conclusion stands in open contradiction to the *Vatsouras* judgment, adopted just a few years earlier. There, the Court excluded that the same benefit could be labelled as 'social assistance', pointing to the fact that its main aim was to promote access to employment. On the basis of this finding the Court held that this benefit cannot be withheld from jobseekers, at least those having a genuine link with the labour market of the host State.[103]

The reason for this shift and, more generally, for the application of the affluence test to SNCBs is to be found in the new *telos* of the Directive. Insofar as these benefits involve public

---

[100] Maria A Panascì, 'Legal Values and Hermeneutic Virtues: The Status Quo of European Social Citizenship' (2017) Politiche Sociali 429, 441.
[101] Case C-160/02 *Skalka* EU:C:2004:269, para. 20.
[102] *Alimanovic*, para. 45.
[103] Joined Cases C-22/08 and C-23/08 *Vatsouras and Koupatantze* EU:C:2009:344, para. 45.

largesse, being paid under general taxation,[104] they fall within the notion of social assistance within the meaning of the Directive, whose primary aim is now to prevent non-self-sufficient individuals from becoming an unreasonable burden. Yet, the evolution is problematic from at least two perspectives. First, the choice to admit that Member States can rely upon the right-to-reside test also with regard to social security benefits encroaches upon the pursuit of one of the objectives of Regulation 883/2004, that is, avoiding the risk that mobile citizens could be left without any protection by falling into the gaps between national systems. Second, the shift has overturned the terms of the compromise between Directive 2004/38/EC and Regulation 883/2004 with regard to SNCBs. The compromise was premised upon, on the one side, the derogation from the principle of exportability for these types of benefits and, on the other, the attribution of the responsibility for their payment to the Member State of residence.[105]

The Court went a step further, allowing Member States to refuse to pay any social benefit, including purely social security ones, to EU citizens failing to pass the right-to-residence test under Directive 2004/38/EC due to lack of financial resources. In *Commission v UK*, a decision adopted just ten days before the Brexit referendum in a desperate attempt to defuse voters' concerns regarding migration issues, it held that EU law does not prevent national authorities from making access to purely social security benefits – such as child benefit and child tax credit – conditional upon the possession of a right to reside. According to the Commission, the 'right to reside' requirement is nowhere to be found in Regulation 883/2004 and it unduly deprives a number of people from having access to the social benefits at issue. In the context of social security coordination, the notion only designates the place where the person has the habitual centre of interests and has nothing to do with its legal status. The Court disagreed, admitting that Member States can rely upon the right-to-reside test in order to restrict the access to certain social benefits.[106]

The main reason underpinning this approach is, once again, the willingness to entrust national authorities with the widest possible margin of manoeuvre when it comes to protecting their welfare systems against the risks posed by intra-EU mobility – even if this entails the adoption of openly discriminatory measures that end up sacrificing 'the last vestiges of EU citizenship to the altar of [...] nativist tendencies'.[107] The Commission purported to bring this evolution full circle, proposing to codify it in the amended version of Regulation 883/2004. According to the proposal presented in December 2016, the new Article 4 would have allowed Member States to 'require that the access of an economically inactive person residing in that Member State to its social security benefits be subject to the conditions of having a right to legal residence as set out in Directive 2004/38/EC'.[108]

---

[104] See *Brey*, para. 61.

[105] Rob Cornelissen, 'EU Regulations on the Coordination of Social Security Systems and Special Non-contributory Benefits: A Source of Never Ending Controversy' in Guild, Carrera and Eisele (eds) (n 92) 82.

[106] Case C-308/14 *Commission v United Kingdom* EU:C:2016:436, para. 68. By so doing, the Court implicitly accepted the argument put forward by the British government according to which the reasoning set out in *Brey* could not be confined exclusively to special non-contributory cash benefits, as demonstrated by the use by the Court of the term 'social benefits', without any further specification.

[107] Charlotte O'Brien, 'The ECJ Sacrifices Citizenship in Vain. *Commission v. United Kingdom*' (2017) 54 CML Rev 209.

[108] Proposal for a Regulation of the European Parliament and the Council amending Regulation (EC) No 883/2004 of 13 December 2016 on the coordination of social security systems and regulation

7. SHORING UP WORKERS' RIGHTS AGAINST THE RIGHT-TO-RESIDE TEST UNDER DIRECTIVE 2004/38/EC: *JOBCENTER KREFELD*

There are some recent signs that the Court has come to realise that making Directive 2004/38/EC, and the restrictive right-to-reside requirement set therein, a sort of a gateway to the receipt of any social benefits by any economically non-self-sufficient citizens is now encroaching upon some of the core elements of free movement and, thus, of one of the *raisons d'être* of the European integration process. This is not to say that the Court has reverted to the old expansive logic of citizenship, but at least it is no longer passively accepting any derogation from the principle of equal treatment justified by the need of protecting national welfare states' financial viability against the perceived risks posed by intra-EU mobility.

Jobcenter Krefeld represents a landmark in this regard. The case concerned the refusal by German authorities to continue to pay basic social security benefits to JD, a Polish national, and his two daughters who were under his exclusive custody. Jobcenter Krefeld motivated the refusal by referring to the status of JD, who at that time had lost his job more than six months earlier and was residing in Germany only to seek new employment. JD brought a judicial action against the refusal and the Sozialgericht Düsseldorf upheld it. The Social Court observed that, while it was true that JD could no longer rely on a right of residence derived from previous employment according to the national legislation transposing Directive 2004/38/EC, he could derive such right from that enjoyed by his daughters on the basis of Article 10 Regulation (EU) 492/2011. Indeed, JD was the sole carer of two children who had commenced school attendance in Germany when he was a worker and who were entitled to reside in the host State regardless of their father subsequently losing his job.[109]

The key question was whether JD was entitled to claim equal treatment with regard to access to the basic social security benefit on the basis of the right of residence derived from Article 10 Regulation 492/2011 or whether national authorities were entitled to deny it on the basis of Article 24 Directive 2004/38/EC, since he no longer met the requirements for lawful residence set in that act. The latter was the position expressed by the German government intervening in the proceedings in front of the Court. As reported by Advocate General Pitruzzella in his Opinion, the national government considered Article 24.2 Directive 2004/38/EC as 'a cross-cutting provision, which regulates exhaustively the issue of equal treatment with regard to social assistance benefits and therefore goes beyond the regulatory scope of Directive 2004/38'.[110] According to the German government, the case at hand was a replica of *Alimanovic* and the Court should have adopted the same solution elaborated there. Admitting

---

(EC) No 987/2009 laying down the procedure for implementing Regulation (EC) No 883/2004, COM (2016) 815 final. The attempt to revise Regulation (EC) 883/2004 has not been successful so far. On 18 April 2019 the European Parliament decided to postpone the work on the dossier to the following legislature, after two and a half years of negotiations. For a detailed analysis, see Marc Morsa, 'The Failure of Negotiations on European Regulations for the Coordination of Social Security Systems: The End of European Solidarity? The Reasons for Failure in an Endeavour that Started Well' in Borelli and Guazzarotti (eds) (n 55) 123–42.

[109] With regard to the autonomous nature of the right of residence, see Case C-310/08 *Ibrahim and Secretary of State for the Home Department* EU:C:2010:80, paras 35, 40–41 and Case C-480/08 *Teixeira* EU:C:2010:83, para. 46.

[110] *Jobcenter Krefeld*, Opinion AG Pitruzzella, para. 35.

that JD could derive a right to equal treatment from the mere fact that his daughters were educated in the host Member State could weaken the wall created by the restrictive interpretation of Directive 2004/38/EC to protect the financial sustainability of national welfare states against the threats posed by benefit tourism.

The Court roundly rejected the position of the German government, refusing to further strengthen the normative status of the Directive. The judgment clarified that the right of residence conferred upon the children of a worker by Article 10 Regulation (EU) 492/2011 triggers the right to equal treatment provided for under Article 7.[111] Being the sole carer of the children, JD enjoyed the same right, even if he had lost the status of worker. Subsequently, and this is a key finding of the judgment, the Court stressed that in this case equal treatment was autonomous from Directive 2004/38/EC and the limits set therein. This conclusion is based on three main arguments. First, the derogation set in Article 24.2 Directive 2004/38/EC makes clear that it operates only with regard to 'all Union citizens residing on the basis of this Directive in the territory of the host Member State'.[112] Second, the Directive was not meant to constitute a gateway to equal treatment for any type mobile citizen, exhaustively codifying limits and conditions to the exercise of the right of free movement.[113] Third, the objective of preserving the financial soundness of national welfare states plays no role here and, thus, it cannot be invoked by national authorities to justify any restriction upon the right of equal treatment with regard to access to social benefits.[114]

The judgment does not represent the rejection of the restrictive approach to access to national welfare states analysed above. Rather it marks a return to the two citizenships model,[115] once again making participation in the market – and contribution to the financing of the national welfare system – the key criterion to distinguish different categories of mobile citizens and to justify differences in the way in which they are treated. The Court put great emphasis on the fact that the position of JD is significantly different from that of short stayers, such as Mr Peña Cuevas, or economically inactive persons moving solely to get access to social benefits in a host State, such as Ms Dano. Indeed, before losing his job, JD had worked and sent his daughters to school in Germany; for those reasons, he deserved to be admitted into the national redistributive community. Less evident was the distinction between the position of JD and that of Nazifa Alimanovic. From a factual perspective, the two cases are very similar: like JD, also Ms Alimanovic moved to Germany with her children – all of whom were born there – worked for a period and then asked for help while she was looking for a new job. All these similarities notwithstanding, the Court resisted the call to apply the conclusion reached there also in this case, by pointing out that the referring judge in the *Alimanovic* case did not refer to Regulation (EU) 492/2011, taking for granted that Directive 2004/38/EC was the only possible basis for their right of residence.

Saying that workers, and their family members, have a right to equal treatment with regard to access to any social advantage is not particularly innovative. However, the judgment is not just a restatement of the obvious, but represents a strong reminder that, at least with regard to workers, solidarity is an in-built feature that national authorities cannot dispense with

---

[111] Case C-181/19 *Jobcenter Krefeld* EU:C:2020:794, paras 34–55.
[112] *Jobcenter Krefeld*, para. 62.
[113] *Jobcenter Krefeld*, paras 63–65.
[114] *Jobcenter Krefeld*, para. 66.
[115] Jean-Michel Belorgey, 'La protection sociale dans une Union de citoyens' (1998) Droit social 159.

by simply raising the spectre of social tourism. To this end, the decision put a check on the seemingly unstoppable ascent of the right-to-reside test under Directive 2004/38/EC and its progressive transformation into a gateway to equal treatment for any mobile citizen not having sufficient financial resources.

Furthermore, the judgment represents a belated attempt to undo some of the damage done by previous decisions, such as *Alimanovic*, that took the counter-reformation of EU mobility law well beyond social tourism.[116] In that regard it is worth observing that the Court did not even mention EU citizenship, focusing instead on the rules on free movement of workers and reviving their solidaristic dimension.[117] The judgment brought back under the protection of Article 45 TFEU second-time jobseekers with precarious employment histories and insufficient financial resources for themselves and their families.[118] Therefore *Jobcenter Krefeld* does not constitute a *stricto sensu* reversal of *Alimanovic*, as the Court managed to reach different conclusions by switching to a different legal framework.

The downside of the judgment is that it concerns only some jobseekers and, in particular, only those having children enrolled in school in the host State. All the others, no matter the strength of their linkage to the national job market or their integration into the societal fabric of the host State, are excluded from it, since they cannot trigger the protection offered by Article 10 Regulation (EU) 492/2011. This is bound to further increase the fragmentation and the arbitrariness of the legal framework on free movement. Moreover, the judgment's capacity to open up an avenue of access to national welfare states for precarious and low-income workers risks being seriously undermined by the widespread – and, so far, largely tolerated – national manipulations of the definition of what counts as work, so as to exclude marginal workers coming from other Member States from access to social benefits. As insightfully reported by O'Brien, Spaventa and De Coninck,[119] this mainly occurs through the imposition of working hours or income thresholds to identify which activities are 'purely marginal and ancillary', designating those workers who fail to meet such requirements as economically inactive persons.

---

[116] O'Brien (n 62) 973.

[117] This approach is strongly reminiscent of the idea of free movement of workers 'as an incipient form of citizenship'. See Richard Plender, 'An Incipient Form of European Citizenship' in FG Jacobs, *European Law and the Individual* (North-Holland Publishing Company 1976). See also Niamh Nic Shuibhne, 'Reconnecting Free Movement of Workers and Equal Treatment in an Unequal Europe' (2018) 43 EL Rev 477.

[118] In a recent decision not concerning the relationship between free movement and access to social benefits, the Court reasserted that also a first-time jobseeker, genuinely seeking work, 'must be classified as "worker"' and thus falls under the protection of Article 45 TFEU. See Case C-710/19 *G.M.A.* EU:C:2020:1037, para. 25.

[119] Charlotte O'Brien, Eleanor Spaventa and Joyce De Coninck, *Comparative Report 2015. The Concept of Worker under Article 45 TFEU and Certain Non-Standard Forms of Employment* (European Commission – FreSsco Free Movement of Workers and Social Security Coordination 2016) 24-25.

8. CONFIRMING THE ROLE AS GATEKEEPER OF DIRECTIVE 2004/38/EC WITH REGARD TO ECONOMICALLY INACTIVE CITIZENS: *GC*

In a judgment[120] adopted in July 2021 the Court confirmed that the approach adopted in *Jobcenter Krefeld* concerns only a limited portion of mobile citizens, thus consolidating the return to the two citizenships model. Indeed, *GC* upheld the decisive role played by Directive 2004/38/EC, and its restrictive conditions, in determining access to social assistance benefits by economically inactive EU citizens. Quite remarkably, this happened in a case where Article 24 Directive 2004/38/EC was not even applicable.

The judgment concerned the refusal by UK authorities to grant a social assistance benefit known as Universal Credit to GC, a dual Croatian and Dutch national living in a women's refuge in Northern Ireland with no resources for her and her two children. GC had a temporary right of residence in the UK, having been granted pre-settled status, which is not subject to any condition as to resources. Yet, according to the Universal Credit Regulations, holding this right of residence is not enough to fulfil the habitual residence requirement and to obtain the benefit. Seized with the matter, the referring judge asked the Court to clarify whether the eligibility conditions set by the national legislation were discriminatory on grounds of nationality and, hence, in breach of Article 18 TFEU.

The reasoning of the Court is premised on the marginalisation of Article 18 TFEU, which 'is intended to apply independently only to situations governed by EU law with respect to which the FEU Treaty does not lay down specific rules on non-discrimination'. The provision is displaced by Directive 2004/38 and, more specifically, by its Article 24, since the latter gives 'concrete expression' to the principle of non-discrimination 'in relation to Union citizens who exercise their right to move and reside within the territory of the member States'.[121] Therefore, argued the Court, the question raised by the referring judge needs to be reformulated. Indeed, 'it is in the light of Article 24 of Directive 2004/38, and not of the first paragraph of Article 18 TFEU, that it is necessary to assess whether that person faces discrimination on the grounds of nationality'.[122]

This is quite a bold move that can hardly be categorised as a mere reformulation of the preliminary question, since it changed the legal framework against which the legality of national authorities' choice to exclude certain EU citizens from social assistance has been assessed. This shift was functional to bring back into play the restrictive reading of the right-to-reside requirement first elaborated in *Dano*, so as to conclude that national authorities were fully entitled to exclude GC from having access to Universal Credit. Being an economically inactive person, without sufficient resources for her and her children, her residence did not comply with the requirements set by Article 7 Directive 2004/38/EC. Therefore, she could not claim entitlement to social benefits on a non-discriminatory basis, as provided for by Article 24 Directive 2004/38/EC.[123]

The problem is that this provision was not applicable in the case at hand. As duly acknowledged by the Court itself, GC's right of residence was based on national law and 'cannot

---

[120] Case C-709/20 *GC* EU:C:2021:602.
[121] *GC*, para. 66.
[122] *GC*, paras 67 and 72.
[123] *GC*, paras 63–82.

[...] be regarded in any way as being granted "on the basis of" Directive 2004/38 within the meaning of Article 24(1) of that directive'. One could expect that the inapplicability of the secondary act setting the limits and the conditions for the enjoyment of the rights established by the Treaty would have led the Court to admit that the principle of non-discrimination established by Article 18 TFEU could operate in full. Instead, it established that Member States are free 'to specify the consequences of a right of residence granted on the basis of national law alone'[124] and, thus, to exclude economically inactive Union citizens who do not have sufficient resources from benefits that are guaranteed to nationals in the same situation. This is a highly questionable conclusion based on the premise that Article 24 Directive 2004/38/EC does not simply give expression to the principle of non-discrimination, but constitutes it, as if Treaty provisions were non-existent.[125]

The tortuous reasoning followed by the Court in *GC* did not end here. The last part of the judgment sought to set some limits to Member States' freedom to keep economically non-self-sufficient citizens, residing on the basis of a national law, out of their social assistance systems. To this end, it established that national authorities are obliged to respect the claimant's fundamental rights by complying with the Charter of Fundamental Rights. In the present case, the Court held that UK authorities must respect human dignity, as protected by Article 1 of the Charter; the right to private and family life, as protected by Article 7 of the Charter; to be read in conjunction with the obligation to take into consideration the best interest of the child, as recognised by Article 24(2) of the Charter.[126] This is a potentially far-reaching reference, especially with regard to the refusal to grant a basic benefit to a woman not having any other resources for her and her children, and it is highly unfortunate that the Court limited itself to mentioning the relevant articles, without providing much guidance with regard to their practical application.

9. CONCLUSION

Given the contested legitimacy of the initial solidarity move of its case-law,[127] the Court of Justice's precipitous retreat from the bold stance taken in the short-lived 'progressive' phase could appear inevitable.[128] This involution can be considered as a – belated, according to some commentators – form of judicial restraint by the Court, which finally decided to accept the limits posed by the legislator to the possibility of constructing European citizenship as a catalyst for transnational solidarity. And yet, it remains very questionable in terms of the

---

[124] *GC*, para. 83.

[125] For a righly critical take of the judgment see Charlotte O'Brien, 'The Great EU Citizenship Illusion Exposed: Equal Treatment Rights Evaporate for the Vulnerable (CG v The Department for Communities in Northern Ireland)' (2021) 46 EL Rev 801.

[126] *GC*, paras 85–92.

[127] Michael Dougan, 'The Bubble that Burst: Exploring the Legitimacy of the Case Law of the Court of Justice on the Free Movement of Union Citizens' in Maurice Adams, Henri de Waele, Johan Meeusen and Gert Straetmans (eds), *Judging Europe's Judges: The Legitimacy of the Case Law of the European Court of Justice* (Hart Publishing 2013) 127; Susanne K Schmidt, *The European Court of Justice and the Policy Process* (OUP 2016) 180 ff.

[128] See Urška Šadl and Suvi Elina Sankari, 'Why Did Citizenship Jurisprudence Change?' in Thym (n 10) 89.

uncomfortable abdication of any ambition towards a constitutional foundation of the social rights attached to European citizenship,[129] since it offers the best possible evidence 'that Union citizenship has staunchly remained a market economy form of citizenship, deeply stratified according to socio-economic class, and inadequate to deliver principles of social justice'.[130] What is highly problematic is that, as aptly observed by O'Brien, 'it is not just the economically inactive who are ill-served, but workers in low-paid, low-status and law-security jobs, and those whose work histories are punctuated by, for example, periods of child care or adult care'. There is a risk that these people 'fall through the gaps' of a 'law-as-lists, rather than law-as-justice'[131] form of citizenship. Rediscovering the solidaristic potential of the rules on free movement of workers, as done in *Jobcenter Krefeld*, can help to reverse this trend, even though, as further demonstrated by *GC*, this may end up increasing the fragmentation and the arbitrariness of the legal framework on free movement.

At the same time, we should not be unaware of the intrinsic limits of a judicially led form of transnational solidarity. Redistributive efforts always rely on some accepted idea of social justice: de-linking the welfare state and national citizenship for the economically inactive is a politically demanding challenge, especially in times of crisis. The quest for a stronger political foundation of European solidarity can no longer be eluded: 'The EU can only become fully legitimate, when the majority of EU citizens are included in each others' scope of justice.'[132] The tragedy of the Covid-19 pandemic crisis gives us a unique opportunity to reinvent solidarity within the EU under a new politically shared paradigm. However, as the example of Next Generation EU clearly indicates, the creation of supranational solidaristic mechanisms, such as a true European social citizenship, requires an unprecedented collective redistributive effort.

---

[129] Niamh Nic Shuibhne, 'Integrating Union Citizenship and the Charter of Fundamental Rights' in Thym (n 10) 209.
[130] O'Brien (n 3) 1.
[131] Ibid.
[132] Dimitry Kochenov, 'The Just World' in Kochenov, De Búrca and Williams (n 24) 455.

15. Progression and retrogression of the ECJ case law on access to social benefits

Ségolène Barbou des Places

1. INTRODUCTION

It is claimed, in political discourse and media reporting, that European welfare states are increasingly threatened by EU citizens' intra-EU mobility. Despite the Commission's efforts to convince Member States and public opinion that movement within the EU is not *per se* detrimental to the welfare systems,[1] Member States continue to denounce the 'welfare tourism' strategies that are deemed to be altering the cohesion of national solidarity systems. Debates over the conditions under which EU citizens should be able to ask for social benefits in a host Member State have exploded in the recent political arena. During the Brexit campaign in particular, claims that EU law did not prevent – or, worse, that it facilitated – welfare tourism had a strong impact on public opinions. The idea that EU citizens could be an economic threat, and that even EU workers could be a drain on public finance, has become an argument of utmost political importance. This was expressed in the letter David Cameron addressed to Donald Tusk, dated 10 November 2015, where the then British Prime Minister tried – and managed – to convince his EU partners that free movement had to be limited in order to provide the UK with the capacity to prevent Eastern EU citizens from 'put[ting] at risk' the precarious balance of the British solidarity mechanisms.[2]

Against this background, the ECJ case law on access to social benefits plays a decisive role for the EU, its Member States and EU citizens. Its judgments come under intense scrutiny, with argument regarding the entity (the legislature or the judiciary) most legitimate to adequately balance free movement rights with the protection of viable national welfare systems. In the absence of EU competence, entitlement to social benefits has indeed been, and remains to this day, a matter of national law. That does not mean, of course, that EU law is irrelevant to the question of access to social rights, as this chapter will show. But welfare systems are mostly organised on a national basis, as they organise solidarity between the members of a cohesive group of people who feel committed to each other.[3] This is the reason why welfare systems are closed to outsiders: access to solidarity is generally conditioned upon previous contribu-

---

[1] Commission, Free movement of people: five actions to benefit citizens, growth and employment in the EU, 25 November 2013, IP/13/1151, https://ec.europa.eu/commission/presscorner/detail/en/IP_13_1151 accessed 8 April 2021.

[2] European Council conclusions, 18–19 February 2016 (A new settlement for the UK within the EU), www.consilium.europa.eu/en/meetings/european-council/2016/02/18-19/ accessed 07 April 2021.

[3] Michael Dougan and Eleanor Spaventa, '"Wish You Weren't Here"… New Models of Social Solidarity in the EU' in Michael Dougan and Eleanor Spaventa (eds), *Social Welfare and EU Law* (Hart Publishing 2005) 181; Ségolène Barbou des Places, 'Solidarité et mobilité des personnes en droit de l'Union européenne: des affinités sélectives?' in Chahira Boutayeb (ed.), *La solidarité dans l'Union européenne. Eléments constitutionnels et matériels* (Dalloz 2011), 218.

tion, legal residence and/or nationality. Unsurprisingly, ECJ cases in which a European judge delineates EU citizens' capacity to access Member States' circle of solidarity and clarifies the Member States' obligations on matters of social benefits trigger intense reactions. This is notably the case when, as it has done in the past decades, the Court adjudicates on the rights of inactive EU citizens, or those of workers with limited incomes or of indigent people asking for social protection. When the Court is dealing with the situations of those people who are at the margins of the European economic market, any obligation to grant access to social benefits equates to imposing a net cost on the welfare system. This is why since the late 1950s there has been a sharp contrast, as regards access to social entitlements, between the situation of workers and that of non-economically active EU citizens. The access to social benefits depends on the type and the category of social benefits asked for by mobile Europeans but, as a general rule, social rights are granted in priority to people contributing to the welfare systems.

The EEC first enacted legal norms, aimed at granting mobile workers the right to social security entitlements,[4] which organise coordination between the Member States' social security mechanisms and institutions. The ambition was to ensure the removal of obstacles to the free movement of persons between the Member States: EU citizens working and residing in a Member State other than their own must not lose some or all of their social security rights. In order to guarantee that EU citizens are insured when two or more countries are involved, the coordination Regulation determines under which country's system they are insured. The Regulation also relies on four main principles that are of utmost importance: the single applicable law, equal treatment, aggregation and exportability.[5]

To reach their protective objective, EU Member States agreed that the material scope of the social security coordination had to be broad: it therefore covers sickness, maternity and equivalent paternity benefits; old-age, survivor's and invalidity benefits; benefits in respect of work-related accidents and occupational diseases; death grants; pre-retirement benefits; unemployment benefits; family benefits; and special non-contributory cash benefits – which, however, are not exportable. Accordingly, the personal scope of the social security coordination was broadened: it now covers workers and their family and dependants but also stateless persons and refugees. The scope was then further extended, to include students and persons not in gainful employment. Finally, in 2003, the scope was extended to cover third country nationals who are legally residing in the EU. Despite the extension of the scope of the social security coordination, a number of social benefits are excluded from the coordination logic.

---

[4] In 1958, the Council adopted two regulations on social security for migrant workers, which were subsequently superseded by Regulation (EEC) No 1408/71 of the Council of 14 June 1971 on the application of social security schemes to employed persons and their families moving within the Community [1971] OJ L 149. In 2004, Regulation (EC) No 883/2004 (OJ L 166) repealed Regulation No 1408/71. A major reform of the system was carried out in 2010 with the adoption of the so-called 'modernised coordination package': Regulation No 988/2009 (Regulation (EC) No 988/2009 of the European Parliament and of the Council of 16 September 2009, OJ L 284, and implementing Regulation (EC) No 987/2009 (OJ L 284)).

[5] The single applicable law means that each beneficiary is covered by the legislation of one country only, and pays contributions in that country only. Under the principle of equal treatment, workers and self-employed persons from other Member States have the same rights and obligations as the host Member State's nationals. Aggregation means that previous periods of insurance, work or residence in other countries are taken into account in the calculation of benefits. Exportability entails that social security benefits can be paid throughout the Union: reserving payment for people who reside in the country is prohibited.

This is the case of the so-called social assistance by the social security Regulation, which covers entitlements that do not depend on previous contributions to the social security system. Social assistance benefits are not governed by the coordination principles, and in particular they remain outside the principle of equal treatment. As it appears from this exclusion, EU law aims at primarily protecting EU workers, that is, persons who are contributing to the welfare system of the host State.

The same holds true for the ECJ, which has played a pivotal role in protecting workers' right to social entitlements. In particular, the Court has used the equal treatment clauses laid down in different regulations for workers as examples of a broader equal treatment clause. The Court has for instance interpreted broadly the personal scope of application of the Treaty provisions on workers' freedom of movement, including persons partially dependent upon social welfare, as long as they exercise a genuine and effective economic activity.[6] In the same line, the Court has broadly interpreted the notion of 'social advantages benefits' generally granted on virtue of nationality yet opened to the moving EU workers by Article 7(2) of Regulation 1612/68, as rights to be granted to EU workers by 'the mere fact of their residence on the national territory'. The Court's rationale is clearly expressed: the extension of social advantages to workers who are nationals of other Member States seems suitable to facilitate their mobility within the Community.[7]

In order not to impose too heavy a burden on welfare systems, this generous interpretation was however complemented with specific limits. The Court hence confirmed, in *Brown*,[8] that assistance given to students for maintenance and training fell in principle outside the scope of the Treaty for the purpose of the principle of non-discrimination. Accordingly, in *Lebon*[9] the judge held that jobseekers were entitled to equal treatment only with regard to access to employment, but not with regard to social assistance benefits. In the same vein, in order to prevent EU citizens burdening Member States' social systems, the three Residence Directives, enacted in 1990, have conditioned residence rights to complete sickness insurance and sufficient economic resources. In sum, the distinction between economically active and non-economically active EU citizens has become central as regards access to social entitlements. Access to social benefits such as jobseeker allowances, minimum subsistence fees or students' maintenance grants was never to be opened – or at least not unconditionally – to economically inactive EU citizens. While EU workers can ground their claim on previous contributions to the host State's welfare system, non-economically active EU citizens can only expect a certain degree of social solidarity from the host society that derives from their 'European citizenship'. Before the intervention of the ECJ in the early 2000s, this remained a much weaker normative ground.

But the Court's case law has 'fleshed the bones' of EU citizenship,[10] and has progressively contributed to giving 'social citizenship' a substance and a real meaning. In the early 1990s the very expression 'social citizenship' was put at odds for a number of constitutional lawyers,

---

[6] Case C-237/94 *John O'Flynn v Adjudication Officer* EU:C:1996:206.
[7] Ségolène Barbou des Places, 'Regulation (EU) 492/2011 on freedom of movement for workers within the Union' in Edoardo Ales, Mark Dell, Olaf Deinert et al. (eds), *International and European Labour Law, Article-by-Article Commentary* (Nomos Verlagsgesellschaft 2018) 785.
[8] Case C-197/86 *Brown v Secretary of State for Scotland* EU:C:1988:323.
[9] Case C-316/85 *Centre public d'aide sociale de courcelles v Lebon* EU:C:1987:302.
[10] Following Siofra O'Leary's expression: Siofra O'Leary, 'Putting Flesh on the Bones of European Citizenship' (1999) 24 ELR, 68.

who generally gave the notion of citizenship a political meaning: citizenship was referred to as the citizens' capacity to participate in the political decision within a democracy. Following this view, citizens were defined as active participants in a State's public affairs: they were not universally defined as the passive recipients of rights. But T.S. Marshall's book[11] has become very influential in the EU law literature. For Marshall, citizenship is a status bestowed upon those who are full members of a community. Those who possess this status are equal with respect to the rights and duties that come with it. Moreover, for Marshall, the history of citizenship can be described as a process: civil rights were granted to citizens during the eighteenth century, while political rights were granted in the nineteenth century and social rights during the twentieth century. For EU lawyers who were searching for an analytical grid in order to account for the Court's role in the construction of EU citizenship, Marshall's notion of 'social citizenship' proved useful: it permitted conceptualising the impact of ECJ case law on the distribution of social rights to mobile EU citizens.

The ambition of this chapter is to describe how the Court has modelled the EU social citizenship. The European judges' case law is not linear and it has significantly evolved over time. This jurisprudential evolution is generally described as developing in a series of waves, with 'revolutionary cases' constituting turning points. But while some authors describe two phases of the ECJ case law – one of progression, followed by a phase of retrogression of social citizenship – there is increasing controversy as to whether the Court's case law has actually changed. It is also the ambition of this chapter to analyse the substance of these debates within the EU legal scholarship.

Section 2 analyses the first phase of the ECJ case law on social benefits: it shows the Court's contribution to the construction of EU social citizenship. Section 3 describes what is deemed to be the retrogression phase, that is, the group of cases whereby the Court takes its inspiration from the letter of Directive 2004/38 which aims to strike a balance between EU citizens' free movement rights and the viability of national welfare systems. As a consequence, the Court tends to be less favourable to mobile citizens who ask for social entitlements. Section 4 focuses on the controversies among EU legal scholars who disagree on the existence of a 'retrogression' phase in the ECJ case law on social benefits. Section 5 provides concluding remarks.

2. CONSTRUCTING EU SOCIAL CITIZENSHIP: THE ROLE OF THE ECJ CASE LAW

Given the central role played by the dichotomy between workers and inactive EU citizens, the *Martínez Sala* case[12] can only be described as a 'revolutionary' judgment in which the Court has furthered the value of Union citizenship by interpreting the law away from its market-based origin. The ECJ had to adjudicate on the German authorities' refusal to grant Ms Martínez Sala, a Spanish national residing lawfully in Germany for more than 20 years, equal treatment with regard to social security benefit, in the form of a child benefit. The German authorities argued that Ms Sala's residence permit on the basis of national law expired and that she was yet to receive a new one. The Court held that if EU citizens are lawfully resident in a host State, they must be treated with full equality, and enjoy equal treatment (with the

---

[11] Thomas H Marshall, *Citizenship and Social Class: And Other Essays* (CUP 1950).
[12] Case C-85/96 *María Martínez Sala v Freistaat Bayern* EU:C:1998:217.

nationals of the host State) as regards rights and benefits in the substantive scope of EU law.[13] To reach this conclusion, the Court built upon the status of European citizen enshrined in the Treaty.

The *Martínez Sala* case was innovative for two main reasons. First, all the parties to the case, including the German government, acknowledged that refusal of the benefits on the basis of the lack of residence document amounted to discrimination based on her nationality. The German government however argued that the case did not fall within the scope of Community law because Ms Sala could not be regarded as a worker. Ms Sala argued that the very fact that she was a EU citizen brought the case within the scope of EU law. Surprisingly, the judge welcomed her argument: it held that, since the creation of EU citizenship, relationships between a Member State and the other Member States' nationals are governed by Community law, even if the said citizens are economically inactive. In so judging, the Court transformed the concept of EU citizenship: it brought all EU nationals – whether economically active or not – under the same banner of EU citizenship.[14] Second, and as importantly, the Court extended the right to equal treatment based on the sole condition of being legally resident. In other words, the ECJ decided that the right to equal treatment had to be granted to every EU citizen as the sole consequence of his or her European nationality coupled with his or her right of residence. For these two reasons the judgment was rightly regarded as particularly progressive, and as a milestone in the construction of EU citizenship.

The Court then gradually eliminated the distinction between workers entitled to full access to social benefits and non-economically active EU citizens, who in principle are only entitled to residence subject to sufficient resources. In a sequence of judgments beginning with the *Grzelczyk* ruling in 2001,[15] the ECJ has relied on EU citizenship as an instrument to extend the scope of equality as regards access to social benefits. M. Grzelczyk was a young French man who went to study at the University of Louvain in Belgium. For the first three years, he supported himself through loans and part-time jobs. Yet, in his fourth and final year, he decided to ask for the benefit of the Belgium *Minimex*, a mechanism intended for those with insufficient income or means. He argued that he had worked hard during his studies, but in his last year he would have to write a time-consuming dissertation and to do a period of training which would make it difficult – if not impossible – to be employed at the same time. As he was a student, his situation was ruled by Directive 93/96, Article 1 of which requires that students assure national authorities that they are in possession of sufficient resources and Article 4 of which states that students have a right of residence only as long as these conditions are met. The Court however held that denying Mr Grzelczyk a right of residence could not be 'the automatic con-

---

[13] For the Court, 'A national of a Member State lawfully residing in the territory of another Member State comes within the scope ratione personae of the provisions of the Treaty on European citizenship and can rely on the rights laid down by the Treaty which Article 8(2) attaches to the status of citizen of the Union, including the right, laid down in Article 6, not to suffer discrimination on grounds of nationality within the scope of application ratione materiae of the Treaty'.

[14] For this reason, many scholars have welcomed the prospect of equal treatment being extended beyond the realms of economic activity: Jo Shaw, 'A View to the Citizenship Classics: Martinez Sala and Subsequent Cases on Citizenship of the Union' in Miguel Poiares Maduro and Loïc Azoulai (eds), *The Past and Future of EU Law: The Classics of EU Law revisited on the 50th Anniversary of the Rome Treaty* (Hart 2010) 356 et seq.

[15] Case C-184/99 *Rudy Grzelczyk v Centre public d'aide sociale d'Ottignies-Louvain-la-Neuve* EU:C:2001:458.

sequence'[16] of a mere request for social assistance. Even more importantly, the Court insisted that the receiving Member State must 'demonstrate a degree of financial solidarity'[17] with the mobile citizen, in particular when the difficulties he meets are temporary, and as long as the individual does not become an 'unreasonable burden' on the public finances of the host State.

The practical outcome of the judgment was somehow obscure for the referring judge: it hence remained unclear how to assess whether Mr Grzelczyk was an 'unreasonable burden' to the welfare system. The case is nonetheless a notable contribution to the development of EU social citizenship, as the Court limited Belgium's capacity to expel Mr Grzelczyk despite his demonstrated lack of resources. From a political perspective, the call to a 'certain degree of solidarity' expected from host Member States was decisive: it allowed some commentators to believe that the ECJ was promoting a new and transnational form of solidarity in the EU. This undeniably gave flesh to the very notion of EU social citizenship.

One year later the Court rendered its judgment in the *Baumbast* case.[18] The Baumbast family had moved from Germany to the UK after Mr Baumbast, a German national, was offered employment. A few years later, he lost his position and worked outside the EU while his wife and children stayed in the UK. Although he was still economically active, Mr Baumbast was not legally an EU worker any more. He was thus asked to prove, subject to the 1990 Residence Directive, that he had sufficient resources and comprehensive sickness insurance for his family and for himself. On these grounds the UK government refused to renew the family residence documents, arguing that the insurance did not cover emergency care in the UK. While the *Baumbast* case does not deal with social benefits, it plays a role in the construction of EU social citizenship, as the British decision was grounded on the fact that Mr Baumbast and his family were a potential burden to British social security. The ECJ hence found that the measure rejecting the right of residence was disproportionate even though Mr Baumbast failed to meet the conditions laid down in the Directive: Mr Baumbast could indeed rely on Article 18 EC (now Article 21 TFEU) to obtain a right to reside. Consequently, he was entitled to equal treatment with British nationals.

The Court developed the same line of argument later on in the *Trojani* judgment.[19] Mr Trojani is a French national who moved to Belgium, where he remained unemployed and spent some time living on a campsite and in a hostel before joining a Salvation Army reintegration programme. As such he was allowed to live in the hostel and received food and pocket money. He was asked to do various jobs for around 30 hours a week. As Mr Trojani was refused the benefit of the *Minimex* for which he had applied, he challenged the Belgian decision. The ECJ first held that a citizen of the European Union who does not enjoy a right of residence in the host Member State as a worker could yet enjoy, 'simply as a citizen of the Union', a right of residence by direct application of Article 18(1) EC. The exercise of that right is evidently subject to the limitations and conditions referred to in secondary and primary law, but the competent authorities must ensure that those limitations and conditions are applied in compliance with the principle of proportionality. The most startling part is however the final one, where the Court held that 'once it is ascertained that a person in a situation such as that of the claimant

---

[16] Case C-184/99, para. 43.
[17] Case C-184/99, para. 44.
[18] Case C-413/99 *Baumbast and R v Secretary of State for the Home Department* EU:C:2002:493.
[19] Case C-456/02 *Michel Trojani v Centre public d'aide sociale de Bruxelles (CPAS)* EU:C:2004:488.

[...] is in possession of a residence permit, he may rely on Article 12 EC in order to be granted a social assistance benefit such as the *Minimex*'.[20] In other words, the Court has accepted that individuals in possession of a residence permit granted on the basis of national law were admissible to social assistance. Finally, in *Collins*[21] the ECJ had to determine whether an Irish–American dual national was entitled to claim jobseekers allowance in Britain. Although the Court held that, in that specific instance, the working period in the UK before a claim for jobseekers' allowance was lodged was too distant to establish a sufficiently close connection with the UK's labour market, such a link could be established through a 'reasonable period' of residence within which the candidate 'genuinely' sought work.

Read together, these different cases form the first wave of the ECJ case law on social benefits. It cannot be denied that there is coherence in the reasoning of the Court as these cases all serve to substantiate EU social citizenship and the rights of non-economically active citizens to claim social benefits. The reasoning of the Court has basically followed one main line:[22] first EU citizenship was declared to be the 'fundamental status of nationals of the member States',[23] enabling those who find themselves in the same situation to enjoy the same treatment under law irrespective of their nationality; then the Court inferred from this statement that a citizen lawfully resident in the territory of a host Member State can rely on the non-discrimination clause of the Treaty in all situations that fall within the *ratione materiae* scope of EU law. At this stage of its reasoning the Court usually referred to some provision whereby the person in question, or the type of activity, was covered by EU law. This allowed the Court to judge that the claimant, although not economically active, may rely on the principle of non-discrimination when he or she has been lawfully resident in the host State for a certain time or when he or she possesses a residence permit. In so doing, the Court has managed to reconcile the conditions imposed by secondary law with the objective of giving real substance to the concept of citizenship mentioned in the Treaty of Maastricht.[24]

The Court has however never ignored the financial imperatives and the necessity to protect the viability of national welfare systems. Already in *Collins*, the Court held that Member States could make the grant of jobseekers' allowance dependent upon a 'genuine link' between the person seeking work and the employment market of that State.[25] In the same vein, in *Ioannidis*[26] – a case about a jobseeker asking for the benefit of tide-over allowances for young people seeking their first employment – the ECJ found that although Belgium was allowed to distinguish on the basis of the existence of a factual connection between the EU citizen and its host State, it was not possible for Belgium to differentiate between individuals on the sole ground that the claimant had completed his secondary education in another Member State. Accordingly, in *Trojani*, the Court allowed Belgium to evaluate if the claimant was (or was not) a reasonable burden on the welfare system. In other words, even in the early case law

---

[20] Case C-456/02, para 39.
[21] Case C-138/02, *Collins v Secretary of State for Work and Pensions* EU:C:2004:172.
[22] As described by Kay Hailbronner, 'The EU Directive on Free Movement and Access to Social Benefits' (2006) CESifo DICE Report 4(4) 8–13.
[23] Case C-184/99, para. 31.
[24] See Vincent Réveillère, *Le juge et le travail des concepts juridiques. Le cas de la citoyenneté de l'Union européenne* (Institut Universitaire Varenne, 2018).
[25] Case C-138/02, para. 69.
[26] Case C-258/04, *Office national de l'emploi v Ioannis Ioannidis* EU:C:2005:559.

on social benefits, the Court acknowledged that EU social citizenship does not equate to an unconditional right to transnational solidarity granted to every mobile inactive EU citizen.

3. THE RETROGRESSION PHASE IN THE ECJ CASE LAW

In 2004 there was a radical change in EU law: the so-called Union Citizenship Directive, Directive 2004/38/EC of 29 April 2004 on the right of citizens of the Union and their family members to move and reside freely within the territory of the Member States,[27] was adopted. For the first time, a norm of EU secondary law was establishing a single legal instrument regulating all EU citizens' circulation regardless of their economic activity. Despite this unifying ambition, the Directive did not eliminate the differences between economically active and inactive EU citizens, as the text created a system of rights based on periods of time.[28]

It is apparent from several provisions of Directive 2004/38 that Member States had the ambition to protect their welfare system from welfare tourism. The text expresses the prevailing political consensus that EU citizens should be free to move within the EU, provided that they are not a burden on the social assistance system of host States. To reach this balance, the directive codifies the balance established by the Court in its previous judgments between free movement and the protection of welfare systems. On the one hand, the directive does not allow Member States to automatically terminate the right of residence to EU citizens that become dependent on social welfare. Accordingly, Article 14 states that the right of residence for up to three months is retained as long as EU citizens do not become an 'unreasonable burden' on the social assistance system of the host Member State. Article 14 makes the retention of the right of residence dependent upon the fulfilment of the conditions contained in Articles 7, 12 and 13 (that is, the condition that EU citizens have sufficient resources and health insurance). This does not imply, however, that residence may immediately be terminated if non-economically active EU citizens no longer fulfil the requirements; as decided by the Court in *Grzelczyk*, an expulsion measure shall not be the 'automatic consequence' if the EU citizen takes recourse to the welfare system of the host Member State (Article 14(3)).

But on the other hand, the directive is also protective of the Member States' welfare systems. While the first paragraph of Article 24 (a clause of equal treatment) grants EU citizens a right to non-discrimination as regards social entitlements, its second paragraph limits the scope of the principle: equal treatment is derogated for the first three months of residence generally or, where appropriate, for a longer period to which jobseekers may be entitled as long as they have continued to look for work and have a genuine chance of being hired. The same limit applies with regard to students concerning maintenance aid, including whether they are obliged to provide maintenance grant for studies, such as student loans, prior to the acquisition of a right to permanent residence.

---

[27] OJ L 158.
[28] For a period of up to three months, all Union citizens have the right of residence, subject to the condition of having a passport. After three months, non-economically active EU citizens are entitled to the right to residence under the condition of proving that they have sufficient resources and health insurance. After five years of continuous and legal residence in one Member State, EU citizens can be granted the right to permanent residence.

The problem is that while the provisions of Directive 2004/38 express a political consensus among Member States that their assistance system has to be protected from intra-EU mobility driven by social assistance motives, the Directive also contains a number of vague provisions such as the notion of 'reasonable/unreasonable burden'. For Hailbronner, who commented on the text shortly after it was adopted, Member States

> in an erroneous perception of the relationship between the legislator and the European Court, have chosen to leave it to the Court to solve their disputes, incorporating in the Directive vague provisions like the clause referring to an unreasonable burden on the social security system of the host member State. In addition, they have chosen a system of rewards for those who have managed to secure a lawful residence for a continuous period of five years [...] Whether this will lead to an instability of the social systems of member States remains to be seen.[29]

In fact, the discretion given to the judiciary has not entailed a deficit in protecting welfare systems. In the 'second wave' of the ECJ case law on social benefits, a new trend has become visible. The ECJ has progressively given more credit to the Member States' concerns regarding the viability of their social assistance systems. This has even led some scholars to describe the cases decided after 2013 as a 'swift dismantling project' of the EU citizenship *acquis*.[30] Undeniably, in four major cases given in a very short sequence (the *Brey*, *Dano*, *Alimanovic* and *Garcia-Nieto* cases), the Court has initiated a new approach.

In September 2013 the Court delivered its judgment in *Brey*.[31] Mr Brey was a German national who moved to Austria with his wife. As they were of retirement age, their income from Germany, which consisted of an invalidity pension for Mr Brey and a care allowance for his wife, amounted to about 1,000 euros per month. Mr Brey applied for a 'compensatory supplement' which consists of extra income paid in Austria to those living on a low retirement or invalidity pension. He was first entitled to an extra 326 euro per month but the Austrian authorities later on decided that Mr Brey should not be entitled to this benefit because he did not have sufficient resources as required by Directive 2004/38. As a consequence he did not have a right of residence in Austria, and therefore could not claim equal treatment with Austrian nationals as regards rights to social assistance. The *Brey* case is deemed to embody an evolution in the ECJ approach, as the Court emphasised the link between Article 7 of Directive 2004/38, which makes the right of residence for more than three months conditional upon work of sufficient resources, and the requirement not to rely on welfare benefits in the country of residence. The Court however specified a limit: automatic denial of social assistance based on presumption of insufficient resources is not permitted. Member States must assess on a case-by-case basis whether the individual places an unreasonable burden on the State's welfare system as a whole, by reference to the personal circumstances of the individual. The Court insisted on the obligation to comply with the principle of proportionality: this requires that national authority assess the financial stability of the national welfare system overall. Although it seemed that, in the name of proportionality, equal treatment could be refused only

---

[29] Kay Hailbronner, 'The EU Directive on Free Movement and Access to Social Benefits' (2006) CESifo DICE Report 4(4) 8–13, 12; see also Kay Hailbronner, 'Union Citizenship and Access to Social Benefits' (2009) 46 CML Rev 1245.

[30] Charlotte O'Brien, 'The ECJ sacrifices Citizenship in Vain: Commission v. United Kingdom' [2017] CML Rev 209, 21.

[31] Case C-140/12 *Pensionsversicherungsanstalt v Peter* Brey EU:C:2013:565.

when the burden was too important on welfare systems, commentators immediately perceived that this latter requirement imposed assessments that administrations in charge of granting social benefits would find it impossible to perform in practice.[32]

The *Brey* case is typically analysed as being the first sign of a change. Only a few months later, the Court gave the highly contested *Dano* ruling.[33] Ms Dano was a Romanian citizen who went to live in Germany with her son. She lived with her sister, who provided for them materially. Ms Dano was neither working nor looking for a job; she did not have sufficient resources and although we have limited information on her situation, she apparently was not very well integrated into German society. Ms Dano received child benefit from the German authorities. She then applied for further social assistance for herself that was refused. The main reason why the ECJ allowed Germany to refuse Ms Dano social minimum assistance benefits was that she did not meet the conditions for legal residence mentioned in Article 7 of Directive 2004/38. She was neither a worker nor did she have sufficient resources. Therefore she could not rely on the right to equal treatment enshrined in Article 24 of Directive 2004/38. The Court decided that Article 24(1) of the directive does not preclude legislation of a Member State under which nationals of other Member States are excluded from entitlement to certain 'special non-contributory cash benefits', although those benefits are granted to nationals of the host Member State who are in the same situation, insofar as those nationals of other Member States do not have a right of residence under Directive 2004/38 in the host Member State.

The case gained notoriety immediately: it was analysed as a shift in the ECJ case law on social benefits. First the Court mentioned that a Member State must have the possibility of refusing to grant social benefits to economically inactive Union citizens 'who exercise their right to freedom of movement solely in order to obtain another Member State's social assistance although they do not have sufficient resources to claim a right of residence'.[34] Second, it held that EU citizens could not claim equal treatment unless they have a right of residence under EU law. The Court did not even consider whether Ms Dano had links with Germany; rather, the judge insisted on the fact that she had to comply with the conditions laid down in the directive. This reasoning was analysed by many scholars as a shift from the *Martínez Sala* approach. In the latter case, Ms Sala indeed did not have sufficient resources for her and her son, but as she was residing legally (that is, in conformity with German law), she could enjoy equal treatment for social benefits. In contrast, in *Dano* the legal residence criterion is defined only by reference to EU law, which requires individuals, subject to Directive 2004/38, either to be a worker or to possess sufficient resources not to be a burden on the social assistance systems of the host State.

A third reason why the *Dano* ruling received criticism is that the Court relied on secondary law only: it ruled that any unequal treatment between EU citizens who have made use of their freedom of movement and residence and nationals of the host Member State with regard to the grant of social benefits

> is an inevitable consequence of Directive 2004/38. Such potential unequal treatment is founded on the link established by the Union legislature in Article 7 of the directive between the requirement to have

---

[32] Niamh Nic Shuibhne, 'Limits Rising, Duties Ascending: The Changing Legal Shape of Union Citizenship' (2015) 52 CML Rev 4, 889 et seq.

[33] Case C-333/13 *Elisabeta Dano and Florin Dano v Jobcenter Leipzig* EU:C:2014:2358.

[34] Case C-333/13, para. 78.

sufficient resources as a condition for residence and the concern not to create a burden on the social assistance systems of the Member States.[35]

This argument allowed the ECJ to avoid mentioning Treaty provisions on citizenship and on the principle of equality. This is why the Court is deemed to have abandoned, with *Dano*, its case law based on primary EU law on the sole basis of provisions found in secondary law, an inferior source of law of the Treaties. The Court indeed mentioned that the principle of non-discrimination laid down generally in Article 18 TFEU 'is given more specific expression in Article 24 of Directive 2004/38 in relation to Union citizens who [...] exercise their right to move and reside within the territory of the Member States'. Nic Shuibhne considers that, in so judging,[36] the Court has poured the content of the equal treatment rule (based upon primary EU law) into a statement in secondary law. As a consequence, the conditions and limits no longer temper equal treatment: they constitute the rights. Under such a perspective, it can be argued that Directive 2004/38 is elevated to the status of a constitutional instrument.

The fourth source of criticism revolved around the use of the notion of 'social assistance'. The social benefit that was refused to Ms Dano was a 'special non-contributory benefit' after Regulation 883/2004 on social security coordination rules. The fact is that this Regulation imposes Member States to apply the equal treatment rule for special non-contributory benefits. Yet, in *Brey* and *Dano*, the Court decided that special non-contributory benefits were also part of the 'social assistance system' mentioned in Directive 2004/38 even if they were not 'social assistance' within Regulation 883/2004. This is a crucial interpretative step because the fact that the same term, 'social assistance', is present in the two texts has thus allowed the Court to shift the reasoning from the application of Regulation 883/2004 to Directive 2004/38 and its residence conditions.

One year later, the ECJ consolidated this approach in the *Alimanovic* judgment.[37] Ms Alimanovic, a Swedish national, had three children who were born in Germany. She had left Germany and returned ten years later. She and her eldest daughter worked in temporary jobs for a little less than a year. They then applied for unemployment benefits and other forms of social assistance for Ms Alimanovic's two other children. As jobseekers they were entitled to a right of residence, but the question for the Court was whether they could also be granted a right to social assistance. The answer was complex. Article 24(2) of the Citizenship Directive provides that by way of derogation from paragraph 1, the host Member State shall not be obliged to confer entitlement to social assistance for jobseekers. But Ms Alimanovic had previously been employed and, after her work ended, had maintained the status of worker for six months under the terms of the Directive; this gave her a right to social assistance. As the six months was over, the national judge asked the ECJ whether, as jobseekers who were formerly employed years ago and for 11 months just prior to their application for social benefit, they should retain the status of worker or be treated as jobseekers. The Court confirmed the link established in the *Brey* and *Dano* rulings between residence under the conditions of Article 7 Directive 2004/38 and equal treatment under Article 24. Again, primary law played no role in its decision. The Court held that Ms Alimanovic and her daughter could not retain worker

---

[35] Case C-333/13, para. 77.
[36] Niamh Nic Shuibhne, 'Limits Rising, Duties Ascending: The Changing Legal Shape of Union Citizenship' (2015) 52 CML Rev 4, 889 et seq.
[37] Case C-67/14 *Jobcenter Berlin Neukölln v Nazifa Alimanovic and Others* EU:C:2015:597.

status for longer than six months. The ECJ also ruled that while they could reside as jobseekers, Article 24(2) allowed Germany to deny them social assistance.

Commentators have stressed the problematic difference between the *Brey* and *Alimanovic* judgments. In *Alimanovic*, the Court found that it was not necessary to establish that each individual claim of social benefit would amount to an unreasonable burden on the national welfare system. Of course, the Court admits, Directive 2004/38 requires a Member State to take account of the individual situation of the person concerned before it adopts an expulsion measure or finds that the residence of that person is placing an unreasonable burden on its social assistance system. But such individual assessment was not deemed necessary by the Court because

> as regards the individual assessment for the purposes of making an overall appraisal of the burden which the grant of a specific benefit would place on the national system of social assistance [...] the assistance awarded to a single applicant can scarcely be described as an 'unreasonable burden' for a Member State, within the meaning of Article 14(1) of Directive 2004/38. However, while an individual claim might not place the Member State concerned under an unreasonable burden, the accumulation of all the individual claims which would be submitted to it would be bound to do so.[38]

The individual assessment requirement, which appeared to be a protection given to the claimant in *Brey*, was hence firmly rejected in *Alimanovic*.

The *Garcia-Nieto* judgment[39] came to be considered as the fourth step[40] in the ECJ's new approach. Mr and Ms Garcia-Nieto, a couple of Spanish nationals, moved to Germany. The couple were not married or in a civil partnership but did have a child together. While the mother left Germany with the child in order to work, the father moved only later, with his child from a previous relationship. He then applied for minimum subsistence social assistance, which was refused on the grounds that he had not been residing in Germany for longer than three months. For the Court, Mr Garcia-Nieto and his son cannot be entitled to this social assistance benefits because of Article 24(2) Directive 2004/38: it follows from its wording that the host state may refuse to grant persons other than workers, self-employed persons or those who retain that status any social assistance during the first three months of residence. Article 24(2), the ECJ held, is consistent with the objective of maintaining the financial equilibrium of the social assistance system of the Member States pursued by Directive 2004/38. Since the Member States cannot require EU citizens to have sufficient means of subsistence and personal medical cover for a period of residence of a maximum of three months in their respective territories, 'it is legitimate not to require those Member States to be responsible for those citizens during that period'.[41]

In this judgment, like in *Alimanovic*, the delicate issue was whether national authorities were required to proceed with individual assessment in order to evaluate if the person is placing an unreasonable burden on the social assistance system. Again, the Court answered negatively. It argued that Directive 2004/38 takes into consideration various factors characterising the

---

[38] Case C-67/14, para. 62.
[39] Case C-299/14 *Vestische Arbeit Jobcenter Kreis Recklinghausen v Jovanna García-Nieto e.a.* EU:C:2016:114.
[40] See also Case C-308/14 *Commission v United Kingdom* EU:C:2016:436.
[41] Case C-299/14, para. 45.

individual situation of each applicant for social assistance and, in particular, the duration of the exercise of any economic activity. Moreover,

> the assistance awarded to a single applicant can scarcely be described as an 'unreasonable burden' for a Member State, within the meaning of Article 14(1) of Directive 2004/38, for an individual claim is not liable to place the Member State concerned under an unreasonable burden, but the accumulation of all the individual claims which might be submitted to it would be bound to do so.[42]

Again, to adjudicate on the claimant's rights the Court relied on a secondary law instrument and not on Treaty provisions, which triggered immediate reaction from EU legal scholars.

4. RETROGRESSION OR TRANSFORMATION OF EU SOCIAL CITIZENSHIP?

The Court's judgment in *Dano* immediately triggered intense and contradictory reactions, both in the legal and the political arenas. More generally, there is no consensus on how to analyse the ECJ recent case law on social benefits: both its coherence and its implications are debated.

Authors strongly disagree on whether the Court, in the cases decided in the 2010s, has changed its conception of EU social citizenship. For a first group of scholars, it cannot be denied that the ECJ has undergone an ideological transformation, retreating from the commitment to transnational citizenship which it used to display.[43] A main explanation given for the 'shift' is that judges 'read the morning papers':[44] the Court proves responsive to the political context. The ECJ indeed mostly aims to prevent welfare tourism; it is also aware that its legitimacy, as an international court, is increasingly debated. Hence the apparent necessity for the ECJ to take Member States' anxieties into consideration, and to adequately balance the interests of mobile EU citizens with the viability of welfare systems supported by a majority of non-mobile nationals.

In contrast with this reading, which argues that the Court has renounced grounding EU social citizenship on equal treatment, a number of authors support the alternative view that there is no radical change in how the ECJ is approaching citizenship. Gareth Davies[45] agrees that in recent cases the Court has sided with Member States against the litigating citizens, and this has created the impression of a change in judicial perspective. But the explanation, he argues, mostly lies in the changing characteristics of the litigants themselves: recent claims for social assistance are based on 'less meritorious facts'. A good example is the comparison between the facts of the *Martínez Sala* and the *Dano* cases. While Ms Sala has always resided legally, the cause of Ms Dano is difficult to justify: she never worked nor looked for a job in

---

[42] Case C-299/14, para. 50.
[43] See among a vast literature Eleanor Spaventa, 'Earned Citizenship – Understanding Union Citizenship through Its Scope' in Dimitry Kochenov (ed.), *EU Citizenship and Federalism: The Role of Rights* (CUP 2017) 204; Anastasia Iliopoulou-Penot, 'Deconstructing the Former Edifice of Union Citizenship? The Alimanovic Judgment' (2016) 53(4) CML Rev 1007.
[44] Michael Blaumberger et al., 'ECJ Judges Read the Morning Papers: Explaining the Turn-around of European Citizenship Jurisprudence' (2018) 25(10) Journal of European Public Policy 1422.
[45] Gareth Davies, 'Has the Court Changed, or Have the Cases? The Deservingness of Litigants as an Element in Court of Justice Citizenship Adjudication' (2018) 25(10) Journal of European Public Policy 1442.

Germany, she never had resources of her own and she did not even speak (nor learn) German. More generally for Davies, the ECJ has always had a 'moderately traditional, mainstream view of when a mobile citizen deserves assistance', and the cases depict this worldview 'consistently applying to changing fact'.

Other authors consider that there is no discontinuity in the ECJ's approach to social benefits. Rather, *Dano* and *Alimanovic* should be viewed as illustrations of a quite ordinary evolution of judicial interpretation.[46] In fact, the disputed cases are the logical consequence of the entry into force of Directive 2004/38: the ECJ could only accept the political choices made by the EU legislature. After the introduction of EU citizenship in 1992, the Court had to fill the gaps in the Treaty provisions and define the relationships between the citizenship provisions with pre-existing secondary law: this led the Court to privilege the teleological interpretation of the law. But in 2004 a major norm of secondary law was adopted, which defined more precisely the status and rights (including equal treatment rights) of mobile EU citizens. Logically, the ECJ has opted for a strict reliance on the terms of the Directive. Moreover, the Court's interpretation would be consistent with the primary law itself, which explicitly mentions that EU citizens can only exercise their rights 'in accordance with the conditions and limits defined by the Treaties and by the measures adopted thereunder': Directive 2004/38 is said to fulfil its constitutional role in defining the conditions and limits mentioned by the Treaty itself. Carter and Jesse[47] argue that the 'second wave' of case law is also coherent with previous case law on social benefits. In particular, the *Förster*[48] and *Ziolkowski*[49] cases would have paved the way for the *Dano* judgement. These two cases would form a continuum: after these judgments the directive emerged as the only frame within which the Court establishes legality of residence of EU citizens, and as a consequence the right to social benefits; *Dano* and *Alimanovic* were the inevitable next step.[50]

But the Court's (in)coherence in reasoning is not the only source of controversy among EU law commentators. The main critiques of the second phase judgments are related to their political consequences. The main question is: do they evidence a deep transformation of the notion of EU social citizenship?

The *Martínez Sala* ruling had major practical and conceptual implications because the Court tied EU citizenship together with the principle of equality. To be a citizen had both a political and a legal meaning: free movement rights and access to social protection were not limited to the happy few who were exercising an economic activity. Rather, the ECJ's ambition, in the early 2000s, was to create a meaningful status of equality. This is the reason why *Dano* is seen as initiating a trend in which illegitimate hierarchies among EU citizens were introduced. Some authors argue that a new distinction is born, between wealthy and

---

[46] Daniel Carter and Moritz Jesse, 'The "Dano Evolution": Assessing Legal Integration and Access to Social Benefits for EU Citizens' [2018] European Papers 3, 1179.
[47] Ibid.
[48] Case C-158/07 *Förster v Hoofdirectie van de Informatie Beheer Groep* EU:C:2008:630.
[49] In *Ziolkowski* the Court held that the definition of 'legal' and 'continuous' residence for five years, mentioned in Article 16, had to be interpreted autonomously from national law: only residence in conformity with the conditions laid down in the Directive can open a right of (permanent) residence.
[50] In *Dano* (n 33) the Court assesses legal residence and equal treatment rights exclusively within the framework created by the residence Directive. It rejects the idea that links between the claimant and the host State must be taken in consideration. In *Alimanovic* (n 37) the Court upholds the link between residence in conformity with Article 7 Directive 2004/38 and equal treatment for social benefits.

indigent people. The decision to rely on Article 7 of Directive 2004/38 as a pre-condition to access social rights would inevitably lead to recreating the distinction between economically active and non-economically active citizens. As a result, Kochenov argues, EU citizenship does not empower but merely informs 'the dogmatic ideal of good market citizen'.[51] Charlotte O'Brien goes as far as to argue that 'welfare nationalism is washing away the traces of EU citizenship':[52] 'Member States are creating an elitist model of free movement – alienating the working poor, and effectively awarding rights on the basis of socio-economic class' and it has 'extinguished citizenship hope'.[53] In short, while EU citizenship offered an interpretative prism though which the fundamental rights of migrant workers should be protected, judicial fervour has now burned out.

There is no denying that *Dano* is a point of inflection in the ECJ case law. Directive 2004/38 is elevated by the Court to the status of a constitutional instrument but, as a secondary law norm, it should be viewed as the result of a political compromise which is susceptible to evolution. When the notion of citizenship was introduced in the Treaty in 1992, Member States agreed to make reference to a very dense concept: citizenship is the status bestowed on those who are full members of a community and with this status comes equality. Moreover, citizenship has always been a process: citizens have conquered rights progressively. Citizenship never was a given: it had to be constructed. This is the reason why *Martínez Sala* was welcomed at the time. The Court was assumed to participate in the enrichment of EU citizenship: the judge was the only one who could impose a dynamic. With *Dano*, the Court has preferred balance, compromise and stability over movement and innovation. This is politically and legally comprehensible but far less enthusiastic. This is probably why the 2010s case law is delusive: it certainly can be explained and justified rationally, but it is engrained in a technical conception of EU law: it lacks inspiration.

Be that as it may, the authors seem to agree – despite their contrasting views – that the ECJ case law on social benefits is indicative of how the EU tries to reconcile conflicting objectives: ensuring that free movement is accessible to EU citizens (and not to workers only) while accepting a certain degree of 'welfare nationalism'. This is probably why the notion of 'deservingness' is now emerging as playing an important role for the access to social benefits. When adjudicating on access to social benefits, the Court will indeed take different elements into account: whether the claim is the product of choice or circumstances; the need and attitude of the claimant (whether he or she behaved 'well' or not); the degree to which the claimant is 'part of' society or distant from it, and so on.[54] Dion Kramer argues that the ECJ case law evidences 'earned citizenship' as a technique of government into a broader political strategy, requiring EU citizens to 'earn' access to welfare system through emphasis on their individual responsibility to fulfil the economic, social and cultural conditions of membership. If any-

---

[51] Dimitry Kochenov, 'The Citizenship of Personal Circumstances' in Daniel Thym (ed.) *Questioning EU Citizenship: Judges and the Limits of Free Movement and Solidarity in the EU* (Hart Publishing 2017) 51. See also Paul E Minderhoud and Sandra Mantu, 'Back to the Roots? No Access to Social Assistance for Union Citizens Who Are Economically Inactive' in Daniel Thym (ed.), *Questioning EU Citizenship: Judges and the Limits of Free Movement and Solidarity in the EU* (Hart Publishing 2017) 191.

[52] Charlotte O'Brien, 'Civis Capitalist Sum: Class as the New Guiding Principle of EU Free Movement Rights' (2016) 53 CML Rev 2016, 937.

[53] Ibid, 939 and 940.

[54] See Gareth Davies (n 45).

thing, the Court has now made clear that the right to freedom of movement is not equal to an unrestricted right to social welfare in other Member States.

This raises a question of central importance: is EU citizenship supposed to introduce a new rationale in free movement law, or is it destined to be limited solely to active, wealthy or deserving citizens? There is, of course, the risk that the notion of equal treatment would become 'mutable and pragmatic, not fundamental and principled'.[55] The whole theory of free movement and the very substance of EU social citizenship are at stake. This explains why the *Dano* case was even commented upon in the media. The ECJ case law on social benefits is not a technical legal issue: it has to do with the meaning and substance of EU citizenship. It also has to do with the meaning of fair movement in EU law, and the possible limits to free movement.[56]

5. CONCLUSION

While social benefits are, to a large extent, conferred upon workers on the basis of the principle of equal treatment with the host States' nationals, the situation of non-economically active EU citizens as regards social entitlements has always been more precarious. This is the reason why the ECJ case law is so crucial: the Court has constructed 'EU social citizenship'. The judge has extended the scope of the principle of equality, and it has imposed on Member States the requirement to provide a robust justification before they can deny social benefits to non-active EU citizens. Solidarity among Member States and among EU citizens has become a central notion of EU citizenship law.

However, in the context of growing welfare protectionism, Member States increasingly tend to restrict access to non-contributory benefits for non-nationals who do not contribute to the welfare system. In this context, the ECJ case law on social benefits has become an issue of both legal and political importance. Since 2016, the Court has initiated what is sometimes viewed as its 'new approach': the Court now makes access to social benefits conditional on a right of residence under the terms of Directive 2004/38. This can have very unsatisfactory consequences: the Court requires indigent people to demonstrate that they have enough resources before they can benefit social benefits. Whether the Court's case law is rightly respecting the balances agreed upon by the legislator when enacting the 2004 Directive is a matter of disagreement among observers. Be that as it may be, the Court's case law on social benefits reveals the tensions in the European construction. The challenge for the judge is to reconcile the imperatives of transnational solidarity, which seems to be required by the very idea of a European citizenship, with the fact that welfare is organised on a national basis.

---

[55] Charlotte O'Brien (n 52).
[56] Catherine Jacqueson and Frans Pennings, 'Equal Treatment of Mobile Persons in the Context of a Social Market Economy' (2019) 15(2) Utrecht Law Review 64.

16. The limits of judicialising transnational welfare: progression and retrogression of the ECJ case law on access to social benefits[1]

Susanne K. Schmidt

European integration has greatly profited from case law of the European Court of Justice, relying on the Treaty's many policy goals under its supremacy and direct effect. After the introduction of EU citizenship rights in the Treaty of Maastricht, case law of the Court pushed European integration towards opening national entitlements of member states' heterogeneous welfare states to EU citizens. In the light of rising political contention, the Court has halted its extensive case law development in recent years, resulting in pronounced criticism from the community of EU law scholars. In this chapter, I challenge the expectation that judicialisation can be an avenue for building Social Europe. This is not only because of the possibility of 'a tragedy of the commons', where the opening of national welfare may risk undermining its financial basis; given the heterogeneity of national welfare regimes, I argue that non-discrimination is a poor guide for the Court in furthering transnational welfare as in fact, new inequalities result. Moreover, the extent of legal uncertainty accompanying policy-making by the Court could imply that individuals are better off with clearly defined rights.

1. INTRODUCTION

EU citizenship was introduced with the Treaty of Maastricht. Article 8a of the Treaty Establishing the European Community (TEC) gave citizens 'the right to move and reside freely within the territory of the Member States, subject to the limitations and conditions laid down in this Treaty and by the measures adopted to give it effect'. With the explicit referral to the subsequent specification in secondary law, member states held EU citizenship to have a more symbolic character.[2] But for the EU law community, for the European Court of Justice and later for the European Commission, the insertion of EU citizenship held the promise to expand to all EU citizens the privileges that the Treaty of Rome includes for workers. These free movement rights of workers were a late addition to the Treaty of Rome, alongside the

---

[1] The chapter draws on research of TransJudFare, funded by Norface, WelfareStateFutures (DFG SCHM 2404/1-1) as well as project B04 of the CRC 1342 Global Dynamics of Social Policy (DFG project-no. 374666841). I am grateful for comments at the ECPR conference in Paris, 13–15 June 2018; at the DVPW Congress in Frankfurt, 25 September 2018; at the Law School of the University of Amsterdam, 9 October 2018; at the CRC 1342 conference in Bremen, 25–26 October 2018; and at the conference 'Mutual solidarity and respect in the domain of EU citizenship', Max Planck Institute for the Study of Religious and Ethnic Diversity, Göttingen, 14 June 2019.

[2] Agustín José Menéndez and Espen DH Olsen, *Challenging European Citizenship: Ideas and Realities in Contrast* (Palgrave Pivot 2020) 91.

other freedoms of goods, services, establishment and capital.[3] The EU is unique among regional organisations in granting unconditional free movement rights for workers. Already in 1958, regulations no 3 and 4 set out rules for the coordination of social security for migrant workers, as the Treaty of Rome left the responsibility for social security in the hands of the member states. The rules on the coordination of social security have been reformed multiple times in the 60-plus years of their existence. For many legislative reforms, the case law of the European Court of Justice was instrumental.[4] Every so often, member states were seen to introduce welfare benefits but attempt to exclude EU workers, despite their obligation to non-discriminatory treatment.

Integration through law has underpinned European integration. Based on the establishment of direct effect and supremacy in the 1960s, the Court could shape European integration, given the over-constitutionalisation of the EU polity, where the Treaty includes many policy goals that are subject to ordinary law in the member states.[5] A broad definition of workers established by case law gives equal treatment to those working fewer hours. Also, extending the rights of EU citizens to nationally financed welfare has been a court-driven process. In this chapter I challenge the expectation that judicialisation, that is, shifting decisions to courts and judicial means,[6] is suited to serve as a major pillar for building Social Europe. Essentially, the prohibition on discrimination along national lines allows the ECJ to open social entitlements that are financed at the national level. A dominant concern of the literature has been that this opening risks undermining the financial basis of national welfare, thereby being akin to a 'tragedy of the commons'.[7] But this concern is substantiated only under adverse conditions (see below). The judicialisation of welfare entitlement, however, faces further problems that are hardly discussed. Given the heterogeneity of national welfare regimes, non-discrimination is a poor guide for the Court to bring about equality, I argue. Building Social Europe on case law can lead to new inequalities among individuals seeking rights in other member states. It is striking that, differently from the situation in the US, EU lawyers have hardly engaged in a critical discussion of how judicial review can further social rights.[8] This is despite the origins of the 'integration through law' project that lie in the comparison with the US system.[9]

In the following, I start by elucidating the background of the promise of EU citizenship and summarise how case law has helped to expand social rights of EU citizens – the scope

---

[3] Catherine Barnard and Sarah Fraser Butlin, 'Free Movement vs. Fair Movement: Brexit and Managed Migration' (2018) 55 CML Rev 203; Federico Romero, 'Migration as an Issue in European Interdependence and Integration: The Case of Italy' in Alan S Milward, Francesco MB Lynch, Federico Romero and Vibeke Sorenson (eds), *The Frontier of National Sovereignty: History and Theory 1945–1992* (Routledge 1993).
[4] Dorte S Martinsen and Gerda Falkner, 'Social Policy: Problem-solving Gaps, Partial Exits, and Court-decision Traps' in Dorte S Martinsen and Gerda Falkner (eds), *The EU's Decision Traps* (OUP 2011).
[5] Dieter Grimm, *The Constitution of European Democracy* (OUP 2017).
[6] Ran Hirschl, 'The Judicialization of Politics' in Keith E Whittington, Roger Daniel Kelemen and Gregory A Caldeira (eds), *The Oxford Handbook of Law and Politics* (OUP 2008).
[7] Russel Hardin, 'The Social Evolution of Cooperation' in Karen Schweers Cook and Margaret Levi (eds), *The Limits of Rationality* (University of Chicago Press 1990).
[8] Alexander Somek, 'Accidental Cosmopolitanism' (2012) 3 Transnational Legal Theory 371.
[9] Mauro Cappelletti, Monica Seccombe and Joseph HH Weiler, *Integration through Law: Europe and the American Federal Experience. Volume 1: Methods, Tools and Institutions* (Walter de Gruyter 1986).

of which has however remained contested. This process of judicialisation has slowed down markedly with the judgments of the Court since late 2014, starting with C-333/13 *Dano*,[10] a judicial backlash that is related to the political backlash to integration that culminated in Brexit.[11] In the following, the problems of judicialisation shall be discussed, starting with the most well-known fear: overuse of welfare. On this basis less obvious disadvantages shall be discussed, particularly with a view to individual citizens.

2. JUDICIALISING SOCIAL RIGHTS: FROM THEORY TO PRACTICE

Like welfare, EU citizenship is tied to member states. It is here that social belonging, redistribution and solidarity are primarily rooted.[12] Not being based on a political community that would allow the forming of such republican values, the EU faces the problem of how it can construct legitimacy only on the basis of individual rights.[13] In the following this question is discussed theoretically; it is then asked which rights are being allocated at the European level.

2.1 EU Constitutional Theory and Citizenship

The unsolved legitimation of European integration is one of the warhorses of European Union research.[14] As long as decisions on integration were taken by member-state governments unanimously, legitimation could be constructed via the democratic political systems of member states. The switch to qualified majority voting with the Single European Act, effective from 1987 onwards, broke this chain of legitimation to the member states, requiring an independent source of legitimacy at the European level. But this legitimation problem existed prior to this, given the Court's role in building Europe. The unanimity requirement among member states had blocked the decision-making process, allowing the Court to foster integration through law uninhibited by political interference, as judicial decisions could hardly be overruled.[15]

While the multi-faceted discussion on the legitimation deficit of European integration does not need to be summarised, the importance of the missing *demos* of the EU is crucial for our

---

[10] Case C-333/13 *Dano v Jobcenter Leipzig* EU:C:2014:2358.
[11] Michael Blauberger, Anita Heindlmaier, Dion Kramer, Dorte S Martinsen, Jessica S Thierry, Angelika Schenk and Benjamin Werner, 'ECJ Judges Read the Morning Papers: Explaining the Turnaround of European Citizenship Jurisprudence' (2018) 25 Journal of European Public Policy 1422; Gareth Davies, 'Has the Court Changed, Or Have the Cases? The Deservingness of Litigants as an Element in Court of Justice Adjudication' (2018) 25 Journal of European Public Policy 1442.
[12] Richard Bellamy and Joseph Lacey, 'Balancing the Rights and Duties of European and National Citizens: A Demoicratic Approach' (2018) 25 Journal of European Public Policy 1403.
[13] Fritz W Scharpf, 'Legitimacy in the Multilevel European Polity' (2009) 1 European Political Science Review 173.
[14] Andreas Follesdal, 'Survey Article: The Legitimacy Deficits of the European Union' (2006) 14 Journal of Political Philosophy 441.
[15] Joseph HH Weiler, 'The Community System: The Dual Character of Supranationalism' (1981) 1 Yearbook of European Law 267; Joseph HH Weiler, 'The Transformation of Europe' (1991) 100 The Yale Law Journal 2402.

topic.[16] The introduction of EU citizenship rights under Maastricht was linked to furthering such a European *demos*. Granting rights to EU citizens as citizens, and not only market participants, would foster allegiance to the EU polity. However, rights to welfare as part of EU citizenship are financed by the member states, implying that the nexus of allegiance of national citizenship and welfare is simultaneously loosened. The legitimation function that welfare plays for the national polity explains the reluctance of member states to cede control over the financing and services of their welfare states to the EU.[17]

The two-level character of the EU polity makes welfare rights for EU citizens particularly challenging. Normative constitutionalism seeks 'to reconcile constitutionalism (the protection of minority and individual rights and particular substantive political values) and democracy (a mode of government that places ultimate political authority in popular majorities)'.[18] Constitutions differ in the extent to which they grant positive rights, with newer constitutions typically including social rights whereas classical constitutions, such as that of the US, rather focus on individual liberties that are being guaranteed against the state. Already in the 1920s, Kelsen highlighted that judicial review puts a constitutional court in a similar position to that of the legislator, albeit a negative legislator drawing out limits.[19] In this view, if constitutional courts have the power of judicial review over legislative acts, broad constitutional rights let courts compete with legislators, granting entitlements. But because positive social rights are conferred by a community to its members, they need to be shaped politically. Redistributive measures are much more closely tied to the power of parliament's purse, so that these positive rights require different legitimation than negative rights constraining the state towards the individual.

Following the New Deal legislation and the civil rights movement, US constitutional theory has seen quite a lively debate on welfare rights.[20] Part of it has related to whether strong social rights can only be paired with weak judicial review as one way to limit interference of the judiciary with the prerogative of the legislature,[21] and its power of the purse. This conflict figures prominently in the seminal writing of Frank Michelman[22] on the topic. Without further summarising this literature here, suffice it to say that welfare rights can only be adjudicated to the extent that there is an indirect legitimation through the legislature.

No comparable discussion has been prominent in the EU. This may be justified by the differences compared to the national level. Whereas in the national context the extent or scope

---

[16] Joseph HH Weiler, 'Does Europe Need a Constitution? Demos, Telos and the German Maastricht Decision' (1995) 1 European Law Journal 219.

[17] Stephan Leibfried, 'Social Policy: Left to the Judges and the Markets?' in Helen Wallace, Mark A Pollack and Alasdair R Young (eds), *Policy-making in the European Union* (OUP 2010).

[18] Keith E Whittington, 'Constitutionalism' in Keith E Whittington, Roger Daniel Kelemen and Gregory A Caldeira (eds), *The Oxford Handbook of Law and Politics* (OUP 2008) 284.

[19] Basil Bornemann, 'Politisierung des Rechts und Verrechtlichung der Politik durch das Bundesverfassungsgericht? Systemtheoretische Betrachtungen zum Wandel des Verhältnisses von Recht und Politik und zur Rolle der Verfassungsgerichtsbarkeit' (2007) 28 Zeitschrift für Rechtssoziologie 75.

[20] William E Forbath, 'The Constitution and the Obligations of Government to Secure the Material Preconditions for a Good Society. Constitutional Welfare Rights: A History, Critique, and Reconstruction' (2001) 69 Fordham Law Review 1821; Goodwin Liu, 'Rethinking Constitutional Welfare Rights' (2010) 61 Stanford Law Review 203.

[21] Mark V Tushnet, 'Alternative Forms of Judicial Review' (2003) 101 Michigan Law Review 2781.

[22] Frank I Michelman, 'Welfare Rights in a Constitutional Democracy' (1979) 1979 Washington University Law Review 659.

of rights may be subject to judicial review, in the European context the Court has a different mandate. It is the political and judicial process of member states that determines social rights, such as whether social assistance is sufficiently high or pensions need to reflect child rearing. The ECJ can only decide on eligibility for these rights, broadening access to rights established by national legislatures in drawing on the prohibition to discriminate along national lines; it cannot decide on the foundation of these rights as such. Courts are well legitimated to adjudicate non-discrimination rights. When adjudicating non-discrimination, courts set limits to the executive and legislature's ability to treat individuals differently. Compared to the US, one could also argue that the normative difficulty of judicialising social rights is heightened in the multi-level context of the EU. Here, the development of social rights through the ECJ constrains not only the EU legislator but also the legislator at the member-state level. The Court is engaged in a dialogue with the European and the member-state legislators. Demands of non-discrimination based on nationality impact member states' heterogeneous social systems differently depending on the design of social benefits. Thus, it is not convincing a priori to consider the judicialisation of EU social rights as not requiring further constitutional debate.

Bellamy has been a long-term critic of judicialising social rights, arguing for the need for parliamentary legitimation.[23] Drawing on the idea of *demoicracy*, he argues that European social rights require attention to stakeholdership in order to balance the sustainability of member states' welfare systems with individual entitlements.[24] According to this perspective there cannot be a 'duty-free citizenship', as advocated by some,[25] because welfare rights have to be financed and therefore depend on solidarity and a sense of belonging.

EU law scholars in contrast, it seems fair to say, have generally welcomed the development of social rights through the ECJ, without much discussion of needed legislative support.[26] Judicially broadened access to national social rights is seen as a way of shifting the integration process from market integration towards social rights, supporting the emergence of a European *demos* while fostering the teleological process of the 'ever closer union'. The lack of judicial means against EU-induced measures of austerity after the financial and euro crises roused negative reactions,[27] which intensified after the ECJ changed track from late 2014 onwards and, to the surprise of the EU law community, allowed member states greater leeway in closing off their welfare states to economically inactive EU citizens. For instance, it was said that the 'ECJ sacrifices EU citizenship'.[28] On the whole, scholars of EU citizenship law saw

---

[23] Richard Bellamy, 'Introduction: Should Europe Adopt the American Way of Law ... and Has It Done So? European Political Science and the Law' (2008) 7 European Political Science 1; Richard Bellamy, *A Republican Europe of States* (CUP 2019).

[24] Richard Bellamy and Joseph Lacey, 'Balancing the Rights and Duties of European and National Citizens: A Demoicratic Approach' (2018) 25 Journal of European Public Policy 1403.

[25] Dimitry Kochenov, 'EU Citizenship without Duties' (2014) 20 European Law Journal 482.

[26] Agustín José Menéndez and Espen DH Olsen (n 2) 101.

[27] Ibid., 109.

[28] Charlotte O'Brien, 'Court of Justice. The ECJ Sacrifices EU Citizenship In Vain: Commission v. United Kingdom' (2017) 54 CML Rev 209; Other scholars have similarly criticised the restrictive stance of the ECJ: Anita Heindlmaier and Michael Blauberger, 'Enter at Your Own Risk: Free Movement of EU Citizens in Practice' (2017) 40 WEP 1198; Dora Kostakopoulou, 'Scala Civium: Citizenship Templates Post-Brexit and the European Union's Duty to Protect EU Citizens' (2018) 56 JCMS 854; Stephanie Reynolds, '(De)constructing the Road to Brexit: Paving the Way to Further Limitations on Free Movement and Equal Treatment?' in Daniel Thym (ed), *Questioning EU Citizenship: Judges and the Limits of Free Movement and Solidarity in the EU* (Hart Publishing 2017); Sandra Seubert, 'Why

the development of social rights through the Court as having positive effects, with little regard to potential drawbacks given the multi-level character of its foundation. Much attention has been given to individual rights as a way to strengthen the Union, but little has been paid to the national origin of rights and to the question of how judicialised rights can be sufficiently legitimated by the legislator.

In the following, I will start by summarising how the coordination of social security has developed between case law and legislative reform widening rights of migrant workers, and then increasingly extending the non-discriminatory access to economically inactive EU citizens. This process raises several normative and positive issues. Among these, I will focus on the practical problems of the chosen avenue to establish welfare rights in the EU, largely leaving aside the normative dimension of constitutional considerations. Behind this choice is the consideration that it is only meaningful to engage in ideas of bolstering the input legitimation of this judicialisation of social rights if the rights established by the ECJ do have a positive outcome for individuals. But before we discuss the effects of these rights at the level of member states and individual citizens, it is necessary to analyse how case law shapes social rights in the EU.

2.2 The Judicial Shaping of Social Coordination and Citizenship Rights

As mentioned, as early as 1958, the coordination regulations no. 3 and 4 were agreed upon in order to back the free movement of labour, although welfare remained under member-state prerogative. The regulations stipulate the responsible member state for social security first by the principle of *lex loci laboris*, the place of work, and second by the place of residence. Social assistance is not covered by the regulation, but left under exclusive national purview.[29] The regulations were later revised into regulation 1408/71 (now 883/2004) and regulation 1612/68 (now 492/2011).

Case law of the Court has constantly shaped these regulations, leading to repeated revisions.[30] Thereby the Court could draw on the support over-constitutionalisation gives to the judicialisation of rights.[31] The rights enshrined in the regulations on the coordination of national social security systems and in the Citizenship Directive (2004/38/EC) have been shaped in a back-and-forth process between the EU's judiciary and its legislature, with the latter not being able to overrule the former's constitutionalised rulings.[32] The following cita-

---

the Crisis of European Citizenship is a Crisis of European Democracy' in Maurizio Ferrera and Rainer Bauböck (eds), *Should EU Citizenship Be Duty-free? EUI Working Papers RSCAS 2017/60* (European University Institute 2017); Francesca Strumia, 'European Citizenship and Transnational Rights: Chronicles of a Troubled Narrative' in Daniel Thym (ed), *Questioning EU Citizenship: Judges and the Limits of Free Movement and Solidarity in the EU* (Hart Publishing 2017).

[29] Dorte S Martinsen and Gerda Falkner, 'Social Policy: Problem-solving Gaps, Partial Exits, and Court-decision Traps' in Gerda Falkner (ed), *The EU's Decision Traps* (OUP 2011) 138.

[30] Dorte S Martinsen, 'Social Security Regulation in the EU. The De-territorialization of Welfare?' in Gráinne De Búrca (eds), *EU Law and the Welfare State: In Search of Solidarity* (OUP 2005); Dorte S Martinsen and Gerda Falkner (n 29).

[31] Dieter Grimm, *The Constitution of European Democracy* (OUP 2017).

[32] Susanne K Schmidt, *The European Court of Justice and the Policy Process: The Shadow of Case Law* (OUP 2018).

tion of the Commission exemplifies the importance of the Court's case law in developing the social protection of free movement rights:

> The rules are now 30 years old, however. Over this period, the Court of Justice has repeatedly ruled on the texts and interpreted them. As a result, a whole corpus of case-law to interpret the wording of the legislation has been created. To strengthen the security and transparency of the law on behalf of the citizen, it is now time to bring the texts (i.e. the regulation, SKS) into line with existing case-law.[33]

The case law is very complex, as are the two regulations. Indeed, when commenting on the attempted revision of social security regulations (COM(2016)815)[34] in 2017 the German Bundesrat alluded to the 'better regulation' programme of the Commission and urged the importance of tackling the complexity of social coordination that is challenging to understand for EU citizens and member-state administrations alike.[35] Therefore, I will only focus here on two related questions, concerning the opening of the so-called SNCBs, special non-contributory benefits for citizens of other member states, and the inclusion of economically inactive EU citizens.

Much conflict between member states and the Court concerned SNCBs, that is, tax-financed social security falling under the responsibility of the country of residence. While the coordination regulations do not apply to social assistance, they do not define the term.[36] Case law concerning these tax-financed, supplementary benefits typically concerned restrictions that member states imposed on the exportability of these benefits. After much haggling between member states and the Court, where the latter repeatedly lifted national restrictions on the exportability of SNCBs, council regulation 1247/92 allocated the responsibility for SNCBs to the country of residence, at the same time declaring these benefits non-exportable to other member states.[37] Martinsen and Falkner take this regulation as an instance of overrule, where the Council took back control over the expansive case law development.[38] Subsequently, the Court initially deferred to the legislator, and the list of SNCBs in the annex of the regulation grew. In 2001 the Court opposed this development and ruled in C-215/99 *Jauch*[39] and C-43/99 *Leclerc*[40] that the Austrian long-term care and the Luxembourg maternity allowance were wrongly included in the annex, and had to be exportable.[41] SNCBs are now regulated in Article 70 of regulation 883/2004 and detailed in its annex X – and have remained conflictual. Access to these social benefits depends on factual residence, which was defined by the Court in case

---

[33] Parliament and Council Regulation [1998] COD 98/0229, 98/0230, 98/0231, COM 98/394, p.4.
[34] Regulation of the European Parliament and of the Council [2016] COD 2016/0397.
[35] Bundesrat 761/1/16 *Empfehlungen* (27 February 2017), p.3 www.bundesrat.de/drs.html?id=761-1-16 accessed 14 January 2020.
[36] Dorte S Martinsen and Gerda Falkner (n 29) 138.
[37] Rob Cornelissen, 'EU Regulations on the Coordination of Social Security Systems and Special Non-Contributory Benefits: A Source of Never-Ending Controversy' in Elspeth Guild, Sergio Carrera and Katharina Eisele (eds), *Social Benefits and Migration: A Contested Relationship and Policy Challenge in the EU* (Centre for European Policy Studies (CEPS) 2013) 92.
[38] Dorte S Martinsen and Gerda Falkner (n 29) 138.
[39] Case C-215/99 *Jauch v Pensionsversicherungsanstalt der Arbeiter* EU:C:2001:139.
[40] Case C-43/99 *Leclere v Caisse nationale des prestations familiales* EU:C:2001:303.
[41] Dorte S Martinsen and Gerda Falkner (n 29) 139.

C-90/97 *Swaddling*⁴² as relating to the place someone 'habitually resides' (No. 29f) and where the person's centre of interest lies.⁴³

SNCBs were important in the long-term contested question of the access of economically inactive EU citizens to social support in member states. The Citizenship Directive (2004/38/EC) was adopted at the same time as regulation 883/2004 but the relationship of both sets of rules remained unclear for a long time. The directive details the rights of EU citizens by establishing a gradual system of rights. For the first three months, EU citizens are free to settle anywhere in the Union, but they have no right to access social benefits in the host member state. After five years of legal residence, EU citizens have equal rights to nationals. Between three months and five years of stay, member states can require EU citizens to have sufficient financial resources and comprehensive sickness insurance. However, if they do require financial assistance, this may not automatically end their right of residence (Article 14 III). This qualification directly reflects the 2002 ruling in *Grzelczyk* (C-184/99) (No. 43).⁴⁴ Grzelczyk was a French student in Belgium, and even though the student directive at the time required financial self-sufficiency for students, the Court argued that member states have to show a 'certain degree of financial solidarity with nationals of other Member States'.⁴⁵ Indeed, that the directive leaves largely open which rights are enjoyed between three months and five years reflects that *Grzelczyk* received assistance after three years.⁴⁶ Member states were not willing to grant equal rights before five years of legal residence but could not insist on these five years because in *Grzelczyk* the Court had demanded some solidarity already after three years, as long as this is not 'an unreasonable burden on the public finances of the host Member State' (No. 6). This inability of the legislature to overrule the judiciary reflects over-constitutionalisation. Consequently, in an important aspect, the directive could not settle the rights of EU citizens.

The unclear relationship between the directive and regulation 883/2004 led to the question of whether economically inactive EU citizens could rely on social security from the host state to cover the financial self-sufficiency that is needed for legal residence following the directive. Until different Court rulings (*Brey*, *Dano*, *Alimanovic* and *Garcia-Nieto*) settled the relationship of both pieces of legislation from late 2013 onwards, allowing member states to restrict access to social benefits for economically inactive citizens who took residence recently, it had been assumed in part that the social security regulations were *lex specialis* to the directive.⁴⁷ In this light, access to benefits depends on the habitual residence of EU citizens, which opens up social security under annex X. These social benefits could then cover the directive's requirement of sufficient financial resources.

---

⁴² Case C-90/97 *Swaddling v Adjudication Officer* EU:C:1999:96.
⁴³ Rob Cornelissen (n 37) 93.
⁴⁴ Case C-184/99 *Grzelczyk v Centre public d'aide sociale d'Ottignies-Louvain-la-Neuve* (No. 43) EU:C:2001:458.
⁴⁵ Case C-184/99 *Grzelczyk v Centre public d'aide sociale d'Ottignies-Louvain-la-Neuve* (No. 44) EU:C:2001:458.
⁴⁶ Fabio Wasserfallen, 'The Judiciary as Legislator? How the European Court of Justice Shapes Policy-making in the European Union' (2010) 17 Journal of European Public Policy 1128.
⁴⁷ Michael Coucheir, Maija Sakslin, Stefano Giubboni, Dorte Martinsen and Herwig Verschueren, *Think Tank Report 2008: The Relationship and Interaction between the Coordination Regulations and Directive 2004/38/EC* (European Commission 2008) 28.

Any other conclusion would make this special coordination system meaningless. If a person first had to prove that her or his residence in the host State is in line with the subsistence requirement under Directive 2004/38/EC before s/he could even claim a minimum subsistence benefit under Regulation 1408/71, it would never be possible for him/her to do so. Indeed when applying for a minimum subsistence benefit s/he would demonstrate that s/he is no longer fulfilling the condition concerning sufficiency of resources under Directive 2004/38/EC.[48]

These arguments can similarly be found in an explanatory note of the Commission on the social security coordination from January 2011.[49] The assessment did not discuss the fact that the regulations do not cover social assistance.

To summarise, the Court has repeatedly opened up national social protection to EU citizens, but has refrained from this path since 2013/14. 'The boundaries of membership to the communities of solidarity-based redistribution defined by national welfare schemes have – thanks to ECJ case law – become more open and permeable, and hence more inclusive, at least for European citizens.' Having given some background to this development, I shall now turn to questioning how this judicialised system works, starting with the most commonly voiced concern of a possible undermining of national welfare through the supranational opening.

3. SHORTCOMINGS OF JUDICIALISING WELFARE

Integration through law has allowed many advances of European integration that would have been difficult or impossible if relying only on political agreement.[50] Yet, as judicialisation builds on individual rights, embodied in the four freedoms and citizenship, it has a bias whereby only certain liberal values and liberalisation can be pushed, while public policy goals and republican values depend on political agreement and are undermined by extensive individual rights[51]. Scharpf sees a double asymmetry, where some redistributive schemes at the national level come under pressure through European equal access requirements, while it is not possible to agree on common policies in the European legislative process.[52] This risk of an under-provision of welfare, reminiscent of a tragedy of the commons, relates to the member-state level. Moreover, judicialising welfare results in problems at the individual level. These are often overlooked but have more immediate relevance. They relate to the difficulty that the Court faces in constructing Social Europe via non-discrimination when conditions in the member states are heterogeneous. From this new inequalities arise, as I will show. Advancing rights via case law, furthermore, implies significant legal uncertainty for the individuals.[53] If rules are in flux and subject to case law development, again individuals will likely

---

[48] Michael Coucheir, Maija Sakslin, Stefano Giubboni, Dorte Martinsen and Herwig Verschueren (n 47) 32.
[49] European Commission, *Explanatory Notes on Modernised Social Security Coordination. Regulations (EC) No 883/2004 & No 897/2009* (European Commission 2011).
[50] Mauro Cappelletti, Monica Seccombe and Joseph HH Weiler (n 9).
[51] Agustín José Menéndez and Espen DH Olsen (n 2) 106.
[52] Fritz W Scharpf, 'The Asymmetry of European Integration, or Why the EU Cannot Be a "Social Market Economy"' (2010) 8 Socio-Economic Review 211.
[53] Jos Hoevenaars, 'The Preliminary Reference Procedure: Challenge or Opportunity?' (2015) 36 Recht der Werkelijkheid 83.

be treated very differently, depending on the authorities they face. This legal uncertainty could imply that individuals are better off with certain, even if more restrictive, rules.

3.1 A Tragedy of the Commons? Opening Welfare and Risking Under-provision

Scharpf[54] has argued that the negative integration via the Court's case law and the lifting of restrictions has very unequal repercussions among the member states of the EU, with their differing capitalist and welfare institutions. Opening up national welfare to EU citizens, or even beyond to third-country nationals, it is feared, could give incentives for cutting down on social benefits in general.[55] Similar concerns of a race to the bottom are known from mutual recognition in the single market, where market actors can settle in the member state with the least stringent requirements.[56] In the realm of market regulation as in the realm of welfare state financing, it is often politically contentious whether there is pressure on high-standard regulation and social services, or whether this is only alleged in order to facilitate liberalisation.

Empirically, there does not seem to be much support for concerns of under-provision. Dustmann and Frattini find positive effects of EU migration for Britain (different to non-EU migration and nationals).[57] Drawing on register data, Martinsen and Pons Rotger similarly show positive fiscal contributions for Denmark.[58] People normally migrate in order to work. Being predominantly of working age, they contribute more than they cost to their host society. Benefits for the host accrue because they profit from the upbringing and education of the migrant's home society, and possibly from lower wages for the migrants' work. If the latter is the case, wage pressure contributes to rising inequalities.[59] Yet, much depends on the skill level and the institutions in the host country. Costs accrue because of language and cultural adaptation. Often migrants take up work below their skill level, leading to a de-skilling effect of migration.[60] While Scharpf[61] expected that liberal market economies could accommodate far-reaching EU free movement rights more easily than social market economies, as the latter's institutions coordinating economic activities would be undermined, this expectation needs to be modified. Contrary to expectations, the Danish welfare state copes well. Conversely, the UK's flexible labour market attracts lower-skilled workers, and in-work benefits of an acti-

---

[54] Fritz W Scharpf (n 52).

[55] Fritz W Scharpf, 'Legitimacy in the Multilevel European Polity' (2009) 1 European Political Science Review 173; Anja Wiesbrock, 'Granting Citizenship-related Rights to Third-country Nationals: An Alternative to the Full Extension of European Union Citizenship?' (2012) 14 European Journal of Migration and Law 63, 93.

[56] Jeanne-Mey Sun and Jacques Pelkmans, 'Regulatory Competition in the Single Market' (1995) 33 Journal of Common Market Studies 67.

[57] Christian Dustmann and Tommaso Frattini, 'The Fiscal Effects of Immigration to the UK' (2014) 124 The Economic Journal F593.

[58] Dorte S Martinsen and Gabriel Pons Rotger, 'The Fiscal Impact of EU Immigration on the Tax-financed Welfare State: Testing the "Welfare Burden" Thesis' (2017) 18 European Union Politics 620.

[59] George J Borjas, *We Wanted Workers: Unraveling the Immigration Narrative* (WW Norton & Co Inc 2016).

[60] Marek Okólski and John Salt, 'Polish Emigration to the UK after 2004; Why Did So Many Come?' (2014) 3 Central and Eastern European Migration Review 11.

[61] Fritz W Scharpf (n 52) 235.

vating welfare state make this immigration more costly.[62] This does not mean that the overall gain from labour migration is low. In fact, Eastern European home states are paying a price for brain drain.[63] Economic benefits from migration are very much mediated by member states' labour market and welfare institutions.[64]

Because of this significant mediating effect of institutions of labour markets and the welfare state, it may not be so surprising that there are few examples of an overuse in social welfare rooted in non-discrimination. One of the rare examples relates to the case of German medical students in Austria.[65] In fact, in May 2017, following many years of controversy, the Commission allowed Austria to apply a quota to German students, effectively restricting free movement rights.[66] Before this the number of German students had grown considerably, making up one quarter of all students in human medicine in the winter of 2016 – and even 42 per cent in psychology (where Austria does not employ a quota).[67] The ECJ had established strict non-discrimination among the member states as early as the mid-1980s.[68] In 2010 the ECJ was more lenient in a ruling regarding Belgium (in a similar situation to Austria but in this case with French students), on the subject of permissible reasons for restrictions.[69] Empirical proof that more than two thirds of German medical students leave Austria after exams to practise in their home country finally convinced the Commission to allow the Austrian quota system. In contrast, it is fully accepted that out-of-state tuition is much higher in the US and in the Canadian university system,[70] so that someone from Colorado pays higher tuition in California, not having contributed taxes there.

Students are a highly mobile group of the population, and as a small country neighbouring a large one with the same language, and not willing to renounce its university policy of unconditional access, Austria was extremely vulnerable to free-riding. There are not many situations in which the opening of a single welfare benefit would motivate EU citizens to move for its cause. Possibly, had the Court required Austria in *Brey* (C-140/12)[71] to open up its compensatory pension unconditionally to all EU pensioners moving to Austria,[72] similar dynamics could

---

[62] Martin Ruhs, 'Free Movement in the European Union: National Institutions vs Common Policies' (2017) 55 International Migration 22.

[63] Ruben Atoyan, Lone Christiansen, Allan Dizioli, Christian Ebeke, Nadeem Ilahi, Anna Ilyina, Gil Mehrez, Haonan Qu, Faezeh Raei, Alaina Rhee and Daria Zakharova, *Emigration and Its Economic Impact on Eastern Europe* (International Monetary Fund 2016).

[64] Frida Boräng, *National Institutions – International Migration: Labour Markets, Welfare States and Immigration Policy* (Rowman & Littlefield 2018).

[65] Angelika Schenk and Susanne K Schmidt, 'Failing on the Social Dimension: Judicial Law-making and Student Mobility in the EU' (2018) 25 Journal of European Public Policy 1522.

[66] European Commission, 'Free movement of students: Commission closes infringement case against Austria' https://ec.europa.eu/commission/presscorner/detail/en/IP_17_1282 accessed 14 January 2020.

[67] Angelika Schenk and Susanne K Schmidt (n 65).

[68] Case C-193/83 *Gravier* EU:C:1986:75.

[69] Case C-73/08 *Bressol v Gouvernement de la Communauté française* EU:C:2010:181.

[70] Willem Maas, 'Boundaries of Political Community in Europe, the US, and Canada' (2017) 39 Journal of European Integration 575.

[71] Case C-140/12 *Brey v Pensionsversicherungsanstalt* EU:C:2013:565.

[72] Gareth Davies, 'Has the Court Changed, or Have the Cases? The Deservingness of Litigants as an Element in Court of Justice Adjudication' (2018) 25 Journal of European Public Policy 1442.

have resulted. It is interesting that in 2011 the Commission had been convinced that a situation like *Brey* would clearly lead to entitlements under regulation 883/2004.[73]

To conclude, while EU citizens moving to other member states typically result in positive fiscal effects, in extreme situations moving can be motivated by a specific benefit, risking under-provision in a 'tragedy of the commons' scenario. Non-discrimination, moreover, also leads to inequalities among individuals moving between systems, to which we turn now.

3.2 New Inequalities at the Individual Level

Given the great heterogeneity of member states' welfare regimes, an approach of non-discrimination is a poor guide for the Court to further social equality. Why? The example of student financial support can illustrate the problem.[74] Member states' schemes show great variety, reflecting their different higher education policies, welfare states and economic development. Some member states do not have any scheme to support students financially, some have loans and some have means-tested support with different repayment requirements. Denmark has the most generous system, with a non-means-tested, non-repayable benefit. Some of these national benefits are portable, to be used for studies in other member states; others are not.

Different criteria derived from EU law determine eligibility for student financial support in host member states. Employment status, whether own or derived (as a family member), grants non-discriminatory treatment to student benefits of the host state. As the free movement of workers encompasses those working only a few hours as long as it is not 'marginal and ancillary',[75] eligibility starts, depending on the member state, at about 10 hours per week. With the ECJ ruling in C-46/12 *L. N. v Styrelsen* in 2013, Denmark was forced to open its study benefit to EU students working 10–12 hours per week[76]. If they do not qualify for equal treatment under the free movement of workers, EU citizens living in other member states acquire equal rights after five years of legal residence, according to the Citizenship Directive. However, the Court often requires an individual assessment of their situation, as seen in the *Grzelczyk* ruling. Consequently, students aiming to access financial support in host member states can find themselves in very different situations, depending on the conditions of their home country (with portable loans or not) and the criteria of eligibility (as workers or EU citizens) on which they draw.

Why is the principle of non-discrimination a poor guide in a situation of such diversity? If we juxtapose the different situations that can result depending on the system in the home and in the host country of study, we see that combinations multiply. The crucial question is whether a person's home state grants portable student support or not. Solely guided by the non-discrimination principle, the Court cannot stop new discriminations arising. A case from November 2015 at the Austrian Federal Administrative Court illustrates this,[77] where a German medical student claimed eligibility for a student grant based on part-time employ-

---

[73] European Commission (n 49) section: R5.
[74] Angelika Schenk and Susanne K Schmidt (n 65).
[75] Case 53/81 *Levin v Staatssecretaris van Justitie* EU:C:1982:105.
[76] Dorte S Martinsen and Benjamin Werner, 'No Welfare Magnets: Free Movement and Cross-border Welfare in Germany and Denmark Compared' (2019) 26 Journal of European Public Policy 637.
[77] Bundesverwaltungsgericht (26.11.2015) Entscheidung BVwG W129 2008055-2.

ment in Austria.[78] The Federal Administrative Court backed denying the application because of the risk of double eligibility in Austria and Germany. The student had only handed in proof of not having applied for a German grant, but (naturally) could not bring proof that such application was not to follow later. The student argued that it was discriminatory that Italian, Polish, Slovakian, Romanian and Czech students did not need to bring such proof – explained by the fact that their countries do not provide (portable) student grants (No. 2.3.11 of the ruling). In heterogeneous settings, non-discrimination alone cannot bring equality. It is for this reason that the world trade regime has the most-favoured nations clause, to compensate for inequalities arising from applying the non-discrimination rule.[79]

Given the complexity of national support schemes, it is notable that the legal principles the Court goes by, related to the free movement of workers, EU citizenship and non-discrimination on the basis of nationality, increase the number of possible eligibility criteria. Eligibility can relate to own or derived employment, length of residence and integration in the host state or the portability of grants in the home state. For the individuals concerned, it is not easy to understand the conditions of case law-based eligibility. It is telling that the official Austrian website for student grants denies giving guidelines for EU citizens, speaking instead of the complexity and rapidly changing case law of the ECJ.[80] Evolving case law implies additional legal uncertainty for EU citizens' rights. This uncertainty also means that chance has more of a say in whether or not EU citizens are granted certain rights derived from ECJ case law in their local courts. It is to this issue that I now turn.

3.3 Up against Chance: Unequal Treatment and Legal Uncertainty

As summarised above, for quite some time it was unclear how regulation 883/2004 and the Citizenship Directive related to each other: could non-economically active EU citizens access social benefits based on their habitual residence, helping them to cover the financial self-sufficiency requirement of the Citizenship Directive, or not? In Germany, it was contentious whether the rule of §7 SGB II (social law book No. 2) that restricted non-Germans' access to basic social support was compatible with the non-discrimination rule of the social coordination regulations. Germany took this basic assistance to be social assistance in the sense of Article 24 II of the Citizenship Directive, and as we have seen, basic social assistance is not included in the coordination regulations. In 2009 the Court had ruled in case C-22-23/08 *Vatsouras*[81] that benefits aiming to facilitate access to employment had to be granted in a non-discriminatory way. But until case C-333/13 *Dano*[82] decided that economically inactive EU citizens could be excluded from social benefits of SGB II, whether the German exclusion could stand against EU non-discrimination was disputed.

---

[78] Angelika Schenk and Susanne K Schmidt (n 65).
[79] Thanks to Fritz Scharpf for pointing this out.
[80] I thank Michael Blauberger for making me aware of this. Österreichische Studienbeihilfenbehörde. www.stipendium.at/studienfoerderung/studienbeihilfe/wer-hat-anspruch accessed 30 March 2021.
[81] Case C-22-23/08 *Vatsouras and Koupatantze v Arbeitsgemeinschaft (ARGE) Nürnberg 900* EU:C:2009:344.
[82] *Dano*.

Table 16.1 Expansive and restrictive verdicts and rulings on social benefits for EU citizens

Year	2006	2007	2008	2009	2010	2011	2012	2013	2014	2015	2016
expansive	3	11	9	8	10	11	30	20	22	39	33
restrictive	6	9	8	10	17	18	64	40	37	54	35

Given these doubts, German social courts increasingly ruled in favour of EU citizens, as Table 16.1, based on an analysis of 543 cases dealing with access of EU citizens to SGB II support between 2006 and 2016, shows.[83]

A further look at regional differences in adjudication, focusing on the higher regional social courts, proves interesting. Figure 16.1 shows significant differences depending on where cases were decided.

Finally, we can look at those cases, verdicts and rulings that were positively decided for EU citizens until 2015 – altogether 248 cases. Here it is striking that increasingly the granting of benefits was justified with reference to the complex legal situation. While in 2009 only two cases were substantiated in this way, there were 20 cases in 2015, and 70 cases over the whole period.

Ongoing European case law development about individual rights, to sum up, implies significant legal uncertainty for the individuals concerned. Legal uncertainty and variance in court rulings are likely to be much higher when European legal entitlements are in flux than in a situation of relatively fixed rules. I will argue in the next section that where individuals and their life chances are concerned, it is questionable whether they are better served with evolving entitlements to more far-reaching rights than with more restrictive but relatively fixed rules allowing greater legal certainty. After all, when rights are developed by the ECJ, case law development may halt (as happened, in fact, with the rulings of *Dano* et al.).

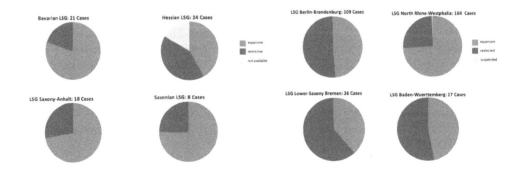

Figure 16.1 Rulings according to region

---

[83] The cases were assembled via the website www.sozialgerichtsbarkeit.de, by choosing all cases that relate to SGB II benefits citing ECJ jurisprudence, and analysed in an Excel sheet according to outcome, court, and until 2015 also according to legal justification for the outcome. I thank Laura Baade for her research assistance.

3.4 Being Unaware of Taking Risks: The Case of Comprehensive Sickness Insurance

The unsettled relationship between the requirements of the Citizenship Directive and the coordination regulations concerned not only the question whether social benefits of the regulation could contribute to the sufficient resources of economically inactive EU citizens, but also the requirement of comprehensive sickness insurance (CSI). Following the Citizenship Directive, EU citizens can settle anywhere provided they have sufficient financial resources and comprehensive sickness insurance in the first five years (Articles 7 and 16). Member states have different health systems, with some having national health systems and others having health insurance. The UK government, with its national health service (NHS), has always held that health cover through the NHS could not meet the requirement of CSI, as this requirement was meant to protect the public finances of the host state. Domestic courts backed the position of the British government.[84] But in line with its approach to sufficient resources, the Commission regarded access to the NHS as following from residence under the coordination regulations.[85] In 2012 the Commission sent a reasoned opinion as part of an infringement procedure, holding that all EU citizens have access to the NHS in the UK, thereby covering their requirement of CSI,[86] derived from the prohibition to discriminate along national lines.[87] The infringement procedure was not handed to the Court, but the Commission noted in 2017 that it was still pending.[88]

With the UK referendum to leave the EU, this question suddenly became very problematic for all EU citizens living in the UK but not falling under free movement of workers. The lack of a CSI implied that the requirement for five years of legal residence under the directive would not be met – even by EU citizens who had spent many more years living in the UK.[89] As in practice EU citizens living in the UK could easily access the services of the NHS, it was only when wanting to clarify their long-term legal residence that many EU citizens learned about their predicament. Under the ordinary residence of regulation 883/2004, access to the NHS had been possible for EU citizens. But this access could hinder ever meeting the legal residence requirement of the directive.

The UK government has agreed to lift this restriction.[90] But the saga of CSI as well as the question of sufficient financial resources shows how the incremental extension of rights by the

---

[84] *Ahmad v Secretary of State for the Home Department* [2014] EWCA Civ 988. Thanks to Stéphanie Reynolds.
[85] European Commission (n 49) 5, fn 8.
[86] 'Under the Free Movement Directive, EU citizens who settle in another EU country but do not work there may be required to have sufficient resources and sickness insurance. The United Kingdom, however, does not consider entitlement to treatment by the UK public healthcare scheme (NHS) as sufficient. This breaches EU law' (IP-12-417_EN).
[87] Grega Strban, Gabriella Berki, Dolores Carrascosa and Filip van Overmeiren, *FreSsco Analytical Report 2016. Access to Healthcare in Cross-border Situations* (European Commission 2017).
[88] www.europarl.europa.eu/sides/getAllAnswers.do?reference=P-2017-003659&language=MT accessed 30 March 2021.
[89] Alexandra Herbeć, *The Scandal of CSI, the Little-Known Loophole Used to Deny EU Citizens Permanent Residency* (LSE Brexit (17 Mar 2017) 2017).
[90] Department of Health United Kingdom, *Guidance on Implementing the Overseas Visitor Hospital Charging Regulations 2015: Ways in which People Can Be Lawfully Resident in the UK* (Department of Health United Kingdom 2016).

Court puts individuals in extremely vulnerable situations. A clear and transparent obligation to take out CSI would have probably been preferable.

4. CONCLUSION

Unlike in the case of single-market policies, the ECJ has not succeeded in becoming an important motor of common social policies. Where case law may result in a regulatory race to the bottom in the single market, there is the analysed risk of under-provision in the social realm. But compared to the regulatory policies of the single market, with recognised high standards in environment and consumer protection, it appears even more unlikely that ECJ case law could be an incentive for member states to agree on common social policies involving distribution.

Yet, the expectation had been for comparable integration dynamics in the social field. 'The ECJ's role in "social engineering" the status of Union citizen to replace entitlement based on market freedoms, is the engine of new forms of cross-border solidarity.'[91] The ECJ, in this respect, is caught in a dilemma resulting from the decision in the EU to leave welfare systems in national competence while opting for unconstrained free movement rights. By applying its non-discrimination adjudication, it automatically opens up national systems of social protection to outsiders. But 'no taxation without representation' belongs to the core of liberal democracies. Courts, accordingly, are much better legitimated to enforce liberal individual rights against the state than to decide on spending decisions, which should be left to parliaments. Judicialised European rights to national welfare are also in danger of undermining transnational solidarity, as has been seen in the context of the Brexit discussion.[92]

EU constitutional theory has not sufficiently reflected on the difficult dialogue between the judiciary and the legislator in the multi-level system. In emphasising the opportunities arising from EU citizenship, the precarious legitimation of judicialised rights to welfare, financed by the member states, has received too little attention. Increasing politicisation of intra-EU migration also reflects this missing link between judicialised rights and legislative legitimation.[93] A positive fiscal balance under conditions of EU free movement insufficiently reflects the difficulties following from coordinating heterogeneous national social protection schemes with the principle of non-discriminatory access. Intra-EU mobility has been low and there has not been a full opening as member states tread carefully, protecting their welfare schemes under the relative openness forced by the ECJ. Determining discriminatory practices requires drawing a distinction – like situations are treated alike and unlike situations are treated differently. But the ECJ is very reluctant to take into account fiscal contributions for publicly financed welfare.

> The cohesion and effectiveness of the tax system, or balanced industrial relations, are not mere appendices to subjective rights, but the very soil on which rights stand. By imagining them as if they were

---

[91] Michael Coucheir, Maija Sakslin, Stefano Giubboni, Dorte Martinsen and Herwig Verschueren (n 47) 33.
[92] Matthew Goodwin and Caitlin Milazzo, 'Taking Back Control? Investigating the Role of Immigration in the 2016 Vote for Brexit' (2017) 19 The British Journal of Politics and International Relations 450.
[93] Laurie Beaudonnet, 'A Threatening Horizon: The Impact of the Welfare State on Support for Europe' (2015) 53 Journal of Common Market Studies 457.

further subjective rights, or subjective-right-like fundamental positions, the European Court of Justice erodes the very foundations of the Democratic and Social state, and in the process, of Democratic and Social citizenship.[94]

Signs of erosion are so far rare. It is rather at the individual level that the analysis has shown how the incremental and iterative extension of social rights resulted in an overly complex set of rights, exemplified with the right to maintenance support for students. Relying on non-discrimination in a heterogeneous setting, the Court can further equal treatment only to some extent, and also establishes new inequalities. If national social courts struggle, moreover, with the complexity of rules, basic tenets of legal certainty under the rule of law are violated. The ongoing case law development puts individuals in a position of significant uncertainty concerning their rights and obligations, with the problem that contradictory rules and legal uncertainty also delegitimise political systems.

Recent scholarship has questioned how the Court shaped citizenship rights and welfare entitlements.[95] As difficult as it may appear, welfare entitlements require political majorities to legitimate the underlying redistribution.

---

[94] Agustín José Menéndez and Espen DH Olsen (n 2) 108.
[95] Martijn van den Brink, 'EU Citizenship and (Fundamental) Rights: Empirical, Normative, and Conceptual Problems' (2019) 25 European Law Journal 21; Agustín José Menéndez and Espen DH Olsen (n 2).

17. The outer limits of transnational solidarity between the EU's Member States in a social security setting

Jaan Paju[1]

1. INTRODUCTION

The point of departure for this chapter is a crucial issue which has been largely ignored in doctrine: the relationship between social assistance, on the one hand, and social security benefits that have a redistributive component, on the other, in the light of Directive 2004/38[2] as well as of Regulation 883/2004[3] that coordinates the Member States' social security systems.[4]

This chapter consists of five sections. After this introduction, in section 2 I set out the Union's system for coordinating the social security benefits of the Member States, and I describe the core concept of the right of residence featured in Directive 2004/38. In Section 3 I discuss the CJEU's decisions in *Brey*,[5] *Dano*,[6] *Alimanovic*,[7] *García-Nieto*,[8] *Commission v UK*[9] and *Jobcenter Krefeld*.[10] Sections 4 and 5 are devoted to an analysis of the consequences of these preliminary rulings for Regulation 883/2004. The chapter ends with section 6, in which I provide a summary and present overarching conclusions.

---

[1] The author would like to thank the Torsten Söderberg Foundation for supporting and enabling this study.

[2] Directive 2004/38/EC of the European Parliament and of the Council of 29 April 2004 on the right of citizens of the Union and their family members to move and reside freely within the territory of the Member States amending Regulation (EEC) No 1612/68 and repealing Directives 64/221/EEC, 68/360/EEC, 72/194/EEC, 73/148/EEC, 75/34/EEC, 75/35/EEC, 90/364/EEC, 90/365/EEC and 93/96/EEC [2004] OJ L 158.

[3] Regulation (EC) No 883/2004 of the European Parliament and of the Council of 29 April 2004 on the coordination of social security systems [2004] OJ L 166.

[4] Cf. however, Herwig Verschueren, 'Preventing "Benefit Tourism" in the EU: A Narrow or Broad Interpretation of the Possibilities offered by the CJEU in Dano?' (2015) 52(2) CML Rev 363, also Bernhard Spiegel, 'Anspruch auf Leistungen der sozialen Sicherheit von nicht aktiven Personen – wer fürchtet sich vor "Sozialtourismus"? Neue EuGH Fälle: C-140/12, Brey, und C-333/13, Dano' [2014] ERA Forum 339.

[5] Case C-140/12 *Brey* EU:C:2013:565.

[6] Case C-333/13 *Dano* EU:C:2014:2358.

[7] Case C-67/14 *Alimanovic* EU:C:2015:597.

[8] Case C-299/14 *García-Nieto* EU:C:2016:114.

[9] Case C-308/14 *Commission v UK* EU:C:2016:436.

[10] Case C-181/19 *Jobcenter Krefeld* EU:C:2020:794.

2. THE PARALLEL REGULATION IN EU LAW OF SOCIAL ASSISTANCE AND OF SOCIAL SECURITY – AND A PARADOXICAL OUTCOME

2.1 Regulation 883/2004

Regulation 883/2004 coordinates the social security systems of the Member States in connection with cross-border situations. Among other things, the social security systems offer sickness benefits, pensions, family benefits and unemployment compensation, as well as ensuring cross-border health care.[11]

The basic idea behind the (then) EEC's first substantive regulation in this area, Regulation 3/58,[12] was to limit – through coordination – the territoriality of the social security benefits provided by the Member States. Migrant workers could thus be sure that, irrespective of national rules, they would always be covered by the social security provisions of a Member State, and that rights which they have earned would not be lost upon moving to another Member State. Regulation 3/58 thus constituted – together with its successor, Regulation 1408/71[13] – an important piece of the puzzle with regard to the free movement of workers. With the adoption of Regulation 883/2004, the personal scope has been extended to all Union citizens who are or ever have been covered by the social security system of a Member State (Article 2(1)).[14] This is important to keep in mind when reading this chapter.

When an economically active Union citizen crosses a border, the Member State in which he or she is employed becomes the competent state under Article 11(3)(a) of the Regulation. That is, the worker will be covered by the social security system of the state in which he/she works. When an economically inactive Union citizen moves to another Member State, Article 11(3)(e) of the Regulation points to the state of residence as the competent state: 'any other person to whom subparagraphs (a) to (d) do not apply shall be subject to the legislation of the Member State of residence.'

The broadening of the personal scope of Regulation 883/2004, in combination with Article 11(3)(e), has led to unforeseen consequences for residence-based, social security systems. States with such systems face the risk, when identified as the competent Member State under Article 11(3)(e), that economically inactive Union citizens resident in the country will become eligible for social security benefits, merely on the basis of residence. This, in combination with Article 4 of the Regulation that foresees equal treatment, leads inevitably to eligibility for those social security benefits.

The scenario certainly provokes questions about the outer boundaries of solidarity in relation to economically inactive Union citizens. The widening of the personal scope exposes thus the residence-based systems in a way probably not foreseen by the Member States when drafting and enacting Regulation 883/2004.

---

[11] See further Jaan Paju, *The European Union and Social Security Law* (Hart, 2017) 10 ff.
[12] Council Regulation 3/58 of 25 September 1958 [1958] OJ No 30.
[13] Council Regulation (EEC) No 1408/71 of 14 June 1971 on the application of social security schemes to employed persons, to self-employed persons and to members of their families moving within the Community [1971] OJ L149.
[14] The personal scope covers also family members of the covered union citizens as well as stateless persons and refugees residing in a Member State.

This outcome certainly may be provocative but it forms a natural part of the coordination of the Member States' social security systems, as Regulation 883/2004 merely coordinates, not harmonises. Hence the national social security systems remain, with their respective strengths and weaknesses. Therefore, it is up to the national legislator to amend its national system, should the outcome of EU coordination pose political challenges.[15]

Although all Member States agree on the importance of coordinating social security so as to support the free movement of persons, their eagerness might be less evident when it comes to social security benefits that involve far-reaching national social ambitions such as *hybrid benefits*.[16]

These hybrid benefits are social security benefits which have been instituted in order to meet specific national needs or to support particularly vulnerable groups in a society. It may be a question of providing income supplements,[17] topping up low guarantee pensions[18] or helping to defray increased living costs for people with disabilities.[19]

These benefits occupy the border zone between social assistance and classic, 'pure' social security benefits. They display elements of social assistance, inasmuch as they have been created in order to meet the special needs of vulnerable groups within the state in question. But they are social security benefits, insofar as they take the form of legally defined rights and are paid out without any individual assessment of need; however, they are non-contributory, that is, tax-financed, benefits. These social security benefits are tightly linked to the specific living conditions prevailing within the Member State and express the political will and idea of solidarity that form the foundation for a state.[20] Such hybrid benefits are not dependent on a work record; instead they reflect a universalist notion, according to which all the residents of a state can benefit from them based simply on residence.

Irrespective of their scent of social assistance, hybrid benefits continue to be governed by Regulation 883/2004.[21] Therefore, when persons falling under the scope of the Regulation move to another Member State, the equal treatment principle of Article 4 of the Regulation ensures that they are not treated worse than citizens of the Member State in question: that is, if nationals of said Member State are entitled to a hybrid benefit on the basis of residence, then

---

[15] For a further analysis of the sovereignty erosion and the possibilities of lessening the impact of such an erosion, see Jaan Paju, *The European Union and Social Security Law* (Hart, 2017).

[16] Regulation 883/2004 talks of special non-contributory cash benefits. I use here the less cumbersome 'hybrid benefits' that such benefits are also named.

[17] Case C-90/97 *Swaddling* EU:C:1999:96.

[18] Case C-160/02 *Skalka* EU:C:2004:269.

[19] Case C-299/05 *Commission v Parliament and Council* EU:C:2007:608.

[20] Cf. Kaarlo Tuori, 'European Social Constitution: Between Solidarity and Access Justice' in Kai Purnhagen and Peter Rott (eds), *Varieties of European Economic Law and Regulation, Liber Amicorum for Hans Micklitz* (Springer, 2014) 374 f.

[21] According to both the present and the former co-ordinating regulations, persons covered by the social security system of a Member State are entitled to social security benefits that fall within the scope of the Regulation, irrespective of whether they reside within the country in question or in another Member State. This was a sensitive issue with regard to the hybrid benefits and led to a derogation introduced by Regulation 1247/92 (Council Regulation (EEC) No 1247/92 of 30 April 1992 amending Regulation (EEC) No 1408/71 on the application of social security schemes to employed persons, to self-employed persons and to members of their families moving within the Community [1992] OJ L136), when a social security benefit is tightly linked to the specific living conditions prevailing within a given Member State, it can be registered as a hybrid benefit (a special non-contributory cash benefit) under Article 70 of the Regulation, and so may be restricted to being granted only within the borders of that Member State.

persons to whom the regulation applies – among them economically inactive Union citizens – are also to be entitled to it upon moving to said Member State. This fact clearly provokes and challenges the notion of solidarity, especially as social assistance can be made conditional upon a right of residence under Union law.

2.2 Parallel Tracks: Directive 2004/38 and Regulation 883/2004

The right of economically inactive Union citizens to reside in another Member State is conditional, in that Directive 2004/38 stipulates – in Article 7(1)(b) – that the right of residence can be made conditional on not becoming a burden on the social assistance system of the host Member State. The legislator has thus sought, through an exemption from the principle of equal treatment set out in Article 24 of the Directive, to balance the principle of free movement of persons against the desire of the Member States not to expose their social assistance systems to the demands of economically inactive Union citizens.

When it comes to the coordination of the Member States' social security systems, on the other hand, we find no corresponding balancing against the right of residence; instead the principle of equal treatment (Article 4) reigns in full.

As Regulation 883/2004 strengthened the freedom of movement for persons by extending the personal scope to all Union citizens who are or have been covered by the social security system of a Member State, economically inactive Union citizens are among those to whom the Regulation applies.

The Regulation states that, when residence has been established (Article 11(3)(e)), the right to residence-based benefits cannot be made subject to any right of residence as the principle of equal treatment applies in full, so that economically inactive Union citizens too may enjoy the right to residence-based social security benefits.

In this way the Regulation, with its aim of strengthening freedom of movement for persons, ends up in sharp conflict with the desire of the Member States to restrict access to social benefits (in its widest sense) by economically inactive Union citizens.[22]

3. THE COURT'S RULINGS

3.1 Introduction

Some years after the widening of the personal scope of Regulation 883/2004, the CJEU faced requests for preliminary rulings by referring Member State courts on the issue of balancing access to social benefits and the free movement of Union citizens. This case law will be dealt with chronologically as doing so follows a logical pattern.

3.2 Fifty Shades of *Brey*

In *Brey*, the Court defines hybrid benefits as a form of social assistance by introducing a legal definition of social assistance so broad as to include most of the benefits furnished by a welfare

---

[22] Cf. *Dano*, para 54.

state.[23] Hence, according to Directive 2004/38, access to hybrid benefits can be restricted, despite Regulation 883/2004 requiring equal treatment.

In the ruling, however, the Court disregards the fact that there are crucial differences between social assistance and social security.

Regulation 883/2004 is a legislative product with roots in the early twentieth century, where labour is the central question it addresses. Union citizenship, on the other hand, is a significantly more recent legal construction – and its essential nature is now less clear than ever – where the Court's case law has sought to balance the right of economically inactive Union citizens to reside in a Member State against the need of the host state to keep control over its social assistance system.[24]

As Union citizenship evolved through the Court's case law, the need to consolidate this evolution grew. Directive 2004/38 of 2004 codified the case law. At nearly the same time,[25] the modernisation of Regulation 1408/71 was achieved after 12 years of negotiations.[26] This modernisation, in the form of Regulation 883/2004, considers the evolution of Union citizenship by extending the personal scope covered by the Regulation to include all Union citizens who are or have been covered by the social security system of a Member State (Article 2(1)).[27]

With the expansion in late April 2004 of the personal scope covered under the Regulation, there were two relevant general instruments of EU law, Directive 2004/38 and Regulation 883/2004, in the area of social benefits.

They overlap in terms of the persons covered, and touch upon one another in terms of subject matter as both cover social benefits.

When legal instruments are tangent to each other, the European legislator has responded by introducing rules clarifying the relationship between them. Regulation 492/2011,[28] for example, includes such a clarification in connection with Regulation 883/2004 as the purpose of Regulation 492/2011, like that of Regulation 883/2004, is to strengthen the free movement of workers.[29] The relationship between Regulation 883/2004 and Regulation 492/2011 is governed by Article 36(2) of the latter, which assigns precedence to the former in areas where the two overlap; that is, Regulation 883/2004 is to be treated as lex specialis.[30] However, no such order of precedence governs the relationship between Regulation 883/2004 and Directive 2004/38.

---

[23] *Brey*, para 61.

[24] Niamh Nic Shuibhne, 'Limits Rising, Duties Ascending: The Changing Legal Shape of Union Citizenship' (2015) 52(4) CML Rev 889, 896 f.

[25] Regulation 883/2004 and Directive 2004/38 were enacted on 29 and 30 April 2004, respectively, only days ahead of the enlargement of the EU with ten new Member States, on 1 May 2004.

[26] The new Regulation was initiated at the European Council in Edinburgh 1992: Eberhard Eichenhofer, 'How to Simplify the Co-ordination of Social Security' (2000) EJSS 231, 232.

[27] See further, Proposal for a Council Regulation (EC) on coordination of social security [1999] C 38/08.

[28] Regulation (EU) No 492/2011 of the European Parliament and of the Council of 5 April 2011 on freedom of movement for workers within the Union [2011] OJ L 141.

[29] Cf. Peter Starup and Matthew J Elsmore, 'Taking a Logical Step Forward? Comment on Ibrahim and Teixeira' (2010) 35(4) EL Rev 571, 571.

[30] On this lex specialis, see Case C-206/10 *Commission v Germany* EU:C:2011:283, para 39.

It may seem strange that two major legislative projects within the Union that have strong points of contact have not been brought into line with one another.[31] Be that as it may, there are fundamental differences that cannot be ignored.

Social assistance involves various benefits to persons who cannot otherwise acquire – through wages, pensions, study stipends and the like – the means for maintaining a decent level of living. The social safety net kicks in when one cannot support oneself.

Social security benefits, by contrast, are based on the payment of social security contributions. They involve a collective arrangement whereby individuals, through paying contributions, become eligible to receive various state or state-regulated social security benefits, resembling insurance. These include pensions, parental benefit, sickness insurance and the like. Depending on historical context and the balance of political forces, social security systems have developed along various lines, of which two main types can be observed: a work-based system (the Bismarck model) and residence-based systems (the Beveridge and Nordic models). Residence-based social security, as its name indicates, is based on residence. It differs from work-based social security in that it aims at redistribution and involves a degree of solidarity vis-à-vis weaker groups.[32] But unlike tax-funded social assistance, it is not disbursed on the basis of means tests. It is instead an insurance-based arrangement with solidaristic elements.

Therefore, no matter how much one wishes it not to be the case, social assistance and social security differ, especially as hybrid benefits are to be registered as special non-contributive social security benefits (and thus being in fact recognised as social security benefits) in order not to be exported, as the general rule is with regard to social security benefits, to another Member State.[33]

Social security benefits cannot therefore be regarded as being social assistance, and thus are not capable of falling under Directive 2004/38.

3.3   *Dano et al.*

Irrespective of this fact, the CJEU's Grand Chamber confirmed this reasoning in *Dano*.[34]

In its request for a preliminary ruling, however, the German court underlined that the German benefit (*Grundsicherung*) was listed as a hybrid benefit, falling under Regulation 883/2004. It was therefore the task of the CJEU to advise in its preliminary ruling whether Article 4 of the Regulation, prescribing equal treatment, prevented the German legislator from distinguishing between German nationals and Union citizens in respect of their right to the benefit.[35]

To begin with, the Court confirms that the coordination called for in Regulation 883/2004 includes hybrid benefits, and that no derogation from the principle of equal treatment is in question with regard to these benefits.[36] The Court then stresses the centrality of the equal

---

[31] Herwig Verschueren, 'Free Movement or Benefit Tourism: the Unreasonable Burden of Brey' (2014) 16(2) Europea Journal of Migration and Law 66.
[32] Gøsta Esping-Andersen, *The Three Worlds of Welfare Capitalism* (Polity Press, 1990) 23 f.
[33] See further note 19.
[34] *Dano*.
[35] Ibid, para 45.
[36] Ibid paras 48–51.

treatment principle and cites the concordance of such an interpretation with the intent of the legislator[37] – namely that hybrid benefits are to be issued in the country of residence without discrimination on grounds of nationality.[38]

The Court thus appears to have set everything up for the conclusion that unlawful discrimination according to the Regulation has occurred, inasmuch as the national legislation in Germany subjects Union citizens resident in the country to more exacting requirements than was the case for German nationals.

However, the CJEU avoids this conclusion by instead reformulating the question asked by the German court[39] – which concerned the requirement of equal treatment set out in the Regulation – so as to allow for legitimate restrictions on said principle.[40]

This (sly) move enabled the CJEU to confirm *Brey* and to rule that, since hybrid benefits have been regarded as social assistance within the meaning of Directive 2004/38, Member States can, according to the Directive, distinguish between their own nationals and similarly situated Union citizens when it comes to granting them.

The Grand Chamber of the Court confirms this understanding of hybrid benefits in *Alimanovic*, stating that 'such [hybrid] benefits are also covered by the concept of "social assistance" within the meaning of Article 24(2) of Directive 2004/38'.[41]

The Court's Grand Chamber confirms this further in *García-Nieto*, where it states that hybrid benefits 'also constitute "social assistance" within the meaning of Article 24(2) of Directive 2004/38'.[42] The Grand Chamber ruling in *Jobcenter Krefeld* confirms this restrictive finding with regard to economically inactive Union citizens,[43] summing up, as case law has it, that hybrid benefits that fall under Regulation 883/2004 are to be considered as social assistance that in parallel falls under Directive 2004/38. This despite, as argued in section 3.2, serious flaws and shortcomings in the CJEU's argument.

3.4   *Commission v UK*: Reaching Out in Vain

In contrast to *Brey*, *Dano*, *Alimanovic*, *García-Nieto* and *Jobcenter Krefeld*, the case brought before the CJEU by the Commission in 2014 – *Commission v UK* – dealt with classic social security benefits (family benefits),[44] to which Directive 2004/38 does not apply as there is not even a reminiscence of social assistance.

---

[37] See Council Regulation (EEC) No 1247/92 of 30 April 1992 amending Regulation (EEC) No 1408/71 on the application of social security schemes to employed persons, to self-employed persons and to members of their families moving within the Community [1992] OJ L136 recital 7.
[38] *Dano*, paras 52–53.
[39] Ibid, para 56.
[40] Cf. Katarina Voss, 'But That's Not What I Asked! The Reformulation of Questions Asked in Preliminary Rulings' [2015] Europarättslig Tidskrift 939.
[41] *Alimanovic*, para. 44.
[42] *García-Nieto*, para 36.
[43] Case C-181/19, *Jobcenter Krefeld*, p.87.
[44] Classic 'pure' social security benefits in the sense falling under the material scope of the Regulation 883/2004, Article 3, as well as to a large extent being financed by social contributions and not taxes.

Regardless of that fact, the CJEU declared – only days ahead of the UK referendum on EU membership of 23 June 2016 – that Regulation 883/2004 in itself does not hinder discriminatory Member State legal requirements on access to residence-based social security benefits.

This outcome is not surprising, given the previous case law and the fact that the Court alluded to 'benefit tourism' at the beginning of its judgment, stating that Article 11(3)(e) could lead to residence-based family benefits being requested by 'in particular, economically inactive persons'.[45]

The key issue when analysing a case is whether a Court ruling can be regarded as, at least, rationally justifiable.[46] With regard to *Commission v UK* the answer is in the negative.

However, to start on a positive note, a welcome development is that the CJEU chose in *Commission v United Kingdom* to respect the essential material differences between Regulation 883/2004 and Directive 2004/38, which was, as seen above, not the case in *Brey*, *Dano*, *Alimanovic*, *García-Nieto* and *Jobcenter Krefeld*. As a result, the CJEU made its decision in the infringement case against the UK on the basis of the Regulation rather than the Directive.[47] By doing so the CJEU recognised that social security is based on a principle of contributions to that end, whereas social assistance is a tax-financed last resort. This distinction is important, since blending the two systems would have enabled Member States to circumvent Regulation 883/2004 and its non-discrimination principle in Article 4 by reference to Directive 2004/38 and its unreasonable burden test. By doing so there would have been no residence-based social security benefits left to co-ordinate.

Furthermore, the $64,000 (constitutional) question would have been whether a directive can prevail over a regulation, and if the directive could deprive those persons falling under the personal scope of Regulation 883/2004 of the right to free movement.

In the light of the CJEU's initial statement that residence-based social security systems are at risk, it is not surprising that the Court adopted a narrow textual interpretation of the Regulation's provisions on the scope of the applicable legislation. By doing so, the CJEU found that the Regulation's conflict rules merely point to the competent Member State, and therefore it is possible to supplement Article 11(3)(e) with material national eligibility requirements, such as requirements for a right to reside alongside the lines of Directive 2004/38.[48]

By doing so the Court, however, disregarded certain fundamentals.

One of the main aims of Regulation 883/2004 is to ensure that a person falling under its personal scope can be assured that, irrespective of where he or she resides, he or she will remain covered by a Member State's social security system. Nonetheless, as a result of the Court's judgment in *Commission v United Kingdom*, economically inactive Union citizens actually end up falling between two stools and the Regulation's aim – to protect those falling under the personal scope of the Regulation, not just economically active Union citizens – becomes a chimera.

---

[45] *Commission v UK*, para 63.

[46] Joxerramon Bengoetxea, Neil MacCormick and Leonor Moral Soriano, 'Integration and Integrity in the Legal Reasoning of the CJEU' in Grainne de Búrca and Joseph Weiler (eds), *The European Court of Justice* (OUP, 2001) 43.

[47] See also Mel Cousins, 'The Baseless Fabric of this Vision: EU Citizenship, the Right to Reside and EU Law' (2016) 23(2) Journal of Social Security Law 89.

[48] *Commission v UK*, paras 64–68.

4. STRIKING A BALANCE THAT RESPECTS REGULATION 883/2004

This ruling was appealing for the UK, but it did not have a decisive impact on the outcome of the Brexit referendum.[49] However, the question remains: has the ruling had a decisive impact on the future role of the coordination of social security? Another question to be considered, in light of the above analysis, is whether the CJEU could at the time have approached the challenge posed by *Brey* in a different way.

In answering the latter question, it is interesting to note that Regulation 883/2004 itself incorporates a balance between the principle of free movement and the need for the Member States to maintain economically sustainable systems.

Soon after the introduction of Regulation 883/2004 and its widened personal scope, the Member States expressed fears that, due to an increase in the number of persons covered, Union citizens would gain access to social security benefits by moving to another Member State. The upshot was a clarification of Regulation 883/2004 in the autumn of 2010, when recital 17a was introduced:[50] 'Once the legislation of a Member State becomes applicable to a person under Title II of this Regulation, the conditions for affiliation and entitlement to benefits should be defined by the legislation of the competent Member State [...]'.

This recital clarifies that EU law does not prevent Member States from introducing additional qualifying requirements for social security benefits (perhaps in particular those based on residence). Thus Article 11(3)(e) of the Regulation only determines, on the basis of stated residence, the competent Member State.

However, the second point in recital 17a states that this possibility may not be exploited in a manner contrary to Union law 'while respecting Community law'.

It may seem that we are back at square one. It must be borne in mind, however, that the equal treatment principle in EU law is not absolute. If a Member State can cite an objective justification for deviating from equal treatment, the CJEU may grant its approval.[51] Any such deviation must be proportionate, however. Therefore, once the Court has found such a justification to be present, an assessment of proportionality then follows, the purpose being to ascertain whether any less far-reaching deviation from equal treatment may be available for achieving the approved goal.

In the area of social security, the CJEU has previously accepted that German restrictions on the receipt of a certain benefit – one designed to encourage childbirth – have an objective justification.[52] Another consideration accepted by the Court as an objective justification is more topical in connection with the *Brey* saga: the importance of ensuring an economic balance of

---

[49] Still, the press did cover the ruling, although not extensively. See Oliver Wright, 'EU Court Backs Government's Right to Restrict Migrant Benefits' *Independent* (London, 14 June 2016); see also Alan Travis, 'EU Court Backs UK Limits on Migrants' Access to Child Benefits' *The Guardian* (London, 14 June 2016).

[50] Regulation (EC) No 988/2009 of the European Parliament and of the Council of 16 September 2009 amending Regulation (EC) No 883/2004 on the coordination of social security systems, and determining the content of its Annexes [2009] OJ L284/43.

[51] Catherine Barnard, *The Substantive Law of the EU: The Four Freedoms* (6th edn, OUP, 2019) 475 ff.

[52] Case C-213/05 *Geven* EU:C:2007:438.

the social security system.⁵³ This objective justification ground was at stake in the infringement proceedings *Commission v UK*.

However, it goes without saying that in order to be able to seek to safeguard economic sustainability, there must be a real threat to the national social security system.

Looking at relevant social security case law, the Court has not been impressed by the Member States' lines of argument on, and evidence of, a threat to their national systems. The Court held in *Kohll* that 'the risk of seriously undermining the financial balance of the social security system may constitute an overriding reason in the general interest capable of justifying a barrier of that kind'.⁵⁴ However, the Member State involved – Luxembourg – did not manage to prove this threat.⁵⁵ Member States have not, in any cross-border health care case,⁵⁶ managed to convince the Court that there would be serious economic disturbance as a result of a broadened right to cross-border health care.⁵⁷

The infringement ruling in *European Commission v Republic of Cyprus* confirms that a Member State can justify unequal treatment if it can prove that the treatment is motivated by ensuring economic balance in the national social security system.⁵⁸ However, this burden of proof demands 'an objective, detailed analysis, supported by figures'.⁵⁹

Given this, it is rather remarkable that the CJEU in *Commission v UK* entirely ignored its previous case law on the burden of proof,⁶⁰ and in the following proportionality test found, with a rather shallow analysis, the restriction in question to be proportionate.⁶¹ The UK could therefore require the right of residence for receipt of social security benefits which are based purely on residence.

In retrospect, and taking the ruling in *Commission v UK* into account, it would therefore have been possible, especially in *Dano* – where the status of the Regulation was the central issue in the questions put by the referring national court – for the CJEU to elaborate along objective justification arguments.

A take on objective justification – if taking such a justification test seriously – would respect the limits on the EU's competence in the area of social security. Further, it would be based on the principle of freedom of movement of persons rather than domestic politics of the Member States, inasmuch as the Member States would have to present well-substantiated macro-level threats to justify restrictions. Furthermore, it would avoid blurring the line between the two sharply different types of benefits: social assistance and social security benefits.

---

⁵³ Case C-158/96 *Kohll* EU:C:1998:171, para 41.
⁵⁴ Ibid.
⁵⁵ Ibid, para 42.
⁵⁶ See e.g. Case C-368/98 *Vanbraekel* EU:C:2001:400, para 51; Case C-157/99, *Smits Peerbooms* EU:C:2001:404, paras 104–105; Case C-385/99 *Müller-Fauré* EU:C:2003:270, para 92; Case C-372/04 *Watts* EU:C:2006:325, paras 75–77.
⁵⁷ Chris Newdick, 'Citizenship, Free Movement and Health Care: Cementing Individual Rights by Corroding Social Solidarity' (2006) 43(6) CML Rev 1645, 1660 f., see also Gareth Davies, 'Legislative Control of the European Court of Justice' (2014) 51(6) CML Rev 1579, 1602 ff.
⁵⁸ Case C-515/14 *European Commission v Republic of Cyprus* EU:C:2016:30, para 53.
⁵⁹ Ibid, para 54, see further Charlotte O'Brien, 'The ECJ Sacrifices EU Citizenship in Vain: Commission v. United Kingdom' (2017) 54(1) CML Rev 209, 230.
⁶⁰ Ibid 227 ff.
⁶¹ *Commission v UK*, paras 80 ff, For a thorough analysis of the objective justification reasoning: Jaan Paju, 'On the Lack of Reasoning in Case C-308/14, European Commission v United Kingdom' (2019) 48(1) Industrial Law Journal 29 ff.

As of December 2021, the confusion remains: does Directive 2004/38 also apply to Regulation 883/2004 despite its latter equal treatment principle with regard to all persons covered by the Regulation?

5. CONSEQUENCES FOR THE COORDINATION OF SOCIAL SECURITY BENEFITS

Residence-based social security models are based on a distributive concept with origins in the early 1900s – a period of poor public health but also ageing populations. Universal welfare systems enabled states to quickly reach the entire population, not just the working population.

Today's challenges for social security benefits are similar. To reach the population as a whole, a residence-based approach is the most suitable.

When systems that provide such universal benefits are faced with Union citizens eligible for rights without corresponding obligations, domestic political pressures arise to change the conditions whereby economically inactive citizens are eligible for social benefits.[62] However, by doing so, the systems are no longer universal.

As *Brey*, *Dano*, *Alimanovic*, *García-Nieto* and *Jobcenter Krefeld* make clear, Member States may restrict the personal scope covered by Regulation 883/2004 to migrant workers as far as hybrid benefits are concerned. Thus, when Directive 2004/38 provides for deviating from equal treatment, the principle of equal treatment set out in Regulation 883/2004 loses its force for the economically inactive Union citizens covered by the Regulation.

Member States are thereby free to establish a 'virtual' territoriality within their borders and to exclusively restrict residence-based hybrid benefits to their own nationals (and to migrant workers who pay social security contributions).[63]

The same seems to be possible, as discussed above in section 3.4, with regard to classic social security benefits, as indicated in *Commission v UK*.

Considering the case law, the Commission proposed an amendment to the equal treatment principle in Article 4 of Regulation 883/2004 by introducing an option for Member States to require legal residence as set out in Directive 2004/38 before granting residence-based social security benefits.[64] Interestingly, the Council negotiation position of 21 June 2018 entails no amendment to Article 4, merely a proposal to add a new recital, which is of no normative character. This suggests that the Council was unwilling to challenge the primary law equal treatment principle, as well as showing an understanding of the underlying logic to Regulation 883/2004, since equal treatment is the key to coordination leaving the Member States' systems untouched. This was still the position of the Council when it presented a final compromise

---

[62] Cf. Stefano Giubboni, 'A Certain Degree of Solidarity? Free Movement of Persons and Access to Social Protection in the Case Law of the CJEU' in Malcolm Ross and Yuri Borgmann-Prebil (eds), *Promoting Solidarity in the European Union* (OUP, 2010), Kay Hailbronner, 'Union Citizenship and Access to Social Benefits' (2005) 42(5) CML Rev 1245.

[63] Migrating workers enjoy a right of residence as of day one, being economically active: Article 7(1)(a), Directive 2004/38.

[64] Proposal for a Regulation of the European Parliament and of the Council amending Regulation (EC) No 883/2004 on the coordination of social security systems and regulation (EC) No 987/2009 laying down the procedure for implementing Regulation (EC) No 883/2004, [2018] 10295/18, 2016/0397 (COD).

text with a view to reaching a first-reading agreement with the European Parliament in March 2019.[65]

The negotiations are cumbersome and complex and there is no indication of when they are likely to come to an end.[66] At this stage, there is no point in speculating on the outcome of the negotiations – it is not over until the fat lady sings.

6. CONCLUSIONS

The national welfare models reflect solidarity based in shared values and a common history and identity.[67] The legislation embodying this solidarity is therefore generally territorial in scope.[68] Solidarity with the neediest is based, inasmuch as the persons concerned have no substantial work record, on residence.[69]

As a result of the Regulation's extension of the circle of persons covered to a majority of Union citizens in 2004, a new category of persons could now obtain hybrid benefits on the basis of residence. This, in combination with the principle of equal treatment enunciated in the Regulation, had results that were unexpected (and undesired): economically inactive Union citizens are eligible for social security benefits when moving to a Member State with residence-based social security benefits.[70]

Aware of the national challenges this presented, the Court designed a bridge between Regulation 883/2004 and the Directive 2004/38 in *Brey*, allowing Member States to require a right of residence before granting hybrid benefits to the persons concerned. The Court then took the same approach in *Dano*, and confirmed it in *Alimanovic*, *García-Nieto* and, in late 2020, *Jobcenter Krefeld*. Furthermore, the Court held in *Commission v UK* that additional national requirements were possible with regard to classic social security benefits as the Regulation merely coordinates the systems.

---

[65] Proposal for a Regulation of the European Parliament and of the Council amending Regulation (EC) No 883/2004 on the coordination of social security systems and regulation (EC) No 987/2009 laying down the procedure for implementing Regulation (EC) No 883/2004, [2019] 7698/19, 2016/0397(COD). At the time of writing there are no further official negotiation positions available.

[66] EU Social security coordination https://ec.europa.eu/social/main.jsp?catId=849&langId=en; see also L&E Global, 'EU: Revision of Regulation 883/2004 on the coordination of social security postponed to the next legislature', https://knowledge.leglobal.org/european-union-revision-of-regulation-883-2004-on-the-coordination-of-social-security-postponed-to-the-next-legislature/ both accessed 30 November 2021.

[67] Kaarlo Tuori, 'European Social Constitution: Between Solidarity and Access Justice' in Kai Purnhagen and Peter Rott (eds), *Varieties of European Economic Law and Regulation: Liber Amicorum for Hans Micklitz* (Springer, 2014) 374 f.

[68] Cf Pieters' Circles of Solidarity being based on territoriality: Danny Pieters, *Social Security: An Introduction to the Basic Principles* (2nd edn, Kluwer, 2006) 21.

[69] Gøsta Esping-Andersen, *The Three Worlds of Welfare Capitalism* (Polity Press, 1990) 27 f.

[70] On solidarity, transnational solidarity and its outer boundaries see Dagmar Schiek, 'Perspectives on Social Citizenship in the EU – from Status Positivus to Status Socialis Activus via Two Forms of Transnational Solidarity' in Dimitry Kochenov (ed.), *EU Citizenship and Federalism: The Role of Rights* (CUP, 2016) and Niamh Nic Shuibhne, 'Limits Rising, Duties Ascending: The Changing Legal Shape of Union Citizenship' (2015) 52(4) CML Rev 889.

However, the CJEU's legal reasoning does not consider that social assistance and social security have different underlying aims. Furthermore, the purpose of the Regulation is to strengthen free movement for the persons covered by its personal scope.

Since the legislative competence of the EU in social policy is limited,[71] the welfare systems of the Member States differ – as do their outcomes (even if this can seem 'unjust'). While it is true that the Regulation's rules determining the applicable legislation only point out which state is the competent one, this does not mean Member States can impose further qualifying requirements that fail to observe the principle of equal treatment set out in EU law.

In sum, the bridge built by the CJEU between Regulation 883/2004 and Directive 2004/38 shows such flaws that it is hard to speak of a well-founded change or at least a rationally justifiable change. This is especially true since Regulation 883/2004 does allow for balancing the principle of free movement against the Member States' concern regarding increased costs for social security should the number of economically inactive Union citizens within their borders increase. This objective justification was at stake in *Commission v UK*. However, the CJEU did not delve into any advanced legal reasoning, instead simply declaring the UK position as good law.

The shift of perspective from the *homo europaeus* back to the original *homo economicus* can, as discussed above in section 5, also be seen in the Commission's proposal to amend the equal treatment principle in Article 4. However, the Council negotiation position is not as far-reaching, merely proposing to include a referral to the case law in a new recital.

Still, it is undoubtedly the case that the encounter with Regulation 883/2004 potentially threatens[72] to undermine the fundamental values and welfare structures of the Member States: what had been universal welfare social security benefits are now denied to economically inactive Union citizens, as national solidarity appears to have reached an outer limit.

Current case law implies that economically inactive Union citizens residing in a Member State, being unable to apply for social security benefits, end up in a grey zone whereby they can live in the Member State in question but have no substantive rights within it.

This inevitably leads to the question – one needing an answer – of where the emphasis in Article 3(3) TEU on a 'social market economy' is to be placed. My contribution suggests that the strengthening of the right to social security benefits that resulted from Regulation 883/2004 – with its expansion of the personal scope – has been curtailed by case law, and that the emphasis is seemingly less on 'social' than on 'market'.

It is obvious that we face challenges with regard to the quest for transnational solidarity. De Witte has proposed that we detach welfare provisions from nation-states and instead consider such questions from a more rational and overarching standpoint, where affiliation with a nation-state no longer constitutes the sole basis for eligibility.[73]

However, contradictory interests are in play here which are hard to reconcile: the Member States' understanding of coordination is limited by the idea of state sovereignty, with domestic

---

[71] Cf. Articles 151, 153 and 156 TFEU.
[72] I write potentially, as the total cost for eligible Union citizens at the time of the ruling in *Brey* was 3.5 million euros out of a total 960 million euros for the specific Austrian social security benefit. Cf. Benedikt Kommenda, 'Urteil: Hürde für Erhalt von Sozialgeld zu hoch' *Die Presse* (Vienna, 19 September 2013).
[73] Florian de Witte, *Justice in the EU: The Emergence of Transnational Solidarity* (OUP, 2015) 214 f.

solidarity applying within an agreed economic framework; by contrast, the EU sees coordination as based on the idea of opening up the territorially based systems of the Member States to an enhanced freedom of movement for persons. This freedom of movement presupposes, however, a transnational solidarity financed by the respective (host) Member States.

Regardless of these standpoints, the right to freedom of movement for all Union citizens remains, and we will continue to see economically inactive Union citizens make their way to other Member States in search of means of subsistence. The question of what solidarity the Member States are prepared to show the most vulnerable members of our societies thus persists, irrespective of the evolution of case law or any new legislation that might be introduced.

Rather, the question is what the EU will do to respect Article 3(3) TFEU and combat social exclusion. Legal arguing does not suffice as the EU's competence is limited when it comes to social security: Article 151 and Article 153 TFEU only give supplementary competences. Hence, since its introduction back in 1958 the Regulation has only ever been merely an instrument for enhancing free movement for workers rather than harmonising the Member States' social security systems, as regulated by Article 45 and Article 48 TFEU. The odd exception is, as this contribution discusses, the widening of the latest personal scope in 2004 to nearly all Union citizens, thus (rather unexpectedly) shedding light on the outer boundaries of transnational solidarity with regard to the national social security systems. As seen in *Brey, Dano, Alimanovic, García-Nieto, Commission v UK* and the Grand Chamber ruling *Jobcenter Krefeld* in late 2020, the outer boundaries are narrower than one could expect from the legislation. In the light of this, the question is whether there is a political will to extend the solidarity? We must wait to see the outcome of the ongoing negotiations on amending Regulation 883/2004.

PART IV

EU CITIZENSHIP POST-BREXIT: DIFFERENTIATED CITIZENSHIP REVISITED

18. Differentiated citizenship in the European Economic Area

Christian Franklin and Halvard Haukeland Fredriksen[1]

1. INTRODUCTION

The aim of this chapter is to analyse the scope and content of substantive citizen rights under the Agreement on the European Economic Area (EEA),[2] and to illustrate how these differ from those which apply under EU law. The starting point for the analysis is the by now generally accepted view that the EEA Agreement, within its scope, puts the three participating EFTA States (Iceland, Liechtenstein and Norway[3]) 'on the same footing as Member States of the European Union'.[4] In its Grand Chamber ruling *I.N.*, the ECJ stated that the EEA Agreement reaffirms 'the special relationship between the European Union, its Member States and the EFTA States, which is based on proximity, long-standing common values and European identity'.[5] It is in the light of that special relationship that the principal objective of the EEA Agreement must be understood – 'to provide for the fullest possible realisation of the free movement of goods, persons, services and capital within the whole EEA, so that the internal market established within the European Union is extended to the EFTA States'.[6] In *I.N.*, the ECJ noted that the EEA/EFTA States (in this case Iceland) are also associated to, for example, the Schengen *acquis*, thereby establishing a special relationship 'which goes beyond economic and commercial cooperation'.[7] In a remarkable statement, the Grand Chamber added that the combination of the EEA Agreement and the association to the Schengen *acquis* rendered the situation of the Icelandic citizen in question 'objectively comparable with that of an EU citizen to whom, in accordance with Article 3(2) TEU, the Union offers an area of freedom, security and justice without internal frontiers, in which the free movement of persons is ensured'.[8]

---

[1] Thanks to research assistant Fredrik Vingsnes for help with formatting and referencing.
[2] Agreement on the European Economic Area (EEA) [1994] OJ L1/3. For a general introduction, see Halvard Haukeland Fredriksen and Christian NK Franklin, 'Of Pragmatism and Principles: The EEA Agreement 20 Years On' (2015) 52(3) CML Rev 629.
[3] The fourth remaining EFTA State, Switzerland, is not a party to the EEA Agreement. For more on Swiss–EU relations, particularly in the field of free movement of persons, see Narin Idriz and Christa Tobler, 'Citizenship of the Association: The Examples of Turkey and Switzerland', Chapter 19 in this book.
[4] Case C-81/13 *UK v Council* EU:C:2014:2449, para 59 (differentiating the EEA Agreement from the EEC-Turkey Association Agreement). For a similar differentiation of the EEA from the 'route of bilateral arrangements' between Switzerland and the EU, see e.g. Case C-351/08 *Grimme* EU:C:2009: 697, para 27.
[5] Case C-897/19 *PPU (Ruska Federacija v I.N.)* EU:C:2020:262, para 50.
[6] Ibid. The origin of this very 'EEA-friendly' approach is to be found in the, for the EEA, seminal Case C-452/01 *Ospelt* EU:C:2003:493, para 29.
[7] *I.N.*, para 44.
[8] *I.N.*, para 58.

Still, in the field of free movement of persons, there exists a quite fundamental difference between the EU and the EEA legal framework: there are no provisions in the EEA Agreement corresponding to Arts 20–25 TFEU on EU citizenship! As explained in no uncertain terms by the Contracting Parties in a Joint Declaration from 2007, '[t]he concept of Union Citizenship [...] has no equivalent in the EEA Agreement'.[9] At the same time, however, the EEA/EFTA States agreed to incorporate Directive 2004/38 on the right of citizens of the Union and their family members to move and reside freely within the territory of the Member States into the EEA Agreement without any substantial adaptations.[10] Unsurprisingly, this rather peculiar political compromise – full incorporation of the Citizenship Directive without any recognition of the underlying concept of Union citizenship – has left the EFTA Court, in particular, with several hard cases.

In those cases, as will be demonstrated below, the EFTA Court has done its utmost to 'remedy' the lack of an EEA parallel to Art. 21 TFEU through dynamic interpretation of the Citizenship Directive. Controversies have ensued, particularly in cases concerning the rights of economically inactive persons to return to their home EEA/EFTA State with accompanying family members from third countries. The Norwegian government has accused the EFTA Court of judicial law-making in breach of recognised methods of interpretation of EEA law, and thus with violating the principles of legality, separation of powers and legal certainty, and even the rule of law![11] The European Commission, on the other hand, has lauded the EFTA Court for taking proper account of the context of the EEA Agreement when interpreting the Directive, arguing that any other approach would have resulted in a situation whereby free movement of persons could not be exercised within the EEA under the same conditions as within the EU, which would 'undoubtedly undermine the development of the association and the realisation of the objectives pursued by the EEA Agreement'.[12]

The latest development in the saga came with the EFTA Court's recent advisory opinion in *Campbell*.[13] Here the Court not only stood its ground concerning the interpretation of the Citizenship Directive, but also paraphrased the ECJ case-law to the effect that the freedom of movement for workers, as enshrined in Art. 28 EEA/Art. 45 TFEU, is (only) 'a specific expression of the general right to move and reside freely within the EEA'.[14] The opinion says nothing about the legal basis for this general right to free movement, which in the context of EU law of course is to be found in Arts 20 and 21 TFEU. However, based on the EFTA Court's approach in other cases, the Court seems poised to reveal a general, unwritten EEA law principle of free movement, deduced from the various provisions in the Main Part of the Agreement on the free movement of workers, self-employed and service providers and recipients; the many EU legal acts in the annexes concerning free movement of other categories of people;

---

[9] Joint declaration by the EEA Contracting Parties to Decision no. 158/2007 incorporating Directive 2004/38/EC into the EEA Agreement.

[10] Decision of the EEA Joint Committee No 158/2007.

[11] See the truly remarkable written observations of the Norwegian government in Case E-4/19 *Campbell* [2020] (nyr), as they are reproduced in the Report for the Hearing, paras 47–53 (available at https://eftacourt.int/cases/e-4-19/).

[12] Written observations of the Commission in Case E-4/19 *Campbell* [2020], as reproduced in the Report for the Hearing, ibid. para 105.

[13] Ibid. paras 48 and 58.

[14] Case C-457/12 *S. and G.* EU:C:2014:136, para 45.

the Citizenship Directive; and, more generally, 'the stated purposes and the legal structure of the EEA Agreement'.[15]

In the following, we will focus on the tensions within the EEA brought about by the decision of the Contracting Parties to incorporate the Citizenship Directive without the underlying concept of Union citizenship. In order not to leave the reader with the wrong impression as to the functionality of the EEA Agreement, however, it must be stressed that the controversies to date have largely been limited to matters where ECJ case-law builds directly on Arts 20 and 21 TFEU. There is by now agreement in EEA literature that the Citizenship Directive gives nationals of the EEA/EFTA States at least the same rights as it gives to EU citizens within the context of EU law. Furthermore, for workers, self-employed persons, providers or recipients of services and other economically active persons protected by provisions of the TFEU that are reproduced in the Main Part of the EEA Agreement, the general rule is certainly that their rights within the EEA are, in law and in fact, the same as within the EU.

Also quite uncontroversial is the status of political rights affiliated with the concept of EU citizenship, but for very different reasons: The Contracting Parties have made very clear that the EEA Agreement does not provide a legal basis for political rights of EEA nationals.[16] The only way in which such rights can be acquired by EFTA State nationals is by the acquisition of nationality of one of the 27 EU Member States, or the accession of that person's State of nationality to the EU itself.[17] The clearest point of differentiation between EU and EEA law in this particular field is therefore to be found in the lack of EEA parallels to the political rights stipulated in Arts 20–25 TFEU.

2. HISTORICAL CONTEXT: THE WIDENING GAP BETWEEN THE EU TREATIES AND THE EEA AGREEMENT

The Treaty of Maastricht's introduction of the concept of EU citizenship has over time transformed EU Member State nationals into true stakeholders of the EU polity through a rather unique fusion of legal and political rights and duties, as spelt out in the EU Treaties and further detailed in several secondary measures. First and foremost of the substantive rights enjoyed by all EU citizens under the EU Treaties today is the right of free movement and residence within the territory of the EU Member States set out in Arts 20 and 21 TFEU.

Despite early claims that it constituted a mere public relations exercise,[18] and notwithstanding the considerable time-lapse before its true exploitation by the ECJ in practice, the impact

---

[15] This is the phrase used in Case E-9/97 *Sveinbjörnsdóttir* [1998] EFTA Ct. Rep. 95, para 47, where the Court deduced an unwritten principle of State liability from the purposes and structure of the Agreement. For other examples of unwritten general principles being deduced in similar ways, see section 3 below.

[16] Joint declaration by the EEA Contracting Parties to Decision no. 158/2007. The lack of political rights appears to be the reason why the EEA Joint Committee decided that, for the purposes of the Agreement, the words 'Union citizen(s)' shall be replaced by the words 'national(s) of EC Member States and EFTA States', thus avoiding the term 'EEA citizens' ('EEA citizenship').

[17] See Elspeth Guild, 'EU Citizenship' in Dennis Patterson and Anna Södersten (eds), *A Companion to European Union Law and International Law* (Wiley 2016) 491.

[18] Joseph Weiler, 'Citizenship and Human Rights' in Jan Winter and others (eds), *Reforming the Treaty on European Union: The Legal Debate* (Kluwer 1996) 57.

that EU citizenship has had on rights of free movement and residence under EU law can hardly be understated. Although the link to some form of economic activity as a prerequisite for enjoying free movement had been effectively severed by secondary law a few years earlier, the introduction of citizenship at Treaty level in 1993 proved the final nail in that particular coffin.[19] Rights of free movement and residence could henceforth be enjoyed by all economically inactive persons not covered by other EU provisions on the basis of Art. 21 TFEU. And while it may be easy to forget that this particular strand of EU citizenship actually grew from more specific rights of free movement, today all EU rights of free movement and residence are instead said to stem from Art. 21 TFEU.[20]

Viewed superficially, the differences between EU citizenship rights and rights of EEA nationals under the EEA Agreement might indeed seem numerous. As highlighted in the introduction, no concept of 'EEA citizenship' is spelt out in the Main Part of the EEA Agreement. Given that formal negotiations on the Maastricht Treaty and the EEA Agreement were being conducted at the same time (from 1990 to 1992), and the Treaty was signed several months before signatures were (finally) attached to the EEA Agreement, the Contracting Parties to the EEA Agreement were surely all well aware of the imminent arrival of EU citizenship. The fact that the drafters of the EEA Agreement chose to not include any mention of citizenship – neither in the Main Part of the Agreement nor in its Preamble – is therefore not insignificant in itself. This is especially so given the drafters' foresight in including certain other amendments which were being introduced by the Treaty of Maastricht.[21]

At the same time, however, the whole point of the EEA is to allow the participating EFTA States not only access to, but – within the scope of the Agreement – full participation in the EU's internal market, without having to lend as much sovereignty as full EU membership would entail.[22] Rights of free movement have played a central role in the creation and devel-

---

[19] Council Directive 90/364 of 28 June 1990 on the right of residence, according to which any national of a Member State with sufficient resources and health insurance coverage may reside in another Member State [1990] OJ L180/26.

[20] According to the ECJ, the Treaty provisions on workers (Art. 45 TFEU), self-employed persons (Art. 49 TFEU) and services (Art. 56 TFEU) are all to be viewed as mere and 'more specific expressions of this right'. See e.g. Case C-233/12 *Gardella* EU:C:2013:449, para 38; and *S. and G.*, para 45.

[21] See e.g. Art. 29 EEA on social security, which includes an express reference to both workers and self-employed persons. The latter was not found in previous versions of the EC Treaties (Art. 42 EC), but was added following the Treaty of Maastricht (what is now Art. 48 TFEU). Further examples of the EEA Contracting Parties anticipating the entry into force of the Maastricht Treaty are found in important statements in the preamble concerning, for example, human rights and the social dimension of the internal market: see further Finn Arnesen and Halvard Haukeland Fredriksen, 'Preamble' in Finn Arnesen and others (eds), *Agreement on the European Economic Area: A Commentary*, (C.H./Beck/Hart/Nomos/Universitetsforlaget 2017) para 3. Still, it needs to be taken into account that the text of the EEA Agreement was agreed upon already in October 1991, whereas the drafting of the Maastricht Treaty was only concluded by the European Council on 9–10 December that year (signed on 7 February 1992). It is perhaps not surprising that the willingness of the EEA Contracting Parties to anticipate the final version and entry into force of the Maastricht Treaty at the very last minute of the EEA negotiations was limited to certain rather uncontroversial statements already supported by established ECJ case-law.

[22] Awareness of the à la carte element of the EEA enshrined in the Agreement's scope is paramount to any attempt to understand why the EEA/EFTA States accept the obvious democratic shortcomings of the Agreement as such: the EEA Agreement gives them full access to the internal market and at the same time allows for far-reaching exemptions when it comes to particularly sensitive fields such as agriculture and fisheries. For Liechtenstein, considerable limitations on the right of free movement of nationals from

opment of the EU, and therefore also constitute a cornerstone of EEA cooperation. The EC Treaty rules as they then stood on workers, establishment and services are reproduced verbatim in the text of the Main Part of the EEA Agreement.[23] Social security rights ancillary to the free movement of persons are also included (Art. 29 EEA), mirroring the content of what is now Art. 48 TFEU.

Since the Main Part of the EEA Agreement has not been revised since its signature in 1992, however, none of the many amendments the EC/EU Treaties introduced by the Treaties of Nice, Amsterdam or Lisbon are reflected in it. The differing objectives of EU and EEA cooperation have therefore been laid rather bare over time: unlike the EU's objective of securing an 'ever closer union between the peoples of Europe', the EEA was designed to be more limited to elements primarily connected to economic integration.[24] While the concept of citizenship signifies the EU's commitment to resist the classification of its beneficiaries on the basis of economic activity, the long-held view of the EEA/EFTA States has been that the link between economic activity and free movement still prevails as a matter of EEA law. Rights of economically inactive persons to move to and from the EEA/EFTA States should generally be viewed as a matter of national immigration policy, and therefore as outside the remit of EEA law.[25]

The fact that the Main Part of the EEA Agreement has been able to remain in stasis for more than 25 years is explained by the dynamism of EEA law secured by the mechanism for incorporating new EU secondary measures into the EEA Agreement's Annexes. The consensus-based decision-making procedure set out in Art. 102 EEA allows the EEA Joint Committee, as the body responsible for ensuring the effective implementation and operation of the Agreement, to make decisions on the incorporation of EEA-relevant EU legal acts into EEA law. Crucial to acceptance of the mechanism in the dualist EEA/EFTA States of Iceland and Norway, the EEA Joint Committee's decisions must then in turn be made part of national law.[26] This allows EEA law to keep more or less up to speed with legislative developments in the EU internal market, while at the same time preserving the formal legislative sovereignty of the EEA/EFTA States.

Many important EU secondary measures concerned with facilitating the free movement of various categories of persons were included in the Annexes to the EEA Agreement from its

---

other EEA states are an important part of this (see further section 7 below); the same is not the case for Iceland and Norway.

[23] Arts. 28, 31 and 36 EEA.

[24] As recalled in several of the Preamble recitals, and highlighted in Art. 1(1) EEA, the aim of the Agreement is to 'promote a continuous and balanced strengthening of trade and economic relations between the Contracting Parties with equal conditions of competition, and the respect of the same rules'.

[25] See, e.g., Johanna Jonsdottir, *Europeanization and the European Economic Area* (Routledge 2013) 107, explaining Iceland's and Liechtenstein's scepticism towards the Citizenship Directive.

[26] Art. 7 EEA, as interpreted by Iceland and Norway and (tacitly) recognised by the EU Commission ever since the entry into force of the Agreement. The ECJ caused quite a stir in the EEA legal community when it suggested in passing in Case C-431/11 *UK v Council* EU:C:2013:589, para 54 and Case C-83/13 *Fonnship* EU:C:2014:2053, para 24, that regulations are directly applicable in the national legal orders of (all of) the EEA states by virtue of Art. 7 EEA, but the EFTA Court quickly reassured the dualist EEA/EFTA States that this is not the case, see, e.g., Case E-15/14 *ESA v Iceland* [2015] EFTA Ct. Rep. 40, para 32. As the EU side has not pursued the matter in the EEA Joint Committee, the EFTA Court's stand is essentially the last word on the matter.

entry into force, such as the Workers Regulation,[27] the Social Security Regulation,[28] various directives providing for the recognition of professional qualifications[29] and several directives providing rights of free movement and residence for specific categories of persons (students, retirees and economically inactive persons).[30] Other secondary measures have been added over time, such as for example the Services Directive,[31] the 'new' Social Security Regulation,[32] the Recognition of Professional Qualifications Directive[33] and – as already mentioned in the introduction – the Citizenship Directive.[34]

The adoption of new secondary EU measures has allowed the scope of the EEA Agreement to be adapted and expanded over time, thereby considerably reducing the potential nexus between the EU and EEA legal spheres. Importantly, unlike in the hierarchical EU legal system, the legal bases of free movement and residence rights are not limited to the provisions of the Main Part of the EEA Agreement – they may also stem directly from EC/EU regulations and directives incorporated into the Agreement.[35] A fitting example is provided by the situation as regards retirees and economically inactive persons. From the very outset of EEA cooperation, both of these categories of persons have enjoyed specific rights of free movement and residence stemming directly from former EC directives incorporated into the EEA Agreement, completely untraceable to any provisions in the Main Part of the EEA Agreement.

---

[27] Regulation (EEC) 1612/68 of 15 October 1968 on freedom of movement for workers within the Community [1968] OJ L257/2; Regulation (EU) No 492/2011 of 5 April 2011 on freedom of movement for workers within the Union [2011] OJ L141/1.

[28] Regulation (EEC) 1408/71 of 14 June 1971 on the application of social security schemes to employed persons and their families moving within the Community [1971] OJ L149/2.

[29] E.g. Council Directive 77/452 of 27 June 1977 concerning formal qualifications of nurses [1977] OJ L176/1; Council Directive 78/686 of 25 July 1978 concerning formal qualifications of practitioners of dentistry [1978] OJ L233/1; Council Directive 78/1026 of 18 December 1978 concerning formal qualifications in veterinary medicine [1978] OJ L362/1; Council Directive 89/48 of 21 December 1988 on a general system for the recognition of higher-education diplomas [1988] OJ L19/16.

[30] Council Directive 93/96 of 29 October 1993 on the right of residence for students [1993] OJ L317/59; Council Directive 90/365 of 18 June 1990 on the right of residence for employees and self-employed persons who have ceased their occupational activity [1990] OJ L180/28; Council Directive 90/364 of 28 June 1990 on the right of residence [1990] OJ L180/26.

[31] Directive 2006/123 of the European Parliament and of the Council of 12 September 2006 on services in the internal market [2006] OJ L376/36.

[32] Regulation 883/2004 of the European Parliament and of the Council of 29 April 2004 on the coordination of social security systems [2004] OJ L166/1.

[33] Directive 2005/36 of 7 September 2005 on the recognition of professional qualifications [2005] OJ L255/22.

[34] Directive 2004/38 of the European Parliament and of the Council of 29 April 2004 on the right of citizens of the Union and their family members to move and reside freely within the territory of the Member States [2004] OJ L158/77.

[35] See Christian NK Franklin, 'Pride and Prejudice: Some Reflections on the (In)discretionary Application of Fundamental Freedoms by Norwegian Courts' in Andreas T. Müller and Werner Schroeder (eds), *25 Jahre Europäischer Wirtschaftsraum* (2020) 1 Europarecht 225, 243. According to Art. 119 EEA, the Annexes and the EU legal acts referred to therein (as adapted for the purposes of the EEA) 'shall form an integral part of this Agreement'. Thus, there is no formal hierarchy between the provisions found in the Main Part of the EEA Agreement and the EU legal acts referred to in the annexes.

3. THE HOMOGENEITY PRINCIPLE AS THE 'GLUE'

Keeping pace with developments under EU law can nevertheless not be ensured by simply including the same rules in the EEA Agreement. In order to secure 'a homogeneous European Economic Area' (Art. 1 EEA), the rules have to be understood and applied in the same way, or at the very least lead to the same results. Crucial to the success of the EEA Agreement in practice is therefore the objective of the Contracting Parties to arrive at, and maintain, a uniform interpretation and application of EEA rules and corresponding EU rules – generally referred to in EEA parlance as the principle of homogeneity.[36]

At its most basic level, as indicated several places in the wording of the EEA Agreement itself, the principle of homogeneity requires provisions of the EEA Agreement that are taken over from EU law to be interpreted and applied in the same way, with deference to their understanding as a matter of EU law.[37] The EFTA Court has invariably given rather short shrift to any attempts by the EEA/EFTA State authorities to argue for a more 'State friendly' interpretation of such provisions of the EEA Agreement than the ECJ's interpretation of the corresponding provisions of EU law.[38] Crucially for the success of the EEA, so have the EU Courts in cases where parties appearing before them have argued for interpretations of EEA rules diverging from their EU law counterparts.[39]

Fairly early in the history of the EEA, however, both the EFTA Court and the ECJ were confronted with cases of treaty changes on the EU side not being reflected in the Main Part of the EEA Agreement. After some initial hesitation, the EFTA Court opted for a broad understanding of the homogeneity principle, allowing it to engage in dynamic interpretation of the Agreement in order to bridge the gaps that had appeared.[40] Crucially, the ECJ was convinced to do the same.[41] Justification was found in the object and purpose of the EEA project, coupled with the fact that the reasons for the lack of an 'update' of the Main Part of the EEA Agreement were of a practical nature only.[42] Although the undertaking gave rise to some academic debate, the Contracting Parties themselves appeared quite pleased with the fact that the courts relieved them from the strenuous work of updating the Main Part of the Agreement. As far as the EEA/EFTA States were concerned, a principled approach to the matter was (and still is) difficult to ascertain. Before the EFTA Court they have sometimes argued for an interpretation of EEA

---

[36] Whether or not uniformity and homogeneity under EU and EEA law are wholly synonymous or a particular means for differentiating between the two legal systems in itself may nevertheless be debated. See e.g. Christian N K Franklin, Ólafur Ísberg Hannesson, Ómar Berg Rúnarsson, Georges Baur and Enya Steiner, 'Norway (including Iceland & Liechtenstein)' in Marleen R Botman (ed.) *National Courts and the Enforcement of EU Law: The Pivotal Role of National Courts in the EU Legal Order* (Eleven International Publishing 2020) 337–82.

[37] Arts 1, 6 and 105 EEA, and e.g. recitals 4 and 15 of the EEA Agreement's Preamble.

[38] See in detail Halvard Haukeland Fredriksen, 'The EFTA Court 15 Years On' (2010) 59 ICLQ 740.

[39] See, in particular, the judgment of the (then) Court of First Instance in Case T-115/94 *Opel Austria* EU:T:1998:166, rejecting pleas by the Council and the Commission(!) for a diverging interpretation of Art. 10 EEA and Art. 12 TEC (now: Art. 30 TFEU).

[40] See in detail Halvard Haukeland Fredriksen, 'Bridging the Widening Gap between the EU Treaties and the Agreement on the European Economic Area' (2010) 18 European Law Journal 868-886.

[41] The seminal case is C-452/01 *Ospelt* EU:C:2003:493, where the ECJ interpreted Art. 40 EEA on the free movement of capital in line with its own interpretation of Art. 56 TEC (now: Art. 64 TFEU), despite the fact that the latter provision had been amended by the Maastricht Treaty.

[42] See Halvard Haukeland Fredriksen (n 40) 877 ff., with further references.

law in light of subsequent amendments to the EU Treaties and at other times warned against this, depending on the desired outcome of the specific case.[43] At the same time, initiatives for an update of the Main Part of the Agreement appear to have been put aside.

In parallel, the EFTA Court has also broadened the scope of homogeneity to include the thorny issue of the effect of EEA law in the legal orders of the dualist EEA/EFTA States. In the seminal *Sveinbjörnsdóttir* case, the principle of homogeneity was instrumental in the deduction of an unwritten principle of State liability akin to that found under EU law.[44] Again, crucial support followed from the ECJ, which endorsed not only the principle as such, but also the EFTA Court's *effect-related* understanding of the principle of homogeneity.[45] Of particular importance for present purposes is the fact that the EFTA Court deduced the principle of State liability from the object and purpose of the EEA Agreement despite the fact that not only both the remaining dualist EEA/EFTA States (Iceland and Norway) but also the EU Commission objected to this, all referring to the alleged common understanding of the Contracting Parties at the time of the signature of the Agreement.[46] Nevertheless, the principle of State liability has since been acknowledged by the highest courts of all of the three EEA/EFTA States, and with it also a very broad understanding of the homogeneity principle.[47]

Over the years, the EFTA Court has in similar ways deduced a number of general principles of EEA law from the object and purpose of the Agreement, mirroring principles already found in EU law.[48] An example of particular interest to the analysis of the EFTA Court's recent recognition of a general right to move and reside freely within the EEA[49] is the deduction of a general EEA law principle of equality. The EFTA Court has not (yet) stated clearly that it sees the general prohibition of discrimination on grounds of nationality in Art. 4 EEA as 'only' a specific expression of a general EEA law principle of equality mirroring that found

---

[43] Examples include Case E-1/01 *Einarsson v Iceland* [2002] EFTA Ct. Rep. 1, Case E-1/02 *ESA v Norway* ('Postdoc') [2003] EFTA Ct. Rep. 1, Case E-8/00 *Landsorganisasjonen* [2002] EFTA Ct. Rep. 114, Case E-12/10, *ESA v Iceland* [2011] EFTA Ct. Rep. 117 (see the Report for the Hearing, para 92) and Case E-14/15 *Holship* [2016] EFTA Ct. Rep. 240 on the one hand; and Case E-10/14 *Deveci* [2014] EFTA Ct. Rep. 1364, Case E-26/13 *Gunnarsson v Iceland* [2014] EFTA Ct. Rep. 254, Case E-28/15 *Jabbi v Norway* [2016] EFTA Ct. Rep. 575 and Case E-4/19 *Campbell v Norway* [2020] (nyr) on the other.

[44] Case E-9/97 *Sveinbjörnsdóttir* [1998] EFTA Ct. Rep. 95, para 60.

[45] Case C-140/97 *Rechberger* EU:C:1999:306, para 39.

[46] Report for the Hearing in *Sveinbjörnsdóttir*, paras 60 (Iceland); 71 (Norway) and 96 (the Commission).

[47] Sceptical on such development, see e.g. Pål Wennerås, who contends that the EFTA Court has thereby 'expanded the scope of these rules and basically substituted them for a principle of homogeneity *sans frontiéres*'. Pål Wennerås, 'Article 6 – Homogeneity' in Finn Arnesen, Halvard Haukeland Fredriksen and others (eds), *Agreement on the European Economic Area: A Commentary* (2018 C.H. Beck/Hart/Nomos/Universitetsforlaget) 210.

[48] Examples include Case E-15/10 *Posten Norge v ESA* [2012] EFTA Ct. Rep. 246, para 86 (principle of effective judicial protection including the right to a fair trial), Case E-14/11, *Schenker v ESA* [2012] EFTA Ct. Rep. 1178, paras 118 ff. (access to documents), Case E-26/13 *Gunnarsson* [2014] EFTA Ct. Rep. 254, para 84 (general principle of equality) and Case E-10/14 *Deveci* [2014] EFTA Ct. Rep. 1364, para 64 (freedom to conduct a business).

[49] As mentioned in the introduction and to which we will also return in sections 4, 5 and 6 below.

in EU law,⁵⁰ but it has nevertheless clearly recognised such a general principle and applied it in several cases.⁵¹

In this way, the EFTA Court has by and large managed to keep EEA law up to date with developments in EU law. However, as will be demonstrated below, the EFTA Court's recent attempts to remedy the lack of EEA provisions mirroring Arts 20 and 21 TFEU through dynamic interpretation of the Citizenship Directive has been met with much harder opposition from (some of) the EEA/EFTA States and revealed fundamental disagreements as to the true meaning of the homogeneity principle. The fight over the proper interpretation of the Citizenship Directive in the context of EEA law is thus not only about the limits of teleological interpretation of a directive, but also, and more fundamentally, about the true meaning of homogeneity as a principle of EEA law. In one corner, the Norwegian government argues that the principle dictates an interpretation of the directive in line with the ECJ's interpretation of it in the context of EU law, no less and certainly no more. In the other corner, the EFTA Court, supported by the European Commission and (eventually) the EFTA Surveillance Authority, argues that in a conflict between *homogeneity as to results in the EU and in the EEA* and *homogeneity as to the interpretation of individual EU/EEA rules*, the former takes precedence.⁵² This does not entail that homogeneity as to results will always be achievable, but rather that the principle of homogeneity militates in favour of such an outcome even if it requires an interpretation of, for example, a directive that diverges from the ECJ's interpretation of it in the context of EU law. Put differently, the need to ensure homogeneity as to results may sometimes trump homogeneity as to interpretation, with a differentiated interpretative approach nevertheless leading to the same results being achieved in practice.

4. DIFFERENTIATION BETWEEN RIGHTS BASED IN EU TREATIES AND THE MAIN PART OF EEA AGREEMENT?

According to the classic understanding of homogeneity, where provisions of EEA law are taken over from EU law a strong presumption exists in favour of their homogenous interpretation and application in practice.⁵³ Given that the provisions in the Main Part of the EEA Agreement on workers, establishment and services are copied almost verbatim from their EC/EU Treaty counterparts, there can be little doubt that they are and should be understood in

---

⁵⁰ Case C-115/08 *ČEZ* EU:C:2009:660, para 89, describing what is now Art. 18 TFEU as 'a specific expression of the general principle of equality, which itself is one of the fundamental principles of Community law'.

⁵¹ See further Páll Hreinsson, 'General Principles' in Carl Baudenbacher (ed.), *The Handbook of EEA Law* (Springer 2016) 360–2, linking the unwritten principle to Art. 4 EEA as well as the Agreement's preamble, other provisions in the Main Part of the Agreement and legal acts referred to in the annexes.

⁵² See also Christa Tobler, 'Free Movement of Persons in the EU v. in the EEA: Of Effect-related Homogeneity and a Reversed Polydor Principle' (2018) 3 *European Papers* 1429–51.

⁵³ See e.g. Hreinsson (n 51) 352–3. For the provisions in the Main Part of the EEA Agreement discussed in this section, there is no conflict between homogeneity as to results and homogeneity as to interpretation of the individual rules.

largely the same way.⁵⁴ In certain cases, however, the fact that there are no provisions in the Main Part of EEA Agreement corresponding to Arts 20 and 21 TFEU may complicate matters.

First, where the ECJ interprets the EU Treaty rules on workers, the self-employed or service providers or receivers in the light of the concept of citizenship, the same method will not be possible under EEA law. A good example is provided by looking at the issue of job-seekers' right to equal treatment, which were historically limited under what is now Art. 45 TFEU to matters concerning access to employment. There was no right to equal treatment as far as social benefits were concerned. In *Collins*, however, the ECJ held that in light of the establishment of EU citizenship, it was no longer possible to exclude social benefits of a financial nature intended to facilitate access to employment.⁵⁵ Without any corresponding citizenship provisions in the EEA Agreement, the same 'citizenship interpretation' of Art. 28 EEA and/or the Workers Regulation would naturally not be possible.

Second, the lack of provisions mirroring Arts 20 and 21 TFEU also means that where the ECJ draws indigenous rights of free movement or residence from these, such rights will not apply outright as a matter of EEA law. The most poignant example of this is provided by the ECJ's case-law stemming from *Zambrano*, to which we shall return in more detail further below, following which the cross-border requirement triggering free movement and residence rights for certain persons may, in highly exceptional circumstances, be removed under reference to the concept of citizenship.⁵⁶ Another interesting example is provided by *Bidar*, where the ECJ held that students could rely on Arts 18 and 21 TFEU to acquire a right to equal treatment in respect of student loans in the host state before the normally prescribed period of five years mandated by the Citizenship Directive.⁵⁷ The Court held that the right to equal treatment with regard to student maintenance grants would apply to any student who was able to show 'a certain degree of integration' in the host State, which in this particular case could be assumed after three years' residence. According to Art. 24 of the Citizenship Directive, however, students are required to have attained permanent residence in the host State before enjoying equal treatment with regards to maintenance grants, and permanent residence will usually require a period of five years' continuous residence before being granted.⁵⁸ The fact that the ECJ based its decision on the citizenship provisions of the Treaty and not on Art. 24 of the Citizenship Directive is not altogether surprising, since the case was decided after the adoption yet before the entry into force of the latter. Whether the result would have been different under the directive is nevertheless far from certain, especially given the ECJ's marked tendency to bypass application of Art. 24 of the Directive in practice in favour of reliance on the general prohibitions against discrimination under Art. 45 TFEU, or Arts 18 and 21 TFEU combined.

The analysis above is not to say that it would be impossible to arrive at the same result or outcome under EEA law as in the cases mentioned. It does mean, however, that such a result must be sought by using different tools. In the case of *Bidar*, for example, a similar outcome

---

⁵⁴ See e.g. Case E-4/19 *Campbell* (workers), Joined Cases E-3/13 and E-20/13 *Fred Olsen and others* [2014] EFTA Ct. Rep. 400 (self-employed persons), and Joined Cases E-11/07 and E-1/08 *Rindal and Slinning* [2008] EFTA Ct. Rep. 320 (service recipients).
⁵⁵ Case C-138/02 *Collins* EU:C:2004:172.
⁵⁶ Case C-34/09 *Zambrano* EU:C:2011:124.
⁵⁷ Case C-209/03 *Bidar* EU:C:2005:169, paras 42–43.
⁵⁸ Art. 18 Citizenship Directive, subject to exceptions concerning former workers and self-employed persons set out in Art. 17.

might potentially be achieved by interpreting the derogations in Art. 24 of the Citizenship Directive in the light of the general principle of non-discrimination contained in Art. 4 EEA, which corresponds almost verbatim to the first sentence of Art. 18 TFEU. Although this route is longer, requiring no small degree of ingenuity on the part of the interpreters, the possibility of finding distinct EEA legal bases allowing one to arrive at the same practical result in such cases should not be dismissed out of hand. Similarly, in the case of *Collins*, one may wonder if the recognition in *Campbell* of a general right to move and reside freely within the EEA would suffice to transfer the ECJ's 'citizenship interpretation' of Art. 45 TFEU to Art. 28 EEA. The principle of homogeneity militates strongly in favour of such a solution.

5. DIFFERENTIATION BETWEEN RIGHTS BASED IN SECONDARY EU MEASURES IN THEIR EU AND EEA CONTEXTS?

Many of the same issues noted in the previous section also arise when looking at the body of secondary EU measures made part of the EEA Agreement concerning rights of workers, establishment and services. Barring any substantive or technical adaptations introduced by the EEA Joint Committee on their incorporation into EEA law, the same strong presumption of homogeneous interpretation and application may also be said to apply to these rules, at least when viewed without the context of citizenship. And the same problems concerning 'citizenship readings' of such secondary measures by the ECJ naturally beg the question as to whether and how the same outcomes might be possible as a matter of EEA law. For example, the case of *Collins* noted above concerned not merely a citizenship interpretation of what is now Art. 45 TFEU, but also certain provisions of the Workers Regulation. In the event that the Workers Regulation was not capable of being construed to the same end in its EEA context, job-seekers would be seen as having attained certain rights to equal treatment regarding certain social advantages under the EU pillar unreciprocated in the EFTA pillar. Simply put, the boundaries of homogeneity would then be reached.

Matters are even more vexed when we consider rights of free movement and residence based in the Citizenship Directive, which endured a rather laboured passage into EEA law.[59] The EU Commission, representing the EU pillar in the EEA Joint Committee, considered the entire Directive to be EEA-relevant. The EEA/EFTA States, bound to speak with one voice on behalf of the EFTA pillar in the Joint Committee, were more sceptical.[60] Although large parts of the directive clearly carried over rights from the measures it was replacing, it also included a number of seemingly new and/or amended rights to the bargain – including a right of permanent residence in the host State after five years, a potentially broader range of derived rights of residence for third country national family members and a new arsenal of procedural safeguards. The issues facing the EEA/EFTA States were plain: To what extent might these

---

[59] For more on the background and an insightful exposé of the politics and discussions involved, see *Jonsdottir* (n 25) 103.

[60] According to *Jonsdottir* (n 25) 105, Iceland and Liechtenstein were far more sceptical than Norway. The Norwegian view was that Norwegian law already was in conformity with the Directive. In light of subsequent case-law from the EFTA Court (see further below), this assessment can only be characterised as rather misguided.

novel rights be attributable to citizenship? Would acceptance of the directive in its entirety lead to a *de facto* broadening of the scope of the EEA Agreement, effectively introducing EU citizenship through the back door? How could one seek to disentangle the parts of the directive which were clearly EEA-relevant from those which were not?

Discussions in the EEA Joint Committee dragged on for more than three years, before the EU Commission finally invoked the six-month conciliation procedure under Art. 102 EEA to force a solution. After almost a year of conciliation talks, the parties reached a compromise solution: full incorporation of the Citizenship Directive, yet with a Joint Declaration clearly seeking to delimit its potential impact.[61] The Declaration, included here in full, states:

> The concept of Union Citizenship as introduced by the Treaty of Maastricht (now Articles 17 seq. EC Treaty) has no equivalent in the EEA Agreement. The incorporation of Directive 2004/38/EC into the EEA Agreement shall be without prejudice to the evaluation of the EEA relevance of future EU legislation as well as future case law of the European Court of Justice based on the concept of Union Citizenship. The EEA Agreement does not provide a legal basis for political rights of EEA nationals.
>
> The Contracting Parties agree that immigration policy is not covered by the EEA Agreement. Residence rights for third country nationals fall outside the scope of the Agreement with the exception of rights granted by the Directive to third country nationals who are family members of an EEA national exercising his or her right to free movement under the EEA Agreement as these rights are corollary to the right of free movement of EEA nationals. The EEA/EFTA States recognise that it is of importance to EEA nationals making use of their right of free movement of persons, that their family members within the meaning of the Directive and possessing third country nationality also enjoy certain derived rights such as foreseen in Articles 12(2), 13(2) and 18. This is without prejudice to Article 118 of the EEA Agreement and the future development of independent rights of third country nationals which do not fall within the scope of the EEA Agreement.

As indicated rather clearly in the EFTA Court's first ruling on the matter in *Wahl*, however, the practical effects of the Declaration have proved to be rather limited.[62] The case concerned the interpretation of the public policy and security justifications set out in Art. 27 of the Citizenship Directive, following a decision by Icelandic authorities to ban entry of a Norwegian citizen who was a member of the Hell's Angels motorcycle club. The Norwegian government intervened in the case, arguing that the Citizenship Directive must be considered as having a more limited scope under EEA law given that the concept of citizenship fell outwith the EEA Agreement. In a few preliminary remarks, the EFTA Court made clear that it disagreed concerning the scope of the directive. While generally recognising that the concepts of EU citizenship and immigration policy fell without the EEA Agreement, it held that these exclusions had no impact on the present case. The Court did admit, however, that the Declaration's impact could vary from one case to another and would therefore need to be assessed on a case-by-case basis. The EFTA Court pointed out explicitly in this regard that such arguments might be particularly relevant in cases concerning Art. 24 of the Directive essentially dealing with the equal treatment of third country national family members of EEA nationals enjoying a right of residence or permanent residence. Such an issue has yet to be brought before the EEA courts in practice.

The relevance of the Joint Declaration was further downplayed in a trilogy of cases on the interpretation of Art. 7 of the Citizenship Directive – *Gunnarsson*, *Jabbi* and *Campbell* – to

---

[61] Joint Declaration by the Contracting Parties to Decision No. 158/2007.
[62] Case E-15/12 *Wahl v Iceland* [2013] EFTA Ct. Rep. 534, paras 74-77.

which we will return in more detail below.⁶³ For present purposes, however, suffice it to note that the EFTA Court in *Gunnarsson* mentioned the Joint Declaration only in passing, acknowledging that 'the incorporation of Directive 2004/38 cannot introduce rights into the EEA Agreement based on the concept of Union Citizenship', but then immediately adding: 'However, individuals cannot be deprived of rights that they have already acquired under the EEA Agreement before the introduction of Union Citizenship in the EU. These established rights have been maintained in Directive 2004/38.'⁶⁴

This was repeated in *Jabbi*, with the important addition that the Joint Declaration shows that 'the Contracting Parties also agreed that rights granted by the Directive to third country nationals who are family members of an EEA national, exercising the right to free movement under the EEA Agreement, must be included since these rights are corollary to the right of free movement of nationals of EU States and EFTA States'.⁶⁵ In its not uncontroversial interpretation of the Joint Declaration, the EFTA Court then added: 'It cannot be assumed that the Contracting Parties intended the introduction of Union citizenship in EU law to restrict further evolution of the free movement of persons in the EEA.'⁶⁶

The final nail in the Joint Declaration's coffin was added in *Campbell*, where the EFTA Court confirmed the approach taken in *Gunnarsson* and *Jabbi* without even mentioning it. Without the EFTA Court making a point of it, the fact that European Commission evidently interpreted the Declaration very differently from the EEA/EFTA States surely helps to explain its demise.

Notwithstanding the limited effects of the Declaration, the fact remains that there are no provisions mirroring Arts 20 and 21 TFEU in the EEA Agreement, meaning that ECJ interpretations of the directive fuelled by the EU Treaty rules on citizenship cannot be automatically transferred to EEA law. The EFTA Court has nevertheless become remarkably adept in seeking to reach the same practical results by using other tools at its disposal. One example is *Clauder*, concerning the interpretation of Art. 16 of the Directive and derived residence rights for family members of retired EEA nationals enjoying permanent residence in another EEA State.⁶⁷ The material content of Art. 16 had been amended by the Citizenship Directive: while two of the previous directives it had replaced had contained general requirements of sufficient resources and health insurance in order to trigger such derived rights, Art. 16 contained no such requirements.⁶⁸ The EFTA Court held that although not expressly stated in the wording of the provision, the right of permanent residence under Art. 16(1) nevertheless conferred a derived right of residence for family members in the host State.⁶⁹ The EFTA Court thereby seemed to

---

⁶³ Case E-26/13 *Gunnarsson* [2014] EFTA Ct. Rep. 254; Case E-28/15 *Jabbi* [2016] EFTA Ct. Rep. 575; Case E-4/19 *Campbell* [2020] (nyr).

⁶⁴ Case E-26/13 *Gunnarsson* [2014] EFTA Ct. Rep. 254, para 80. The first sentence of this quote could be interpreted to suggest that the EEA Joint Committee cannot amend the EEA Agreement in ways that limit existing EEA rights, but that is obviously not the case. The EFTA Court's point, as demonstrated in the final sentence, is that the relevant free movement rights found in the various EU legal acts that were repealed and replaced by Directive 2004/38 were in fact maintained in the latter directive.

⁶⁵ Case E-28/15 *Jabbi* [2016] EFTA Ct. Rep. 575, para 64.

⁶⁶ Ibid.

⁶⁷ For more details on the facts surrounding the case, which need not concern us here, see e.g. Thomas Burri and Benedikt Pirker, 'Constitutionalization by Association? The Doubtful Case of the European Economic Area' (2013) 32 (1) Yearbook of European Law 207, 218–20.

⁶⁸ Art. 1 of Directive 90/364, and Art. 1 of Directive 90/365.

⁶⁹ Case E-4/11 *Clauder* [2011] EFTA Ct. Rep. 216, paras 43–48.

imply that even though novel rights found in the Citizenship Directive could well be linked to the concept of citizenship as such and might therefore be expected to be given an extensive 'citizenship reading' by the ECJ, this would not prevent the EFTA Court from reaching the same result based on a highly dynamic and teleological interpretation of the directive as such.[70]

A futile attempt to limit the reach of the Citizenship Directive under EEA law was made by the Norwegian government in *Gunnarsson*, arguing that the Joint Declaration demonstrated that the parts of the directive based on Art. 21 TFEU were not part of EEA law, and further that the directive's implementation into Annex V on the free movement of workers and Annex VIII on the right of establishment proved that it only gave rights to economically active persons.[71] The EFTA Court rejected both arguments, noting that previous EU secondary law giving rights to (certain categories of) economically inactive persons had been incorporated into the EEA Agreement, and indeed (presumably in want of a better alternative) in Annex VIII on freedom of establishment.[72]

6. THE CRUX OF THE MATTER: FREE MOVEMENT RIGHTS BASED IN ARTS 20 AND 21 TFEU

More testing are situations where the ECJ builds free movement rights directly on Arts 20 and 21 TFEU. The above-mentioned trilogy of EFTA Court cases centring on the interpretation of Art. 7 of the Citizenship Directive – *Gunnarsson*, *Jabbi* and *Campbell* – are highly illustrative in this regard. Subject to a number of conditions, Art. 7 provides for a right of residence for up to five years for EEA nationals and their family members on the territory of *another Member State*. The private individuals involved in all three cases were not seeking to enforce their rights against a *host EEA State* to which they had moved, however, but rather against their *home states*. According to the ECJ's ruling in *O and B* and confirmed in many cases since, while no such right flows from the Directive in its EU setting, such a right does flow from Art. 21 TFEU.[73] Unable to simply follow the ECJ's lead, the EFTA Court therefore sought a different interpretative route with a view to arriving at the same result. Its reasoning in these cases has already been subjected to some academic scrutiny and has developed somewhat from one case to the next. To summarise the EFTA Court's position today, however, we can say the following:

The EFTA Court has stressed that the line of ECJ case-law starting with *O and B* is distinguishable from the situations in *Gunnarsson*, *Jabbi* and *Campbell*. The EU and EEA legal contexts within which the Directive finds itself quite simply differ.[74] According to the EFTA Court, *O and B* therefore is to be read in its proper (that is, EU) legal context, which encompasses the concept of citizenship. And since neither *O and B* nor any of the cases following it were concerned with the interpretation of the Citizenship Directive in its EEA context, the

---

[70] For more, see Christian N K Franklin, 'Square Pegs and Round Holes: The Free Movement of Persons Under EEA Law' (2017) 19 Cambridge Yearbook of European Legal Studies, 165–86.
[71] Case E-26/13 *Gunnarsson* [2014] EFTA Ct. Rep. 254, paras 48–50.
[72] Ibid., paras 75–80.
[73] Case C-456/12 *O and B* EU:C:2014:135; confirmed in e.g. Case C-133/15 *Chavez-Vilchez* EU:C:2017:354; Case C-89/17 *Banger* EU:C:2018:570; Case C-230/17 *Altiner and Ravn* EU:C:2018:497.
[74] Franklin (n 35) 241–4. See also Ólafur Jóhannes Einarsson, in: Finn Arnesen and others (eds) (n 21) 2018, comments on Art. 31 EEA, paras 46–49.

ECJ's case-law cannot just be transposed to the EEA.[75] The EFTA Court also called particular attention to the fact that citizenship as a concept could not be considered synonymous with free movement in any event – indeed, the latter quite clearly only forms one (albeit integral) part of the former.

Furthermore, and crucially, the EFTA Court considers the homogeneity principle to encompass and require homogeneity as to the practical results achieved in the EU and in the EEA, that is, that similar cases of free movement should lead to the same outcomes in EU and EEA law, despite the fact that the legal bases for reaching those results might differ, and even if it requires a provision of a directive to be interpreted differently in the EEA than in the EU.[76]

Building on this understanding of homogeneity, the question confronting the EFTA Court was essentially whether Art. 7 of the Citizenship Directive could, within recognised methodological principles, be interpreted to achieve the same result that the ECJ deduced from Art. 21 TFEU in *O and B*.

In reaching an affirmative answer, the EFTA Court has emphasised that the free movement of persons lies at the heart of the EEA Agreement, and that '[t]he consideration of homogeneity therefore carries substantial weight'.[77] The latter is EEA parlance to suggest that a rather dynamic interpretation may be justified. The objection by the EEA/EFTA States that what lies at the core of the EEA Agreement is free movement of *economically active persons* was refuted by highlighting that certain rights of free movement and residence were also bestowed on at least certain categories of economically inactive EEA nationals, including their family members, from the very outset. Further, by making the Citizenship Directive a part of EEA law, the Contracting Parties agreed to extend the scope of free movement rights to *all* EU/EEA nationals. In short, the distinction between economically active and inactive persons is toned down, culminating in the finding in *Campbell* of a general right to move and reside freely within the EEA.

Building particularly on the ECJ's decisions in *Singh* and *Eind*,[78] the EFTA Court found in *Jabbi* that the right of economically inactive persons to move freely from one's home State under Art. 7(1)(b) of the Citizenship Directive could not be fully achieved if EEA nationals were deterred from exercising their rights to free movement by their home states placing obstacles in the way for a return with accompanying third country national spouses. The Court concluded the point in *Jabbi* by stating that the provisions of the Directive which open for a derived right of residence for third country national family members in another EEA State

---

[75] Case E-28/15 *Jabbi* [2016] EFTA Ct. Rep. 575, paras 60–67; Case E-4/19 *Campbell* [2020], paras 56–58.

[76] See, implicitly, E-28/15 *Jabbi* [2016] EFTA Ct. Rep. 575, para 68; E-4/19 *Campbell* [2020], paras 55 and 58. In Case E-26/13 *Gunnarsson* [2014] EFTA Ct. Rep. 254, the EFTA Court did not take issue with the narrower understanding of homogeneity advocated by Iceland, Norway and (then) the EFTA Surveillance Authority. When the Court introduced the principle of homogeneity into its reasoning in *Jabbi* and *Campbell*, it did so without explaining the legal basis for its broad, result-oriented understanding of it. It is submitted here that the EFTA Court ought to have addressed the issue concerning the right understanding of homogeneity head on, and explained why it thinks that the overarching object and purpose of the EEA Agreement, as expressed in Art. 1 EEA and the fourth recital of the preamble, should prevail over the narrower understanding of homogeneity suggested in, e.g., Arts 6 and 105 EEA and the 15th recital of the preamble. See also Tobler (n 52) 2018, pp. 1444 and pp. 1447f.

[77] Case E-28/15 *Jabbi* [2016] EFTA Ct. Rep. 575, para 60.

[78] Case C-370/90 *Singh* EU:C:1992:296; Case C-291/05 *Eind* EU:C:2007:771.

will therefore apply 'by analogy' in situations where the EEA national returns home with a third country national family member.[79]

The conclusion reached in *Jabbi*, and the reasoning underlying it, failed to convince the Norwegian government, which continued to argue for an interpretation of the directive in line with *O and B* in the national courts. Unsurprisingly, therefore, the matter eventually ended up before the Supreme Court of Norway in *Campbell*, which decided to refer it back to the EFTA Court. In a tellingly brief opinion, however, the EFTA Court noted firm support from both the European Commission and the EFTA Surveillance Authority and stated that it saw no reason to depart from 'the understanding of homogeneity and effectiveness' as expressed in *Jabbi*.[80]

At the time of writing, it remains to be seen if Norway, as the last of the EEA/EFTA States,[81] will come around and accept the EFTA Court's stand.[82] The ECJ's view in *O and B* that it follows from 'a literal, systematic and teleological interpretation of Directive 2004/38 that it does not establish a derived right of residence for third-country nationals who are family members of a Union citizen in the Member State of which that citizen is a national' certainly demonstrates that the EFTA Court's stand is rather daring. To characterise its stance as untenable and as violating the rule of law is nevertheless going too far, in our opinion. After all, the ECJ has long considered the effectiveness of other provisions of EU law, including Art. 45 TFEU on the free movement of workers, to justify interpretations obliging home states not to hinder free movement by placing obstacles in the way for a return with accompanying third country national spouses.[83] Transferring this approach to the Citizenship Directive can hardly be considered *ultra vires*.

7. THE SPECIAL CASE OF LIECHTENSTEIN

In a chapter aiming to provide an overview over the right to free movement and residence under EEA law, the far-reaching derogations that exist for Liechtenstein must also be mentioned.[84] The derogations are explained by Liechtenstein's very small and rural inhabitable area, with an unusually high percentage of non-national residents and employees, and related concerns as to the preservation of national identity. With exceptions for persons providing cross-border services and for residence of less than three months per year that does not include work or other permanent economic activity, nationals from Iceland, Norway and the EU Member

---

[79] Case E-28/15 *Jabbi* [2016] EFTA Ct. Rep. 575, para 82. For an explanation and defence of the EFTA Court's use of analogous reasoning, see Franklin (n 35), 236–45.

[80] Case E-4/19 *Campbell* [2020], para 58. For an early analysis of *Campbell*, see Christina Neier, 'The right to come home – within or outside the scope of the EEA Agreement?' (EFTA-Studies.org) www.efta-studies.org/post/the-right-to-come-home accessed 19 April 2021.

[81] Given the lack of any intervention by Iceland or Liechtenstein in *Campbell*, it seems reasonable to assume that they have accepted the EFTA Court's views on the matter.

[82] *Campbell* itself will not clarify this as Ms Campbell withdrew her appeal to the Supreme Court following the EFTA Court's advisory opinion. Her application for family reunification with her Norwegian wife was accepted by the immigration authorities on other grounds, leaving her case before the Supreme Court moot.

[83] This point was made by the Commission already in Case E-26/13 *Gunnarsson* [2014] EFTA Ct. Rep. 254, para 65.

[84] For the details, see Ólafur Jóhannes Einarsson in: Finn Arnesen and others (eds) (n 21) 2018, comments on Art. 31 EEA, paras 30–39.

States may only take up residence in Liechtenstein after receiving a permit from Liechtenstein authorities.[85] The number of permits provided is very low – only 56 new residence permits for economically active EEA nationals and 16 permits for other EEA nationals. Importantly, family members of EEA nationals who reside lawfully in Liechtenstein have the right to obtain a permit of the same validity as that of the person upon whom they depend. They also have the right to take up economic activity, but they will then be counted towards the yearly quota for economically active EEA nationals.

The derogations obtained by Liechtenstein were recognised by the EEA Joint Committee when incorporating the Citizenship Directive into the EEA Agreement, considerably limiting the practical impact of the directive in the principality.[86] For EEA nationals holding a valid Liechtenstein residence permit, however, the directive will apply in full. A recent confirmation is to be found in *D and E*, in which Liechtenstein argued that a permit issued to a German citizen *outside* the EEA quota system explained above could not give rise to a right of family unification under Art. 7(1)(d) of the directive. The EFTA Court replied that while Liechtenstein is not under any obligation to grant residence permits to EEA nationals outside the quota system, the sectoral adaptations could not preclude the EEA rights of EEA nationals to whom Liechtenstein has in fact granted such residence permits.[87]

8. PEEKING INTO THE FUTURE – CONVERGENCE OR (TRUER) DIFFERENTIATION?

Taking a brief look at what lies ahead, it seems that issues concerning the free movement of persons are likely to continue to colour the dockets of the national courts of the EEA/EFTA States and the EFTA Court itself for some time. The following section will address only some of the most pressing issues, starting with the EEA-relevance of the ECJ's case-law on cross-border requirements in the light of *Zambrano*, continued reticence to accept dynamic interpretations of the Citizenship Directive, various free movement and residence issues raised by the ongoing social security scandal in Norway and the relationship between fundamental rights and free movement under EEA law.

8.1 Cross-border Requirements: *Zambrano*

A first issue concerns the EEA-relevance of the ECJ's case-law on cross-border requirements as developed following the ECJ's controversial decision in *Zambrano*.[88] As we recall, the main question in that case was whether Mr Zambrano, as a third country national, could

---

[85] Sectoral adaptations to Annex V (Free movement of workers) and Annex VIII (Right of establishment).

[86] Recital 12 of EEA Joint Committee Decision No 158/2007 amending Annex V (Free movement of workers) and Annex VIII (Right of establishment) to the EEA Agreement [2007] OJ L 124: 'The incorporation of Directive 2004/38/EC into the Agreement shall be without prejudice to these sectoral adaptations with regard to Liechtenstein.'

[87] Case E-2/19 *D and E* [2019] (nyr), para 57. The residence permit of D was issued outside the EEA quota system because it was based on family reunification with a third country national resident in Liechtenstein.

[88] Case C-34/09 *Ruiz Zambrano* EU:C:2011:124.

derive rights under EU law on the basis of his two children's status as EU citizens. The family had been resident in Belgium and never at any point exercised their right to move to another Member State. Without going so far as giving up the 'wholly internal' rule altogether, the ECJ nevertheless found a way around it. The Court held that denying Mr Zambrano a residence and/or work permit would effectively force two EU citizens (his children) to leave the EU altogether. The ECJ concluded that denial of a residence and/or work permit in this case could not be accepted, as it would leave two EU citizens 'unable to exercise the substance of the rights conferred on them by virtue of their status as EU citizens', contrary to Art. 20 TFEU.[89] Although a number of subsequent ECJ decisions have reined in some of the potential effects of *Zambrano*, it has not been overruled.[90]

Looking at the EEA context, all rights of free movement and residence under EEA law have traditionally been understood as requiring fulfilment of a cross-border requirement in order to be triggered. Where the EEA national physically moves from one State to another, this will usually be rather unproblematic. But what about so-called wholly internal situations, where the facts appear confined to one EEA State alone – do EEA nationals enjoy rights of free movement and residence in such situations? According to the Norwegian Supreme Court in *Case of A* (also known as 'the *Maria* case'), the answer was no.[91] The case concerned a decision by Norwegian authorities to deport a Kenyan lady (A) for breaches of Norwegian immigration laws, among other reasons for providing misleading information on her date of birth, and hence residing illegally in Norway for many years. She had a four-year-old daughter who was a Norwegian citizen. The Norwegian father was no longer in the picture. A therefore argued that refusing her a residence permit would effectively mean that her daughter would be deported as well – thereby depriving her daughter of any potential enjoyment of rights of free movement and/or residence under EEA rules. One of the questions raised was whether the Citizenship Directive could apply to resolve the issue in favour of A, allowing her to derive a right of residence on the basis of her daughter's Norwegian nationality.[92] The Norwegian Supreme Court did not accept the argument, pointing to the EEA Joint Committee's Joint Declaration that neither EU citizenship nor immigration policy was ever intended to be a part of EEA law. Crucially, the Court seemed to contend that the EEA rules only applied to those who had physically exercised their right of free movement. This was a 'wholly internal situation' altogether outwith the scope of the Directive. It therefore held that the ECJ's case-law on Arts 20 and 21 TFEU, including *Zambrano* more particularly, could have no effects for EFTA State nationals. The case was nevertheless decided in A's favour on other (human rights) grounds.[93]

---

[89] Ibid., para 44.
[90] Cf. e.g. Case C-434/09 *McCarthy* EU:C:2011:277, and Case C-356-357/11 *O. and S.* EU:C:2012:776; with Case C-165/14 *Rendon Marin* EU:C:2016:675, and Case C-133/15 *Chavez-Vilchez* EU:C:2017:354.
[91] HR-2015-206-A.
[92] It is worth pointing out that the Norwegian Immigration Act expressly provides for sectoral monism in this field, meaning that the provisions of, for example, the Citizenship Directive will enjoy precedence over divergent rules contained in the national (transposing) measure. See Section 3 of the Norwegian Immigration Act of 15 May 2008 (on the entry of foreign nationals into the Kingdom of Norway and their stay in the realm).
[93] Arts 102 and 104 of the Norwegian constitution (the right of family life and the rights of children); Art. 8 ECHR and Art. 3 of the UN Convention on the rights of the child.

Looking at the EEA dimension of the case, the Supreme Court's *obiter* indication that actual physical movement must take place in order to trigger rights under the Citizenship Directive sits rather poorly with the very liberal approach taken by the ECJ in other parts of its case-law.[94] The EEA-relevance of the ECJ's approach in such cases is likely to come under closer scrutiny in a related (yet slightly different) ongoing case, concerning children's residence rights under EEA law.[95] As explained in the next section, however, the outcome of this pending case may well prove telling on a completely different issue, too – namely the Norwegian authorities' final acceptance of the EFTA Court's opinions in *Gunnarsson*, *Jabbi* and *Campbell*.

8.2   Accepting Dynamic Interpretations of the Citizenship Directive

At the time of writing, the EFTA Surveillance Authority (ESA) has opened formal proceedings against Norway in a case concerning children's residence rights under EEA law.[96] The complaints were borne from the situation of a third country national mother who had resided in Norway with her two Greek children on the basis of a right derived from her Greek husband. The husband, who was the children's stepfather, subsequently left Norway, and the mother applied to stay in Norway. Her application was turned down on the grounds that neither she nor the children could retain their rights of residence under Norwegian immigration rules or the Citizenship Directive. In its so-called pre-Article 31 letter,[97] the ESA raised two legal issues for the Norwegian authorities to address: first, to explain why a child could not enjoy an independent right of residence under Art. 7(1)(b) of the Citizenship Directive and to be accompanied by their primary carer in the process; second, why the mother and her two children were not able to retain a right of residence under Art. 12(3) of the Citizenship Directive despite the children being stepchildren of the EEA-national sponsor.

In its initial reply, the Norwegian Ministry of Labour and Social Affairs admitted that there was little reason on the basis of Art. 2(2)(c) not to consider an EEA national's stepchildren as family members within the meaning of the Directive, and that the Norwegian immigration authorities had now taken this understanding onboard. Concerning the first question raised by the ESA, however, the Ministry was not so certain. It argued that third country national immigration and the concept of citizenship fall outside the scope of the EEA Agreement and that Art. 21 TFEU does not apply to EEA nationals, and had doubts as to whether the Directive viewed in isolation could serve as a legal basis for the residence rights claimed. Although the Ministry had instructed the immigration authorities to suspend processing cases related to

---

[94] See e.g. Case C-200/02 *Zhu and Chen* EU:C:2004:639, where the Court deemed a child's different EU Member State nationality than the host state where she was residing enough to bring the situation within the remit of EU law, thereby triggering derived rights for the child's Chinese parents; and case C-86/12 *Alokpa and Mondoulou* EU:C:2013:645, where the fact that the twin children of a Togolese citizen were French nationals living in another EU Member State (Luxembourg) was considered sufficient to bring the matter potentially within the territorial scope of both Art. 21 TFEU and the Citizenship Directive – in spite of the fact that no physical movement between the countries had taken place.

[95] Case No. 84397; Doc. No. 1103071, 19 December 2019.

[96] Case No. 84397; Doc. No. 1103071, 19 December 2019.

[97] This is a reference to Art. 31 SCA, which vests the EFTA Surveillance Authority with the power to institute infringement proceedings if it considers that an EFTA State has failed to fulfil an obligation under the EEA Agreement. It mirrors the powers of the EU Commission under what is now Art. 258 TFEU.

children's rights of residence under Art. 7 of the Directive, it will be interesting to see what happens next – especially since the Ministry's reply was written prior to the EFTA Court's decision in *Campbell*, which – if accepted – would most likely resolve the issue in favour of the complainant. Given the Norwegian authorities' reticence at times in accepting potentially controversial rulings of the EFTA Court without the blessing of the Norwegian courts (and particularly the Supreme Court), it will be interesting to see how the issue pans out in the end. An answer may well be forthcoming in the not-so-distant future, as the Oslo District Court has referred the matter for an advisory opinion following a legal challenge to the immigration authorities' decision to deport the mother and her two children.[98]

8.3 Exportability of Social Security Rights

The Citizenship Directive and the general right to free movement also lurk in the background in the judicial and political scandal related to Norway's systemic violations of the exportability of certain categories of social security cash benefits.[99] The case is multifaceted and complex, but at its core lies a statutory requirement of 'stay' in Norway as an entitlement criterion, subject to prior authorisation and with only limited grounds for exception. For reasons that are yet to be fully understood, Norwegian authorities considered EEA-based exportability of sickness benefits, work assessment allowances and attendance allowances to be limited to cases where the recipient transferred his residence to another EEA State, thus excluding all other stays abroad. The mistake seems to have affected mainly (but not exclusively) Norwegian nationals who were met with hefty reimbursement claims in cases where the authorities revealed that they had been in other EEA States while receiving benefits. More than 40 cases resulted in criminal convictions for social security fraud, including 36 cases of imprisonment.

In the ongoing investigation into the affair, and the parallel attempts of the authorities and public prosecutors to right the wrongs, most of the attention thus far has focused on the principle of exportability of cash sickness benefits under Art. 21(1) of Regulation 883/2004. However, as some of the cases stem from before the entry into force of this regulation in the EEA in 2012, questions have also been asked about the state of the law under the former Social Security Regulation 1408/71. As Art. 22 of the 'old' regulation only regulated exportability in cases of transfer of residence, attention has shifted to other possible legal bases. One such basis is Art. 36 EEA on the freedom to provide services. As recently confirmed by the ECJ in *I.N.*, Art. 36 EEA is to be interpreted in line with Art. 56 TFEU, thus giving all EEA nationals the right to go to another EEA State in order to receive, for example, tourist services there.[100]

---

[98] E-16/20, *Q and others v The Norwegian Government, represented by The Immigration Appeals Board*.

[99] For an overview in the English language, see the Letter of formal notice to Norway from the EFTA Surveillance Authority, 25 November 2020 (Case No. 84329, Doc. No. 1138850).

[100] Case C-897/19 *PPU, I.N.* EU:C:2020:262, paras 52–53. With Art. 36 EEA as the legal basis, the ECJ held that the EEA Agreement offers an Icelandic citizen the same protection from extradition to a third State that the ECJ, in Case C-182/15 *Petruhhin* EU:C:2016:630, concluded that EU citizens enjoy based on Articles 18 and 21 TFEU. The judgment highlights that the EEA relevance of ECJ case-law cannot be decided solely by looking at the legal basis used. At first glance, one may well think that *Petruhhin* is a clear example of 'future case law of the European Court of Justice based on the concept of Union Citizenship', within the meaning of the joint declaration discussed in section 5 above. After *I.N.*, however, it seems clear that *Petruhhin* could have been based on any of the specific expressions of the

However, for cases where the stay abroad was 'only' about visiting family or friends, there seems to be no way around Arts 4 and 6 of the Citizenship Directive in particular, and the question whether they give rise to a general right to leave the country for shorter stays and to move and reside freely within the EEA. Notably, a majority of the governmentally appointed investigative committee tasked with getting to the bottom of the scandal seemed set in its first findings on sweeping any issues connected to the Citizenship Directive under the carpet.[101] The Supreme Court of Norway has now picked up this point and referred it – together with a host of other questions related to exportability of cash benefits – to the EFTA Court.[102] To say the EFTA Court's reply in this, and other related cases,[103] is awaited with considerable interest would be an understatement.

8.4 Fundamental Rights

Another area of considerable textual difference between EU and EEA law is the field of fundamental rights: there is no provision in the EEA Agreement mirroring the fundamental rights clause now found in Art. 6 TEU, and the EU Charter of Fundamental Rights has not been incorporated into the EEA Agreement or in any other way formally recognised by the EEA/EFTA States either. Given the impact which the Charter has had on ECJ case-law since it acquired binding force through the Treaty of Lisbon, EU lawyers might be excused for thinking that its absence from the EEA Agreement must pose a considerable problem to the functioning of the EEA. So far, however, the EFTA Court has managed to bridge the gap by relying on other legal sources, thereby preserving homogeneity while at the same time side-stepping the sensitive issue of the legal significance of the EU Charter as such.[104]

Quite unproblematic are the situations where provisions of the EU Charter merely reproduce provisions of the European Convention on Human Rights. All the EEA States are parties to the ECHR and there is general agreement in case-law and literature that provisions of the EEA Agreement are to be interpreted and applied in a manner which is consistent with the Contracting Parties' obligations under the Convention.

Quite unproblematic also are the many EU legal acts which include references to the EU Charter in their preambles, as indeed the Citizenship Directive does. Even if it is true that the preambles are not adapted for the purposes of the EEA Agreement, it follows from Protocol 1 EEA that they are 'relevant to the extent necessary for the proper interpretation and application, within the framework of the Agreement, of the provisions contained in such acts'.

---

general right to move and reside freely within the EU that are to be found in the EU treaties. Whether the EFTA Court's stand in *Campbell* can convince the ECJ to extend *Petruhhin* also to a case of an EEA/EFTA national who is not economically active remains to be seen.

[101] *Trygd, oppholdskrav og reiser i EØS-området*, report of 4 March 2020, available (Norwegian only) at www.regjeringen.no/no/dokumenter/trygd-oppholdskrav-og-reiser-i-eos-omradet/id2692285/ accessed 19 April 2021.

[102] Case E-8/20 *A* (pending). From a methodological point of view, it is nevertheless interesting to see how the Supreme Court in the framing of its referral seems to indicate that application of Art. 36 EEA should be ventured (and hence be deemed preferable) before considering potential application of any provisions of the Citizenship Directive.

[103] Two further referrals have also since been made by Norwegian courts concerning exportability of unemployment benefits (E-13/20, *O v Norwegian Labour and Welfare Administration (NAV)*; E-15/20, *Criminal Proceedings Against P*).

[104] See further Fredriksen and Franklin (n 2), pages 646 ff.

More problematic are cases where neither the ECHR nor the preambles offer any help, but so far the EFTA Court has been able to preserve homogeneity by relying on, for example, constitutional traditions common to the EEA States.[105] Of course, future ECJ case-law may interpret provisions of the Charter to include rights which the EFTA Court will have to acknowledge are not reflected in international legal instruments to which all of the EEA States are bound, or easily linked to constitutional traditions common to them. However, most of the provisions of the Charter without any parallel in the ECHR 'only' contain principles that need to be implemented by EU secondary law to become judicially cognisable. Since the social dimension, including in relation to labour law, health and safety at work and gender equality, is an important part of the EEA Agreement,[106] most of the EU legal acts implementing the so-called European Pillar of Social Rights must be presumed to be of EEA-relevance.

8.5 Brexit

As the EEA Agreement integrates the EEA/EFTA States into the internal market, Brexit will affect free movement and residence between the UK and the EEA/EFTA States in much the same way as that between the UK and the EU. The UK, Norway, Iceland and Liechtenstein have signed an EEA EFTA Separation Agreement which largely mirrors the EU–UK Withdrawal Agreement, protecting acquired rights for EEA/EFTA nationals in the UK and UK nationals in the EEA/EFTA States.[107]

9. CONCLUSIONS

To briefly summarise what we have seen in this chapter, it seems clear that notwithstanding the lack of EEA rules directly mirroring Arts 20–25 TFEU, the situation of EEA EFTA State nationals is today largely comparable to that of EU citizens, at least as far as free movement and residence rights are concerned. This has been ensured by gradually expanding the rights of free movement by incorporating secondary EU measures into EEA law, the EFTA Court's highly dynamic interpretation of such rights, and most recently its apparent institution of a general, unwritten principle of free movement under EEA law. The latter development may naturally seem somewhat out of tune with the traditional, category-based approach to free movement rights under the EFTA pillar of the EEA system. To the extent that it may also be viewed as an expression of the gradual erosion of the requirement of economic activity as a precondition

---

[105] Case E-14/11 *Schenker v ESA* [2012] EFTA Ct. Rep. 1178, para 118. EU lawyers will not miss the parallel with Art. 6(3) TEU and ECJ case-law.

[106] As noted, for example, in the Joint statement of the members of the EEA Council, 25 May 2020. Available at www.efta.int/sites/default/files/documents/eea/eea-news/EEA-Council-2020-05-25-Joint-Statement.pdf accessed 19 April 2021.

[107] Agreement on arrangements between Iceland, the Principality of Liechtenstein, the Kingdom of Norway and the United Kingdom of Great Britain and Northern Ireland following the withdrawal of the United Kingdom from the European Union, the EEA Agreement and other agreements applicable between the United Kingdom and the EEA EFTA States by virtue of the United Kingdom's membership of the European Union, 28 January 2020. For details on the EU–UK Withdrawal Agreement, see Oliver Garner, 'Does Member State Withdrawal Automatically Extinguish EU Citizenship?', Chapter 13 in this book.

to free movement under EEA law, however, then it seems rather spot on. The inclusion of the Citizenship Directive in the EEA Agreement has proven key in allowing the EFTA Court to paper over the cracks which have appeared between the EU and EEA legal spheres in this area. The cases which it has given rise to have also served to further cement the effects-based understanding of the principle of homogeneity as a key tool for ensuring an exceptionally high degree of convergence between EU and EEA law. As we have seen, sometimes uniform interpretations must make way for uniform results. The only significant differentiation between EU and EEA law in the field is therefore seemingly to be found in the lack of EEA parallels to the political rights bestowed upon EU citizens under Arts 20–25 TFEU.

19. 'Citizenship of the Association': the examples of Turkey and Switzerland

Narin Idriz and Christa Tobler

1. INTRODUCTION

This chapter focuses on the issue of Union citizenship seen in the context of association agreements, focusing specifically on the agreements concluded by the European Union (EU) with Turkey and Switzerland. One might argue that the issue is not an obvious one – after all, Union citizenship is a concept of European Union law which, according to Art. 20(1) TFEU, is linked to the nationality of an EU Member State. As such, it cannot be extended to cover the citizens of non-Member States. However, citizenship is a multifaceted concept. While the political rights attached to the concept are, in principle, to be enjoyed by the nationals of Member States who are Union citizens,[1] that is not the case regarding the economic rights attached to it.

Art. 20(2) TFEU states that citizens of the Union shall enjoy the rights and be subject to the duties provided for in the Treaties, including, for example, the free movement of persons and services. It is a fact that the Union rules on these freedoms have been transposed either fully – at least in principle – or partially to the external relations of the EU with certain non-Member States. Turkey and Switzerland are cases in point: for example, in the case of Turkey a prohibition of discrimination on grounds of nationality applies to Turkish persons lawfully present in an EU Member State under the Ankara Agreement[2] – a prohibition the meaning of which has, essentially, proven to be the same as under EU law, even though the Ankara Agreement does not provide for the free movement of persons. This is different in the case of Switzerland, where the EU–Swiss agreement on the Free Movement of Persons (AFMP) has explicitly been modelled on EU law: according to its preamble, the parties to the agreement are 'resolved to bring about the free movement of persons between them on the basis of the rules applying in the [then] European Community'.[3]

In other words, such agreements contain *parts* of the rules that relate, under present EU law, to Union citizenship. However, how far do such rules reach, as compared to EU law? Further, do such legal regimes mean that Union citizenship as such has been transposed to these agreements; that is, can or even should we speak of 'differentiated citizenship'? And

---

[1] The Court ruled in Case C-145/04 *Spain v UK* EU:C:2006:543, paras 79–80 that extending the right to vote and stand as a candidate in the European Parliament elections to Commonwealth citizens resident in Gibraltar, who are not Union citizens, did not violate the Treaties. In other words, even political rights linked to the citizenship concept, which are in theory exclusive to Union citizens, can in practice be extended to non-EU citizens.

[2] Agreement establishing an Association between the European Community and its Member States, of the one part, and the Republic of Turkey, of the other part, [1963] OJ 1964 217/3687 (German, Italian, French, Dutch) [1973] OJ C113/1 ('Ankara Agreement'), as amended.

[3] Agreement between the European Community and its Member States, of the one part, and the Swiss Confederation, of the other, on the free movement of persons, [1999] OJ 2002 L114/6, as amended.

what about agreements with other countries, such as that with Ukraine, which provides for the temporary presence of natural persons to provide services but not for free movement of workers or freedom of establishment for natural persons?[4] Could one qualify this as a form of citizenship too? Where does one draw the line?

Defining what citizenship entails is a complicated task, as it is an ever-changing concept.[5] The hallmark of modern citizenship is seen as striving towards equality and the fulfilment of 'basic civil rights', which include, together with one's family, 'the right to reside, to enter, to emigrate, to conduct an economic activity, and to move freely on the state's territory'.[6] To be able to enjoy these rights one needs a strong link to a state, which goes beyond a short-term visit or temporary stay in order to receive or provide services. One has to have the possibility to participate in the social and economic life of that state on an equal and permanent basis and in return to be granted access to the social services and benefits granted to other members of that society.[7] In short, to call it a 'citizenship' of some form or degree, one has to have access to the territory of a state, to have the prospect of settling there with one's family, and to participate on equal terms with the locals in the social and economic life of the host state.

In light of the various components of these definitions, one could conclude that only the citizens of the EEA, Switzerland and Turkey have such a strong link and enjoy the rights mentioned above to various degrees.[8] The most extensive rights have been granted to EEA nationals, whose legal status is almost equivalent to that of Union citizens, followed by the status of Swiss nationals under the AFMP. Since Chapter 18 of this book deals exclusively with the rights of the EEA nationals, the present chapter focuses on the rights of Swiss and Turkish nationals. The rights of Turkish nationals are weakest, even though the main objective of the Ankara Agreement is quite ambitious. The Ankara Agreement does not provide Turkish nationals with a right to access the territory of Member States; however, in practice, Turkish workers, the self-employed and their family members have a right to access the territory of some of the Member States due to the application of standstill clauses, the operation of which will be explained in more detail below.

In the following, this chapter provides an overview of the rights enjoyed by Turkish nationals and their family members under the framework of the Ankara Agreement (section 2) and by Swiss nationals and their family members under the AFMP (section 3). This is followed by some concluding remarks, including on the question of whether one of these models or aspects

---

[4] Association Agreement between the European Union and its Member States, of the one part, and Ukraine, of the other part [2014] OJ L161/3. See Art 18 of the Agreement on the mobility of workers; Art 85(5) on establishment; and Arts 97–102 under the title 'Temporary presence of natural persons for business purposes' on the scope of the freedom to provide services.

[5] Magleby Sørensen, *The Exclusive European Citizenship: The Case for Refugees and Immigrants in the European Union* (Avebury 1996) 3.

[6] Ibid, 28 and 31.

[7] According to Siofra O'Leary, *The Evolving Concept of Community Citizenship: From the Free Movement of Persons to Union Citizenship* (Kluwer Law International 1996) 13, citizenship is about 'membership of and participation in a defined community or State [carrying] with it a number of rights and duties which are, in themselves, an expression of the political and legal link between the State and the individual'.

[8] The Association Agreement with Ukraine is one of the most advanced and comprehensive agreements signed by the EU in the recent years (n 4). However, it is not covered in this chapter since it does not fulfil the criteria for citizenship as defined above.

thereof could serve as inspiration for the rights of nationals of other third countries that might seek to establish close ties with the EU (section 4).

2. RIGHTS OF TURKISH NATIONALS AND THEIR FAMILY MEMBERS UNDER THE EEC–TURKEY ASSOCIATION LAW

2.1 Introductory Remarks

The EEC–Turkey Association Agreement, also called the Ankara Agreement (AA), has formed the basis of relations between the EU and Turkey since its entry into force in 1964. While the main priority of the Agreement was to establish a Customs Union between the parties, it also contained provisions envisaging the establishment of the freedom of movement for workers (Art. 12 AA), freedom of establishment (Art. 13 AA) and freedom to provide services (Art. 14 AA). The relevant provisions of the EEC Treaty were to provide guidance in achieving those objectives,[9] which were to be realised step by step by decisions taken by the Association Council (AC), the main decision-making body of the Association (Arts 22–23 AA).

An Additional Protocol (AP), which laid down more detailed rules and timetables for establishing the Customs Union and free movement of workers,[10] entered into force on 1 January 1973.[11] While it set 1986 as the deadline for establishing free movement of workers, it contained only a standstill clause on the freedom to provide services and freedom of establishment. With the changing political and economic realities of the 1970s and 1980s, establishing free movement of workers was no longer a desirable or realistic goal for both sides. Therefore, the AC adopted decisions that granted rights only to workers and their family members who were already legally resident on the territory of Member States. Decision 2/76 was the first decision adopted on the matter and was replaced later by Decision 1/80, which is still in

---

[9] Art 12 AA refers to Arts 48, 49, 50 of the Treaty establishing the Community, while Art 13 AA refers to Arts 52, 56 and 58, and Art 14 AA refers to Arts 55, 56, 58, and 65 of the Treaty. It was this wording of Art 12 AA that provided the basis for the CJEU to interpret concepts and rights of Turkish workers in parallel to those of Community/EU workers. See Daniel Thym, 'The Constitutional Foundations of the Judgments on the EEC–Turkey Association Agreement' in Daniel Thym and Margarite Zoetewij-Turhan (eds), *Rights of Third-country Nationals under EU Association Agreements: Degrees of Free Movement and Citizenship* (Brill/Nijhoff 2015) 17; Kees Groenendijk, 'The Court of Justice and the Development of EEC–Turkey Association Law' in Daniel Thym and Margarite Zoetewij-Turhan (eds), *Rights of Third-country Nationals under EU Association Agreements: Degrees of Free Movement and Citizenship* (Brill/Nijhoff 2015) 42; Anne Pieter van der Mei, 'The Bozkurt-Interpretation Rule and the Legal Status of Family Members of Turkish Workers under Decision 1/80 of the EEC–Turkey Association Council' (2009) 11 EJML 367, 367–8; and Narin Tezcan/Idriz, 'Free Movement of Persons between Turkey and the EU: To Move or not to Move? The Response of the Judiciary' (2009) 46 CML Rev 1621, 1623.

[10] The Customs Union was put in place as planned by the adoption of Decision No 1/95 of the EC–Turkey Association Council on implementing the final phase of the Customs Union [1996] OJ L35/1.

[11] The Additional Protocol (AP) is a mixed agreement and forms an integral part of the AA, [1973] OJ C113/17.

force.¹² What ensured that the rights granted in these decisions did not remain a dead letter was the jurisprudence of the CJEU establishing that it had jurisdiction to interpret these decisions.¹³

It is the relevant provisions of these instruments – the AA, the AP and the AC Decisions – together with their corresponding interpretation by the CJEU that constitute the so-called Ankara *acquis* or EEC–Turkey Association Law. It is important to note from the outset that the regime of free movement between the EU and Turkey is a peculiar one. Its peculiarity stems from the combination of its grandiose ambitions (integrating Turkey into EU's internal market by gradually establishing the four freedoms before its accession into the EU) with the minimal and modest steps taken to make these ambitions a reality. These rules bear the mark of the era in which they were taken and the instruments that served as their source of inspiration; that is, they reflect the spirit of the 1960s and 1970s. Therefore, these rules comprise the free movement rights of economically active Turkish nationals and their families, that is, workers, the self-employed and service providers. The self-sufficient and recipients of services do not fall within the scope of Association Law.¹⁴

2.2 Market Access, the Right to Employment and Legal Residence

The Court ruled in *Demirel* that Art. 12 AA, according to which Arts 48, 49 and 50 of the EEC Treaty were to provide guidance in securing the freedom of movement for workers, did not have direct effect,¹⁵ despite the fact that the deadline laid down in the AP had expired. However, Turkish workers and their family members could rely on other provisions of the AA or the AC decisions that did fulfil the conditions of direct effect.¹⁶ These decisions put some flesh on the bones of Art. 12 AA. They specified the rights to residence, employment and non-discrimination that Turkish workers and their family members have on the territory of a host Member State, as well as the grounds for limiting these rights. They also introduced a standstill obligation on the conditions of access to employment of Turkish workers and their family members. The fact that some provisions in these decisions were inspired by the provisions of the first Regulation adopted on the free movement of workers in the EEC's transition period¹⁷ illustrates the peculiarity of Association Law, in terms of both its ambition and its limitations.

---

¹² Decision No 2/76 of the Association Council on the implementation of Article 12 of the Ankara Agreement, not published in the Official Journal. It laid down the rules for the implementation of the first stage of Art 36 AP, which was to last for four years. It was replaced by Decision No 1/80 of the Association Council of 19 September 1980 on the development of the Association, not published in the Official Journal.

¹³ For an overview of the case law of the CJEU, see Groenendijk (n 9).

¹⁴ There are no rights for the self-sufficient in Association law as those did not exist within the EEC legal framework, but developed later in the 1990s. Regarding the limited scope of the free movement of services, it was the Court's *Demirkan* judgment that established that service recipients are not covered by Art 41(1) AP. See Case C-221/11 *Leyla Ecem Demirkan v Bundesrepublik Deutschland* EU:C:2013: 583.

¹⁵ Case C-12/86 *Meryem Demirel v Stadt Schwäbisch Gmünd* EU:C:1987:400, para 23.

¹⁶ Case C-192/89 *S. Z. Sevince v Staatssecretaris van Justitie* EU:C:1990:32, para 26.

¹⁷ cf Art 6 of Decision 1/80 to Art 6 of Regulation No. 15 on the first steps for attainment of freedom of movement for workers within the Community [1961] OJ 57/1073 (German, French, Italian, Dutch language versions; no longer in force).

The most invoked provision of Decision 1/80, which is still applicable, provides for the gradual integration of Turkish workers into the labour force of a Member State. According to the first indent of Art. 6, Turkish workers are entitled to the extension of their work permit with the same employer after one year, if the job is available. They can change employer after three years of legal employment, subject to priority being given to the workers of that Member State and on the condition that they practise the same occupation. It is only after four years of legal employment that Turkish workers can enjoy free access to any employment in that Member State. What breathed life into this provision and made it functional was the Court's jurisprudence establishing that the right to employment necessarily implied a right to legal residence. According to the Court, any other interpretation would deprive the right to access to the labour market and the right to work of all effect.[18]

The Court's finding in *Demirel* regarding the lack of direct effect could also be extended to the provisions of the AA on freedom of establishment and freedom to provide services.[19] The absence of any specific AC decision on these freedoms does not mean that there are no Turkish nationals providing services or that there are no self-employed Turkish nationals in the Member States. It merely means that in the absence of the direct effect of these two provisions, they need to rely on other provisions to claim rights under Association Law, such as the standstill clause prohibiting the introduction of any new restrictions on these freedoms or the general prohibition of non-discrimination on the basis of nationality in the AA. In addition, it is worth noting that the Court acknowledged that the principles it established in the context of free movement of workers 'must also apply, by analogy, in the context of the provisions of that Association Agreement concerning the right of establishment'.[20]

2.3 Access to the Territory of Member States

There is no provision in Association Law that explicitly grants Turkish nationals access to the territory of Member States. However, the objective of the AA, and of the AP in particular, was to achieve freedom of movement for workers and service providers and freedom of establishment gradually over time, by keeping markets open where they were already so (by introducing standstill obligations) and by opening them, by way of decisions of the AC, where they were not yet open. As mentioned above, the deadline for opening Member States' employment markets to establish free movement of workers was 1986. There was no such deadline for the realisation of the freedom to provide services and freedom of establishment, but a broad standstill obligation prohibited the parties from introducing any new restrictions to these freedoms.[21] Such a standstill clause was also laid down in Art. 7 of Decision 2/76, which was later replaced by Art. 13 of Decision 1/80. Cases brought before the CJEU on the standstill clauses are relevant regarding market access, as they reveal these clauses apply on rules of first entry into a Member State, that is, they help to determine whether there is a right to access the territory of a particular Member State regarding a particular freedom.

---

[18] *Sevince* (n 16) para 29; and Case C-1/97 *Mehmet Birden v Stadtgemeinde Bremen* EU:C:1998:568, para 20.
[19] The Court already ruled that Art 13 AA has no direct effect in Case C-37/98 *The Queen v Secretary of State for the Home Department, ex parte Abdulnasir Savas* EU:C:2000:224, para 45.
[20] *Savas* (n 19) para 63.
[21] See Art 41(1) AP.

The Court established that the standstill obligation applies to procedural and substantive rules on first entry into an EU (formerly: Community) Member State with regard to freedom of establishment, freedom to provide services and freedom of movement for workers.[22] According to the Court, these provisions, which have direct effect, do not grant any substantive rights on individuals, but are merely quasi-procedural rules helping one identify which particular rule or law of a Member State is applicable to a situation.[23] The obligation not to act or not to introduce new restrictions becomes operative as of the entry into force of the instrument containing the standstill clause with regard to that state. Moreover, once a restriction is lifted, it may not be reintroduced.[24] In short, the standstill provisions aim to freeze the most favourable legal framework for the three freedoms after their entry into force in a particular Member State. Unfortunately, this leads to a fragmented picture across the EU.[25] While the free movement rules were quite liberal in the old Member States when the standstill obligations became applicable in the 1970s, that was not usually the case with the states that joined the Community/Union in the 1990s and 2000s.[26]

Another peculiarity of Association Law is the evolution of the case law on the standstill clauses. While the Court initially defined the standstill obligation as 'an absolute prohibition' on creating any new obstacles,[27] it changed its interpretation in the face of harsh critique and the realisation that such an approach might not be sustainable.[28] In *Demir*, it acknowledged the possibility of Member States to derogate from the standstill obligation on public policy, public security and public health grounds, as well as on grounds of overriding reasons in the public interest, on the proviso that the restriction introduced respected the principle of proportionality.[29]

With this development the case law on the freedom of movement for workers, services and establishment in Association Law came closer to resembling the case law of the Court on the

---

[22] See respectively, Case C-16/05 *The Queen, Veli Tum and Mehmet Dari v Secretary of State for the Home Department* EU:C:2007:530; Case C-228/06 *Mehmet Soysal and Ibrahim Savatli v Bundesrepublik Deutschland* EU:C:2009:101; and Case C-225/12 *C. Demir v Staatssecretaris van Justitie* EU:C:2013: 725.

[23] *Tum and Dari* (n 22) para 55.

[24] Joined cases C-300/09 and 301/09 *Staatssecretaris van Justitie v F. Toprak and I. Oguz* EU:C: 2010:756.

[25] Steve Peers, 'EC Immigration Law and EC Association Agreements: Fragmentation or Integration?' (2009) 34 EL Rev 628; Mustafa T Karayigit, 'Vive la Clause de Standstill: The Issue of First Admission of Turkish Nationals into the Territory of a Member State within the Context of Economic Freedoms' (2011) 13 European Journal of Migration and Law 411, 433–40.

[26] See Kees Groenendijk and Elspeth Guild, *Visa Policy of Member States and the EU towards Turkish Nationals After Soysal* (3rd edn, Economic Development Foundation No. 257 2012).

[27] *Tum and Dari* (n 22) para 61.

[28] See Kay Hailbronner, 'The Stand Still Clauses in the EU–Turkey Association Agreement and Their Impact upon Immigration Law in the EU Member States' in Daniel Thym and Margarite Zoetewij-Turhan (eds), *Rights of Third-country Nationals under EU Association Agreements: Degrees of Free Movement and Citizenship* (Brill/Nijhoff 2015) 197–8.

[29] *Demir* (n 22) paras 40–41. On *Demir*, see Narin Tezcan, 'The Puzzle Posed by *Demir* for the Free Movement of Turkish Workers: A Step Forward, a Step Back, or Standstill' in Daniel Thym and Margarite Zoetewij-Turhan (eds), *Rights of Third-country Nationals under EU Association Agreements: Degrees of Free Movement and Citizenship* (Brill/Nijhoff 2015) 221–47.

four freedoms of the internal market.³⁰ In addition to prohibiting rules discriminating on the basis of nationality, restrictions on the respective freedoms are prohibited under Association Law. While that is the case by virtue of the standstill clause regarding the rights of workers and their family members, regarding the freedom of establishment (Art.13 AA) and the freedom to provide services (Art. 14 AA), it is also the case by virtue of the wording of these two provisions, which aim at 'abolishing restrictions' between the parties. However, since these provisions lack direct effect,³¹ individuals are able to rely on the principles enshrined in them only indirectly, by invoking the respective standstill clauses, which is only possible for measures adopted after the entry into force of the standstill clauses.³² Notably, there is no such temporal limitation in EU law.

2.4 Non-discrimination Rights

Art. 9 AA contains a general provision prohibiting any discrimination on the basis of nationality, in line with the principle laid down in Art. 18 TFEU. This provision applies without prejudice to the more specific non-discrimination provisions that were laid down later in the AP and AC decisions. The first such provision was Art. 37 AP, which prohibited discrimination on the basis of nationality for Turkish workers with regard to conditions of work and remuneration. This provision was replicated in Art. 10(1) of Decision 1/80. Another specific non-discrimination provision that is important in terms of the rights enjoyed by Turkish workers and their families applies in the area of social security, namely Art. 3(1) of Decision 3/80.³³ It is worth taking a brief look at the case law of the Court to understand the scope of these prohibitions.

In determining the scope of the prohibition of discrimination contained in Art. 10(1) of Decisions 1/80, the Court reiterated that it has consistently inferred from the wording of Arts. 12 AA and 36 AP that principles laid down in Arts. 45, 46 and 47 TFEU 'must be extended, so far as possible, to Turkish nationals who enjoy the rights conferred by Decision No 1/80'.³⁴ The prohibition in Art. 10(1) specifically targets 'remuneration and other conditions of work'. According to the Court, 'other conditions of work' must be interpreted to have a broad scope as far as Art. 45(2) TFEU 'provides for equal treatment in all matters directly and indirectly

---

[30] The development of the case law in that direction was predicted by İlke Göçmen, 'To Visa, or Not to Visa: That Is the (Only) Question, Or Is It?' (2010) 37 Legal Issues of Economic Integration 149, 158–61. See also Thym (n 9) 24; Tezcan (n 29) 246.

[31] Since the wording of Art 13 AA is almost identical to that of Art 14 AA, the Court's ruling in *Savas* (n 19) para 45 regarding the lack of direct effect of that provision can also be transposed to Art 14 AA.

[32] The relevant date is 1 January 1973 for the freedom to provide services and freedom of establishment (art 41(1) AP), 20 December 1976 for the freedom of movement for workers (Art 7 of Decision 2/76) and 1 December 1980 for the rights of workers' family members (Art 13 of Decision 1/80). For Member States joining the EU after these dates, the entry into force of these instruments is the date they acceded to the EU.

[33] Association Council Decision 3/80 of 19 September 1980 on the application of the social security schemes of the Member States of the European Communities to Turkish workers and members of their families, not published in the Official Journal.

[34] Case C-171/01 *Wählergruppe 'Gemeinsam Zajedno/Birlikte Alternative und Grüne GewerkschafterInnen/ UG', and Bundesminister für Wirtschaft und Arbeit and Others* EU:C:2003:260, para 72.

related to the exercise of activity as an employee in the host Member State'.[35] All these statements led the Court to establish that Art. 10(1) lays down for Turkish workers 'a right to equal treatment as regards conditions of work and remuneration of the same extent as that conferred in similar terms by [Art. 45(2) TFEU] on nationals of the Member States'.[36]

The broad interpretation of the prohibition of non-discrimination with regard to remuneration and other conditions of work was matched by an equally strong equal treatment obligation in the field of social security, enabling Turkish workers and their family members to have access to a variety of social security benefits on the same terms as the nationals of the host Member State.[37] This development was of particular significance given the fact that Decision 3/80 required further implementing measures, which were never taken.[38] The case law of the Court contributed to creating a stable and secure status for Turkish workers and their families, enabling them to enjoy almost full equality regarding conditions of work and access to social security benefits in the host Member State, which led some scholars to coin the term 'citizenship of the Association'[39] or 'Association citizenship'.[40]

2.5   Right to Family Reunification

There is no substantive right to family reunification for Turkish workers and the self-employed in Association Law. AC Decisions grant rights to the family members of Turkish workers who have been authorised to join them. Until the introduction of the Family Reunification Directive (FRD),[41] the basis of that authorisation was not EU law but the national law of the Member States. Currently, like all third country nationals (TCNs), Turkish nationals are also able to rely on the provisions of the FRD.[42] In addition to the right granted in the Directive, in some

---

[35]   Ibid para 85.

[36]   Ibid para 89.

[37]   For the list of the benefits covered under Decision 3/80 see its Art 4. See also Case C-262/96 *Sema Sürül v Bundesanstalt für Arbeit* EU:C:1999:228; Joined cases C-102/98 and 211/98 *Ibrahim Kocak v Landesversicherungsanstalt Oberfranken und Mittelfranken and Ramazan Örs v Bundesknappschaft* EU:C:2000:119; Case C-373/02 *Sakir Öztürk v Pensionsversicherungsanstalt der Arbeiter* EU:C:2004: 232.

[38]   For more details see Paul Minderhoud, 'Social Security Rights under Decision No 3/80 of the EEC–Turkey Association Council: Developments in the EU and in the Netherlands' (2016) 18 Eur J Soc Sec 268, 269.

[39]   See Annette Schrauwen and Thomas Vandamme, 'Towards a Citizenship of the Association? On the Future of Non-Discrimination, Preferential Treatment and the Standstill Clauses in the EU–Turkey Association Regime' in Elspeth Guild, Cristina Gortázar Rotaeche and Dora Kostakopoulou (eds), *The Reconceptualization of European Union Citizenship* (Brill/Nijhoff 2014) 89–109.

[40]   Julinda Beqiraj and Francesca Ippolito, 'Conceptualizing an "Association Citizenship" for Children of Turkish Workers' in Daniel Thym and Margarite Zoetewij-Turhan (eds), *Rights of Third-country Nationals under EU Association Agreements: Degrees of Free Movement and Citizenship* (Brill/Nijhoff 2015) 277.

[41]   Directive 2003/86/EC on the right to family reunification (FRD) [2003] OJ L251/12.

[42]   For an analysis of the interaction between the FRD and Ankara Association Law, see Steve Peers, 'EU Migration Law and the EU/Turkey Association Agreement' in Daniel Thym and Margarite Zoetewij-Turhan (eds), *Rights of Third-country Nationals under EU Association Agreements: Degrees of Free Movement and Citizenship* (Brill/Nijhoff 2015) 205–12.

cases there might be a right to family reunification by virtue of the application of the standstill clauses, which according to the Court also apply to the rules on family reunification.[43]

In all the five family reunification cases brought before the CJEU up to the time of writing, it found that the rules have been made more stringent: in one case by introducing the requirement to hold a residence permit to enter and reside for TCNs under the age of 16;[44] in two cases by introducing a requirement to establish sufficient ties with the host Member State that will enable future integration;[45] and in two other cases by introducing a pre-entry language requirement.[46] Even though all five applicants were successful in challenging the laws that prevented them to stay with or join their loved ones, in most cases this success was due to their particular circumstances. The new rules failed the proportionality test because of the specificities of each case. As far as the objectives of these laws were concerned, the Court ruled that 'prevention of forced marriages',[47] 'achieving successful integration'[48] and 'efficient management of migration flows'[49] may constitute overriding reasons in the public interest. This means that these rules may no longer be considered as 'new restrictions', which are prohibited, but as new rules that are justified in the light of the public interests they pursue. The implication of this finding for future applications is that only exceptional cases that fail the proportionality test will succeed.[50]

2.6 Rights Granted to Family Members of Turkish Workers

Decision 1/80 strengthened the rights of Turkish workers in the host Member States and granted more rights to their family members.[51] The only right granted to family members in Decision 2/76 was the right of Turkish children to have access to courses of general education.[52] That right was upgraded in Art. 9 of Decision 1/80 to provide for the admission of Turkish children 'to courses of general education, apprenticeship and vocational training under the same educational entry qualifications as the children of nationals of that Member State'. The provision added further that they might also be eligible for advantages provided in the area of education. The Court interpreted this provision as a full-blown non-discrimination

---

[43] See Narin Idriz, 'Hierarchies of Privilege: Juxtaposing Family Reunification Rights, Integration Requirements, and Nationality in EU Law' in M Jesse (ed), *European Societies, Migration and the Law: The 'Others' amongst 'Us'* (CUP 2020) ch 7.

[44] Case C-652/15 *Furkan Tekdemir v Kreis Bergstraße* EU:C:2017:239, paras 28–30.

[45] Case C-561/14 *Caner Genc v Integrationsministeriet* EU:C:2016:247, para 50; and Case C-89/18 *A v Udlændinge- og Integrationsministeriet* EU:C:2019:580. For the annotation of *Genc*, see Narin Tezcan/Idriz, 'Family Reunification under the Standstill Clauses of EU–Turkey Association Law: *Genc*' (2017) 54 CML Rev 263.

[46] Case C-138/13 *Naime Dogan v Bundesrepublik Deutschland* EU:C:2014:2066; Case C-123/17 *Nefiye Yön v Landeshauptstadt Stuttgart* EU:C:2018:632.

[47] *Dogan* (n 46) para 38.

[48] *Genc* (n 45) para 55. See also *A* (n 45) para 33.

[49] *Tekdemir* (n 44) para 39; *Yön* (n 46) para 77; *A* (n 45) para 33.

[50] This conclusion does not hold for cases where the law itself is not suitable for achieving the objective it pursues, as was the case with the Danish law that gave rise to two preliminary references, namely *Genc* (n 45) and *A* (n 45). For the Court's ruling to that effect, see *A* (n 45), paras 35–46.

[51] For an example, cf Art 2 of Decision 2/76 to Art 6 of Decision 1/80. For an analysis of the case law on the rights of family members, see van der Mei (n 9); Tezcan/Idriz (n 9) 1642–5, 1660–4; Groenendijk (n 9) 43–4.

[52] See Art 3 of Decision 2/76.

provision covering the area of education, including university education and extending to related benefits and advantages provided under national law. According to the Court, any other interpretation would make the non-discriminatory access to education of Turkish children 'purely illusory'.[53]

Art. 7(2) of Decision 1/80 also provides children of Turkish workers 'who have completed a course of vocational training in the host country' access to the labour market of the host state under more favourable conditions compared to other members of the worker's family. These children can respond to any offer of employment, 'provided one of their parents has been legally employed in the Member State concerned for at least three years'. Other family members can respond to an offer of employment only after three years of legal residence in the host Member State and subject to priority being given to nationals of other Member States. They have free access to any employment only after five years of legal residence. These rights were important at the time they were introduced; however, they are *de facto* defunct since the introduction of the FRD, which provides that all family members of a TCN who were allowed to join him have a right to access the labour market of the host Member State after a residence period of maximum 12 months.[54]

2.7 Limitations on the Rights of Turkish Workers and Their Family Members

Turkish workers' right to residence might be terminated on three grounds. First, if they cease to belong to the labour force of the host Member State, either because they retire or they become permanently incapacitated;[55] second, if they do not strictly observe the requirements of Art. 6(1) and change their employer before they are allowed to;[56] last, 'on grounds of public policy, public security or public health'.[57] Regarding the interpretation and application of the latter concepts, the Court ruled that to ensure the effectiveness of the rights of Turkish workers 'it is essential to grant those workers the same procedural guarantees as those granted by Community law to nationals of Member States'.[58] Accordingly, the protection provided under Arts 8 and 9 of Directive 64/221 was to be extended both to Turkish workers and to their family members enjoying rights under Decision 1/80.[59]

While it was easier to extend the rights of Community workers to Turkish workers, the underlying rationale of the free movement rights of both categories being economic, the situation changed with the introduction in the European Union of the concept of Union citizenship and Directive 2004/38/EC.[60] Under this Directive, nationals of Member States of the EU were

---

[53] Case C-374/03 *Gaye Gürol v Bezirksregierung Köln* EU:C:2005:435, para 39.
[54] See Art 14 FRD.
[55] Case C-434/93 *Ahmet Bozkurt v Staatssecretaris van Justitie* EU:C:1995:168, para 39.
[56] Case C-4/05 *Hasan Güzeli v Oberbürgermeister der Stadt Aachen* EU:C:2006:670.
[57] See Art 14 of Decision 1/80.
[58] Case C-136/03 *Georg Dörr v Sicherheitsdirektion für das Bundesland Kärnten and Ibrahim Ünal v Sicherheitsdirektion für das Bundesland Vorarlberg* EU:C:2005:34, para 67.
[59] Ibid, paras 67–68. See also Directive 64/221/EEC on the co-ordination of special measures concerning the movement and residence of foreign nationals which are justified on grounds of public policy, public security and public health [1963–1964] OJ Spec Ed 117 (no longer in force).
[60] Directive 2004/38/EC on the right of citizens of the Union and their family members to move and reside freely within the territory of the Member States amending Regulation (EEC) No 1612/68 and repealing Directives 64/221/EEC, 68/360/EEC, 72/194/EEC, 73/148/EEC, 75/34/EEC, 75/35/EEC, 90/364/EEC, 90/365/EEC and 93/96/EEC [2004] OJ L158/77 (as corrected).

given free movement rights and extra protections by virtue of their status as Union citizens. In *Ziebell*, the Court established that it was not possible to extend the extra protection granted to Union citizens against expulsion under that Directive to Turkish workers.⁶¹ In other words, Turkish workers are no longer automatically comparable to Union workers by virtue of the additional status of the latter as Union citizens, the basis of which is political and no longer economic.

It is worth noting that the rights of Turkish versus Union workers were never entirely comparable, despite the CJEU's extension to the former of some of the principles underlying the rights of the latter. One of the most important differences is the fact that Turkish workers enjoy rights only in their host Member State.⁶² They have never had the right to move between Member States.⁶³ An additional limitation engrained in Association Law is Art. 59 AP, which provides that Turkish nationals cannot be treated more favourably than nationals of the Member States – which occurs very rarely.⁶⁴

The gap between the rights of Turkish nationals and those of Union citizens is likely to get bigger over time,⁶⁵ as Union citizenship becomes the 'fundamental status of nationals of the Member States'.⁶⁶ This is also visible in the Court's *Demirkan* ruling, in which it established the scope of the freedom to provide services in Association Law to exclude the freedom to receive services, as the receipt of services according to the Court comes too close to establishing 'freedom of movement for persons of general nature which may be compared to that afforded to European Union citizens under Article 21 TFEU'.⁶⁷ Another justification for the restrictive interpretation of the freedom to provide services, according to the Court, is the 'essentially economic purpose' of the Ankara Agreement, which it established to be different from that of the Union, which is to establish an internal market.⁶⁸

After *Ziebell*, *Demirkan* is the second case in which, by looking at the context and purpose of the Ankara Agreement,⁶⁹ the Court deviates from its classic approach of parallel interpreta-

---

⁶¹ Case C-371/08 *Nural Ziebell v Land Baden-Württemberg* EU:C:2011:809.
⁶² Case C-325/05 *Ismail Derin v Landkreis Darmstadt-Dieburg* EU:C:2007:442, para 66.
⁶³ Now that is possible for all TCNs who fulfil the conditions of Dir. 2003/109/EC concerning the status of third-country nationals who are long-term residents (Long-term Residents Directive) [2004] OJ L16/44.
⁶⁴ See *Derin* (n 62); Case C-485/07 *Raad van bestuur van het Uitvoeringsinstituut werknemersverzekeringen v H. Akdas and Others* EU:C:2011:346.
⁶⁵ This gap is to some extent filled by secondary EU law that grants rights to TCNs, such as the Family Reunification Directive (n 41) and the Long-term Residents Directive (n 63). See also Peers (n 42).
⁶⁶ See Case C-184/99 *Rudy Grzelczyk v Centre public d'aide sociale d'Ottignies-Louvain-la-Neuve* EU:C:2001:458, para 31.
⁶⁷ *Demirkan* (n 14) para 53.
⁶⁸ *Demirkan* (n 14) para 56.
⁶⁹ In the interpretation of a provision of the Ankara Agreement, in addition to its wording, the Court has also been looking into 'the nature and purpose of the agreement itself' since its earliest cases. See *Demirel* (n 15) para 14. Thus, what is novel in *Ziebell* (n 61) and *Demirkan* (n 14) is not the Court's general approach to interpreting the provisions of Association law, but the downgrading of the objective of the association to one of 'purely' or 'essentially economic nature'. In the past, the Court did not shy away from acknowledging the ultimate aim of the association is 'accession'. For two examples, see *Savas* (n 19) para 52; Case C-416/96 *Nour Eddline El-Yassini v Secretary of State for Home Department* EU:C:1999:107, para 49.

tion,⁷⁰ and the first in which it explicitly mentions its *Polydor* ruling as a justification for doing so.⁷¹ In both cases the Court ignores the accession objective of the Ankara Agreement⁷² and downgrades it to 'purely' or 'essentially' economic.⁷³ While the Court's reasoning in *Ziebell* could be defended in light of the accession objective of the agreement,⁷⁴ its reasoning in *Demirkan* is problematic even if one were to ignore that objective. As argued by Hatzopoulos, the difference between the economic objective of the Ankara Agreement and the EU's internal market is 'one *of degree not of nature*',⁷⁵ and as such there is no legal or economic basis to justify the Court's approach.⁷⁶ In this respect it is worth underlining that the objective of the Ankara Agreement is Turkey's accession to the EU, until the parties decide otherwise, which entails full integration into the EU and its internal market. This objective is also the only meaningful explanation of its Customs Union with the EU.⁷⁷

---

⁷⁰ See the literature cited in n 9.
⁷¹ According to the principle developed in the *Polydor* case, similarity in wording does not suffice for parallel interpretation of provisions of international agreements: the context and purpose of these agreements has to be taken into account. See Case 270/80 *Polydor Limited and RSO Records Inc. v Harlequin Records Shops Limited and Simons Records Limited* EU:C:1982:43, paras 14–15. For an in-depth discussion of the use of this principle in the context of the Ankara Agreement, see Christa Tobler, 'Context-related Interpretation of Association Agreements. The Polydor Principle in a Comparative Perspective: EEA Law, Ankara Association Law and Market Access Agreements between Switzerland and the EU' in Daniel Thym and Margarite Zoeteweij-Turhan (eds), *Rights of Third-country Nationals under EU Association Agreements: Degrees of Free Movement and Citizenship* (Brill/Nijhoff 2015) 112 –14; Thym (n 9) 16–27.
⁷² The Ankara Agreement explicitly states the objective of accession in the fourth recital of its preamble and its Art 28 AA.
⁷³ See respectively *Ziebell* (n 61) para 72 and *Demirkan* (n 14) para 56.
⁷⁴ Arguably, there is a qualitative difference between rights granted by virtue of being an economic actor and rights granted by virtue holding a political status/citizenship. However, in this context, it should be noted that the Court also ruled that the Ankara Agreement 'has the objective of bringing the situation of Turkish nationals and citizens of the Union closer together through the progressive securing of free movement for workers and the abolition of restrictions on freedom of establishment and freedom to provide services'. See Case C-92/07 *European Commission v Kingdom of the Netherlands* EU:C:2010: 228, para 67.
⁷⁵ See Vassilis Hatzopoulos, 'Turkish Service Recipients under the EU–Turkey Association Agreement: *Demirkan*' (2014) 51 CML Rev 647, 659. Cf Thym (n 9) 14–27.
⁷⁶ Hatzopoulos (n 75) 663. It should be noted that there is nothing in the wording of Art 14 AA to justify a more limited scope or the application of a different interpretation method when compared to Art 12 AA on the freedom of movement of workers. Similarly, there is nothing in the Court's former case law to provide clues to that effect. See, Joined cases C-317/01 and 369/01 *Eran Abatay and Others* (C-317/01) and *Nadi Sahin* (C-369/01) *v Bundesanstalt für Arbeit* EU:C:2003:572, para 112.
⁷⁷ Decision 1/95 (n 10).

3. RIGHTS OF SWISS NATIONALS AND THEIR FAMILY MEMBERS UNDER THE EU–SWISS AGREEMENT ON THE FREE MOVEMENT OF PERSONS

3.1 Introductory Remarks

In comparison with the Ankara law, the EU–Swiss Agreement on the Free Movement of Persons (AFMP) is not only much younger but also rather different in terms of its substantive reach. In the view of the political institutions of the EU, Switzerland is participating in the EU's extended internal market, and thus is a partner in a multilateral project.[78] At the same time, it is important to note that the economic part of the present EU–Swiss agreement relates only to three of the four freedoms of the internal market – there is no agreement about the free movement of capital – and then only to parts of these freedoms. These limits are crucial to an understanding of the legal relationship between the EU and Switzerland, and also with respect to the movement of persons, which is the focus of the present contribution.[79]

On the one hand, being modelled on EU free movement law, it is unsurprising that AFMP provides for the usual categories of free movement rights, namely market access (for the economically active), movement and residence rights (also for persons who are not economically active) and derived family rights. In addition, there are rules relating to social security and professional qualifications. According to Art. 1 AFMP, it is the objective of the Agreement, for the benefit of nationals of the EU Member States and of Switzerland:

(a) to accord a right of entry, residence, access to work as employed persons, establishment on a self-employed basis and the right to stay in the territory of the Contracting Parties;
(b) to facilitate the provision of services in the territory of the Contracting Parties, and in particular to liberalise the provision of services of brief duration;
(c) to accord a right of entry into, and residence in, the territory of the Contracting Parties to persons without an economic activity in the host country;
(d) to accord the same living, employment and working conditions as those accorded to nationals.

On the other hand, there are important limits both in terms of scope and in terms of rights, as will be shown below. In fact, in certain areas such differences exist even though Art. 16(2) AFMP states the principle of parallel interpretation. According to the wording of this provision, CJEU case law handed down prior to the signature of the agreement is to be taken

---

[78] See e.g. Council conclusions on a homogeneous extended single market and EU relations with Non-EU Western European countries of 16 December 2014, para 44, www.consilium.europa.eu/uedocs/cms_data/docs/pressdata/en/er/146315.pdf accessed 29 May 2020.

[79] For a brief, general introduction to the EU–Swiss legal relationship in the English language, see Matthias Oesch, *Switzerland and the European Union: General Framework, Bilateral Agreements, Autonomous Adaptation* (Dike 2018). For more extensive information from a legal point of view, see notably Thomas Cottier, Nicolas Diebold, Isabel Kölliker, Rachel Liechti-McKee, Matthias Oesch, Tetyana Payosova and Daniel Wüger, *Die Rechtsbeziehungen der Schweiz und der Europäischen Union* (Stämpfli 2014). For a political science perspective see Sandra Lavenex and René Schok, 'The Swiss Way: The Nature of Switzerland's Relationship with the EU' in EO Eriksen and JE Fossum (eds), *The European Union's Non-members. Independence under Hegemony?* (Routledge 2015) 36. For a historical perspective, see Clive H Church (ed), *Switzerland and the European Union: A Close, Contradictory and Misunderstood Relationship* (Routledge 2007), and Johnathan Steinberg, *Why Switzerland?*, 3rd edition (CUP 2015), ch. 8 'Switzerland and the European Union'.

into account when concepts of Union law are at issue.[80] While the CJEU tends to stick to this wording,[81] the Swiss Federal Tribunal takes a broader approach and, as a matter of principle, also looks at more recent CJEU case law.[82] Even so, differences may emerge.

3.2 Market Access Rights of Economic Operators

Under the AFMP, economically active persons enjoy market access rights. However, compared to EU law, these are more limited both in terms of the field of application of the Agreement and in terms of the substantive meaning of those rights.

On the level of scope, according to Art. 18 Annex I AFMP, service providers covered by the Agreement can be companies formed in accordance with the law of a Member State of the EU or Switzerland and having their registered office, central administration or principal place of business in the territory of a Contracting Party; such companies may post workers in another country. However, outside Art. 18 Annex I AFMP the AFMP covers only natural persons and is thus more limited than is EU law on the free movement of persons and services. Notably, there is no freedom of establishment for companies under the AFMP[83] (but rather only under other and specific sectoral agreements).[84]

With respect to services, there is a limitation to services of 'brief duration' (for both natural persons and companies), which relates to activities for 'a period not exceeding 90 days of actual work in a calendar year' (Art. 5(1) AFMP), which is again different from EU law. Further, while the CJEU in its EU case law went beyond the wording of Arts 56 and 57 TFEU to extend market access rights also to service recipients,[85] the same is not true for the AFMP, as stated first by the Swiss Federal Tribunal[86] and subsequently also by the CJEU.[87] Under the AFMP, natural persons who are service providers merely enjoy movement and residence rights, to the exclusion of substantive market access rights. In this respect, the Swiss Federal Tribunal argued that the bilateral agreements do not lead to an integral participation of Switzerland in the EU's internal market. Interestingly, the relevant passage also contains a reference to Union citizenship:

---

[80] Art 16(2) AFMP states: 'Insofar as the application of this Agreement involves concepts of Community law, account shall be taken of the relevant case-law of the Court of Justice of the European Communities prior to the date of its signature. Case-law after that date shall be brought to Switzerland's attention. To ensure that the Agreement works properly, the Joint Committee shall, at the request of either Contracting Party, determine the implications of such case-law.'

[81] For a recent example, see Case C-581/17 *Martin Wächtler v Finanzamt Konstanz* EU:C:2019:138, para 45.

[82] The Federal Tribunal has decided that there is an obligation to 'take into consideration' also younger CJEU cases. Deviation from it is allowed if there are cogent reasons to do so; case law as of BGE 136 II 5; see Oesch (n 79), 33.

[83] See notably Case C-351/08 *Christian Grimme v Deutsche Angestellten-Krankenkasse* EU:C:2009: 697.

[84] Namely the Agreement between the European Economic Community and the Swiss Confederation on direct insurance other than life assurance, [1991] OJ 1991 L205/3, and the Agreement between the European Community and the Swiss Confederation on Air Transport, [1999] OJ 2002 L114/73, both as amended.

[85] Case 286/82 *Graziana Luisi and Giuseppe Carbone v Ministero dello Tesoro* EU:C:1984:35.

[86] BGE 133 V 624.

[87] Case C-70/09 *Alexander Hengartner and Rudolf Gasser v Landesregierung Vorarlberg* EU:C: 2010:430.

In order to be able to fully assess the scope of the relevant ECJ rulings for Switzerland, it should be borne in mind that the AFMP is part of a series of seven agreements, which are not only sectoral, but also concern only partial areas of the four freedoms which are the free movement of persons, goods, capital and services; it is therefore not a question of full participation in the Community internal market [...] CJEU judgments based on concepts or considerations expressed outside this relatively narrow context cannot therefore, without further examination, be transposed into Swiss law. This is the case, for example, for the notion of European citizenship, which is absent from the AFMP and which cannot apply to Switzerland.[88]

On the level of the substantive meaning of market access under the AFMP, too, the Agreement is more limited than EU law, even though many of its basic provision are modelled on EU law and even though Art. 16(2) AFMP states the principle of parallel interpretation. Instead, the case law in this field reflects the application of the Polydor principle, according to which different contexts may lead to different interpretations of otherwise identical or similar provisions.[89]

Within the EU internal market and based on CJEU case law, the right of market access has developed into a far-reaching regime that relates both to actual access to the relevant market (employment, self-employment, services) and to the treatment while active on that market. In this context, CJEU case law defines market access rights under EU law not only as a right to equal treatment with respect to nationality, prohibiting both direct and indirect discrimination (which approach also applies in the context of the AFMP), but also as a right to be free from any other restriction that would make free movement more difficult or less attractive. Thus, even though the wording of Art. 45 TFEU only mentions discrimination on grounds of nationality, the Court also included the prohibition of restrictions.[90] The same is true for the EEA Agreement due to its extension of the, in principle, full internal market rules to the non-EU states Iceland, Liechtenstein and Norway.[91] In both legal orders, the relevant rules also prohibit the state of origin from hindering free movement.

Conversely, it has been a long-debated issue whether, in addition to the prohibition of discrimination on grounds of nationality, the AFMP also includes a prohibition of restrictions in this broad sense.[92] At the time of writing (spring 2020) there is no explicit case law that would address the issue as a matter of principle. There are, however, bits and pieces that result in a picture that is both complicated and intriguing. It is worth taking a somewhat closer look, and offering a comparison with the Ankara law.

It has been noted above that the standstill provisions of the Ankara law have been interpreted by the CJEU as prohibiting restrictions and that these provisions fulfil a crucial role in the legal framework of this law. Conversely, in the context of the AFMP, the standstill provision of Art. 13 AFMP is less important in practice due to the existence of other, substantive provisions that give rights to individuals. It is nevertheless interesting to note that, even though the Contracting Parties under Art. 13 AFMP undertake 'not to adopt any further restrictive

---

[88] BGE 133 V 624, consideration 4.3.4, translation from the original Italian language of the judgment.
[89] See above under 2.7.
[90] E.g. in Case C-19/92 *Dieter Kraus v Land Baden-Württemberg* EU:C:1993:125.
[91] See the EEA chapter in the present volume.
[92] See in this context in particular the PhD thesis by Chantal Delli, Verbotene Beschränkungen für Arbeitnehmende. Überlegungen zur Tragweite des Personenfreizügigkeitsabkommens zwischen der Schweiz sowie der EG und ihren Mitgliedstaaten (Helbing Lichtenhahn 2009), with further references.

measures' vis-à-vis each other's nationals in fields covered by the Agreement, the Swiss Federal Tribunal has interpreted this as covering discriminatory measures only – without taking into account the development of the CJEU law on EU law or (from a comparative perspective) on the Ankara law.[93] It is submitted that a broader interpretation is called for also under the AFMP.[94]

To turn to the substantive rights of workers, the CJEU held in *Grimme* that Art. 9 Annex I AFMP guarantees (emphasis added):

> [E]qual treatment of employed persons who are nationals of a Contracting Party in the territory of another Contracting Party. Thus, they may not be treated differently in the territory of the other Contracting Party from national employed persons as regards conditions of employment and working conditions, especially as regards pay, dismissal, or reinstatement or re-employment if they become unemployed. Therefore, that Article only concerns the case of discrimination by reason of nationality against a national of a Contracting Party *in the territory of another Contracting Party*.[95]

This is, therefore, a more limited approach than under EU law. However, subsequent case law shows that, in certain specific constellations, workers can indeed rely on the provisions of the AFMP against their own Member State. This includes notably the situation where they are employed or self-employed frontier workers.[96] However, according to Advocate General (AG) Mengozzi's opinion in *Picart*,[97] such cases concern very specific situations and do not mean that market access under the AFMP goes beyond the prohibition of discrimination on grounds of nationality. In support of this view, the AG refers to consistent CJEU case law according to which Switzerland did not join the (full) internal market of the EU, as a consequence of which the interpretation given to the provisions of EU law concerning that market cannot be automatically applied by analogy to the interpretation of the AFMP, unless there are express provisions to that effect laid down by the agreement itself.[98] The CJEU in *Picart* did not address the question of whether the AFMP includes a prohibition of restrictions.

However, there is more recent case law that appears to point in a different direction than that advocated by AG Mengozzi. In *Wächtler*, the Court confirms its previous finding according to which the scope *ratione personae* of the provisions in the AFMP on the self-employed is limited to situations where the person in question 'has become established in the territory of another contracting party and pursues a self-employed activity in the territory of that other

---

[93] BGE 130 I 26.

[94] See already Christa Tobler, *Grundzüge des bilateralen (Wirtschafts-)Rechts. Systematische Darstellung in Text und Tafeln text volume* (Dike 2013) para 190. On the EU side, Case C-506/10 *Rico Graf und Rudolf Engel v Landratsamt Waldshut* ECLI:EU:C:2011:643 involved indirect discrimination on grounds of nationality contrary to Art 13 AFMP. The CJEU did not address the question of whether the standstill provision goes further than discriminations.

[95] *Grimme* (n 83) para 47 et seq, emphasis added.

[96] E.g. BGE 136 II 241 (Swiss Federal Tribunal); Case C-425/11 *Katja Ettwein v Finanzamt Konstanz* EU:C:2013:121, and Case C-241/14 *Roman Bukovansky v Finanzamt Lörrach* EU:C:2015:766 (both CJEU). Regarding social security law, see n 119.

[97] Case C-355/16 *Christian Picart v Ministre des Finances et des Comptes publics*, Opinion of AG Mengozzi, EU:C:2017:610, para 49 et seq.

[98] Beginning with *Grimme* (n 83) para 27; Christa Tobler, 'Die EuGH-Entscheidung *Grimme* – Die Wiederkehr von *Polydor* und die Grenzen des bilateralen Rechts' in A Epiney and N Gammenthaler (eds), *Schweizerisches Jahrbuch für Europarecht 2009/2010* (Stämpfli and Schulthess 2010) 369.

party'.⁹⁹ But then it adds that the right of establishment, within the meaning of EU law, has the aim not only of ensuring that foreign nationals are treated in the host Member State in the same way as nationals of that state, but also of preventing restrictions on that right issuing from the Member State of origin of the national concerned. The Court then proceeds to apply this also to the AFMP (though it should be remembered that this is only within the framework of the above-mentioned requirement of having to be established 'in the territory of another Contracting Party'):

> Accordingly, in certain circumstances and in the light of the applicable provisions, nationals of a Contracting Party of the AFMP may claim rights under that agreement not only against the State to which they exercise freedom of movement but also against their State of origin […]. The free movement of persons guaranteed by the AFMP would be impeded if a national of a Contracting Party were to be placed at a disadvantage in his State of origin solely for having exercised his right of free movement […]. It follows that the principle of equal treatment, laid down in Article 15(2) of Annex I to the AFMP, read together with Article 9 of that annex, can also be relied on against his State of origin by a self-employed person who falls within the scope of that agreement.¹⁰⁰

The Court finds that a case such as *Wächtler* involves 'an unjustified restriction on the right of establishment provided for by the AFMP'.¹⁰¹ In other words, while the Court refers to equal treatment on grounds of nationality, in fact its finding is much closer to that of a restriction within the meaning of EU law. However, commentators note that it remains open whether the Court indeed meant to recognise a prohibition of restrictions with relation to the self-employed.¹⁰²

Finally, it also remains open whether the Court's findings in *Grimme* preclude workers under the AFMP from making use of the approach reflected in EU law case law such as *Angonese*.¹⁰³ In that case, which concerned Art. 45 TFEU, the Court referred to indirect discrimination on grounds of nationality against the background of a situation where an Italian had brought an action against his own Member State. Based on this case law, where a rule amounts to indirect discrimination on grounds of nationality (rather than a mere restriction), persons affected by the rule in question may rely on the prohibition of discrimination even against their own Member State and in spite of not holding the foreign nationality.¹⁰⁴ While this approach appears to have been successful in a tax dispute in Switzerland in which Christa

---

[99] *Wächtler* (n 81) para 49.
[100] Ibid, paras 51–54.
[101] Ibid, para 67.
[102] Benedit Pirker and Livia Matter, 'Recent Practice: Europarecht: Schweiz–Europäische Union' (2020) 30 SRIEL 75, 88.
[103] Case C-281/98 *Roman Angonese v Cassa di Risparmio di Bolzano SpA* EU:C:2000:296. Conversely, in the more recent Case C-710/18 *WN v Land Niedersachsen* ECLI:EU:C:2020:299 the Court found that the concept of discrimination cannot be relevant in a case involving a national complaining about action of the state of this person's nationality.
[104] See also Case C-419/92 *Ingetraut Scholz v Opera Universitaria di Cagliari and Cinzia Porcedda* EU:C:1994:62, and Case C-224/01 *Gerhard Köbler v Austria*, EU:C:2003:513. The same approach can be found in the field of social law: Case C-83/14 *CHEZ Razpredelenie Bulgaria AD v Komisia za zashtita ot diskriminatsia (third parties: Anelia Nikolova, Darzhavna Komisia za energiyno i vodno regulirane)* EU:C:2015:480.

Tobler was involved, it should be noted that the decision in her case was handed down unreasoned, meaning that the legal grounds on which the case was decided are not known.[105]

3.3 Movement and Residence Rights; Family Rights

In addition to market access rights, the AFMP provides for rights in relation to movement and residence and family members. However, it is important to note that, in this respect, the agreement is still on the level of the EU law at the time of signing the AFMP in 1999, both for economic and for non-economic actors. In other words, the AFMP does not reflect the present EU law under Directive 2004/38. Indeed, in this respect, there is a particularly marked gap between EU law and the EU–Swiss AFMP.

This raises the question of how to interpret the AFMP in the areas where the Swiss courts are bound by CJEU case law under Art. 16(2) of the Agreement, particularly in a situation where much free movement case law of that Court relates to Union citizenship or to Directive 2004/38. The Swiss Federal Tribunal has been flexible in this respect. For example, it followed the Court's *Metock* case law,[106] even though it dates from after the time of the signature of the FMPA, is based on Directive 2004/38 and deviates from previous case law.[107]

In fact, the EU would like to see the content of Directive 2004/38 integrated into the AFMP. However, in 2011 the Swiss government refused to enter into negotiations on this matter. In a media release the government stated that, compared to the free movement of persons as laid down in the AFMP, Directive 2004/38 leads to additional claims, especially in the area of social assistance and family reunification, and that Switzerland considered the rules currently in force to be sufficient.[108] While the government did not mention Union citizenship explicitly in this context, the fact remains that the entitlement to equal treatment with respect to social assistance under Art. 24 of the Directive is rooted in previous CJEU case law where the Court recognised such a right based on Union citizenship in combination with other provisions, for which it had previously denied such an interpretation.[109] As the Swiss Federal Tribunal rightly notes, the anchoring of Union citizenship in EU primary law was accompanied by an expansion to include rights that went beyond those that existed under the previous law.[110]

From 2014 onwards, the issue of updating the AFMP in the light of Directive 2004/38 returned to the table in negotiations between the EU and Switzerland about a new institutional arrangement for some of their economic agreements, among them the AFMP. While the EU demanded that Directive 2004/38 be incorporated into the AFMP on the same terms as in

---

[105] *Christa Tobler v Schweizerische Eidgenossenschaft und Staat Zürich*, decision of the *Steuerrekursgericht* of 31 January 2020.

[106] Case C-127/08 *Blaise Baheten Metock and Others v Minister for Justice, Equality and Law Reform* EU:C:2008:449.

[107] BGE 136 II 5; see in particular Francesco Maiani, 'La "saga Metock", ou des inconvénients du pragmatisme helvétique dans la gestion des rapports entre droit européen, droit bilatéral et droit interne' [2011] I Revue de droit suisse 27.

[108] Swiss Federal Government, *Schweiz-EU: Elftes Treffen des Gemischten Ausschusses zum Freizügigkeitsabkommen*, 14 June 2011, www.admin.ch/gov/de/start/dokumentation/medienmitteilungen.msg-id-39604.html accessed 29 May 2020.

[109] E.g. *Grzelczyk* (n 66), with respect to the right to equal treatment relating to social assistance for the economically non-active. See generally Daniel Thym, 'The Elusive Limits of Solidarity: Residence Rights of and Social Benefits for Economically Inactive Union Citizens' (2015) 52 CML Rev 17.

[110] BGE 141 II 35, consideration 5.2.

the EEA[111] in the framework of a new, dynamic mechanism of continuous updating of the Agreement in order to keep it in line with the relevant EU law, the Swiss government stuck to its line that this is not necessary and should not happen. As a result of these differences, Directive 2004/38 is not explicitly mentioned in the draft text for an Institutional Agreement as published in 2018,[112] and the parties to the negotiations appear to disagree on what this means.

In a letter sent to the European Commission following an internal Swiss consultation on the draft text, the federal government stated that while it believes the outcome of the negotiations to be largely in Switzerland's interests, it will be necessary, in order to present the draft Institutional Agreement to the Swiss Federal Parliament, to clarify certain points. With respect to Directive 2004/38, the letter states that 'Switzerland wishes to clarify that no provision of the institutional agreement shall be interpreted as an obligation for Switzerland to adopt the directive, or any related further developments, and that a possible adoption of the directive by Switzerland shall only be achieved by means of negotiations between the parties'.[113] However, in May 2021 the Swiss government decided not to sign the Institutional Agreement.

It is submitted that the Directive would indeed have fallen under the new dynamic updating mechanism but that including it into the AFMP would still have required a formal treaty revision. This is due to the fact that the AFMP provides for a simplified way of amendment only with respect to Annexes II and III that deal with the coordination of the social security systems and with the mutual recognition of professional qualifications, respectively, to the exclusion of the main body of the Agreement and of Annex I, which deals with free movement. In that respect, a formal treaty revision is required. Christa Tobler[114] had therefore suggested that the following Joint Declaration be added to the Institutional Agreement: 'The parties note that an adaptation of the Agreement on the Free Movement of Persons to the relevant provisions of Directive 2004/38 must be made in accordance with Art. 18 FMPA by way of a formal revision of the Agreement.'

In practice, the negotiations between the parties would have provided scope for substantive discussions on the extent to which the Directive should be incorporated into the AFMP, based on whether or not a particular part of the Directive can or cannot be traced back to Union citizenship. In addition to the issue of equal treatment under Art. 24 of Directive 2004/38, which

---

[111] See the EEA chapter in this volume.

[112] Draft text of 23 November 2018, in the original French language: Accord facilitant les relations bilatérales entre l'Union Européenne et la Confédération Suisse dans les parties du marché intérieur auxquelles la Suisse participe, www.eda.admin.ch/dam/dea/fr/documents/abkommen/Acccord-inst-Projet-de-texte_fr.pdf accessed 29 May 2020. On the draft agreement, see Christine Kaddous, 'Switzerland and the EU: Current Issues and New Challenges under the Draft Institutional Framework Agreement' in S Gstöhl and D Phinnemore (eds), *Proliferation of Privileged Partnerships: The Proliferation of Privileged Partnerships between the European Union and its Neighbours* (Routledge 2019) 68, in the German language e.g. Astrid Epiney, 'Der Entwurf des Institutionellen Abkommens Schweiz – EU', Jusletter 17 December 2018; Christa Tobler and Jacques Beglinger, Tobler/Beglinger-Brevier zum Institutionellen Abkommen Schweiz-EU, edition 2020-02.1 of 16 February 2020 (continuously updated), www.brevier.eur-charts.eu accessed 29 May 2020.

[113] Letter to Commission President Juncker of 7 June 2019, unofficial English translation, www.eda.admin.ch/dam/dea/en/documents/bericht_konsultationen_insta/20190607_Lettre-CF-President-Commission-europeenne_en.pdf accessed 29 May 2020.

[114] Christa Tobler, 'Wie weiter mit dem Institutionellen Abkommen? Varianten zum Umgang mit den drei heiklen Punkten' (2020) *Jusletter*, para 55 et seq https://jusletter.weblaw.ch/juslissues/2020/1007/wie-weiter-mit-dem-i_c32d05eeef.html__ONCE&login=false accessed 31 March 2021.

is clearly rooted in Union citizenship, in formal negotiations Switzerland might have pointed to the CJEU's finding that the concept of citizenship is a feature of EU law which justifies the recognition, 'for Union citizens alone, of guarantees which are considerably strengthened in respect of expulsion, such as those provided for in Article 28(3)(a) of Directive 2004/38'.[115] On a more general level, the Court held that 'a particularly restrictive interpretation of the derogations [from free movement] is required by virtue of a person's status as a citizen of the Union'.[116] On the Swiss side, the Federal Tribunal has expressed the view that not only Art. 28(3) of Directive but also Art. 6 (residence up to three months) and Art. 16 (permanent residence) are linked to Union citizenship.[117] Referring to all of these points, Switzerland could have argued that it should be left out of any update of the AFMP in light of Directive 2004/38.

Conversely, it is submitted that no such argument could be made with regard to the more widely defined family circle under Art. 2(2) of the same Directive, which now also includes registered partners. There is no indication whatsoever that this change is due to Union citizenship. Instead, it is simply a more modern version of the previous law on derived family rights and as such should also be part of an updated AFMP. In fact, this would not change anything on the Swiss side, as Swiss law recognises a right to residence of registered same-sex partners.[118]

3.4 Social Security and Professional Qualifications

When the AFMP was signed in 1999, it incorporated the then valid EU law on matters of social security and on professional qualifications by referring to it in Annexes II and III to the Agreement. According to Art. 18 AFMP, these annexes may be updated, in light of more recent EU law in the relevant fields, by the Joint Committee that is in charge of the AFMP. This happened after the EU had adopted new legislation in these fields.[119] Since then, a process of updating the AFMP has been ongoing in light of more recent changes to that legislation. The parallelism with EU law is also reflected in the CJEU case law on social security matters in cases with a Swiss element.[120] As a result, in the fields of social security and professional qualifications, the AFMP is particularly close to EU law.

---

[115] *Ziebell* (n 61) para 73.

[116] Joined Cases C-482/01 and 493/01 *Georgios Orfanopoulos and Others v Land Baden-Württemberg* EU:C:2004:262, para 65.

[117] BGE 142 II 35, consideration 5.2. In academic writing, see in particular Astrid Epiney and Sian Affolter, 'Das Institutionelle Abkommen und die Unionsbürgerrichtlinie', (2019) *Jusletter* https://jusletter.weblaw.ch/juslissues/2019/971/das-institutionelle-_327cb6c5be.html__ONCE&login=false accessed 31 March 2021.

[118] Aliens and Integration Act of 16 December 2005, in German: *Bundesgesetz über die Ausländerinnen und Ausländer und über die Integration* (Ausländer- und Integrationsgesetz, AIG), SR 142.20, Art 52.

[119] Reg. 883/2004/EC on the coordination of social security systems [2004] OJ L166/1, Reg. 987/2009/EC laying down the procedure for implementing Regulation (EC) 883/2004 on the coordination of social security systems [2009] OJ L284/1 and Directive 2005/36/EC on the recognition of professional qualifications [2005] OJ L255/22.

[120] See e.g. Case C-29/19 *ZP v Bundesagentur für Arbeit* EU:C:2020:36: This case, like the earlier Case C-257/10 *Försäkringskassan v Elisabeth Bergström* EU:C:2011:839, concerns an EU national complaining about rules of the state of origin.

3.5 Free Movement of Persons under Political Pressure

The above shows that, in terms of its content, how close the AFMP in its present form is to the modern EU free movement and EU citizenship law depends on the various sub-fields involved. Even so, it is certainly much closer to EU law than is the Ankara Association law. At the same time, the political accession objective of the latter is much more ambitious – there is no such objective in the AFMP. It is true that the Swiss government had requested negotiations on potential Community membership in 1992, but this was put on ice following a negative popular referendum on EEA membership later in the same year and the request was formally withdrawn in 2016. Since then, the Swiss government has focused on the 'Bilateral Way' (as it is often called in Switzerland).

At the same time, the current way of managing the legal relationship with the EU and, more particularly, the free movement of persons appears to be under constant political pressure. On the Swiss side, the country's political system of semi-direct democracy[121] has led to a number of popular initiatives that aim at limiting, or even doing away with, the free movement of persons. The initiative 'For a moderate immigration (Limitation Initiative)' was put to the vote on 27 September 2020 and was rejected. The initiative was opposed by the Swiss federal government which, overall, is in favour of the system of free movement.[122] If accepted, the initiative would have meant the end of not only the free movement of persons between Switzerland and the EU,[123] but also of a number of other EU–Swiss agreements that are legally linked to the AFMP, with which they form a package called the 'Biterals I'. In addition, accepting the initiative would already then have dealt a deathblow to the draft Institutional Agreement. Further, the EU had announced that, without an Institutional Agreement, it would not be prepared to conclude new market access agreements with Switzerland or to update certain existing market access agreements in favour of Switzerland.[124]

The above shows the importance of the free movement of persons in the overall picture of the relationship between the EU and Switzerland. Given the factors at issue in summer 2020, Schwok has concluded that the Bilateral Way finds itself in 'a fragilized position'.[125] Indeed, the question 'EU–Switzerland: quo vadis', raised by Maresceau in 2011,[126] is still relevant and will remain so in the future.

---

[121] On EU–Swiss relations and the Swiss political system see Marius Wahl and Nina Grolimund, *Integration without Membership: Switzerland's Bilateral Agreements with the European Union* (Centre for European Policy Studies 2006), 8; Alexander Trechsel, 'Direct Democracy and European Integration: A Limited Obstacle?' in Clive H Church (ed), *Switzerland and the European Union: A Close, Contradictory and Misunderstood Relationship* (Routledge 2007), 36.

[122] See media release by the Swiss Federal Government: www.ejpd.admin.ch/ejpd/de/home/themen/abstimmungen/begrenzungsinitiative.html accessed 29 May 2020.

[123] And further, in the context of the EFTA Agreement, between Switzerland and the other EFTA States.

[124] See most recently Council conclusions on EU relations with the Swiss Confederation, 19 February 2019, www.consilium.europa.eu/en/press/press-releases/2019/02/19/council-conclusions-on-eu-relations-with-the-swiss-confederation/ accessed 29 May 2020.

[125] René Schwok, 'Switzerland–EU Relations: The Bilateral Way in a Fragilized Position' (2020) 25(2) European Foreign Affairs Review 159.

[126] Marc Maresceau, 'EU–Switzerland: Quo Vadis?' 39 (2011) Georgia Journal of International & Comparative Law 727.

4. CONCLUDING REMARKS

The above discussion has shown that both the Ankara Association law and the EU–Swiss AFMP provide for certain rights that, in the different context of EU law, are part of the package of rights of Union citizens. However, it was also noted that CJEU case law emphasises certain limits of the two models with respect to the legal position of natural persons. Against this background, some academic writers use terms such as 'citizenship of the Association'.[127]

As for the AFMP, from the point of EU law it is indeed an association agreement within the meaning of Art. 217 TFEU and as such establishes 'special, privileged links [of the EU] with a non-member country which must, at least to a certain extent, take part in the [Union] system'.[128] It was shown that the Agreement provides for important substantive rights of natural persons. Still, these rights are more limited than under EU law. In some cases this is due to the fact that the AFMP reflects old EU law (movement and residence, family rights). In others it has to do with limitation of scope as set out in the Agreement (such as the limitation of services to those of 'brief duration'), and still other limits result from a comparatively narrow interpretation of the existing rights by the courts (market access). What results is a picture of meaningful yet, in comparison with Union citizenship, limited rights. In fact, if the most important components of the concept of citizenship were to be defined as rights to access to territory, the right to be accompanied by one's family and the right to equal treatment while residing in a state (see introduction), it becomes clear that, in the case of the AFMP and compared to Union citizenship, one could speak about 'partial' Union citizenship at most. But then perhaps it is better to adhere to 'a citizenship of the Association' or 'differentiated citizenship' as *sui generis* concepts.

The same is true for the Ankara law, which, from the point of EU law, is also an association regime, but a much more limited one as far as rights of natural persons are concerned. Compared to Union citizenship, one might speak of 'crippled' citizenship at best: there is no right to access the territories of Member States or to be accompanied by one's family in the Ankara Association law outside the standstill provisions. The differences between the rights of Turkish nationals and those of Union citizens do not end once the former has accessed the territory of a host Member State. Turkish workers need to strictly follow the rules of Art. 6 of Decision 1/80 for the initial four years of employment if they do not want to jeopardise their right to residence. Similarly, their family members are allowed to respond to an offer of employment only after three years of legal residence, subject to priority being given to workers of the Member States. Clearly, this is not comparable to the rights of economically active or self-sufficient Union citizens who have the right to be accompanied by their family members, and whose family members have immediate access to the labour market of the host state. Conversely, rights that can be compared to some extent, thanks to the interpretation of the CJEU, are the right to equal treatment with regard to remuneration and other conditions of work, access to education for children and access to social security benefits covered by Decision 3/80.

---

[127] Schrauwen and Vandamme (n 39).
[128] *Demirel* (n 15) para 9. From a political scientist's perspective, Lavenex overall speaks about a 'fragmented system of association'; Sandra Lavenex, 'Switzerland's Flexible Integration in the EU: A Conceptual Framework' (2009) 14 Swiss Political Science Review 547, 550.

In the case of the Ankara Association law, the changing political and economic environment, coupled with the changing aspirations of the parties regarding their relationship, have prevented the freedoms from developing to their full potential. The result is an idiosyncratic (or – again – *sui generis*) system of rules that can be explained in the context of EU–Turkey relations, but are far from forming a model or example for relations with any other third country.

This last remark relates to the question of whether any of these two models, or at least some of their elements, could serve as a template or an example for the rights to be enjoyed by the nationals of other third countries, and could have included UK nationals post-Brexit. Arguably, neither of the two models was very attractive to the UK in its entirety: the Turkish model is outdated and too complicated/impractical due to the standstill rules, and the Swiss model bears too much resemblance to the existing free movement regime within the EU, which was one of the important reasons behind the UK's decision to leave the EU. Indeed, the UK's strong emphasis on control over its immigration laws explains why no market access rights are provided for in the EU-UK Trade and Cooperation Agreement for workers and the self-employed.[129] In fact, the UK had ruled out any form of association that would have tied it to EU legislation and CJEU case law.

However, some aspects of the two models might be used as a source of inspiration in the context of the EU's relations with third countries that look for establishing close commercial links with the EU. This is particularly true for the equal treatment rights granted to individuals once they are legally resident on the territory of a Member State, the rules under the AFMP for the provision of services of short duration and the rules on the coordination of the social security systems and the mutual recognition of professional qualifications.

In particular, equal treatment for legally resident TCNs is one element that could be secured without difficulty, as the EU grants this right in many of its agreements with third countries.[130] As was already mentioned, that right is now also part of the EU's Charter of Fundamental Rights. However, whether the rights of nationals of a particular country amount to a form of 'associated' or 'differentiated citizenship' as defined in this chapter depends on whether there is some form of market access right for workers and the self-employed, even if limited or conditional.

---

[129] Trade and Cooperation Agreement between the European Union and the European Atomic Energy Community, of the one part, and the United Kingdom of Great Britain and Northern Ireland, of the other Part, OJ 2021 L 149/10.

[130] For a recent example, see Art 17 of the Association Agreement with Ukraine. For another example see Case C-265/03 *Igor Simutenkov v Ministerio de Educación y Cultura and Real Federación Española de Fútbol* ECLI:EU:C:2005:213.

20. Employment and social rights of labour migrants post-Brexit

Herwig Verschueren

1. INTRODUCTION

Now that the UK has left the European Union, the legal positions of EU citizens going to work in the UK and of UK citizens going to work in an EU Member State are no longer regulated by the Union law on the free movement of workers. Nevertheless, labour migration between the UK and the EU will not stop. On the contrary, workers from the EU will continue to go and work in the UK, and vice versa. But this will no longer take place as part of the EU system of free movement. The UK will subject this economic migration to certain conditions and the EU Member States will do the same. As far as the EU is concerned, this will partly be done jointly by applying the European directives with regard to labour migration from third countries.

In this chapter we will specifically pursue the question as to which employment and social security rights workers migrating between the UK and the remaining EU Member States could invoke. In this respect we will have a look at the various legal instruments that could play a role in this.

First of all, we will briefly expound on the currently applicable EU law on the free movement and posting of workers (section 2). Post-Brexit, this system will only be applicable to those workers who already used the right to free movement before the end of the transition period as provided for in the Withdrawal Agreement. In section 3, we will expand on the content of this agreement. For persons migrating as workers between the UK and the EU after that period, other rules will apply. For UK citizens going to work in an EU Member State, the EU directives on labour migration will be the main rules. These contain a number of provisions on the employment and social security rights of these individuals (section 4). In section 5 we will discuss a few examples of agreements concluded by the EU with third countries and, in particular, will examine what exactly has been provided for with regard to the employment and social security rights of labour migrants. In section 6 we will analyse the relevance of the EU–UK Trade and Cooperation Agreement in this respect. We will end with some concluding remarks (section 7).

2. EMPLOYMENT AND SOCIAL RIGHTS OF EU MIGRANT WORKERS: SHORT OVERVIEW[1]

Within the internal market EU citizens have the right to freely seek and take up employment in another Member State and to be treated equally to the workers of that State. These rights are

---

[1] For a more detailed analysis of the matters dealt with in this section see: Mijke Houwerzijl and Herwig Verschueren, 'Free movement of (posted) workers and applicable labour and social law' in

laid down in Article 45 TFEU and are further implemented in secondary law – since 2011, by EU Regulation 492/2011.[2] These instruments guarantee the right to equal treatment in the host State regarding, in particular, access to employment, terms and conditions of employment, social and fiscal advantages and housing.

Special rules govern the status of workers who are temporarily posted by an employer established in a certain Member State to carry out work on behalf of this employer in another Member State. This situation is first and foremost subject to the rules on the freedom to provide services across the border (Article 56 TFEU), which prohibit all restrictions on such freedom. A special directive on the posting of workers was adopted in 1996 to balance workers' protection, fair competition and the freedom to provide services.[3] This directive does not impose the application of all of the labour law provisions of the receiving State, but only of those provisions that constitute the core of mandatory rules for minimum protection (the so-called hard core), including, *inter alia*, maximum work and rest periods, minimum number of paid annual holidays and remuneration.

In addition, the employment rights for migrant and posted workers in the context of the free movement of workers and the freedom to provide services interact with the Private International Law rules applicable to the employment contract. The rules governing the determination of the applicable law are laid down in the Rome I Regulation.[4] In the absence of a choice of law, the principle is that the employment contract is subject to the law of the country where the employee habitually carries out his/her job (or from where he/she usually carries out his/her job), even when he/she is temporarily employed in another country.[5]

An important element in guaranteeing the right to free movement for workers is the necessity to avoid workers losing social security rights when looking for or accepting a job

---

Teun Jaspers and others (eds), *European Labour Law* (Intersentia 2019) 45–130; Catherine Barnard, *Substantive Law of the EU: The Four Freedoms* (5th edn, OUP 2016) 237–89; Anne Pieter van der Mei, 'Free movement of workers and coordination of social security' in Pieter Jan Kuijper and others (eds), *The Law of the European Union* (Wolters Kluwer 2018) 587–610; Paul Minderhoud, 'Free movement of workers' in Carolus Grütters and others (eds), *Migration on the Move* (Brill 2017) 54–75.

[2] European Parliament and Council EU Regulation (EU) 492/2011 of 5 April 2011 on freedom of movement for workers within the Union (EU Regulation 492/2011) [2011] OJ L141/1.

[3] European Parliament and Council Directive (EC) 96/71 of 16 December 1996 concerning the posting of workers in the framework of the provision of services (EC Posting of Workers Directive) [1997] OJ L18/1, as amended by European Parliament and Council Directive 2018/957 of 28 June 2018 amending Directive (EC) 96/71 concerning the posting of workers in the framework of the provision of services [2018] OJ L173/16. For a more specific analysis of this directive: Jens Arnholtz and Nathan Lillie (eds), *Posted Work in the European Union. The Political Economy of Free Movement* (Routledge 2020) and Piet Van Nuffel and Sofie Afanasjeva, 'The Posting of Workers Directive Revised: Enhancing the Protection of Workers and the Cross-border Provisions of Services' (2018) 3 European Papers 3 1401.

[4] European Parliament and Council Regulation (EC) 593/2008 of 17 June 2008 on the law applicable to contractual obligations (EC Rome I Regulation) [2008] OJ L177/6.

[5] See on the issue of applicable employment legislation in cross-border situations in the EU: Magdalena Bernaciak (ed.), *Market Expansion and Social Dumping in Europe* (Routledge 2015); Aukje Van Hoek, 'Re-embedding the Transnational Employment Relationship: A Tale about the Limitations of (EU) Law?' (2018) 55 CML Rev 2 449; Aukje van Hoek and Mijke Houwerzijl, 'Where do EU mobile workers belong, according to Rome I and the (E)PWD' in Herwig Verschueren (ed.), *Residence, Employment and Social Rights of Mobile Persons: On How EU Law Defines Where They Belong* (Intersentia 2016) 215–53; Herwig Verschueren, 'The European Internal Market and the Competition between Workers' (2015) 6 European Labour Law Journal 2 128.

in another Member State. This kind of loss can be a consequence of the application of the Member States' social security systems and more specifically of their territorial scope and waiting periods. Therefore, the Union legislature set up an EU system of coordination of the national social security schemes, which is currently laid down in EC Regulation 883/2004[6] and EC Regulation 987/2009.[7] This coordination system applies not only to EU citizens but also to third-country nationals.[8] The main principles of this system are the equal treatment of nationals of other Member States (Article 4 EC Regulation 883/2004); the aggregation of periods of insurance, employment or residence in the various Member States concerned (Article 6 EC Regulation 883/2004); and the waiving of residence requirements in the legislation of the Member States, so as to allow the export of benefits (Article 7 EC Regulation 883/2004). These principles are laid down in detailed provisions of these regulations, including some exceptions.

This coordination system also determines the applicable legislation in a cross-border situation. This is based on the State-of-employment principle for economically active persons and on the State-of-residence principle for economically inactive persons (Article 11 *et seq* EC Regulation 883/2004). As far as economically active persons are concerned, there are special rules for, *inter alia*, posting and situations in which the person concerned works in more than one Member State at the same time. For unemployed frontier workers, the legislation of the State of residence applies. These provisions do not aim only at preventing the simultaneous application of different national legal regulations and the possible complications, but also at ensuring that persons in cross-border situations between Member States are not left without social security coverage because there is no legislation that is applicable to them. These rules are imperative and do not leave any choice to the Member States or the persons concerned. At all relevant times, the legislation of only one Member State applies.[9]

3. EMPLOYMENT AND SOCIAL RIGHTS FOR MIGRANT WORKERS IN THE EU–UK WITHDRAWAL AGREEMENT

Since the UK has left the EU, these rules on the employment and social rights of labour migrants between the EU Member States have ceased to apply in cross-border situations between the EU and the UK. However, in the first period after the withdrawal of the UK,

---

[6] European Parliament and Council (EC) Regulation 883/2004 of 29 April 2004 on the coordination of social security systems (EC Regulation 883/2004) [2004] OJ L 200/1.

[7] European Parliament and Council Regulation (EC) 987/2009 of 16 September 2009 laying down the procedure for implementing Regulation (EC) No 883/2004 on the coordination of social security systems (EC Regulation 987/2009) [2009] OJ L 294/1.

[8] See European Parliament and Council Regulation (EU) 1231/2010 of 24 November 2010 extending Regulation (EC) No 883/2004 and Regulation (EC) No 987/2009 to nationals of third countries who are not already covered by these Regulations solely on the ground of their nationality [2010] OJ L344/1. For a detailed analysis of this regulation, see: Rob Cornelissen, 'Regulation 1231/2010 on the Inclusion of Third-country Nationals in EU Social Security Coordination: Reach, Limits and Challenges' (2018) 20 European Journal of Social Security 2 86.

[9] For more detail on this EU social security coordination system see: Maximilian Fuchs and Rob Cornelissen (eds), *EU Social Security Law: A Commentary on EU Regulations 883/2004 and 987/2009* (Beck-Hart-Nomos 2015); Jaan Paju, *European Union and Social Security Law* (Hart 2017); Frans Pennings, *European Social Security Law* (6th edn, Intersentia 2015).

transition rules applied as laid down in the Withdrawal Agreement, which entered into force on 1 February 2020.[10] From this date until the end of the transition period (which was set at 31 December 2020), EU law continued to be applied to and in the United Kingdom.

As regards the period after 31 December 2020, the Withdrawal Agreement safeguards free movement rights derived from EU law exercised by EU27 citizens residing or working in the UK and by UK nationals residing or working in the EU27 at the end of the transition period (Part Two).[11] Title II of Part Two concerns the rights of these persons related to residence, the rights of workers and self-employed persons and professional qualifications. As far as the rights of workers are concerned, Article 24 stipulates that EU law on the free movement for workers continues to apply to the workers covered by this part of the Withdrawal Agreement. It states explicitly that this includes the right to equal treatment in respect of employment and work, the right to social and tax advantages and the right to take up and pursue an economic activity.

Title III concerns the coordination of social security (Articles 30–36). These provisions are very complex and can be summarized as follows.[12] Article 31 confirms that the rules and objectives set out in Article 48 TFEU, EC Regulation 883/2004 and EC Regulation 987/2009 shall continue to apply to the persons as defined in Article 30.

Article 30 lists the persons to whom the EU regulations continue to apply. They primarily concern Union citizens who are, pursuant to EC Regulation 883/2004, subject to the social security legislation of the UK and mutatis mutandis to UK citizens who are subject to the social security legislation of a Member State at the end of the transition period.[13] The EU regulations also continue to apply to economically active persons who are not subject to the social security legislation of the UK or an EU Member State respectively, despite being economically active in the UK or that Member State respectively. This is the case, for instance, for Union citizens who are posted to the UK by their employers in a Member State and who remain subject to the legislation of the posting State during the posting period (application of

---

[10] Agreement on the withdrawal of the United Kingdom of Great Britain and Northern Ireland from the European Union and the European Atomic Energy Community (Withdrawal Agreement) [2020] OJ L29/1.

[11] Article 10 of the Withdrawal Agreement specifies the personal scope of these provisions. See for an earlier account of the labour mobility issues raised by Brexit: Carolus Grütters and others, *Brexit and Migration: Study for the LIBE Committee of the European Parliament* (European Parliament 2018); Elspeth Guild, *Brexit and Its Consequences for UK and EU Citizenship or Monstrous Citizenship* (Brill Nijhoff 2017); Yves Jorens and Grega Strban, 'New forms of social security for persons moving between the EU and the UK?' in Nazaré da Costa Cabral and others (eds), *After Brexit* (Palgrave Macmillan 2017) 271–321; Herwig Verschueren, 'Scenarios for Brexit and Social Security' (2017) 24 Maastricht Journal of European and Comparative Law 3 367.

[12] For more detail on how these provisions should be interpreted and for concrete examples of situations that might occur, see: European Commission, *Guidance Note relating to the Agreement on the withdrawal of the United Kingdom of Great Britain and Northern Ireland from the European Union and the European Atomic Energy Community. Part two – Citizen's rights*, C(2020) 2939 final of 12 May 2020, 32-54. This note has been prepared by staff of the European Commission, and specifies that the views contained therein should not be interpreted as stating an official position of the European Commission. For more details on the social security provisions in the Withdrawal Agreement see: Herwig Verschueren, 'The Complex Social Security Provisions of the Brexit Withdrawal Agreement, to be Implemented for Decades' (2021) 23 European Journal of Social Security 1, 7.

[13] This 'being subject to' is set by the rules on the determination of the applicable legislation in Articles 11 to 16 EC Regulation 883/2004.

Article 12 EC Regulation 883/2004). Although they do work in the UK, they are not subject to its legislation, nor do they reside there. Family members and survivors of all the persons in this list are covered as well.

All these persons shall be covered by the provisions on social security in the Withdrawal Agreement for as long as they continue, without interruption, to be in one of the situations in which both an EU27 Member State and the UK are involved at the same time (Article 30(2)). This means that when the cross-border situation between the UK and an EU27 Member State stops after the end of the transition period, the persons involved will no longer be covered by these provisions of the agreement. This also seems to be the case should these persons find themselves once again in such a cross-border situation at a later stage.

The exact scope of this is, however, not very clear. The situations mentioned above refer to situations of being subject to the legislation of the UK or a Member State. So these situations would continue so long as the subjection continues. This might be the case when a person changes employment within the same country, for instance when a UK citizen who works in Germany at the end of the transition period changes employment within Germany after the transition period and therefore continues to work in Germany. This UK citizen remains subject to the German social security legislation, which means that the situation remains unchanged.

Another situation concerns a Dutch worker who is posted to the UK and who remains subject to the Dutch legislation pursuant to Article 12 EC Regulation 883/2004 for the duration of the posting, and who is still subject to the Dutch legislation at the end of the transition period. In that case, the social security regulations remain applicable to this person (and his family members and survivors) for the duration of the posting (in accordance with Article 30(1)(e)(i)). However, this situation ends when the person goes back to work in the Netherlands at the end of his/her posting period. If this person were to be reposted to the UK a couple of months later, the regulations would no longer apply to him/her. It is remarkable, though, that if this were to concern a UK citizen who was posted from the Netherlands to the UK and who would continue to work in the Netherlands at the end of this posting period, this person would still fall within the scope of Article 31 and the social security regulations at the end of the posting period. Indeed, he/she would remain in the situation as intended in Article 30(1)(b), that is, that of UK citizens who are covered by the legislation of a Member State (the Netherlands in this case) at the end of the transition period. That situation does not change at the end of the posting period. The person in question remains subject to the Dutch legislation and is therefore covered by Article 30(1)(b), so the regulations remain applicable to him/her.

Regarding family members and survivors, Article 30(5) specifies that those persons shall be covered by this Title only to the extent that they derive rights and obligations in that capacity under EC Regulation No 883/2004. This provision signifies that these persons fall within the scope of Article 31, but only for the rights that are derived from their capacity as family member or survivor and not for rights they can claim on their own account.[14] Incidentally, these family members do not have to be in a cross-border situation themselves at the end of the transition period, as would be the case, for instance, for the children (residing in Belgium)

---

[14] However, this does not mean that these persons cannot fall within the scope of Article 31 on their own account. This is the case, for instance, for an economically non-active UK citizen who resides in Belgium at the end of the transition period. Pursuant to Article 11(3)(e) Regulation (EC) 883/2004 this person is subject to the Belgian legislation. As a result, he/she is in the situation mentioned in Article 30(1)(b) of the Withdrawal Agreement.

of a Belgian employee who works in the UK. It may even concern family members who are born after the end of the transition period or who are entitled to a benefit in the future, such as a survivor's pension. These family members can, *inter alia*, invoke the provisions in the regulations regarding the settlement of medical expenses by the competent Member State. If the entitling family member works in the UK, the competent Member State is the UK (application of Articles 17 and 18 Regulation (EC) 883/2004). However, the rights of these family members and survivors under the regulations only apply for as long as the entitling family member is in a situation as listed in Article 30.

In this respect, Article 31(2) states: 'by way of derogation from Article 9 of this Agreement, for the purposes of this Title, the definitions in Article 1 of Regulation (EC) No 883/2004 shall apply.' This reference to the definition of Article 1 EC Regulation 883/2004 also concerns the definition of family member. Consequently, the concept of 'family member' has to be interpreted in conformity with the provisions of this regulation[15] and not with the definition in Directive 2004/38.[16]

For persons who were not in a cross-border situation between the UK and the EU27 at the end of the transition period (31 December 2020), Article 32 governs some rights deriving from the social security coordination rules that need to be protected. More specifically, Article 32(1)(a) protects existing and future rights based on past periods of insurance, employment, self-employment or residence, including obligations deriving from such periods. It also ensures that EU citizens with previous periods in the UK, and vice versa, will be able to claim benefits and rely on the aggregation of periods if needed. The coordination rules will apply to periods completed before the end of the transition period as well as to those completed after that date. For instance, this provision applies to an EU27 citizen who worked in the UK but returned to his/her country of origin before the end of the transition period (and therefore is not in a cross-border situation on 31 December 2020 to which Articles 30 and 31 apply) and who retires after that date. His/her entitlement to an old-age pension based on his/her periods of insurance in the UK will continue to be covered by the EU social security coordination regulations.

In addition, Article 32(2) guarantees that the coordination rules on sickness benefits and family benefits will also apply to these persons (and their family members and survivors) when they receive a benefit under Article 32(1). This might include the obligation for the UK or for the EU27 Member State involved to cover the costs for the healthcare of such a person if he/she receives an old-age pension from the UK or from the EU27 Member State involved, as well to pay family benefits for children not living in the State paying the pension.

Furthermore, Article 32(1)(d) also guarantees the continuation of the payment of family benefits by the UK or an EU27 Member State for children not residing in the relevant State, if such benefits are paid by that State on 31 December 2020. In addition, Article 32(1)(e) protects the derived rights of family members existing at that date.

Finally, Article 39 confirms that the persons covered by Part Two on citizens' rights shall enjoy the rights provided for in the relevant titles of this part for their lifetime, unless they

---

[15] See Art. 1(i) Regulation (EC) 883/2004. In principle, this definition refers to the definitions in the applicable national social security legislation.

[16] See Art. 2 Directive 2004/38. This provision itself defines which persons can be regarded as family members and does not refer to the definitions in the national legislations of the Member States. See, inter alia, Case C-673/16 *Coman* EU:C:2018:385.

cease to meet the conditions set out in these titles. This may be a long time. For instance, pursuant to Article 32 of the Withdrawal Agreement, a 25-year-old Union citizen who has already worked in the UK for five years at the end of the transition period and who was to return to a Member State after that period can invoke the EU regulations 40 years after Brexit (so in 2060) in order to obtain and calculate a retirement pension from the UK. This person shall also be able to invoke all derived rights. Another illustration concerns the situation of a Union citizen, born in 1995, who has already worked and resided in the UK for six years at the end of the transition period and who remains there for the rest of his/her life, maybe as a pensioner later. In accordance with Articles 30 and 31 of the Withdrawal Agreement, the regulations shall remain applicable to this person. For instance, if this person were to return to his/her country of origin for a short holiday in 2070, and were to require medical care in that country, the European regulations in place at that moment would still apply with regard to the settlement of the costs between that country and the UK.

4.   UK CITIZENS AS THIRD-COUNTRY NATIONALS

The Withdrawal Agreement will only cover persons who were in a cross-border situation between the UK and an EU Member State at the end of the transition period or before that date (31 December 2020). Persons moving after that date shall not be able to rely on the provisions of this agreement. They may possibly rely on the Trade and Cooperation Agreement that will be discussed in section 6.

Notwithstanding the existence and content of such an agreement, UK citizens will, post-Brexit, be treated as third-country nationals under EU law and be protected as such by a number of EU directives regulating labour migration of third-country nationals to the EU. These directives also contain provisions on the employment and social security rights of third-country nationals. In this section we will briefly analyse these provisions.[17]

The first relevant directive is EC Directive 2009/50, which intends to facilitate the admission and mobility of highly qualified migrants and their family members by harmonizing, to a certain extent, entry and residence conditions throughout the EU and by providing a legal status and a set of rights.[18] These rights include equal treatment with the nationals of the host Member State, which is explicitly guaranteed in Article 14 for all employment conditions,

---

[17]   For a more detailed analysis see: Katharina Eisele, *The External Dimension of the EU's Migration Policy: Different Legal Positions of Third-country Nationals in the EU* (Wolf Legal Publishers 2013); Bjarney Friðriksdóttir, *What Happened to Equality? The Construction of the Right to Equal Treatment of Third-country Nationals in European Union Law on Labour Migration* (Brill 2017); Dimitri Kochenov and Martijn van den Brink, 'Pretending there is no Union: non-derivative *quasi*-citizenship rights of third-country nationals in the EU' in Daniel Thym and Margarite Zoeteweij-Turhan (eds), *Rights of Third-Country Nationals under EU Association Agreements: Degrees of Free Movement and Citizenship* (Brill Nijhoff 2015) 65–100; Herwig Verschueren, 'Employment and Social Security Rights of Third-country Labour Migrants under EU Law: An Incomplete Patchwork of Legal Protection' (2016) 18 European Journal of Migration and Law 4 373; Herwig Verschueren, 'Employment and Social Security Rights of Third-country Nationals under the EU Labour Migration Directives' (2018) 20 European Journal of Social Security 2 100.

[18]   Council Directive (EC) 2009/50 of 25 May 2009 on the conditions of entry and residence of third-country nationals for the purpose of highly qualified employment (EC Blue Card Directive) [2009] OJ L155/17.

including the freedom to join workers' organizations, as well as for the branches of social security as defined in EEC Regulation 1408/71 (now EC Regulation 883/2004). It also applies to payment of pensions to former 'EU Blue Card' holders when they move to a third country (Article 14(1)(f)).

Of particular importance for employment and social security rights of labour migrants is the so-called Single Permit EU Directive 2011/98.[19] This directive does not create a right for third-country national workers to enter a Member State for the purpose of employment. It only introduces a single application procedure and a single permit for both residence and access to employment on the territory of the host State. In addition, the directive guarantees a set of rights for third-country workers legally admitted to the Member States, including an elaborate provision on the right to equal treatment (Article 12). It stipulates that third-country workers covered by this directive shall enjoy equal treatment with nationals of the Member State where they reside with regard to employment conditions (including freedom of association and affiliation with and membership of an organization representing workers) as well as for branches of social security, as defined in EC Regulation 883/2004.[20] Article 12(4) also guarantees equal treatment with a State's own nationals for the payment of statutory old-age, invalidity and death pensions to third-country workers moving to a third country as well as to their survivors residing in a third country. However, Member States may limit equal treatment for social security rights, except for persons who are in employment or who have been employed for a minimum period of six months and are registered as unemployed. In addition, Member States may decide that equal treatment relating to family benefits does not apply to third-country nationals who have been authorized to work in the territory of a Member State for a period not exceeding six months, to third-country nationals who have been admitted to that territory for the purpose of study or to third-country nationals who are allowed to work there on the basis of a visa (Article 12(2)(b)). In addition, recital 24 of the directive specifies that the directive should not grant rights in situations which lie outside the scope of Union law, such as in relation to family members residing in a third country. This means that the directive does not guarantee the right to family benefits for children residing in a third country.

Next, EU Directive 2014/36 on seasonal workers[21] determines the conditions of entry, stay and access to the labour market for a limited period for third-country seasonal workers in the

---

[19] European Parliament and Council Directive (EU) 2011/98 of 13 December 2011 on a single application procedure for a single permit for third-country nationals to reside and work in the territory of a Member State and on a common set of rights for third-country workers legally residing in a Member State (EU Single Permit Directive) [2011] OJ L343/1. For a detailed analysis of the various aspects of this directive, see the contributions in: Paul Minderhoud and Tinneke Strik (eds), *The Single Permit Directive: Central Themes and Problem Issues* (Wolf Legal Publishers 2015). See also: Ana Beduschi, 'An Empty Shell? The Protection of Social Rights of Third-country Workers in the EU after the Single Permit Directive' (2015) 17 European Journal of Migration and Law 2/3 210.

[20] See on the application of this directive regarding the right to family benefits: Case C-449/16 *Martínez Silva* EU:C:2017:485. In this judgment the CJEU explicitly stated that derogations from the equal treatment provision can be relied on only if the national authorities responsible for the implementation of that directive have stated clearly that they intended to rely on them. See also Case C-302/19 *INPS* EU:C:2020:957.

[21] European Parliament and Council Directive (EU) 2014/36 26 February 2014 on the conditions of entry and stay of third-country nationals for the purpose of employment as seasonal workers (EU Seasonal Workers Directive) [2014] OJ L94/375. For a more detailed analysis of this directive see, inter alia: Judy Fudge and Petra Herzfeld Olsson, 'The EU Seasonal Workers Directive: When Immigration

EU Member States, and defines their rights. It provides for a simplified and uniform procedure for the admission of seasonal workers from third countries. As regards employment and social security rights, this directive also contains an equal treatment clause (Article 23). It guarantees the seasonal worker admitted to the host Member State under this directive equal treatment with nationals of this State with regard to all terms of employment, the right to strike and the right to take industrial action, as well as the right to freedom of association. It also provides for equality of treatment with nationals of the host country regarding back payments concerning any outstanding remuneration to be made by the employers to the third-country national.

Equal treatment for the branches of social security, as defined in EC Regulation 883/2004, is also provided for. However, as far as social security is concerned, Article 23(2)(i) allows Member States to restrict equal treatment for social security by excluding family benefits and unemployment benefits, meaning that Member States may deny seasonal workers entitlement to these benefits even if they meet the conditions imposed on the nationals of the Member States with regard to these benefits and even if they themselves or their employer paid contributions for the financing of these benefits. The final paragraph of Article 23(1) guarantees the payment of statutory pensions to seasonal workers moving to a third country as well as to their survivors residing in a third country, provided the export to the third country involved is also guaranteed to the nationals of the Member State in question.

EU Directive 2014/66 on the so-called intra-corporate transferees (ICTs)[22] has a very specific scope since it concerns temporary assignments by companies of highly skilled third-country nationals, in particular managers, specialists or trainee employees, to subsidiaries in the EU.[23] It aims at facilitating such transfers by setting up harmonized conditions for admission, residence and work, including speedy application procedures. It also provides for the possibility for the holders of an ICT permit issued by a Member State to enter, stay and work in one or several other Member States for a short or a long period.

This directive contains a provision on the right to equal treatment of these workers, but in a rather conditional way. As far as employment conditions are concerned, Article 18(1) provides that ICTs admitted under this directive shall enjoy at least equal treatment with persons covered by the EC Posting of Workers Directive with regard to the terms and conditions of employment in accordance with Article 3 of this directive in the Member State where the work is carried out. Compared with the equal treatment provisions in the other directives discussed above, it is clear that ICTs shall not be treated fully equally with workers of the host State in comparable situations.

Controls Meet Labour Rights' (2014) 16 European Journal of Migration and Law 4 439 and Mariya Gromilova, 'Can the EU Seasonal Workers' Directive Alleviate the Pending Crisis of Climate-Induced Displacement?' (2015) 6 European Labour Law Journal 4 292; European Migration Network, *Attracting and Protecting the Rights of Seasonal Workers in the EU and the United Kingdom – Synthesis Report* (European Migrations Network 2020).

[22] European Parliament and Council (EU) Directive 2014/66 of 15 May 2014 on the conditions of entry and residence of third-country nationals in the framework of an intra-corporate transfer (EU Intra-Corporate Transferees Directive) [2014] OJ L157/1. For more details see: Herwig Verschueren, 'The role of employment and social security rights in the Intra-Corporate Transferee Directive' in Paul Minderhoud and Tesseltje De Lange (eds), *The Intra Corporate Transferee Directive: General Themes, Problem Issues and Implementation in Selected Member States* (Wolf Legal Publishers 2018) 35–54.

[23] See the definitions in Article 3(b).

In fact, the provisions of the EU Intra-Corporate Transferees Directive leave open the extent to which the employment protection of the host State is applicable as well as the question of which law is applicable to the employment relationship. The latter is indeed a matter to be decided by the rules of Private International Law, as laid down in EC Rome I Regulation (see section 2). The employment contracts of ICTs who are sent temporarily to a subsidiary in the EU by an employer established in a third country, while maintaining their habitual place of work in that third country, will, on the basis of the EC Rome I Regulation, normally remain subject to the employment law of this third country and not to the employment law of the receiving State.

On the other hand, Article 18(2)(c) of the EU Intra-Corporate Transferees Directive provides that ICTs shall enjoy (unconditionally) equal treatment to nationals of the Member State where the work is carried out as regards the branches of social security as defined in EC Regulation 883/2004. However, for the latter matter the entitlement to equal treatment is made subject to the application of bilateral agreements or the national law of the Member State. This provision means in practice that it is possible that the ICT is not at all subject to the social security legislation of the host Member State, but, by virtue of the law of that Member State or of a bilateral social security agreement concluded by that Member State with a third country, is subject to the social security legislation of another country, and more specifically the country of origin. In addition, Article 18(3) of the EU Intra-Corporate Transferees Directive allows Member States to decide that the right to equal treatment with regard to family benefits shall not apply to ICTs who have been authorized to reside and work in the territory of a Member State for a period not exceeding nine months. On the other hand, Article 18(2)(b) guarantees the export of statutory old-age pensions and invalidity and death pensions to a third country under the same conditions and at the same rates as provided for in national law or in bilateral agreements for the nationals of the Member State concerned when they move to a third country.

Finally, EU Directive 2016/801 regulates the conditions of entry and residence of third-country nationals for the purposes of research, studies, training, voluntary service, pupil exchange schemes or educational projects and au pairing.[24] Article 22 of this directive contains equal treatment clauses, one for researchers and one for trainees, volunteers and au pairs, the latter categories only to the degree that they are considered to be in an employment relationship in the Member States concerned. Article 22(1) guarantees equal treatment with nationals of the host Member State as provided for by Articles 12(1) and 12(4) of the EU Single Permit Directive. In addition, this right to equal treatment includes the export of old-age pensions to a third country, but only insofar as this has been provided for nationals of the Member State involved (Article 12(4) of the EU Single Permit Directive). However, Article 22(2)(b) EU Researchers Directive allows Member States to restrict equal treatment as regards researchers, *inter alia*, by not granting family benefits to researchers who have been given the right to reside in the territory of the Member States concerned for a period not exceeding six months.

None of these migration directives contain provisions regarding aggregation of periods of insurance, employment or residence. As a result, third-country migrant workers coming from a non-EU State where they have fulfilled such periods cannot bring these into account

---

[24] European Parliament and Council (EU) Directive 2016/801 of 11 May 2016 on the conditions of entry and residence of third-country nationals for the purposes of research, studies, training, voluntary service, pupil exchange schemes or educational projects and au pairing (recast) (EU Researchers Directive) [2016] OJ L132/21.

in order to obtain the right to benefits for which the national social security legislation of the host Member State requires the fulfilment of such waiting periods. For instance, for the right to an unemployment benefit the legislation of the Member States often requires the worker to have paid contributions or have worked for a certain period of time, sometimes more than one year. A third-country national who has worked in that Member State for a period shorter than that required for obtaining the right to an unemployment benefit will not acquire such a benefit, even if a provision in a directive or in national law would guarantee this worker equal treatment, including for unemployment benefits. The same problem could also occur for other benefits, such as invalidity and old-age pensions.

The exceptions concerning the right to equal treatment for social security benefits in these migration directives are striking. In particular, for third-country labour migrants who have only worked in an EU Member State for a short period, several exceptions to the equal treatment rule are allowed. However, it is doubtful whether the exclusion of the entitlement to benefits, such as family benefits or even unemployment benefits, is in line with other European and international instruments on the rights of labour migrants or on human rights in general. As far as the European Convention on Human Rights (ECHR) is concerned, the European Court of Human Rights (ECtHR) has repeatedly found that, in principle, all forms of discrimination on grounds of nationality regarding the right to social security benefits are contrary to the ECHR, unless they are duly justified by 'very weighty reasons'.[25] The European Charter of Fundamental Rights, which is applicable when the implementation of EU law is at stake, contains a general anti-discrimination clause in its Article 21. Pursuant to Article 52(3) of the EU Charter, the interpretation of this clause must be in line with the case law of the ECtHR.[26] ILO Migrant Workers Conventions Nos 97 and 143 and the Equal Treatment (Social Security) Convention No 118 also include the right to equal treatment for social security.[27]

The principles of equal treatment and non-discrimination are indeed fundamental to the body of international instruments and are at the centre of the human rights discourse.[28] This would argue for at least a very restrictive interpretation of the possibilities the various directives offer the Member States to provide for exceptions to equal treatment for social benefits of migrants coming from third countries. It also advocates implementation of these possibilities by the Member States only when it is duly justified. Since those restrictions are indeed exceptions to the principle of equal treatment, as enshrined in Article 21(1) of the EU Charter

---

[25] See for instance *Koua Poirez v France* App no 40892/98 (ECHR, 19 September 2003), para. 46 and *Andajeva v Latvia* App no 55707/00 (ECHR, 18 February 2009), para. 87.

[26] See also: Ana Beduschi, 'An Empty Shell? The Protection of Social Rights of Third-country Workers in the EU after the Single Permit Directive' (2015) 17 European Journal of Migration and Law 2–3 224 and Ulrike Davy, 'Für Drittstaatsangehörige weniger Gleichheit? Zum eingeschränkten Zugang zu sozialen Rechten für langfristig Aufenthaltsberechtigte im Unionsreht' in Stamatia Devetzi and Constanze Janda (eds), *Freiheit-Gerechtigkeit-Sozial(es) Recht. Festschrift für Eberhard Eichenhofer* (Nomos 2015) 13744.

[27] See Article 6(1)(a)(i) of Convention No 97; Articles 9(1), 10 and 12 (g) of Convention No 143 and Article 3 of Convention No 118. However, so far these conventions have only been ratified by a limited number of Member States.

[28] For a more recent and detailed analysis of the relevant international law instruments on the legal position of migrant workers and in particular on non-discrimination clauses (with special focus on the ILO instruments) see: Shauna Olney and Ryszard Cholewinski, 'Migrant workers and the right to non-discrimination and equality' in Cahtryn Costello and Marc Freedland (eds), *Migrants at Work* (OUP 2014) 259–81.

of Fundamental Rights as well, they must be interpreted strictly and in conformity with other principles of EU law or other provisions of the Charter, such as Articles 30 and 31.[29] Otherwise they would deprive the directives of their effectiveness.[30]

5. EMPLOYMENT AND SOCIAL RIGHTS FOR MIGRANT WORKERS IN INTERNATIONAL AGREEMENTS CONCLUDED BY THE EU

The legal position of workers migrating between the UK and the EU Member States after the end of the transition period is dealt with, to some extent, in the Trade and Cooperation Agreement concluded between the EU and the UK. Before this agreement is analysed in section 6, what follows gives an overview of the provisions on employment and social rights for migrant workers in some of the international agreements previously concluded by the EU and third countries.[31]

5.1 EEA and Switzerland

On the basis of the Treaty establishing the European Economic Area,[32] the nationals of Norway, Iceland and Liechtenstein have the same rights as the nationals of the Member States, in particular regarding the free movement of workers (Article 24). The same applies to the nationals of Switzerland, a country with which a separate agreement was concluded.[33] These agreements provide for the right to free movement of workers between these countries and the EU, and also guarantee equal treatment with regard to employment and social rights. For

---

[29] Kees Groenendijk, 'Equal treatment of workers from third countries: the added value of the Single Permit Directive' in Paul Minderhoud and Tineke Strik (eds), *The Single Permit Directive: Central Themes and Problem Issues* (Wolf Legal Publishers 2015) 28–9. Articles 30 and 31 of the Charter guarantee all workers the right to protection against unjustified dismissal and working conditions which respect workers' health, safety and dignity, to limitation of maximum working hours, to daily and weekly rest periods and to an annual period of paid leave.

[30] Ana Beduschi, 'An Empty Shell? The Protection of Social Rights of Third-country Workers in the EU after the Single Permit Directive' (2015) 17 European Journal of Migration and Law 2–3 227 and Kees Groenendijk, 'Equal treatment of workers from third countries: the added value of the Single Permit Directive' in Paul Minderhoud and Tineke Strik (eds), *The Single Permit Directive: Central Themes and Problem Issues* (Wolf Legal Publishers 2015) 34. Compare Case C-578/08 *Chakroun* EU:C:2010:117, para 64. See also the recitals in the various directives stating that they respect the fundamental rights and observe the principles recognized by the Charter: recital 31 of the Single Permit Directive, recital 26 of the Blue Card Directive, recital 61 of the Researchers and Student Directive, recital 52 of the Seasonal Workers Directive (which explicitly refers to Articles 7, 15(3), 17, 27, 28, 31 and 32(2) of the EU Charter) and recital 45 of the Intra-Corporate Transferees Directive (which explicitly refers to 'the Social Charters adopted by the Union and the Council of Europe').

[31] See in general on this issue: Katharina Eisele, *The External Dimension of the EU's Migration Policy: Different Legal Positions of Third-country Nationals in the EU* (Wolf Legal Publishers 2013). Regarding social security see also the different contributions in the special issue on the external dimension of EU social security coordination of the European Journal of Social Security (2018) issue 20(2).

[32] Agreement of 2 May 1992 on the European Economic Area [1994] OJ L1/3.

[33] Agreement of 21 June 1999 [2002] OJ L114/6.

EEA nationals, the EEA Joint Committee decided to extend the scope of the EU social security coordination in Regulation 883/2004 to the EEA States and its nationals.[34]

As far as Switzerland is concerned, a series of (joint) agreements has been concluded between the EU and the Member States and Switzerland, among which is an agreement pertaining to the 'free movement of persons'.[35] This agreement with Switzerland includes a special provision with regard to the coordination of social security (Article 8) which stipulates that pursuant to Annex II, the contracting parties coordinate their social security systems with a view to equal treatment, determination of the applicable legislation, aggregation of periods, export of benefits and mutual administrative support and collaboration. This provision does not contain substantive rules or any indication of the objectives that should be aimed at. It is nothing more than a list of the classic coordination techniques. Subsequently, in Annex II reference is made to the EU social security coordination instruments that apply between the Member States (the abovementioned regulations), although with a number of special provisions, specifications and exceptions regarding the relations with Switzerland.[36]

5.2   Turkey

The EEC concluded an Association Agreement with Turkey as early as 1963.[37] According to Article 36 of the Additional Protocol of 1970,[38] freedom of movement for workers between EU Member States and Turkey shall be secured in progressive stages. However, the Court of Justice did not recognize the direct effect of this provision[39] and it was never implemented by other legally binding texts either. Accordingly, a Turkish national's first admission to the territory of a Member State is, as a rule, still governed exclusively by that State's own domestic law.[40] On 19 September 1980 the Association Council adopted Decision 1/80 to implement the agreement. This decision regulates the situation of Turkish workers already integrated into the labour market of a Member State. It also contains a provision on equal treatment of these Turkish migrant workers. Article 10 provides that the Member States shall, as regards remuneration and other conditions of work, grant Turkish workers who are duly registered as belonging to their labour force treatment involving no discrimination on the basis of nationality between them and EU workers. The CJEU has recognized the direct effect of this provision.[41]

On 19 September 1980 the EU–Turkish Association Council also adopted Decision 3/80 on the application of the social security schemes of the Member States of the European Communities to Turkish workers and members of their families.[42] However, the Court of

---

[34]   Decision no 76/2011 of 1 July 2011 [2011] OJ L62/33.
[35]   Agreement of 21 June 1999 between the European Community and its Member States, on the one part, and the Swiss Confederation, on the other, on the free movement of persons [2002] OJ L114/6.
[36]   See also on the institutional aspects of the relations between the EU and Switzerland: Christa Tobler, 'One of Many Challenges after "Brexit". The Institutional Framework of an Alternative Agreement – Lessons from Switzerland and Elsewhere?' (2016) 23 Maastricht Journal of European and Comparative Law 4 575.
[37]   [1963] OJ 3685.
[38]   [1972] OJ L293/1.
[39]   Case C-12/86 *Demirel* EU:C:1987:400.
[40]   Case C-37/98 *Savas* EU:C:2000:224, para. 65.
[41]   Case C-171/01 *Wählergruppe* EU:C:2003:260.
[42]   [1983] OJ C110/60. For a more detailed analysis of this decision see: Paul Minderhoud, 'Decision 3/80 of the EEC–Turkey Association Council: significance and developments' in Daniel Thym and

Justice ruled that in the absence of any measures to implement Decision 3/80 its legal effect is limited.[43] Still, the Court of Justice recognized the direct effect of the equal treatment provision of Article 3 of Decision 3/80 and of the provision on the export of benefits to Turkey of Article 6.[44] This means that Turkish workers in the EU Member States can claim equal treatment with nationals of the host State as regards social security benefits and that Turkish nationals who acquired rights to social security benefits in a Member State are, in principle, entitled to the export of these benefits when they return to Turkey.

5.3 Agreements with the Maghreb Countries

The next series of relevant agreements concluded by the EU consists of the Association Agreements with the so-called Maghreb countries (Morocco, Tunisia and Algeria). Currently applicable are the Euro-Mediterranean Agreements signed in 1995, 1996 and 2002.[45]

These agreements include provisions on the rights of workers who are nationals of these countries. They are entitled to equal treatment with the nationals of the host Member State with regard to working conditions, remuneration and dismissal.[46] They also enjoy equal treatment in the field of social security.[47,48] Moreover, the provision on social security also determines that the workers in question shall be able to claim export of pensions, including invalidity pensions, when they return to their home country. However, the right to receive family benefits is limited to those members of their families who are resident in the EU.

These agreements authorize the Association Council to adopt provisions to implement the principles with regard to social security, in particular as regards the coordination between the social security schemes of the EU Member States on the one hand and those of the three other countries on the other.[49] For this purpose, and on the proposal of the European Commission, the EU Council of Ministers has in the meantime adopted the positions to be taken on this issue by the European Union within the different Association Councils.[50] These Council decisions contain, for each of these third countries, draft decisions to be negotiated on in the relevant Association Councils. These draft decisions confirm the right to equal treatment for

---

Margarite Zoeteweij-Turhan (eds), *Rights of Third-country Nationals under EU Association Agreements: Degrees of Free Movement and Citizenship* (Brill-Nijhoff 2015) 169–85; Herwig Verschueren, 'Social security co-ordination in the Agreements between the EU and Mediterranean countries' in Danny Pieters and Paul Schoukens (eds), *The Social Security Co-ordination Between the EU and Non-EU Countries* (Intersentia 2009) 19–55.

[43] Case C-277/04 *Taflan-Met* EU:C:1996:315. In 1983 the Commission presented a proposal for a Council Regulation implementing Decision 3/80 within the Community OJ 1983 C110/1, but this decision was never adopted by the Council.

[44] Case C-262/96 *Sürül* EU:C:1999:228 and Case C-485/07 *Akdas* EU:C:2011:346.

[45] Agreement with Tunisia of 17 July 1995 [1998] OJ L97/1; Agreement with Morocco of 26 February 1996 [2000] OJ L70/1; Agreement with Algeria of 22 April 2002 [2005] OJ L265/1.

[46] Article 64 Agreement with Tunisia, Article 64 Agreement with Morocco and Article 67 Agreement with Algeria.

[47] Article 65 Agreement with Tunisia, Article 65 Agreement with Morocco and Article 68 Agreement with Algeria.

[48] The CJEU has confirmed the direct applicability of these equal treatment provisions. See Case C-18/90 *Kziber* EU:C:1991:36.

[49] Article 67 Agreement with Tunisia, Article 67 Agreement with Morocco and Article 70 Agreement with Algeria.

[50] Decisions of 21 October 2010 [2010] OJ L306/8.

social security benefits as well as the right to export old-age and invalidity benefits. They also propose to set up mechanisms of cooperation, such as for administrative checks and medical examinations. However, they do not contain any further rules on social security coordination, such as the determination of the applicable legislation or rules on aggregation of periods of insurance, payment of contributions or employment for obtaining or calculating social security benefits. But even so, after more than ten years, these proposals are still awaiting final approval from the Association Councils. This means that the social security coordination between the systems of the EU Member States and these third countries continues to be governed by the bilateral social security agreements, if any, concluded between these States.[51]

5.4 Association and Partnership Agreements Concluded by the EU with Third Countries

Apart from these specific agreements, the EU has also concluded a large number of agreements with third countries, such as Partnership Agreements, Partnership and Cooperation Agreements and Stabilization and Association Agreements. Most of these agreements contain provisions on the right to equal treatment with nationals of the host State as regards working conditions, remuneration and dismissal.[52] The CJEU has explicitly recognized the direct effect of such clauses.[53] However, in a series of other agreements the equal treatment clause has been worded in weaker terms, referring to the commitment of the EU Member States to 'endeavour to ensure' equal treatment as regards working conditions.[54] Such clauses do not seem to qualify for direct effect in line with the case law of the CJEU. Their weak wording may even be inspired by the latter's broad interpretation of employment rights in other international agree-

---

[51] For a more detailed analysis see: Katharina Eisele, *The External Dimension of the EU's Migration Policy: Different Legal Positions of Third-country Nationals in the EU* (Wolf Legal Publishers 2013) 287321; Laetitia Razé, *Union européenne et Maghreb: protection sociale des travailleurs migrants* (Bruylant 2016); Herwig Verschueren, 'Social security co-ordination in the Agreements between the EU and Mediterranean countries' in Danny Pieters and Paul Schoukens (eds), *The Social Security Co-ordination Between the EU and Non-EU Countries* (Intersentia 2009) 19-55.

[52] See for instance the following agreements and their provisions on equal treatment as regards working conditions: Agreement of 16 December 1991 on Cooperation and Customs Union with San Marino [2002] OJ L84/43, art 20; Partnership and Cooperation Agreement of 24 June 1994 with Russia [1997] OJ L327/1, art 23; the Cotonou Partnership Agreement of 23 June 2000 with the members of the African, Caribbean and Pacific Group (the so-called ACS States, 79 in total [2000] OJ L317/1, art 13(3); Stabilisation and Association Agreement of 03 March 2004 with FYR of Macedonia [2004] OJ L84/13, art 44; Stabilisation and Association Agreement of 12 June 2006 with Albania [2009] OJ L107/166, art 46); Stabilisation and Association Agreement of 15 October 2007 with Montenegro [2010] OJ L108/3; art 49; Stabilisation and Association Agreement of 29 April 2008 with Serbia [2013] OJ L278/16, art 49; Association Agreement of 21 March 2014 with Ukraine [2014] OJ L161/3, art 17.

[53] See Case C-265/03, *Simutenkov* EU:C:2005:213 (on the Agreement with Russia).

[54] See for instance the following agreements and their relevant clauses: Partnership and Cooperation Agreement of 28 November 1994 with Moldova [1998] OJ L181/3; art 23; Partnership and Cooperation Agreement of 23 January 1995 with Kazakhstan [1999] OJ L196/3, art 19; Partnership and Cooperation Agreement of 9 February 1995 with the Kyrgyz Republic [1999] OJ L196/48, art 19; Partnership and Cooperation Agreement of 22 April 1996 with Georgia [1999] OJ L205/3, art 20; Partnership and Cooperation Agreement of 22 April 1996 with Azerbaijan [1999] OJ L246/3, Art 20; Partnership and Cooperation Agreement of 22 April 1996 with Armenia [1999] OJ L239/3, art 20; Partnership and Cooperation Agreement of 21 June 1996 with Uzbekistan [1999] OJ L229/3, art 19; Partnership and Cooperation Agreement of 11 October 2004 with Tadzhikistan [2009] OJ L350/3, art 17.

ments, which would have caused the Member States to avoid phrasing subsequent agreements in a similarly strong way.[55]

Except for the agreement with San Marino, these agreements do not contain any non-discrimination clause with regard to social security benefits. Moreover, only a few of these agreements also provide for a mandate for the relevant Association Councils (created in the context of these agreements) to decide on provisions to coordinate the social security schemes applicable to workers of the third countries involved who are legally employed in an EU Member State. Such coordination measures should, *inter alia*, deal with the aggregation of periods of insurance, employment or residence completed by such workers in the various Member States for entitlement to benefits such as pensions, medical care and family benefits, and should also regulate the portability of pensions to these third countries.[56] In the meantime, the EU Council of Ministers has adopted the positions to be taken by the European Union within some of the relevant councils set up by these agreements.[57] These positions have more or less the same (limited) scope as the ones referred to above for the Maghreb countries. But again, after more than or almost ten years these proposals are still awaiting final approval from the various Association Councils. So, despite the mandate given in some of these agreements to adopt coordination rules between the social security systems of the Member States and the third countries involved, no such coordination rules have been adopted so far.

5.5 Trade Agreements

The EU concluded a number of trade agreements with third countries. In some of these agreements provisions have been included with regard to labour migration and the rights of the labour migrants falling under these provisions. We will now analyse a number of recent examples of these.[58]

The 'comprehensive economic and trade agreement' (CETA) between Canada and the EU[59] and its Member States contains a specific chapter on the 'temporary entry and stay of natural persons for business purposes' (Article 10). As a general obligation each party shall allow temporary entry to natural persons for business purposes of the other party (Article 10(3)(1)). This applies to measures concerning entry and stay of key personnel, contractual services suppliers, independent professionals and short-term business visitors, as defined in Article 10(1). For these categories, specific conditions and limitations are laid down in this chapter (Article 10(7)–10(9)) as well as in the detailed commitments of the parties in the annexes to the agreement. It is explicitly stated that this chapter does not apply to natural persons seeking

---

[55] Katherina Eisele, *The External Dimension of the EU's Migration Policy: Different Legal Positions of Third-country Nationals in the EU* (Wolf Legal Publishers 2013) 274, 281 and 294–85.

[56] See agreement with San Marino (art 21); with Russia (art 24); with Albania (art 48); with Montenegro (art 51); with FYR Macedonia (art 46) and also the Euro-Mediterranean Agreement of 20 November 1995 with Israel [2000] OJ L147/3, art 64.

[57] See Council Decisions of 21 October 2010 [2010] OJ L306 (for the agreements with Israel and with the FYR Macedonia) and the Decisions of 6 December 2012 [2012] OJ L340 (for the agreements with San Marino, with Montenegro and with Albania).

[58] See in general on such agreements: Rafael Leal-Arcas, *EU Trade Law* (Edward Elgar Publishing 2019).

[59] [2017] OJ L 1/23.

access to the employment market of a party, nor shall it apply to measures regarding citizenship, residence or employment on a permanent basis (Article 10(2)(2)).[60]

As far as the employment and social rights of these persons are concerned, Article 10(2)(5) stipulates that all requirements of the parties' laws regarding employment and social security measures shall continue to apply, including regulations concerning minimum wages as well as collective wage agreements. This provision only refers to the national laws of the parties without there being any additional substantive requirement. However, more substantive provisions can be found in chapter 23 on 'Trade and labour'. Under Article 23(3) the parties must ensure that their labour law and practices embody and provide protection for the fundamental principles and rights at work, in particular those guaranteed by the instruments of the ILO, which include the elimination of discrimination in respect of employment and occupation and non-discrimination in respect of working conditions, including for migrant workers.[61] The latter does not seem to apply to persons covered by the chapter on the 'temporary entry and stay of natural persons for business purposes', since that chapter is not applicable to natural persons seeking access to the employment market of a party.

Another example is the free trade agreement between the EU and Korea.[62] It also contains a section on the 'temporary presence of national persons for business' (Article 7(17)–7(20)). This section applies to key personnel, graduate trainees, business services sellers, contractual service suppliers and independent professionals as defined in Article 7(17). It includes specific conditions for the temporary entry and stay of these persons as well as references to the reservations by the parties in the annexes (Article 7(18)–7(20)). However, this agreement does not mention the applicable employment or social security law for this category of person. Still, the chapter on 'Trade and sustainable development' (Chapter 13) contains some provisions on 'multilateral labour standards and agreements'. The parties commit to respect, promote and realize in their laws and practices the principles concerning the fundamental rights, including the elimination of discrimination in respect of employment and occupation (Article 13(4)(3)).

A third example is the provisions relating to what is called a 'Deep and Comprehensive Free Trade Area' in the abovementioned Association Agreement between the EU and Ukraine.[63] In this agreement there is also a section on the 'temporary presence of natural persons for business purposes' which applies to key personnel, graduate trainees, business services sellers, contractual services suppliers and independent professionals. It allows under specific conditions and reservations in the relevant annexes the temporary employment and activities of these persons in the context of the cross-border provision of services. But this agreement does

---

[60] For more detail see, inter alia, Ase Odin Ekman and Samuel Engblom, 'Expanding the Movement of Natural Persons through Free Trade Agreements? A Review of CETA, TPP and ChAFTA' (2019) 35 International Journal of Comparative Labour Law and Industrial Relations 2 176.

[61] On the impact of trade agreements on labour standards, see Franz Christian Ebert, 'The Comprehensive Economic and Trade Agreement (CETA): Are Existing Arrangements Sufficient to Prevent Adverse Effects on Labour Standards?' (2017) 33 International Journal of Comparative Labour Law and Industrial Relations 2 295 and Lore Van den Putte and Jan Orbie, 'EU Bilateral Trade Agreements and the Surprising Rise of Labour Provisions' (2015) 31 International Journal of Comparative Labour Law and Industrial Relations 3 263. For a recent account of the weaknesses in the enforcement of the provisions on labour standards and proposals to strengthen it: Marco Bronckers and Giovanni Gruni, 'Taking the Enforcement of Labour Standards in the EU's Free Trade Agreements Seriously' (2019) 56 CML Rev 6 1591.

[62] [2011] OJ L127/6.

[63] Note 52.

not contain any provisions on the employment or social security rights of these persons either. Still, it also has a chapter on 'Trade and sustainable development' (chapter 13) in which the parties commit to promoting and implementing in their laws and practices the internationally recognized core labour standards, including the elimination of discrimination in respect of employment and occupation (Article 291(2)(d)). However, in Article 291(4) the parties stress that labour standards should not be used for protectionist trade purposes and they 'note' that their comparative advantage should in no way be called into question.

These examples of recent free trade agreements concluded by the EU with third countries show that such agreements regulate labour migration only for a very limited category of workers in the context of the temporary provision of services. Moreover, they do not contain any substantive employment or social security rights of these persons, except in the reference to international standards on non-discrimination. References to specific international instruments on the legal position of migrant workers are absent.

As a consequence, the provisions in these agreements do not interfere with the existing instruments on conflicts of law, which are specifically relevant to the forms of temporary labour migration to which these agreements apply. The rules of Private International Law that determine the law applicable to the employment contract continue to apply, such as the EU Rome I Regulation (see section 2). It may well be the case that according to these rules the employment law of the State where these persons are temporarily working is not at all applicable, since that State is not the habitual place of work (Article 8 EC Rome I Regulation). Furthermore, the determination of the applicable social security law depends on the existing bilateral agreements between States and, failing these, on the national conflict rules of each of the States involved.

6. THE EU–UK TRADE AND COOPERATION AGREEMENT

On 24 December 2020, the EU and the UK reached an agreement on their future relations and concluded a Trade and Cooperation Agreement.[64] This agreement applies as of 1 January 2021 to persons and situations not covered by the Withdrawal Agreement, in particular to persons moving between the EU and the UK after this date.

This Agreement contains only very few provisions on the movement of natural persons between the UK and the EU27. Free movement for workers has ended and access to the UK labour market for EU nationals – and, vice versa, access for UK nationals to the labour market of the Member States – will in principle depend on the domestic law of these States. As far as the EU Member States are concerned, this also depends on the implementation of the EU labour migration directives as discussed above in section 4.

The only provisions on access to the territory and the labour market are those on the entry and temporary stay of natural persons for business purposes. These provisions apply to business visitors for establishment purposes, contractual service suppliers, independent professionals, intra-corporate transferees and short-term business visitors, as defined by the agreement.[65] For each of these categories, these provisions define the conditions under which the parties have to allow these categories of persons to enter and stay in their territory and to

---

[64] [2021] OJ L 149/10.
[65] Articles 140 *et seq.*

exercise economic activities there. The application of these provisions is subject to the very detailed commitments undertaken by each of the States involved and the conditions of which are specified in Annex 21 of the Agreement.

With regard to the employment rights of these persons, Article 140(3) specifies that all requirements provided for in the law of a party regarding work and social security measures shall continue to apply, including laws and regulations concerning minimum wages and collective wage agreements. This means that in principle domestic employment law of the parties will apply. However, as far as the EU Member States are concerned, the Private International Law rules as laid down in the Rome I Regulation (see section 2) continue to be applicable.[66] Indeed, these rules have universal application, meaning that any law specified by this regulation shall be applied whether or not it is the law of a Member State.[67] In the absence of a choice of law, this directive makes applicable the employment law of the country where the employee habitually carries out his/her job. For the persons covered by the chapter on entry and temporary stay of natural persons for business purposes, this will mostly be the sending State.

As far as the EU Member States are concerned, they also have to apply the labour migration directives discussed in section 4 to UK nationals who are now third-country nationals. The Intra-Corporate Transferee Directive may be particularly relevant. The Posting of Workers Directive (see section 2) does not apply to postings from third countries, but it provides in its Article 1(4) that the Member States must not give more favourable treatment to undertakings established in a non-Member State than undertakings established in a Member State. This would mean that the employment protection guaranteed by this directive (as recently amended) must also be ensured for workers posted from a third country such as the UK. The combination of the provisions in the Trade and Cooperation Agreement, the Rome I Regulation, the ICT Directive, the Posting of Workers Directive and the domestic law of the States involved may give rise to complex issues.

Regarding employment rights, it is remarkable that Article 140(4) additionally confirms that commitments on the entry and temporary stay of natural persons for business purposes do not apply in cases where the intent or effect of the entry and temporary stay is to interfere with or otherwise affect the outcome of any labour or management dispute or negotiation, or the employment of any natural person who is involved in that dispute.

The agreement also has some general provisions on substantive employment rights in its Article 399 on 'Multilateral labour standards and agreements'. With regard to migrant workers, the parties commit to promoting 'non-discrimination in respect of working conditions, including for migrant workers'.[68]

These provisions on employment rights are comparable to the ones in the trade agreements mentioned in section 5.

Contrary to these rather general provisions on employment rights of persons migrating between the EU and the UK after 31 December 2020, the Trade and Cooperation Agreement contains an extensive system of coordination of the social security systems of the parties. Its scope is defined in Articles 489 and 499 of the Agreement and refers to persons legally resid-

---

[66] The UK is not bound by the Rome I Regulation but continues to be bound by the Rome I Convention of 19 June 1980 on the law applicable to contractual obligations ([1998] OJ C27/36) whose provisions on the applicable employment law are comparable to the provisions of the Rome I Regulation.
[67] Article 2 Rome I Regulation and Article 2 Rome I Convention.
[68] Article 399(6)(c) of the Agreement.

ing in a Member State or the UK and who are in a cross-border situation between a Member State and the UK.

A detailed coordination system is laid down in a Protocol on Social Security Coordination, which is 247 pages long. This Protocol applies to persons who are or have been subject to the legislation of one or more States[69] as well as to their families and survivors. So it has a very wide personal scope, which is not limited to persons who are entitled under the agreement to move between the UK and the EU and is irrespective of the exercise of an economic activity or the residence status of the persons involved. The Protocol itself does not provide for a right to enter, reside or work in a State. Moreover, the definition of the personal scope of the Protocol is not limited to nationals of the Parties, so it also applies to nationals of States that are not part of the Agreement.

It is a self-standing coordination system, which, contrary to the chapter on the social security coordination in the Withdrawal Agreement, does not refer to the provisions of EC Regulations 883/2004 and 987/2009 and their future amendments, but mirrors them and takes them over in part. This is the case with the general principles of the EU coordination system, such as the right to equal treatment, the aggregation of periods of insurance, employment, self-employment or residence completed under the legislations of the States and the waiving of residence clauses (export of benefits).[70] It also includes a system of determination of the applicable legislation which is based on the EU coordination system.[71] Furthermore, it contains detailed provisions on the rights and calculations of various benefits, including a number of annexes with special provisions regarding the social security systems of the States. There is also an annex with an implementing part. All these detailed provisions are identical or comparable to the provisions in the EU regulations.

However, there are some striking differences. First, some benefits included in the EU coordination system are excluded from the material scope of the Protocol, such as family benefits, special non-contributory benefits with characteristics of social assistance, long-term care benefits, assisted conception benefits and expenses for heating in winter. The exclusion of family benefits is striking, since it means not only that equal treatment for these benefits is not guaranteed, but neither is the payment of such benefits for children living in another State (export).[72] Next, the export of invalidity benefits and unemployment benefits for those seeking employment in another State is excluded. In addition, the chapter on unemployment benefits does not contain any special rules on entitlement to unemployment benefits for frontier workers. This means that workers who resided in an EU Member State when they became unemployed after having worked in the UK, and vice versa, will not be covered by the Protocol. Their rights will depend solely on the domestic legislation of the States involved. Still, UK workers in the EU can also rely on the EU labour migration directives discussed in section 4, which contain several provisions on the social security rights of these persons by referring to the provisions of the EU social security coordination regulations. These directives may fill in the loopholes in the EU–UK Trade and Cooperation Agreement, as far as UK workers in the EU are concerned. In addition, Council Decision (EU) 2020/2252 of 29 December 2020 explicitly allows

---

[69] 'States' means both the EU Member States and the UK. See Article 6(e) of the Agreement.
[70] Articles SSC.4 to SSC.8 of the Protocol.
[71] Articles SSC.10 to SSC.14 of the Protocol.
[72] Article SSC.3(4) of the Protocol.

Member States to conclude bilateral agreements with the UK as regards matters not covered by this Protocol.[73]

Nonetheless, this coordination system in the Protocol is unique. Apart from the EEA Agreement and the Agreement with Switzerland, which largely took over the EU social security coordination system, no other agreement concluded by the EU with a third country has such an extensive and self-standing social security coordination system.

7. CONCLUDING REMARKS

It is apparent from the foregoing analysis that the rights of workers migrating between the UK and the EU27 post-Brexit will depend on a number of legal instruments. The Withdrawal Agreement guarantees the continuous application of Union law on the free movement of workers and the EU regulations on the social security coordination to workers who found themselves in a cross-border situation between the UK and the EU27 at the end of the transition period (31 December 2020) or prior to that date. The rights of labour migrants who will migrate between the UK and the EU after this period depend on the EU directives on labour migration from third countries and on the EU–UK Trade and Cooperation Agreement. The latter does not include any rights to move between the EU and the UK, except for some limited categories of persons moving for business purposes. Their employment protection is scarcely dealt with – contrary to a detailed and elaborate social security coordination system, which moreover applies to all persons in a cross-border situation between the EU and the UK, irrespective of their residence status.

This complex set of agreements and rules will undoubtedly give rise to many legal issues in the years or even decades to come – a tremendous task for administrations, lawyers and courts lies ahead.

---

[73] See Articles 7 and 8 of Council Decision (EU) 2021/689 of 29 April 2021 on the signing, on behalf of the Union, and on provisional application of the Trade and Cooperation Agreement between the European Union and the European Atomic Energy Community, of the one part, and the United Kingdom of Great Britain and Northern Ireland, of the other part, and of the Agreement between the European Union and the United Kingdom of Great Britain and Northern Ireland concerning security procedures for exchanging and protecting classified information [2021] OJ L 149/2.

21. Irish citizenship law after Brexit: implications for Northern Ireland

Clemens M. Rieder[1]

1. INTRODUCTION

In 1998 the Good Friday Agreement (GFA) ended open violence in Northern Ireland (NI).[2] Despite this, it seems that Northern Irish society has failed to take full advantage of this opportunity to fully integrate its two communities, that is, Protestant/Unionist/British and Catholic/Nationalist/Irish. In this context, a fundamental error was made by the political elites and society as a whole in assuming that a culture of tolerance would emerge in the wake of the GFA. In fact, 20 years after its ratification, 90 per cent of children continue to be educated in either Protestant or Catholic schools.[3] It is also telling that only 10 per cent of marriages in NI are 'mixed', that is, between a Protestant/Unionist/British person and a Catholic/Nationalist/Irish person.[4] All of this suggests that communities remain largely separated from each other. In many ways, one has the impression that NI 'has been suspended in time since the Good Friday Agreement was signed, the region and its people entirely frozen at the moment the parties put their pens to the document'.[5]

This 'frozen' status may have always constrained NI's development into a more modern, open and welcoming society. However, maintaining the status quo was at least an option as long as both the United Kingdom and the Republic of Ireland (Ireland) were members of the EU. It was, perhaps, also because of this somewhat external stability that NI has been able for so long to entertain what Denis Bradley, Vice Chairman of NI Policing Board and a Co-Chairman of the Consultative Group on the Past, has described as a 'really small, petty, inward-looking kind of conflict'.[6] With the advent of Brexit, however, the situation has significantly changed.[7] Since the Brexit vote, there has been considerable discussion on the island of Ireland regarding the implications of the UK's withdrawal from the EU, not only for the Irish border but also for Irish EU citizens living in NI. In line with the identity navel-gazing which

---

[1] I am grateful for the careful reading by, and helpful feedback I received from, Professor Dora Kostakopoulou and Professor Colin Harvey. All errors remain mine.
[2] For a legal analysis of the Good Friday Agreement in the Brexit context, see Richard Humphreys, *Beyond the Border: The Good Friday Agreement and Irish Unity after Brexit* (Merrion Press 2018).
[3] Department of Education, 'Integrated Schools' www.education-ni.gov.uk/articles/integrated-schools accessed 14 September 2019.
[4] Siobhán Fenton, *The Good Friday Agreement* (Biteback Publishing 2018) ch 2.
[5] Ibid 3.
[6] Denis Bradley, Vice Chairman of NI Policing Board and a Co-Chairman of the Consultative Group on the Past, quoted in Tony Connelly, *Brexit and Ireland* (Penguin 2017) 272.
[7] For a critical analysis of the UK Supreme Court reasoning on the NI dimension in *R (Miller) v Secretary of State for Exiting the European Union*, see Christopher McCrudden and Daniel Halberstam, 'Miller and Northern Ireland: A Critical Constitutional Response' (2017) U of Michigan Public Law Research Paper no 575.

is predominant in NI society, there has been little discussion of the implications for non-Irish EU citizens, who often find themselves in a far more vulnerable situation, as their very right to remain may be contested.

In this chapter I want to focus on one particular question which to date has received no scholarly attention, namely whether Irish citizenship law, as it applies in NI, conflicts with Ireland's obligations under EU law. Specifically, I will focus on the principle of 'sincere cooperation' as it is established in Article 4(3) of the Treaty on European Union (TEU). As Irish citizenship law currently stands, a baby born in NI to an Irish or British parent or a person who is 'entitled to reside in Northern Ireland without any restriction on his or her period of residence' qualifies for British and/or Irish citizenship and consequently is also an EU citizen by virtue of Irish citizenship.[8]

While it is true that under EU law Member States enjoy considerable sovereignty over their national citizenship laws,[9] it is also the case that Member States, as emphasised by the European Court of Justice (ECJ) in *Micheletti* and subsequently in *Rottmann*, have a 'duty to exercise those powers having *due regard to European Union law*'.[10] Although this chapter is focused on NI, the issues discussed may have more general relevance. Take, for example, the case of Cyprus,[11] or broader questions of independence and segregation, which are gaining increasing traction across the EU. One might wonder, for example, whether Spain could offer the application of its citizenship laws to an independent Catalonia, while at the same time blocking its accession to the EU.

This chapter is structured as follows. Section 2 examines the dominant principles on the basis of which citizenship can be acquired. Here I will differentiate between the two archetypical categories of *jus sanguinis* and *jus soli*. Section 3 asks whether the Republic of Ireland has given 'due regard to European Union law' when it comes to the application of its citizenship law in NI. Here, I will focus specifically on the question of whether Irish national law violates the duty of 'sincere cooperation' as outlined in Article 4(3) TEU. Finally, in section 4 I will investigate possible solutions to any violations of EU law. My proposal for institutional reform involves a two-pronged approach: one evolutionary, based on the idea that national citizenship law of Ireland changes; the other revolutionary, in which EU citizenship is reconceptualised as partly independent from national citizenship.

2. BOUNDARIES

Thomas Humphrey Marshall, whose work is a frequent reference point in Anglo-American writing on the subject of citizenship, divided citizenship into three categories: civil, political and social.[12] Since the days of Marshall's writing, there has been 'a definite shift from a strict

---

[8] Irish Nationality and Citizenship Act (2004) s 6; see also Article 2 of the Constitution of Ireland (as amended in 1999). For a detailed legal and historical analysis, see Bernard Ryan, 'The Ian Paisley Question: Irish Citizenship and Northern Ireland' (2003) 25 Dublin University Law Journal 145.
[9] Case C-369/90, *Mario Vicente Micheletti a.o. v Delegación del Gobierno en Cantabria* EU:C:1992:295, para 10.
[10] Case C-135/08, *Janko Rottmann v Freistaat Bayern* EU:C:2010:104, para 62 (emphasis added).
[11] Yiannis Papadakis and others (eds), *Divided Cyprus: Modernity, History, and an Island in Conflict* (Indiana UP 2006).
[12] Thomas Humphrey Marshall and Tom Bottommore, *Citizenship and Social Class* (Pluto 1992) 8.

political definition of a citizen [...] to a broader, somewhat more sociological definition, which implies greater emphasis on the relationship of the citizen with society as a whole'.[13] For the purpose of this chapter, I am interested especially in territory and the role it plays in the acquisition of citizenship.

Traditionally, the acquisition of citizenship has been based either on *jus sanguinis* or on *jus soli*. In more recent times, we find a combination of both.[14] According to *jus sanguinis*,[15] an individual acquires citizenship because at least one of their parents is a citizen of that country.[16] Here the territorial boundaries of a nation-state are irrelevant. The principle of *jus sanguinis* is in operation across continental Europe.[17] One extreme example is Austria, which confers citizenship exclusively based on the principle of *jus sanguinis*.[18] Such an exclusive application of the *jus sanguinis* principle is problematic, because although people may remain entitled to citizenship even when their ancestors have not lived in the country for generations, actual residents may face considerable obstacles to becoming citizens because they lack the correct 'bloodline'.

The second principle which governs the acquisition of citizenship and which is of particular relevance to the discussion here is the *jus soli* principle. According to *jus soli*, a person who is born within the specific territorial boundaries of a given country is entitled to citizenship of that country, irrespective of whether or not they have any prior connection to that country.[19] As Brubaker argues, '[j]us soli defines the citizenry as a territorial community';[20] it has also been described as 'a more inclusive conception of citizenship'.[21] The principle of *jus soli* dates back to Calvin's Case, a 1608 English legal decision which established a person's entitlement to legal benefits based on the place of their birth.[22] Under the *jus soli* principle, the only question which is relevant for the acquisition of citizenship is 'whether the child was born *within* the territory over which the state maintains (or in certain cases has maintained or wishes to extend) its *sovereignty*'.[23] The link between *jus soli* and sovereignty is no coincidence: *jus soli* 'is historically linked with the feudal doctrine of perpetual allegiance to a *sovereign* lord'.[24]

One consequence of the application of the *jus soli* principle is that membership boundaries, which are so important in the *jus sanguinis* context, have no role to play. One prominent example of a country in which the *jus soli* principle operates unconditionally is the United

---

[13] Bart van Steenbergen, 'The Condition of Citizenship: An Introduction' in Bart van Steenbergen (ed.), *The Condition of Citizenship* (Sage 1994) 1, 2.
[14] James Brown Scott, 'Nationality: Jus Soli or Jus Sanguinis' (1930) 24 *The American Journal of International Law* 58.
[15] Rainer Bauböck, 'Jus *Filiationis*: A Defence of Citizenship by Descent' in Rainer Bauböck (ed.) *Debating Transformations of National Citizenship* (Springer 2018) 83.
[16] Gerad-René de Groot and Oliver Vonk, 'Acquisition of Nationality by Birth on a Particular Territory or Establishment of Parentage: Global Trends Regarding *Ius Sanguinis* and *Ius Soli*' (2018) 65 *Netherlands International Law Review* 319, 321.
[17] Dora Kostakopoulou, *The Future Governance of Citizenship* (CUP 2008) 26.
[18] § 7 Staatsbürgerschaftsgesetz 1985, BGBl. Nr. 311/1985 (as currently amended).
[19] Rogers Brubaker, *Citizenship and Nationhood in France and Germany* (Harvard UP 1992) 81.
[20] Ibid 122–3.
[21] Kostakopoulou (n 17) 26.
[22] Calvin's Case (1572) 77 ER 377.
[23] Ayelet Shachar, 'Children of a Lesser State: Sustaining Global Inequality through Citizenship Laws' (2003) Jean Monnet Working Paper no 2/03, 9 (emphasis added).
[24] Kostakopoulou (n 17) 117 (emphasis added).

States. The US Constitution stipulates that '[a]ll persons born or naturalized in the United States, and subject to the jurisdiction thereof, are citizens of the United States and of the state wherein they reside'.[25] In Europe, too, an unconditional *jus soli* principle has been in operation, for example, in Ireland until 2005. Until then, anyone born on the island of Ireland was automatically granted Irish citizenship.[26] This applied not only to the Republic of Ireland but also to NI, which is under the sovereign authority of the United Kingdom.

The case of *Chen* showed the implications of unconditional *jus soli* under EU law.[27] The case was important because it was the first in a series of cases in which the ECJ bolstered the effects of EU citizenship. In this case, a Chinese mother gave birth in NI to a baby girl who became an Irish and an EU citizen based on the unconditional and extraterritorial *jus soli* principle that was in force in Ireland at the time. As far as can be seen from the facts of the case, the Chen family had never shown any intention of residing in Ireland. Their only interest was in living in the UK. The development in the case law of the Court, which allowed third-country nationals to remain in EU territory in order to take care of EU citizens, forcefully brought home the (obvious) point that Irish citizenship law by virtue of EU citizenship could have significant implications on residency rights, not necessarily for Ireland but for another Member State, in this case the UK.

In the aftermath of *Chen*, Ireland changed its law on citizenship and narrowed the scope of its *jus soli* approach.[28] As a consequence, a child now born in Ireland will only be entitled to Irish citizenship if one parent is Irish or British or has a right of indefinite leave to remain.[29] Adopting this mixed approach of *jus soli* and *jus sanguinis* brought Ireland in line with the rest of Europe, as a recent briefing report for the European Parliament on the *Acquisition and Loss of Citizenship in EU Member States* suggests. The report outlined key trends and issues, and clearly stated that '[n]o country in the EU grants automatic and unconditional citizenship to children born in their territories to foreign citizens'.[30]

While it is true that the field of national citizenship is at the heart of state sovereignty, the existence of EU citizenship, at least to some extent, limits the ability of Member States to exclude or include individuals at will. This limitation of sovereignty through EU citizenship has both a doctrinal and a political dimension, as the case of Ireland shows. While one may engage in extensive speculation as to why Ireland changed its law, it seems reasonable to assume that *Chen* played a role in this change. It is plausible that Ireland eventually changed its citizenship law following political pressure from other Member States.[31] It is noticeable

---

[25] 14th Amendment to the US Constitution (1968).

[26] Karolina Rostek and Gareth Davies, 'The Impact of Union Citizenship on National Citizenship Policies' (2006) 10 EIoP, 1. 16-21, eiop.or.at/eiop/pdf/2006-005.pdf accessed 15 September 2019.

[27] Case C-200/02, *Kunqian Catherine Zhu and Man Lavette Chen v Secretary of State for the Home Department* EU:C:2004:639.

[28] Identifying the mix of reasons: Bernard Ryan, 'The Celtic Cubs: The Controversy over Birthright Citizenship in Ireland' (2004) 6 *European Journal of Migration and Law* 173, 187–90.

[29] Irish Nationality and Citizenship Act (2004) s 6.

[30] Maria Mentzelopoulou and Costica Dumbrava, 'Acquisition and Loss of Citizenship in EU Member States: Key Trends and Issues' (2018) European Parliamentary Research Service (PE625.116) 2 www.europarl.europa.eu/RegData/etudes/BRIE/2018/625116/EPRS_BRI(2018)625116_EN.pdf accessed 15 September 2019.

[31] Ryan (n 28) 186, and Dimitry Kochenov, 'EU Influence on the Citizenship Policies of the Candidate Countries: The Case of the Roma Exclusion in the Czech Republic' (2006) 3 Journal of Contemporary European Research 124, 129–31.

that with the advent of EU citizenship, Member States have developed an increasing interest in each other's citizenship laws.

There are two main reasons why Member States have become especially concerned about the citizenship laws of other Member States. First, national citizenship law may generate significant numbers of citizens beyond the territorial boundaries of the EU.[32] Second, some Member States have begun to sell citizenship to rich individuals based on the nascent concept of *jus pecuniae* principle.[33] This raises concerns not only in relation to security but also regarding the preservation of identity, because some of these schemes provide pathways to naturalisation with no requirement that the individual has ever lived within the national territory (or that of the EU). I will examine both reasons in turn, because the principles at stake will also play a role in the debate over Irish citizenship.

Particular criticism about the handling of citizenship was raised in relation to some post-Communist countries before they joined the EU.[34] Romania especially was singled out for its citizenship laws in relation to Moldova. Based on the principle of *jus sanguinis*, Romania allowed the restoration of Romanian citizenship to all former Romanians who had lost their citizenship as a consequence of the Soviet annexation of Bessarabia.[35] Consequently, some of Moldova's 4.4 million people are of Romanian descent.[36] Romania's citizenship law was criticised by other Member States because they feared that it would create a backdoor to EU citizenship, which would suddenly be wide open to otherwise third-country nationals.[37]

In response the EU Commission simply adopted a purely doctrinal and formalistic position, namely that citizenship is an internal issue for Romania to determine. Other EU agencies, however, shared the concern raised by Member States regarding Romania's citizenship law.[38] Between 1991 and 2001 a steady increase in the rate of citizenship restitution in Romania was observed, with a noticeable and exponential jump in 2001,[39] the year when Romanian citizens were granted visa-free travel to the Schengen Area. Between 2002, before Romania joined the EU, and 2011, after almost a decade as a Member State, there were 118,507 restitution cases, with significantly higher numbers from 2009 onwards;[40] I will return to this point later.

By contrast, the *jus pecuniae* principle enables citizenship to be sold, which usually does not require a link between either the individual and identity (*jus sanguinis*) or the individual and territory (*jus soli*). While this route to the acquisition of citizenship has been in the media spot-

---

[32] Maarten Peter Vink and Gerad-René de Groot, 'Birthright Citizenship: Trends and Regulations in Europe' (2010) EUDO Citizenship Observatory Comparative Report No. RSCAS/EUDO-CIT-Comp. 2010/8. https://ssrn.com/abstract=1714975 accessed 15 September 2019.

[33] Jelena Džankić, *The Global Market for Investor Citizenship* (Palgrave Macmillan 2019).

[34] Generally on ethnic citizenship laws of the new Member States: Myra A Waterbury, 'Making Citizens Beyond the Borders: Nonresident Ethnic Citizenship in Post-Communist Europe' (2014) 61(4) Problems of Post-Communism 36.

[35] Constantin Iordachi, 'Country Report: Romania' (2010) EUDO Citizenship Observatory 1 https://cadmus.eui.eu/bitstream/handle/1814/19633/Romania.pdf?sequence=1 accessed 15 September 2019.

[36] 'EU worries about Romanian offer of citizenship to Moldovans' (*Deutsche Welle*, 17 April 2009) www.dw.com/en/eu-worried-about-romanian-offer-of-citizenship-to-moldovans/a-4185592 accessed 15 September 2019.

[37] Constantin Iordachi, 'Romanian Citizenship Offer to Moldovans: Exaggerated Fears in the European Union' (2009) *EUDO Citizenship Observatory* 1, 2.

[38] Iordachi, 'Country Report: Romania' (n 35) 17.

[39] Ibid.

[40] Ibid 23.

light more recently, it is not entirely new. In the Middle Ages, for example, foreign merchants would pay higher customs duties in order to gain access to certain liberties.[41] Today, when the conventional process of naturalisation is becoming more and more burdensome, under currently available investor schemes 'the applicant's wallet is the core, if not sole criterion determining whether gates of admission will open'.[42]

These schemes have become especially lucrative in the EU, where it is possible for smaller Member States to add significant value to their otherwise less marketable national citizenships. Currently, approximately 'half of Member States now have dedicated immigrant investor routes'[43] which contribute to the '*marketization of citizenship*'.[44] Malta has been especially criticised in this context because it granted naturalisation for a sum of €650,000 originally, rising subsequently to €1.15 million.[45] For the purpose of this chapter I am not interested in the question of whether the selling of citizenship is in itself ethical,[46] but rather in the fact that for some groups of people, the acquisition of citizenship is no longer governed by the archetypical principles of *jus sanguinis* or *jus soli*. This development indicates a seismic shift in the meaning of citizenship away from belonging and has been criticised not only by Member States but also now by the EU Commission.

In response to the developments taking place in some Member States, in 2019 the Commission issued its first *Report on Investor Citizenship and Residence Schemes in the European Union*, in which it outlined the situation in the Member States but also highlighted the risks for the EU as a whole.[47] So-called citizenship-for-sale schemes raise difficult questions due to the close link between national and supranational citizenship. In this context, one is inevitably reminded of Weiler's famous 'Eros and civilisation' dichotomy. The absence of a requirement to reside within the territory of a Member State for any length of time seems especially problematic for national citizenship (that is, Eros), which is assumed to instil a sense of 'belonging' that could be eroded if citizenship is sold to individuals who may have formed no connection to the community.[48]

Having outlined the core principles of *jus sanguinis* and *jus soli* which usually determine the acquisition of citizenship and having briefly outlined the concept of *jus pecuniae* and related issues, I will now focus on the question of how Irish citizenship law, as it is currently applied in NI, fits into this existing framework. According to Article 2 of the Irish Constitution, 'It is the entitlement and birthright of every person born in the island of Ireland, which includes its islands and seas, to be part of the Irish Nation. That is also the entitlement of all persons otherwise qualified in accordance with law to be citizens of Ireland.'

---

[41] Keechang Kim, *Aliens in Medieval Law: The Origins of Modern Citizenship* (CUP 2000) 40–1.
[42] Ayelet Shachar, 'Citizenship for Sale?' in Ayelet Shachar et al (eds) *The Oxford Handbook of Citizenship* (OUP 2018) 789, 794.
[43] Madeleine Sumption and Kate Hooper, *Selling Visas and Citizenship: Policy Questions from the Global Boom in Investor Immigration* (Migration Policy Institute 2014) 2.
[44] Shachar (n 42) 793 (original emphasis).
[45] Ibid 795.
[46] Džankić (n 33) ch 3.
[47] EU Commission, 'Report from the Commission to the European Parliament, the Council, the European Economic and Special Committee and the Committee of the Regions on investor citizenship and residence schemes in the European Union' COM (2019) 12 final.
[48] Joseph HH Weiler, 'To Be a European Citizen – Eros and Civilization' (1997) 4 Journal of European Public Policy 495, 511.

The relevant law in operation is the Irish Nationality and Citizenship Act of 2004, to which I now turn.

In relation to NI, Section 6A(2) of the Irish Nationality and Citizenship Act of 2004 stipulates that babies whose parents are either Irish or British or are 'entitled to reside in Northern Ireland without any restriction on his or her period of residence' are citizens of Ireland. This is in line with the British–Irish Agreement, which also acknowledges that it is the birthright of the people of NI

> to identify themselves and be accepted as Irish or British, or both, as they may so choose, and accordingly confirm that their right to hold both British and Irish citizenship is accepted by both Governments and would not be affected by any future change in the status of Northern Ireland.[49]

Brexit, however, introduces a significant change in relation to EU citizenship, because the territory of NI will no longer be under the jurisdiction of the EU.

While the Republic of Ireland can, of course, confer citizenship beyond its territorial boundaries based on the *jus sanguinis* principle, the issue becomes controversial, at least from an EU perspective, to the extent that Ireland applies an extraterritorial *jus soli* principle in NI. Given that the Republic does not have sovereignty over NI, at best it could be said that it 'wishes to extend its sovereignty'. Unsurprisingly, it is difficult to find examples of other Member States which grant citizenship based on an extraterritorial *jus soli* principle.[50] The closest example, albeit obviously different in its detail and probably weaker in its territorial connotation, is Germany prior to reunification in 1990.

Based on Article 11 of the German Basic Law, which protects freedom of movement of German citizens, Germany applied a unitary German citizenship which, according to the German Constitutional Court,[51] covered both the Federal Republic of Germany and the German Democratic Republic (GDR).[52] This interpretation of the law, pursued by the Federal Republic of Germany, was disputed by the USSR and the GDR.[53] Leaving aside the restrictions imposed on emigration from the GDR, the fact that Germany was unified before the introduction of EU citizenship limits its relevance as a precedent. Nevertheless, the crucial question remains of whether, and if so how, an extraterritorial *jus soli* principle violates Article 4(3) TEU, which specifically stipulates a duty of 'sincere cooperation'.

3. 'SINCERE COOPERATION'

In the previous section I outlined the different ways in which a person can acquire citizenship of a state. To this end I distinguished between two archetypical principles, *jus soli* and *jus sanguinis*, noting that many states now apply a mix of the two. I also discussed the concept of

---

[49] Good Friday Agreement, s 2, para 1 (vi).
[50] Overseas countries and territories differ in this regard; see Loïc Azoulai, 'Transfiguring European Citizenship: From Member State Territory to Union Territory' in Dimitry Kochenov (ed.), *EU Citizenship and Federalism: The Role of Rights* (CUP 2017) 178, 178–82.
[51] BVerfGE 2, 266 – Notaufnahme.
[52] Ferdinand Weber, *Staatsangehörigkeit und Status. Statik und Dynamik politischer Gemeinschaftsbildung* (Mohr Siebeck 2018) 163, FN 8, 10–11.
[53] Ibid 165, para 20.

jus pecuniae and its implications for national identity and cohesion. I then examined how the law governing Irish citizenship, as it applies in NI, fits into the existing framework. Noting that the island of Ireland will no longer be undivided EU territory following Brexit, I argued that Irish citizenship law, at least as it applies to those in NI who are not covered by *jus sanguinis*, expresses an extraterritorial *jus soli* principle, which constitutes a conceptual anomaly.

This section will examine the possible implications of this finding in relation to Ireland's duty of 'sincere cooperation' under EU law. The principle of sincere cooperation is protected under Article 4(3) TEU, which stipulates that 'the Union and the Member States shall, in full mutual respect, assist each other in carrying out tasks which flow from the Treaties'. This duty has both positive and negative faces. On the one hand, a Member State should not engage in any activity that jeopardises the attainment of the objectives of the Union; on the other hand, it is required to actively engage in activities that advance those objectives. Before examining whether the application of Irish citizenship law in NI is at odds with the duty of 'sincere cooperation' as it is outlined and protected in Article 4(3) TEU, we must consider whether that duty can limit the sovereignty of Member States in relation to citizenship, despite the fact that this area of law is largely within the competence of the Member States.

This specific question has already been addressed by the Court, albeit in a different context. In *Commission v Luxembourg*, the Court clarified that a 'duty of genuine cooperation is of general application and does not depend either on whether the Community competence concerned is exclusive or on any right of the Member States to enter into obligations towards non-member countries'.[54] In other words, 'the scope *ratione materiae* of the principle of sincere cooperation extends also to areas of intervention in domains of "overlapping" competence between the Union and national arenas, or even in domains where Member States retain the monopoly of action'.[55]

The aim of this section is to examine whether Irish citizenship law, as it is applied in NI, amounts to a violation of the principle of sincere cooperation. Because the focus of my analysis in this chapter is on the extraterritorial application of the *jus soli* principle in NI, my argument has implications primarily for members of the Protestant/Unionist/British community, who were encouraged by Ian Paisley Jr, an MP for the Democratic Unionist Party (DUP),[56] to apply for an Irish passport following Brexit (an outcome consistently promulgated by the DUP).[57]

More generally, however, the question of a possible link between national citizenship law and the obligation of 'sincere cooperation' was addressed by Advocate General Maduro in the seminal citizenship case of *Rottmann*, in which he argued that the obligation of sincere cooperation '*could* be affected if a Member State were to carry out, without consulting the Commission or its partners, an unjustified mass naturalisation of nationals of non-member

---

[54] Case C-266/03 *Commission v Luxembourg* EU:C:2005:341, para 58.
[55] Sergio Carrera, 'The Price of EU Citizenship: The Maltese Citizenship-for-sale Affair and the Principle of Sincere Cooperation in Nationality Matters' (2014) 21 Maastricht Journal of European and Comparative Law 406, 420; also, with further references, Marcus Klamert, *The Principle of Loyalty in EU Law* (OUP 2014) 24.
[56] The DUP is the main Unionist party in NI, which often receives media attention for its ultra-conservative, misogynistic, right-wing and racist views.
[57] Casey Eagan, 'Ian Paisley, Jr. Dismissed Irish Passport as "an EU Document with a Harp Stuck On"' (*Irish Central*, 11 August 2016) www.irishcentral.com/news/politics/ian-paisley-jr-dismissed-irish-passport-as-an-eu-document-with-a-harp-stuck-on accessed 21 September 2019.

States'.[58] Although clearly Ireland engaged in discussions with the Commission during the drafting of the Withdrawal Agreement,[59] this may not be sufficient to avert a violation of the principle of sincere cooperation. Carrera claims that '[t]he mere act of informing or consulting the European counterparts and institutions' would not constitute a sufficient excuse.[60] Ultimately, even the Commission cannot simply negotiate away core principles of the EU Treaty. In any case, more flesh needs to be put on the bones of sincere cooperation.

The obvious starting point for a substantive debate on the meaning of sincere cooperation is Article 4(3) TEU: its positive face requires Member States to 'facilitate the achievement of the Union's tasks', whereas its negative face requires Member States to 'refrain from any measure which could jeopardise the attainment of the Union's *objectives*'.[61] In other words, Member States jeopardise the attainments of these objectives when they undermine the interests of the EU.[62] In this section, I will highlight especially three different types of interest which the EU has, which may be challenged through the application of Irish citizenship law in NI. First, the EU has an interest in reinforcing its territorial boundaries and integrity in order to protect its single market. Second, the EU has an interest in providing security to the people living in its territory, which is critical for the functioning of Schengen. Third, the EU has an increasing interest in preserving the integrity of EU citizenship in order to develop a shared identity, which is important for generating a feeling of solidarity.

Let me begin with the sensitive issue of preserving boundaries, which may be challenged through the rules on the acquisition of citizenship. Whatever one makes of the Romanian extraterritorial naturalisation figures cited in the previous section, they are dwarfed by the more recent figures coming from Ireland in the post-Brexit environment. In 2018 alone, Ireland, a country of around 5 million people, issued 84,855 passports to people in NI and another 98,544 to people living in the UK. This amounts to an increase of 22 per cent in comparison to the previous year.[63] NI has a population of around 1.8 million people, most of whom are entitled to Irish and, at least as the law currently stands, EU citizenship. Thus, unless countries such as Romania and Ireland have a somewhat different status, one would expect at least a political discourse about Ireland's citizenship law, simply because it produces, in a consistent and perpetual manner, significant numbers of EU citizens outside the EU's territorial boundaries.

Another crucial interest of the EU is the preservation of its security. For example, security concerns were a core argument against investor schemes, as a report by the European Parliament shows.[64] They are also cited regularly by Member States to undermine the Schengen

---

[58] Case C-135/08 *Janko Rottmann v Freistaat Bayern* EU:C:2010:104 Opinion of AG Maduro, para 30 (emphasis added).

[59] Agreement on the Withdrawal of the United Kingdom of Great Britain and Northern Ireland from the European Union and the European Atomic Energy Community [2020] OJ 2019/66 I/01 and Political declaration setting out the framework for the future relationship between the European Union and the United Kingdom [2019]OJ 2019/C 66 I/02.

[60] Carrera (n 55) 425.

[61] Emphasis added.

[62] Klamert (note 55) 123.

[63] Lisa O'Carroll, 'Record Number of Britons Seek Irish Passports before Brexit' *The Guardian* (London, 31 December 2018) www.theguardian.com/politics/2018/dec/31/record-number-of-britons-seeking-irish-passports-ahead-of-brexit accessed 21 September 2019.

[64] European Parliament, P8_TA-PROV(2019)0240 Report on financial crimes, tax evasion and tax avoidance. European Parliament resolution of 26 March 2019 on financial crimes, tax evasion and tax avoidance (2018/2121(INI)) paras 182-201.

framework.⁶⁵ As a consequence, the idea of a Union offering its citizens 'an area of freedom, security and justice without frontiers' as promoted in Article 3(2) TEU has increasingly come under pressure. Irrespective of whether we consider these security concerns justified or not, they are a political reality and they undermine the core objectives of the EU. The question which needs to be addressed next is in what sense the Irish question raises security concerns.

When it comes to NI, it must not be forgotten that there are still active paramilitary groups on both sides of the political spectrum.⁶⁶ These groups constitute 'the most disturbing and dangerous threats to the peace process in modern-day Northern Ireland'.⁶⁷ Their existence has broader, possibly destabilising implications for society. On the Catholic side, there are successors to the IRA such as the New IRA, which sent a chilling message by killing 29-year-old journalist Lyra McKee in Derry in 2019.⁶⁸ On the Protestant side, the Ulster Volunteer Force also has engaged in killings; one of their most recent victims was Ian Ogle, also in 2019.⁶⁹

To be clear, I am not suggesting that NI terrorist groups would necessarily attack targets within the EU, but members of these groups would enjoy free movement. Were the conflict to heat up again, this may increase an unspecified feeling of threat within the EU and among its populations, to be further exploited by political populists. What is more relevant in the context of this chapter is that, even when they do not kill, such groups terrorise communities as quasi-police forces, punishing those whom they suspect of breaking the law by shooting them in the arms and legs.⁷⁰ Paramilitaries fuel a sectarian society which holds NI back in many ways; for example, there appears to be a close correlation between paramilitary activity and poverty.⁷¹ This highlights another significant characteristic of NI society, which is its considerable poverty.

On a macro-economic level, it is estimated that the Troubles account for a reduction in GDP of 15–20 per cent if one excludes the post-1968 subventions.⁷² In this context it is interesting to note that when it comes to citizenship law, the Republic of Ireland treats the territory of NI as if it were part of the Irish State through the application of the *jus soli* principle, and yet seems

---

⁶⁵ European Commission, 'Temporary Reintroduction of Border Control' https://ec.europa.eu/home-affairs/what-we-do/policies/borders-and-visas/schengen/reintroduction-border-control_en accessed 21 September 2019.

⁶⁶ Ann Marie Gray and others, *Northern Ireland Peace Monitoring Report No 5* (Northern Ireland Community Relations Council 2018) 106–14.

⁶⁷ Fenton (n 4) 92.

⁶⁸ Matthew Weaver and Kevin Rawlinson, 'Lyra McKee: New IRA Says its Activists Killed Journalist' *The Guardian* (London, 23 April 2019) www.theguardian.com/uk-news/2019/apr/22/lyra-mckee-friends-stage-protest-derry-offices-saoradh accessed 21 September 2019.

⁶⁹ Rory Carroll, 'Belfast Murder of Ian Ogle "Not in the Name of Loyalism", says UVF' *The Guardian* (London, 29 January 2019) www.theguardian.com/uk-news/2019/jan/29/belfast-of-ian-ogle-not-in-the-name-of-loyalism-says-uvf accessed 21 September 2019.

⁷⁰ Henry McDonald, 'Northern Ireland "Punishment" Attacks Rise 60% in Four Years' *The Guardian* (London, 12 March 2018) www.theguardian.com/uk-news/2018/mar/12/northern-ireland-punishment-attacks-rise-60-in-four-years accessed 21 September 2019.

⁷¹ Goretti Horgan and Marina Monteith, 'What Can We Do to Tackle Child Poverty in Northern Ireland?' (*Viewpoint*, November 2009) 1, 14 https://pure.ulster.ac.uk/ws/portalfiles/portal/11497252/tackling-child-poverty-Northern-Ireland-summary_%281%29.pdf accessed 21 September 2019.

⁷² Richard Dorsett, 'The Effect of the Troubles on GDP in Northern Ireland' (2013) 29 European Journal of Political Economy 119, 130.

unwilling to make significant transfer payments to NI in order to support citizens there.[73] Even cross-border investments seem to be rather limited in scope, if one takes the Belfast–Dublin train line as a focal point. The journey takes more than twice as long as comparable routes on the Continent, with far fewer journeys available each day.[74] It is astonishing that such a poor service between two major cities exists anywhere in Western Europe. Generally, one has the impression that the Republic is not serious in pursuing the project of reunification.

Even in the midst of the dramatic constitutional change and crisis created by Brexit, the Irish government still seems unwilling to prepare for the possibility of reunification. Ireland's apathy has been frequently criticised by Colin Harvey, who has rightly characterised the Irish government's position as 'constitutional negligence'.[75] My point is that if Ireland were actively engaging in any constitutional planning for reunification, one could argue that the violation of the principle of sincere cooperation is temporary and, when balanced against another constitutional principle – proportionality – could be justified. However, if Ireland's aim is merely to spread the risk and draw the EU into a bilateral conflict with the UK, without having a clear plan for the future, then it seems to me that these two principles cannot be balanced.

In effect, Irish citizenship law gives a third country, the UK, a say in who can become an EU citizen, even if only indirectly. A person born in NI is entitled to Irish/EU citizenship if born to a UK parent or to a person who is 'entitled to reside in Northern Ireland without any restriction'. The conditions under which a person becomes a UK citizen or has permanent residency rights in NI are for the UK to decide, however, and neither Ireland nor the EU have any influence over that decision.

Finally, I want to focus on the integrity of EU citizenship and the solidarity it engenders, both of which are undermined by the current situation.

Originally, '[t]he traditional extended family gave a wide range of kinfolk, and at times neighbours and villagers […] some economic responsibilities for each other'.[76] In some ways citizenship serves a similar function, in that the State assumes economic responsibility for its citizens. This begs the question of in what sense Irish citizenship law requires the EU to assume responsibility for those in NI based on their EU citizenship. In other words, the extent to which the EU may be responsible for providing remedies for the difficulties that exist in NI society must be discussed. Towards this end I want to draw on Pogge's seminal book *World Poverty and Human Rights*, in which he describes a pyramid of duties, each of which implies some degree of responsibility;[77] after all, a duty makes us answerable.

Negative duties, according to Pogge, are those which require 'that others are not unduly harmed (or wronged) through one's own conduct'; all others ('the remainder') are positive Negative duties, so the conventional moral argument goes, trump any and all positive duties

---

[73] Nancy Fraser and Linda Gordon, 'Civil Citizenship against Social Citizenship? On the Ideology of Contract-versus-Charity' in Bart van Steenbergen (ed.), *The Condition of Citizenship* (Sage 1996) 90, 99.
[74] Cormac McQuinn, 'Faster Rail Link between Dublin and Belfast Needed to Tackle Brexit Challenges, Says Report' (*Herald.ie*, 12 December 2018) www.herald.ie/news/faster-rail-link-between-dublin-and-belfast-needed-to-tackle-brexit-challenges-says-report-37617843.html accessed 21 September 2019.
[75] He used the phrase in a talk at St Mary's University College, Belfast, on 7 August 2019.
[76] Fraser and Gordon (n 73) 99.
[77] Thomas Pogge, *World Poverty and Human Rights* (Polity Press 2011, 2nd) 138.

one may have, including the duty to support our next of kin or our fellow citizens.[78] For example, while it may be acceptable that we give preferential treatment to our parents in a rescue operation, we nevertheless must not (directly) harm others in attempting to rescue them.[79] The negative duty not to harm others is at the top of Pogge's pyramid.[80]

At the bottom of this pyramid are positive duties, those we have towards people who are unrelated to us.[81] This lack of relationship explains why people feel relatively less responsibility to provide help beyond their identity boundaries. Identity boundaries, which circumscribe our family, friends and, many would argue, even our nation, are in the middle of the pyramid. Given the importance of identity, it is unsurprising that it plays such a prominent role. Recall that one of the reasons why Member States and the EU Commission were critical of the investor schemes was that applicants were not required to live in the territory of a specific Member State or the EU.[82] The European Parliament specifically made the point that 'EU citizenship implies the holding of a stake in the Union and depends on a person's ties with Europe and the Member States or on personal ties with EU citizens'.[83]

As Pogge's pyramid indicates, those inside our identity boundaries feature most prominently in relation to our sense of responsibility. It follows that the arguments of civic nationalists such as David Miller, who contend that our positive duties toward those within our identity boundaries rank higher than our duties to those outside them, are at least normatively plausible.[84] For Miller, a sense of community is a prerequisite for remedial responsibility.[85] After Brexit, however, NI will no longer constitute a territory of the EU and it is difficult to see how the situation of those who acquired Irish citizenship solely based on extraterritorial *jus soli* in NI is any different from those who acquired citizenship based on *jus pecuniae* when it comes to the issue of identity.

The point can be made that citizenship influences boundaries of responsibility. 'We assume an established group and a fixed population', Michael Walzer argued, 'and so we miss the first and most important distributive question: *How is that group constituted?*'[86] It is because of Irish citizenship law, so we can argue, that the people who live in the territory of NI move from the bottom to the middle of the pyramid in terms of positive obligations. Once repositioned, the EU no longer has merely a general negative duty to do them no harm. Rather, it has a positive duty to provide support and seek solutions for those people as if they were not only inside our identity boundaries but also, as a consequence of the fiction applied to NI territory through the principle of extraterritorial jus soli, within the territorial boundaries of the EU.

While Irish society has had its say on the Irish law on citizenship through a national political discourse, there has been no political debate at the EU level. Though it may be a slight

---

[78] Ibid.
[79] Valentin Beck, *Eine Theorie der globalen Verantwortung: Was wir Menschen in extremer Armut schulden* (Suhrkamp 1996) 90.
[80] Pogge (n 77) 138.
[81] Ibid.
[82] European Commission (n 47) 4.
[83] European Parliament Resolution of 16 January 2014 on EU citizenship for sale (2013/2995(RSP)) point 7.
[84] Pogge (n 77) 136.
[85] David Miller, *National Responsibility and Global Justice* (OUP 2007) 97.
[86] Michael Walzer, *Spheres of Justice: A Defense of Pluralism and Equality* (The Pitman Press 1983) 31 (emphasis added).

exaggeration, one could argue that what is taking place in front of our eyes is an unapproved quasi-enlargement of the EU, or at least a spreading of the political risk from one Member State to the rest of the EU. In other words, Ireland is creating additional responsibilities for the EU, and there is a risk that other Member States and EU citizens may lose trust in the European project if, as a consequence of the legal status quo, they are called upon to honour those responsibilities without ever having had a political discourse on the implications of the Irish–UK conflict. Germany's unilateral act during the 'refugee crisis', while morally praiseworthy, has shown that the EU has limited resilience when defending its core pillars while under pressure; Schengen, for example, has still not recovered. Creating facts without having a political discussion will hurt the European project as a whole. In the next section, I offer institutional recommendations which may help to remedy the violation of the principle of sincere cooperation.

4. RECOMMENDATIONS

The conflict identified in this chapter is between the duty of sincere cooperation and the application of Irish citizenship law in NI. I want to suggest two possible solutions to this conflict: amending the national citizenship law of Ireland and/or adapting the supranational law which governs EU citizenship. Before examining these options in detail, however, it is necessary to identify Ireland's obligations under international law. Of particular relevance are the Good Friday Agreement (GFA) concluded between Ireland and the UK in 1998, which makes specific reference to Irish citizenship in NI, and the Withdrawal Agreement which was concluded between the EU and the UK in 2018 and which makes specific reference to EU citizenship.

I want to begin my discussion with the GFA, which is an agreement between a Member State, that is, Ireland, and a third country, that is, the UK. The GFA is 'extraneous to Union law' but forms 'part of the *national* law' of Ireland, which concluded this agreement.[87] While the issue of agreements concluded by the EU has been examined closely, much less has been said about agreements which are concluded by individual Member States and the relevance they have for EU law.[88] In EU primary law there are a variety of Treaty provisions which recognise the right of Member States to conclude international agreements.[89] In particular, two types of agreement can be distinguished: those which have been concluded before a Member State joined the EU and those concluded by a state that is already a member of the EU. The GFA belongs to the latter group.

An important provision which aims to resolve any conflicts that may emerge between national law and international agreements is Article 351(2) of the Treaty on the Functioning of the European Unity (TFEU), which constitutes 'an application of the general duty of cooperation laid down in Article 4(3) TFEU'.[90] The provision stipulates:

---

[87] Allan Rosas, 'The Status in EU Law of International Agreements Concluded by EU Member States' (2011) 34 Fordham International Law Journal 1304, 1310 (original emphasis).
[88] Ibid.
[89] Ibid 1313.
[90] Klamert (n 55) 16.

> The rights and obligations arising from agreements concluded before 1 January 1958 or, for acceding States, *before the date of their accession*, between one or more Member States on the one hand, and one or more third countries on the other, shall not be affected by the provisions of the Treaties.[91]

Clearly this provision does not apply to the GFA, which came into force in 1998, 25 years after Ireland and the UK joined the EU.

The Treaty expressly states that agreements which were concluded before a Member State joined the EU must be compatible with EU law, and Klamert argues that the same principle should apply to agreements which were concluded after a state becomes a member of the EU. If compatibility cannot be achieved, then the agreement must be renegotiated.[92] However, a literal interpretation of the GFA shows that there exists no conflict between Ireland's obligations under EU law and its obligation under the GFA. The GFA only stipulates that the people of NI can 'identify themselves and be accepted as Irish or British, or both'.[93] It makes no specific reference to EU citizenship.

The situation is different in relation to the Withdrawal Agreement. References to both Irish citizenship and EU citizenship are found in the Protocol on Ireland and Northern Ireland of the Withdrawal Agreement. The relevant passage states that

> Irish citizens in Northern Ireland, by virtue of their Union citizenship, will continue to enjoy, exercise and have access to rights, opportunities and benefits, and that this Protocol should respect and be without prejudice to the rights, opportunities and identity that come with citizenship of the Union for the people of Northern Ireland who choose to assert their right to Irish citizenship as defined in Annex 2 of the British–Irish Agreement 'Declaration on the Provisions of Paragraph (vi) of Article 1 in Relation to Citizenship'.[94]

The paragraph is opaque and an example of particularly poor drafting. Three questions in particular stand out. First, why is there this emphasis on Irish citizens? What about the rights of EU citizens from other EU Member States? It almost seems as if the Withdrawal Agreement invited the introduction of first- and second-class EU citizenship in NI, which is not only highly problematic but also not without irony. After all, Irish citizens in NI, who have never activated their EU citizenship by exercising their right of free movement,[95] apparently have entitlements under EU law, whereas EU citizens who have exercised that right deserve no special mention in the view of the Commission. Second, it remains entirely unclear to which rights the Withdrawal Agreement is alluding, given that, after Brexit, NI is no longer part of EU territory. Finally, there is the question of whether the wording of the Protocol of the

---

[91] Emphasis added.
[92] Klamert (n 55) 280.
[93] GFA (n 49) s 2, para 1 (vi).
[94] Agreement on the withdrawal of the United Kingdom of Great Britain and Northern Ireland from the European Union and the European Atomic Energy Community, as endorsed by leaders at a special meeting of the European Council on 25 November 2018, Protocol on Ireland/Northern Ireland, 302.
[95] In Case C-434/09 *Shirley McCarthy v Secretary of State for the Home Department* EU:C:2011: 277, para 56, together with Case C-165/16 *Toufik Lounes v Secretary of State for the Home Department* EU:C:2017:862, paras 49–62. From the perspective of EU law, it is certainly peculiar, to say the least, that the NI First-Tier Tribunal did not request a preliminary ruling from the ECJ on the case of Emma de Souza.

Withdrawal Agreement can be construed to guarantee that Irish citizens in the North will retain EU citizenship also in the future.

In relation to this last question, I want to make the following points. The first sentence of the passage in question is cryptic and yet also expresses a banality, namely that Irish citizens retain rights 'by virtue of their Union citizenship', wording which *per se* does not guarantee that they retain Union citizenship. The reference to identity and Union citizenship also seems peculiar, given that it is possible that some people will adopt Irish/EU citizenship who have no relationship with the EU whatsoever, either through a Member State or the territory of the EU. In light of previous observations, one can only wonder why the Commission is critical of citizenship based on *jus pecuniae* on the grounds that those who acquire citizenship in this way lack sufficient identity with the Union, while at the same time apparently having no issue with Irish citizenship law. Finally there is the reference to the GFA agreement, which, as previously noted, makes no mention of EU citizenship. All in all, it would be useful to seek an Opinion from the ECJ based on Article 218(11) TFEU.

In addition to questions of interpretation, it may be helpful to undertake a conceptual analysis by asking about the position of international law in the context of EU law. Given the opacity of the Protocol of the Withdrawal Agreement, it remains an open question whether it would fulfil the requirements of direct effect, under which, according to EU law, a provision must be sufficiently clear, precise and unconditional, but also must not be precluded by the 'nature and structure' or 'broad logic' of the Treaty.[96] As outlined above, the provision in question seems to be neither clear and precise nor in line with the logic of the Treaty, if one considers the following question: if Ireland exited the EU tomorrow, could Irish citizens successfully claim that they had retained EU citizenship based on the Withdrawal Agreement? There is little doubt that the answer to this question is no. Moreover, even if the Protocol has direct effect, international law 'generally does not rank more highly than EU primary law (EU Treaty provisions)'.[97] In other words, core principles of the EU cannot simply be overwritten by international agreements.

Some of the problems discussed in this chapter stem from the close relationship between national and EU citizenship. That relationship follows from the wording of Article 20 TFEU, which states that 'Citizenship of the Union is hereby established. Every person holding the nationality of a Member State shall be a citizen of the Union.' The close relationship between national identity and supranational citizenship was also echoed in the case of *Tjebbes*.[98] Coutts identified the core of the judgment as follows: 'The absence of a genuine link with one of the Member States is sufficient to justify loss of Union citizenship; being a member of a national political community is necessary to be a Union citizenship.'[99] If one considers this close

---

[96] Case C-308/06, *Intertanko a.o.* EU:C:2008:312, para 45.

[97] Katja Ziegler, 'The Relationship between EU Law and International Law' (2015) University of Leicester School of Law Research Paper No 15-04, 1, 11 https://papers.ssrn.com/sol3/papers.cfm?abstract_id=2554069 accessed 21 September 2019.

[98] Case C-221/17, *M.G. Tjebbes a.o. v Minister van Buitenlandse Zaken* EU:C:2019:189, paras 35–36.

[99] Stephen Coutts, 'Bold and Thoughtful: The Court of Justice Intervenes in Nationality Law Case C-221/17 Tjebbes' (*European Law Blog*, 25 March 2019) https://europeanlawblog.eu/2019/03/25/bold-and-thoughtful-the-court-of-justice-intervenes-in-nationality-law-case-c-221-17-tjebbes/ (original emphasis) accessed 21 September 2019.

relationship as axiomatic, then Ireland must amend its citizenship law in order to achieve a conceptually plausible solution.

In this context it should be recalled that when Ireland replaced its citizenship law in 2004, abandoning an unconditional *jus soli* approach, the Tánaiste (Deputy Prime Minister) argued that 'it was not the number of persons coming to Ireland which mattered, but the fact that [...] "our constitutional provisions are being used in a way we did not intend"'.[100] If Ireland changed its citizenship law then to protect the integrity of its citizenship, it should change its citizenship law now, because Brexit changes the situation dramatically in relation to EU citizenship, thereby undermining Ireland's integrity. The only question is in what way Irish citizenship should be changed.

I suggest the introduction of a 'special EU protected citizen status'. The idea for such a status under EU citizenship law was developed by Kostakopoulou in the context of Brexit,[101] but the origins of the concept of a 'special status of British protected person' date back to the British Nationality Act of 1948 and therefore have their roots in Britain's colonial past, when Britain created a variety of 'sub-citizenships'.[102] Of course, the irony is not lost on me that it is primarily people from the Unionist community who, if they wished to avail of EU citizenship in the future, would need to resort to this status, which was originally designed for use by residents of Britain's former colonies. In some ways, the former colonisers would finally be governed by their own colonial rules.

The special status of British protected persons under the British Nationality Act 1948 'was granted to individuals from territories which were originally British protectorates or protected states or states over which the Crown had exercised jurisdiction without their inclusion into the Crown's dominions'.[103] The status recognises a certain lack of national identity which is also absent in the cases governed by the extraterritorial *jus soli* principle but which seems to be pivotal under EU law, as the foregoing discussion of the *jus pecuniae* principle suggested. Protected status simply 'demonstrates a generalized awareness of the responsibility of a political unit to protect individuals following political change as well as an acceptance of its complementarity with other nationality statuses'.[104] This type of citizenship is different in kind from, and does not amount to, full citizenship. It would apply only to those who have been granted Irish citizenship based on the extraterritorial *jus soli* principle.

The protected status simply recognises that the link to the EU is weaker for those people who have been granted citizenship based on the extraterritorial *jus soli* principle than for those people who have been granted their Irish citizenship based on *jus sanguinis*. The Court accepted a divided form of national citizenship already when it held in *Kaur* that

> On the basis of that principle of customary international law, the United Kingdom has, in the light of its imperial and colonial past, defined several categories of British citizens whom it has recog-

---

[100] Ryan (n 28) 189.
[101] Dora Kostakopoulou, '*Scala Civium*: Citizenship Templates Post-Brexit and the European Union's Duty to Protect its Citizens' (2018) 56 Journal of Common Market Studies 854, 862–6.
[102] Prakash Shah, 'British Nationals under Community Law: The Kaur Case' (2001) 3 European Journal of Migration 271.
[103] Kostakopoulou (n 101) 863–4.
[104] Ibid 864.

nised as *having rights which differ* according to the nature of the ties connecting them to the United Kingdom.[105]

While some of these categories would come with EU citizenship, others will not. My point is simply that certain groups of people in NI, while still qualifying for a form of Irish citizenship based on the idea of a protected status, would no longer automatically qualify for EU citizenship. This protected status could be applied either *ex nunc* or preferably *ex tunc*.

The changes suggested on the national level could then be complemented by detaching EU citizenship from national identity/citizenship under certain circumstances and making it autonomous. This would allow the EU to introduce its own terms and conditions for the acquisition of EU citizenship based on a specified identity nexus which has nothing to do with national identity. While this may seem radical at first, it should not be forgotten that the close link between citizenship and nationhood is a consequence of the French Revolution. During that period, at least, the nation developed at the expense of guilds, provinces and other subnational groups.[106] Even so, the French Revolution remained remarkably cosmopolitan and in line with the *Ancien Régime* for some time. As Brubaker points out, however, '[i]t was in the xenophobic nationalism of its radical phase, not in the cosmopolitanism of its liberal phase, that the Revolution was genuinely revolutionary'.[107] One of the achievements of the nation was that the boundaries that existed below the level of the nation-state were finally abolished, whereas boundaries among nation-states were reinforced.[108]

Habermas also dates the interconnectedness between citizenship and national identity back to the French Revolution and identifies a similar purpose. He contends that nationalism played a 'functional role' that helped to broaden the reach of citizenship, which was otherwise 'never conceptually tied to national identity'.[109] Thus, detaching EU citizenship from national citizenship would free EU citizenship from the requirement of national identity. In order to detach EU citizenship from national identity/citizenship, again I want to refer to Kostakopoulou, who has suggested that Article 20 TEU be amended as follows: '*every person holding the nationality of a Member State or declared as an EU citizen shall be a citizen of the Union.*'[110]

While adopting the idea of 'declaring EU citizens', I would like to make a slightly different suggestion. My aim is to keep any changes to citizenship to a minimum while changing the concept of EU citizenship. Towards this end, the starting point of my approach is for all Member States to apply a form of *jus soli* or *jus sanguinis*. In my view, Article 20 TEU should read that an EU citizen is 'any person holding the nationality of a Member State, granted on a *jus sanguinis* or *jus soli* basis, or who has become a national in any other way and has lived on the EU territory for at least one year'. This approach not only overcomes the issues of identity noted in the context of *jus pecuniae* but would also solve the problem created by Irish

---

[105] Case C-192/99, *The Queen v Secretary of State for the Home Department, ex parte: Manjit Kaur* EU:C:2001:106, para 20 (emphasis added).
[106] Brubaker (n 19) 44.
[107] Ibid 45.
[108] Ibid 47–8.
[109] Jürgen Habermas, 'Citizenship and National Identity: Some Reflections on the Future of Europe' in Ronald Beiner (ed.), *Theorizing Citizenship* (Suny 1995) 255, 259.
[110] Dora Kostakopoulou, 'Who Should Be a Citizen of the Union? Toward an Autonomous European Union Citizenship' in Liav Orgad and Jules Lepoutre (eds), *Should EU Citizenship Be Disentangled from Member State Nationality? EUI Working Papers* (RSCAS 2019/24) 3 (original emphasis).

citizenship law, since people who had received Irish citizenship on the basis of an extraterritorial *jus soli* principle would fall under the third category and therefore would be required to spend one year on the territory of the EU before they could be declared EU citizens.

While *national* identity would no longer play an exclusive role in relation to EU citizenship, the issue of identity, albeit more broadly, would remain significant. Together with Simmel, we would still need to ask the fundamental question, 'How is society possible?'[111] The answer Kostakopoulou provides is that people become part of a society through their work and the social relations they develop.[112] Capitalism can play a functional role in overcoming existing boundaries: 'the growth of exchange relationships, the expansion of markets and the development of a modern system of money [make] possible the growth of autonomous individuals and [undermine] the importance of local, religious or particularistic definition of the social person.'[113]

Attempting to preserve EU identity by virtue of Irish identity in NI presents a genuine conceptual problem. What differentiates a UK citizen living in Germany and the Irish citizen living in NI is that only the former can develop this type of identity because only she lives in the territory of the EU. As currently formulated, however, the law engenders the perverse situation in which the former is excluded from EU citizenship while the latter can gain access to EU citizenship at will. This situation also has a political dimension. Citizens in NI are largely excluded from the decision-making processes in the Irish Republic and the EU. This exclusion has significant implications for identity building. Preuß has argued that the 'egalitarian dynamics of the idea of citizenship' helped to extend the concept to all adult nationals.[114] What is more, '[i]t is not identity which determines citizenship; rather, it is citizenship which creates (political) identity'.[115]

In some ways, my suggestion is less radical than Kostakopoulou's because it would leave nationality intact as the main link to citizenship, while at the same time restricting the ability of Member States to grant citizenship only modestly. My suggestion could be considered an additional moderate step. What both of our suggestions share, however, is that they enable Member States 'to retain their definitional monopoly over nationality but [end] their definitional monopoly over EU citizenship and thus giv[e] European institutions a say in determining the EU's citizenry'.[116] This seems justified, given that it is the EU which may be asked to shoulder additional responsibility as a consequence of EU citizenship in NI.

The aim of this section was to identify possible solutions to the problem of Irish citizenship law, which, as it currently stands, may violate Article 4(3) TEU, which stipulates an obligation of sincere cooperation. Focusing on two international agreements which deal specifically with NI, the GFA and the Withdrawal Agreement, it was determined that the solutions proposed in this section are consistent with a literal interpretation of both agreements. In other words, there is no need to renegotiate either. The proposed solutions would require only modest changes

---

[111] Georg Simmel, *Soziologie* (Suhrkamp 1992) 42–61.
[112] Kostakopoulou (n 101) 858.
[113] Bryan S Turner, *Citizenship and Capitalism: The Debate over Reformism* (Allen & Unwin 1986) 26.
[114] Ulrich K Preuß, 'Citizenship and Identity: Aspects of a Political Theory of Citizenship' in Richard Bellamy and others (eds), *Democracy and Constitutional Culture in the Union of Europe* (Lothian Foundation Press 1997) 107, 118.
[115] Ibid 119.
[116] Kostakopoulou (n 110) 4.

at the national and/or on the supranational level. On the national level, Ireland would need to introduce a different category of citizenship, such as special protection status, which would be available to those who have no *jus sanguinis* link with Ireland. Alternatively, those who have not acquired citizenship on the basis of either *jus sanguinis* or *jus soli* could nevertheless be declared EU citizens provided they met a specified residency requirement.

5. CONCLUSION

The aim of this chapter was to discuss whether there is a conflict between the duty of sincere cooperation as it is established in Article 4(3) TEU and Irish citizenship law as it is applied in NI. I distinguished between people in NI who acquire Irish citizenship based on *jus sanguinis* and those who do so based on an extraterritorial *jus soli* principle. It is the latter scenario, so I argued, that creates conceptual problems, because Ireland by definition does not have sovereign authority over NI, which is a precondition for the application of the *jus soli* principle. Thus, to the extent that the application of Irish citizenship law in NI is based on an extraterritorial jus soli principle, it would appear that this violates the principle of sincere cooperation because it thwarts the interests of the EU, which has implications for trust and consequently the willingness to cooperate.

Nevertheless, it could be argued that the principle of sincere cooperation would not be violated if the Republic of Ireland had a clear plan or policy agenda for how it aims to achieve political reunification with NI. In that case, the disconnect between territory and sovereignty would only be temporary. However, despite the enormous political flux created by Brexit, the Irish government has not engaged in any significant planning for a possible border poll.[117] Indeed, the Republic's generally lacklustre approach to reunification suggests an intention to spread the risk of NI to the EU and other Member States with no clear commitment or even a willingness to accept political or financial responsibility for a project which is first and foremost in the interest of Ireland, north and south. This is not to say that these interests cannot be transferred to the supranational level at some stage, but this must go hand in hand with a political discussion on that level.

Nevertheless, in the current political climate, I would suggest a moratorium on the implementation of my suggestion until a border poll has been conducted. There has been considerable uncertainty regarding the circumstances under which a border poll must be called by the Secretary of State.[118] It seems to me that one possible indicator for a change would be once 50 per cent of the citizens born in NI have applied for an Irish passport. As shown above, EU citizenship, as currently conceptualised, is linked to national identity. In other words, EU citizenship is currently acquired through national identity even if, for some communities in NI, the link is tenuous. Unionist representatives are conceptually wrong to assume that EU

---

[117] Mark Bassett and Colin Harvey, 'The Future of Our Shared Island: A Paper on the Logistical and Legal Questions Surrounding Referendums on Irish Unity' (*BrexitLawNI*, February 2019) https://brexitlawni.org/library/resources/the-future-of-our-shared-island/ accessed 21 September 2019.

[118] GFA (n 49) sch 1, s 1.

citizenship can be claimed without first accepting de facto Irish identity.[119] By rejecting Irish identity, they are rejecting EU citizenship.

---

[119] Simon Carswell, "'We Are Not Going to be Bribed Out of the United Kingdom' – Orange Order Chief' *The Irish Times* (Dublin, 10 July 2019) www.irishtimes.com/news/ireland/irish-news/we-are-not-going-to-be-bribed-out-of-the-united-kingdom-orange-order-chief-1.3951739 accessed 21 September 2019.

22. Epilogue: on guest houses and institutional reconfigurations

Dora Kostakopoulou

The thirteenth-century poet Jalal al-Din Rumi (1207–73)[1] described the individual as a 'guest house', that is, as a dwelling with expanding space as new life experiences, which are personified as guests who might not always be welcome, knock on the door and come to live within the self. As he put it:

> This being human is a guest house
> Every morning a new arrival.
>
> A joy, a depression, a meanness,
> Some momentary awareness comes
> as an unexpected visitor.
>
> Welcome and entertain them all!
> Even if they're a crowd of sorrows,
> who violently sweep your house
> empty of its furniture,
> Still, treat such guest honourably.
> He may be clearing you out
> for some new delight…

Rumi's 'guest house' metaphor applies to almost everything in life, including to life itself. Institutions are guest houses,[2] countries are guest houses and creative works are guest houses too! And all of us are privileged to witness, and live in, guest houses where we must 'treat each guest honourably'.

This sentiment of gratitude embraces me while I am writing the epilogue to this Research Handbook. A significant number of researchers dedicated months to examining various dimensions of EU citizenship in detail and to carefully unravelling the past, present and future of EU citizenship. Within a few hundred pages, they have managed to describe 30 years of a historically unique institution which has captured the political and scholarly imagination since the early 1990s.

They have carefully dispelled myths and falsehoods perpetuated in political as well as academic narratives, such as the presentation of EU citizenship as an existential threat to national citizenships and certain narratives about national identities. For EU citizenship has not been designed to erase, but only to add; as Article 20 TFEU states: 'Citizenship of the

---

[1] Rumi was a Persian poet and Sufi mystic.
[2] Dora Kostakopoulou, *EU Citizenship Law and Policy: Beyond Brexit* (Edward Elgar Publishing, 2020); *Institutional Constructivism in Social Sciences and Law: Frames of Mind, Patterns of Change* (Cambridge University Press, 2018), *Citizenship, Identity and Immigration in the EU: Between Past and Future* (Manchester University Press, 2001).

Union shall be additional to and not replace national citizenship.' Another falsehood exposed in this volume is that EU citizenship has simply opened up opportunities for 'market citizens', that is, selfish individuals from a privileged class background seeking to exploit opportunities for self-gratification and betterment. All the authors of the chapters, in their own unique ways, have emphasised the connections and relations fostered by the activation of EU citizenship among individuals, families, professional groups, societal sectors and home and host Member States. Every movement sparks a relation of various dimensions and facilitates a connection that enriches human lives, institutions, societies and polities. Connections and relations also give rise to tensions – in Rumi's poetic expression, to 'a crowd of sorrows' – but tensions and sorrows are nevertheless important because, as Rumi noted, they may be clearing an entity for some new (de)light.

And this is precisely how both historic and contemporary challenges to EU citizenship (and to our worlds) have been treated by the scholars who have contributed to this volume. As anatomists of EU citizenship's journey (see Maas) and its remarkable evolution as well as endurance, they have paid equal attention to existing weaknesses and limitations as well as to possibilities for greater socio-political change in the European Union and its members, states and peoples, but also in the way that we live and relate to other human beings. Readers will appreciate the theoretical lenses of the first part of the Handbook, ranging from Wesemann's view of EU citizenship as a constitutional rights norm to Yiannakou's social empathy lens, Steinfeld's social constructivist approach and Thym's and Schmidt's pleas for a thicker normative understanding and for more guidance and legal certainty to be provided by the Court of Justice of the EU, respectively. And while certain chapters remind us of the role of power relations and intergovernmental negotiations, such as those by Coutts, Boitos and Kellebauer and van den Brink, there are many insights in them as well as in the contributions by Yong, Ziegler, Garner and Kroeze which suggest that leaps to other institutional designs of EU citizenship are not only possible but also necessary. Van den Brink advances the proposal for the EU to enact shared minimum rules regulating access to national citizenship and thus to EU citizenship. Garner, on the other hand, supports the idea of a fully autonomous EU citizenship drawing inspiration from emancipative political constitutionalism, and Yong, Kroeze and Ziegler support a more principled EU citizenship paradigm that protects fundamental rights, family reunification in the European territory as a whole and academic freedom.

By reflecting on 'what EU citizenship should be', the contributors have set new agendas for scholarly investigations in this area. As the discussion shifts seamlessly from the theoretical, civil and political dimensions of EU citizenship to social perspectives, social rights and the challenges generated by Brexit and the Covid-19 pandemic, readers have the opportunity to obtain a deeper understanding of the dynamics of EU citizenship as well as existing discords and possible solutions. Costamagna and Giubboni, Barbou des Places and Paju's chapters seem to capture the 'social positioning school' of EU citizenship by exploring the limits as well as possibilities for social solidarity in the EU. They convincingly make the case for a stronger political foundation of European solidarity and the lessening of welfare nationalism. They correctly point out that the language games of 'earned citizenship' or 'deserved citizenship' do not cohere with the dimensions of equality and universality characterising citizenship, at least on paper.

The last part of the Handbook is devoted to an exploration of ideas about the configuration or reconfiguration of citizenship following Brexit. Franklin and Frediksen, Tobler and Idriz, Verschueren and Rieder provide a panoramic account of differentiated citizenship paradigms and divergence in the rights enjoyed by different publics (EEA EFTA state nationals, Turkish and Swiss nationals) or sections of the public (migrant workers and Northern Irish citizens). They make suggestions and recommendations for reform. None of them favours a reactive EU citizenship; on the contrary, their insightful chapters point out that the management of differentiation needs to continue in a strategic as well as visionary manner.

It is important to highlight here the volume's wide-ranging discussions of the various impacts generated by what I wish to call 'the nationality of injustice' and the need to strengthen the connections among (i) EU citizenship, (ii) fundamental rights and the protection of human dignity and (iii) the European Pillar of Social Rights.[3] In this respect, 'the new delight' in Rumi's sense might well be a fuller and more dynamic EU citizenship which, by defying populist and nationalist challenges to it and rigid mindsets, enshrines, realises and promotes respect for human dignity and non-discrimination in all its activities for the benefit of Europe's citizens and residents and, in particular, the younger generations who have not witnessed much other than economic recession, digital surveillance and, in the past months, death and severe disruption of normal life.

2021 is, without a doubt, a turning point for EU citizenship. We are just beginning to gain a glimpse of an end to the global pandemic which has caused a seismic shift in our perceptions and political and economic priorities, including the idolatry of market forces and the belief in limited state interference with them. The focus of the EU citizenship project in the third decade of the new millennium cannot be other than that of transformation through greater cooperation and delivery of services to EU citizens and residents.

As the contributors to this Research Handbook have observed, the phases of EU citizenship 'breaking the mould', its subsequent entrapment in needless and monotonous discursive games on the alleged democratic deficit of the EU or the limited significance of market citizenship, and speculation about and/or tests of its endurance in the light of populist neo-nationalism and Brexit have been superseded by a fresh urgency and opportunity – the urgency to make EU citizenship better engaged with the experiences of EU citizens and more focused on realising its full institutional potential, tackling obstacles and inequality and improving human living. An opportunity mindset and motivated action will thus reconfigure EU citizenship as a process of transformation of the conditions of living for EU citizens and residents irrespective of their mobility status.

Transformation embraces the chipping away of false representations and narratives, intergovernmental obstacles, wasteful restrictions, unnecessary hardship and some appalling cruelties which render human personality invisible or, even worse, disposable in the twenty-first century. It also requires engagement with citizens' disrupted lives, growing inequality, poverty and homelessness and ecological sustainability. Finally, it necessitates a sustained and principled resistance to forces of authoritarianism and coercive control reminiscent of a past that the

---

[3] European Commission, The European Pillar of Social Rights, 24 October 2017 (https://ec.europa.eu/commission/priorities/deeper-and-fairer-economic-and-monetary-union/european-pillar-social-rights_en). On 5 October 2017 the Commission also adopted a proposal for a Council Recommendation on the European Framework for Quality and Effective Apprenticeships (COM (2017) 563 final). This initiative complemented the European Pillar of Social Rights, which envisages a right to quality and inclusive education, training and lifelong learning. The Commission formulated 14 criteria which Member States and stakeholders could use to develop quality apprenticeships with a view to increasing employability and high skills.

EU has shaken off, and the condemnation of regressions in the protection of rights which we have witnessed in the first two decades of the new millennium.

1. A NORMIC EU CITIZENSHIP: INSTITUTIONAL INTERVENTIONS

1.1 The European Parliament's Report on the Implementation of the Treaty Provisions related to EU Citizenship

On 29 January 2019 the European Parliament's Report on the Implementation of the Treaty Provisions related to EU Citizenship sought the activation of EU citizenship through successive and connected reforms to realise its potential and to close gaps in the protection of EU citizens.[4] The point of departure of the report of the Committee on Constitutional Affairs was the centring of EU citizenship, that is, its elevation into a central edifice in the European integration process and the (timely) extension of its scope and effectiveness. As the EP's report stated, 'European citizenship is a construction that has no equivalent anywhere in the world. Its introduction is an achievement of the European project, but it is undeniable that it has not reached its full potential.'[5] A number of factors are responsible for this, including shortcomings in the implementation of the Citizens' Rights Directive (2004/38) by the Member States as well as citizens' deficient awareness of their rights in the European Union and when they travel abroad. But Article 25 TFEU provides opportunities for the enrichment of EU citizenship and the EP took the initiative to stimulate reflection on various issues which could lead to the future evolution of EU citizenship rights.[6]

Among its proposals, the abolition of the disenfranchisement of expatriates in elections to national parliaments because of their residence in other EU Member States, the extension of voting to national parliamentary elections in the Member State of residence for EU citizens, the introduction of e-democracy tools, the adoption of the horizontal EU Anti-discrimination Directive (which has been delayed by the Council), increasing the political participation of young people and people with disabilities and enhancing the effectiveness of the EU Charter on fundamental rights are noteworthy. After all, 'the successful exercise of EU Citizenship rights presupposes that Member States uphold all rights and freedoms enshrined in the Charter of Fundamental Rights',[7] and 'non-discrimination is a cornerstone of European citizenship, in addition to being a general principle of EU law and a fundamental value under Article 2 TEU'.[8]

The EP's report also notes the links between EU citizenship rights and the European Pillar of Social Rights and encourages the Commission to take concrete measures to implement it – for free movement and residence in the EU cannot be ensured without supporting legislation on equal opportunities and equal access to the labour market, fair working conditions and

---

[4] A8-0041/2019 EP Report of 29 January 2019, PE631.784v02-00.
[5] Ibid 3.
[6] Ibid 7.
[7] Ibid 23.
[8] Ibid 31.

social protection and inclusion across the EU.[9] To this end, the EP's motion for a European Parliament Resolution[10] suggested the consolidation of citizen-specific rights and freedoms under an EU Statute of Citizenship by activating the procedure laid down in Article 25 TFEU. The EU Statute is envisaged to include both the EUCFR's provisions and the social rights set out in the European Pillar of Social Rights and the values of the EU under Article 2 TEU,[11] thereby offering unprecedented resonance in the protection of EU citizens. By so doing, it would correct chronic uncertainties and the missed past connections. It is envisaged that the EP will repeat the call for EU Statute of Citizenship when it delivers its opinion on the Commission's 2020 EU Citizenship Report, which is examined below.

1.2 EU Citizenship Report 2020

In the European Commission's EU Citizenship Report 2020, which was published on 16 December 2020,[12] I discern elements of both repair and configuration. I say 'repair' because the Commission situates the report within the political landscape of Covid-19 and the concomitant restrictions imposed on free movement, and in the context of social movements for climate change, racism and equality, challenges to democracy and the (positive) developments that have taken place since the previous 2017 Citizenship Report.[13] It also contains a strategy of configuration since it sets out priorities and actions (18 actions) to empower and protect EU citizens, thereby acknowledging the impact of externally imposed vulnerabilities in their life worlds.

As Mr Didier Reynders, Commissioner for DG Justice, stated: 'EU citizenship is at the core of the European project. And yet we have seen unprecedented challenges to some of the basic rights we tend to take for granted in Europe – from restrictions to free movement because of the pandemic to challenges to our democratic institutions.'[14] The time is thus ripe to introduce protective measures which contribute to the chain that better citizens' lives. No one seriously believes that citizens will be healed by ideology or rhetorical promises.

Functioning as a complement to the action plan on the European democracy and the new strategy for strengthening the application of the Charter of Fundamental Rights published by the Commission in early December 2020,[15] the new EU citizenship report envisages a number of concrete actions and priorities for EU citizens in four priority areas, namely:

---

[9] Ibid, para 21 of the Opinion of the Committee on Petitions (21 November 2018), 34.
[10] 2018/2111(INI), para 53, p.20.
[11] The values are: respect for human dignity, freedom, democracy, equality, the rule of law and respect for human rights, including the rights of persons belonging to minorities.
[12] Empowering Citizens and Protecting Their Rights, European Commission, European Union: 2020. My analysis of the report first appeared in the European Law Blog in January 2021 and is replicated here.
[13] Ibid 4, 5. The Report notes that 9 out of 10 European citizens are now familiar with the term 'citizen of the Union' and that support for free movement is at its highest rate in 12 years; p.4.
[14] See at europeansting.com/2020/12/16/eu-citizenship-report-empowering-citizens-and-protecting-their-rights/.
[15] European Commission, Communication from the Commission to the European Parliament, the Council, the European Economic and Social Committee and the Committee of the Regions, Strategy to strengthen the application of the Charter of Fundamental Rights in the EU, COM(2020) 711 Final, Brussels 2.12.2020; Communication from the Commission to the European Parliament, the Council,

(a) in the fields of democratic participation, citizen empowerment and inclusion in the EU;
(b) the facilitation of free movement and residence rights and the simplification of daily life;
(c) the protection and promotion of EU citizenship by asserting that EU citizenship 'is not for sale', thereby addressing Member States' investment citizenship schemes, and monitoring the impact of Covid-19 restrictions; and
(d) protecting EU citizens in Europe and abroad, including in times of crisis/emergency.

To this end, the Commission is fully committed to a multi-actor and multi-dimensional strategy; that is, to a strategy of partnership with the Member States, national local and regional authorities, other EU institutions, the civil society and citizens themselves. Accordingly, the Citizenship Report does not posit enemies. Nor does it escape the burden of the present. Instead, it delineates connections and coordinated action in order to protect and empower EU citizens. In a balanced way, the protection of EU citizens' civil rights (free movement and residence) is also linked to their political rights and the updating of the rules on voting rights for mobile EU citizens as well as to social rights through the building of a European Health Union.[16] Furthermore, the internal face of EU citizenship is intimately connected with its external face, that is, with the protection of EU citizens abroad who may face situations of emergency or crisis, such as the difficulties of return to the EU, owing to the restrictions associated with Covid-19. According to the Report, as many as 600,000 EU citizens had to be repatriated to the EU between February and May 2020.[17]

'Empowering citizens and protecting their rights' is a priority for the Commission given that around 13.3 million EU citizens have exercised their free movement and residence rights and continue to face a host of challenges and obstacles. Some of these are new, such as border-related closures and restrictions due to Covid-19. But one cannot sidestep the longstanding problem of Member States' compliance with Directive 2004/38[18] involving national administrative authorities, national courts, border security agencies and subnational governance, including municipalities. In this respect, the Commission's intention to simplify cross-border work and travel, including citizens' tax obligations, and to review and update the Guidelines it issued in 2009 on the implementation of free movement[19] are important.

There have been calls over the years for a systematic examination of the transposition of Directive 2004/38 by the Member States and the national interpretations of various legal terms contained in it which restrict the scope of the fundamental freedoms of movement and residence in the European Union.[20] Here, one could hope that the publication of the new Guidelines on free movement will be followed by an EU-wide study on the role and the effectiveness of national courts in exercising oversight over the implementation and enforcement of EU law by national authorities. In national courts, EU citizens expect to get justice. However, this is often

---

the European Economic and Social Committee and the Committee of the Regions on the European Democracy action plan, COM(2020) 790 Final, Brussels, 3.12.2020.
[16] See ec.europa.eu/info/strategy/priorities-2019-2024/promoting-our-european-way-life/European-health-union_en.
[17] 2020 Citizenship Report, 5, 40.
[18] OJ L158/77 [2004], 30.4.2004.
[19] COM(2009) 313 final.
[20] See, for example, ECAS's policy papers: https://ecas.org/wp-content/uploads/2020/06/Towards-a-Citizen-Centric-European-Union.pdf; https://ecas.org/wp-content/uploads/2020/02/Policy-paper-final-07022020.pdf.

no more than an expectation, particularly in those national arenas where corruption affects the independence and impartiality of the judiciary.[21]

The Citizenship Report's references to the provision of support to EU citizens who might resort to rough sleeping in the Member State of residence, as well as the Commission's pledge to protect the rights of all EU citizens (EU citizens in the UK and UK nationals in EU Member States) affected by Brexit, are welcome. In fact, a specific action (Action 8) reflects the Commission's explicit commitment to 'continue to support the protection of the rights of EU citizens who, as a result of exercising their right to free movement while the UK was still a member of the EU, were resident in the UK before the end of the transition period'.[22] The correct implementation of the citizens' rights part of the Withdrawal Agreement is pronounced to be a 'top priority for the Commission'.[23]

The environment in certain host Member States also contributes to an ineffective exercise of EU political rights at local and regional level, as detailed in the Report. Difficulties in the electoral registration process; lack of awareness of the relevant rules, deadlines and processes; insufficient awareness of rights; underrepresented categories of voters, such as persons with disabilities and of a minority racial or ethnic background – all contribute to creating obstacles in the exercise of political rights. In an attempt to overcome this problem, the Commission will update the directives on voting rights of mobile EU citizens in municipal and European elections[24] (Action 1) and has announced the 'possibility of creating a dedicated shared resource to support EU citizens in exercising their electoral rights' (Action 2). Equally important is increased involvement by citizens at all stages of the democratic process; hence the Commission's proposed Action 4 on the promotion of the active participation of citizens in the democratic process, including their possible involvement in the legislative process. Innovations in the design of deliberative democratic avenues in our digital age and the forthcoming Conference on the Future of Europe[25] will provide opportunities for inclusive, bottom-up participation and for transnational debates on the future of Europe.

Under the thematic area 'Protecting and Promoting EU Citizenship', the Report explicitly acknowledges the interconnection between EU citizenship and fundamental rights: 'EU citizenship is underpinned by common values, encompassing the respect for democracy, rule of law, equality and fundamental rights.'[26] This is a very important acknowledgement and a guidepost for citizens' protection and empowerment. The common values referred to above are none other than the values stated in Article 2 TEU[27] and the realisation of those values is aligned with the Commission's actions with respect to 'golden passports', the creation of a rule of law culture, the support of citizenship education and Erasmus+, the forthcoming action plan for social economy and ongoing work in the fields of equality and non-discrimination.

The final thematic area focuses on the protection of EU citizens in the EU and abroad. The recovery programme of EUR 750 billion, as well as targeted reinforcements to the 2021–7 EU budget, will address aspects of the impact of the pandemic, but more needs to be done to

---

[21] Dora Kostakopoulou, 'Justice, Individual Empowerment and the Principle of Non-Regression in the EU' (2021) 46 *European Law Review* 92–104.
[22] 2020 Citizenship Report, 25.
[23] Ibid 25.
[24] Council Directive 94/80/EC and Directive 93/109/EC.
[25] www.consilium.europa.eu/en/meetimgs/gac/2021/01/18/.
[26] 2020 Citizenship Report, 29.
[27] Ibid 33.

prepare the EU and the Member States for health crises in the future. The Commission has been laying the foundations for a resilient 'European Health Union' by proposing a new EU health programme, EU4Health;[28] by implementing the European Pillar of Social Rights; and by helping young EU citizens. Action 17 states: 'the Commission will increase its support for young EU citizens, including those from disadvantaged groups, to help them access education, training and finally the labour market through the strengthened Youth Guarantee scheme.' And as regards the protection of EU citizens abroad, the Commission acknowledges the lessons of the Covid-19 crisis and the need to protect EU citizens travelling abroad. For this reason, it pledges the review of the Consular Protection Directive[29] as well as the possibility of using Article 25(2) TFEU[30] in order to expand the citizenship right to consular protection under Article 23 TFEU (Action 18).

In comparison to previous EU citizenship reports, it seems to me that the present one is much more explicit in the actions the Commission intends to take, more holistic in its content, and more protective of EU citizens' rights, 'lives and livelihoods'.[31] It is also more attuned to the 'time identity' of the EU and the need to use the experiences of Covid-19 as a means of developing a new role and effective agenda for EU citizenship. I would have liked to see more explicit commitments to combating poverty and homelessness in the EU as well as to the prevention of Member States' 'creative interpretations' of legal terms that securitise intra-EU mobility and procure the deportability of EU citizens from Member States of residence. One can only hope that the 18 Actions of the 2020 EU Citizenship Report will reverse the present trend of rights erosion in Europe and will lead to transformative changes in the lives and experiences of EU citizens in the next three years. This is, in fact, a wider invitation to all institutions and layers of governance, beyond borders, strife and ideology, to value, protect and respect human beings and their fundamental rights.

The EU citizenship institutional design has evolved considerably since Maastricht and will continue to evolve gradually, feature by feature, dimension by dimension, in a series of stages and steps that make it more discussion-worthy and special each time. The contributors to this volume have shed ample light on those features and dimensions. But at the end of those modifications and future institutional changes, EU citizenship will still be a simple institutional structure validating that non-discrimination on the ground of nationality creates associates, unites, and enriches human lives, societies and polities.

---

[28] Ibid 38.
[29] Council Directive 2015/637, OJ L106, 24.4.2015.
[30] Article 25 TFEU.
[31] Ibid 45.

Index

academic freedom
    academic citizenship 187, 195–7
    definition 188
    Erasmus program 186
    ethnic discrimination 185
    gender studies 185, 191
    grants and funding access 187, 189–90
    institutional funding 190–91
    protection of
        EU citizenship role in 187, 195–7
        EU competence 186–7
        fundamental rights-based issue, as 188, 197–200
    qualifications, recognition of 186–7
    religious discrimination 189
    research, cooperation in 187, 189–90
    researchers, rights of 187, 189–90
    restrictions on
        banned studies 185, 191–2
        Central European University, at 194–5
        freedom of thought or speech, and 185, 191–2
        grants and funding 189–91
        Hungary and Poland, in 184–5, 188–95
        quota systems 193–4
        research cooperation, and 189–90
        scholarship contracts 193–4
    UK citizens post-Brexit, for 352–3
Adler, Emanuel 33, 36
adoption, recognition of 157, 162, 175–8
Alexy, Robert 13–19, 23, 31
Algeria, EU Association Agreement 2002 356–7
Alimanovic 8, 56–7, 86, 158, 237–9, 243–5, 259–60, 262, 272, 288–9, 293
Alokpa 180
Altiner and Rayn 156
Angonese 141, 143, 336
Arendt, Hannah 117–18
armed forces, free movement principle exception 137–8
association agreements
    Ankara Agreement (*see* Turkey)
    EU-Swiss Agreement on the Free Movement of Persons (*see* Switzerland)
    EU-UK Trade and Cooperation Agreement 133, 342, 360–63
    Euro-Mediterranean Agreements (Maghreb countries) 356–7
    third-country partnership agreements, generally 357–8
    trade agreements 358–60
Augenstein Daniel 207–8
Austria, citizenship 366
Azoulai, Loïc 120, 178

B and Vomero 159
Baumbast 229, 254
Bellamy, Richard 269
Bidar 230, 232, 306–7
Bloch, Ernst 10
border controls
    external borders, perceptions of 121, 127
    free movement principle derogations 122–3
    internal border controls and EU citizenship, relationship between 121, 127–8
    reintroduction during Covid-19 pandemic, legality of 123–5
Borneman, Jonas 125
Bouchereau 160
Brexit (withdrawal of UK from EU) 7
    EU citizens' rights, impacts on
        comprehensive sickness insurance 279–80
        coordination regulation 279–80, 288–9
        EEA citizens, implications for 318
        family member rights 347–8
        family unity 206
        financial stability requirement, and 279–80
        freedom of movement 205
        pensions 348–9
        political rights 206
        qualifications, recognition of 205
        removal, procedures for 203–4
        residence rights 205–6
        substance of rights, protection of 206–7
        third-country nationals 208
        welfare benefits, access to 8, 226, 249, 279–80, 288–9, 348–9
    EU citizenship, and
        acquired or derivative rights 213–16
        Amsterdam Appeal Court ruling 210–20
        Amsterdam District Court preliminary ruling 201–2, 210–20
        associate citizenship proposal 208
        automatic loss, perspectives on 209–20

Commission Decision (2017) 210
conditional loss or retention 219–20
dual citizenship 29–30, 214–17
European Citizens Initiatives (ECIs) 209–10
implications for 85, 100, 104, 107–9, 133, 148, 201–2, 207
nationality condition, relevance of 213–16
preservation of, academic debate on 207–10
referendum debate, role in 13
Treaty provisions, teleological interpretation 216–18
Treaty provisions, textual interpretation 213–16
welfare benefits, access to 348–9
EU-UK Trade and Cooperation Agreement 133, 342, 360–63
European Citizens Initiatives (ECIs) 209–10
free movement principle, and
EU-UK Trade and Cooperation Agreement 360–63
immigration conflicts 67, 131
removal of rights 131, 133, 148, 203–5
Withdrawal Agreement provisions 204–6
Independent Monitoring Authority, role and powers 206
migrant workers' rights, impacts on
cross-border situation 346–8
EU law, continuing provisions 346–7
EU workers in UK 345–9
family member rights 347–8
free movement principle, applicability 345–9, 363
generally 343, 363
international agreements, protections under 354–60
pensions 348–9
posted workers 346–7, 361–2
seasonal workers 350–51
social security and employment rights 345–9
transition period provisions 345–8
UK agreements with third-countries 349–54
UK workers in EU Member States 351–4
Withdrawal Agreement provisions 345–9
Northern Ireland, implications for
British protected persons status 379–80
Irish citizenship *vs.* EU citizenship conflicts 376–82

Irish passport application trends 372, 382
sincere cooperation principle, and 365, 370–82
Withdrawal Agreement provisions 372, 377–8, 381–2
referendum debate issues 8, 13, 29–30, 202–3
UK citizens, impacts on
academic freedom 352–3
aggregation of employment or residence periods 352–3
business purposes, entry and temporary stays for 361
equal treatment, applicable EU Directives 349–54
EU residence permits 350
family member rights 350–51
non-discrimination on grounds of nationality 353–4
posted workers 351–2, 361–2
seasonal workers 350–51
third-country nationals, status as 349–54
UK workers in EU Member States, rights of 349–54
welfare benefits, access to 350–52, 361–3
UK status following 205–6
Withdrawal Agreement
family member rights 347–8
Ireland, treatment of 372, 377–8, 381–2
legality of 207
migrant workers in UK, applicable provisions 345–9
negotiation issues 202–3
protected rights, scope of 204–6, 346–7
protection of UK citizens in EU Member States 207–8
purpose 204–5, 220, 363
removal of rights, procedures for 203–4
sincere cooperation principle, and 372
transition period 205–6, 345–8
welfare benefits coordination 362
withdrawal procedures, generally 203–4
Brey 54–5, 236–7, 241, 257–8, 272, 275–6, 285–9, 293
Brown 251
Brubaker, Rogers 118, 366, 380

Calvin's case 366
Campbell 298–9, 308–10, 312, 315
Canada-EU Comprehensive Economic and Trade Agreement (CETA) 358–9
caregivers, rights of 89–90, 155–6, 176–7

Carpenter 152–3, 169–70
Carter, Daniel 262
Central European University 194–5
Chambon, Adrienne 46
Chavez-Vilchez 28–9, 89, 156, 162
Chen 153, 169–70, 367
children *see also* family member rights
    adoption, recognition of 157, 162, 175–8
    best interests of the child 29, 89–90, 155–6, 162
    caregivers, rights of 89–90, 155–6, 176–7
    child benefits, indexation of 240
    education, right to 188
    family reunification 88–9, 103–5, 153, 155–6, 161–2
    residence rights, under EEA Agreement 315–16
    rights of name 103–5, 153
    welfare benefits, access limitations 89
citizens' rights, EU
    caregivers, of 89–90, 155–6, 176–7
    citizenship, relationship with 25–6
    constitutional trends, influences of 49
    deprivation of, conflicts of law and policy 26–8
    derivative rights 15–16, 22–3
        family member rights (*see* family member rights)
    development, background to 70–73
    duties, pyramid of 374–5
    education and research 188, 198–9
    emancipatory nature of 65
    fundamental rights, and
        best interest of the child 89–90, 155–6, 162
        family reunification 88–9, 103–5, 153, 155–6, 161–2, 165–73
        limitations on 88–90
        right to protection of family life 88–9, 153, 182–3
        significance of 97–8
    genuine enjoyment test 24–9, 60, 89, 120, 153–4, 156, 172, 178–9
    identity, territoriality of 118–19
    implementing infrastructure, need for 62–3
    marginalised citizens 85–6, 88–9, 95–6, 248
    models for
        access to social benefits, and 54–6
        constitutional context, influences of 56–8, 61–4, 66–7
        judicial interpretation 64–8
        methodology, basis for 51–2
        political participation, and 59–64
        residence model 49, 52, 54–5, 59–60, 64–5
        social empathy 93–9
        social integration model 49, 52–3, 55–6, 60–61, 65–7
    political controversies 7–8, 31
    pregnancy and childbirth 89–90
    proportionality 90, 254–5, 257–8
    right to vote
        European Parliament elections, in 109
        national elections, in 387
        transnational rights 59–60, 387, 390
    social context, influences of 50
    structural obstacles to 97–8
    substance of rights test 60–61, 120, 172–3
    transnational solidarity, and 57–8, 96–7, 230–31, 234–5, 249–50, 269, 283–5, 293–5
    Treaty safeguards, role of 96–7
    welfare benefits, access to 8, 54–6, 86–8, 158–9, 162, 250, 256
citizenship, generally *see also* EU citizenship; national citizenship
    acquisition, methods of 101, 107, 365–70
    citizen empowerment, and 20–21
    civic identity, role of 20
    conceptions of 4, 51, 64, 321, 365–70
    constructivist approaches 32–8
    EEA membership, and (*see* European Economic Area)
    identity, link with 37–8, 117–19, 128–9, 380
    jurisdiction, and 117–18
    jus sanguinis vs. jus soli approaches 365–70, 379–80
    multiplicity of 38
    nodal points 42–6
    principles and purpose of 4, 116–19
    rights and duties, pyramid of 374–5
    social cohesion, and 52–3, 117
    stakeholder citizenship 49, 52
    territory, relationship with 116–19
Clauder 309–10
Collins 239, 255, 306–7
Coman 157–8, 174–6
Commission v. Luxembourg 371
Commission v. UK 86, 242, 288–9, 291–4
connexio rerum model of citizenship 91–2, 94
constitutional rights
    constitutional quality of 14–15
    constitutional rights norms
        EU citizenship, and 22–31, 25–8
        genuine enjoyment test 24–9, 60, 120, 178–9
        multiplicity of 31
        purpose of 268
        radiating effects of 27–9
        welfare benefits, and 268–9

definition of 14–15
derivative rights norms, and 15–16, 22–3
    family member residence rights 28–9,
        65–6, 153, 155–7, 169–70,
        177–8, 367
EU citizenship, and
    academic freedom 186–7
    constitutional rights norm, as 22–31,
        25–8
    constitutional significance of 20–23
    doctrinal interpretation 51–2
    integration element 29–31
    judicial interpretation, role of 23,
        30–31, 272
    purpose of 31
    residential rights of spouses 29–31,
        180–82
law of competing principles 18–19, 289
optimization requirements 17, 26–31
principles and rules
    characteristics of 13, 16–17
    conflicts/ collisions 18–19, 289
    EU citizenship concept, and 23–6
    EU law general principles, role of 97–8,
        199–200
    judicial interpretation, creation by
        258–9
theory of 13–19, 27–8
Constitutional Treaty 7, 62, 68
constructivism
    EU citizenship research, and
        benefits of 46–8
        conventional approaches, compared
            with 38–40, 46–8
        failures and resistance, analysis of 45–6
        ideas, role of 33–4
        identity construct, as 36–8, 43–4
        incremental policy development
            perspectives 44–5
        institutional constructivist approach 84,
            90–93
        interdisciplinarity in 39–40
        methodological perspectives 40–48
        nodal points of citizenship,
            identification of 42–6
        norms as discourses perspective 41–8
        norms, linkages between existing and
            emerging norms 43–4
        othering, relevance of 47
        repetition and imitation, role of 44
        role in, generally 33, 35–6, 38–40
        textual interpretation, importance of
            41–2
    generally
        assumptions, role of 40
        benefits of 32, 40
        discourse theory 41–8
        dynamic imitation 44
        ideational turn 33–4, 40
        identity, role of 39
        individualism, and 35–6
        institutions, interpretation of 35–6
        interdisciplinary approach to law, and
            39–40
        intersubjectivity 33, 44
        norm diffusion processes 36–7
        purpose of 33, 35
        social change theory, and 37–8
    institutional constructivist approach
        EU citizenship, to 84–5
        EU integration, to 84, 90–93
consular protection 391
Covid-19 pandemic
    equal treatment principle conflicts 124–5
    EU citizenship debate, impact on 116–30,
        386
    border controls, and 121, 127–8
    EU territory, relationship with 119–21
    EU travel bans, and 126–9
    national identities vs. EU membership,
        128–9
    national territory, safety perspective on
        123–6, 129
    national travel bans, and 124–6
    territory, general perceptions of
        116–19, 125–6
    free movement principle
        external borders, perceptions of 121,
            127
        intra- vs. inter-movement policy
            variations 123–30
        Member State restriction measures 116,
            122–5, 129
        public health restriction applicability
            122–4
        reintroduction of borders, legality of
            123–5
        repatriations 389
        restrictions, proportionality of 124–5
        Schengen Border Code derogations, use
            of 116, 122–3
        spread facilitation perception of 116
criminal offenders, expulsion of 8, 159–60, 162,
    181–2
C.S. 155–6
Cyprus, investor citizenship schemes 101, 107

D and E 313
D v. Sweden 174

Dano 8, 54–7, 86–7, 158, 162, 236–7, 239, 246, 258–9, 261–4, 272, 277, 287–9, 291
Dawson, Mark 207–8
De Witte, Floris 58, 294
Demir 323, 325
Demirkan 330–31
democracy, EU citizenship role in 20–21
dependency requirement 89–90, 155–6, 176–7
Dereçi 177, 196
derivative residence rights 28–9, 65–6, 153, 155–7, 169–70, 177–8, 367
Derrida, Jacques 47
d'Hoop 193, 217
Dias 61
dignity 93, 95, 97
discrimination *see also* equal treatment principle
  forms of 142–3
Dougan, Michael 228–9
Doyle, Oran 118
Duff, Andrew 208
Dustmann, Christian 274

E. 159
economic crises 83
  access to welfare systems, influences on 86–8, 233–4, 269–70
education *see also* academic freedom
  ethnic discrimination 185
  EU and national competences 186–8
  EU Charter rights 195, 198–200
  fundamental right to 188
Egenberger 104–5
Eind 311
Eleftheriadis, Pavlos 20
employment contracts, applicable law 344, 353, 360
employment relationship
  definition 142–3
  duration of employment 134–5
  employment under direction of another 135–6
  free movement principle applicability, and 133–40
  jobseekers 137
  marginal or ancillary activities 136–7
  payment for services 136–7
  posted workers 344, 346–7
  scope of, compared with other economic activities 133–5
  self-employment, interpretation of 135
  unemployed persons 137
  working conditions 142–3
equal treatment principle
  access to employment 141

asymmetries and inequalities caused by 276–8
comparison, scope of 266
constitutional implications of 258–9, 263–4
Covid-19 pandemic, and 124–5
direct and indirect discrimination 142–3
discriminatory national measures, right to challenge 229
EU Charter of Fundamental Rights and Freedoms, and 353–4, 387–8
EU citizenship, and 104–5, 151
family member rights 245
free movement principle, overlap and conflicts 52–3, 57–8, 141–3, 276–7
jobseekers 8, 56–7, 86, 137, 139, 158, 237–40, 243–7, 251, 255–6, 259–60, 306
judicial interpretation (*see under* judicial interpretation)
legal uncertainty, and 277–8
Member State interpretation, scope for 246
nationality, employment criteria based on 142–3
recognised qualifications 75, 77–8, 80–82, 139, 141, 143
reintroduction of border controls in Covid-19 pandemic 124–5
residence model of EU citizenship, and 54–5
residence rights, and 229, 256–8
secondary law, use of 258–60
social integration model of EU citizenship, and 57–8
students 229–32, 253–4, 256, 272, 276–7, 306
unemployed workers 141, 350
welfare benefits, access to (*see* welfare benefits, access to)
working conditions 141–2
EU Charter of Fundamental Rights and Freedoms
  applicability and effect 153, 188, 198, 342, 353–4
  education and research rights 188, 198–200
  equal treatment principle, and 353–4, 387–8
  grounds for action under 195
  third-country nationals, applicability to 188, 342
EU citizenship *see also* citizens' rights
  academic citizenship, relationship between 187, 195–7
  association agreements (*see* association agreements)
  consular protection 391
  Covid-19 pandemic, impacts on debate (*see* Covid-19 pandemic)
  definition of

challenges 4–5, 111
conceptual development 20–22, 251–2, 384–6
social citizenship 151–2
development
    fundamental rights-based approach 149–54
    political and economic influences on 70–74, 85
    research perspectives 85, 386
    social change in context 83–4
EEA membership, and (*see under* European Economic Area)
equal treatment principle, and 104–5, 151
EU territory, relationship with
    free movement rights, and 119–21
    judicial interpretation 120–21
free movement principle, and
    fundamental rights protection, and 149–52, 163–4, 387–8
    national citizenship, relationship between (*see* national citizenship)
    relationship between 57, 119–21, 272–3, 285–7, 387–8
fundamental rights-based approach (*see* fundamental rights and freedoms)
ideal subject concept 92–3
implementation of
    background 20–22
    Commission Citizenship Report 2020 388–91
    European Parliament Report 2019 387–8
    infrastructure, need for 62–3
integrity, need for protection of 111–13
interpretation
    constitutional significance 22–3
    unique concept of 19–20
    variations, implications of 8–9
introduction of, Treaty provisions 1, 3, 6, 22, 57, 265–6, 299–300
investor citizenship schemes 101, 107, 369, 372–3
Irish citizenship, relationship with 376–82
judicial interpretation (*see under* judicial interpretation)
legal and conceptual ambiguity, reasons for 49
legal construction and social construction, relationship between 63
marginalised citizens 85–6, 88–9, 95–6, 248
marketisation 101, 107, 369
models for
    access to social benefits, and 54–6
    constitutional context, influences of 56–8, 61–4, 66–7
    human-centred approach 84, 90–93
    implementing infrastructure, need for 62–3
    instrumentalist approach 88
    interdisciplinary perspective 84, 90–93
    judicial interpretation 64–8
    methodology, basis for 51–521
    political participation, and 59–64
    residence model 49, 52, 54–5, 59–60, 64–5
    rights-based perspective 70–72, 152–4
    self-determination 202, 222–3
    social empathy 93–9
    social integration model 49, 52–3, 55–6, 60–61, 65–6
    social justice, and 92–3
national citizenship, relationship with (*see* national citizenship)
naturalisation, and 10, 21, 24, 29–30, 101–7, 110–13, 171–2, 213, 215, 368, 369, 371–2
social constructivist approaches 32–48
social justice, and 85
substance of rights test 60–61, 120, 172–3
transformative potential of 3–4
Treaty provisions 1, 3, 6, 22, 57, 265–6, 299–300
    implementation, European Parliament Report on 387–8
welfare state, relationship with 225–6, 272–3, 279
EU Single Permit Directive 352
EU territory
    concept, scope of 119–20, 178–9
    EU citizenship, relationship with
        Area of Freedom, Security and Justice, recognition of 122
        derived residence rights, and 177–8
        EU travel bans 126–9
        free movement derogations 122–3
        family reunification rights perspective 177–82
        hard *vs.* soft territoriality 119–21, 129–30
    national territory
        Covid-19 influences on perspective of 116–19, 123–6, 129
        status of 122–3
    protective *vs.* systemic policy approaches 181–2
EU-UK Trade and Cooperation Agreement 133, 342, 360–63
European Citizens Initiatives (ECIs) (Brexit-related) 209–10

European Coal and Steel Community Treaty
    free movement principle, and 71, 74–8
    purpose 83
    ratification 76–8
    recognised qualifications 75, 81–2
European Commission v. Cyprus 291
European Convention on Human Rights
    EEA incorporation 90, 317–18
    right to protection of family life 88–90, 157–8, 162, 174–6, 182–3, 213–14
European Economic Area (EEA)
    Agreement
        amendments 301–5
        Annexes, secondary measures incorporation into 301–2
        EEA/ EFTA court interpretation 303–5
        EU Treaties, relationship with 299–301
        generally 133, 297–301
        homogeneity principle, and 303–5, 307, 317–18
        purpose 301
        TFEU Arts 20 and 21, lack of comparable provisions 299, 305–6, 309–10, 318–19
    citizenship, generally 300, 308–9, 321
    citizenship rights
        Brexit, implications of 318
        children, residence rights of 315–16
        Citizenship Directive, incorporation 298–9, 308–9
        cross-border requirements 312–15
        derivative rights 308–10, 311–16
        EEA/ EFTA court interpretation 298–9, 305
        eligibility conditions, and 307–10, 318–19
        EU Treaty rights, interpretation of 305–7
        free movement rights, and 300–302, 307–8, 310–12
        fundamental rights incorporation 317–18
        homogeneity principle, and 307, 311, 317–18
        Joint Declaration 308–10, 314
        non-workers 311–12
        political rights of EEA nationals 299, 307–8
        residence requirement 310, 315–16
        rights comparison 297, 300
        rights differentiation, EU Treaty-based rights 310–12
        rights differentiation, secondary measure-based rights 307–10
        third-country nationals, family member rights of 308–9, 311–16
    EU, special relationship with
        citizenship, comparability of 297–8, 300
        free movement principle, framework differences 298–300
        sovereignty, implications for 300–301
    free movement principle, and
        framework differences 298–300
        incorporation 301–2, 354–5
        judicial interpretation by EEA/ EFTA court 298–9, 304–5, 310–15
        Liechtenstein, special derogations 312–13
    judicial interpretation, by EEA/ EFTA court
        children, residence rights of 315–16
        citizenship, on 298–9, 305
        free movement principle, on 298–9, 304–5, 310–15
        homogeneity principle, on 303–5, 311
        third-country nationals, family member rights of 308–9, 311–16
        welfare benefits, access to 316–17
    status of participating states 297
European Health Union 390–91
European integration *see also* social integration model of EU citizenship
    ambiguities of 52–3
    changing attitudes regarding/ towards 1–2
    employment mobility, incentives for 131
    EU citizenship role in 33, 49, 52–3
    historical background 70–4
    human-centred approach 90–93
    institutional constructivist approach 84, 90–93
    integration through law concept 5–7, 9, 62–3, 68
    interpretation, challenges of 4–5
    judicial interpretation, influences on 63–4
    legitimation of 266–70
    mobile *vs.* immobile citizens, perceptions of 63–4
    political influences on 52–3
    rights-based approach 70–4
    Schuman Plan 70–3
    self-determination, role of 202, 222–3
    Treaty modification stages 5–6
European Parliament
    EU Citizenship Report 2019 387–8
euroscepticism 7, 62–3
"ever closer union" concept 178–9
    development of 3–4, 30–31
    implications of 49, 131, 269–70

Index 399

expulsion, protection from 61, 158–60, 162, 181–2, 256

family member rights
  adoption, recognition of 157, 162, 175–8
  best interest of child, and 29, 89–90, 155–6, 162
  definition of family member 348
  derived residence rights 28–9, 65–6, 153, 155–7, 169–70, 177–8, 180–82, 367
  divorce, residence rights after 65, 155–6, 162
  equal treatment principle, and 245
  EU rights and Convention rights, minimum protection compared 175–6
  expulsion, protection from 61, 158–60, 162
  family reunification (*see* family reunification rights)
  free movement principle, applicability 88–9, 103–5, 152–3, 155–6, 161–2, 165–73
  genuine enjoyment test 120, 153–4, 156, 172, 178–9
  non-traditional families 157, 161–2, 174–6
  residence model of citizens' rights, and 65
  same-sex marriages 157, 174–6
  social integration model of citizens' rights, and 65–7
  spouses, rights of 174–6
  substance of rights test 60–61, 172–3
  third-country nationals, of (*see* third-country nationals)
family reunification rights
  applicable law variations 165
  caregiving requirement 89–90, 155–6, 176–7
  constitutional context 166–8, 172–7
  cross-border situations 168–72, 174–6
  dependency requirement 89–90, 155–6, 176–7
  derived rights 174–8
  EU citizens' eligibility 169–73
  EU law applicability 167–73, 182
  EU territory perspective, implications of 177–82
  exercise of free movement rights, lack of 171–2
  family members, eligibility criteria 173–7
  free movement principle, applicability to 152–3, 155–6, 161–2, 165–73
  fundamental rights-based approach 88–9, 103–5, 153, 155–6, 161–2
  internal market, relationship with 165–6
  judicial interpretation of 166, 168, 172–3, 177–82

  Member State competence conflicts 166–8, 172–3, 182
  naturalisation 171–2
  non-cross-border situations 168, 172–3
  post-cross-border situations 168, 170–72, 174
  return situations 171–2
  right to protection of family life, and 162, 181–2
  spouses, rights of 174–6
  Treaty provisions, eligibility under 172–7
Faulkner, Gerda 271
Ferguson, James 41–2
Ferreira, Nuno 84, 94, 99
Fineman, Martha 96
Finnemore, Martha 36–7, 40–41, 43–6
Förster 55–6, 232–3, 262
Foucault, Michel 40–42, 46–7, 91
France, national identity and citizenship 380
Frattini, Tommaso 274
Free Movement Directive
  judicial interpretation, codification of 235–8, 256–61, 285–6
  limitations of 256–7
  principles of 256
  reform, calls for 389–90
  Social Security Coordination Regulation, relationship with 283–94, 344–5
  status of 259, 285–6
  welfare benefits, access to 231–3
    non-workers, by 232, 235–8, 243–7, 256–61, 277–8, 285, 292–4
    restrictions 256, 285
    right to residence test, and 243–7
    unreasonable burden test 236–7, 253–8, 260–61, 264, 289, 291
free movement principle
  academic freedom, protection of (*see* academic freedom)
  association agreements 8, 61, 67
  border controls, and
    abolition of 121
    free movement principle derogations 122–3
    perceptions of 121, 127–8
    reintroduction during Covid-19 pandemic, legality of 123–5
  choice of law, applicable provisions 344
  constitutional analysis, need for 51, 57
  Covid-19 pandemic, impacts on (*see* Covid-19 pandemic)
  cross-border requirement 139–40, 153–4, 164
  development of 6, 70–82, 265–6, 299–300
    Benelux support for 79–81

common market approach 72, 76–7, 79–81
ECSC Treaty provisions 71, 74–81
institutional competence 78–81
Italian support for 72–9
Member State support for and opposition to 72–81
recognised qualifications 75, 77–8, 80–81
sectoral approach 71, 74–9
Spaak Committee 80, 131
Treaty of Rome/ EEC proposals 71, 79–82, 265–6
effective exercise of 66
employment contracts, applicable provisions 344
equal treatment principle, overlap and conflicts 52–3, 141–3, 276–7
EU citizenship, and
fundamental rights-based approach, distinction from 150–54, 163–4
relationship with 57, 119–21, 263–4, 285–7
expulsion, protection from 61, 158–60, 162, 181–2, 256
family member rights, applicability to 132–3
family reunification, and 152–3, 155–6, 161–2, 165–73
return situations 171–2
freedom to provide services, cross-border 344
jobseekers 8, 56–7, 86, 137, 139, 158, 237–40
judicial interpretation of (*see under* judicial interpretation)
labour efficiency goal of 72–80
limitations of 2, 7, 65–6, 74–5, 265–6
appropriateness 146–7
cross-border requirement 139–40, 164
discriminatory measures 141–3
horizontal direct effect 141
jobseekers 137, 239
justifications for 145–7
legality of 132
necessity 147
obstacles 144–5
public health 74–5, 80, 122–3, 146–7
public interest or policy 146–7
public service exception 138–9
recognised qualifications 75, 80–82, 139, 141, 143
self-employed persons 135–6
unemployment 137
vertical direct effect 140–41

mobile *vs.* immobile citizens, perceptions of 63–4
national citizenship restrictions, relevance for 106–7
non-discrimination principle, and 141–3
non-workers, restrictions on 7, 57–8, 137, 285, 300
parent-subsidiary company relationships, and 140
perspectives on 78–9, 91
posted workers 333, 344, 346–7, 361–2
proportionality 146–7, 257–8
residence model of citizens' rights 49, 52, 54–5, 65, 180–82
social affiliation *vs.* territorial presence 61
social integration model of citizens' rights 49, 52–3, 55–6
social tourism implications 8, 67, 158, 226, 233–8, 249, 289
students, and 227, 256, 275–6
Treaty provisions 71, 79–82, 132
applicability of 132–40
cross-border requirement 139–40
direct effect, implications of 140–41
duration of employment 134–5
employers, extension of personal scope to 137–8
employment relationship *vs.* other economic activities 133–5
EU citizenship requirement 132–3
family members, applicability to 132–3
freedom to provide services cross-borders 344
jobseekers, and 137
payment for services requirement 136–7
personal scope 132–40
prohibited measures, justifications for 145–7
public service exception 138–40
self-employed persons, relevance to 132–3, 135–6
unemployed workers, and 137
worker status, scope of definition 133–40
unemployed persons 137, 345
welfare benefits, access to 231–3, 285, 288–9
judicial interpretation (*see under* judicial interpretation)
frontier workers 240, 345, 362
fundamental rights and freedoms
citizens' rights
best interest of the child 89–90, 155–6, 162

derived rights for family members 28–9, 65–6, 153, 155–7, 161–2, 177–8
divorce, residence rights after 65, 155–6, 162
limitations on 88–90
political influences on 160–61
right to protection of family life 88–9, 157–8, 162, 182–3, 213–14
significance of 97–8
duties, pyramid of 374–5
EEA membership, and 317–18
EU Charter (*see* EU Charter of Fundamental Rights and Freedoms)
EU citizenship, rights-based approach
cross-border test 153–4, 164
development 152–4
free movement principle, and 149–54, 163–4, 387–8
genuine enjoyment test 153–4, 156, 172
judicial interpretation, political influences on 160–61
legal gateway for rights-protection, as 152–4, 161–4
limitations of 150–152, 160
model 70–72
non-workers, protection from expulsion 159–60, 162
international law, non-discrimination clauses 353
restrictions on
academic freedom, and 188, 197–200
justifications for 146
right to education 188
right to protection of family life 88–9, 157–8, 162, 182–3, 213–14
world poverty, and 374–5

G. 61
Garcia Avello 103–5, 153
Garcia Nieto 86, 158, 162, 238, 260–61, 272, 288–9, 293
G.C. (access to benefits) 247–8
Gebhard 144
genuine enjoyment test 24–9, 60, 89, 120, 153–4, 156, 172, 178–9
genuine link requirement 101–2, 107, 163, 255–6, 378–9
Germany, citizenship 370
Giddens, Andrew 91
Goerens, Charles 208–9
Good Friday Agreement 364–5, 376–7
Graf 145, 193–4
Grimme 335–6

Grzelczyk 55, 57, 217, 229–30, 232, 253–4, 256, 272, 276
Gunnarsson 308–10, 315
Gusa 158–9, 162

Haas, Peter 35–6
Hailbronner, Kay 257
Haltern, Ulrich 39
Holocaust 192
homeland narrative 117
Humbel 195
Hungary
academic freedom, restrictions on 184–5, 188–9
banned studies 191–2
Central European University 194–5
freedom of thought and speech, on 191–2
institutional funding 190–91
research institution reforms 189
scholarship contracts 193–4
autocratic legalism, implications of 184–5

Iceland *see* European Economic Area
Iglesias Sánchez, Sara 179
immigration policy *see also* border controls
social integration model of citizens' rights, and 66–7
inactive citizens *see* non-workers
I.N. 315–16
institutional constructivism
EU citizenship, and 84–5
European integration, and 84, 90–93
integration through law concept 5–7, 9
constitutional limitations 62–3, 68
international law, generally
employment contracts, applicable law 344, 353, 360
non-discrimination clauses 353
Intra-Corporate Transferees Directive 351–2, 361
investor citizenship schemes 101, 107, 369, 372–3
Ioannidis 255
Ireland
Good Friday Agreement, influences of 364–5, 376–7, 381–2
Irish citizenship
citizens resident in Northern Ireland, Brexit implications for 364–5, 372
EU citizenship, relationship between 376–83
Irish passport application trends 372, 382

jus sanguinis vs. jus soli approaches
    365–70, 379–80
  political debate 375–6
  sincere cooperation, duty of 365,
    370–82
 reunification, possibility of 374
Italy, free movement of workers 73–8

Jabbi 308–12, 315
Jakab, András 19, 198
Janah v Libya, Benkharbouche v Sudan 198
Jauch 271
Jesse, Moritz 262
Jobcenter Krefeld 243–8, 288–9, 293
jobseekers
  free movement principle, limitations of 137,
    239–40
  welfare benefits, access to 8, 56–7, 86, 137,
    139, 158, 237–9, 243–7, 251, 255–6,
    259–60, 306
judicial interpretation
  equal treatment principle, and
    welfare benefits coordination 55–6,
      250, 270–73, 287–93
  equal treatment principle, on 53
    access to employment 141
    asymmetries and inequalities caused by
      276–8
    constitutional implications of 258–9,
      263–4
    criticism of 258–9, 261–3
    employment conditions 141–3
    EU citizenship, and 151
    financial stability requirement 253–61,
      257–9, 272, 277–9
    importance of 264
    jobseekers 8, 56–7, 86, 137, 139, 158,
      237–9, 243–7, 251, 255–6,
      259–60, 306
    legal uncertainty, and 277–8
    non-workers 8, 54–7, 86–7, 158, 162,
      236–7, 239, 246, 258–9, 264,
      277–8, 292–4
    secondary law, use of 258–60
    welfare benefits, access to 8, 54–7,
      86–7, 151, 158, 162, 229, 235–9,
      243–7, 252–3, 252–64, 292–3
    welfare benefits coordination 55–6,
      250, 270–73, 287–93
  EU citizenship, of
    automatic loss on withdrawal from EU
      201–2, 210–20
    background 251–2
    Citizenship Directive as violation of EU
      Treaties 57

CJEU jurisdiction 24
conflict of norms, and 26–8
constitutional powers, and 268–9
constitutional rights norms
  characteristics, on 13, 19, 23
criticism of 8, 150, 269–70
cross-border test 8, 24–9, 60, 65, 67,
  89, 120, 153–4, 164
development stages 9–10, 24–6, 44–5,
  86–7, 251–2, 285–6
EEA Agreement, under (*see* European
  Economic Area)
EU territory, relationship with 120–21
extension of rights to family members
  10, 24–8
free movement principle, and 151–2,
  285–7
generally 97, 280–81
genuine enjoyment test 24–9, 89, 120,
  172, 178–9
genuine link requirement 101–2, 107,
  163, 255–6, 378–9
importance of 264, 280–81
legal certainty, and 86–7, 234–5
loss of citizenship, rights implications
  of 24–6
Member State competence, on 24
national citizenship, relationship
  between 100, 102–5, 107, 114
non-discrimination principle 151
non-worker protection from expulsion
  159–60, 162
political climate, influences of 160–61
political participation, on 10, 21
protection from extradition, on 10–11
restrictions on 10, 50, 151
right to acquire EU citizenship, on 10
rules and principles, interpretation of
  23–6
social change, role in 6–7, 10–11, 21–2,
  24, 251–2
social citizenship concept 264
TFEU arts 20 and 21, reliance on 23–5,
  29–31
transnational citizenship, on 1–4, 8
welfare benefits, access to 7–8, 57–8,
  68, 86–8, 158–9, 162, 227–9,
  232, 235–8, 243–7, 250, 252–64
withdrawal from EU, implications of
  201–2, 210–20
family member rights, of
  EU territory perspective 177–82
  kafala adoption, recognition of 157,
    162, 175–8
  same-sex marriages 157, 174–6

welfare benefits, access to 7–8, 54–6, 68, 86–8, 158–9, 162, 256–61
free movement principle, on 3, 8, 21, 147–8, 151–3
  access to employment restrictions 141
  codification 235–8, 256–61, 285–6
  EU citizenship, and 151–2
  Free Movement Directive 235–47, 256–61
  fundamental rights protection, and 151–3
  jobseekers 137, 239–40
  obstacles to 144–5
  public interest exception 146
  social, economic and political rights, need for balance 152–3
  welfare benefits, access to 232–3, 256
  worker, definition 136–7
loss of EU citizenship on withdrawal from EU 201–2, 210–20
  acquired or derivative rights 213–16
  admissibility of case 210–12
  Amsterdam Appeal Court ruling 201–2
  Amsterdam District Court preliminary ruling 201–2, 210–20
  automatic loss, argument against 216–18
  automatic loss, arguments for 214–16
  conditional loss or retention 219–20
  constitutional relevance of 221–3
  nationality condition, relevance of 213–16
  right to protection of family life, and 213–14
  substance of the question 214–20
  Treaty provisions, teleological interpretation 216–18
  Treaty provisions, textual interpretation 214–16
welfare benefits, access to 235–40
  automatic exclusion of 237–8
  criticism of 250, 258–9, 261–4, 266, 268–9
  EEA Agreement, under 315–16
  equal treatment principle, and 55–6, 243–7, 250, 252–61, 270–73
  EU citizenship, and 7–8, 57–8, 68, 86, 158–9, 162, 227–9, 232, 235–8, 243–7, 250, 252–64
  family members, of 7–8, 54–6, 68, 86–8, 158–9, 162, 256–61
  frontier workers 240, 345
  jobseekers, by 237–40, 243–7, 251, 255–6, 259–60
  judicial review, restrictions on 268–9

  legal certainty, and 234–5
  limitations, emphasis on 235–8, 256, 264
  non-workers, by 229, 232, 236–7, 243–7, 250, 252–64, 277–8, 292–4
  policy development stages 249–64
  residence rights and restrictions 86, 158, 162, 229, 232, 236–7, 238, 241–7, 252–8
  social assistance, interpretation 241–2, 251, 259–61, 287–9, 291, 293
  special non-contributory cash benefits 241–2, 258–9, 271–2
  students, by 55, 57, 227, 229–32, 251, 253–4, 256, 272, 276–7, 306
  unreasonable burden test 236–8, 253–7, 260–61, 264, 289, 291
jurisdiction, territoriality and citizenship, relationship between 118–19
jus pecuniae 368–9, 379
jus sanguinis 365–70, 379–80
jus soli 365–70, 379–80
J.Y. v. Wiener Landesregierung 103

K and H.F. 159
K.A. 89–90, 156–7
kafala adoption, recognition of 157, 162, 175–8
Karran, Terence 199
Kaur 379–80
Kendall, Gavin 41
Klamert, Marcus 377
Kochenov, Dimtry 178, 198, 263
Kohll 291
Korea-EU Trade Agreement 359
Kostakopoulou, Dora 38, 83–4, 90–92, 94, 99, 208, 279–380
Kramer, Dion 263
Kreil 104–5

language, discrimination on grounds of 141, 143
Lawrie-Blum 134–5, 137
Lebon 251
Leclerc 271
Liechtenstein, free movement principle derogations 312–13, 354
linear progress, perceptions of 2–4
Linklater, Andrew 19–20
L.N. v. Styrelsen 276
Loughlin, Carl 14
Lounes 29–31, 105, 156–7, 217

McCarthy (Shirley) 180, 196
MacCormick, Neil 20
McCrea, Ronan 221

Malta, investor citizenship schemes 101, 107
Mantu, Sandra 121
marginalised citizens 85–6, 248
   definition of 88
   social cruelty, and 95–6
   vulnerability, definition of 96
Maria 314
Marshall, Thomas Humphrey 365
Marshall, T.S. 152
Martinez Sala 55, 151, 229, 252–3, 261–3
Martinsen, Dorte 271, 274
Metock 67, 153, 337
Micheletti 103–5, 365
Michelman, Frank 268
Milan Programme 72
Miller, David 375
Morocco, EU Association Agreement 1995 356–7
Motomurta, Hiroshi 50

N.A. (ex-spouses' rights) 155
national citizenship
   EU citizenship, relationship between
      access requirements 102, 111–13
      acquisition of citizenship, controls over 101–8, 111–13
      associate citizenship proposal, challenges of 109
      autonomous of EU citizenship, proposal implications 108–10
      balancing, challenges of 101
      Brexit, implications of 85, 100, 104, 107–9
      CJEU interpretation of 100, 102–5, 107, 114
      conditionality 105–6
      conflicts between 8–9, 59–60, 100
      decoupling, implications of 108–10, 208
      democratic fairness, need for 112–13
      derivation requirement 102
      EU law general principles, relevance of 106–7
      free movement principle, and 106–7
      genuine link requirement 101–2, 107, 163, 255–6, 378–9
      investor citizenship schemes 101, 107, 369, 372–3
      judicial interpretation 100, 102–5, 107, 114
      legal and normative relationships 100–101
      loss of citizenship, controls over 101–8, 111–13
      Member State competences 101–6, 114
      neutrality, lack of 111–12
      non-discrimination principle, and 104–5
      proportionality, and 103, 105–6
      recognition of nationality 103–5
      reform approaches 108–13
      shared minimum standards of access proposal 111–13
      sincere cooperation, duty of 107, 112, 365, 370–76
      supplementary nature of EU citizenship 72, 102, 105, 107–8
      third-country nationals, recognition of social membership 112–13
      Treaty provisions 102, 107
naturalisation 10, 21, 24, 29–30, 101–7, 110–13, 171–2, 213, 215, 367–9, 371–2
necessity test, free movement restrictions 147
Nic Shuibhne, Niamh 121, 181, 259
non-discrimination principle *see* equal treatment principle
non-linear evolutionary path 2–3, 9–10
non-workers *see* family members; jobseekers; students; welfare benefits, access to
norms as discourses perspective 41–8
Northern Ireland
   Brexit implications for (*see under* Brexit)
   Good Friday Agreement, influences of 364–5, 376–7, 381–2
   Irish citizenship, and 365–70, 372–4, 376–83
   paramilitary group activity 373–4
   reunification, possibility of 374
   UK citizenship, and 374
Norway *see* European Economic Area
Nussbaum, Martha 93

O and B 310–12
O'Brien, Charlotte 87–8, 90, 94, 248, 263

Paltridge, Brian 42, 46
part-time employment 134–5
partnership agreements 357–8
Petruhn 181–2
Picart 335
Pisciotti 182
Pogge, Thomas 374–5
Poland
   academic freedom, restrictions on 184–5, 188–9
   freedom of thought and speech, and 192
   institutional funding 191
   research institution reforms 189–90
   autocratic legalism, implications of 184–5
   gender discrimination 192
political participation

EU citizenship, and 10, 21
residence model of EU citizenship 59–60
right to vote
    European Parliament elections, in 109
    national elections, in 387
    transnational rights 59–60, 387, 390
self-determination, and 202, 207, 222–3
social integration model of EU citizenship 60–61
Pons Rotger, Gabriel 274
posted workers 7, 333, 344, 346–7, 361–2
poverty 374–5
power, perceptions of 91
proportionality
    citizens' rights, of 90, 254–5, 257–8
    Covid-19 pandemic restrictions, of 124–5
    free movement principle restrictions 146–7
    loss of EU citizenship after withdrawal from EU 212
    loss of nationality, and 103, 105–6
    social empathy, and 98
    welfare benefits, access by non-workers 228–9, 236–8, 254–5, 257–8
public health, free movement principle exception 74–5, 80, 122–3, 146
public policy
    expulsion of criminal offenders 8, 159–60
    free movement principle exception 74–5, 80, 122–3, 146–7
public services, free movement principle exception 137–8
Pullano, Teresa 119

qualifications, recognition of
    Brexit, and 205
    equal treatment principle, and 75, 77–8, 80–82, 139, 141, 143
    EU competence 186–7
    free movement principle, and 75, 80–82, 139, 141, 143

Rawls, John 92
Rendón Marín 155–6, 180–81
residence model of EU citizenship 49, 52
    access to social benefits, judicial interpretation 54–5
    free movement principle, and 49, 52, 54–5, 65–7
    habitual residence 54–5
    judicial interpretation 65–6
    political participation, and 59–60
residence rights
    Brexit, implications of 205–6
    caregivers, of 89–90, 155–6, 176–7
    changing perspectives 180–82

    comprehensive sickness insurance, and 279–80
    criminal offenders, of 8, 159–60
    derived rights, as 28–9, 65–6, 153, 155–7, 169–70, 177–8, 180–82, 367
    equal treatment principle, and 229, 256–8
    EU territory concept, and 178–9
    expulsion, protection from 61, 158–60, 162, 181–2, 256
    naturalization, and 171–2
    non-workers, of 229, 232, 236–7, 252–61, 300
    refusal, implications of 180–82
    return situations 171–2
    right to residence test 241–7
    welfare benefits, access to 236–7, 241–2, 252–61, 271–2
R.H. 156–7
right to protection of family life 88–90, 157–8, 162, 182–3
    loss of EU citizenship after withdrawal from EU, and 213–14
    same-sex marriages 174–6
right to vote
    European Parliament elections, in 109
    national elections, in 387
    transnational rights 59–60, 387, 390
Risse, Thomas 41, 44, 45–6
Roma people 8, 185
Romania, citizenship 368
Rottmann 24–6, 60, 103–6, 163, 215, 217, 365, 371–2
Ruggie, John 35
Ruiz Zambrano see Zambrano
Rumi, Jalal al-Din 384–5
Runevi?-Vardyn and Wardyn [#symbol] 217m

S and G 170
same-sex marriages 157, 174–6
San Marino partnership agreement 358
Sangiovanni, Andrea 95–7
Sargentini Report 185
Scharpf, Fritz 273–4
Schengen Area
    EU travel bans 126–9
    external border controls, perceptions of 121
    free movement principle derogations 122–3
    internal border controls and EU citizenship, relationship between 121
    reintroduction of border controls, legality of 123–5
Scheppele, Kim Lane 198
Schmitt, Carl 14–15
Schuman Plan 71–3
Segal, Elizabeth 93–5

self-employment
    EU-Swiss Agreement on the Free Movement of Persons 335–6
    free movement principle, applicability to 132–3, 135–6
    interpretation of 135
    Turkish association agreement, access to EU under 323–4
    welfare benefits, access to 88, 232
Shindler v European Commission 202, 207, 212
short-term employment 134–5
Sikkink, Kathryn 36–7, 40–41, 43–6
sincere cooperation, duty of
    national citizenship and EU citizenship, relationships between 107, 112, 365, 370–76
Singh 311
S.M. 157–8, 177
Smith, Adam 92–3
social assistance, interpretation 241–2, 251, 259–61, 284–5, 287–9, 291, 293
social change
    constructivist approaches 32, 37–8
        conventional research methods, compared with 38–40
    influences on 83–4
    perspectives on 2–4, 83
social cohesion 52–3
    EU territory as place for 120–21
    homeland narratives, and 117
social cruelty 95–6
social empathy 99
    conceptual scope of 93–4
    development and cultivation approaches 94
    dignity, role of 93, 95, 97
    EU citizenship, role in 95–7
    EU law general principles, application of 97–8
    proportionality, role of 98
    sense of self 95, 97
    solidarity, and 96–7, 249–50
    systemic barriers, understanding of 94–5, 97–8
    vulnerability, recognition of 96–7
social integration model of EU citizenship 49, 52, 55–6
    free movement principle, and 49, 52–3, 55–6, 66–7
    immigration policy, and 66–7
    integration through law, limitations of 62–3
    judicial interpretation 65–8
    welfre benefits access, judicial interpretation 54–5
social justice

human-centred approach to citizenship, and 92–3
    marginalised citizens 85–6, 88–9, 95–6, 248
    social protection, relationship with 225
social learning concept 37–8
Social Security Coordination Regulation
    Free Movement Directive, relationship with 283–94
social tourism 8, 67, 158, 226, 233–8, 249, 289
solidarity
    social empathy, and 96–7, 249–50
    transnational citizens' rights, and 57–8, 96–7, 249–50, 283–5, 293–5
    welfare benefits, access to 230–31, 234–5, 249–50, 269, 283–5, 293–5
Solomon Robert 93
sovereignty, citizenship approaches 366–7, 379–80
Spaak Committee 80, 131
spouses *see also* family member rights
    dual citizenship rights, and 29–31
    residence rights after divorce 65, 155–6, 162
Stillar, Glenn, 43
students
    benefits, access to 55, 57, 227, 229–33, 250–51, 253–4, 256, 272, 276–7, 306
    financial stability requirement 253–4, 272, 276–7
    free movement principle, and 187, 256
    quota systems, validity of 275–6
    residence requirement 232–3, 253–4, 256
substance of rights test 60–61, 120, 172–3
Sveinbjörnsdóttir 304
Swaddling 272
Switzerland
    EU-Swiss Agreement on the Free Movement of Persons
        amendments to 337–9
        Annexes 339, 355
        background 332
        criticism of 341–2
        EU Citizenship Directive, incorporation of 337–9
        family member rights 337–9
        free movement rights, generally 320, 332–3, 354–5
        freedom of establishment and to provide services 333–7
        limitations and restrictions 332–3, 340–41
        market access rights 333–7
        migrant workers 354–5
        non-discrimination on grounds of nationality 334–7
        political influences on 340

posted workers 333
provisions, generally 332–3, 341
qualifications, recognition of 339
residence rights 339
self-employment 335–6
standstill clauses 334–5
substantive reach 332
welfare benefits, access to 339, 355
workers' rights 335

Tarola 158–9, 162
Taviani, Paolo 73
territory, generally *see also* EU territory
    citizenship, relationship with 116–19
    hard *vs.* soft territoriality 119–22
    homeland narrative 117
    identity and community, links with 117
    jurisdiction, and 117–18
    law, territoriality of 117–18
    state, definition of 119, 122
TFEU arts 20 and 21
    constitutional rights norms
        application as 13, 25–6
        EU citizenship, establishment of 22–3, 120–21, 214–20
        EU citizenship, loss of 214–20
        EU territory concept, and 178–9
        family reunification, and 167–8, 172–3
        free movement rights *vs.* national competence conflicts 167–8
        genuine enjoyment test 178–9
        radiating effect of 27–9, 384–5
        residence rights of spouses 29–31
        rules and principles, differentiation 23–6
    EEA/ EFTA Agreement
        citizens' rights, relevance to 305–6
        lack of comparable provisions, implications of 299, 305–6, 309–10
    judicial interpretation, influences on 13, 23–5
third-country nationals
    Brexit, implications for 208, 349–54
    citizens' rights ambiguities 52, 113
    constitutional rights norms, and conflicts 26–7, 120–21
    genuine enjoyment test 24–9, 60, 120
    radiating effect 27–9
    EU Charter rights, applicability to 188, 342
    EU citizenship, and
        associate citizenship proposal, implications of 109
        denial of access 112–13, 120–21
        social membership of EU, recognition of 112–13
    family member rights
        best interest of child, and 29, 89–90, 155–6, 162
        conflicts regarding 7–8, 26–9, 367
        dependency relationships 89–90
        derived residence rights 28–9, 65–6, 153, 155–7, 169–70, 177–8, 367
        divorce, residence rights after 65, 155–6, 162
        domestic law conflicts 28–9, 60
        expulsion, protection from 61, 158–60, 162
        family reunification 152–3, 155–6, 161–2, 165–73
        free movement principle, and 132–3, 165–6
        genuine enjoyment test 120, 153–4, 156, 172, 178–9
        international agreements regarding 133, 357–8
        judicial interpretation 10–11, 24–9, 60–61
        non-traditional families 157–8, 161–2, 174–5, 174–6
        residence model of citizens' rights, and 65
        social affiliation *vs.* territorial presence 60–61
        social integration model of citizens' rights, and 65–6, 65–7
        substance of rights test 60–61, 172–3
        welfare benefits, access to 28–9, 158–9, 162, 250, 357–8
Thym, Daniel 86, 125
Titscher, Stefan 43
Tjebbes 103–6, 163, 378
Torfing, Jacob 40, 42, 43, 47
trade agreements
    Canada-EU Comprehensive Economic and Trade Agreement (CETA) 358–9
    EU-UK Trade and Cooperation Agreement 133, 342, 360–63
trainee workers 134, 136
transnational citizenship, generally *see also* EU citizenship
    statal communities, suitability for 50
Treaty of Maastricht 1, 3, 6, 22, 57, 151, 391
Trojani 55, 254–6
Tunisia, EU Association Agreement 1996 356–7
Turkey
    Ankara Agreement 8, 61, 67, 355
    access to EU territory, rights of 324–6

access to labour market 323–4, 329, 355
background 322–3
children of Turkish workers, rights of 328–9
criticism of 341–2
education, rights to 328–9
equal treatment principle 320, 325–7, 355–6
expulsion, protection from 330
family member rights 326–31
family reunification rights 327–8
free movement of workers 323–6, 355–6
free movement principle, applicability of 320–21, 323, 329–30, 355–6
freedom of establishment and to provide services 324–6, 330
judicial interpretation 330–31
limitations and restrictions 323, 325, 329–31, 341
non-discrimination on grounds of nationality 320, 325–7
political influences on 342
provisions, generally 322–3, 341
self-employment 323–4
standstill clauses 321, 324–5, 334
termination of rights, grounds for 329
welfare benefits, access to 326, 355–6

UK withdrawal from EU *see* Brexit
Ukraine-EU Trade and Association Agreements 321, 359–60
unemployed workers
    equal treatment principle, and 141, 350
    free movement principle, applicability to 137, 345
    marginalisation of 88
    welfare benefits, access to 241, 250, 254–5, 259–60, 335, 345, 353
        Brexit, implications of 350–51, 362–3
United States
    citizenship, basis for 367
    constitutional theory and welfare rights debate 268
    immigration policies, perspective development 50
unreasonable burden test 236–7, 253–8, 260–61, 264, 289, 291

Van Gend en Loos 208
Vatsouras 57, 241, 277
Verhofstadt, Guy 208
von Bogdandy, Armin 51
vulnerability, definition of 97

Wächtler 335–6
Waever, Ole 41–2
Wahl 308
Walzer, Michael 375
Weiler, Joseph 105
welfare benefits, access to
    automatic exclusion 8, 56–7, 86, 158, 237–8
    child benefits, indexation of 240
    compensatory pensions 54–5, 236–7, 241, 257–8, 272, 275–6
    comprehensive sickness insurance 279–80
    concerns and conflicts 8, 68, 87–8, 142, 158, 226
    constitutionalism, relationship with 268–9
    coordination
        applicability 345
        challenges of 292
        comprehensive sickness insurance 279–80
        cross-border situations, in 345
        development of 270–71
        eligibility conditions 227, 236–8, 270, 285, 289–90, 293, 345
        equal treatment principle, interpretation 55–6, 250, 270–73, 285–93
        EU competence 295
        free movement principle, overlap with 285–92
        hybrid benefits 284–6, 287–8, 293
        judicial interpretation 55–6, 270–73, 285–93
        limitations, justification for 290–92
        mechanisms for 283–5, 345
        Member State competence and powers 284, 290, 292–5
        multiplicity of approaches 285
        non-workers, access by 283, 292–4, 345
        personal scope 283, 288–9
        Regulation, role and scope of 283–94, 344–5
        scope and purpose of 250, 283
        unreasonable burden test 291
    economic crises, influences of 86–8, 233–4, 269–70
    EEA Agreement, under 316–17
    eligibility conditions 227, 236–8, 270, 285, 288–90, 293
    equal treatment principle, and 243–7, 250–61, 292–3
        challenges of 269–70
        coordination, judicial interpretation 55–6, 250, 270–73, 287–93
        deservingness 159–60, 162–4, 263–4
        hybrid benefits 284–5, 287–8, 293

jobseekers, by 8, 56–7, 86, 137, 139, 158, 237–40, 243–7, 251, 255–6, 259–60, 306
non-workers, by 87–8, 142, 227–9, 246–7, 252–61, 277–8, 283, 285, 292–4
residence rights and restrictions 243–7, 252–8, 283–5, 292–3
restrictions on 87–8, 227–9, 237–8, 251–3, 252–3, 256–8, 285, 287–8
social assistance 284–5, 287–9, 291, 293
students, by 187, 227, 229–32, 250–51, 253–4, 256, 272, 276–7, 306
family members, by 260–61
third-country nationals, of 28–9, 158–9
workers, of 227, 238, 250
financial stability requirement 253–61, 257–9, 272, 277–9
free movement principle, and 231–3, 285, 288–9
frontier workers, by 240, 345
hybrid benefits 284–6, 287–8, 293
integration model of citizens rights, and 55–6
jobseekers 8, 56–7, 86, 137, 139, 158, 237–40, 243–7, 251, 255–6, 259–60, 306
judicalisation of
  asymmetries and inequalities caused by 273–4, 276–7
  general implications of 266, 268–73, 280–81
  limitations of 273–81
  tragedy of the commons, as 273–6
judicial interpretation (*see under* judicial interpretation)
legislative limitations on 227–8, 230–31
marginalised citizens 88–9, 248
Member State competence and powers 249, 284, 290, 292–5
Member State variations in
  impacts of 249, 271–2, 274–5, 294–5
  under-provision, risks of 274–6
non-discrimination principle, and 87–8, 142, 227–9, 246–7
non-workers 7–8, 57–8, 68, 87–8, 158–9, 162, 227–9, 232–3, 235–8, 243–7, 250, 252–61, 277–8, 283, 285, 292–4, 345
personal scope, expansion of 283–4
proportionality 228–9, 236–8, 254–5, 257–8
residence-based approach, reasons for 292–3
residence model of citizens rights, and 54–5

residence requirement 232–3, 236–7, 241–7, 251–6, 271–2, 283–5, 292–3
self-employed persons, by 88, 232
social assistance, interpretation 241–2, 251, 259–61, 284–5, 287–9, 291, 293
special non-contributory cash benefits 241–2, 258–9, 271–2
students, by 55, 57, 227, 229–33, 250–51, 253–4, 272, 276–7, 306
third-country nationals, by 250
third-country partnership agreement provisions 357–8
trade agreement provisions 358–60
transnational solidarity, and 57–8, 230–31, 234–5, 249–50, 269, 283–5, 293–5
under-provision, risks of 274–6
unemployed workers 241, 250, 254–5, 259–60, 335, 345, 353
  Brexit, implications of 350–51, 362–3
unreasonable burden test 236–7, 253–8, 260–61, 264, 289, 291
welfare tourism 8, 67, 158, 226, 233–8, 249, 289
welfare state, generally
  access to benefits (*see* welfare benefits, access to)
  EU citizenship, relationship with 225–6, 272–3, 279
  Member State solidarity, and 57–8, 230–31, 234–5, 249–50, 269, 283–5, 293–5
  social inclusion goal of 225
  welfare nationalism, rise of 226, 263–4
Wickham, Gary 41
Wiener, Antje 45–6
Wightman 201–2, 216
Wijsenbeek 121
withdrawal from EU membership
  loss of EU citizenship, implications for academic debate regarding 207–10
  Amsterdam District Court and Appeal Court rulings on 201–2, 210–220
  automatic loss, perspectives on 209–20
  CJEU preliminary reference 201–2
  Commission Decision (2017) 210
  constitutional context, in 220–4
  procedures for 203
  UK, by (*see* Brexit)
Wittgenstein 217
women's rights
  caregiving 89–90, 155–6, 176–7
  pregnancy and childbirth 89
  third-country nationals, derived rights 89–90, 155–6, 162
workers, definition 133–40, 266

Young, Marion 88

Zambrano 8, 24–9, 60, 65, 67, 89, 120, 153–4, 156, 164, 168, 172, 177–9, 181, 183, 195–6, 306, 313–14
Ziebell 330
Ziolkowski 262